Improve the probability of your success!

We understa... ...of an accounting
student. It ... ...of subjects, but
statistics ha... ...been ...the learning package from OUP,
designed with you in mind.

We all know that practice makes perfect, so you can't go wrong with your very own numerical skills workbook, featuring over 180 examples and 40 exercises to equip you with the skills you need to study the topics in the textbook, and to go on to successfully apply your learning in the world of business.

Don't worry, though, you don't have to know it all yet; for every statistical procedure featured there's a visual walkthrough with author commentary. So take advantage of this unique resource now and make sure that when it matters you'll know your histogram from your box plot.

As you can see we've got all bases covered: from grasping the basics with our self-test questions and gaining a real understanding of the subject with relevant web links, to excelling in your exam with our focused revision tips, OUP is with you at every stage, always just a click away!

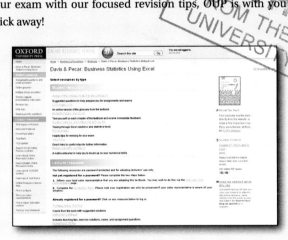

www.oxfordtextbooks.co.uk/orc/davis_pecar/

Lecturers – interact with your students and track their progress both inside and outside the class:

» **PowerPoint slides for every chapter**

» **Assignment and exam style questions**

» **Fully customizable test bank**

All uploadable to your unive...

business statistics using Excel®

business statistics
using Excel®

Glyn Davis & Branko Pecar

OXFORD

UNIVERSITY PRESS

OXFORD
UNIVERSITY PRESS

Great Clarendon Street, Oxford ox2 6DP

Oxford University Press is a department of the University of Oxford.
It furthers the University's objective of excellence in research, scholarship,
and education by publishing worldwide in

Oxford New York

Auckland Cape Town Dar es Salaam Hong Kong Karachi
Kuala Lumpur Madrid Melbourne Mexico City Nairobi
New Delhi Shanghai Taipei Toronto

With offices in

Argentina Austria Brazil Chile Czech Republic France Greece
Guatemala Hungary Italy Japan Poland Portugal Singapore
South Korea Switzerland Thailand Turkey Ukraine Vietnam

Oxford is a registered trade mark of Oxford University Press
in the UK and in certain other countries

Published in the United States
by Oxford University Press Inc., New York

British Library Cataloguing in Publication Data

Data available

Library of Congress Cataloging in Publication Data

Davis, Glyn.
Business statistics using Excel / Glyn Davis & Branko Pecar.
p. cm.
ISBN 978-0-19-955689-2
1. Microsoft Excel (Computer file) 2. Commercial statistics.
3. Commercial statistics–Computer programs. 4. Business–Computer programs.
I. Pecar, Branko, 1953- II. Title.
HF5548.4.M523D38 2009
005.54–dc22
2009031333

Typeset by MPS Ltd, A Macmillan Company
Printed in Italy by L.E.G.O S.p.A

ISBN 978-0-19-955689-2

1 3 5 7 9 10 8 6 4 2

Aims of the book

It has long been recognized that the development of modular undergraduate programmes coupled with a dramatic increase in student numbers has led to a reconsideration of teaching practices. This statement is particularly true in the teaching of statistics and in response a more supportive learning process has been developed. A classic approach to teaching statistics, unless one is teaching a class of future professional statisticians, can be difficult and is often met with very little enthusiasm by the majority of students. A more supportive learning process based on method application rather than method derivation is clearly needed. The authors thought that by relying on some commonly available tools, Microsoft Excel in particular, such an approach is possible.

To this effect, a new programme relying on the integration of workbook based open learning materials with information technology tools has been adopted. The current learning and assessment structure may be defined as:

a. To help students 'bridge the gap' between school and university

b. To enable a student to be confident in handling numerical data

c. To enable students to appreciate the role of statistics as a business decision making tool

d. To provide a student with the knowledge to use Excel to solve a range of statistical problems

This book is aimed at students who require a general introduction to business statistics that would normally form a foundation level business school module. The learning material in this book requires minimal input from a lecturer and can be used as a self-instruction guide.

The growing importance of spreadsheets in business is emphasized throughout the text by the use of the Excel spreadsheet. The use of software in statistics modules is more or less mandatory at both diploma and degree level and the emphasis within the text is on the use of Excel to undertake the required calculations. The textbook uses Excel 2003, but Excel 2007 solutions to all examples are available online.

How to use the book effectively

The sequence of chapters has been arranged so that there is a progressive accumulation of knowledge. Each chapter guides students step by step through the theoretical and spreadsheet skills required. Chapters also contain exercises that give students the chance to check their progress.

Hints on using the book

a. Be patient and work slowly and methodically, especially in the early stages when progress may be slow.

b. Do not omit or 'jump around' between chapters; each chapter builds upon knowledge and skills previously gained. You may also find that the Excel applications that you develop require earlier ones in order to work.

c. Try not to compare your progress with others too much. Fastest is not always best!

d. Don't try to achieve too much in one session. Time for rest and reflection is important.

e. Mistakes are part of learning. Do not worry about them. The more you repeat something, the fewer mistakes you will make.

f. Make time to complete the exercises, especially if you are learning on your own. They are your best guide to your progress.

g. The visual walkthroughs have been developed to explore using Excel to solve a particular statistical problem. If you are not sure about the Excel solution then use the visual walkthrough as a reminder.

Business Statistics Using Excel is an independent publication and is not affiliated with, nor has it been authorized, sponsored, or otherwise approved by Microsoft Corporation.

Brief contents

Detailed contents

2 Numerical Skills Revision 31

8   Chi Square and Non-Parametric Hypothesis Testing   352

9   Factorial Experiments   393

10   Linear Correlation and Regression Analysis   454

Learning Objectives

Each chapter identifies the key learning objectives that you will be able to achieve after completing the unit. They also serve as helpful recaps of the important concepts when revising.

Worked examples

Detailed worked examples run throughout each chapter to show you how theory relates to practice. The authors break concepts down into clear step-by-step phases, which are often accompanied by a series of Excel screenshots to enable you to assess your progress.

Step-by-step Excel guidance

Excel screenshots are fully integrated throughout the text, and regular boxes showing the Excel formulas, functions, and solutions, provide you with clear step-by-step guidance on how to solve the statistical problems posed.

Interpretation boxes

Interpretation boxes appear throughout the chapters, providing you with further explanations to aid your understanding of the concepts being discussed.

Note boxes

The note boxes, featured throughout each chapter, present additional information such as important points to remember, areas where extra care should be taken, or to point out certain exceptions to the rules.

Student Exercises

Throughout each chapter you are regularly given the chance to test your knowledge and understanding of the topics covered, through student exercises after each section. You can then monitor your progress by checking the answers at the back of the textbook.

Techniques in Practice

Techniques in practice exercises appear at the end of each chapter and reinforce learning by presenting questions to test the knowledge and skills covered in that unit. You can use these to check your understanding of a topic before moving on to the next chapter.

Chapter summary

Each chapter ends with an overview of the techniques covered, an ideal tool for you to check your understanding of the key areas in this topic.

Key Terms

Key terms are highlighted in green where they first appear in the text, and the definition placed in the margin. These terms are also then listed at the end of each chapter as a quick reference tool.

Further Reading

A list of recommended reading is included to allow you to explore a particular subject area in more depth. Annotated web links are also provided to help you locate further resources in statistics.

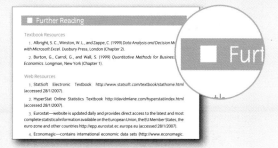

How to use the Online Resource Centre

www.oxfordtextbooks.co.uk/orc/davis_pecar/

For students

Multiple choice questions

A bank of self-marking multiple choice questions accompany each chapter, ideal for you to test your understanding of a topic before progressing to the next stage.

Data from exercises in book

Raw data from the textbook is available for you to use in your ongoing learning and revision.

Web links

A series of annotated web links explaining why each site is relevant has been provided to help you locate further resources useful to your study.

Glossary of key terms

Key glossary terms from the textbook have also been placed online, along with their definitions, for use as a quick revision tool.

Revision tips

The authors provide you with helpful revision tips to help consolidate your learning and to assist you when preparing for your exams.

Visual walkthroughs

Visual walkthroughs, complete with audio explanations, are provided for each statistical procedure described in the text, and guide you through each Excel solution. This resource enables you to work at your own pace, ensuring that you fully understand each concept before progressing. It can also be used as an ideal revision tool.

Numerical skills workbook

The authors provide you with a numerical skills refresher, packed with over 180 examples and 40 exercises, equipping you with the skills needed to study the topics in the textbook with confidence.

For lecturers

Lecturer's manual

A chapter-by-chapter guide to structuring lectures and seminars, including teaching tips, has been provided by the authors in this helpful guide for instructors. The manual also contains worked answers to all the exercises and techniques in practice cases set in the textbook, available in both Excel 2003 and Excel 2007.

The authors have also put together a comprehensive set of assignment and examination questions for you to set your students, enabling them to practise answering both in-depth and exam style questions.

PowerPoint lecture slides

A suite of fully customizable PowerPoint slides has been designed by the authors for use in your lecture presentations.

Test bank

For each chapter the authors have designed a set of fully customizable questions to test your students' knowledge and understanding of statistics. Automated grading allows you to assess your students' progress via your university's Virtual Learning Environment, and instant feedback shows students the areas where they need to improve.

Introduction to Microsoft Excel 2003

1

Microsoft Excel provides a series of tools that can be used to undertake the analysis of data sets as well as a presentation tool for reporting your results. This chapter describes Excel 2003, which is part of the *Office 2003* suite of programs. It is assumed that you are familiar with *Microsoft Windows* and know how to perform tasks such as accessing commands from the menus on the menu bar, selecting items, and entering information into a dialog box. This chapter will describe the Excel skills required to enable the Excel user to undertake the statistical tests described within each chapter of this textbook.

» Overview «

A *spreadsheet* is a table of cells arranged in *rows* and *columns*. The data values in each cell can take many forms, such as text, dates, times, and numbers (including currency and percentages).

The relationships between cells are called formulae. If you change the value in a cell, the contents of any cells that depend on that value will change automatically. This enables you to study what-if scenarios.

Excel can create and manipulate spreadsheets (which are called *worksheets*). It can also produce *graphs* (known as *charts*, see Figure 1.1) and can link one worksheet to another.

Furthermore, Excel can be used to solve a variety of mathematical, statistical, and financial problems. This textbook is concerned with the application of the Excel spreadsheet to solve business statistics focused problems.

» Learning Objectives «

On successful completion of this chapter, you will be able to:

- » Create a new Excel workbook and worksheets.
- » Save and close workbooks.
- » Format cells.

» Select a cell or a range of cells.

» Enter data into a cell or a range of cells, e.g. numbers, text.

» Create and modify cell formulae.

» Create and apply names to a cell range.

» Print worksheets and workbooks and apply preview before printing worksheets.

» Understand that Excel can create a table and chart.

» Apply Excel functions to solve statistical problems.

» Load Excel Analysis ToolPak add-in to solve a range of statistical problems.

» Insert an Excel worksheet and chart into Microsoft Word.

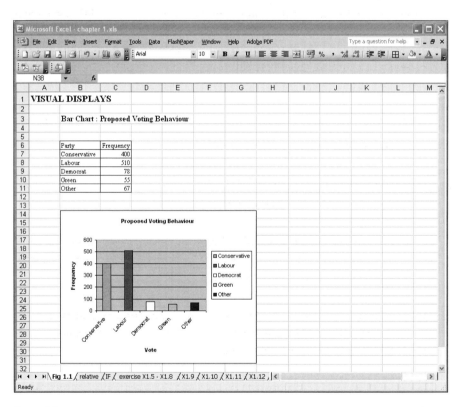

Figure 1.1

1.1 Introduction to Microsoft Excel 2003

A spreadsheet is basically a document which has been divided into rows and columns.
Excel is designed to ease the management of numbers and calculations. Various menu
commands and buttons make it easy to arrange and format columns of numbers and to

calculate totals, averages, percentages, financial, statistical, and scientific formulae. The look of a spreadsheet application derives from the account ledgers that have been used to keep records for centuries. Ledger pages are lined off into rows and columns to record such things as items in inventory, income and expenses, debits and credits. The biggest advantage of a spreadsheet over these paper-based ledgers is the ability to update calculations automatically as new data is added to the worksheet.

1.1.1 Components of an Excel spreadsheet

- **Worksheets**

  Worksheets can be used to store, manipulate, calculate, analyse data, and create tables and charts.

- **Workbooks**

  These are a collection of sheets stored in the same file on the disk. By keeping related worksheets in the same workbook, it is easy to make simultaneous changes and edits to all workbook sheets at one time, or to consolidate related sheets or to do calculations involving multiple sheets. Excel 2003 contains a maximum of 255 worksheets.

- **A row**

  A row is a line of horizontal cells within a spreadsheet, e.g. A3, B3, C3, D3, E3, etc.

  Within each worksheet there are 65536 rows.

- **A column**

  A column is a line of vertical cells within a spreadsheet e.g. A1, A2, A3, A4, A5, etc.

  Within each worksheet there are 256 columns.

- **A cell**

  A cell is the intersection of a row and a column, which has a unique address or reference. For example where column C and row 8 intersect is cell C8. You use cell references when you write formulae or refer to cells.

- **Absolute cells**

  A reference such as $A$2 tells Excel how to find a cell based on the exact location of that cell in the worksheet. An absolute reference is designated by adding a dollar sign ($) before the column letter and the row number.

- **A range**

  A selection of multiple cells is referred to as a range. A single cell in some circumstances may represent a range.

- **Charts**

  Excel can create charts quickly to visually represent a data set stored in a worksheet. A range of chart types can be created, including: *pie charts*, *bar charts*, *line graphs*, and *scatter plots*.

- **Macros**

  Excel can be used to develop and store macros that can be used to undertake frequently applied tasks.

- **Presentations**
  Excel as a range of drawing and formatting tools that can be used to create high-quality presentations. These presentations can then be printed or copied to a word processing or presentation software package.

1.1.2 Loading Excel

Select Start to display the Start menu > Select All Programs > Select Office > Select Excel. Excel opens and displays an empty workbook as illustrated in Figure 1.2 below:

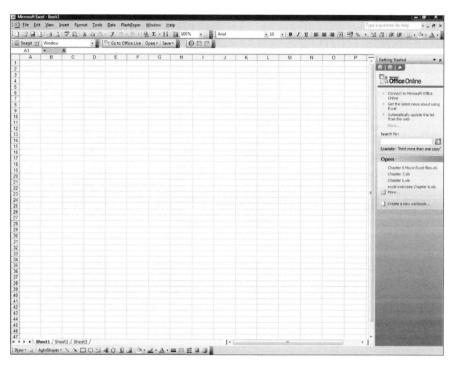

Figure 1.2

In Excel, the normal file type is referred to as a workbook. The first blank workbook displayed by Excel is called Book 1 (see Figure 1.2). Each workbook contains sheets that are referred to as worksheets if they contain a spreadsheet and as chart sheets if they contain just a graph. A new workbook usually has three worksheets but more can be added if required. The screen display is made up of the worksheet which is divided into rows (with headings 1, 2, 3 …) and columns (with headings A, B, C …). Although you cannot see them there are 255 columns and 65536 rows. This means that there are more than 16 million individual cells in one worksheet. At the top of the Excel workspace is the title bar displaying Microsoft Excel followed by the name of the current workbook (Book 1 in this case). Below that is the menu bar and toolbars. Then, just above the row of column headings, are the Name box containing the address of the active cell (A1 at the moment) and the Formula Bar displaying the contents of the active cell (blank at the moment).

1.1.3 Task panes

On the View menu, there is now a Task Pane option. When this is ticked, a pane appears on the right-hand side of your screen as illustrated in Figure 1.3.

Figure 1.3

The Getting Started task pane provides easy ways of accessing Office information, creating new workbooks, and opening recently used workbooks. Next to the Close button of the New Workbook task pane is the Other Task Panes down-arrow. This gives access to facilities for online help, inserting clip art, searching for files, and copying multiple items. To close a task pane, either click on its Close button or de-select Task Pane in the View menu option.

1.1.4 Help

Excel has a comprehensive, easy-to-use help system. The Office Assistant (Figure 1.4) can be employed to ask questions or ask for help from the Help menu (Figure 1.5):

Figure 1.4

Figure 1.5

1.1.5 Saving a workbook

Your workbook can be saved to a local hard disk or stored on an external storage device, e.g. USB memory stick.

1. Click on File and then Save.

2. A Save As box will appear—with the File Name Box highlighted. Type into this box a file name and save to an appropriate location on the storage drive. It is very important to save any work created at regular time intervals.

Figure 1.6

3. Press Delete Key on key board to delete the default file name.

4. Enter the name of your workbook (e.g. chapter 1). Excel will automatically give it a file extension (.xls). The file extension (.XLS) denotes the file to be an Excel spreadsheet.

5. Click on ⌄ in the Dri<u>v</u>es box and select the appropriate drive (e.g. (E:) Corsair).

Figure 1.7

6. Click on SAVE. The name of the document is displayed at the top of the screen.

However, if you wish to make some alteration to the original document and save the altered version *as well as* keeping the original version, carry out the following procedures:

1. Click on <u>F</u>ile and then Save <u>A</u>s.

2. The Save As box appears—with the File <u>N</u>ame Box highlighted, containing the documents original name with the cursor flashing.

3. Press Delete Key on key board to delete the default file name.

4. Enter the new name of your document.

5. Click on OK. The new name of the document is displayed at the top of the screen. If you use the Save command the original document will be over written.

1.1.6 Opening an existing workbook

1. Click on open button 🖼 in the toolbar, or click on <u>F</u>ile and then <u>O</u>pen. The screen shown in Figure 1.8 will appear.

2. Select the drive you require (i.e. C:\) by clicking on ⌄ in the Dri<u>v</u>es box and selecting the C: drive.

3. Click on the directory the file is in (if any).

4. Click on the file you wish to open.

5. Click on Open.

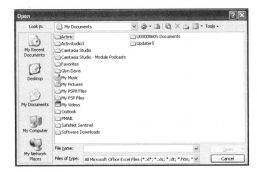

Figure 1.8

1.1.7 Closing a workbook

You can close a workbook at any time. From the File menu, select Close. If you have made any changes to the workbook since it was last saved, you will be asked whether you wish to save those changes. Click Yes to keep the changes or No to discard them. You can rename the file if you wish to keep the changes made but save it to a different Excel file.

1.1.8 Switch to a new worksheet

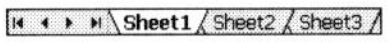

Click on the tab at the bottom of the screen to select the next sheet. Since you have up to 255 worksheets available in a workbook, it is advisable to use them in sequential order to avoid confusion. Worksheets (sheet 1, sheet 2 . . .) can be moved by dragging the worksheet tab to the left or right to reorder the worksheets.

Figure 1.9

1.1.9 Creating a new worksheet

To create a new worksheet in your workbook select Insert > New Worksheet.

1.1.10 Opening a new workbook

Click on the New Workbook button ▭ in the toolbar, or Click on File and then New, in the menu bar. A new workbook will appear on the screen. Note: the original book also remains open behind the new one until you close it.

1.1.11 Printing and print preview

The print preview function allows you to preview your worksheet exactly as it will be printed.

1. Click on the print preview button 🔍. A similar screen to that shown below will appear:

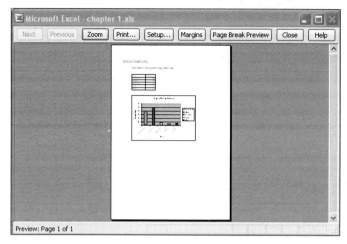

Figure 1.10

Table 1.1 shows the options that are available within preview:

Option	Description
Next	When the worksheet has more than one page, Next displays the next page.
Previous	This will display the previous page.
Zoom	Allows you to enlarge the display to see more detail and reduce it again.
Print	Calls up the print window.
Setup	Calls up the Setup window.
Margins	Shows the position of the page margins and indicates where the columns and rows are. You can directly change margins from Print Preview display.
Page Break Preview	Shows the page breaks in documents.
Close	Exits Print Preview and returns you to the worksheet.

Table 1.1

Once you are satisfied with the page layout, you may print the worksheet as follows:

•   Click on the print button in the Toolbar 🖨, the worksheet will print using the default settings.

•   Click on the print button from within the print preview window, or click on File in the menu bar and then click on Print. The following menu is displayed:

Figure 1.11

The printer you are connected to is displayed in the Printer Name. Table 1.2 shows which options are available in the Print what section:

Option	Description
Selection	Prints a selected range of cells.
Active Sheet(s)	Prints a current or selected worksheet(s), this is also a default setting.
Entire Workbook	Prints all sheets in the workbook.

Table 1.2

To change the number of copies to be printed:

1. Click on the up arrow in the Copies box to increase the number of copies to be printed.
2. Click on the down arrow to decrease the number of copies to be printed.

To print selected pages:

1. Click on Page(s).
2. Enter the page number you wish to start printing from in the From box.
3. Enter the last page in the range you wish to print in the To box.
4. Click on OK to start printing.

1.1.12 What to do if you encounter a damaged Excel file

If an Excel file is corrupted due to a computer crash (or other problem) then Excel will automatically attempt to save a file. The *Document Recovery* task pane shows the files that were open at the time of the computer crash. It identifies the original version of the file and the recovered version of the file. After you open the recovered version, you can then save its changes by choosing File > Save on the Excel menu bar. The *AutoRecover* feature is set to automatically save changes to your workbook (provided that the file has already been saved) every ten minutes. You can modify this time by choosing Tools > Options > Save on the Excel menu bar. The *Open and Repair* command can be used to recover corrupt Excel files (choose File > Open and Repair).

1.2 Entering Data and Formatting

Data is entered into the worksheet by moving the cursor to the appropriate position on the screen, clicking the left mouse button to select the cell, and then typing the information required. The characters you type will then appear in the active cell and on the formula bar. When you have finished typing data into a cell you should signal the end of that data by pressing the enter key. There are two basic types of information that can be entered into a worksheet: constants and formulae. The constants are of four types: numeric values, text values, date values, and time values. Two special types of constants, called logical values and error values, are also recognized by Excel but are not discussed in this textbook. Numeric values include only the digits 0–9 and some special characters such as:

| + | − | E | e | (|) | . | , | £ | % | / |

A numeric cell entry can maintain precision up to 15 digits. If you enter a number that is too long, Excel converts it to scientific notation. For example, if you type 97867985685859300, it will be stored as 97867985685859300, and displayed as 9.7868E+16. Sometimes, although the number is stored correctly in the cell, the cell is not wide enough to display it properly. In those cases, Excel will round the number off or display a string of # signs. To solve this problem increase the width of the column. A text entry can contain up to 32767 characters but only 1024 characters will display in the cell and all will be displayed in the formula bar. If the text you enter will not fit in the particular width of your cell, Excel lets it overlap the adjacent cell unless that cell already contains an entry, in which case the extra text can be thought of as being tucked behind the adjacent cell. By default, text is left-justified in a cell whereas numbers are right-justified.

1.2.1 Entering data in a cell

1. Select a cell in which you want to enter data.

	A	B	C
1	1	2	
2	2	3	
3	3	4	1
4	4	5	
5	5	5	

Figure 1.12

2. Type in the entry. The entry will appear in the formula bar as it is typed.

3. To enter what you have typed press the Return key, or click on the Green Tick to enter.

1.2.2 Modifying data in a cell

If you are in the process of entering data in a cell and you notice that you have made a mistake, it is easy to correct it. Press the Backspace key to delete a character to the left of the cursor or the Delete key to delete a character to the right of the cursor. If you want to edit the contents of a cell then you should double-click on the cell and make the required alterations either in the cell itself or on the formula bar. If you want to clear the cell of its contents (formula and data), formats, comments, or all three, you can select that cell with a single click of the left mouse button, select Clear from the Edit menu and then click on Contents, Formats, Comments, or All.

1.2.3 Entering data into a range

In Excel, any rectangular area of cells is known as a *range*. The range is defined by the top-left and bottom-right corner cell references separated by a colon (:). So, C8:G15 represents the range of cells cornered by C8 and G15. To enter the same data into a range of cells:

(a) Select the range.

(b) Enter the data.

(c) Hold down the CTRL key and press Return. All of the cells in the range should now contain the same data, or

- Select the cell containing the data.

- Move the mouse pointer to the bottom right corner of the cell until the pointer changes to a cross.

(d) Hold down the left mouse button and drag the cross in the direction you wish to fill, and then release the mouse button.

1.2.4 Cancelling a cell entry

To cancel a cell entry before you have pressed return, press the Escape key (Esc), or click on the red cross to cancel the entry.

C3		▾ X ✓ ƒ×	1
	A	B	C
1	1	2	
2	2	3	
3	3	4	1
4	4	5	
5	5	5	

Figure 1.13

1.2.5 Undoing a cell entry

To undo a cell entry after you have pressed the return key:

1. Click on Edit in the menu bar.

2. Click on Undo Entry from the drop down menu. The cell will be returned to its previous state.

1.2.6 Entering numbers

Numbers are constant values containing only the following characters: 1 2 3 4 5 6 7 8 9 0 − + / . E e £ $ % , ( ). Once a number has been entered into a cell, it may then be formatted by using the following buttons:

	Currency Style	Applies the currently defined Currency style to selected cells
%	Percent Style	Applies the currently defined Percent style to selected cells
,	Comma Style	Applies the currently defined Comma style to selected cells
	Increase Decimal place	Adds one decimal place to the number format each time you click the button
	Decrease Decimal place	Removes one decimal place from the number each time you click the button

1.2.7 Entering dates or times

If you type a date or time (e.g. 13/4/8 or 16:21) directly into a cell Excel should automatically recognize it as such and changes the cell formatting from general to the appropriate date or time format. The program will normally align it to the right of the cell and display it in the formula bar in a standard format (e.g. 13/04/2008 or 16:21:00).

If you type	Excel formatting
12/06/8	dd/mm/yy
12-June-8	dd-mmm-yy
31-Oct	dd-mmm
Oct 13 2008	Mmm d, yyyy
24/05/08 3:21	dd/mm/yy hh:mm
3:45 PM	h:mm AM/PM
3:35:30 PM	h:mm:ss AM/PM
13:50	hh:mm
13:50:35	hh:mm:ss

Table 1.3

The displayed formats in particular cells can be modified using Format > Cells > Number menu option. You can either choose a date format from the Category box or select Custom to define your own cell format. Regardless of how the date (or time) is displayed, the actual value stored in the cell is a long numeric value e.g. the date variable 13/04/2008 would be stored under general format as 39752.

1.2.8 Entering text

To enter text, select a cell and type the text. A cell can hold up to 255 characters. You can format the characters within a cell individually but note that if there are more than 255 characters in the cell then the cell will show '#########'. This problem can be resolved by applying text wrapping to the cell.

1.2.9 Formatting a worksheet

You can use many formatting options in Excel to add emphasis to your data, or make the worksheet easier to read. To apply cell formats you can either use the Toolbar or the Menu bar. You can change the format of the text by using the following parts of the toolbar:

• To apply or change font size

   1. Click on the down arrow to the right of the font size selection box ⌗ 10 ▾ .

   2. To select the size you require use the scroll bar arrows to move up or down the list of available sizes, then click on a number.

   3. The selected font size will appear in the font size box.

- To apply or change font type
    1. Click on the down arrow to the right of the font box ⊞ Times New Roman ▾ .
    2. To select the font you require use the scroll bar arrows to scroll through the list of available fonts, then click on a font type.
    3. The selected font type will appear in the font box.
- To bold text
    1. Click on ⒷButton on the tool bar to enable **bold** type.
    2. Enter text and click on Ⓑ button again to return to normal.
- To apply italic text
    1. Click on Ⓘ button on the tool bar to enable *Italic* type.
    2. Enter text and click on Ⓘ button again to return to normal.
- To apply underlined text
    1. Click on Ⓤ button on the tool bar to enable <u>Underlined</u> text.
    2. Enter text and click on Ⓤ button again to return to normal.
- Aligning text
    1. Highlight the cell.
    2. Click on one of the following alignment boxes in the toolbar, to apply the desired alignment:

▤	Left Alignment
▥	Centred
▦	Right Alignment
▧	Centre Across Columns (When a number of columns are highlighted)

1.2.10 Column widths and row heights

In a new worksheet all columns and rows are set to a standard size. Rows automatically adjust to the largest font entered into the row. You may need to adjust the column width if you are entering more than 8 characters.

- Column width

    You can format one or a number of columns in the following manner:

    1. Highlight the columns you wish to alter.
    2. Click on Fo_rmat from the menu bar.
    3. Select C_olumn from the drop down menu. An additional menu box will appear.
    4. Click on W_idth … The following box will appear.
    5. Enter the column width you require.
    6. Click on OK.

Figure 1.14

- Row height

To adjust the row height:

1. Select the rows.

2. Click on Format from the menu bar.

3. Select Row from the drop down menu. An additional menu box will appear.

4. Click on Height … The following box will appear.

Figure 1.15

5. Enter the row height you require.

6. Click on OK.

1.2.11   Naming a worksheet

The information on sheet1 might refer to a particular project. It would make sense to name the sheet (or worksheet) accordingly.

1. Right-click on sheet1.

2. Select Rename from the menu that appears.

3. Type your project name into the text box and press Enter key.

1.2.12   Inserting and deleting rows and columns

Extra rows and columns can be inserted whenever you wish. As an example, insert a row between row 8 and 9.

1. Click with the right mouse click on the row name 8.

2. Select Insert.

Now, try inserting a column between column B and C.

1. Click with the right mouse click on the column name B.

2. Select Insert.

To delete a row or column, right click on its name and select Delete from the menu which appears.

1.2.13   The clear command

When you use the Clear command you will clear the contents, formats, or notes but leave the cells on the worksheet. Unlike delete which removes the cell from the worksheet and the surrounding cells shift to take their place.

1. Select the range of cells you want to clear.

2. Click on Edit in the menu bar.

3. Select drop down menu and click on Clear. An additional menu box will appear.

4. Click on one of the following, depending on what you want to clear:

All	Removes contents, formats, and notes from the selected cells
Formats	Removes formats only, cell contents and notes are unchanged. Returns cells to a general format
Contents	Removes the contents from selected cells without affecting the formats or notes
Comments	Removes notes from selected cells, but leaves contents and formats intact

Table 1.4

1.2.14 Spell checking

Excel allows you to check the spelling of your work.

1. Select a cell with text.

2. Select the Spelling button on the toolbar .

If a spelling mistake is found Excel will prompt and provide an opportunity to correct the error.

1.2.15 AutoFormat

This applies a built in format (table) to a range of cells. To apply AutoFormat:

1. Highlight a range.

2. Click on Format in the menu bar.

3. Select drop down menu and click on AutoFormat. The following box will appear:

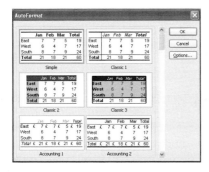

Figure 1.16

4. From the tableformat box highlight one of the formats, a sample of which will be shown in the Sample box.

5. Click on OK to apply the format.

1.3 Performing Calculations

Excel can be used to develop simple solutions to business data problems. The nature of these problems can be mathematical, statistical, and financial. This textbook will explore how you solve statistical problems using Excel.

1.3.1 Entering formulae

Using a formula can help you analyse data on a worksheet. With a formula you can perform operations, such as addition, multiplication, and comparison on worksheet values. Excel formulae always begin with an equals sign, e.g. =7/8, =3*5+4/7, =3*A3, and =A3*A3.

1. Select cell in which you want to enter formula.
2. Type an equals sign (=) to activate the formula bar. If you forget to type an equals sign the rest of the line will be treated as text.
3. Enter the formula.
4. Press Enter, or click on the Green Tick to the left of the formula bar.

1.3.2 Understanding operators

Table 1.5 shows some of the mathematical operators that can be used to create formulae:

%	Percent
^	Exponentiation
* and /	Multiplication and division
+ and −	Addition and subtraction (or negation when placed before a value i.e. -1)
&	Text joining
=	Equal
>	Greater than
<	Less than
>=	Greater than or equal to
<=	Less than or equal to
<>	Not equal to

Table 1.5

It should be noted that the list is listed in order of priority starting with Percent (highest priority) and ending with Comparisons (lowest priority) e.g. =, >,..., <>. If you want to alter the order of priority, use parentheses (brackets) to group expressions, e.g. (i) 9 + 3/2 is equal to 10.5 and not equal to 6, (ii) (9+3)/2 is equal to 6.

1.3.3 Selecting cells and moving around worksheet

Selecting a cell

To select a cell:

1. Position the cursor over the cell.
2. Click the left mouse button once.

The cell will then become highlighted with a dark border, with the cell reference number appearing in the upper left portion of the screen.

Selecting a range of cells

If you wish to select more than one cell in a work sheet:

1. Click on the first cell in the range.
2. Holding the left mouse button down, drag the cursor to the last cell in the range and release the mouse button. The area of the range will be highlighted.

Select an entire row

Click the cursor in the row heading i.e. the numbers running down the left hand side of the worksheet.

Select an entire column

Click the cursor in the column heading i.e. the alphabetic letters on the top of the worksheet.

Select all the cells within a worksheet

Click on the Select All button. The entire worksheet will then become highlighted.

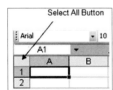

Figure 1.17

1.3.4 Reference operators

There are three types of reference operators: *Range, Union,* and *Intersection.*

Range (Colon :)

Produces one reference to all the cells between and including the two references.

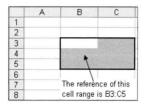

Figure 1.18

Union (Comma ,)

Produces one reference that includes the two references.

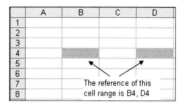

Figure 1.19

Intersection (Space)

Produces one reference to cells common to the two references.

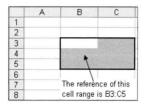

Figure 1.20

1.3.5 Editing a formula

To edit an existing formula:

1. Click on the cell containing the formula. The formula will then appear in the formula bar.

2. Press the F2 function key. You may now edit the formula, or position the cursor in the formula bar at the point you wish to change.

3. Press the Return key.

1.3.6 Creating and applying names

Names make formulae easier to read, understand, and maintain. You can change or delete names that have been defined previously and define a constant or computed value that you intend to use later. Names appear in the reference area of the formula bar when you select a named cell or an entire named range. In the example below we will name the monthly sales data in cells C3:E3 and name this range Sales_Quarterly.

1. Select the Range you wish to name e.g. C3:E3

	A	B	C	D	E
1					
2			January	February	March
3		Sales	£234,000	£456,000	£120,000
4		Expenses	£124,000	£30,900	£234,000
5		Profit	£110,000	£425,100	-£114,000

Figure 1.21

2. Click on Insert from the menu bar.

3. Select drop down menu and click on Name. An additional menu box will appear.

4. Click on Define.

5. Enter the name to be applied to the range e.g. Sales_Quarterly.

6. Click on the Add button. The name is then added to the workbook's list of names.

7. Click on OK.

The name may then be used in a formula, instead of using the cell locations and is easier to interpret and remember, e.g. SUM(Sales_Quarterly) instead of SUM(C3:E3).

1.3.7 Copying formulae to adjacent cells

Rather than retyping a formula in each of the adjacent cells it is much more convenient to copy the formulae across.

1. Position the cursor over the cell containing the formula.

2. Hold down the left mouse button and drag the cursor across the cells so that they become highlighted.

3. Click on Edit in the menu bar.

4. Select drop down menu and click on Fill. An additional menu box will appear.

5. Click on the direction you have highlighted, e.g. If you have highlighted to the left click on Left. If you have highlighted to the right click on Right.

1.3.8 Using absolute and relative references

The $ sign in a cell will tell Excel how to treat your references when copying the content of a cell. To illustrate this concept consider what happens to the following formulae in Cell C14 that are copied to D15:

- =C14 becomes =D15
- =$C14 becomes =$C15
- =C$14 becomes =D$14
- =$C$14 becomes =$C$14

This simple example illustrates the $ sign acts as an 'anchor' to fix the row number or column letter. You will find when creating a spreadsheet solution (or model) that a term in the equation can be considered to be constant. To illustrate this concept consider an example where you would like to calculate price (p) based upon demand for a product

(d) where the relationship between price and demand is given by the equation p = 2d. We can see that no matter what the value of p, or d, the number 2 does not change. The number 2 is fixed (or constant) and in a spreadsheet this value would be fixed using the $ sign.

Example 1.1

Consider solving this problem for price when the demand undergoes a unit change from 1–4.

We can see from the equation in cell B2 that price =2*A2. When we copy the formula down then the price is calculated for a demand change from 1, 2, 3, and 4.

B2		fx	=2*A2
	A	B	C
1	Demand	Price	
2	1	2	
3	2	4	
4	3	6	
5	4	8	

Figure 1.22

Example 1.2

This same problem can be solved by fixing the value of the number 2 in the spreadsheet (cell C3) shown. In this case the price in cell C7 is given by the formula price =C3*B7. When we copy the formula down from C7 to C10 the price value is calculated for the demand change.

We note from the spreadsheet solution that the price in cell C8 is zero and not the correct value of 4. Inspecting the equation in cell C8 we note that the formula is price =C4*B8. The B8 reference is correct but C4 is incorrect and should read C3, which represents the position of the number 2.

C7		fx	=C3*B7
	A	B	C
1			
2			
3		Constant =	2
4			
5			
6		Demand	Price
7		1	2
8		2	0
9		3	0
10		4	#VALUE!

Figure 1.23

Example 1.3

To solve this problem we fix the cell position of the number 2 and we achieve this using the Excel $ sign. Therefore, in cell C7 we insert the correct price equation =$C$3*B7.

The use of $C$3 is to fix the value of the number 2. If we now copy the formula down from C7 to C10 we can now see that we have the correct values for price based upon changing demand.

C7		fx	=$C$3*B7
	A	B	C
1			
2			
3		Constant =	2
4			
5			
6		Demand	Price
7		1	2
8		2	4
9		3	6
10		4	8

Figure 1.24

1.3.9 IF function

The *IF* function is very useful in solving numerical problems and enables the user to ask questions of the type 'Is this true or false' and then undertake a particular action.

The technique can be illustrated by exploring the marks for two examination tests in which the tutor would like to find out which students obtained a higher mark for test 1 compared to test 2.

Student	Test 1	Test 2
A	46	56
B	67	65
C	34	67
D	78	66

This problem can be solved by using the IF function.

→ Excel function

=IF(condition, value_if_true, value_if_false)

To solve this problem we insert the data into Excel (Figure 1.25). Test 1 (C4:C7) and Test 2 (D4:D7). In cell E4, insert =IF(c4>d4,"Larger","Smaller"). This will place the text 'Smaller' in cell E4 (46 < 56).

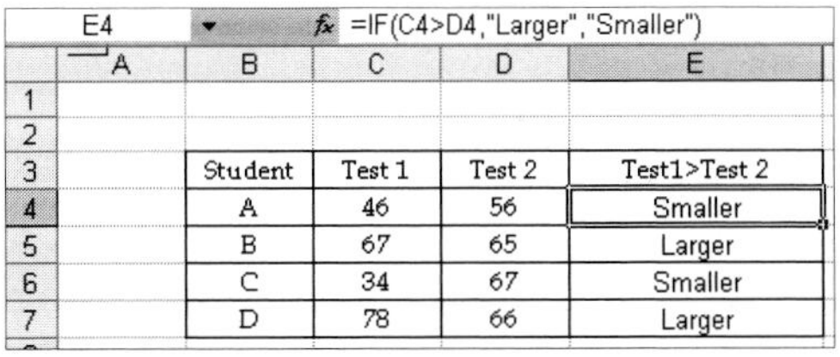
E4 fx =IF(C4>D4,"Larger","Smaller")

	A	B	C	D	E
1					
2					
3		Student	Test 1	Test 2	Test1>Test 2
4		A	46	56	Smaller
5		B	67	65	Larger
6		C	34	67	Smaller
7		D	78	66	Larger

Figure 1.25

Now complete for the other three students by copying the formula down from cell E4 to E7.

Interpretation Two students (B and D) obtained higher marks for test 1 compared to test 2.

1.3.10 Adding a column of numbers using AutoSum

To add the demand values together from example 1.3 we can make use of the Excel AutoSum function.

1. Click in B7.

2. Click on the AutoSum button on the toolbar Σ ▾. The AutoSum suggests a range that is to be summed, in this case B7:B10.

3. Press the Enter key.

You can achieve this by using the Excel function SUM e.g. total demand =SUM(B7:B10). The use of Excel functions will be explored briefly in the next section and in detail throughout the textbook.

1.3.11 What if analysis

What-if analysis in Microsoft Excel can be used to check what happens if you modify a value in a formula. For example, what-if analysis can be used to modify a student module mark given a recent change to the mark after external examiner comments, or, what would happen to the profit/loss account if we modified a particular variable cost.

> ▷ **Example 1.4**
>
> To illustrate this concept consider the situation where a student would like to achieve an A grade in an economics module. The student requires a minimum overall mark of 70% with the module assessments consisting of three parts with individual weights: in course assignment 1 (weight 25%), in course assignment 2 (weight 25%), and end examination (weight 50%). The student has received the assignment marks and was awarded 66% and 72% respectively. What mark will the student need to obtain from the examination to achieve an A grade? To solve this problem the student set up a simple Excel worksheet with the two assignment marks included and the overall mark calculated from the stated formula (value in cell E6 and formula in cell F6).

	E6	▾	f_x =0.25*B6+0.25*C6+0.5*D6		
	A	B	C	D	E	F
1	Grade calculation for economics module					
2						
3						
4		Assign 1	Assign 2	Exam	Overall	
5						
6		66	72	71	70	=0.25*B6+0.25*C6+0.5*D6

Figure 1.26

Click in cell D6 and enter a series of examination mark values, one at a time:

- Examination mark 90%. The effect of this change will be to ripple through the worksheet formulae. In this case, the overall mark is now 79.5%. In this case the student would achieve an A grade (>70%) but the student would have to obtain more marks in the examination (90%) than is required to achieve an A grade (70% +).

- Examination mark 70%. This would achieve an overall mark of 69.5%, or 70%, if the examination board rules allow for rounding up to 70%. If we are in doubt we could modify the examination mark to 71%.

- Examination mark 71%. This would achieve the required overall mark of 70% and the student would achieve an A grade.

1.3.12 Insert function

Excel provides the user with a range of built in functions which will allow a range of statistical techniques to be applied to a data set. A range of functions will be employed in later chapters but for the time being we will be content with being able to call the function, Select Insert > Select Function (see Figure 1.27). You can find a detailed list of all the Excel functions in Chapter 2.

Figure 1.27

1.3.13 Copying formulae and values

To copy formulae and values use the copy 📄 and paste 📋 buttons on your Formatting toolbar.

1.3.14 Excel arrays

In earlier sections formulae were input into a cell and then copied to adjacent cells by using relative cell references. An alternative method is to use an Excel array formula which allows a formula to be input once and would be copied to the cells within the array. This topic is discussed in Section 2.2.2.

1.3.15 Install Excel ToolPak add-ins

Together with individual functions, Excel provides the Data Analysis ToolPak add-in. To install this add-in Select Tools > Add-ins.

Figure 1.28

Choose Analysis ToolPak, and Click OK.

When installed you will find an extra menu on the Tools menu in Excel called Data Analysis. This will be used to conduct a range of statistical tests.

1.4 Presenting Results

This section explores the methods used to insert a worksheet or chart into your word processed report. The information provided below assumes that you are planning to insert into Microsoft Word.

1.4.1 Inserting Excel features into Microsoft Word

Inserting a Worksheet

You may insert Excel worksheets into a Word document:

1. Open Microsoft Word.
2. Click on Insert in the menu bar.
3. Select drop down menu and click on Object. The following menu will appear:

Figure 1.29

4. Click on the Create from File tab. The following menu will appear:

Figure 1.30

5. Find and select the file that contains your worksheet and/or chart.

6. Click on OK. The worksheet will appear in your document.

1.4.2 Inserting a chart from an Excel worksheet into Microsoft Word

A chart is a graphical representation of the data in your spreadsheet. You can create an embedded chart, which appears on the worksheet beside the data, or, you can create a chart sheet as a separate sheet in the workbook. The use of Excel charts will be explored in detail in Chapter 3. Once you have created a chart within Excel it is then possible to export it into another application such as Microsoft Word. The chart in the Word document will be automatically updated every time a change is made in the Excel document.

1. Ensure that Excel and the file containing the data and chart is open and displayed on the screen.

2. Click on the chart you wish to appear in the Word document.

3. Click on Edit in the menu bar.

4. From the drop down menu click on Copy.

5. Click on the minimise button ⁻ in the top right hand corner of the screen.

6. Open MS Word.

7. Open the document you wish to insert the chart into.

8. Position the cursor at the point you wish the chart to appear.

9. Select Paste Special. The following menu box will appear:

Figure 1.31

10. Click on the circle next to Paste Link. This will establish a link between the Word document and the Excel worksheet that the chart is being copied from, allowing the automatic updating of the chart.

11. Click on OK. The chart will now be displayed in the document at the chosen location.

🖱 Student Exercises

Which of the following answers are correct for the questions X1.1–X1.3?

X 1.1 The cell entry =SUM(V5:V23):

(a) Computes the sum of cells V5 and V23

(b) Computes the sum of cells V5, V^, V&..., V22, V23

(c) Computes the sumproduct for cells V5 and V23

(d) None of the above

X1.2 The Save command undertakes the following operation:

(a) Stores the workbook on the storage device

(b) Opens a workbook from the identified location on the storage device

(c) Deletes a workbook already saved on the storage device

(d) Copies and saves the new workbook on the storage device

X1.3 A formula containing the reference =C$9 is copied to a cell three columns across and 8 rows down. How will the cell entry appear in its new location?

(a) =%G13

(b) =G13

(c) =F$9

(d) =C13

Use the worksheet below to answer questions X1.4–X1.8

	A	B	C	D	E	F
1	Year 1 Module Results for Econometrics Cohort 1					
2	Exercise X1.4 - X1.8					
3						
4		Student	ICA1 (25% weight)	ICA2 (25% weight)	Exam (50% weight)	Overall
5		Adams, Joe	63	58	76	68.25
6		Buckton, Mike	42	62	54	53.00
7		Alonso, Fred	67	76	63	67.25
8		Grangou, Kate	72	67	78	73.75
9		Jacobson, Sarah	54	56	52	53.50
10		Juninho, Glyn	80	76	81	79.50
11						
12		Module average =	63.00	65.83	67.33	65.88

Figure 1.32

X1.4 Fred Alonso's overall mark is calculated from the formula?

(a) =0.25*E7

(b) =0.25*C7+0.25*D7+0.5*E7

(c) =0.25*D7+0.25*E7+0.5*D7

(d) =0.5*E10

X1.5 The contribution to Sarah Jacobson's overall mark from the in-course assessments can be calculated from the formula?

    (a) =0.25*(C9–D9)

    (b) =0.25*E9+0.25*D9

    (c) =0.25*C9+0.25*D9

    (d) =0.5*E9–0.25*C9–0.25*D9

X1.6 The formula to calculate the average for the first in-course assessment (ICA1) is given by the formula?

    (a) =(C5+C6+C7+C8+C9+C10)/6

    (b) =(C5+C6+D7+C8+C9+C10)/6

    (c) =(D5+D6+D7+D8+D9+D10)/6

    (d) =(C5+C6+C7+C8+C9+C10)/F12

X1.7 The formula to calculate the overall average is given by the formula?

    (a) =SUM(F5:F9)/6

    (b) =SUM(F5:F10)

    (c) =SUM(F5:F10)/6

    (d) =SUM(C12:E12)

X1.8 What happens to Joe's overall average if his examination mark is changed to 81% after an assessment appeal?

Use the worksheet below to answer questions X1.9–X1.12

	A	B	C	D	E	F	G	H	I
1	Exercise X1.9 - X1.12 Staff Pay								
2									
3		Assumptions:							
4		Income tax =	20%						
5		NI =	6%						
6		Pay rate =	£7						
7		Overtime rate =	£10.00						
8									
9		Staff name	Employee ID	Hours	Overtime	Gross	Income Tax	National Insurance	Net Pay
10									
11		Adamson, K	S101	36	1	£262.00	£52.40	£15.72	£193.88
12		Bradburn, P	S102	36	5	£302.00	£60.40	£18.12	£223.48
13		Fredson, D	S103	36	2	£272.00	£54.40	£16.32	£201.28
14		Jacobson, K	S104	36	3	£282.00	£56.40	£16.92	£208.68
15		Kano, T	S105	36	4	£292.00	£58.40	£17.52	£216.08

Figure 1.33

X1.9 The gross pay formula in cell F13 is calculated using the formula:

    (a) =$C6*D11+$C$7*E13

    (b) =$C$6*D13+$C$7*E13

    (c) =$C$6*D13+$C$7*E11

    (d) =$C$6*D13–$C$7*E13

X1.10 If we modify the overtime hours for K Jacobson from 3 to 8 hours what is the change in overall tax payable?

(a) £50

(b) £67

(c) £10

(d) £80

X1.11 The income tax rate and national insurance tax have both been increased to 21% and 7% respectively. K Adamson's net pay will now be:

(a) £217.44

(b) £188.64

(c) £302.00

(d) £243.66

X1.12 K Adamson requests that her pay earned in exercise X1.11 is paid in euros. The currency rate on Friday 16th May 2008 is £1: 1.25935 euro. How much will K Adamson receive?

(a) €149.79

(b) €137.56

(c) €329.95

(d) €237.56

■ Techniques in Practice

1. Coco S.A. supplies a range of computer hardware and software to 2000 schools within a large municipal region of Spain. Coco S.A. uses Microsoft Excel to manage data and undertake a range of statistical analyses of the company's data sets, including:

- Storing company data in Excel workbooks.
- Run queries to sort and filter data.
- Share Excel workbooks between staff members.
- Undertake the creation of statistical reports.
- Use Excel templates to visually present data in summary form so that managers can make quick and effective decisions.

2. Bakers Ltd runs a chain of bakery shops and is famous for the quality of its pies. Bakers Ltd uses Microsoft Excel to manage data and undertake a range of statistical analyses of the company's data sets, including:

- Store financial data on company performance e.g. company payroll.
- Undertake financial forecasting and planning using financial and time series analysis.

3. Skodel Ltd is a small brewery which is undergoing a major expansion after a take-over by a large European brewery chain. Skodel Ltd produces a range of beers and lagers and is renowned for the quality of its beers; winning a number of prizes at trade fairs throughout the European Union. Skodel Ltd uses Microsoft Excel to manage data and undertake a range of statistical analyses of the company's data sets, including:

- Store personnel details.
- Calculate employee monthly pay based upon normal and overtime hours worked.
- Undertake what-if analysis using a range of statistical and financial functions.

■ Summary

This chapter provided the reader with an introduction to the Microsoft Excel spreadsheet that will be required in later chapters to aid understanding in using Excel to undertake the statistical analysis of data sets. The chapter answered the question of what a spreadsheet is used for and described the basic techniques used to apply spreadsheet skills to particular problems. The skills covered in this chapter included: creating a new workbook and worksheets, entering data into worksheet cells, formatting cells, and entering formula to allow what-if analysis. In the next chapter we will provide the reader with a refresher course in mathematics.

■ Key Terms

Absolute reference	Double-click	List box
Alignment	Drag	Maximize
Analysis ToolPak	Drag-and-drop	Menu bar
Cell	Drop-down list	Merge cells
Cell pointer	Exit	Minimize
Cell range	File menu	Mouse pointer
Cell reference	File name	Move command
Check box	Format cells	Name box
Clear	Formatting toolbar	Number format
Click	Formula	Office assistant
Close	Formula bar	OK button
Constant	Function	Page setup
Copy command	General format	Percentage format
Currency format	Help	Print command
Custom format	Home tab	Question-mark button
Date format	IF	Range
Delete	Insert command	Relative reference
Dialog box	Launch button	Right-click

Save As command	Spreadsheet	Time format
Save command	Standard toolbar	Toolbars
Scientific format	Status bar	Undo command
Scroll bars	Tab	Workbook
Select	Task pane	Worksheet
Sheet tab	Text format	Workspace area
Split cells		

■ Further Reading

Textbook Resources

1. Grauer, R. and Barber, M. (2007) *Exploring Microsoft Excel 2003* (10th Edition). Pearson. ISBN: 9780131791237.

2. Reisner, T. (2003) *Sams Teach Yourself Microsoft Office Excel 2003 in 24 Hours*. Pearson. ISBN: 9780672325519.

Web Resources

1. Microsoft Office Excel Official web site http://office.microsoft.com/en-us/excel/FX100487621033.aspx.

2. Excel User http://www.exceluser.com/index.htm.

3. Vertex 42—range of Excel templates http://www.vertex42.com.

Numerical Skills Revision

The aim of this chapter is to provide the reader with a set of tools which can be used to study the topics in this book and will be useful to you throughout your studies. This chapter will allow you to apply a range of mathematical tools that can be used to solve a range of business related problems. These business problems range from calculating percentages to modelling the relationship between one variable and another variable via fitting a line to a data set. For the reader who requires practice in the topics described in this chapter you will find a numerical skills workbook online.

» Overview «

In this chapter we shall look at a range of methods that will be useful in helping us to solve problems using Excel, including: solving number and algebraic problems, using Excel mathematical and statistical functions.

» Learning Objectives «

On successful completion of this chapter, you will be able to:

- » Feel confident in using notation and symbols to represent variables.
- » Use Excel to solve number problems.
- » Identify and apply a range of Excel functions to solve algebraic problems.
- » Identify and apply a range of Excel functions to solve mathematical problems.
- » Identify and apply a range of Excel functions to solve statistical problems.
- » Solve a series of financial problems using Excel functions.
- » Use Excel to plot straight line graphs.
- » Identify and use Excel to fit an equation to line data points.

2.1 Excel and Solving Algebraic Problems

In this section we will explore the concept of a power of a number using Excel to solve a range of problems.

2.1.1 Excel scientific notation

When you enter numbers into an Excel cell which has more than 12 characters (e.g. 563728193324423000) then Excel will display the number using scientific notation. Figure 2.1 illustrates this process using the number example 563728193324423000.

> ### ▷ Example 2.1
>
> We can see from the screenshot that the number is displayed as 5.63728E+17. The cell will still display using scientific notation even if you modify the cell width. The E+17 is just shorthand for 'move the decimal places 17 places to the right'.
>
> | B2 | ▼ | _fx_ | 563728193324423000 |
> | --- | --- | --- | --- |
> | | A | B | C | D |
> | 1 | | | | |
> | 2 | | 5.63728E+17 | | |
>
> Figure 2.1

> 📎 **Note**   To display the number in a format other than scientific notation, you need to reformat the cell(s):
>
> 1. Select the cells that will hold the larger values.
> 2. Right-click the selection.
> 3. Select Format.
> 4. Select Cells.
> 5. In the Number tab, select the desired format (e.g. number) but change Decimal places to zero.
> 6. Click OK.

2.1.2 Squares

The square of a number is that number multiplied by itself. For example, consider the term 'three squared' which is written as 3 x 3 = 9. This can be written using power notation as 3 to the power 2 or $3^2 = 3 \times 3 = 9$.

Example 2.2

Calculate the square of the number 0.3?

$$(0.3)^2 = 0.3 \times 0.3 = 0.09$$

Example 2.3

Excel uses the symbol ^ to calculate the power of a number. The value of the power term when we square a number is 2. In the example we have number 0.3 in cell B2 and in cell B3 we have the value of the square of 0.3 which equals 0.09. The formula in cell B3 is =B2^2.

B3		▾	f_x =B2^2
	A	B	
1			
2		0.3	
3	Value =	0.09	=B2^2

Figure 2.2

→ **Excel Formula Method**

Square = Cell B3   Formula: =B2^2

Excel has a function called POWER that enables you to calculate the power of any number. Repeating Example 2.3 using POWER gives the value of the square of 0.3 as 0.09.

B3		▾	f_x =POWER(B2,2)
	A	B	C
1			
2		0.3	
3	Value =	0.09	=POWER(B2,2)

Figure 2.3

→ **Excel Function Method**

Square = Cell B3   Function: =POWER(B2,2)

2.1.3 Square roots

The sign $\sqrt{}$ means 'the square root of', and you must find a number which when multiplied by itself gives the answer in the sign.

Example 2.4

$$\sqrt{16} = \sqrt{4 \times 4} = 4$$

👆 Example 2.5

$$\sqrt{0.25} = \sqrt{\frac{25}{100}} = \frac{\sqrt{25}}{\sqrt{100}} = \frac{5}{10} = 0.5$$

👆 Example 2.6

We can use Excel to calculate the square root of 16 which is written using mathematical notation as $\sqrt{16}$.

Excel uses the function SQRT to calculate the square root of a number. In the example we have number 16 in cell B2 and in cell B3 we have the value of the square root of 16 which equals 4. The formula in cell B3 is =SQRT(B2).

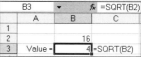

Figure 2.4

The value of the power term when we calculate the square root is the number 1/2. If we use Excel and substitute this formula =B2^(1/2) for the square root we would still obtain the answer 4.

➡ Excel Function Method

Square Root = Cell B3   Formula: =SQRT(B2)

2.1.4 Indices or the power of a number

The index is the power of a number. The number 2^3 is said 'two to the power three' or 'two cubed' and means $2 * 2 * 2 = 8$. The number 3^2 is said 'three to the power two' or 'three squared' and means $3 * 3 = 9$. We could use the method described earlier to calculate 2^3 or we could use the Excel function called POWER to undertake the calculation.

👆 Example 2.7

Excel uses the symbol ^ to calculate the power of a number.

The value of the power term in this example is 3. In the example we have number 2 in cell B2 and in cell B3 we have the value of the cube of 2 which equals 8. The formula in cell B3 is =B2^3 (see Figure 2.5).

The alternative method is to use the Excel function POWER. In cell B2 we have number 2, which we want to take to the power 3, which is in cell C2. The result is given in cell B3, and this is 8 (see Figure 2.6).

Figure 2.5

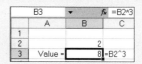

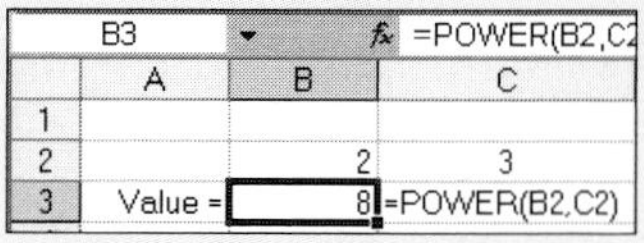

Figure 2.6

→ **Excel Function Method**

Power = Cell B3   Formula: =POWER(B2,C2)

Note   Square root is an inverse function of the power function.

For readers who are interested in practising their skills in solving these types of problems you can find extra notes and exercises within the numerical skills workbook available online.

Student Exercises

X2.1 Use Excel to solve: (a) 3^3 (b) 3^{-3} (c) $16^{\frac{1}{2}}$ (d) $32^{\frac{1}{5}}$.

2.2 Excel Mathematical and Statistical Functions

Excel provides a range of mathematical and statistical functions that we will use within
later chapters of this textbook. A list of these functions is provided below together with
examples of their use:

2.2.1 Mathematical functions

Excel contains a range of mathematical functions that are useful in solving business related problems:

Excel Function	Description
ABS	Returns the absolute value of a number. Consider calculating the absolute value of −4. We can see from the Excel function that ABS(−4) = 4. 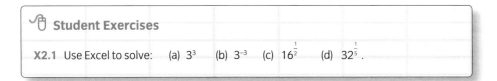 Figure 2.7

Excel Function	Description
COMBIN	Returns the number of combinations for a given number of objects. Consider calculating the number of times that you can pair 2 from a total of 4 numbers. We can see from Excel that COMBIN(4,2) = 6. 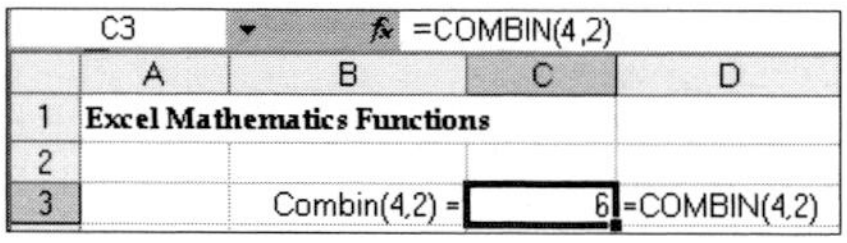 Figure 2.8
DEVSQ	Returns the sum of squares of deviations of data points from their sample mean, DEVSQ = $\sum \left(x - \overline{x} \right)^2$. We can see from Excel that DEVSQ(1,2,3) = 2. 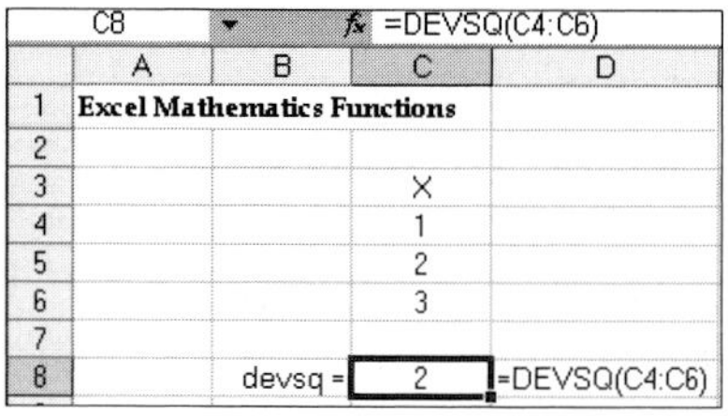 Figure 2.9
FACT	Returns the factorial of a number. Consider calculating factorial 4 = 4 * 3 * 2 * 1. We can see from Excel that FACT(4) = 24. 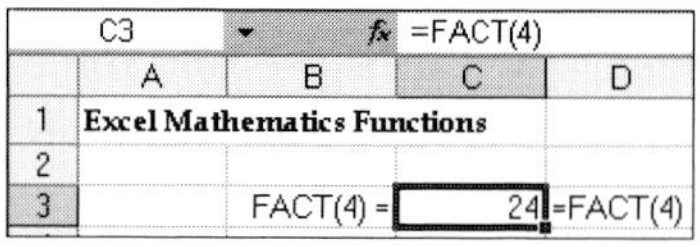 Figure 2.10
INT	Rounds a number down to the nearest integer. Consider calculating INT(2.3). We can see from Excel that INT(2.3) = 2. 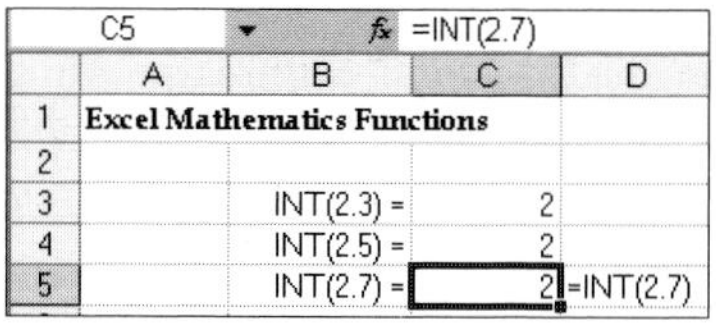 Figure 2.11
LN	Returns the natural logarithm of a number. Consider calculating LOG(4). We can see from Excel that LOG(4) = 1.386294. 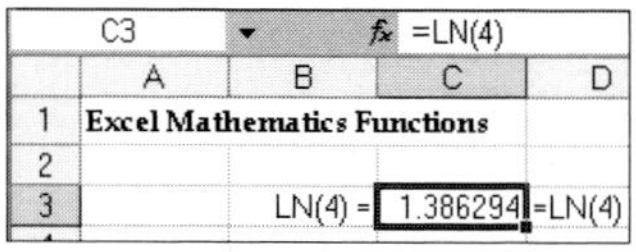 Figure 2.12
LOG	Returns the log of a number to the base you specify. Consider calculating LOG(10,10). We can see from Excel that LOG(10,10) = 1. 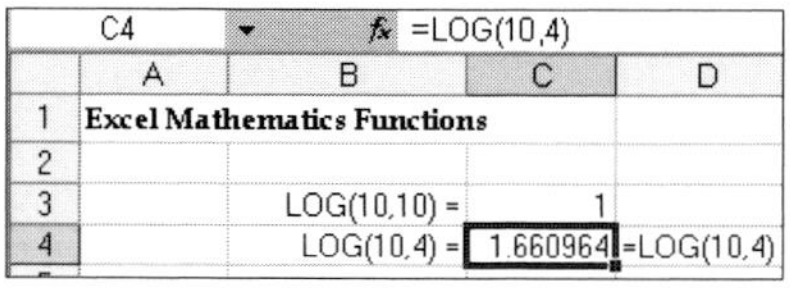 Figure 2.13

Excel Function	Description
LOG10	Returns the base-10 logarithm of a number. Consider calculating LOG10(10). We can see from Excel that LOG10(10) = 1.
	Figure 2.14
PI( )	Returns the value of π. The Excel function PI () is accurate to 15 digits and requires no arguments in the function.
	Figure 2.15
Power	Returns the result of a number raised to a power. Consider calculating 4^3. This can be written in Excel notation as 4 to the power 3 = 4 * 4 * 4. We can see from Excel that POWER(4,3) = 64.
	Figure 2.16
SQRT	Returns a positive square root. Consider calculating the square root of 16. We can see from Excel that SQRT(16) = 4.
	Figure 2.17
SUM	Adds all the numbers in a range of cells. Consider calculating the sum of the numbers 4, 6, 7. These numbers have been inserted into Excel in cells C3, C4, and C5 respectively. We can see from Excel that SUM(C3:C5) = 17.
	Figure 2.18

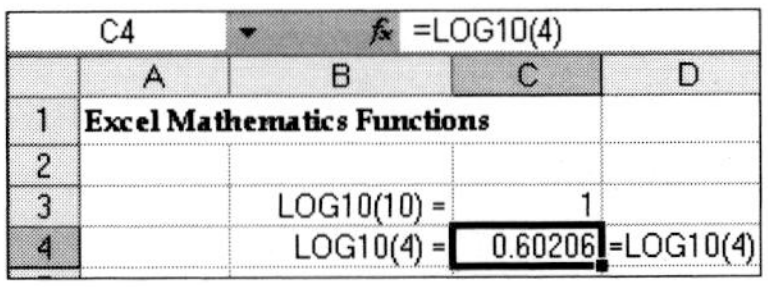

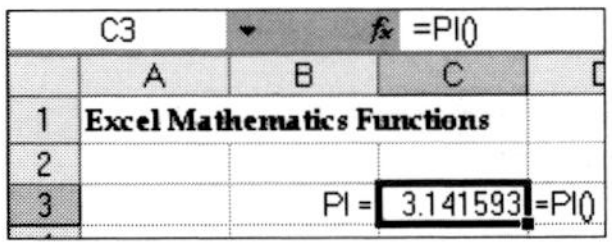

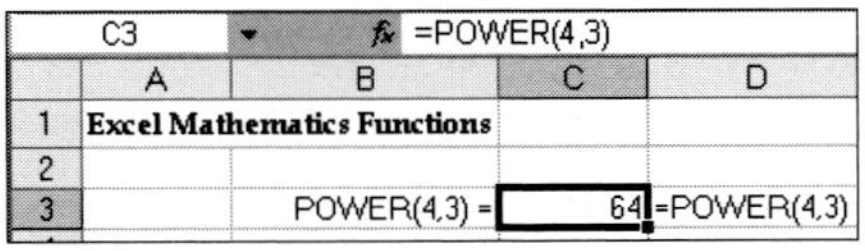

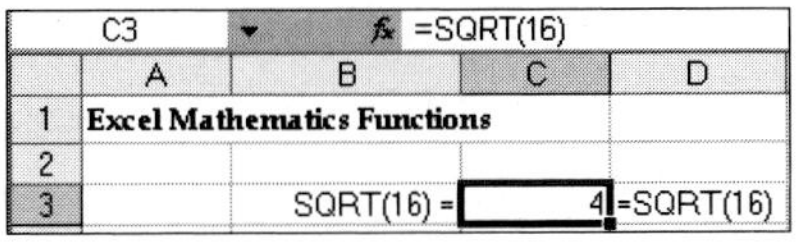

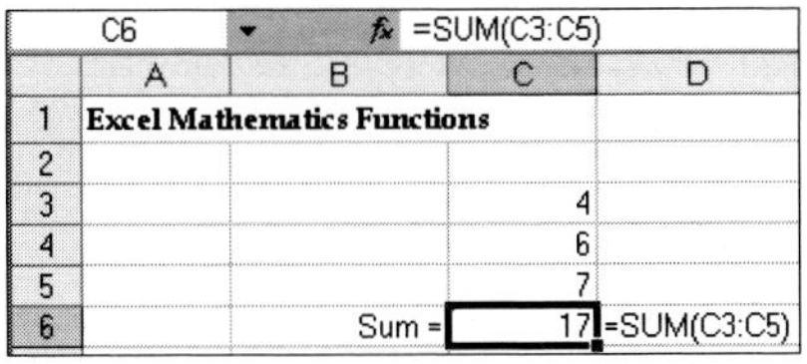

<table>
<tr><th>Excel Function</th><th>Description</th></tr>
<tr><td>SUMPRODUCT</td><td>Multiplies corresponding components in the given arrays, and returns the sum of those products. Consider calculating the SUMPRODUCT for the two arrays X: 1, 2, 3, 4 and Y: 3, 2, 3, 2. These numbers have been inserted into Excel in cells B4:B7 and C4:C7. We can see from Excel that SUMPRODUCT(B4:B7,C4:C7) = 24.

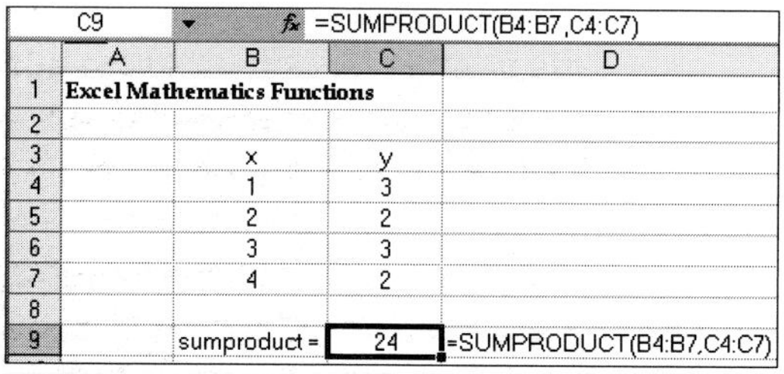
C9 =SUMPRODUCT(B4:B7,C4:C7)
<table><tr><th></th><th>A</th><th>B</th><th>C</th><th>D</th></tr><tr><td>1</td><td>Excel Mathematics Functions</td><td></td><td></td><td></td></tr><tr><td>2</td><td></td><td></td><td></td><td></td></tr><tr><td>3</td><td></td><td>x</td><td>y</td><td></td></tr><tr><td>4</td><td></td><td>1</td><td>3</td><td></td></tr><tr><td>5</td><td></td><td>2</td><td>2</td><td></td></tr><tr><td>6</td><td></td><td>3</td><td>3</td><td></td></tr><tr><td>7</td><td></td><td>4</td><td>2</td><td></td></tr><tr><td>8</td><td></td><td></td><td></td><td></td></tr><tr><td>9</td><td></td><td>sumproduct =</td><td>24</td><td>=SUMPRODUCT(B4:B7,C4:C7)</td></tr></table>
Figure 2.19</td></tr>
<tr><td>SUMSQ</td><td>Returns the sum of the squares of the arguments. Consider calculating the SUMSQ for the two numbers 3 and 5. These numbers have been inserted into Excel in cells B4:B5. We can see from Excel that SUMSQ(B4:B5) = 34.

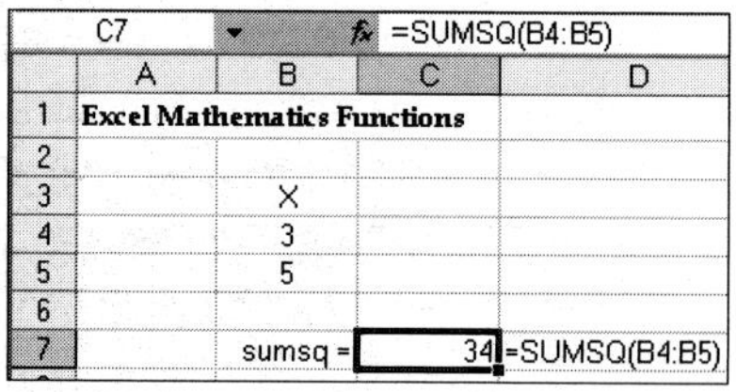
C7 =SUMSQ(B4:B5)
<table><tr><th></th><th>A</th><th>B</th><th>C</th><th>D</th></tr><tr><td>1</td><td>Excel Mathematics Functions</td><td></td><td></td><td></td></tr><tr><td>2</td><td></td><td></td><td></td><td></td></tr><tr><td>3</td><td></td><td>X</td><td></td><td></td></tr><tr><td>4</td><td></td><td>3</td><td></td><td></td></tr><tr><td>5</td><td></td><td>5</td><td></td><td></td></tr><tr><td>6</td><td></td><td></td><td></td><td></td></tr><tr><td>7</td><td></td><td>sumsq =</td><td>34</td><td>=SUMSQ(B4:B5)</td></tr></table>
Figure 2.20</td></tr>
<tr><td>SUMX2MY2</td><td>Returns the sum of the difference of squares of corresponding values in two arrays, SUMX2MY2 = $\sum\left(X^2 - Y^2\right)$. Consider calculating the SUMX2MY2 for the two arrays X: 1, 2, 3, 4 and Y: 3, 2, 3, 2. These numbers have been inserted into Excel in cells B4:B7 and C4:C7. We can see from Excel that SUMX2MY2(B4:B7,C4:C7) = 4.

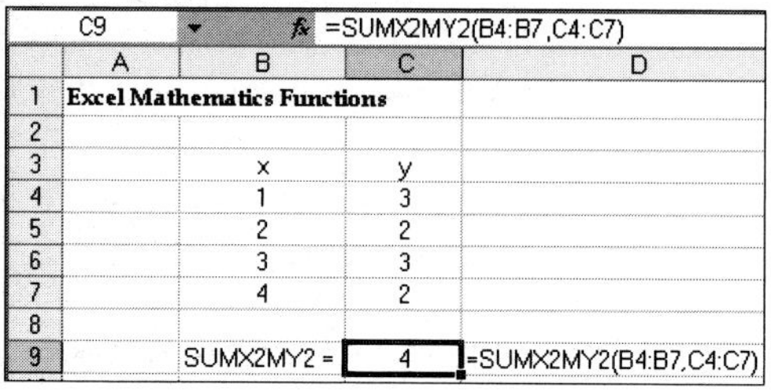
C9 =SUMX2MY2(B4:B7,C4:C7)
<table><tr><th></th><th>A</th><th>B</th><th>C</th><th>D</th></tr><tr><td>1</td><td>Excel Mathematics Functions</td><td></td><td></td><td></td></tr><tr><td>2</td><td></td><td></td><td></td><td></td></tr><tr><td>3</td><td></td><td>x</td><td>y</td><td></td></tr><tr><td>4</td><td></td><td>1</td><td>3</td><td></td></tr><tr><td>5</td><td></td><td>2</td><td>2</td><td></td></tr><tr><td>6</td><td></td><td>3</td><td>3</td><td></td></tr><tr><td>7</td><td></td><td>4</td><td>2</td><td></td></tr><tr><td>8</td><td></td><td></td><td></td><td></td></tr><tr><td>9</td><td></td><td>SUMX2MY2 =</td><td>4</td><td>=SUMX2MY2(B4:B7,C4:C7)</td></tr></table>
Figure 2.21</td></tr>
</table>

Excel Function	Description
SUMX2PY2	Returns the sum of the sum of squares of corresponding values in two arrays, $SUMX2PY2 = \sum\left(X^2 + Y^2\right)$. The sum of the sum of squares is a common term in many statistical calculations. Consider calculating the SUMX2PY2 for the two arrays X: 1, 2, 3, 4 and Y: 3, 2, 3, 2. These numbers have been inserted into Excel in cells B4:B7 and C4:C7. We can see from Excel that SUMX2PY2(B4:B7,C4:C7) = 56. 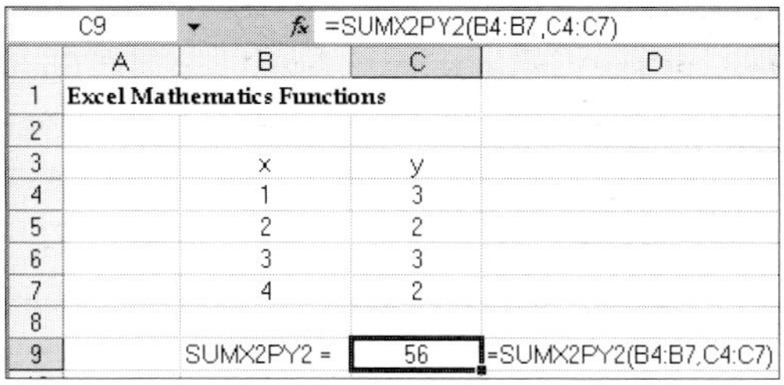

Figure 2.22

Excel Function	Description
SUMXMY2	Returns the sum of squares of differences of corresponding values in two arrays, $SUMXMY2 = \sum\left(X - Y\right)^2$. Consider calculating the SUMXMY2 for the two arrays X: 1, 2, 3, 4 and Y: 3, 2, 3, 2. These numbers have been inserted into Excel in cells B4:B7 and C4:C7. We can see from Excel that SUMXMY2 (B4:B7,C4:C7) = 8. 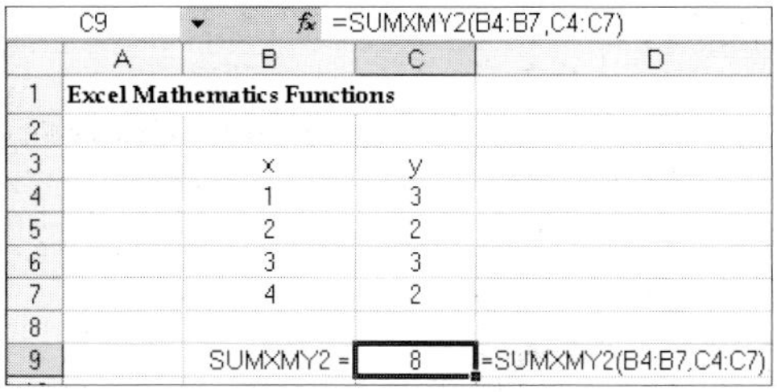

Figure 2.23

Table 2.1

2.2.2 Excel arrays

Section 1.3.14 mentioned that Excel contains an alternative method to copy formulae. This alternative method is to use an array function which allows a formula to be input once but be copied to all the cells within the array. Consider the problem of calculating the pay for employees who are on a different hourly pay rate (Figure 2.24).

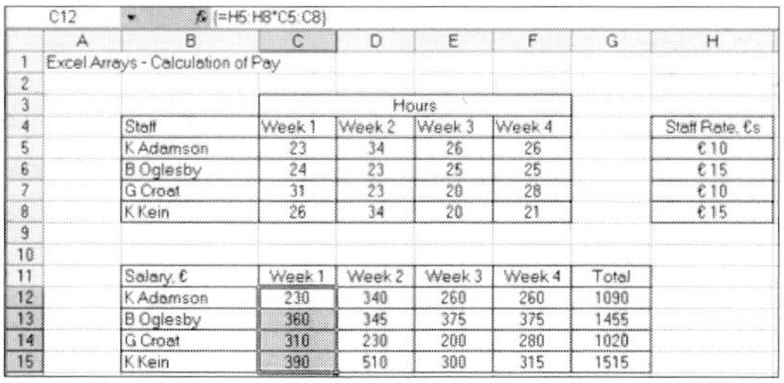

Figure 2.24

This problem can be solved using the standard method or by using array functions:

Standard solution

In the standard method we multiply the hourly rate by the number of hours worked. For K Adamson, input in cell C12 the formula =H5*C5 = €230. For the other members of staff we would then copy the formula down from C12 to C15.

Array solution

This problem can be solved using an array formula: ={H5:H8*C5:C8}. This array formula multiplies each of the hourly rates in the 4 x 1 array in the range H5:H8 with each of the hours worked in the 4 x 1 array in the range C5:C8. This same formula is entered into all cells of the array range (C12:C15) as soon as you complete the formula in the active cell C12.

Step 1   Select cell C12 to C15 and type '=' to start the array formula.
Step 2   Select the range H5:H8 (staff pay rate) and type '*' and select C5:C8 (staff hours).
Step 3   Press Ctrl + Shift + Enter to complete the formula. Excel will automatically insert the curly brackets { }.
Step 4   Repeat steps 1–3 for weeks 2–4 (arrays).

Figure 2.25 shows the weekly pay for weeks 2–3 after completing the array formulae using arrays D5:D12, E5:E12, and F5:F12.

F12	▾	fx {=H5:H8*F5:F8}					
	A	B	C	D	E	F	G	H
1	Excel Arrays - Calculation of Pay						
2							
3					Hours		
4		Staff	Week 1	Week 2	Week 3	Week 4		Staff Rate, €s
5		K Adamson	23	34	26	26		€ 10
6		B Oglesby	24	23	25	25		€ 15
7		G Croat	31	23	20	28		€ 10
8		K Kein	26	34	20	21		€ 15
9							
10							
11		Salary, €	Week 1	Week 2	Week 3	Week 4	Total	
12		K Adamson	230	340	260	260	1090	
13		B Oglesby	360	345	375	375	1455	
14		G Croat	310	230	200	280	1020	
15		K Kein	390	510	300	315	1515	

Figure 2.25

The total pay for each staff member can be calculated using the Excel formula: =SUM (cell range).

2.2.3 Excel statistical functions

Excel contains a range of statistical functions that are useful in solving business related problems. As many of these functions are subject of this book, we will just list them here and return to them through the remaining chapters of the book.

Excel Function	Description
AVEDEV (number1, number2,...)	Returns the average of the absolute deviations of data points from their mean.
AVERAGE (number1, number2,...)	Returns the average of its arguments.
BINOMDIST (number_s, trials, probability_s, cumulative)	Returns the individual term binomial distribution.
CHIDIST (x,degrees_freedom)	Returns the one-tailed probability of the chi square (χ^2) distribution.
CHIINV (probability, degrees_freedom)	Returns the inverse of the chi square (χ^2) distribution.
CHITEST (actual_range, expected_range)	Returns the test for independence.
CONFIDENCE (alpha, standard_dev, size)	Returns a confidence interval for a normal population.
CORREL (array1, array2)	Returns the correlation coefficient between two data sets.
COUNT (value1, value2,...)	Counts how many numbers are in the list of arguments.
COUNTA (value1, value2,...)	Counts how many non-blank values in the list of arguments.
COVAR (array1, array2)	Returns the covariance, the average of the products of paired deviations.
CRITBINOM (trials, probability_s, alpha)	Returns the smallest integer value for which the cumulative binomial distribution is less than or equal to a criterion value.
DEVSQ (number1, number2,...)	Returns the sum of squares of deviations.
FDIST (x, degrees_freedom1, degrees_freedom2)	Returns the F probability distribution.
FINV (probability, degrees_freedom1, degrees_freedom2)	Returns the inverse of the F probability distribution.
FORECAST (x, known_y's, known_x's)	Returns a value along a linear trend.
FREQUENCY (data_array, bins_array)	Returns a frequency distribution as a vertical array.
FTEST (array1, array2)	Returns the result of an F-test.
GEOMEAN (number1, number2,...)	Returns the geometric mean.
GROWTH (known_y's, known_x's, new_x's, const)	Returns values along an exponential trend.
HARMEAN (number1, number2,...)	Returns the geometric mean.

Excel Function	Description
HYPGEOMDIST(sample_s, number_sample, population_s, number_population)	Returns the hypergeometric distribution (used in sampling without replacement from a finite population).
INTERCEPT (known_y's, known_x's)	Returns the intercept of the linear regression line.
KURT (number1, number2,…)	Returns the kurtosis of a data set.
LARGE (array, k)	Returns the kth largest value in a data set.
LINEST (known_y's, known_x's, const, stats)	Returns the parameters of a linear trend.
MAX (number1, number2,…)	Returns the maximum value in a list of arguments.
MEDIAN (number1, number2,…)	Returns the median of the given numbers.
MIN (number1, number2,…)	Returns the minimum value in a list of arguments.
MODE (number1, number2,…)	Returns the most common value in a data set.
NORMDIST (x, mean, standard_dev, cumulative)	Returns the normal cumulative distribution.
NORMINV (probability, mean, standard_dev)	Returns the inverse of the normal cumulative distribution.
NORMSDIST (Z)	Returns the standard normal cumulative distribution.
NORMSINV (probability)	Returns the inverse of the standard normal cumulative distribution.
PEARSON (array1, array2)	Returns the Pearson product moment correlation coefficient.
PERCENTILE (array, k)	Returns the kth percentile of values in a range.
PERCENTRANK (array, x, significance)	Returns the percentage rank of a value in a data set.
PERMUT (number, number_chosen)	Returns the number of permutations for a given number of objects.
POISSON (x, mean, cumulative)	Returns the Poisson probability distribution.
PROB (x_range, prob_range, lower_limit, upper_limit)	Returns the probability that values in a range are between two limits.
QUARTILE (array, quart)	Returns the quartile of a data set.
RANK (number, ref, order)	Returns the rank of a number in a list of numbers.

Excel Function	Description
RSQ (known_y's, known_x's)	Returns the r^2 value of the linear regression line.
SKEW (number1, number2,....)	Returns the skewness of a distribution.
SLOPE (known_y's, known_x's)	Returns the slope of the linear regression line.
SMALL (array, k)	Returns the kth smallest value in a data set.
STANDARDIZE (x, mean, standard_dev)	Returns a normalized value.
STDEV (number1, number2,....)	Estimates standard deviation based on a sample.
STDEVP (number1, number2,....)	Calculates standard deviation based on the entire population.
STEYX (known_y's, known_x's)	Returns the standard error of the predicted y-value for each x in the regression.
TDIST (x, degrees_freedom, tails)	Returns the Student's t-distribution.
TINV (probability, degrees_freedom)	Returns the inverse of the Student's t-distribution for the specified degrees of freedom.
TREND (known_y's, known_x's, new_x's, const)	Returns values along a linear trend.
TRIMMEAN (array, percent)	Returns the mean of the interior of a data set.
TTEST (array1, array2, tails, type)	Returns the probability associated with a Student's t test.
VAR (number1, number2,....)	Estimates variance based on a sample.
VARP (number1, number2,....)	Calculates variance based on the entire population.
ZTEST (array, x, sigma)	Returns the two-tailed P-value of a z test.

Table 2.2

2.2.4 Excel statistical macro functions

These macro functions will require that the Data Analysis add-in is installed.

DESCR (inprng, outrng, grouped, labels, summary, ds_large, ds_small, confid)	Generates descriptive statistics for data in the input range.
EXPON (inprng, outrng, damp, stderrs, chart)	Predicts a value based on the forecast for the prior period.
FTESTV (inprng1, inprng2, outrng, labels)	Performs a two-sample F test.
HISTOGRAM (inprng, outrng, binrng, pareto, chartc, chart)	Calculates individual and cumulative percentages for a range of data and a corresponding range of data bins.
MCORREL (inprng, outrng, grouped, labels)	Returns the correlation coefficient of two or more data sets that are scaled to be independent of the unit of measurement.
MCOVAR (inprng, outrng, grouped, labels)	Returns the covariance between two or more data sets.
MOVEAVG (inprng, outrng, interval, stderrs, chart)	Returns values along a moving average trend.
PTTESTM (inprng1, inprng2, outrng, labels, alpha, difference)	Performs a paired two-sample Student's t test for means.
PTTESTV (inprng1, inprng2, outrng, labels, alpha)	Performs a two-sample Student's t test, assuming unequal variances.
RANDOM ().	Generates random numbers from a given distribution, including: normal, binomial, and poisson distributions.
RANKPERC (inprng, outrng, grouped, labels)	Returns a table that contains the ordinal and percent rank of each value in a data set.
REGRESS (inpryrng, inpxrng, constant, labels, confid, soutrng, residuals, sresiduals, rplots, lplots, routrng, nplots, poutrng)	Performs multiple linear regression analysis.
TTESTM (inprng1, inprng2, outrng, labels, alpha, difference)	Performs a two-sample Student's t test for means, assuming equal variances.
ZTESTM (inprng1, inprng2, outrng, labels, alpha, difference, var1, var2)	Performs a two-sample z test for means, assuming variances.

Table 2.3

2.3 Excel Financial Functions

Excel contains a number of functions that allow the calculation of a number of financial measures. In many circumstances it is important for individuals and organizations to compare different investments to maximize the potential return, e.g. if offered would you accept €5000 now or €5000 in 6 months. In an ideal world the €5000 now would be worth exactly the same value in 6 months. Unfortunately, we do not live in the ideal world and the original €5000 would be reduced due to the effect of inflationary changes in the value of money, e.g. inflation. To counteract this inflationary effect banks (and other financial institutions) will pay for people, or institutions, to invest their money and will charge people, or institutions, for borrowing money. The online numeracy workbook contains information on the following topics: commission, hire purchase, bank loans, profit and loss, discounting, and value added tax (VAT). This section will focus on calculating financial statistics involving: simple interest, compound interest, increasing the sum invested, sinking funds or future value of an ordinary annuity, the concept of present value, trust funds and loan repayments or present value of an ordinary annuity, and the present value of a stream of earnings.

2.3.1 Simple interest

If you borrow money from a bank or building society, you will be charged interest on the amount of money, which you borrow. The sum of money which you borrow is called the principal (P). The time (T) over which you borrow the money is given in years, e.g. 2 years 6 months, must be converted to 2.5 years or 2 1/2 years. The rate (R) at which you borrow the money is given as a percentage, e.g. 5% means that £5 will have to be repaid on every £100 which you borrow. The simple interest (SI) which you pay can be calculated by using the following formula:

$$SI = \frac{PRT}{100} \tag{2.1}$$

Another quantity which is sometimes given is called the amount, where amount = principal + simple interest.

⌕ Example 2.8

If the bank paid 8 % p.a. on deposits, then a deposit of £250 left in the bank for 4 years would earn

$$SI = \frac{250*8*4}{100} = £80$$

Before we examine the implications of this calculation it will be convenient to modify it somewhat. Rather than expressing the rate as a percentage, let us instead express it as a proportion r. To do this, we divide the percentage rate by 100. So, for example if R = 8% then r = 8/100 = 0.08. Our formula for calculating interest now becomes

$$SI = P \times T \times r \tag{2.2}$$

From now on, we shall use r as the rate of interest. Of course, this would in no way affect the result of our calculation: SI = 250 * 4 * 0.08 = £80. Whichever way we express the rate of interest, we still predict that £250 deposited for four years at 8% per annum would earn us £80. But is this figure correct? We would earn £80 only if we withdrew the interest each year. Over the four years we would have earned what is called simple interest. The Excel spreadsheet solution is given in Figure 2.26 below.

Initial Data: P = Cell C5   T = Cell C6   R = Cell C7

Figure 2.26

Calculations:

r = Cell F5

Formula: =C7/100

SI = Cell F6

Formula: =C5*C6*F5

☝ **Student Exercises**

X2.2

(a) Find the simple interest on £700 at 5% for 3 years.

(b) Find SI on £500 at 2.5% for 3 years.

(c) Find SI on £650 at 3% for 2 years 6 months.

(d) Find the rate, if the principal is £1000, the time is 6 years and the SI is £200.

(e) Find the time if the SI on £440 at 8% per annum is £88.

(f) If the SI on an amount of money is £30, and the rate is 6% over 6 months, what is the amount of money?

2.3.2 Compound interest

But suppose we did not withdraw our interest from the bank. If this is so, then the interest on deposit would itself earn interest. We would then be earning what is called compound interest.

▷ **Example 2.9**

Let us now compare the two methods of earning interest on a year by year basis.

Year	Simple Interest		Compound Interest	
	Deposit (£)	Interest (£)	Deposit (£)	Interest (£)
1	250	250 * 0.08 = 20	250	250 * 0.08 = 20
2	250	250 * 0.08 = 20	270	270 * 0.08 = 21.60
3	250	250 * 0.08 = 20	291.60	291.60 * 0.08 = 23.33
4	250	250 * 0.08 = 20	314.93	314.93 * 0.08 = 25.19
Total Interest Earned (£)		80		90.12

Table 2.4

From Table 2.4 the £250 earns £90.12 of interest during the 4 years of the investment. Therefore, the investment is now worth £340.12. So we see that there is a considerable difference between the two methods. Compound interest is the method that is invariably used in the business world, and you would be well advised to forget all about simple interest. If we are going to calculate compound interest on a year to year basis, then the calculation will be tedious to say the least. What we require is a formula for compound interest, and to obtain this we shall use our example, though this time from a slightly different angle. We shall calculate the value of the deposit at the end of each year if £P is invested at an interest rate r and left for n years. The value of the deposit at the end of the year equals the value of the deposit at the beginning of the year *plus* the interest earned during the year. So if we call S the sum of the deposit after n years then

$$S = P(1+r)^n \qquad (2.3)$$

And the total interest earned would be

$$I = P(1+r)^n - P \qquad (2.4)$$

In Excel, the FV function returns the future value of an investment based on an interest rate and a constant payment schedule. The Excel function is *FV(interest_rate, number_payments, payment, PV, type)* where:

- interest_rate is the interest rate for the investment;
- number_payments is the number of payments for the annuity;
- payment is the amount of the payment made each period;
- pv is optional. It is the present value of the payments. If this parameter is omitted, the FV function assumes PV to be 0;
- type is optional. It indicates when the payments are due. Type can be one of the following values: 0—payments are due at the end of the period; (default) and 1—payments are due at the beginning of the period.

The term S in the equation is called the *future value* of an investment based on an interest rate and a constant payment schedule. It is important to remember that *Excel follows the Cash Flow Sign Convention*. This is simply a way of keeping the direction of the cash flow straight. Cash inflows are entered as positive numbers and cash outflows are entered as negative numbers.

▷ Example 2.10

To illustrate application of this equation reconsider Example 2.9.

→ Excel Function Method

=FV(interest_rate, number_payments, payment, PV, type)
Where

- interest_rate = 8% per annum.
- number_payments = 4.
- payment = 0.
- PV = −250. The PV is negative in the Excel function since we have deposited £250 (cash outflow).
- type = 1. The payment is made at the beginning of the period.

Substituting these values into Excel the future value is £340.12 after 4 years. This can be reproduced by directly substituting the values into the FV function in Excel =FV(8%, 4, 0, −250, 1) = £340.12.

C9		f_x =FV(C2,C3,C4,C5,C7)	
	A	B	C	D
1				
2		interest_rate, R =	8%	
3		number_payments, n =	4	
4		payment =	£0	
5		pv, p =	−£250	
6		fv =		
7		type =	1	
8				
9		FV=	£340.12 =FV(C2,C3,C4,C5,C7)	

Figure 2.27

✳ **Interpretation**   The future value of £250 invested for 4 years at 8% per annum is £340.12.

Note   Manual Solution

Now let us repeat our earlier calculation using equation (2.4) to calculate S. In Example 2.28, P = £250, n = 4 yrs, R = 8%. Then S = 250 * $(1.08)^4$ = £340.125.

↳ **Example 2.11**

Consider the future value of an investment where you deposit £5000 into a savings account that earns 7.5% annually. You are going to deposit £250 at the beginning of the month, each month, for 2 years. If we substitute these values into the FV function we obtain S =FV (interest_rate, number_payments, payment, PV, type) =FV(7.5%/12, 2 * 12, −250, −5000, 1) = £12298.46. The future value of this investment is £12298.46 after 2 years.

➜ **Excel Function Method**

=FV(interest_rate, number_payments, payment, PV, type)
Where

- interest_rate = 7.5/12% per month. Since each payment is made monthly.
- number_payments = 2 * 12 months. Since 12 payments per year over 2 years.
- payment = −£250. Payment of £250 at the beginning of each month (cash outflow).
- PV = −£5000. The PV is negative in the Excel function since we have deposited £5000 (cash outflow).
- type = 1. The payment is made at the beginning of the period.

Substituting these values into Excel the future value is £12298.46 after 2 years. This can be reproduced by directly substituting the values into the FV function in Excel =FV(7.5%/12, 2*12, −250, −5000, 1) = £12298.46.

C9	▼	*fx* =FV(C2,C3,C4,C5,C7)		
	A	B	C	D
1				
2		interest_rate, R =	0.625000%	
3		number_payments, n =	24	
4		payment =	−£250	
5		pv, p =	−£5,000	
6		fv =		
7		type =	1	
8				
9		FV=	£12,298.46	=FV(C2,C3,C4,C5,C7)

Figure 2.28

❋ **Interpretation**   The future value of an investment of £5000 invested at 7.5% with £250 deposited at the beginning of the month for 2 years is £12298.46.

Note   Microsoft Excel has a range of financial functions to enable the calculation of key financial measures, including:

- The NPER() function calculates the number of periods of an investment or a loan =NPER(interest_rate, payment, PV, FV, type).
- The PMT() function is used to calculate the regular payment of a loan or an investment =PMT(interest_rate, number_payments, PV, FV, type).
- The PV() function calculates the total amount that a future investment is worth currently =PV(interest_rate, number_payments, payment, FV, type).
- The RATE() function is used to calculate the interest applied on a loan or an investment =RATE(number_payments, payment, PV, FV, type, Guess). Note that the Guess argument is rarely required and is optional. In most cases, you can just leave it out. It is included for those times (only when dealing with annuities) when there are two or more solutions to the problem. Typically, this only happens when you are dealing with uneven cash flows and there are sign changes in the cash flow stream. It can occasionally happen in annuity problems, when the FV has a different sign than PMT.
- The NPV() function uses a series of cash flows to calculate the present value of an investment =NPV(interest_rate, Value1, Value2, ...).
- The IPMT() function is used to calculate the amount paid as interest on a loan during a period of the lifetime of a loan or an investment =IPMT(interest_rate, period, number_payments, PV, FV, type), where the period specifies the year you want to find out the interest earned in.

2.3.3 Increasing the sum invested

So far, we have examined how an initial deposit would grow if it earned compound interest. But suppose we added to the amount deposited at the end of each year. Specifically, suppose we deposited £1000 on the first of January of a certain year, and decided to deposit £100 at the end of each year. If interest is compounded at 10% p.a., then we can use equation (2.1) to deduce the sum at the end of each year, as follows:

sum on deposit at the end of the first year is

$$1000(1 + 0.1) + 100$$

sum on deposit at the end of the second year is

$$1000(1 + 0.1)^2 + 100(1 + 0.1) + 100$$

sum on deposit at the end of the nth year is

$$1000(1 + 0.1)^n + 100(1 + 0.1)^{n-1} + 100(1 + 0.1)^{n-2} + ...+100$$

If we generalize the quantities, then we can derive a formula to solve problems like this swiftly and efficiently. If we let P be the initial deposit, r the interest rate and a the amount that we deposit at the end of each year, then after n years the sum available would be $S = P(1 + r)^n + a(1 + r)^{n-1} + a(1 + r)^{n-2} +........+ a$. Now it can be shown that this expression is equivalent to

$$S = P(1+r)^n + \frac{a(1+r)^n - a}{r} \tag{2.5}$$

▷ Example 2.12

Suppose we deposit £20000 at the beginning of a year at 5% p.a. compound. We withdraw £2000 at the end of each year. What would be the sum available after 4 years? Excel can be used to solve this problem by making use of the FV function.

→ Excel Function Method

=FV(interest_rate, number_payments, payment, PV, type)
Where

- interest_rate = 5% per annum.
- number_payments = 4 years.
- payment = 2000. The value is + since we remove £2000 at the end of the year (cash inflow).
- PV = –20000. The PV is negative in the Excel function since we have deposited £20000 (cash outflow).
- type = 0. The payment is made at the end of the period.

Substituting these values into Excel the sum after 4 years will be £15690. This can be reproduced by directly substituting the values into the FV function in Excel =FV(interest_rate, number_payments, payment, PV, type) =FV(5%, 4, 2000, −20000, 0) = £15689.

C9	▼	f_x =FV(C2,C3,C4,C5,C7)		
	A	B	C	D
1				
2		interest_rate, R =	5%	
3		number_payments, n =	4	
4		payment =	£2,000	
5		pv, p =	−£20,000	
6		fv =		
7		type =	0	
8				
9		FV=	£15,689.88 =FV(C2,C3,C4,C5,C7)	

Figure 2.29

✳ **Interpretation**   The sum after 4 years will be £15690.

Note   Manual Solution

$$S = P(1+r)^n + \frac{a(1+r)^n - a}{r} \quad \text{with } P = £20000, r = 0.05, a = -£2000, \text{ and } n = 4.$$

$$S = 20000(1.05)^4 + \frac{(-2000*(1.05)^4 - (-2000)}{0.05}$$

$$= 20000*1.2155 + \frac{-2000*1.2155 - (-2000)}{0.05}$$

$$S = 24310 - 8620 = £15690.$$

Sum available after 4 years is £15690

2.3.4 Sinking funds or future value of an ordinary annuity

We will now suppose that the accountant is instructed to set aside a sum of money at the end of each year to replace an asset. Using equation (2.5) with P = 0 (problem involves zero initial investment) gives

$$S = \frac{a(1+r)^n - a}{r} \tag{2.6}$$

If we now make 'a' the subject of this formula, we will have an expression telling us how much we must set aside at the end of each year to achieve a specified sum S

$$a = \frac{rS}{(1+r)^n - 1} \tag{2.7}$$

We have derived what is called the *sinking fund* formula (final payment at start of year n).

Example 2.13

Suppose a machine is expected to last 8 years and its replacement price is estimated at £5000. What annual provision must be made to ensure sufficient funds are available if money can be invested at 8% per annum? Excel can be used to solve this problem by making use of the PMT function.

→ Excel Function Method

=PMT(interest_rate, number_payments, pv, fv, type)
Where

- interest_rate = 8% per annum.
- number_payments = 8 years.
- PV = 0. The pv is zero in the Excel function since we start with zero initial investment.
- FV = –£5000. The FV is negative in the Excel function since we will remove the £5000 (cash outflow).
- type = 0. The payment is made at the end of the period.

Substituting these values into Excel then an annual deposit of £470.07 will need to be made at the end of the year for 8 years. This can be reproduced by directly substituting the values into the PMT function in Excel =PMT(interest_rate, number_payments, PV, FV, type) =FV(5%, 4, 0, –5000, 0) = £470.07.

C9 f_x =PMT(C2,C3,C5,C6,C7)

	A	B	C	D
1				
2		interest_rate, R =	8%	
3		number_payments, n =	8	
4		payment =		
5		pv, p =	£0	
6		fv =	-£5,000	
7		type =	0	
8				
9		PMT =	£470.07	=PMT(C2,C3,C5,C6,C7)

Figure 2.30

Interpretation Annual deposit £470.07 will need to be made at the end of the year for 8 years.

> **Note**   Manual Solution
>
> 1. Payment 'a' at the end of the year
> Using equation (2.7)
>
> $$a = \frac{0.08 * 5000}{(1.08)^8 - 1} = \frac{400}{1.85093021... - 1} = £470.09 \text{ to the nearest penny}$$
>
> So £470.09 deposited at the end of the year would be sufficient to yield the required sum of £5000.
>
> 2. Payment 'a' at start of the year
> But suppose (as is more likely) the firm wishes to start the fund now and add to it at annual intervals then equation (2.7) will not do. We will have to use the expression
>
> $$S = a(1 + r)^n + a(1 + r)^{n-1} + a(1 + r)^{n-2} + ... + a(1 + r)$$
>
> Now it can be shown that this expression is equal to
>
> $$S = a\frac{(1+r)^{n+1} - (1+r)}{r} \qquad (2.8)$$
>
> and again re-arranging this formula to make 'a' the subject
>
> $$a = \frac{rS}{(1+r)^{n+1} - (1+r)} \qquad (2.9)$$

2.3.5 The concept of present value

Suppose you were offered the choice of receiving £1000 now or £1000 in 12 months' time—which would you choose? It is almost certain that you would take the money now, even if you had a cast iron guarantee of receiving the money in the future. It would appear that we have strong preference for holding cash now against receiving cash in the future, and economists call this preference 'liquidity preference'. Now why is this preference so universally held? Almost certainly, inflation will have something to do with it. After all, if prices are rising then £1000 in 1 year's time will buy less than it will now, and so it will have less value than it has now. During inflation, then, it would make more sense to take the £1000 now. But suppose we had stable prices then we would still almost certainly choose to take the money now. Why? The great advantage of taking the money now is that it can be invested and earn interest. With inflation, over £1000 invested now at 10% would grow to $£1000 * (1.1) = £1100$ in one year's time and to $£1000 * (1.1)^2 = £1210$ in two years' time. Given stable prices, then, we should be indifferent between £1000 now, £1100 in one year's time and £1210 in two years' time. In other words, £1000 receivable today has the same value as £1100 receivable in one year and £1210 receivable in two years.

So we can now see why we would prefer the £1000 now: if £1000 now is worth £1100 in one year's time, it follows that £1000 in one year's time has a *present value* of less than £1000. We have introduced a very important concept—that of present value and this concept needs defining carefully. The present value of a sum of money receivable in the future is the sum you would be prepared to accept now, rather than have to wait for it. We use the interest earning capacity of money to enable us to calculate the present value. As £1000 invested at 10% p.a. would grow to £1100 in one year's time we would say that £1100 in one year's time has a present value of £1000. We reduce (or discount) the value of a sum receivable in the future to find its present value, and the *discount factor* that we use to do this is the current rate of interest. How can we do this?

▷ Example 2.14

What is the present value of £1000 receivable in two years' time if money can be invested at 10% p.a. compound? Excel can be used to solve this problem by making use of the PV function.

→ Excel Function Method

=PV(interest_rate, number_payments, payment, FV, type)
Where

- interest_rate = 10% per annum.

- number_payments = 2 years.

- payment = 0

- FV = −£1000. The FV is negative in the Excel function since we will remove the £1000 (cash outflow).

- type = 0. The payment is made at the end of the period.

Substituting these values into Excel then the present value is £826.45. This can be reproduced by directly substituting the values into the PMT function in Excel =PV(10%, 2, 0, −1000, 0) = £826.45.

	C9	▼	f_x =PV(C2,C3,C4,C6,C7)	
	A	B	C	D
1				
2		interest_rate, R =	10%	
3		number_payments, n =	2	
4		payment =	£0	
5		pv, p =		
6		fv =	−£1,000	
7		type =	0	
8				
9		PV =	£826.45 =PV(C2,C3,C4,C6,C7)	

Figure 2.31

> ❊ **Interpretation**   The present value is £826.45.

So £1000 receivable in two years' time has a present value of £826.45 now at the current interest rate it would grow to £1000 in two years. We should be indifferent between receiving £1000 in two years' time and £826.40 now.

> **Note**   Manual Solution
>
> Equation (2.3) can be used to calculate how a sum invested now would grow under compound interest $S = P(1+r)^n$. If S is the sum receivable in the future, then P must be its present value.
>
> $$P = \frac{S}{(1+r)^n} = S(1+r)^{-n} \qquad (2.10)$$
>
> The quantity $(1+r)^{-n}$ is the discounting factor reducing the value of the sum.
> For Example 2.14 $S = £1000$, $R = 10\%$ p.a., $r = 0.1$, $n = 2$
>
> $$P = S(1+r)^{-n} = 1000 * (1.1)^{-2} = 1000 * 0.826446281\ldots\ldots = £826.45$$

2.3.6 Trust funds and loan repayments or present value of an ordinary annuity

Let us suppose that we deposit a certain sum of money now, and from this we wish to withdraw at the end of each year a fixed amount. We will continue to withdraw until nothing is left on deposit. In equation (2.5) the terminal sum S would be zero, and because we are withdrawing 'a' would be negative, therefore we can rewrite equation (2.5) as

$$P = a\frac{1-(1+r)^{-n}}{r} \qquad (2.11)$$

$$a = \frac{rP}{1-(1+r)^{-n}} \qquad (2.12)$$

> **Example 2.15**
>
> A father decided to set up a trust fund for his son. He requires the fund to pay him £2000 per year for the next 10 years. How much will this fund cost him if money can be invested at 10% p.a. compound? This problem involves finding P, the initial investment, so equation (2.11) is the one required. Excel can be used to solve this problem by making use of the PV function.

→ **Excel Function Method**

=PV(interest_rate, number_payments, payment, FV, type)
Where

- interest_rate=10% per annum
- number_payments = 10
- payment = −£2000. The value is negative since you will remove (cash outflow) £2000 at the end of every year for 10 years.
- FV = £0. The FV is zero at the end of the 10 years.
- type = 0. The payment is made at the end of the period.

Substituting these values into Excel then an initial investment of £12289.13 is required to be made at the end of the year for 10 years. This can be reproduced by directly substituting the values into the PMT function in Excel =PV(10%, 10, −2000, 0, 0) = £12289.13.

	C9	▼	f_x =PV(C2,C3,C4,C6,C7)	
	A	B	C	D
1				
2		interest_rate, R =	10%	
3		number_payments, n =	10	
4		payment =	-£2,000	
5		pv, p =		
6		fv =	£0	
7		type =	0	
8				
9		PV =	£12,289.13	=PV(C2,C3,C4,C6,C7)

Figure 2.32

✳ **Interpretation** An initial investment of £12289.13 is required to be made at the end of the year for 10 years.

📎 **Note** Manual Solution
From equation (2.11):

$$P = a\frac{1-\left(1+r\right)^{-n}}{r} = 2000 \times \frac{1-\left(1+0.1\right)^{-10}}{0.1} = 12289.13$$

2.3.7 The present value of a stream of earnings

Let us suppose that we have been promised £1000 in one year, £2000 in two years, £4000 in three years, and £3000 in four years' time. We would call this a stream of earnings, and if we wished to find the present value of such a stream we would find the sum of the individual present values. If the current rate of interest is 12%, then the present value would be

$$P = 1000(1.12)^{-1} + 2000(1.12)^{-2} + 4000(1.12)^{-3} + 3000(1.12)^{-4}$$

Excel can be used to solve this problem by making use of the NPV function.

↳ Example 2.16

Consider the problem where we have been promised £1000 in one year, £2000 in two years, £4000 in three years, and £3000 in four years' time. The interest rate is 12% and the present value can be calculated using the Excel NPV function.

→ Excel Function Method

=NPV(interest_rate, Range Reference)
Where

- interest_rate = 12% per annum
- range reference = value 1, value 2, ... are 1 to 29 payments and income, equally spaced in time and occurring at the end of each period.

Substituting these values into Excel then the net present value would be £7240.92. This can be reproduced by directly substituting the values into the NPV function in Excel =NPV(12%, C8:C11) = £7240.92.

C10		▼	f_x =NPV(C2,C5:C8)	
	A	B	C	D
1				
2		R =	12%	
3				
4		Year	Earnings	
5		1	£1,000	
6		2	£2,000	
7		3	£4,000	
8		4	£3,000	
9				
10		NPV =	£7,240.92 =NPV(C2,C5:C8)	

Figure 2.33

✳ Interpretation   The net present value would be £7240.92.

So the stream of earnings has a present value of £7240.92. In other words, if we deposited £7240.92 now at 12% p.a. then we could draw £1000 at the end of the first year, £2000 at the end of the second year, £4000 at the end of the third year and £3000 at the end of the fourth year. The value of the deposit would then be zero (you should use equation (2.3) to prove this yourself). So if you were offered an asset, which yielded the above stream of earnings and the current interest rate, was 12% p.a., then you should be prepared to pay £7241.10 for it. Now it is perfectly possible to have a constant stream of earnings, and an asset that yields a constant stream is called an *annuity*. We could use the same method as above to calculate the present value of an annuity, but it would be easier to use equation (2.11), which would give exactly the same results.

Note   Manual Solution

In general the net present value formula can be written as:

$$NPV = \sum_{i=1}^{n} \frac{values_i}{(1+rate)^i}$$

(2.13)

It is convenient to perform this calculation in a tabular form

YEAR	EARNING (£)	DISCOUNT FACTOR $(1.12)^{-n}$	PRESENT VALUE (£)
1	1000	0.8930	892.86
2	2000	0.7972	1594.39
3	4000	0.7118	2847.12
4	3000	0.6355	1906.55
			P = 7240.92

The NPV investment begins one period before the date of the value1 cash flow and ends with the last cash flow in the list. The NPV calculation is based on future cash flows. If your first cash flow occurs at the beginning of the first period, the first value must be added to the NPV result, not included in the values arguments. NPV is also related to the IRR function (internal rate of return). IRR is the rate for which NPV equals zero: NPV(IRR(...), ...) = 0. Note: NPV is similar to the PV function (present value). The primary difference between PV and NPV is that PV allows cash flows to begin either at the end or at the beginning of the period. Unlike the variable NPV cash flow values, PV cash flows must be constant throughout the investment.

2.3.8 Compound annual growth rate

The compound annual growth rate (CAGR) describes the rate at which an investment or expenditure would have grown if it grew during a period of time at a steady rate. Thus, if the cost of electricity was €5000 in 2004 and three years later was €10000, then its spending grew 100%. This is the growth for the three years but what is the growth per year? Excel allows the calculation of the CAGR by making use of the Rate and XIRR functions.

Example 2.17

Consider the problem of calculating what constant growth rate results in sales figures growing from €18718 to €35678 during the five year period. To calculate this value we will use the Rate function in Excel.

Period	1	2	3	4	5
Sales (€)	18718	22861	28142	30218	35678

→ **Excel Function Method**

=RATE(number_payments, payment, PV, FV, type)
Where

- number_payments = 4 – 4 payments after initial payment
- payment = 0
- PV = 18718
- FV = –35678
- type = 0

Applying the Rate function we have Rate =RATE(4, 0, C5, –C9, 0).

	A	B	C	D
			C12	f_x =RATE(4,0,C5,-C9,0)
1	Calculate a compound annual growth rate (CAGR)			
2				
3				
4		Period	Sales	
5		1	€ 18,718.00	
6		2	€ 22,861.00	
7		3	€ 28,142.00	
8		4	€ 30,218.00	
9		5	€ 35,678.00	
10				
11				
12		CAGR =	17.4993%	=RATE(4,0,C5,-C9,0)

Figure 2.34

✳ **Interpretation**   The compound annual growth rate of 17.5% will result in growth of €18718 to €35678 during the 5 year period.

Example 2.18

Consider the problem of calculating the compound annual growth rate that consists of an initial expenditure of €4500 and results in a series of interest payments on the dates specified below.

Date	21/2/2008	5/4/2008	22/8/2008	1/10/2008	1/2/2009
Payment (€)	– 4500	3200	2250	4850	1750

→ **Excel Function Method**

=XIRR(B6:B10,C6:C10)

The CAGR can be calculated for this problem using the Excel function XIRR.

$$CAGR = XIRR(B6:B10, C6:C10)$$

From Figure 2.35 we have the compound annual growth rate of 11.7%.

	C12	▼	f_x =XIRR(B6:B10,C6:C10)	
	A	B	C	D
1	Calculate a compound annual growth rate (CAGR)			
2				
3				
4		Sales (€)	Date	
5				
6		-4,500.00	21/02/2008	
7		3,200.00	05/04/2008	
8		2,250.00	22/06/2008	
9		4,850.00	01/10/2008	
10		1,750.00	01/02/2009	
11				
12		CAGR =	11.71352625 =XIRR(B6:B10,C6:C10)	

Figure 2.35

❋ **Interpretation**   Compound annual growth rate 11.7%.

Note

1. The Rate function cannot be used for this problem since it requires regular investment (or expenditure) periods for payments.

2. The XIRR function requires that at least one value must be positive and one negative value.

Student Exercises

X2.3

(a) Calculate the compound interest on £3000 invested for 2 years at 6% per annum?

(b) Calculate the amount when £5000 is invested for 2 years at 8% per annum compound interest?

(c) Suppose £9500 is invested on the first of January of a certain year at 12% compound and £800 is withdrawn at the end of each year. How much would remain after 12 years?

(d) A machine costing £12500 now will need replacing in 6 years' time.

    (a) Estimate its replacement price if the rate of inflation is 11% p.a.

    (b) How much must be set aside

        (i) at the end of each year

        (ii) at the beginning of each year

    to replace the machine, if money can be invested at 9% p.a.

(e) Find the present value of £100 received in 2 years' time if the interest rate is 12%.

(f) Which is the greatest sum of money if the interest rate is 14%: (a) £1500 received in 3 years' time or (b) £2000 received in 5 years' time?

(g) If money can be invested at 9% p.a., how much must be invested now to yield an income of £5000 per year, paid at the end of each year for eight years?

(h) Suppose £6500 is borrowed at 18% p.a. compound. Find the annual repayment necessary to pay off the loan in 12 years.

(i) Given a discount rate of 14% p.a., find the present value of an annuity, which yields: (a) £650 per year for 8 years, and (b) £650 per year in perpetuity?

(j) A machine costs £150,000 and its estimated running costs over its life of 5 years are given in the table. Assume all running costs are paid at the end of each year, and that money can be invested at 12% p.a. compound.

Year	Running Costs
1	1250
2	2250
3	3000
4	3100
5	3200

   (a) How much must be set aside to cover running costs?

   (b) How much must be set aside to cover running costs and replace the machine?

2.4 Coordinate Geometry

In the next chapter Microsoft Excel will be used to create a range of graphs that can be used to help to visualize data, e.g. bar charts, pie charts, histograms, and scatter plots. In this section we will explore the concept of coordinate geometry and how Excel can be used to plot algebraic relationships between two variables in the form $y = mx + c$. Before we do this we now need to understand the concept of a coordinate of a point and the Excel method we can use to plot a series of points. This section will then conclude by looking at equations of the form $y = mx + c$ and the Excel method to calculate the terms 'm' and 'c' in the equation.

2.4.1 The coordinates of a point

The coordinates of any point can be written as an ordered pair (x, y).

▷ Example 2.19

Point P in Figure 2.36 has coordinates (2, 3). Its horizontal distance along the x axis from the origin 0 is 2 units so the x coordinate is 2.

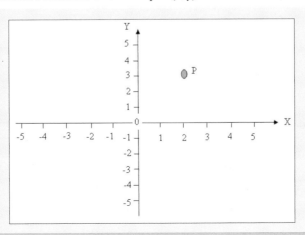

Figure 2.36

Its vertical distance along the y axis from the origin 0 is 3 units so the y coordinate is 3. Remember the x coordinate is always written first. Often points have one or both coordinates which are negative:

- Positive values of x are to the right of the origin.
- Negative values of x are to the left of the origin.
- Positive values of y are upwards from the origin.
- Negative values of y are downwards from the origin.

Student Exercises

X2.4

Use the coordinate graph (Figure 2.37) to complete this list:

- P is (–3, 1)
- Q is ()
- R is ()
- S is ()
- T is ()

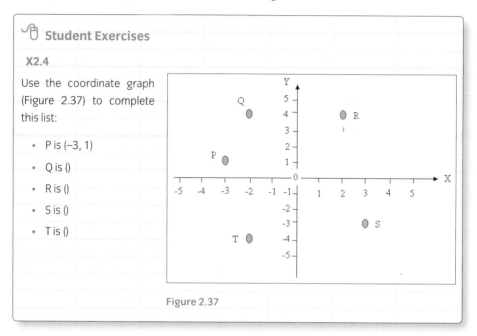

Figure 2.37

2.4.2 Excel and plotting straight line graphs from an equation

If we are given an equation of the form $y = mx + c$ (e.g. $y = 2x - 3$) and calculate values of y for a range of x values then we will find if we plot the points onto a graph that a straight line will fit through every coordinate point (x, y). Any values of x can be chosen to draw the graph but it is best to choose x values not too large or too small. To illustrate this concept consider Example 2.20 where $y = 2x - 3$.

Example 2.20

If we are given a linear equation, such as $y = 2x - 3$, we can draw the graph of this equation and it will be a straight line (linear). Any values of x can be chosen to draw the graph but it is best to choose x values not too large or too small. In this case we will choose x values from –3 to +3.

C5	▼	*fx* =2*B5-3	
	A	B	C	D
1				
2		Line fit to y = 2x - 3		
3				
4		x	y	
5		-3	-9	=2*B5-3
6		-2	-7	=2*B6-3
7		-1	-5	=2*B7-3
8		0	-3	=2*B8-3
9		1	-1	=2*B9-3
10		2	1	=2*B10-3
11		3	3	=2*B11-3

Figure 2.38

Figure 2.38 illustrates the method used to input a range of x values (−3, −2, −1, 0, 1, 2, 3) and the calculation of the value of y at each value of x. For example, when x equals 2 the value of y = 2x − 3 = 2 * 2 − 3 = 4 − 3 = 1.

The next stage is to use Excel to plot the values of y and x using Excel scatter plot graph. This graph method is explained in detail in Chapter 3 'Visualizing and Presenting Data'.

B4	▼	*fx* x	
	A	B	C	D
1				
2		Line fit to y = 2x - 3		
3				
4		x	y	
5		-3	-9	=2*B5-3
6		-2	-7	=2*B6-3
7		-1	-5	=2*B7-3
8		0	-3	=2*B8-3
9		1	-1	=2*B9-3
10		2	1	=2*B10-3
11		3	3	=2*B11-3

Figure 2.39

Step 1 Highlight cells B4:C11

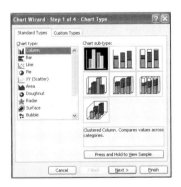

Figure 2.40

Step 2 Select Chart Wizard 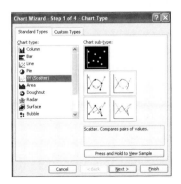 from Excel menu

Step 3 Choose XY (Scatter)
Click <u>N</u>ext

Figure 2.41

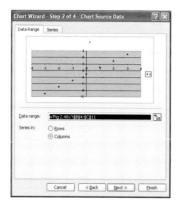

Figure 2.42

Step 4 Choose Series in Columns
Click <u>N</u>ext

Figure 2.43

Step 5 Input chart titles

- Chart <u>T</u>itle: Plot of y − 2x − 3 for x = −3 to +3
- Val<u>u</u>e (X) axis: x
- Value (Y) axis: y

Click <u>N</u>ext

Figure 2.44

Step 6 Choose chart location
Choose As <u>o</u>bject in: and click <u>F</u>inish.

Figure 2.45 illustrates the Excel solution.

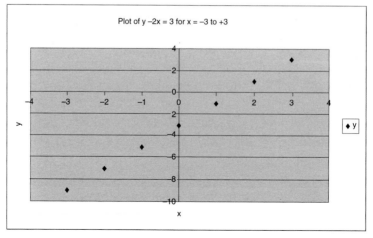

Figure 2.45

We can see from this graph that the coordinate points are plotted onto the scatter plot graph. From the graph we can observe that the points are lined up and it is likely that a straight line will pass through these points. Remember this is what we would expect to occur. We can use Excel to fit a straight line through the points by editing the graph in Excel.

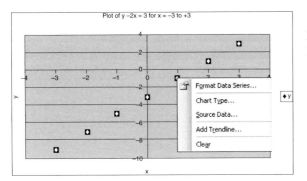

Figure 2.46

Step 7 Click on a point and all points should be highlighted. Right-click on a point.

Figure 2.47

Step 8 Choose Add Trendline Click OK

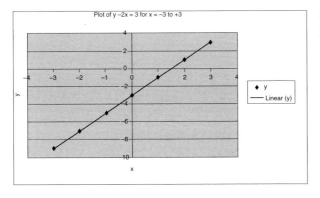

Figure 2.48

Figure 2.48 illustrates the Excel solution.

We can see from Figure 2.48 that all data points do indeed fit on the same straight line.

Note   Manual Solution

If we are given a linear equation, such as y = 2x − 3, we can draw the graph of this equation and it will be a straight line (linear). Any values of x can be chosen to draw the graph but it is best to choose x values not too large or too small. In this case we will choose values x from −3 to +3. First we make a table of values as shown below to calculate y.

X	−3	−2	−1	0	1	2	3
2x	−6	−4	−2	0	2	4	6
−3	−3	−3	−3	−3	−3	−3	−3
y	−9	−7	−5	−3	−1	1	3

Table 2.3

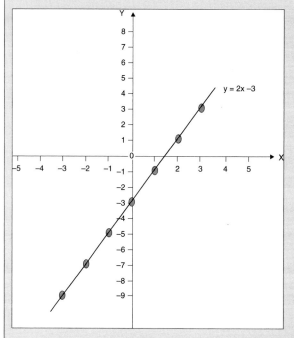

The graph can now be plotted using the coordinates (values of x and y) obtained from the table.

- (−3, −9)
- (−2, −7)
- (−1, −5)
- (0, −3)
- (1, −1)
- (2, 1)
- (3, 3)

Figure 2.49

Figure 2.49 illustrates the points plotted for y = 2x − 3.

1. From the graph of the plotted points for the equation y = 2x − 3 we observe that the line passes through the x axis line (y = 0 line) at y = −3. This value is called the y intercept.
2. It is important to note that all straight lines are graphs of linear equations (i.e. only x and y, no powers of x and y).

X2.5

- Complete the table of values for the equation y = 3x + 1.
- Draw the graph.
- Identify the intercept on the graph and state the coordinates of the y intercept point.

X	−2	0	+2
3x		0	6
+1		1	
y	−5		

2.4.3 Linear equation parameters m and c

In Example 2.18 we calculated the coordinate points for (x, y) based upon an equation of the form y = mx + c. Furthermore, we then used Excel to plot the points onto the graph and superimposed a straight line onto the graph (Figure 2.48). It was noted that the y-intercept is the value of y when x is zero. From the graph we note that this occurs when y = −3. Further observation notes that y = c when x = 0. The y-intercept in the equation y = mx + c is represented by the term 'c'. But what is 'm'?

Example 2.21

The gradient of a straight line can be found by constructing a right angled triangle (Figure 2.50).

$$\frac{BC}{AC} = \frac{12-4}{4-0} = \frac{8}{4} = 2$$

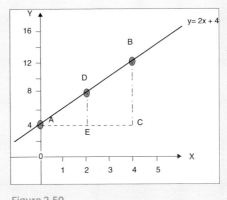

Figure 2.50

We observe that this value of gradient (or slope) of 2 is the same number that multiplies the 'x' variable in the general line equation y = mx + c. Therefore, 'm' represents the gradient of the line.

Examples 2.20 and 2.21 illustrate the concept that all equations of the form $y = mx + c$ will provide a straight line graph when y is plotted against x. It is important to note that the power of y and x is linear only. The general form of this equation is

$$y = mx + c \qquad\qquad (2.14)$$

Where 'm' represents the gradient (or slope) of the line and 'c' represents the y-intercept (or the position where the line cuts the y axis when $x = 0$).

Example 2.22

Figure 2.51 illustrates a line with a positive gradient.

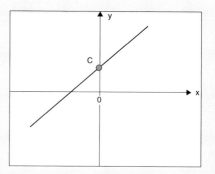

Figure 2.51

Example 2.23

Figure 2.52 illustrates a line with a gradient of 0.

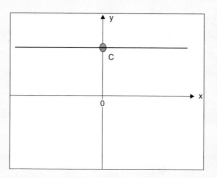

Figure 2.52

⟋ Example 2.24

Figure 2.53 illustrates a line with a negative gradient (or slope).

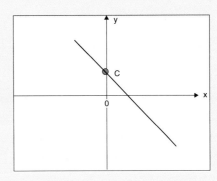

Figure 2.53

⟋ Example 2.25

Figure 2.54 illustrates a line with an infinite gradient (or slope).

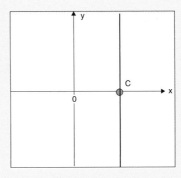

Figure 2.54

⟋ Example 2.26

Consider $y = 2x + 3$. From this equation we can state the value of 'm' and 'c' by comparing with the general form, $y = mx + c$. Compare $y = 2x + 3$ with $y = mx + c$. We can see that m = 2 (gradient of line = 2 and the line slopes upwards since the 2 is a positive number) and c = 3 (intercept of line is 3).

🖱 Student Exercises

X2.6 State the gradient and the intercept of these line equations: (a) $y = 5x + 1$, (b) $y = -3x + 5$, (c) $y = \dfrac{1}{2}x + 3$.

2.4.4 Use Excel to calculate the equation of the line given data points

We can use Excel to calculate the gradient of the line and y intercept if we know the data point values by employing two Excel functions: intercept and slope.

⌕ Example 2.27

Consider Example 2.20 where we were required to plot a graph of y against x for equation $y = 2x - 3$. In this example the values of x were varied between -3 to $+3$ and the values of y were calculated. These data values have been inserted into the Excel workbook for x (B5:B11) and y (C5:C11). Excel has two functions 'intercept' and 'slope' which provide a value of intercept = -3 and slope = 2. This would give an equation of the line of $y = 2x - 3$ (see Figure 2.55). This agrees with the equation in Example 2.20.

C14		▼	f_x =SLOPE(C5:C11,B5:B11)	
	A	B	C	D
1				
2		Data points for equation y = 2x - 3		
3				
4		x	y	
5		-3	-9	
6		-2	-7	
7		-1	-5	
8		0	-3	
9		1	-1	
10		2	1	
11		3	3	
12				
13		intercept =	-3	=INTERCEPT(C5:C11,B5:B11)
14		slope =	2	=SLOPE(C5:C11,B5:B11)

Figure 2.55

→ Excel Function Method

Intercept = Cell C13   Formula: =INTERCEPT(C5:C11,B5:B11)
Slope = Cell C14   Formula: =SLOPE(C5:C11,B5:B11)

Note   The Excel functions 'intercept' and 'slope' are based upon a technique for fitting lines to data sets called least squares regression. Least squares regression will be discussed in greater detail in Chapter 10 (Linear Correlation and Regression Analysis). In these data sets the data points do not always lie on the same line and least squares fits a line based on minimizing the degree of error between the line y value and the data value at a data point x value.

Student Exercises

X2.7 In Exercise X2.6 we stated the gradient and the intercept of these line equations:
(a) $y = 5x + 1$, (b) $y = -3x + 5$, (c) $y = \frac{1}{2}x + 3$.

(a) Use Excel to plot the data points and fit a straight line.

(b) Use Excel to calculate the intercept and slope of this line.

(c) Do these answers agree with your answers to Exercise X2.6?

■ Techniques in Practice

1. Coco S.A. supplies a range of computer hardware and software to 2000 schools within a large municipal region of Spain. When Coco S.A. won the contract the issue of financial investment was discussed and a decision made to purchase new land to build a new factory. The investment plan consisted of making regular monthly payments over a 5 year period with the estimated purchase cost of the land at €1500000. The financial director used Excel to estimate the required monthly payment to achieve this amount over the 5 years by employing the Excel PMT() function =PMT(interest_rate, number_payments, PV, FV, type), with interest rate assumed to be 6% per annum.

- Interest_rate = 6%/12
- Number_payments = 5 * 12
- PV = 0
- FV = –1500000 (negative, cash outflow)
- type = 1 (assumption: paid at beginning of time period)

Substituting these values into the PMT() function gives =PMT(6%/12, 5 * 12, 0, –1500000, 1). From Excel this gives the monthly payment of 21392.24 (cash outflow). A monthly cash payment of €21392.24 will provide the required €1500000 at the end of the 5 year period to purchase the land if the interest rate is 6% per annum.

2. Bakers Ltd runs a chain of bakery shops and is famous for the quality of its pies. The company management accountant has advised that the cost of re-building a shop in 18 years will be £100000 and the company owners have requested that a lump sum be paid in now to provide this re-build costs. After careful consideration the accountant has identified a suitable investment vehicle paying 8% per annum. The lump sum required can be calculated from the Excel present value function =PV(interest_rate, number_payments, payment, FV, type), where:

- Interest_rate = 8%
- Number_payments = 18

- PV = 0
- FV = –100000 (negative, cash outflow)
- type = 1 (assumption: paid at beginning of time period)

Substituting these values into the Excel PV() function gives =PV(8%, 18, 0, –100000, 1). From Excel this gives the monthly payment of 25024.90 (cash outflow). An initial lump sum of £25025 will be worth £100000 after 18 years assuming an interest rate of 8% per annum.

3. Skodel Ltd is a small brewery that is undergoing a major expansion after a take over by a large European brewery chain. Skodel Ltd produces a range of beers and lagers and is renowned for the quality of its beers; winning a number of prizes at trade fairs throughout the European Union. The new parent company plans to invest €350000 in a new bottling plant in 15 years. The finance director has authorized €140000 to be invested now and will use the Excel RATE() function to estimate the rate per annum required to reach the investment target. The RATE() function is used to calculate the interest applied on a loan or an investment =RATE(number_payments, payment, PV, FV, type), where:

- Number_payments = 15
- Payment = 0
- PV = 140000 (positive, cash inflow)
- FV = –350000 (negative, cash outflow)
- type = 1

Substituting these values into the Excel RATE() function gives =RATE(15, 0, 140000, –350000, 1). From Excel this gives a rate of 6.2990%. A rate of 6.3% per annum will achieve €350000 after 15 years if we invest €140000 now.

Summary

In this chapter we have provided the reader with a set of tools that can be used to aid their understanding of applying mathematical concepts in solving problems. The skills developed in this chapter will be used in all other chapters within this text book. The next chapter will explore visualizing data sets using charts and graphs.

Key Terms

Absolute	Combination	Directed numbers
Addition	Compound interest	Division
Algebra	Coordinate geometry	Equation of a line
Annuity	Coordinate of a point	Excel scientific notation
Brackets	Decimal	Exchange

Factorial
Financial functions
Foreign currency
Fraction
Future value
Increasing the sum invested
Indices
Integer
Intercept
Logarithm
Logarithm base 10
Mathematical functions
Multiplication

Natural Logarithm
Negative numbers
Net present value
Percentages
Pi
Plotting straight line graphs
Positive numbers
Power
Present value
Present value of a stream of
  earnings
Simple interest

Sinking funds or future value
  of an annuity
Slope
Square roots
Squares
Statistical functions
Substitution
Subtraction
Sum
Trend line
Trust funds or present value
  of an ordinary annuity

■ Further Reading

Gaulter, B. and Buchanan, L. (2000) *GNVQ Key Skills: Application of Number* (2nd Edition). Oxford University Press. ISBN-13: 978-0-19-914796-0.

■ Formula Summary

$$SI = \frac{PRT}{100} \tag{2.1}$$

$$SI = P \times T \times r \tag{2.2}$$

$$S = P(1 + r)^n \tag{2.3}$$

$$I = P(1 + r)^n - P \tag{2.4}$$

$$S = P(1+r)^n + \frac{a(1+r)^n - a}{r} \tag{2.5}$$

$$S = \frac{a(1+r)^n - a}{r} \tag{2.6}$$

$$a = \frac{rS}{(1+r)^n - 1} \tag{2.7}$$

$$S = a\frac{(1+r)^{n+1} - (1+r)}{r} \tag{2.8}$$

$$a = \frac{rS}{(1+r)^{n+1} - (1+r)} \tag{2.9}$$

$$P = \frac{S}{(1+r)^n} = S(1+r)^{-n} \tag{2.10}$$

$$P = a\frac{1 - (1+r)^{-n}}{r} \tag{2.11}$$

$$a = \frac{rP}{1 - (1+r)^{-n}} \tag{2.12}$$

$$NPV = \sum_{i=1}^{n} \frac{values_i}{(1 + rate)^i} \tag{2.13}$$

$$y = mx + c \tag{2.14}$$

Visualizing and Presenting Data 3

The display of various types of data or information in the form of tables, graphs, and diagrams is quite a common spectacle these days. Newspapers, magazines, and television all use these types of displays to try and convey information in an easy to assimilate way. In a nut shell what these forms of displays aim to do is to summarize large sets of raw data such that we can see at a glance the 'behaviour' of the data.

THE WORST OFFENDERS

Bank	Account	Cut	Mortgage rate cut
A&L	Direct Saver	−4.95%	−2.20%
Abbey	50+	−4.65%	−2.85%
Halifax	Web Saver	−4.65%	−3.50%
Nationwide	e-Savings	−4.60%	−3.99%
Northern Rock	E-Saver	−4.00%	−2.70%

SOURCE: Moneyfacts.co.uk

Table 3.1 'No better off after rate cuts', Elizabeth Colman, *The Sunday Times* — Money, 12th April 2009, p. 6

This chapter and the next will use a variety of techniques that can be used to present the data in a form that will make sense to people.

In this chapter we will look at using tables and graphical forms to represent the raw data and in Chapter 4 we will explore methods that can put a summary number to the raw data.

» Overview «

In this chapter we shall look at methods to summarize data using tables and charts:

» Tabulating data

» Graphing data

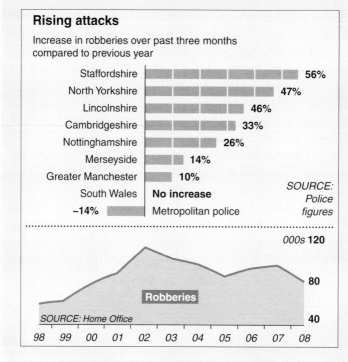

Figure 3.1
'Muggings soar as recession bites', David Leppard, *The Sunday Times*, 12th April 2009, p. 11.

» Learning Objectives «

On successful completion of this chapter, you will be able to:

» Understand the different types of data variables that can be used to represent a specific measurement.

» Know how to present data in table form.

» Present data in a variety of graphical forms.

» Construct frequency distributions from raw data.

» Distinguish between discrete and continuous data.

» Construct histograms for equal and unequal class widths.

» Understand what we mean by a frequency polygon.

» Solve problems using Microsoft Excel.

x

Histogram A histogram is a way of summarizing data that are measured on an interval scale (either discrete or continuous).

Frequency polygon A graph made by joining the middle-top points of the columns of a frequency histogram.

3.1 The Different Types of Data Variable

A **variable** is any measured characteristic or attribute that differs for different subjects. For example, if the height of 1000 subjects were measured, then height would be a variable. Variables can be *quantitative* or *qualitative* (sometimes called '**categorical variables**'). **Quantitative variables** (or numerical variables) are measured on one of three scales: **interval**, **ratio**, or **ordinal**. **Qualitative variables** are measured on a **nominal** (or categorical) scale. If a group of business students were asked to name their favourite browser to browse the web, then the variable would be qualitative. If the time spent on the computer to research a topic were measured, then the variable would be quantitative. *Nominal* measurement consists of assigning items to groups or categories. No quantitative information is conveyed and no ordering of the items is implied. Nominal scales are therefore qualitative rather than quantitative. Football club allegiance, sex or gender, degree type, courses studied are all examples of nominal scales. **Frequency distributions**, covered in Chapter 4, are usually used to analyse data measured on a nominal scale. The main **statistic** computed is the mode. Variables measured on a nominal scale are often referred to as *categorical* or *qualitative* variables. It is very important that you understand the type of data variable that you have since the type of graph or summary statistic calculated will be dependent upon the type of data variable that you are handling.

Measurements with *ordinal scales* are ordered in the sense that higher numbers represent higher values. However, the intervals between the numbers are not necessarily equal. For example, on a five-point rating scale measuring student satisfaction, the difference between a rating of 1 ('very poor') and a rating of 2 ('poor') may not represent the same difference as the difference between a rating of 4 ('good') and a rating of 5 ('very good'). The lowest point on the rating scale in the example was arbitrarily chosen to be 1 and this scale does not have a 'true' zero point. The only conclusion you can make is that one is better than the other (or even worse) but you cannot say that one is twice as good as the other.

On **interval** measurement scales, one unit on the scale represents the same magnitude of the characteristic being measured across the whole range of the scale. For example, if student stress was being measured on an interval scale, then a difference between a score of 5 and a score of 6 would represent the same difference in anxiety as would a difference between a score of 9 and a score of 10. Interval scales do not have a 'true' zero point, however, and therefore it is not possible to make statements about how many times higher one score is than another. For the stress measurement, it would not be valid to say that a person with a score of 6 was twice as anxious as a person with a score of 3.

Ratio scales are like interval scales except they have true zero points. For example, a weight of 100 g is twice as much as 50 g. Interval and ratio measurements are also called **continuous variables**. Table 3.1 provides an example of a table published in an English newspaper. Table 3.2 below summarizes the different measurement scales with examples provided of these different scales.

Variable A variable is a symbol that can take on any of a specified set of values.

Categorical variable A set of data is said to be categorical if the values or observations belonging to it can be sorted according to category.

Quantitative variable Variables can be classified using numbers.

Ratio variable Ratio data are continuous data where both differences and ratios are interpretable and have a natural zero.

Ordinal variable A set of data is said to be ordinal if the values belonging to it can be ranked.

Qualitative variable Variables can be classified as descriptive or categorical.

Nominal scale A set of data is said to be nominal if the values belonging to it can be assigned a label rather than a number.

Frequency distributions Systematic method of showing the number of occurrences of observational data in order from least to greatest.

Statistic A statistic is a quantity that is calculated from a sample of data.

Interval scale An interval scale is a scale of measurement where the distance between any two adjacent units of measurement (or 'intervals') is the same but the zero point is arbitrary.

Continuous variable A set of data is said to be continuous if the values belong to a continuous interval of real values.

Measurement Scale	Recognizing a measurement scale
Nominal data	1. Classification data e.g. male or female, red or black car. 2. Arbitrary labels e.g. m or f, r or b, 0 or 1. 3. No ordering e.g. it makes no sense to state that r > b.
Ordinal data	1. Ordered list, e.g. student satisfaction scale of 1, 2, 3, 4, and 5. 2. Differences between values are not important e.g. political parties can be given labels: far left, left, mid, right, far right etc.
Interval data	1. Ordered, constant scale, with no natural zero e.g. temperature, dates. 2. Differences make sense, but ratios do not e.g. temperature difference.
Ratio data	1. Ordered, constant scale, and a natural zero e.g. length, height, weight, and age.

Table 3.2

3.2 Tables

Presenting data in tabular form can make even the most comprehensive descriptive narrative of data more readily intelligible. Apart from taking up less room, a table enables figures to be located quicker; easy comparisons between different classes to be made and may reveal patterns which cannot otherwise be deduced. The simplest form of table indicates the frequency of occurrence of objects within a number of defined categories. Microsoft Excel provides a number of tables that can be constructed using raw data or data that is already in summary form.

3.2.1 What a table looks like

Tables come in a variety of formats, from simple tables to frequency distribution, that allow data sets to be summarized in a form that allows users to be able to access important information. Table 3.1 compares the interest rate and mortgage rate cuts for 5 leading bank accounts that appeared in *The Sunday Times* newspaper on the 12th April 2009. We can see from the table information on lender, account, interest rate cut, and mortgage rate cut . This table will have been created from a data set collected by the researcher.

▷ Example 3.1

When asked the question 'if there was a general election tomorrow, which party would you vote for', 1110 students responded as follows: 400 said Conservative, 510 Labour, 78 Democrats, 55 Green and the rest some other party. We can put this information in a table form indicating the frequency within each category either as a raw score, or as a percentage of the total number of responses.

Proposed voting behaviour by 1110 university students
(*Source:* University Student Survey October 2008)

Party	Frequency		Party	Frequency %
Conservative	400		Conservative	36
Labour	510		Labour	46
Democrat	78	or	Democrat	7
Green	55		Green	5
Other	67		Other	6
Total	1110		Total	100

Table 3.3 Proposed voting behaviour

Note
- When secondary data source is used it is acknowledged.
- The title of the table is given.
- The total of the frequencies is given.
- When percentages are used for frequencies this is indicated together with the sample size, n.

Sometimes categories can be subdivided and tables can be constructed to convey this information together with the frequency of occurrence within the subcategories. For example the following table indicates the frequency of half yearly sales of two cars produced by a large company with the sales split by month.

Example 3.2

Half-yearly sales of XBAR Ltd							
Month	January	February	March	April	May	June	Total
Pink	5200	4100	6000	6900	6050	7000	35250
Blue	2100	1050	2950	5000	6300	5200	22600
Total	7300	5150	8950	11900	12350	12200	57850

Table 3.4 Half yearly sales of XBAR Ltd

Further subdivisions of categories may also be displayed as indicated in the table in Example 3.3 below, showing a sample of the television viewing behaviour of adult males.

Example 3.3

Tabulated results from a survey undertaken to measure the television viewing habits of adult males by marital status and age.

	Single		Married	
	Under 30	30+	Under 30	30+
Less than 15 hrs per week	330	358	1162	484
15 hrs or more per week	1719	241	643	1521
Total	2049	599	1805	2005

Table 3.5 Viewing habits of adult males

3.2.2 Creating a frequency distribution

When data is collected by survey or by some other form we have initially a set of unorganized *raw data* which, when viewed would convey little information. A first step would be to organize the set into a *frequency distribution* such that 'like' quantities are collected and the frequency of occurrence of the quantities determined.

Example 3.4

Consider the set of data that represents the number of insurance claims processed each day by an insurance firm over a period of 40 days: 3, 5, 9, 6, 4, 7, 8, 6, 2, 5, 10, 1, 6, 3, 6, 5, 4, 7, 8, 4, 5, 9, 4, 2, 7, 6, 1, 3, 5, 6, 2, 6, 4, 8, 3, 1, 7, 9, 7, 2.

SCORE	TALLY	FREQUENCY, f
1	111	3
2	1111	4
3	1111	4
4	1111	5
5	1111	5
6	1111 11	7
7	1111	5
8	111	3
9	111	3
10	1	1
		Σf = 40

The frequency distribution can be used to show how many days it took for one claim to be processed, how many days to process two claims and so on. The simplest way of doing this is by creating a *tally chart*. Write down the range of values from lowest (1) to the highest (10) then go through the data set recording each score in the table with a tally mark. It's a good idea to cross out figures in the data set as you go through it to prevent double counting. Table 3.6 illustrates the frequency distribution for Example 3.4 data set.

Table 3.6

In this example there were relatively few cases. However, we may have increased our survey period to one year and the range of claims may have been between 0 and 30. Since our aim is to summarize information we may find it better to group 'likes' into *classes* to form a **grouped frequency distribution**. The next example illustrates this point.

▷ Example 3.5

Consider the following data set of miles recorded by 120 salesmen in one week

403	407	407	408	410	412	413	413
423	424	424	425	426	428	430	430
435	435	436	436	436	438	438	438
444	444	445	446	447	447	447	448
452	453	453	453	454	455	455	456
462	462	462	463	464	465	466	468
474	474	475	476	477	478	479	481
490	493	494	495	497	498	498	500
415	430	439	449	457	468	482	502
416	431	440	450	457	469	482	502
418	432	440	450	458	470	483	505
419	432	441	451	459	471	485	508
420	433	442	451	459	471	486	509
421	433	442	451	460	472	488	511
421	434	443	452	460	473	489	515

This mass of data conveys little in terms of information. Because there would be too many value scores, putting the data into an ungrouped frequency distribution would not portray an adequate summary. Grouping the data, however, provides the following:

MILEAGE	TALLY	FREQUENCY, f
400–419	‖‖‖ ‖‖‖ 11	12
420–439	‖‖‖ ‖‖‖ ‖‖‖ ‖‖‖ ‖‖‖ 11	27
440–459	‖‖‖ ‖‖‖ ‖‖‖ ‖‖‖ ‖‖‖ ‖‖‖ 1111	34
460–479	‖‖‖ ‖‖‖ ‖‖‖ ‖‖‖ 1111	24
480–499	‖‖‖ ‖‖‖ ‖‖‖	15
500–519	‖‖‖ 111	8
		$\Sigma f = 120$

Table 3.7 Grouped frequency distribution data for Example 3.5 data

X
Grouped frequency distributions Data arranged in intervals to show the frequency with which the possible values of a variable occur.

Excel spreadsheet solution—frequency distribution using Example 3.5 data

The Excel spreadsheet solution can be obtained using the following instructions:

Step 1 Input data into cells A6:H20

	A	B	C	D	E	F	G	H
1								
2	Histogram							
3								
4	Miles Recorded by 120 Salesmen							
5								
6	403	407	407	408	410	412	413	413
7	423	424	424	425	426	428	430	430
8	435	435	436	436	436	438	438	438
9	444	444	445	446	447	447	447	448
10	452	453	453	453	454	455	455	456
11	462	462	462	463	464	465	466	468
12	474	474	475	476	477	478	479	481
13	490	493	494	495	497	498	498	500
14	415	430	439	449	457	468	482	502
15	416	431	440	450	457	469	482	502
16	418	432	440	450	458	470	483	505
17	419	432	441	451	459	471	485	508
18	420	433	442	451	459	471	486	509
19	421	433	442	451	460	472	488	511
20	421	434	443	452	460	473	489	515

Figure 3.2

Step 2 Excel spreadsheet macro command—using Analysis ToolPak

Excel can construct grouped frequency distributions from raw data by using a special macro called Analysis ToolPak. Before we use this add-in we have to input the lower and upper class boundaries into Excel. Excel calls this the Bin Range. In this example we have decided to create a Bin Range that is based upon equal class widths. Let us choose the following groups with the Bin Range calculated from these group values.

MILEAGE	LCB–UCB	Class Width	Bin Range
			399.5
400–419	399.5–419.5	20	419.5
420–439	419.5–439.5	20	439.5
440–459	439.5–459.5	20	459.5
460–479	459.5–479.5	20	479.5
480–499	479.5–499.5	20	499.5
500–519	499.5–519.5	20	519.5

Table 3.8 Class and Bin Range

We can see that the class widths are all unequal and the corresponding Bin Range is 399.5, 419.5, …, 519.5. We can now use Excel to calculate the grouped frequency distribution.

Bin Range: Cells B24:B30 (with the label in cell B23).

	A	B	C	D	E	F	G	H
1								
2	Histogram							
3								
4	Miles Recorded by 120 Salesmen							
5								
6	403	407	407	408	410	412	413	413
7	423	424	424	425	426	428	430	430
8	435	435	436	436	436	438	438	438
9	444	444	445	446	447	447	447	448
10	452	453	453	453	454	455	455	456
11	462	462	462	463	464	465	466	468
12	474	474	475	476	477	478	479	481
13	490	493	494	495	497	498	498	500
14	415	430	439	449	457	468	482	502
15	416	431	440	450	457	469	482	502
16	418	432	440	450	458	470	483	505
17	419	432	441	451	459	471	485	508
18	420	433	442	451	459	471	486	509
19	421	433	442	451	460	472	488	511
20	421	434	443	452	460	473	489	515
21								
22								
23		Bin Range						
24		399.5						
25		419.5						
26		439.5						
27		459.5						
28		479.5						
29		499.5						
30		519.5						

Figure 3.3

Figure 3.4

Now create the histogram.
Select Tools.
Select Data Analysis menu.
Click on Histogram.
Click OK.

Figure 3.5

Input Data Range: Cells A6:H20
Input Bin Range: Cells B24:B30
Choose location of Output range: Cell D23.
Click OK.

Excel will now print out the grouped frequency table (Bin Range and frequency of occurrence) as presented in cells D23–E31.

	A	B	C	D	E	F	G	H
1								
2	Histogram							
3								
4	Miles Recorded by 120 Salesmen							
5								
6	403	407	407	408	410	412	413	413
7	423	424	424	425	426	428	430	430
8	435	435	436	436	436	438	438	438
9	444	444	445	446	447	447	447	448
10	452	453	453	453	454	455	455	456
11	462	462	462	463	464	465	466	468
12	474	474	475	476	477	478	479	481
13	490	493	494	495	497	498	498	500
14	415	430	439	449	457	468	482	502
15	416	431	440	450	457	469	482	502
16	418	432	440	450	458	470	483	505
17	419	432	441	451	459	471	485	508
18	420	433	442	451	459	471	486	509
19	421	433	442	451	460	472	488	511
20	421	434	443	452	460	473	489	515
21								
22								
23		Bin Range		Bin	Frequency			
24		399.5		399.5	0			
25		419.5		419.5	12			
26		439.5		439.5	27			
27		459.5		459.5	34			
28		479.5		479.5	24			
29		499.5		499.5	15			
30		519.5		519.5	8			
31				More	0			

Figure 3.6

The grouped frequency distribution would now be as follows:

Bin Range	Frequency
399.5	0
419.5	12
439.5	27
459.5	34
479.5	24
499.5	15
519.5	8
More	0

Table 3.9 Bin and frequency values

From this table we can now create the grouped frequency distribution:

Bin Range	Frequency	MILEAGE
419.5	12	400–419
439.5	27	420–439
459.5	34	440–459
479.5	24	460–479
499.5	15	480–499
519.5	8	500–519

Table 3.10 Grouped frequency distribution

3.2.3 Types of data

Data can exist in two forms: *discrete* and *continuous*. Discrete data occurs as an integer (whole number) e.g. 1, 2, 3, 4, 5, 6, ... etc. Continuous data occurs as a continuous number and can take any level of accuracy, e.g. the number of miles travelled could be 440.3 or 440.34 or 440.342 and so on.

A	B
5–under 10	5–9
10–under 15	10–15

Table 3.11

It is important to note that whether data is discrete or continuous depends not upon how it is collected but how it occurs in reality. Thus height, distance, and age are all examples of continuous data although they may be presented as whole numbers. *Class limits* are the extreme boundaries. The class limits given in a frequency distribution are called the **stated** limits. Two common types are illustrated in Table 3.11. To ensure that there are no gaps between classes and to help locate data in their appropriate class, we devise what are known as *true* or *mathematical limits*. All calculations are based on these true/mathematical limits. Their definition is determined by whether we are dealing with continuous or discrete data. The following table indicates how these limits may be defined:

| | STATED LIMIT | MATHEMATICAL LIMIT | |
		DISCRETE	CONTINUOUS
A	5–under 10 10–under 15	4.5–9.5 9.5–15.5	5–9.999999' 10–14.999999'
B	5–9 10–15	4.5–9.5 9.5–15.5	4.5–9.5 9.5–15.5

Table 3.12 Example of mathematical limits

Placing of discrete data into an appropriate class usually provides few problems. If the data is continuous and stated limits are as style A then a value of 9.9 would be placed in the 5–under 10 stated class, conversely if style B were used then it would be placed in the 10–15 stated class. Using the true mathematical limits the width of a class can be found.

Stated limits The lower and upper limits of a class interval.

If CW = Class width, UCB = Upper class boundary, and LCB = Lower class boundary, then the class width is calculated using equation (3.1).

$$CW = UCB - LCB \qquad\qquad (3.1)$$

In Example 3.4, the true limits would be 0.5–1.5, 1.5–2.5, and the class width = 1.5–0.5 = 1.0. In Example 3.5, the true limits would be 395.5–419.5, 419.5–439.5, and the class width = 419.5 – 395.5 = 20. Open ended classes are sometimes used at the two ends of a distribution as a catch-all for extreme values and stated as, for example up to 40, 40–50, ..., 100 and over. There are no hard and fast rules for the number of classes to use although the following should be taken into consideration.

(a) Use between 5 and 12 classes. The actual number will depend on the size of the sample and minimizing the loss of information.

(b) Class widths are easier to handle if in multiples of 2, 5, or 10 units.

(c) Although not always possible, try and keep classes at the same widths within a distribution.

(d) As a guide the following formula can be used to calculate the number of classes given the class boundaries and the class width. Based upon this calculation we would construct with six classes.

$$\text{Class Width} = \frac{\text{Highest Value} - \text{Lowest Value}}{\text{Class With}} = \frac{120}{6} = 20$$

3.2.4 Creating a table using Excel Pivot Table

What is a Pivot Table?

A Pivot Table is a way to extract data from a long list of information, and present it in a readable form. To rearrange the worksheet, simply drag and drop column headings to a new location on the worksheet, and Microsoft Excel re-arranges the data accordingly. To begin, you first need raw data to work with. The general rule is you need more than two criteria of data to work with—otherwise you have nothing to pivot. Figure 3.7 depicts a typical Pivot Table where we have tabulated department spends against month. Notice the black down-pointing arrows in the Pivot Table. On Row 1 we have Department.

Sum of Department Budget (euros)	Month			
Department	Apr	May	Jun	Grand Total
ADVERTISING	12377	12377	12422	37176
MARKETING	7046	7046	7246	21338
SALES	11100	11700	10800	33600
Grand Total	30523	31123	30468	92114

Figure 3.7

If the black arrow were clicked, a drop-down box would appear showing a list of the departments.

We could click on a department and view the departmental spend for the three months measured, or we could select which departments to view, or choose only one month. But Excel does most of the work for you, and puts in those drop-down boxes as part of the wizard. In the example we can see the advertising budget spend in June was 12422 euros.

Example 3.6

This example consists of a set of data that has been collected to measure the departmental spend of individuals within three departments of CoCo S.A.

The budgets spend (in euros) have been measured for April, May, and June 2007.

	A	B	C	D
1	Name	Department	Month	Department Budget (euros)
2	PAUL	MARKETING	Apr	2345
3	PAUL	MARKETING	May	2345
4	PAUL	MARKETING	Jun	2345
5	ALAN	MARKETING	Apr	1500
6	ALAN	MARKETING	May	1500
7	ALAN	MARKETING	Jun	1700
8	JANE	MARKETING	Apr	3201
9	JANE	MARKETING	May	3201
10	JANE	MARKETING	Jun	3201
11	KIM	ADVERTISING	Apr	5500
12	KIM	ADVERTISING	May	5500
13	KIM	ADVERTISING	Jun	5500
14	PETRA	ADVERTISING	Apr	2987
15	PETRA	ADVERTISING	May	2987
16	PETRA	ADVERTISING	Jun	2987
17	TONY	ADVERTISING	Apr	1300
18	TONY	ADVERTISING	May	1300
19	TONY	ADVERTISING	Jun	1345
20	BRIAN	ADVERTISING	Apr	2590
21	BRIAN	ADVERTISING	May	2590
22	BRIAN	ADVERTISING	Jun	2590
23	JULIA	SALES	Apr	1600
24	JULIA	SALES	May	1600
25	JULIA	SALES	Jun	1800
26	NOREEN	SALES	Apr	5000
27	NOREEN	SALES	May	5600
28	NOREEN	SALES	Jun	5600
29	KAREN	SALES	Apr	4500
30	KAREN	SALES	May	4500
31	KAREN	SALES	Jun	3400

Figure 3.8

Excel spreadsheet solution—Pivot Table using Example 3.6 data

The Pivot Table wizard

To create a Pivot Table, place the cursor anywhere in the data area and then start the Pivot Table wizard from the data menu as shown in Figure 3.9. The Pivot Table wizard will walk you through the process of creating an initial Pivot Table. While there are many advanced options available to use, in this example, we will simply click the Finish button to create a quick Pivot Table. Select PivotTable and PivotChart Report and follow instructions.

Figure 3.9

Click Next.
Note that every column that contains data MUST have the column heading, otherwise PivotTable cannot be created.

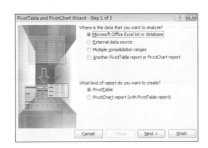

Figure 3.10

Data area A1:D31 is automatically inserted if the cursor is placed within the data area. Use  to browse and highlight the data set if you forget to click inside the data area. Click <u>N</u>ext.

Figure 3.11

Choose F10 to insert the Pivot Table in the existing worksheet. Click Finish.

Figure 3.12

Dragging and dropping data

Excel creates a blank Pivot Table and the user must then drag and drop the various fields from the items, the resulting report is displayed 'on the fly':

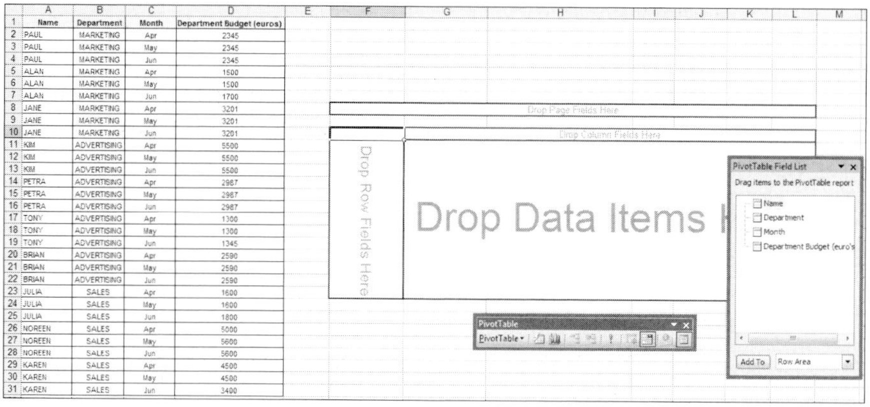

Figure 3.13

Presented in Figure 3.14 are but a few examples of hundreds of possible reports that could be viewed with this data through the Pivot Table format.

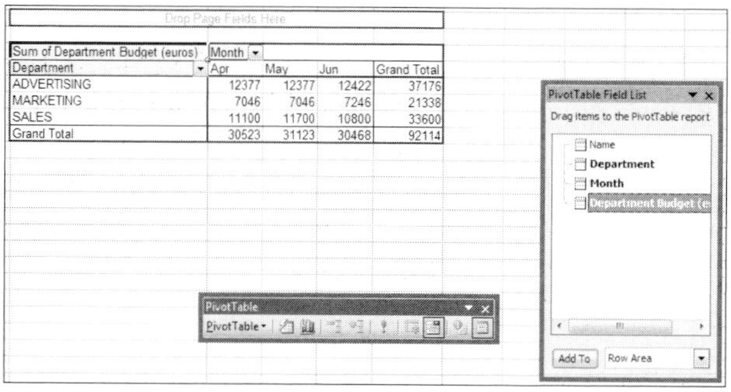

Sum of Department Budget (euros)	Month			
Department	Apr	May	Jun	Grand Total
ADVERTISING	12377	12377	12422	37176
MARKETING	7046	7046	7246	21338
SALES	11100	11700	10800	33600
Grand Total	30523	31123	30468	92114

Figure 3.14

For Figure 3.13 choose:

- Department—drop row fields here.
- Month—drop column fields here.
- Department budget—drop data items here.

Modifying reports

The Pivot Table field dialog box allows changes to be made to the Pivot Table e.g. we can change this report to display percentages of total, instead of total amounts (see Figure 3.15).

Figure 3.15

This particular Pivot Table can be modified to display different results such as averages, counts, minimums, maximums, etc.

Figure 3.16

Expand the box by clicking the options button .
The resulting expanded dialog box is shown on the left.
In this advanced options section, we then pull down the 'Show data as' field and select '% of total'.

Sum of Department Budget (euros)	Month			
Department	Apr	May	Jun	Grand Total
ADVERTISING	13.44%	13.44%	13.49%	40.36%
MARKETING	7.65%	7.65%	7.87%	23.16%
SALES	12.05%	12.70%	11.72%	36.48%
Grand Total	33.14%	33.79%	33.08%	100.00%

Figure 3.17

The resulting report is shown here.

Auto formatting

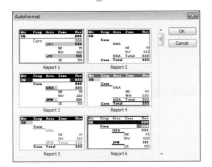

Figure 3.18

The next step in mastering Pivot Tables is to understand how the automatic formatting controls can make data clean-up easy. Simply pull down the Format menu and select AutoFormat. Excel provides an assortment of 22 formats to choose from. Simply choose a format, and your data is now more readable.

In this example choose report 6.

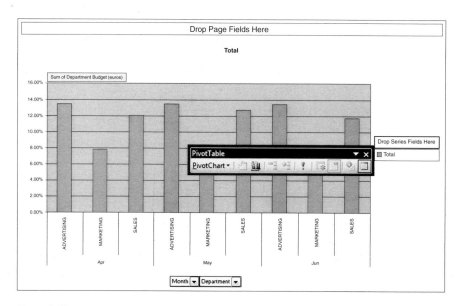

Figure 3.19

Pivot charts

The next step is to create a chart using almost the same technique described above, but this time select the Chart option rather than the Table option from the Pivot Table wizard 👖 (see Figure 3.20).

This default chart can be modified by clicking on 👖 on selecting a new chart type.

Figure 3.20

3.2.5 Principles of table construction

From the above, we can conclude that when constructing tables, good principles to be adopted are as follows: (a) aim at simplicity, (b) the table must have a comprehensive and explanatory title, (c) the source should be stated, (d) units must be clearly stated, (e) the headings to columns and rows should be unambiguous, (f) double counting should be avoided, (g) totals should be shown where appropriate, (h) percentages and ratios should be computed and shown where appropriate, and (i) overall use your imagination and common sense.

Student Exercises

X3.1 Criticize the following table

Castings	Weight of Metal	Foundry
Up to 4 ton	60	210
Up to 10 ton	100	640
All Other Weights	110	800
Other	20	85
Total	290	2000

X3.2 The following represents the number of customers visited by a salesman over a 80 week period

68	64	75	82	68	60	62	88	76	93	73	79	88	73	60	93
71	59	85	75	61	65	75	87	74	62	95	78	63	72	66	78
82	75	94	77	69	74	68	60	96	78	89	61	75	95	60	79
83	71	79	62	67	97	78	85	76	65	71	75	65	80	73	57
88	78	62	76	53	74	86	67	73	81	72	63	76	75	85	77

Use Excel to construct a grouped frequency distribution from the above data set and indicate both stated and mathematical limits (start at 50–54 with class width of 5).

3.3 Graphical Representation of Data

The next stage of analysis after the data has been tabulated is to graph the data using a variety of methods to provide a suitable graph. In this section we will explore: bar charts, pie charts, histograms, frequency polygons, scatter plots, and time series plots. The type of graph you will use to graph the data depends upon the type of variable you are dealing with within your data set e.g. category (or nominal), ordinal, or interval (or ratio) data:

Data type	Which graph to use?
Category or nominal	Bar chart, Pie chart, Cross tab tables (or contingency tables)—see Chapter 8.
Ordinal	Bar chart, Pie chart, Scatter plots.
Interval or ratio	Histogram, Frequency polygon. Cumulative frequency curve (or ogive), Scatter plots, Time series plots.

Table 3.13 Deciding which graph type given data type

3.3.1 Bar charts

Graph and *chart* are terms that are often used to refer to any form of graphical display. *Categorical* data is represented largely by bar and pie charts. *Bar charts* are very useful in providing a simple pictorial representation of several sets of data on one graph. Bar charts are used for categorical data where each category is represented by each vertical (or horizontal) bar.

In bar charts each category is represented by a bar with the frequency represented by the height of the bar. All bars should have equal width and the distance between each bar is kept constant.

It is important that the axes (X and Y) are labelled and the chart has an appropriate title. What each bar represents should be clearly stated within the chart. Figure 3.21 represents a component bar chart for half yearly car sales.

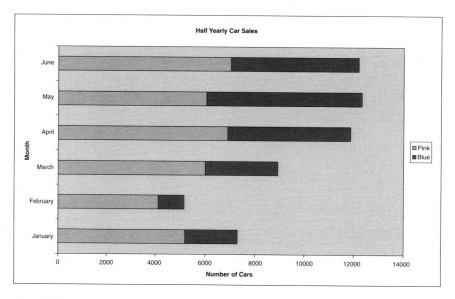

Figure 3.21

Example 3.7

Consider the categorical data in Example 3.1 which represents the proposed voting behaviour of a sample of university students. Excel can be used to create a bar chart to represent this data set. For each category a vertical bar is drawn with the vertical height representing the number of students in that category (or frequency) with the horizontal distance for each bar, and distance between each bar, equal.

Each bar represents the number of students who would vote for a particular United Kingdom political party. From the bar chart you can easily detect the differences of frequency between the five categories (conservative, labour, democrat, green, and other). Figure 3.22 represents a bar chart for the proposed voting behaviour.

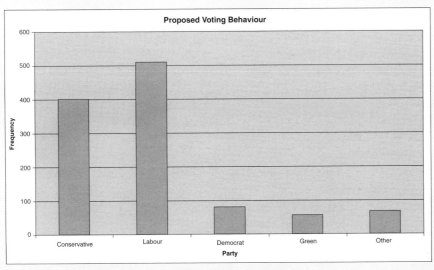

Figure 3.22

⌕ Example 3.8

If you are interested in comparing totals then a *component* (or stacked) *bar chart* is constructed. Figure 3.23 represents a component bar chart for the half yearly car sales (Example 3.2).

In this component bar chart you can see the variation in total sales from month to month, and the split between car type category per month.

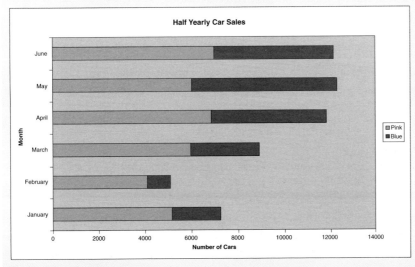

Figure 3.23

Example 3.9

A *multiple bar chart* is used when you want to compare each component over time but the totals are of little importance.

Figure 3.24 represents a multiple bar chart for the half yearly car sales.

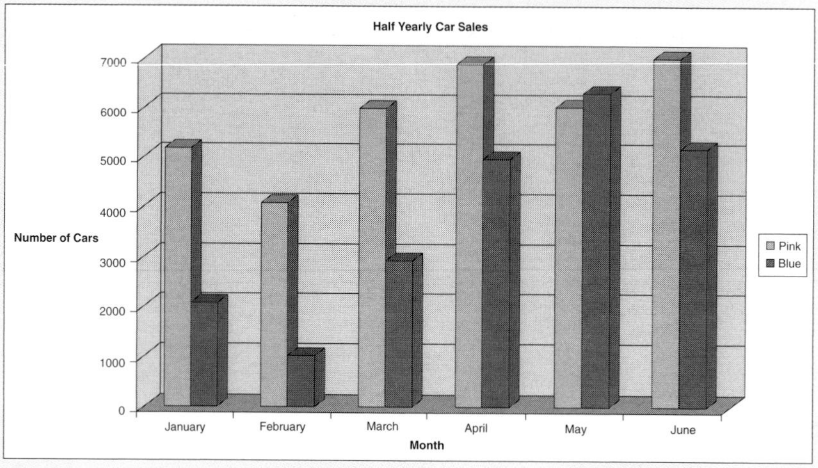

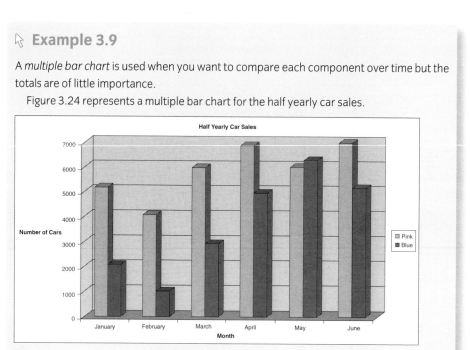

Figure 3.24

Excel ChartWizard solution—bar chart using Example 3.1 data

Step 1 Input Data Series

The data in Example 3.1 consists of two columns of data. Column 1 represents party membership and column 2 represents the number of students proposing to vote for a particular political party (also called frequency of occurrence). We can use Excel to create a bar chart for this data by placing the data in Excel as follows.

Party: Cells B7:B11 (includes label Party, B6)

Frequency: Cells C7:C11 (includes label Frequency, C6)

Figure 3.25 represents the Excel worksheet.

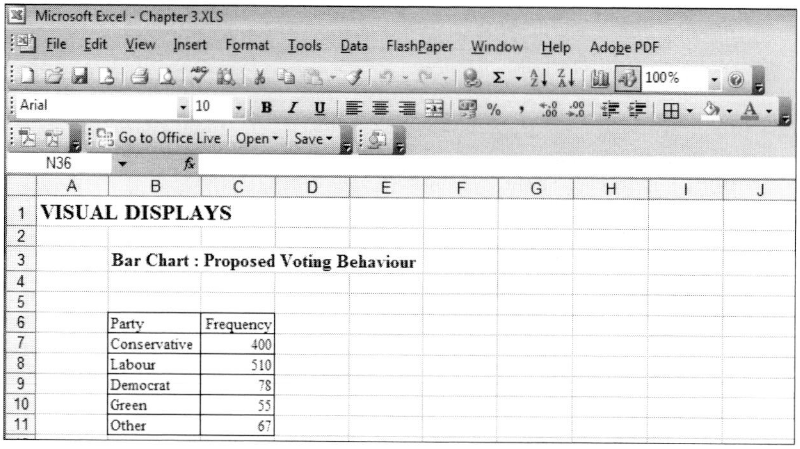

Party	Frequency
Conservative	400
Labour	510
Democrat	78
Green	55
Other	67

Figure 3.25

Step 2 Highlight B6:C11

Step 3 Activate the ChartWizard by Clicking on the ChartWizard Button 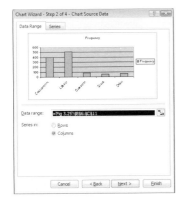 and follow the instructions

ChartWizard—Step 1 of 4: Chart Type

Figure 3.26 illustrates the Excel menu.

You can view the sample chart at this stage by clicking on 'Press and Hold to View Sample'. Choose your chart type.

Click <u>N</u>ext.

Figure 3.26

ChartWizard—Step 2 of 4: Chart Source Data

Click <u>N</u>ext.

Figure 3.27

ChartWizard—Step 3 of 4: Chart Options

Input the chart title: Proposed Voting Behaviour.

Category (X) axis: Party.

Value (Y) axis: Frequency.

Click <u>N</u>ext.

Figure 3.28

ChartWizard—Step 4 of 4: Chart Location

Click on <u>F</u>inish.

Figure 3.29

This will place the bar chart in the location specified. The bar chart will look like the chart in Figure 3.30.

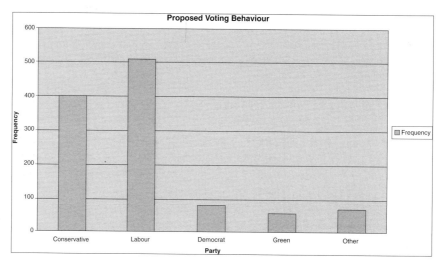

Figure 3.30

Optional: Colour bars

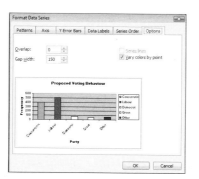

If you double click on one of the bars within the chart then you can then modify the chart. The Option tab will allow you to use different colours for each bar. This is achieved by checking the 'Vary colours by point' box. Click on OK and the bar chart will now appear on the worksheet.

Figure 3.31

Student Exercises

X3.3 Draw a suitable bar chart for the following data

Industrial Sources for Consumption and Investment Demand (thousand million)		
Producing Industry	Consumption	Investment
Agriculture, mining	1.1	0.1
Metal manufacturers	2.0	2.7
Other manufacturing	6.8	0.3
Construction	0.9	2.7
Gas, electricity & water	1.2	0.2
Services	16.5	0.8
Total	28.5	7.8

3.3.2 Pie charts

In a *pie chart* the relative frequencies are represented by a slice of a circle. Each section represents a category, and the area of a section represents the frequency or number of objects within a category. They are particularly useful in showing relative proportions, but their effectiveness tends to diminish for more than eight categories.

Example 3.10

Consider Example 3.1 proposed voting behaviour data as illustrated in Table 3.14.

Political Party	Voting Behaviour
Conservative	400
Labour	510
Democrat	78
Green	55
Other	67

Table 3.14

This data can then be represented by a pie chart.

Figure 3.32 represents a pie chart for proposed voting behaviour.

We can see that different slices of the circle represent the different choices that people have when it comes to voting.

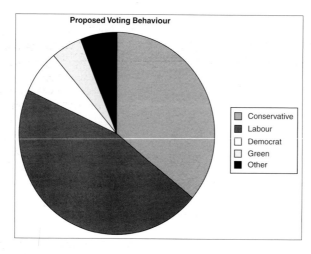

Figure 3.32

Note   Manual Solution

A set of instructions is provided below if you would like to calculate the angles of each slice in the circle that represents each voting category. From the table we can calculate that the total number of students = 400 + 510 + 78 + 55 + 67 = 1110. Given that 360° represents the total number of degrees in a circle, then we can now calculate how many degrees would be represented by each student. For this example we have 360° = 1110 students. Therefore, each student is represented by (360/1110) degrees. Based upon this calculation we can now calculate each angle for each political party category (see Table 3.15).

Political Party	Voting Behaviour	Angle Calculation	Angle (1 decimal place)
Conservative	400	(360/1110) * 400	129.7^0
Labour	510	(360/1110) * 510	165.4^0
Democrat	78	(360/1110) * 78	25.3^0
Green	55	(360/1110) * 55	17.8^0
Other	67	(360/1110) * 67	21.7^0
Total =	1110		359.9

Table 3.15

The size of each slice (sector) depends on the angle at the centre of the circle which in turn depends upon the number in the category the sector represents. Before drawing the pie chart you should always check that the angles you have calculated sum to 360°. A pie chart may be constructed on a percentage basis, or the actual figures may be used.

Excel spreadsheet solution—pie chart using Example 3.1 data

Step 1 Input Data Series

	A	B	C
1	**VISUAL DISPLAYS**		
2			
3		**Pie Chart**	
4			
5			
6		Party	Frequency
7		Conservative	400
8		Labour	510
9		Democrat	78
10		Green	55
11		Other	67

Figure 3.33

The data in Example 3.1 consists of two columns of data. Column 1 represents party membership and column 2 represents the number of students proposing to vote for a particular political party (also called frequency of occurrence). We can use Excel to create a pie chart for this data by placing the data in Excel as illustrated in Figure 3.33. Party: Cells B7:B11 (includes label Party, B6), and Frequency: Cells C7:C11 (includes label Frequency, C6).

Step 2 Highlight B6:B11

Step 3 Activate the ChartWizard by Clicking on the ChartWizard Button

ChartWizard—Step 1 of 4: Chart Type

Figure 3.34

Choose pie chart type.
Click <u>N</u>ext.

ChartWizard—Step 2 of 4: Chart Source Data

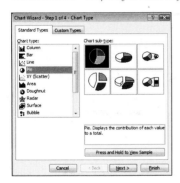

Click <u>N</u>ext.

Figure 3.35

ChartWizard—Step 3 of 4: Chart Options

Input the chart title: Proposed Voting Behaviour.
Click Next.

Figure 3.36

ChartWizard—Step 4 of 4: Chart Location

Click Finish.

Figure 3.37

If you double click on one of the pie chart slices within the chart you can then modify the chart. Click OK and the pie chart will now appear on the worksheet.

Figure 3.38

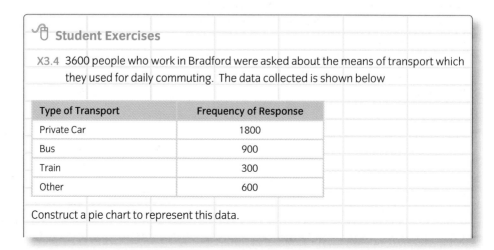

Student Exercises

X3.4   3600 people who work in Bradford were asked about the means of transport which they used for daily commuting. The data collected is shown below

Type of Transport	Frequency of Response
Private Car	1800
Bus	900
Train	300
Other	600

Construct a pie chart to represent this data.

X3.5 The results of the voting in an election were as follows:

Mr P	2045 votes
Mr Q	4238 votes
Mrs R	8605 votes
Ms S	12012 votes

Represent this information on a pie diagram.

3.3.3 Histograms

We have already mentioned the idea of a frequency distribution via the displaying of *category level* data with *tables* and *bar charts*. This concept can now be extended to higher levels of measurement. A point to remember when displaying any form of data is the aim of summarizing information clearly and in such a form that information is not distorted or lost. The method used to graph a *group frequency table* (or distribution) is to construct a *histogram*. A histogram looks like a bar chart but they are different and should not be confused with each other.

Histograms are constructed on the following principles: (a) the horizontal axis (x-axis) is a continuous scale, (b) each class is represented by a vertical rectangle, the base of which extends from one true limit to the next, and (c) the area of the rectangle is proportional to the frequency of the class. This is very important since it means that the area of the bar represents the frequency of each category. In the bar chart the frequency is represented by the height of each bar. This implies that if we double the class width for one bar compared to all the other classes then we would have to halve the height of that particular bar compared to all other bars.

In the special case where all class widths are the same then the height of the bar can be taken to be representative of the frequency of occurrence for that category. It is important to note that either frequencies or relative frequencies can be used to construct a histogram but the shape of the histogram would be exactly the same no matter which variable you chose to graph.

⊳ Example 3.11

Example 3.4 represents the number of insurance claims processed each day by an insurance firm over a period of 40 days (see Table 3.6).

The data variable 'score' is a discrete variable and the frequency distribution is constructed as illustrated in Table 3.16.

SCORE	FREQUENCY, f
1	3
2	4
3	4
4	5
5	5
6	7
7	5
8	3
9	3
10	1
	$\Sigma f = 40$

Table 3.16

Discrete variable A set of data is said to be discrete if the values belonging to it can be counted as 1, 2, 3, …

SCORE	LCB–UCB	Class Width	FREQUENCY, f
1	0.5–1.5	1	3
2	1.5–2.5	1	4
3	2.5–3.5	1	4
4	3.5–4.5	1	5
5	4.5–5.5	1	5
6	5.5–6.5	1	7
7	6.5–7.5	1	5
8	7.5–8.5	1	3
9	8.5–9.5	1	3
10	9.5–10.5	1	1
			$\Sigma f = 40$

We can see from the table that all the class widths are of the same value 1 (constant, class width = UCB − LCB). In this case the histogram can be constructed with the height of the bar representing the frequency of occurrence.

Table 3.17

To construct the histogram we would plot frequency (y-axis, vertical) against score (x-axis) with the boundary between the bars determined by the upper and lower class boundaries (see Figure 3.39).

Figure 3.39 illustrates the class boundary positions for each bar.

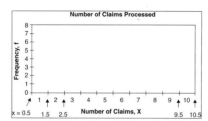

Figure 3.39

The completed histogram is illustrated in Figure 3.40.

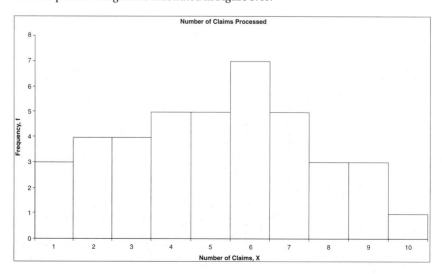

Figure 3.40

We can use the histogram to see how the number of claims varies in frequency from the lowest claims value of 1 to the highest claims value of 10. If we look at the histogram we note:

- Looking along the x-axis we can see that the claims are evenly spread out (1–10).
- The claims rise (1–6) with a maximum of six claims per day which occurred on seven days.
- The claims drop (6–10) with a minimum of 10 claims per day which occurred on one day.

These ideas will lead to the idea of average (central tendency) and data spread (dispersion) which will be explored in Chapter 4.

Example 3.12

Example 3.5 represents the miles recorded by 120 salesmen in one week as illustrated in Table 3.18.

MILEAGE	FREQUENCY, f
400–419	12
420–439	27
440–459	34
460–479	24
480–499	15
500–519	8
	$\Sigma f = 120$

Table 3.18

Figure 3.41 represents the histogram for miles recorded by 120 salesmen.

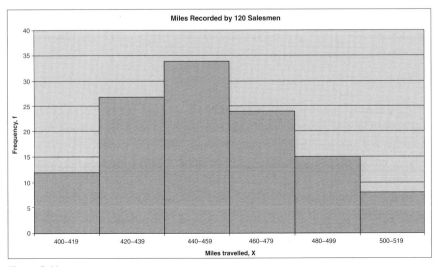

Figure 3.41

Excel spreadsheet solution—histogram with equal class widths using Example 3.5 data

Step 1   Data series

Input data into cells A6:H20

	A	B	C	D	E	F	G	H
1								
2	**Histogram**							
3								
4	Miles Recorded by 120 Salesmen							
5								
6	403	407	407	408	410	412	413	413
7	423	424	424	425	426	428	430	430
8	435	435	436	436	436	438	438	438
9	444	444	445	446	447	447	447	448
10	452	453	453	453	454	455	455	456
11	462	462	462	463	464	465	466	468
12	474	474	475	476	477	478	479	481
13	490	493	494	495	497	498	498	500
14	415	430	439	449	457	468	482	502
15	416	431	440	450	457	469	482	502
16	418	432	440	450	458	470	483	505
17	419	432	441	451	459	471	485	508
18	420	433	442	451	459	471	486	509
19	421	433	442	451	460	472	488	511
20	421	434	443	452	460	473	489	515

Figure 3.42

Step 2   Excel spreadsheet macro command—using Analysis ToolPak

Check that Analysis ToolPak is installed—see Section 1.3.15. Now we can use Excel to create the histogram. Before we use this technique we have to input the lower and upper class boundaries into Excel. Excel calls this the *Bin Range*. In this example we have decided to create a Bin Range that is based upon equal class widths. Let us choose the following groups with the Bin Range calculated from these group values as illustrated in Table 3.19:

MILEAGE	LCB–UCB	Class Width	Bin Range
			399.5
400–419	399.5–419.5	20	419.5
420–439	419.5–439.5	20	439.5
440–459	439.5–459.5	20	459.5
480–499	479.5–499.5	20	499.5
500–519	499.5–519.5	20	519.5

Table 3.19

We can see from Table 3.19 that the class widths are all equal and the corresponding Bin Range is 399.5, 419.5, ..., 519.5. We can now use Excel to create the grouped frequency distribution and corresponding histogram for equal classes. If you want, you can leave the Bin Range box blank. The Histogram tool then automatically creates evenly distributed bin intervals using the minimum and maximum values in the input range as beginning and end points. The number of intervals is equal to the square root of the number of input values (rounded down).

	A	B	C	D	E	F	G	H
1								
2	**Histogram**							
3								
4	Miles Recorded by 120 Salesmen							
5								
6	403	407	407	408	410	412	413	413
7	423	424	424	425	426	428	430	430
8	435	435	436	436	436	438	438	438
9	444	444	445	446	447	447	447	448
10	452	453	453	453	454	455	455	456
11	462	462	462	463	464	465	466	468
12	474	474	475	476	477	478	479	481
13	490	493	494	495	497	498	498	500
14	415	430	439	449	457	468	482	502
15	416	431	440	450	457	469	482	502
16	418	432	440	450	458	470	483	505
17	419	432	441	451	459	471	485	508
18	420	433	442	451	459	471	486	509
19	421	433	442	451	460	472	488	511
20	421	434	443	452	460	473	489	515
21								
22								
23		Bin Range						
24		399.5						
25		419.5						
26		439.5						
27		459.5						
28		479.5						
29		499.5						
30		519.5						

Bin Range: Cells B24:B30 (with the label in cell B23).

Figure 3.43

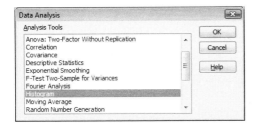

Figure 3.44

Now create the histogram.
Select Tools.
Select Data Analysis Menu.
Click on Histogram.
Click OK.

Figure 3.45

Input Data Range: Cells A6:H20
Input Bin Range: Cells B24:B30
Choose location of Output Range: Cell D23.
Press OK.

Excel will now print out the grouped frequency table (Bin Range and frequency of occurrence) as presented in cells D23–E31 (see Figure 3.46).

	A	B	C	D	E	F	G	H
1								
2	**Histogram**							
3								
4	**Miles Recorded by 120 Salesmen**							
5								
6	403	407	407	408	410	412	413	413
7	423	424	424	425	426	428	430	430
8	435	435	436	436	436	438	438	438
9	444	444	445	446	447	447	447	448
10	452	453	453	453	454	455	455	456
11	462	462	462	463	464	465	466	468
12	474	474	475	476	477	478	479	481
13	490	493	494	495	497	498	498	500
14	415	430	439	449	457	468	482	502
15	416	431	440	450	457	469	482	502
16	418	432	440	450	458	470	483	505
17	419	432	441	451	459	471	485	508
18	420	433	442	451	459	471	486	509
19	421	433	442	451	460	472	488	511
20	421	434	443	452	460	473	489	515
21								
22								
23		Bin Range		Bin	Frequency			
24		399.5		399.5	0			
25		419.5		419.5	12			
26		439.5		439.5	27			
27		459.5		459.5	34			
28		479.5		479.5	24			
29		499.5		499.5	15			
30		519.5		519.5	8			
31				More	0			

Figure 3.46

We can now use Excel to generate the histogram for equal class widths.

Step 3 Input data series

	A	B	C	D
85	**Example 3.12 Solution Histogram - Using Bar Chart**			
86				
87		Mileage	Frequency	
88		400–419	12	
89		420–439	27	
90		440–459	34	
91		460–479	24	
92		480–499	15	
93		500–519	8	

Mileage: Cells B87:B93 (includes data label)
Frequency: Cells C87:C93 (includes data label)
Highlight B87:C93.

Figure 3.47

Step 4 Activate the ChartWizard by Clicking on the ChartWizard Button 📊

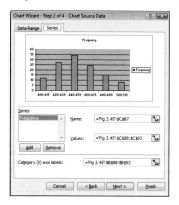

ChartWizard—Step 1 of 4: Chart Type

Choose Column.
Click <u>N</u>ext.

ChartWizard—Step 2 of 4:

Select Chart Format.
Choose Series tab (see Figure 3.48).
Click <u>N</u>ext.

Figure 3.48

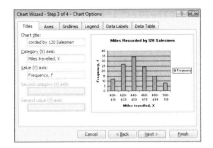

Figure 3.49

ChartWizard—Step 3 of 4: Chart Options

Input chart title: Miles Recorded by 120 Salesmen.
Category (X) axis: Miles travelled, X.
Value (Y) axis: Frequency, f.
Click Next.

Figure 3.50

ChartWizard—Step 4 of 4

Click Finish.

Figure 3.51 represents the resulting chart.

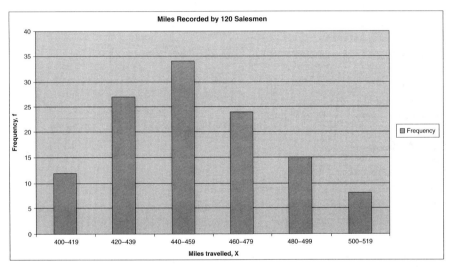

Figure 3.51

Step 5 Transformation of the Bar Chart to a Histogram

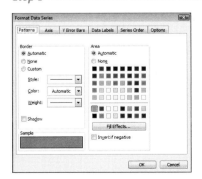

Double click on one of the bars in the chart.

Figure 3.52

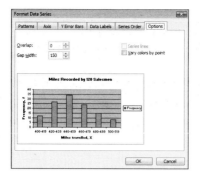

Select Options.

Figure 3.53

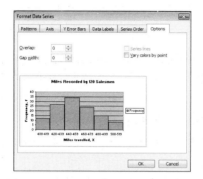

Reduce Gap Width to Zero.

Click OK and the histogram will appear on the worksheet.

Figure 3.54

> ## Note   Manual Solution
>
> The data variable 'mileage' is a grouped variable and the histogram is constructed as follows.
>
> | MILEAGE | LCB–UCB | Class Width | FREQUENCY, f |
> |---------|---------|-------------|--------------|
> | 400–419 | 399.5–419.5 | 20 | 12 |
> | 420–439 | 419.5–439.5 | 20 | 27 |
> | 440–459 | 439.5–459.5 | 20 | 34 |
> | 460–479 | 459.5–479.5 | 20 | 24 |
> | 480–499 | 479.5–499.5 | 20 | 15 |
> | 500–519 | 499.5–519.5 | 20 | 8 |
> | | | | $\Sigma f = 120$ |
>
> Table 3.20 Calculation procedure to identify class limits for the histogram
>
> We can see from the table that all the class widths are of the same value 20 (constant, class width = UCB – LCB). In this case the histogram can be constructed with the height of the bar representing the frequency of occurrence.

To construct the histogram we would plot frequency (y-axis, vertical) against score (x-axis) with the boundary between the bars determined by the upper and lower class boundaries (see illustration).

Figure 3.55 illustrates the class boundary positions for each bar. Figure 3.56 illustrates the completed histogram for miles recorded by 120 salesmen.

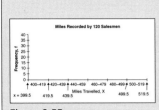

Figure 3.55

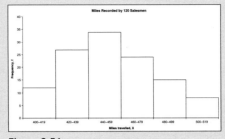

Figure 3.56

We can use the histogram to see how the frequency changes as the miles travelled changes from the lowest group (400–419) to the highest group (500–519). If we look at the histogram we can note:

- Looking along the x axis we can see that the miles recorded are evenly spread out.
- The miles recorded rise (400–419 to 440–459) with a maximum at 440–459 miles recorded.
- The miles recorded drop (440–459 to 500–519) with a minimum at 500–519 miles recorded.

These ideas will lead to the idea of average (central tendency) and data spread (dispersion) which will be explored in Chapter 4.

Student Exercises

X3.6 Create a suitable histogram to represent the number of customers visited by a salesman over a 80 week period.

68	64	75	82	68	60	62	88	76	93	73	79	88	73	60	93
71	59	85	75	61	65	75	87	74	62	95	78	63	72	66	78
82	75	94	77	69	74	68	60	96	78	89	61	75	95	60	79
83	71	79	62	67	97	78	85	76	65	71	75	65	80	73	57
88	78	62	76	53	74	86	67	73	81	72	63	76	75	85	77

X3.7 Create a suitable histogram to represent the spending on extra-curricular activities for a random sample of university students during the ninth week of the first term.

16.91	9.65	22.68	12.45	18.24	11.79	6.48	12.93	7.25	13.02
8.10	3.25	9.00	9.90	12.87	17.50	10.05	27.43	16.01	6.63
14.73	8.59	6.50	20.35	8.84	13.45	18.75	24.10	13.57	9.18
9.50	7.14	10.41	12.80	32.09	6.74	11.38	17.95	7.25	4.32
8.31	6.50	13.80	9.87	6.29	14.59	19.25	5.74	4.95	15.90

3.3.4 Histograms with unequal class intervals

It may be necessary because of the way a set of data is distributed to use *unequal class intervals*. In this case, special care needs to be taken in constructing the histogram, given that each bar (or rectangle) of the histogram is proportional to the frequency. Which of the two histograms for the following distribution is correct?

Class	0–2	2–4	4–6	6–8	8–12
Frequency	3	3	3	3	3

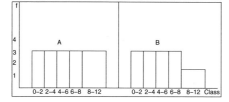

If we plot these values onto graph paper then Figure 3.57 could result.

Although class (8–12) is twice the width of the other classes, histogram A gives equal weighting to the frequency for all classes.

Figure 3.57

Histogram A is therefore incorrect. Keep in mind that area of a rectangle is proportional to frequency and thus

$$\text{Height} = \frac{\text{Class Frequency}}{\text{Class With}} \qquad (3.2)$$

Histogram B indicates the correct weighting to the class (8–12). Since the class width is twice the width of the other classes, the height of the rectangle is halved. In general if we choose a standard class width, a class having twice the width will have a height of one half of its frequency; three times the width a height of one third of its frequency, and so on.

▷ Example 3.13

Construct a histogram for the following distribution of discrete data.

Class	118–121	122–128	129–138	139–148	149–158	159–178
Frequency	2	6	14	31	63	28

Taking the class (129–138) as our standard class width (class width = 10) then we can use the following formula to calculate the heights of each individual bar (or rectangle).

$$h = \frac{CW_s}{CW} f \qquad\qquad (3.3)$$

Where CW_s = Standard Class Width = 10, CW = Class Width, f = Class Frequency, and h = Class height (height of rectangle).

Class	118–121	122–128	129–138	139–148	149–158	159–178
Frequency	2	6	14	31	63	28
LCB	117.5	121.5	128.5	138.5	148.5	158.5
UCB	121.5	128.5	138.5	148.5	158.5	178.5
Class width	4	7	10	10	10	20
Calculation of Height	(10/4) * 2	(10/7) * 6	(10/10) * 14	(10/10) * 31	(10/10) * 63	(10/20) * 28
Height	5	8.6	14	31	63	14

Table 3.21 Calculation process to calculate the class height

Figure 3.58 illustrates the completed histogram for the Example 3.13 data set.

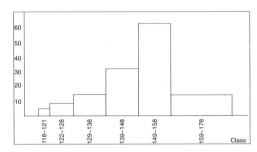

Figure 3.58

> **Note**   It is important to note that:
>
> (a) Since the height of the rectangle is proportional to class frequency and class width we can use the term *frequency density* rather than frequency.
>
> (b) Total area is proportional to total frequency.
>
> Unfortunately you *cannot* create a histogram with unequal class widths using Excel but you can create the frequency distribution by inputting the upper and lower class intervals. These are called *Bins in Excel*.

3.3.5 Frequency polygon

A frequency polygon is formed from a histogram by joining the mid-points of the tops of the rectangles by straight lines. The mid-points of the first and last class are joined to the x-axis to either side at a distance equal to (1/2)th the class interval of the first and last class.

$$\text{Mid-point of class} = \frac{\text{UCB} + \text{LCB}}{2} \tag{3.4}$$

Where UCB = Upper Class Boundary and LCB = Lower Class Boundary.

▷ Example 3.14

Table 3.22 illustrates the frequency polygon for Example 3.5 data set.

Class	True Limits	Class Mid-Point	Frequency
400–419	399.5–419.5	409.5	12
420–439	419.5–439.5	429.5	27
440–459	439.5–459.5	449.5	34
460–479	459.5–479.5	469.5	24
480–499	479.5–499.5	489.5	15
500–519	499.5–519.5	509.5	8

Table 3.22

Figure 3.59 illustrates the frequency polygon for the travelling salesmen problem.

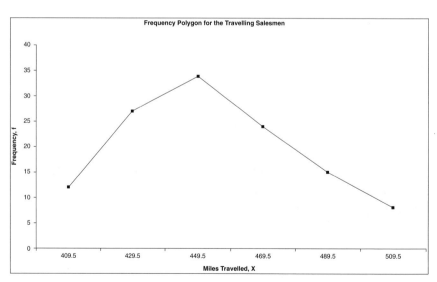

Figure 3.59

Excel spreadsheet solution—frequency polygon using Example 3.14 data

The Excel spreadsheet solution can be obtained using the following instructions:

Step 1 Data series

Class Mid-Point: Cells B114:B120 (includes data label)
Frequency: Cells C114:C120 (includes data label)
Highlight B114:C120

Step 2 Activate the ChartWizard by clicking on the ChartWizard button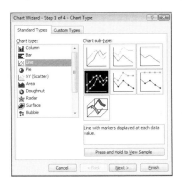

ChartWizard—Step 1 of 4: Chart Type
Choose Line.
Click Next.

Figure 3.60

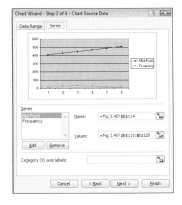

ChartWizard—Step 2 of 4: Chart Source Data
Choose Series tab.
Click Next.

Figure 3.61

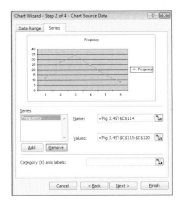

Remove Series Mid-Point
Choose Category (X) axis labels: B115:B120.
Click Next.

Figure 3.62

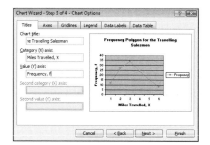

ChartWizard—Step 3 of 4: Chart Options
Chart title: Frequency Polygon for the Travelling Salesmen.
Category (X) axis: Miles Travelled, X.
Value (Y) axis: Frequency, f.
Click Finish.

Figure 3.63

ChartWizard—Step 4 of 4
Click Finish.

Figure 3.64

Figure 3.65 illustrates the frequency polygon after a degree of reformatting (removed border, horizontal gridlines, and gray border).

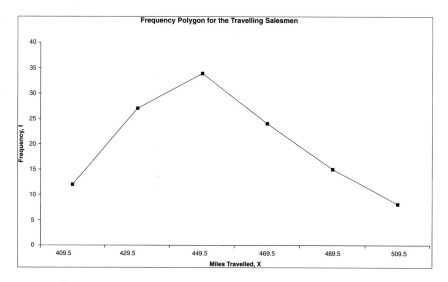

Figure 3.65

🖰 **Student Exercises**

X3.8 Create a frequency polygon (line graph) for the data in X3.2

68	64	75	82	68	60	62	88	76	93	73	79	88	73	60	93
71	59	85	75	61	65	75	87	74	62	95	78	63	72	66	78
82	75	94	77	69	74	68	60	96	78	89	61	75	95	60	79
83	71	79	62	67	97	78	85	76	65	71	75	65	80	73	57
88	78	62	76	53	74	86	67	73	81	72	63	76	75	85	77

3.3.6 Scatter and time series plots

Scatter plots

A scatter plot is a graph which helps us assess visually the form of relationship between two variables. To illustrate the idea of a scatter plot consider the following problem.

⬙ Example 3.15

A manufacturing firm has designed a training programme that is supposed to increase the productivity of employees.

The personal manager decides to examine this claim by analysing the data results from the first group of 20 employees that attended the course.

The results are provided in Table 3.23.

Employee Number	Productivity, X	% Raise in Productivity, Y
1	47	4.2
2	71	8.1
3	64	6.8
4	35	4.3
5	43	5.0
6	60	7.5
7	38	4.7
8	59	5.9
9	67	6.9
10	56	5.7
11	67	5.7
12	57	5.4
13	69	7.5
14	38	3.8
15	54	5.9
16	76	6.3
17	53	5.7
18	40	4.0
19	47	5.2
20	23	2.2

Table 3.23

Figure 3.66 illustrates the scatter plot. As can be seen from the scatter plot there would seem to be some form of relationship; as productivity increases then there is a tendency for the percentage raise in productivity to increase. The data, in fact, would indicate a positive relationship. We will explore this concept in more detail in Chapter 10 when discussing measuring correlation.

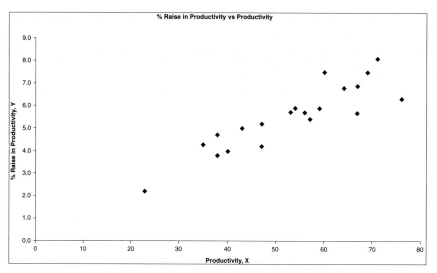

Figure 3.66

Time series plots

Time series analysis is concerned with data collected over a period of time. It attempts to isolate and evaluate various factors which contribute to changes over time in such variable series as imports and exports, sales, unemployment, and prices. If we can evaluate the main components which determine the value of, say, sales for a particular month then we can project the series into the future to obtain a forecast.

▷ Example 3.16

Consider the following time series data and resulting graph.

Sales of Pip Ltd 2001–2004 (tons)				
Year	Quarter 1	Quarter 2	Quarter 3	Quarter 4
2001	654	620	698	723
2002	756	698	748	802
2003	843	799	856	889
2004	967	876	960	976

Table 3.24 Time series data for Example 3.16

X

Time series plot A chart of a change in variable against time.

Time series A variable measured and represented per units of time.

The first step in analysing the above data is to create the time series plot, using the technique discussed in the previous section.

Figure 3.67 illustrate the up and down pattern with the overall sales increasing between the beginning of 2001 and the end of 2004.

This pattern consists of an upward trend and a seasonal component that repeats between individual quarters (Q1–Q2–Q3–Q4).

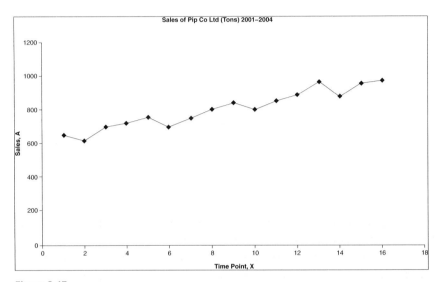

Figure 3.67

We shall explore these ideas of trend and seasonal components in Chapter 11. In the previous two sections we looked at creating scatter plots and time series plots that visually may provide information about the relationship between one measured variable and another measured variable.

Modifying graph axes

Care needs to be taken when using graphs to infer what this relationship may be. If we modify the y-axis scale then we have a very different picture of this potential relationship. We noted that in Example 3.15 that the % raise in productivity increases as the productivity increases. We can change the y-axis so that the minimum value of y-axis is 0 but the maximum value is now increased to 60. Figure 3.68 illustrates the effect on the graph of modifying the vertical scale.

In this rescaled graph the data points are hovering around the x-axis and the upward trend does not look so obvious any more. Any further rescaling of the graph would impact the visual impression of the pattern. Ultimately, the pattern would be impossible to observe.

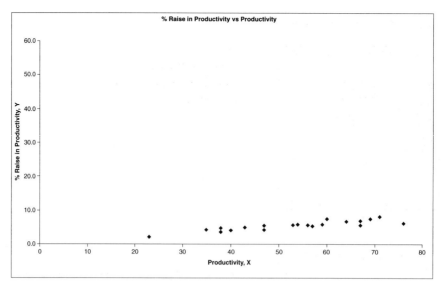

Figure 3.68

In Figure 3.67 we note that the time series plot indicated that the sales were increasing with time (upward trend) and that we have a pattern within the data that repeats between individual quarters (Q1–Q2–Q3–Q4). We can change the y-axis so that the minimum value of y-axis is 0 but the maximum value is now increased to 2000. We are not showing this graph, but if we did, we would be able to see the pattern in the data still shows an upward trend but the distinct pattern is not as pronounced as in the first graph. If we further increased the y-axis scale then this pattern would be diminished even further.

Excel spreadsheet solution—scatter plots using Example 3.15 data

	A	B	C	D
1		Scattergram - % Raise in Production vs Old Production		
2				
3		Employee	Old Production	% Raise in Production
4		Number	X	Y
5		1	47	4.2
6		2	71	8.1
7		3	64	6.8
8		4	35	4.3
9		5	43	5.0
10		6	60	7.5
11		7	38	4.7
12		8	59	5.9
13		9	67	6.9
14		10	56	5.7
15		11	67	5.7
16		12	57	5.4
17		13	69	7.5
18		14	38	3.8
19		15	54	5.9
20		16	76	6.3
21		17	53	5.7
22		18	40	4.0
23		19	47	5.2
24		20	23	2.2

Figure 3.69

The Excel ChartWizard spreadsheet solution can be obtained using the following instructions.

Input Data Series
X: Cells C5:C24
Y: Cells D5:D24
Highlight C4:D24.

Click the ChartWizard Icon

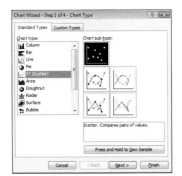

Figure 3.70

ChartWizard—Step 1 of 4
Select XY (Scatter).
Choose default selection.
Click Next.

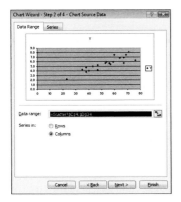

Figure 3.71

ChartWizard—Step 2 of 4
Select the Data range and choose Series in Columns.
Click Next.

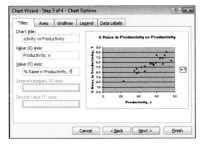

Figure 3.72

ChartWizard—Step 3 of 4
Type in chart title (% Raise in Productivity vs Productivity), x-axis title (Productivity, X) and y-axis title (% Raise in Productivity, Y).
Click Next.

Figure 3.73

ChartWizard—Step 4 of 4
Click Finish.

Figure 3.74 represents the time series plot for % raise in productivity vs productivity (graph formatted).

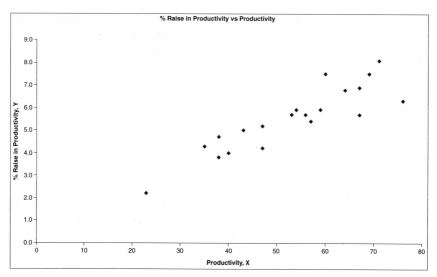

Figure 3.74

We can now ask Excel to fit a straight line (linear) to this data as can be seen in Figures 3.75–3.77 below. We will look at fitting lines (trend line) and curves in Chapters 10 and 11.

Excel spreadsheet solution—Excel ChartWizard solution—fitting line using Example 3.15 data

The Excel spreadsheet solution can be obtained using the following instructions.

Excel ChartWizard Solution—Fitting line
Right click on a data point.

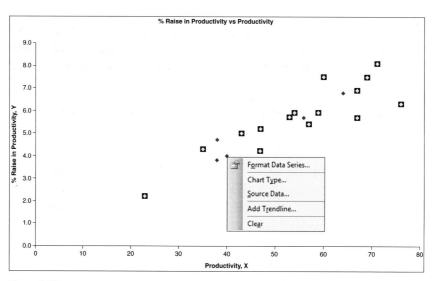

Figure 3.75

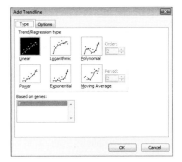

Figure 3.76

Select Add Trendline and choose Linear.
Click OK.

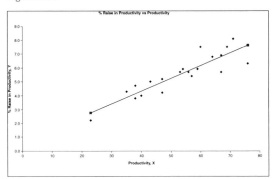

Figure 3.77

Figure 3.77 represents the line fit to the data points.

3.3.7 Superimposing two sets of data onto one graph

In certain circumstances we may wish to combine different data sets onto the same Excel graph.

▷ Example 3.17

A market researcher has collected a set of data that measures the distance travelled by eight salesmen. The market researcher has calculated the average and standard deviation and requires a graph of mileage travelled against ID and the two error measurements provided in the table below.

ID	Mileage	Average + error	Average – error
1	220	239	208
2	210	239	208
3	230	239	208
4	200	239	208
5	250	239	208
6	238	239	208
7	219	239	208
8	220	239	208
Average =	223.38		
Standard deviation =	15.74		

Table 3.25

Excel spreadsheet solution—superimposing two data sets onto one graph (Example 3.17 data)

Figure 3.78 illustrates the spreadsheet solution. Highlight all three columns (including labels).

	A	B	C	D
1	Superimposing different data sets onto one graph			
2				
3				
4		Mileage	Average + error	Average - error
5		220	239	208
6		210	239	208
7		230	239	208
8		200	239	208
9		250	239	208
10		238	239	208
11		219	239	208
12		220	239	208
13				
14	Average =	223.375		
15	SD =	15.73837439		

Figure 3.78

Select column graph.

Figure 3.79 illustrates the column graph.

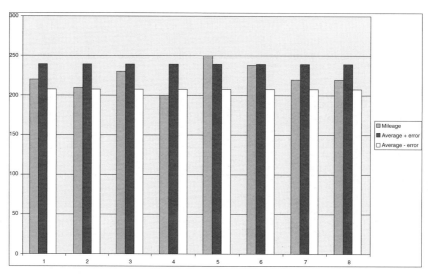

Figure 3.79

Right-click on Average + error bars.

Select Chart Type: Line.

Figure 3.80 illustrates the column graph with error (standard deviation) lines fitted to the graph (average + error, average – error).

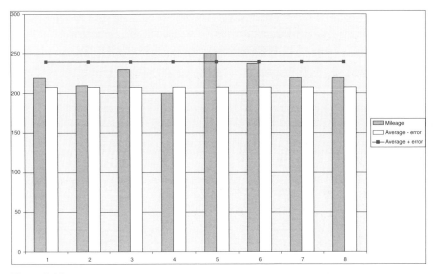

Figure 3.80

Right-click on Average – error bars.

Select Chart Type: Line.

Double click on newly formed Average – error yellow line.

Change colour to the same as Average + error line. See Figure 3.81.

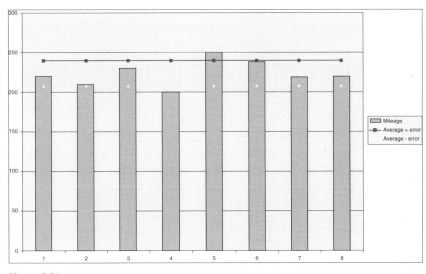

Figure 3.81

🖱 **Student Exercises**

X3.9 Obtain a scatter plot for the data in the table and comment on whether there is
a link between road deaths and the number of vehicles on the road. Would you
expect this to be true? Provide reasons for your answer.

Countries	Vehicles per 100 population	Road Deaths per 100000 population
Great Britain	31	14
Belgium	32	30
Denmark	30	23
France	46	32
Germany	30	26
Ireland	19	20
Italy	35	21
The Netherlands	40	23
Canada	46	30
U.S.A.	57	35

X3.10　Obtain a scatter plot for this data that represents the passenger miles flown by a UK based airline (millions of passenger miles) during 2003–2004. Comment on the relationship between miles flown and quarter.

Year	Quarter 1	Quarter 2	Quarter 3	Quarter 4
2003	98.9	191.0	287.4	123.2
2004	113.4	228.8	316.2	155.7

■ Techniques in Practice

1. Coco S.A. supplies a range of computer hardware and software to 2000 schools within a large municipal region of Spain. When Coco S.A. won the contract the issue of customer service was considered to be central to the company being successful at the final bidding stage. The company has now requested that its customer service director creates a series of graphical representations of the data to illustrate customer satisfaction with the service. The following data has been collected during the last six months and measures the time to respond to the received complaint (days).

5	24	34	6	61	56	38	32
87	78	34	9	67	4	54	23
56	32	86	12	81	32	52	53
34	45	21	31	42	12	53	21
43	76	62	12	73	3	67	12
78	89	26	10	74	78	23	32
26	21	56	78	91	85	15	12
15	56	45	21	45	26	21	34
28	12	67	23	24	43	25	65
23	8	87	21	78	54	76	79

(a) Form a grouped frequency table.

(b) Plot the histogram.

(c) Do the results suggest that we have a great deal of variation in time to respond to customer complaints?

(d) What conclusions can you draw from these results?

2. Bakers Ltd runs a chain of bakery shops and is famous for the quality of its pies. The management of the company are concerned at the number of complaints from customers who complain it takes too long to serve customers at a particular branch. The motto of the company is 'Have your pies in 2 minutes'. The manager of the branch concerned has been told to provide data on the time it takes for customers to enter the shop and be served by the shop staff.

0.70	0.70	0.70	0.70	0.70	0.70	0.70	0.70	0.70	0.70
0.99	0.99	0.99	0.99	0.99	0.99	0.99	0.99	0.99	0.99
0.12	0.12	0.12	0.12	0.12	0.12	0.12	0.12	0.12	0.12
0.70	0.70	0.70	0.70	0.70	0.70	0.70	0.70	0.70	0.70
1.88	1.88	1.88	1.88	1.88	1.88	1.88	1.88	1.88	1.88
0.55	0.55	0.55	0.55	0.55	0.55	0.55	0.55	0.55	0.55
1.38	1.38	1.38	1.38	1.38	1.38	1.38	1.38	1.38	1.38
0.80	0.80	0.80	0.80	0.80	0.80	0.80	0.80	0.80	0.80
1.25	1.25	1.25	1.25	1.25	1.25	1.25	1.25	1.25	1.25
1.48	1.48	1.48	1.48	1.48	1.48	1.48	1.48	1.48	1.48

(a) Form a grouped frequency table.

(b) Plot the histogram.

(c) Do the results suggest that we have a great deal of variation in time to serve customers?

(d) What conclusions can you draw from these results?

3. Skodel Ltd is a small brewery which is undergoing a major expansion after a take-over by a large European brewery chain. Skodel Ltd produces a range of beers and lagers and was renowned for the quality of its beers—winning a number of prizes at trade fairs throughout the European Union. The new parent company are reviewing the quality control mechanisms being operated by Skodel Ltd and are concerned at the quantity of lager in its premium lager brand which should contain a mean of 330 ml and a standard deviation of 15 ml. The bottling plant manager provided the parent company with quantity measurements from 100 bottles for analysis.

326	326	326	326	326	326	326	326	326	326
344	344	344	344	344	344	344	344	344	344
333	333	333	333	333	333	333	333	333	333
346	346	346	346	346	346	346	346	346	346
339	339	339	339	339	339	339	339	339	339
353	353	353	353	353	353	353	353	353	353
310	310	310	310	310	310	310	310	310	310
351	351	351	351	351	351	351	351	351	351
350	350	350	350	350	350	350	350	350	350
348	348	348	348	348	348	348	348	348	348

(a) Form a grouped frequency table.

(b) Plot the histogram.

(c) Do the results suggest that we have a great deal of variation in quantity in the bottles?

(d) What conclusions can you draw from these results?

■ Summary

The methods described in this chapter are very useful for describing data using a variety of tabulated and graphical methods. These methods allow one to make sense of data by constructing visual representations of numbers within the data set. Table 3.26 provides a summary of which table/graph to construct given the data type.

	Which table or chart to be applied?	
	Numerical data	Categorical data
Tabulating data	Frequency distribution. Cumulative frequency distribution (see Chapter 4).	Summary table.
Graphing data	Histogram. Frequency polygon.	Bar chart. Pie chart.
Presenting a relationship between data variables	Scatter plot. Time series graph.	Contingency table.

Table 3.26 Which table or chart to use?

In the next chapter we will look at summarizing data using measures of average and dispersion.

■ Key Terms

Bar chart
Categorical
Class boundaries
Class limits
Class midpoint
Classes
Continuous
Cross tabulation
Discrete
Frequency distributions
Frequency polygon
Graph or chart

Grouped frequency
   distributions
Histogram
Histogram with unequal
   class intervals
Interval
Nominal
Ordinal
Pie chart
Qualitative
Quantitative
Ratio

Raw data
Scatter plot or
   scattergrams
Stated limits
Statistic
Table
Tally chart
Time series plot
True or mathematical
   limits
Variable
Visual displays

■ Further Reading

Textbook Resources

1. Albright, S. C., Winston, W. L., and Zappe, C. (1999) *Data Analysis and Decision Making with Microsoft Excel*. Dusbury Press, London (Chapter 2).

2. Burton, G., Carrol, G., and Wall, S. (1999) *Quantitative Methods for Business and Economics*. Longman, New York (Chapter 1).

Web Resources

1. StatSoft Electronic Textbook http://www.statsoft.com/textbook/stathome.html (accessed 28/1/2007).

2. HyperStat Online Statistics Textbook http://davidmlane.com/hyperstat/index.html (accessed 28/1/2007).

3. Eurostat—website is updated daily and provides direct access to the latest and most complete statistical information available on the European Union, the EU Member States, the euro-zone and other countries http://epp.eurostat.ec.europa.eu (accessed 28/1/2007).

4. Economagic—contains international economic data sets (http://www.economagic.com) (accessed 28/1/2007).

5. The ISI glossary of statistical terms provides definitions in a number of different languages.

4 Data Descriptors

Although tables, diagrams, and graphs provide easy to assimilate summaries of data they only go part way in describing data. Often a concise numerical description is preferable which enables us to interpret the significance of the data. Measures of central tendency (or location) attempt to quantify what we mean when we think of the 'typical' or 'average' value for a particular data set. The concept of central tendency is *extremely important* and it is encountered in daily life. For example:

- What is the average CO_2 emission for a particular car compared to other similar cars?
- What is the average starting salary for new graduates starting employment with a large city bank?

A further measure that is employed to describe a data set is the concept of dispersion (or spread) about this middle value.

» Overview «

In this chapter we shall look at three key statistical measures that enable us to describe a data set:

» The central tendency is the amount by which all the data values coexist about a defined typical value. A number of different measures of central tendency exist, including mean (or *average*), median, and mode that can be calculated for both *ungrouped* (individual data values known) and *grouped* (data values within class intervals) data sets.

» The dispersion is the amount that all the data values are dispersed about this typical value. A number of different measures of dispersion exist, including range, interquartile range, semi interquartile range, standard deviation, and variance that can be calculated for both ungrouped and grouped data sets.

» The *shape* of the distribution is the pattern that can be observed within the data set. This shape can be classified into whether the distribution is symmetrical (or skewed) and whether or not there is evidence that the shape is *peaked*. Skewness is defined as a measure of the lack of symmetry in a distribution and Kurtosis is defined as a measure of the degree of peakedness in the distribution.

» Exploratory data analysis can be used to explore data sets and provide answers to questions involving central tendency, spread, skewness, and the presence of outliers.

X

Central tendency Measures the location of the middle or the centre of a distribution.

Mean The mean is a measure of the average data value for a data set.

Median The median is the value halfway through the ordered data set.

Mode The mode is the most frequently occurring value in a set of discrete data.

Dispersion The variation between data values is called dispersion.

Range The range of a data set is a measure of the dispersion of the observations.

Interquartile range The interquartile range is a measure of the spread of or dispersion within a data set.

Standard deviation Measure of the dispersion of the observations (a square root value of the variance).

Variance Measure of the dispersion of the observations.

Symmetrical A data set is symmetrical when the data values are distributed in the same way above and below the middle value.

Skewness Skewness is defined as asymmetry in the distribution of the data values.

Kurtosis Kurtosis is a measure of the 'peakedness' of the distribution.

» Learning Objectives «

On successful completion of this chapter, you will be able to:

» Understand the concept of an average.

» Recognize that three possible averages exist (mean, mode, and median) and calculate them using a variety of graphical and formula methods in number and frequency distribution form.

» Recognize when to use different measures of average.

» Understand the concept of dispersion.

» Recognize that different measures of dispersion exist (range, quartile range, semi-interquartile range, standard deviation, and variance) and calculate them using a variety of graphical and formula methods in number and frequency distribution form.

» Recognize when to use different measures of dispersion.

» Understand the idea of distribution shape and calculate a value for symmetry and peakedness.

» Apply exploratory data analysis to a data set(s).

» Use Excel to calculate data descriptors.

4.1 Measures of Central Tendency

When reading market reports, newspapers, or undertaking a web search to collect information you will read about a term called the average. The average is an idea that allows us to visualize or put a measure on what is considered to be the most representative value of the group. This value is usually placed somewhere in the middle of the group and as such is the best approximation of all other values. The mean (also called an *average* or *arithmetic average*), mode, and median are different measures of central tendency. Sections 4.1.1 and 4.1.3 will explore the calculation of these measures for ungrouped and grouped data respectively.

4.1.1 Mean, median, and mode

The three most commonly used measures of central tendency (or average) are: **mean** (or arithmetic mean), *median*, and *mode*. If the *mean* is calculated from the entire population of the data set then the mean is called the population mean. If we sample from this population and calculate the mean then the mean is called the *sample mean*. The population and sample mean would be calculated using the same formula: mean = sum of data values/total number of data values. For example, if KC GmbH were interested in the mean time for a consultant to travel by train from Munich to Hamburg and if we assume that KC GmbH has gathered the time (rounded

X

Arithmetic Mean The sum of a list of numbers divided by the number of numbers.

Population mean The population mean is the mean value of all possible values.

to the nearest minute) for the last five trips (645, 638, 649, 630, 647), then the mean time would be:

$$\text{Mean} = \frac{645 + 638 + 649 + 630 + 647}{5} = \frac{3209}{5} = 641.8$$

The mean time to travel between Munich and Hamburg was calculated to be 642 minutes. We can see that the mean uses all the data values in the data set (645 + 638 + ... + 647) and provides an acceptable average if we do not have any values that can be considered unusually large or small. If we added an extra value of one trip that took 1000 minutes then the new mean would be 701.5 minutes, which cannot be considered to be representative of the other data values in the data set that range in value from 630–649. These extreme values are called **outliers** which have a tendency to skew the data distribution. In this case we would use a different measure to calculate the value of central tendency.

An alternative method to calculate the average is the *median*. The median is literally the 'middle' number if you list the numbers in order of size. The median is not susceptible to extreme values to the extent of the mean, but this method of determining the average should only be used with ordinal data and is not suitable for continuous data variables. The final method for determining average is the *mode*. The mode is defined as the number that occurs most frequently in the data set and can be used for both numerical and categorical (or nominal) data variables. A major problem with the mode is that it is possible to have more than one modal value representing the average for numerical data variables and therefore the mean and median are used to provide averages for numerical data variables. Several examples are provided to demonstrate how these are calculated.

Example 4.1

Suppose the marks obtained in the statistics examination were

24	27	36	48	52	52	53	53	59	60	85	90	95

We can describe the overall performance of these 13 students by calculating an 'average' score using the mean, median, and mode.

Excel spreadsheet solution for Example 4.1: mean, median, mode

	A	B	C	D	E
1	Set of Numbers				
2			Formula Method		
3	Statistics				
4	Marks x		n =	13	=COUNT(A5:A17)
5	24		sum x =	734	=SUM(A5:A17)
6	27				
7	36		mean =	56.4615	=D6/D5
8	48				
9	52				
10	52		Excel Function Method		
11	53				
12	53		mean =	56.4615	=AVERAGE(A5:A17)
13	59		median =	53.0000	=MEDIAN(A5:A17)
14	60		mode =	52.0000	=MODE(A5:A17)
15	85		25th Percentile =	48	=PERCENTILE(A5:A17,0.25)
16	90		First Quartile =	48	=QUARTILE(A5:A17,1)
17	95		Third Quartile =	60	=QUARTILE(A5:A17,3)

Data Series input into Cells A5:A17

Figure 4.1 illustrates the Excel solution.

Figure 4.1

X
Outlier An outlier is an observation in a data set which is far removed in value from the others in the data set.

✻ **Interpretation** The above values imply that, depending what measure we use, the average mark for this group can be 56% (the mean), 53% (median), or 52% (mode). The choice of the measure will depend on the type of numbers within the data set.

The mean

The explanation of the Excel spreadsheet solution is as follows:

→ **Excel Function Method**

Mean =Cell D12 Formula: =AVERAGE(A5:A17)

In general the mean can be calculated using the formula:

$$\text{Mean}\ (\bar{X}) = \frac{\text{Sum of Data Values}}{\text{Total Number of Data Values}} = \frac{\sum X}{\sum f} \tag{4.1}$$

Where $\bar{X}$ (X bar) represents the mean value for the sample data, $\sum X$ represents the sum of all the data values, and $\sum f$ represents the number of data values.

Note For the statistics marks example,

$$\text{Mean}\ (\bar{X}) = \frac{\sum X}{\sum f} = \frac{24 + 27 + \ldots + 90 + 95}{13} = 734/13 = 56.4615$$

We can see from the formula method (cell D7) and Excel function method (cell D12) that the mean examination mark is 56%.

The median

The explanation of the Excel spreadsheet solution is as follows:

→ **Excel Function Method**

Median =Cell D13 Formula: =MEDIAN(A5:A17)

The median is defined as the middle number when the data is arranged in order of size. The position of the median can be calculated as follows:

$$\text{Position of Percentile} = \frac{P}{100}(N + 1) \tag{4.2}$$

Where P represents the percentile value and N represents the number of observations in the data set.

> **Note** A percentile is a value on a scale of one hundred that indicates the percent of a distribution that is equal to or below it.

Consider the data from Example 4.1 (note that the data is written in order of size—*rank*. If it wasn't ranked, the data would have to be put in the correct order before this method is used manually).

24	27	36	48	52	52	53	53	59	60	85	90	95

The position of the median number is calculated with P = 50 (middle number, 50%) and N = 13. Position of Median = $\frac{50}{100}(13 + 1)$ = 7th number. We can see from the manual method above and Excel function method (cell D13) that the median mark for the examination is 53%.

> ✻ **Interpretation** From the ordered list of numbers we can see that the median statistics examination mark is 53%. We can see from this example that the mean and median are reasonably close (56% compared to 53%) and the distance between the lowest mark and the median (53 − 24 = 29) is less than the distance between the largest value and the median (95 − 53 = 42). It should be noted that the median is not influenced by the presence of very small or very large data values in the data set (extreme values or outliers). If we have a small number of these extreme values (or *outliers*) we would use the median instead of the mean to represent the measure of central tendency. This issue will be explored in greater detail when discussing measuring *skewness*.

> **Note** In this example the median was calculated to be the 7th number in the ordered list of data values. If we created an extra value then the calculation would be a little more complex. For example, if we had 14 numbers (N = 14) then the position of the median would now be
>
> $$\text{Position of Median} = \frac{50}{100}(14 + 1) = 7.5\text{th number}$$
>
> The position of the median would now be the 7.5th number in the data set. To help us understand what this means we can rewrite this into a slightly different form:
>
> $$\text{Position of Median} = \frac{8\text{th number} + 7\text{th number}}{2} = \frac{53 + 53}{2} = 53$$
>
> The median statistics examination mark would then be 53%.

The mode

The explanation of the Excel spreadsheet solution is as follows:

> **→ Excel Function Method**
>
> Mode = Cell D14   Formula: =MODE(A5:A17)

The mode is defined as the number which occurs most frequently (the most 'popular' number).

> **Note**   We can see that Excel provides only one solution for the mode (52) even though we have two modal values in the data set (two numbers 52 and 53 occurred twice).

⌕ Example 4.2

Example 3.1 consists of category data that provide a measure of proposed student voting behaviour at a university. We can see from the frequency count that Labour was the most popular party for the students. The Labour party would represent the mode for this data set.

4.1.2 The percentile and quartile

Excel spreadsheet solution for Example 4.1: percentiles and quartiles

Returning to Example 4.1, the explanation of the Excel spreadsheet solution is as follows:

> **→ Excel Function Method**
>
> 25th Percentile = Cell D15   Formula: =PERCENTILE(A5:A17,0.25)
> First Quartile = Cell D16   Formula: =QUARTILE(A5:A17,1)
> Third Quartile = Cell D17   Formula: =QUARTILE(A5:A17,3)

The median represents the middle value of the data set, which corresponds to the 50th percentile (P = 50) or the second quartile (Q_2). A data set would be ranked in order of size and we can then use the technique described above to calculate the values that would represent individual *percentile* or quartile values.

First quartile, Q_1

The first quartile corresponds to the 25th percentile and the position of this value within the ordered data set is given by equation 4.2.

X

Quartiles   Quartiles are values that divide a sample of data into four groups containing an equal number of observations.

$$\text{Position of 25th Percentile} = \frac{25}{100}(13+1) = \frac{1}{4}(14) = 3.5\text{th number}$$

We therefore take the 25th percentile to be the number ½ the distance between the 4th and 3rd numbers. To solve this problem we use linear interpolation between the two nearest ranks: Position of 25th Percentile = 3rd number + 0.5 * (4th number – 3rd number). From the list of ordered data values the 3rd number = 36 and 4th number = 48.

$$Q_1 = 36 + 0.5 * (48 - 36) = 36 + 0.5 * (12) = 36 + 6 = 42$$

The first quartile statistic examination mark is 42%.

> ✱ **Interpretation**   You interpret the 25th percentile of 42 to indicate that 25% of students obtained a mark of less than or equal to 42.

Third quartile, Q_3

The third quartile corresponds to the 75th percentile and the position of this value within the ordered data set is given by equation (4.2).

$$\text{Position of 75th Percentile} = \frac{75}{100}(13+1) = \frac{3}{4}(14) = 10.5\text{th number}$$

We therefore take the 75th percentile to be the number ½ the distance between the 10th and 11th numbers. To solve this problem we use linear interpolation between the two nearest ranks: Position of 75th Percentile = 10th number + 0.5 * (11th number – 10th number). From the list of ordered data values the 10th number = 60 and 11th number = 85.

$$Q_3 = 60 + 0.5 * (85 - 60) = 60 + 0.5 * (25) = 60 + 12.5 = 72.5$$

The third quartile statistic examination mark is 73.

> ✱ **Interpretation**   You interpret the 75th percentile of 73 to indicate that 75 % of students obtained a mark of less than or equal to 73.

Notes

1. Remember the 25th percentile is equivalent to the first quartile and 75th percentile is equivalent to the third quartile.
2. Using Excel the first quartile value is 48 and the third quartile value is 60. The manual method provides a first quartile value of 42 and third quartile value of 73. Unlike the median that has a standard calculation method, there is no one standard for the calculation of the quartile. A number of definitions for the quartile exist, which results in a number of different calculation procedures to calculate the value of the quartiles. The method used by Excel is method 1 of Freund, J. and Perles, B. (1987) 'A New Look at Quartiles of Ungrouped Data', *The American Statistician*, 41(3), 200–3.

Excel function wizard solution for Example 4.1

Figure 4.2 illustrates the Excel solution.

	A	B	C	D	E
1	Set of Numbers				
2			Formula Method		
3	Statistics				
4	Marks x		n =	13	=COUNT(A5:A17)
5	24		sum x =	734	=SUM(A5:A17)
6	27				
7	36		mean =	56.4615	=D6/D5
8	48				
9	52				
10	52		Excel Function Method		
11	53				
12	53		mean =	56.4615	=AVERAGE(A5:A17)
13	59		median =	53.0000	=MEDIAN(A5:A17)
14	60		mode =	52.0000	=MODE(A5:A17)
15	85		25th Percentile =	48	=PERCENTILE(A5:A17,0.25)
16	90		First Quartile =	48	=QUARTILE(A5:A17,1)
17	95		Third Quartile =	60	=QUARTILE(A5:A17,3)

Figure 4.2

Figure 4.3

Mean = Cell D12

Select Insert, Select Function, and Select Statistical from the drop-down menu.
Select Average.
Click OK.

Figure 4.4

Input data range: A5 to A17.
Click OK.

Figure 4.5

Median = Cell D13

Select Insert, Select Function, and Select Statistical from the drop-down menu.
Select Median and click OK.
Input data range: A5 to A17.
Click OK.

Mode = Cell D14

Select Insert, Select Function, and Select Statistical from the drop-down menu.
Choose MODE and click OK.
Input data range: A5 to A17.
Click OK.

Figure 4.6

25th Percentile = Cell D15

Select Insert, Select Function, and Select Statistical from the drop-down menu.
Choose PERCENTILE from the Function Name.
Input Data Range: A5 to A17 and input K value for the 25th percentile, k = 0.25.
Click OK.

Figure 4.7

First Quartile = Cell D16

Select Insert, Select Function, and Select Statistical from the drop-down menu.
Choose QUARTILE from the Function Name.
Input Data Range: A5 to A17.
Input Quartile value for first quartile, Quart = 1.
Click OK.

Figure 4.8

Third Quartile = Cell D17

Select Insert, Select Function, and Select Statistical from the drop-down menu.
Choose QUARTILE from the Function Name.
Input Data Range: A5 to A17.
Input Quartile value for third quartile, Quart = 3.
Click OK.

Figure 4.9

Student Exercises

X4.1 In 12 consecutive innings a batsman's scores were: 6, 13, 16, 45, 93, 0, 62, 87, 136, 25, 14, and 31. Find his mean score and the median.

X4.2 The following are the IQs of 12 people: 115, 89, 94, 107, 98, 87, 99, 120, 100, 94, 100, 99. It is claimed that 'the average person in the group has an IQ of over 100'. Is this a reasonable assertion?

X4.3 A sample of 6 components was tested to destruction, to establish how long they would last. The times to failure (in hours) during testing were 40, 44, 55, 55, 64, and 69. Which would be the most appropriate average to describe the life of these components? What are the consequences of your choice?

X4.4 Find the mean, median, and mode of the following set of data: 1, 1, 1, 1, 1, 2, 2, 2, 2, 2, 2, 3, 3, 3, 3, 3, 4, 4, 4, 4, 5, 5, 5, 5, 5.

X4.5 The average salary paid to graduates in three companies is: £7000, £6000, and £9000 p.a. respectively. If the respective number of graduates in these companies is 5, 12, 3, find the mean salary paid to the 20 graduates.

4.1.3 Averages from frequency distributions

In this section we shall extend the calculation of data descriptors for a set of numbers to the situation where we are dealing with frequency distributions. A frequency distribution is a simple data table that shows how many times entities, or frequencies, fall into every category. When data has been arranged into a frequency distribution, a number of methods are available to obtain averages: mean, median, and mode.

Averages from frequency distributions where X is known

Knowing the value of X implies that the data values are predefined and given as a single number (not as a member of a group), as in the example below.

▷ Example 4.3

The distribution of insurance claims processed each day is as follows:

Claims (X)	1	2	3	4	5	6	7	8	9	10
Frequency (f)	3	4	4	5	5	7	5	3	3	1

Excel spreadsheet solution for Example 4.3

Figure 4.10 illustrates the Excel solution.

	A	B	C	D	E	F	G	H	I	J	K	L
1		Example 4.3 Insurance claims processed each day										
2												
3		Number of Claims per day,	Frequency, f	fX								
4		1	3	3		Formula Method						
5		2	4	8								
6		3	4	12		Sum f =	40	=SUM(C4:C13)				
7		4	5	20		Sum fX =	206	=SUM(D4:D13)				
8		5	5	25		Mean =	5.15	=G7/G6				
9		6	7	42								
10		7	5	35		Excel Function Method						
11		8	3	24								
12		9	3	27		Mean =	5.15	=SUMPRODUCT(B4:B13,C4:C13)/SUM(C4:C13)				
13		10	1	10								

Figure 4.10

The mean

→ **Excel Function Method**

Mean = Cell G12   Formula: =SUMPRODUCT(B4:B13,C4:C13)/SUM(C4:C13)

✳ **Interpretation**   The value of the summary statistic, the mean, is as follows:

Mean = 5.15   (Cells G8 and G12)

As claims cannot be partially processed, we ignore the values behind the decimal point and say that on average 5 claims are processed per day.

Note   According to the table, a number of claims corresponding to 'one' occurs 3 times which will contribute 3 to the total, 'two' claims occur 4 times contributing 8 to the sum, and so on. This can be written as follows:

$$\text{Mean } (\bar{X}) = \frac{(3*1)+(4*2)+\dots\dots+(1*10)}{3+4+4+5+5+7+5+3+3+1} = 206/40 = 5.15$$

As already pointed out, since we are dealing with discrete data we would indicate a mean as approximately 5 claims. Equation (4.3) can now be used to calculate the mean for a frequency distribution data set:

$$\bar{X} = \frac{\sum fX}{\sum f}$$

(4.3)

The following indicates a manual method of setting out the calculation for finding $\bar{X}$ using the above data set.

Claims, X	Frequency, f	fX
1	3	3
2	4	8
3	4	12
4	5	20
5	5	25
6	7	42
7	5	35
8	3	24
9	3	27
10	1	10
	$\Sigma f = 40$	$\Sigma fX = 206$

Table 4.1 Frequency distribution for Example 4.3

$$\bar{X} = \frac{\Sigma fX}{\Sigma f} = \frac{206}{40} = 5.15 \text{ claims per day.}$$

Clearly, the number corresponds to the one obtained using the Excel Function method, as expected.

The mode

Since the mode is the most frequently occurring score it can be determined directly from a frequency distribution or a histogram. If we consider the distribution given in Example 4.3, the most frequently occurring score is 6; it has the highest frequency of seven.

> ✳ **Interpretation**   On average, if the mode is used as the central tendency, 6 claims are processed per day.

The median and cumulative frequencies

Finding the mean and modal class from a frequency distribution should now cause little difficulty. However, finding the median involves some further calculations. To this end the **cumulative frequency distribution** is now introduced. If we consider the distribution given in Example 4.3, the median of the 40 values is given by the $(40 + 1)/2$ value (or 20½th). To find out which is the 20½th value we would list all the scores in order of size and create the cumulative frequency distribution.

X
Cumulative frequency distribution The cumulative frequency for a value x is the total number of scores that are less than or equal to x.

Claims, X	Frequency, f	Mathematical Limit	Upper Limit	Cumulative Frequency, CF
1	3	0.5–1.5	1.5	3
2	4	1.5–2.5	2.5	7
3	4	2.5–3.5	3.5	11
4	5	3.5–4.5	4.5	16
5	**5**	**4.5–5.5**	**5.5**	**21**
6	7	5.5–6.5	6.5	28
7	5	6.5–7.5	7.5	33
8	3	7.5–8.5	8.5	36
9	3	8.5–9.5	9.5	39
10	1	9.5–10.5	10.5	40

Table 4.2 Cumulative frequency distribution

The median value of the above distribution lies at the 20½th item which lies at 5 claims. We know this because 21 items are below 5.5.

> ✳ **Interpretation**   If the median is used as the measure of central tendency, on average 5 claims a day are processed, which in this case coincides with the mean.

Averages from frequency distributions where X is class mid-point

Unlike the previous section, where X was given in advance, certain frequencies can apply to a number of classes, or a range of values.

▷ Example 4.4

Consider the distribution of miles travelled by salesmen. The layout is very similar to Example 4.3, except the mid-point value is shown for 'X'.

Mileage	Class Mid-Point, X	Frequency, f	f X
400–419	409.5	12	4914
420–439	429.5	27	11596.5
440–459	449.5	34	15283
460–479	469.5	24	11268
480–499	489.5	15	7342.5
500–519	509.5	8	4076
		$\Sigma fx = 120$	$\Sigma fx = 54480$

Table 4.3 Frequency distribution for Example 4.4

Excel spreadsheet solution for Example 4.4

Figure 4.11 illustrates the Excel solution.

	A	B	C	D	E	F	G	H	I
1	**Frequency Distribution**								
2									
3	Mileage			Mid-Point	Frequency		Cum. Frequency		
4		LCB	UCB	x	f	fx			
5	400-419	399.5	419.5	409.5	12	4914.00	12		
6	420-439	419.5	439.5	429.5	27	11596.50	39		
7	440-459	439.5	459.5	449.5	34	15283.00	73		
8	460-479	459.5	479.5	469.5	24	11268.00	97		
9	480-499	479.5	499.5	489.5	15	7342.50	112		
10	500-519	499.5	519.5	509.5	8	4076.00	120		
11									
12	**Mean**								
13	sum f =	120.00	=SUM(E5:E10)		mean =	454.00	=B14/B13		
14	sum fx =	54480.00	=SUM(F5:F10)		mean =	454.00	=SUMPRODUCT(D5:D10,E5:E10)/SUM(E5:E10)		
15									
16	**Median**				**Mode**				
17	N =	120.00	=SUM(E5:E10)		Class Width c =	20.00	=C7-B7		
18	Pos. of Med.	60.50	=(B17+1)/2						
19	Median class is 440-459				Modal Class 440-459				
20	L =	439.5000	=B7		L =	439.50	=B7		
21	c =	20.0000	=C7-B7		f1 =	34.00	=E7		
22	F =	39.0000	=G6		f0 =	27.00	=E6		
23	f =	34.0000	=E7		f2 =	24.00	=E8		
24	Median =	452.1471	=B20+B21*((B17+1)/2-B22)/B2		Mode =	447.74	=F20+(F21-F22)*F17/(2*F21-F22-F23)		

Figure 4.11

The mean

The explanation of the Excel spreadsheet solution is as follows:

> **→ Excel Function Method**
>
> Mean = Cell F14   Formula: =SUMPRODUCT(D5:D10,E5:E10)/SUM(E5:E10)

The mean mileage is 454 miles.

> **Note**   The Mean is calculated using equation (4.3):
>
> $$\text{Mean } (\bar{X}) = \frac{\sum fX}{\sum f} = \frac{54480}{120} = 454 \text{ miles}$$
>
> 1. The value of X is the class mid-point which is computed using the true limits of each class. This assumes that the data values within each class vary uniformly between the lowest and highest data values within the class.
> 2. Even if a distribution has unequal class widths the same procedure is followed.
> 3. This form of layout transforms very easily to a spreadsheet.

The mode

Since the mode is the most frequently occurring score it can be determined directly from a frequency distribution or a histogram. If we consider the distribution given in Example 4.4, we can see that the most frequently occurring class is the class 440–459 miles. This class is known as the *modal class*. If we look at the histograms associated with these two examples the mode is very apparent: it is the class with the highest rectangle. We can estimate the mode using a formula or graphical method:

(i) Formula method

Having established which is the class interval with the highest frequency (the modal class), then the mode can now be estimated using equation (4.4):

$$\text{Mode} = L + \frac{\left(f_1 - f_0\right)}{\left(2f_1 - f_0 - f_2\right)}C$$

(4.4)

Where: L = lower class boundary of the modal class, f_0 = frequency of the class below the modal class, f_1 = frequency of the modal class, f_2 = frequency of the class above the modal class, and C = modal class width.

> **Note**   Please note that this formula only works if the modal class and the two adjacent classes are of equal width. Therefore, using Example 4.4 we have L = 439.5, f_0 = 27, f_1 = 34, f_2 = 24, and c = 20.

$$\text{Mode} = 439.5 + \frac{\left(34 - 27\right)}{2\left(34\right) - 27 - 24} \times 20 = 448 \text{ miles to the nearest mile}$$

The modal distance travelled is 448 miles.

(ii) Graphical method

We can estimate the mode graphically by constructing the histogram. For Example 4.4 the data set class widths are of the same size (constant) and therefore the height of the column will represent the frequency of occurrence (f). We can see from the histogram that class 440–459 is the modal class and the mode will lie within this class. The frequencies of the two adjacent classes (420–439, 460–479) can be used to estimate the value of the mode: (a) construct the two crossed diagonals (see dashed lines in histogram), (b) drop a perpendicular from where these two lines meet to the horizontal axis, and (c) read from the horizontal axis the value estimate for the mode.

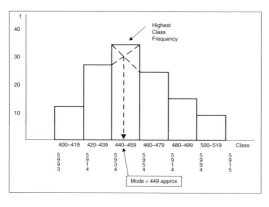

Figure 4.12 illustrates the graphical solution to estimate the modal value.

The modal value is estimated from the histogram to be 449 miles travelled.

Figure 4.12

The median

Just as with the cases where X is known, finding the median from a frequency distribution where X is class mid-point involves some further calculations. *The cumulative frequency distribution* and *cumulative frequency polygon* (ogive) are used. If we consider the distribution given in Example 4.4, the median of the 120 values is given by the $(120 + 1)/2$th value (or $60\frac{1}{2}$th value) and this value lies in the class $(440\text{--}459)$ miles.

Mileage	Frequency	Cumulative Frequency Distribution	
		Upper Class Limit UCL, X_{CF}	Cumulative Frequency, CF
400–419	12	< 419.5	12
420–439	27	< 439.5	39
440–459	34	< 459.5	73
460–479	24	< 479.5	97
480–499	15	< 499.5	112
500–519	8	< 519.5	120

Table 4.4 Cumulative frequency distribution for Example 4.4

An estimate of the value of the median within that class can be determined either by calculation or by using a graphical method:

(i) Formula method

Equation (4.5) can be used to estimate the median:

$$\text{Median} = L + C\frac{(N+1)/2 - F}{f} \tag{4.5}$$

Where: L = true lower class boundary of the median class, C = median class width, F = cumulative frequency before the median class, f = frequency within the median class, N = total frequency.

Position of Median = $60\frac{1}{2}$th item

Median Class = 440–459

From the table L = 439.5, C = 459.5 − 439.5 = 20, F = 39, f = 34, and N = 120.

$$\text{Median} = 439.5 + 20\frac{(120+1)/2 - 39}{34} = 452 \text{ miles}$$

The median number of miles travelled is 452 miles. This is quite close to the value obtained for the mean (454 miles) and we would expect this given that the histogram for miles travelled looks quite *symmetrical*. The concept of symmetry and a measure of how symmetrical a distribution is will be explored when discussing the concept of skewness (see Section 4.2.5).

X
Ogive (or cumulative frequency polygon)
A distribution curve in which the frequencies are cumulative.

(ii) Graphical method

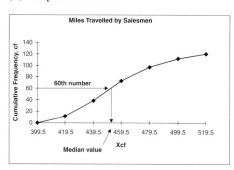

Figure 4.13

Figure 4.13 represents a cumulative frequency curve (or ogive) for the miles travelled example.

We can use this curve to provide an estimate of the median. The median is then the value which corresponds to half of the total frequency.

Therefore, the Position of the Median = $\frac{50}{100}(120 + 1) \approx$ 60th number. We can now use the cumulative frequency curve to estimate the value of the median. From the graph the median is approximately 452 miles.

Percentiles and quartiles

Individual percentiles can be estimated using the following two methods: (i) formula method and (ii) graphical method.

(i) Formula method

Equation (4.6) can be used to estimate the value at a particular percentile:

$$\text{Percentile Value } P = L + \frac{(N+1)P/100 - F}{f}C \tag{4.6}$$

Where: L = true lower class boundary of the percentile class, C = percentile class width, F = cumulative frequency before the percentile class, f = frequency within the percentile class, and N = total frequency. For example, if we want to calculate the 10th percentile, then P = 10. Position of 10th percentile = $\frac{10}{100}(120 + 1) \approx$ 12th number. Therefore, the 10th percentile is in the (400–419) class. From the table: L = 399.5, C = 419.5 − 399.5 = 20, F = 0, f = 12, N = 120.

$$\text{10th percentile } = 399.5 + 20 \times \frac{10}{100}(120 + 1) - 0 = 419.5 \text{ miles}$$

The 10th percentile number of miles travelled is approximately 420 miles.

(ii) In the previous example we have used the cumulative frequency curve (or ogive) to find the median. Other statistics can also be obtained from it and revolve around the idea of *percentiles*. As the name suggests the 10th percentile for the above example will occur at P = 10. Position of 10th percentile = $\frac{10}{100}(120 + 1) \approx$ 12th number. Therefore, the 10th percentile is in the (400–419) class. The estimated value can, like the median (the median is the 50th percentile), can be read off the ogive curve (or cumulative frequency curve).

❊ **Interpretation**   Ten percent of all the data in this data set have the value equal or below 420 miles.

Two important percentiles are the 25th and 75th percentiles. These are known as the *lower quartile* (LQ) and the *upper quartile* (UQ) respectively.

$$\text{Position of 1st Quartile} = \frac{25}{100}(120+1) \approx 30\text{th number}$$

$$\text{Position of 3rd Quartile} = \frac{75}{100}(120+1) \approx 90\text{th number}$$

Figure 4.14 illustrates the 1st and 3rd quartile positions on the cumulative frequency curve. We observe that Q_1 and Q_3 are approximately 430 and 470 respectively.

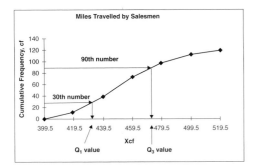

Figure 4.14

❊ **Interpretation**   Twenty-five percent of all the values in this data set are equal or below 430, whilst seventy-five percent are equal or below 470.

4.1.4 Weighted averages

In the previous examples we have calculated the mean using equation 4.1 which assumes that each value of X is of equal importance to all other values of X. In many cases we are faced with a situation where this is not true, e.g. module grades are often computed using a weighted average since a different weighting is applied to different assessments. However, from the calculation point of view, this is no different to the method of calculating averages from frequency distributions. The weighted average is calculated using equation (4.7) (which is identical to equation (4.2)):

$$\bar{X} = \frac{w_1 X_1 + w_2 X_2 + w_3 X_3}{w_1 + w_2 + w_3} = \frac{\sum wX}{\sum w} \tag{4.7}$$

Where w is the level of importance placed on each assessment element and X is the actual mark associated with this weight. This can be laid out in a table format to aid the calculation process.

Example 4.5

Suppose that Karen's statistics module is assessed via a series of assessments (multiple choice questions—mcq, in-course assignment—ica, end assignment—ea) with a weighting of 20 %, 30 %, and 50 % respectively. Figure 4.15 illustrates the Excel solution.

	A	B	C	D	E	F
1	**Weighted Average**					
2						
3						
4						
5			Weights, w	Mark (%), X	wX	
6		mcq	0.2	74	14.8	=C6*D6
7		ica	0.3	66	19.8	=C7*D7
8		ea	0.5	88	44	=C8*D8
9		Totals	1		78.6	=SUM(E6:E8)
10						
11			Weighted average=		78.6	=SUMPRODUCT(C6:C8,D6:D8)

Figure 4.15

Excel Function Method

Mean = Cell E11 Formula: =SUMPRODUCT(C6:C8,D6:D8)

Interpretation Karen's weighted average and therefore module grade would be approximately 79%.

If we wanted to solve the problem manually, and assuming as above that Karen obtained 74%, 66%, and 88% for each assessment, then her weighted average would be: Weighted average = (0.2) * (74) + (0.3) * (66) + (0.5) * (88) = 14.8 + 19.8 + 44 = 78.6. This problem can also be solved manually by using the method outlined in Table 4.5:

	Weights, w	Mark (%), X	Calculation, wX	wX
mcq	0.2	74	0.2 * 74	14.8
ica	0.3	66	0.3 * 66	19.8
ea	0.5	88	0.5 * 88	44.0
Totals	$\sum w = 1$			$\sum wX = 78.6$

Table 4.5

As above, the weighted average is rounded to 79 %.

Note

1. If all the weights are equal, then the weighted mean is the same as the arithmetic mean.
2. As emphasized before, Excel does not contain a built in function to calculate a weighted average. Again, the SUMPRODUCT() function is used.
3. If the weights are given in percentages then the formula would be modified to SUMPRODUCT(C6:C8,D6:D8)/SUM(C6:C8).

Student Exercises

X4.6 Cameos Ltd is employed by a leading market research organization based in Berlin. The company is discussing with the firm to expand the catering facilities provided to its employees to include a greater range of products. The initial research by Cameos has identified the following set of weekly spend (€) by individual employees:

22	16	26	33	33	37	9	23	32	17
20	13	12	18	19	10	21	22	25	22
22	22	34	24	23	21	38	31	41	20

(a) Plot the histogram and visually comment on the shape of the weekly expenditure. Hint: use class width of 5.

(b) Calculate the values of the mean and median.

(c) Use descriptive statistics in conjunction with the histogram to comment on weekly expenditure.

X4.7 Form a frequency distribution of the following data with intervals centred at 10, 15, 20, 25, 30, 35, 40, and estimate the mean value.

9	26	33	24	41	24	37	39	30	28	34	19	32
24	42	17	26	18	33	40	28	31	20	23	18	21
32	21	39	25	16	17	26	11	30	28	24	27	40

X4.8 The frequency distribution of the length of a sample of 98 nails, measured to the nearest 0.1 mm is shown

(a) Find the mean length of this sample by hand and by using a spreadsheet.

(b) Construct the cumulative frequency graph and use this to estimate the median.

(c) Check the value of the median using the formula method.

Length	Frequency
4.0–4.2	4
4.3–4.5	9
4.6–4.8	13
4.9–5.1	20
5.2–5.4	34
5.5–5.7	18

X4.9 The distribution of marks of 400 candidates in an A-level examination are given below

(a) Calculate the mean value.

(b) Construct the cumulative frequency curve and estimate the median, lower and upper quartile values.

Marks	Frequency, F
0–10	6
11–20	15
21–30	31
31–40	80
41–50	93
51–60	69
61–70	54
71–80	33
81–90	12
91–100	7

4.2 Measures of Dispersion

In Section 4.1 we looked at the concept of central tendency that provides a measure of the middle value of a set of data values, including: mean, median, and mode. This, however, only gives a partial description. A fuller description can be obtained by also obtaining a measure of the spread of the distribution. This kind of measure indicates whether the values in the distribution group closely about an average or whether they are more dispersed. These measures of dispersion are particularly important when we wish to compare distributions.

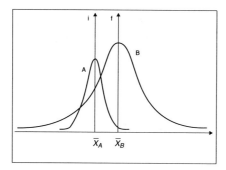

To illustrate this consider the two hypothetical distributions in Figure 4.16 which measure the value of sales per week made by two salesmen in their respective sales areas.

Let us say the means of the two distributions, A and B, were 4000 and 5000 respectively. But as you can see their shapes are very different, with B being far more spread out.

Figure 4.16

What would you infer from the two distributions given about the two salesmen and the areas that they work in? We can see that both distributions, A and B, have different mean values with distribution B being more spread out (or dispersed) than distribution A. Furthermore, distribution B is taller than distribution A. In this section we shall explore methods that can be used to put a number to this idea of dispersion. The methods we will explore include: range, interquartile range, semi interquartile range, variance, standard deviation, coefficient of variation, skewness, and kurtosis.

⌖ Example 4.6

Consider the marks obtained in the statistics examination (Example 4.1)

24	27	36	48	52	52	53	53	59	60	85	90	95

Excel spreadsheet solution to Example 4.1

Figure 4.17 illustrates the Excel solution.

	A	B	C	D	E	F	G
1	MEASURES OF DISPERSION						
2							
3		Set of Numbers			Formula Method		
4					n =	13	=COUNT(B7:B19)
5		Statistics			sum x =	734	=SUM(B7:B19)
6		Marks x	x^2		sum x^2 =	47362	=SUM(C7:C19)
7		24	576		mean =	56.4615	=F5/F4
8		27	729		variance =	455.3254	=F6/F4-F7^2
9		36	1296		standard deviation =	21.3384	=F8^0.5
10		48	2304				
11		52	2704				
12		52	2704		Excel Function Method		
13		53	2809		Range =	71	=MAX(B7:B19)-MIN(B7:B19)
14		53	2809		Q1 =	48.0000	=QUARTILE(B7:B19,1)
15		59	3481		Median =	53.0000	=MEDIAN(B7:B19)
16		60	3600		Q3 =	60.0000	=QUARTILE(B7:B19,3)
17		85	7225		QR =	12.0000	=F16-F14
18		90	8100		SIQR =	6.0000	=(F16-F14)/2
19		95	9025		Mean =	56.4615	=AVERAGE(B7:B19)
20					varp =	455.3254	=VARP(B7:B19)
21					sdp =	21.3384	=STDEVP(B7:B19)

Figure 4.17

4.2.1 The range

The range is the simplest measure of distribution and indicates the 'length' a distribution covers. It is determined by finding the difference between the lowest and highest value in a distribution. The explanation of the Excel spreadsheet solution is as follows:

→ **Excel Function Method**

Range = Cell F13   Formula: =MAX(B7:B19)−MIN(B7:B19)

A formula for calculating the range, depending on the type of data, is:

$$\text{RANGE (ungrouped data)} = \text{Highest Extreme Value} - \text{Lowest Extreme Value} \quad (4.8)$$

$$\text{RANGE (grouped data)} = \text{UCB Highest Class} - \text{LCB Lowest Class} \quad (4.9)$$

Where UCB represents the upper class boundary and LCB represents the lower class boundary. Thus for the statistics examination example (Example 4.1): ungrouped data, lowest value = 24 and highest value = 95, and range = 95 − 24 = 71 marks.

> ❋ **Interpretation**   The range for the statistics examination marks implies that the achieved marks are scattered over 71 marks between the highest and the lowest mark.

If we have data that is in the form of a grouped frequency distribution then we would use the upper and lower class boundaries of the largest and smallest class values to calculate the range. Thus for the miles travelled by salesmen example (Example 4.4): grouped data, LCB = 399.5, UCB = 519.5. Thus, range = 519.5 − 399.5 = 120 miles.

4.2.2 The interquartile range and semi interquartile range

The interquartile range represents the difference between the third and first quartile and can be used to provide a measure of spread within a data set which includes extreme data values. The interquartile range is little affected by extreme data values in the data set and is considered to be a good measure of spread for skewed distributions. The interquartile range is defined as:

$$\text{Interquartile range} = Q_3 - Q_1 \qquad\qquad (4.10)$$

The semi interquartile range (SIQR) is defined as:

$$\text{Semi interquartile range} = \frac{Q_3 - Q_1}{2} \qquad\qquad (4.11)$$

The semi interquartile range is another measure of spread and is computed as one half of the interquartile range which contains half of the data values. With Excel the first quartile value is 48% and the third quartile value is 60%. The manual method provides a first quartile value of 42% and third quartile value of 73%. The explanation of the Excel spreadsheet solution is as follows:

> ➜ **Excel Function Method**
>
> | | |
> |---|---|
> | Q1 = Cell F14 | Formula: =QUARTILE(B7:B19,1) |
> | Median = Cell F15 | Formula: =MEDIAN(B7:B19) |
> | Q3 = Cell F16 | Formula: =QUARTILE(B7:B19,3) |
> | QR = Cell F17 | Formula: =F16–F14 |
> | SIQR = Cell F18 | Formula: =(F16–F14)/2 |

> ❋ **Interpretation**   Interquartile range is a measure of variation that ignores the extremes and focuses on the middle 50% of the data, i.e. only the data between Q_3 and Q_1.

📎 **Note**

1. Excel Solution: The interquartile range $= Q_3 - Q_1 = 60 - 48 = 12$ and the semi interquartile range is 6.
2. Manual method: The interquartile range $= Q_3 - Q_1 = 73 - 42 = 31$ and the semi interquartile range is 16.

The interquartile and semi interquartile ranges are more stable than the range because they focus on the middle half of the data values and, therefore, can't be influenced by extreme values. The semi interquartile range is used in conjunction with the median to a highly skewed distribution or to describe an ordinal data set. The interquartile range (and semi interquartile range) are more influenced by sampling fluctuations in normal distributions than is the standard deviation, and therefore not often used for data that are approximately normally distributed. Furthermore, the actual data values aren't used and we will now look at a method that provides a measure of spread but uses all the data values within the calculation.

4.2.3 The standard deviation and variance

Standard deviation is the measure of spread most commonly used in statistics when the mean is used to calculate central tendency. The variance and standard deviation provide a measure of how dispersed the data values (X) are about the mean value ($\bar{X}$). Because of its close links with the mean, the standard deviation can be greatly affected if the mean gives a poor measure of central tendency.

If we calculated for each data value $(X - \bar{X})$, then some would be positive and some negative. Thus, if we were to sum all these differences then we would find that $\sum(X - \bar{X}) = 0$ i.e. the positive and negative values would cancel out. To avoid this problem we would square each individual difference before undertaking the summation. This would provide us with the squared average difference which is known as the *variance* (VAR(X)). The explanation of the Excel spreadsheet solution is as follows:

➜ **Excel Function Method**

VARP = Cell F20   Formula: =VARP(B7:B19)

Equation (4.12) is used to provide the value of the variance:

$$\text{Variance, VAR(X)} = \frac{\sum(X - \bar{X})^2}{\sum f} \tag{4.12}$$

To provide us with an average difference we take the square root of the variance to give the *standard deviation* (SD(X)):

$$\text{Standard Deviation, SD(X)} = \sqrt{\frac{\sum(X - \bar{X})^2}{\sum f}} \tag{4.13}$$

The explanation of the Excel spreadsheet solution is as follows:

> **→ Excel Function Method**
>
> SDP = Cell F21   Formula: =STDEVP(B7:B19)

By algebraic manipulation we can simplify equation (4.12) to provide an equation that is easier to use within a manual solution:

$$\text{Variance, VAR(X)} = \frac{\sum x^2}{\sum f} - \left(\overline{X}\right)^2 \tag{4.14}$$

$$\text{Standard deviation, SD(X)} = \sqrt{\frac{\sum x^2}{\sum f} - \left(\overline{X}\right)^2} \tag{4.15}$$

> ✳ **Interpretation**   Variance describes how much the data values are scattered around the mean value, or to put it differently, how tightly are the data values grouped around the mean. In a way, the smaller the variance, the more representative the mean value is.
>
> Unfortunately the variance does not have the same dimension as the data set, or the mean. In other words, if the values are percentages, inches, degrees C, or any other measure, the variance is not expressed in the same values, because it is expressed in squared units. As such, it is very useful as a comparison measure between the two data sets, as we will discover later. To bring the variance into the same units of measure as the data set, the standard deviation needs to be calculated. Although the standard deviation is less susceptible to extreme values than the range, standard deviation is still more sensitive than the semi interquartile range. If the possibility of outliers presents itself, then the standard deviation should be supplemented by the semi interquartile range.

Excel function wizard solution for Example 4.6

Figure 4.18 illustrates the Excel solution.

	A	B	C	D	E	F	G
1	**MEASURES OF DISPERSION**						
2							
3		**Set of Numbers**			**Formula Method**		
4					n =	13	=COUNT(B7:B19)
5		Statistics			sum x =	734	=SUM(B7:B19)
6		Marks x	x^2		sum x^2 =	47362	=SUM(C7:C19)
7		24	576		mean =	56.4615	=F5/F4
8		27	729		variance =	455.3254	=F6/F4-F7^2
9		36	1296		standard deviation =	21.3384	=F8^0.5
10		48	2304				
11		52	2704				
12		52	2704		**Excel Function Method**		
13		53	2809		Range =	71	=MAX(B7:B19)-MIN(B7:B19)
14		53	2809		Q1 =	48.0000	=QUARTILE(B7:B19,1)
15		59	3481		Median =	53.0000	=MEDIAN(B7:B19)
16		60	3600		Q3 =	60.0000	=QUARTILE(B7:B19,3)
17		85	7225		QR =	12.0000	=F16-F14
18		90	8100		SIQR =	6.0000	=(F16-F14)/2
19		95	9025		Mean =	56.4615	=AVERAGE(B7:B19)
20					varp =	455.3254	=VARP(B7:B19)
21					sdp =	21.3384	=STDEVP(B7:B19)

Figure 4.18

VARP = Cell F20

Select Insert Function.
Choose Statistical.
Select Function VARP.
Click OK.

Figure 4.19

Input Data Range: B7:B19.
Click OK.

Figure 4.20

SDP = Cell F21

Select Insert Function.
Choose Statistical.
Select Function STDEVP.
Click OK.

Figure 4.21

Input Data Range: B7:B19.
Click OK.

Figure 4.22

▷ Example 4.7

The mean and variance can be calculated for Example 4.6 data set using equations (4.1) and (4.14) respectively:

$$\text{Mean}\,(\overline{X}) = \frac{\sum X}{\sum f} = \frac{24 + 27 + \ldots + 90 + 95}{13}$$

$$= 734/13 = 56.46$$

$$\text{Variance, VAR(X)} = \frac{\sum X^2}{\sum f} - \left(\overline{X}\right)^2$$

From this table we can show that $\sum X = 734$ and $\sum X^2 = 47362$.

Variance

$$\text{VAR(X)} = \frac{47362}{13} - \left(56.4615\right)^2 = 455.33$$

Standard Deviation

$$\text{SD(X)} = \sqrt{\text{VAR(X)}} = \sqrt{455.3254438}$$
$$= 21.34$$

From the calculations we can now summarize the results:

X	X²
24	576
27	729
36	1296
48	2304
52	2704
52	2704
53	2809
53	2809
59	3481
60	3600
85	7225
90	8100
95	9025
ΣX = 734	ΣX² = 47362

Table 4.6

Mean = 56.5%, Standard deviation = 21.3, Median = 53%, Q_3 = 73, Q_1 = 42, SIQR = 15.5.

❋ **Interpretation**   A large proportion of the marks obtained in the statistical examination, as per Example 4.6, are clustered within 21.3 marks around the mean mark of 56.4. We will explain later how large this proportion is. Most of the marks are between 35.1 (56.4 − 21.3) and 77.7 (56.4 + 21.3). 8 out of 13 marks are in this interval, which is 61 % of all the marks.

Note   It is very important to note that Excel contains two different functions (VAR, VARP) to calculate the value of the variance. The function that you use is dependent upon whether the data set represents the complete population or is a sample from the population being measured.

1. If the data set is the complete population then the population variance (σ^2) is given by the Excel function VARP.
2. If the data set is a sample from the population then the sample variance (s^2) is given by the Excel function VAR.

These issues will be explored in greater detail in Chapter 6 when discussing the issue of sampling from populations and estimating population values from the sample data.

▷ Example 4.8

The frequency distribution of the length of a sample of 98 nails, measured to the nearest 0.1 mm is shown in Table 4.7. Calculate the following summary statistics: (a) mean, (b) standard deviation, (c) mode, (d) median, and (e) semi interquartile range.

The explanation of the Excel Spreadsheet solution to Example 4.8 is as illustrated in Figure 4.23.

Length, X	Frequency, f
4.0–4.2	4
4.3–4.5	9
4.6–4.8	13
4.9–5.1	20
5.2–5.4	34
5.5–5.7	18

Table 4.7

	A	B	C	D	E	F	G	H
1	**Frequency Distribution**							
2								
3	Length			Mid-Point	Frequency			Cum. Frequency
4		LCB	UCB	x	f	fx	fx^2	
5	4.0-4.2	3.95	4.25	4.1	4	16.40	67.24	4
6	4.3-4.5	4.25	4.55	4.4	9	39.60	174.24	13
7	4.6-4.8	4.55	4.85	4.7	13	61.10	287.17	26
8	4.9-5.1	4.85	5.15	5.0	20	100.00	500.00	46
9	5.2-5.4	5.15	5.45	5.3	34	180.20	955.06	80
10	5.5-5.7	5.45	5.75	5.6	18	100.80	564.48	98
11								
12	**Mean**					mean =	5.08	=B14/B13
13	sum f =	98.00	=SUM(E5:E10)			variance =	0.1686	=B15/B13-G12^2
14	sum fx =	498.10	=SUM(F5:F10)			standard deviation =	0.4106	=G13^0.5
15	sum fx^2 =	2548.19	=SUM(G5:G10)			variability =	8.0781	=100*G14/G12
16								
17	**Median**				**Mode**			
18	N =	98.00	=SUM(E5:E10)		Class Width c =	0.3000	=C5-B5	
19	Pos. of Med. =	49.50	=(B18+1)/2					
20	Median class is 440-459				Modal class 5.2-5.4			
21	L =	5.1500	=B9		L =	5.15	=B9	
22	C =	0.3000	=C9-B9		f1 =	34.00	=E9	
23	F =	46.0000	=H8		f0 =	20.00	=E8	
24	f =	34.0000	=E9		f2 =	18.00	=E10	
25	Median =	5.1809	=B21+B22*((B18+1)/2-B23)/B24		Mode =	5.29	=F21+(F22-F23)*F18/(2*F22-F23-F24)	
26								
27	**Quartiles**	Q1			Q3			
28	stion of Quartiles	24.7500	=(B18+1)/4		74.2500	=(B18+1)*3/4		
29	Q1 class is 4.6-4.8				Q3 class is 5.2-5.4			
30	L1 =	4.5500	=B7		L3 =	5.1500	=B9	
31	C1 =	0.3000	=C7-B7		C3 =	0.3000	=C9-B9	
32	F =	13.0000	=H6		F =	46.0000	=H8	
33	f1 =	13.0000	=E7		f3 =	34.0000	=E9	
34	Q1 =	4.8212	=B30+B31*((B18+1)/4-B32)/B33		Q3 =	5.3993	=F30+F31*(3*(B18+1)/4-F32)/F33	
35	SIQR =	0.2891	=(F34-B34)/2					

Figure 4.23

(a) Mean

As for any grouped frequency distribution the *true limits* provide an estimate for x by determining the mid-point for each class.

Length, X	Mid-Point, X	Frequency, f	fX	fX²
4.0–4.2	4.1	4	16.4	67.24
4.3–4.5	4.4	9	39.6	174.24
4.6–4.8	4.7	13	61.1	287.17
4.9–5.1	5.0	20	100.0	500.00
5.2–5.4	5.3	34	180.2	955.06
5.5–5.7	5.6	18	100.8	564.48
		98	498.1	2548.19

Table 4.8 Frequency distribution table for Example 4.8

$$f = 98, fX = 498.1, fX^2 = 2548.19$$

$$\text{Mean } \overline{X} = \frac{\sum fX}{\sum f} = \frac{498.1}{98} = 5.0826 \text{ mm}$$

✳ **Interpretation**   Average nail length is 5.08 mm.

(b) Standard deviation

When dealing with a frequency distribution then the frequency of each value within the distribution has to be taken into consideration:

$$SD(X) = \sqrt{\frac{\sum fX^2}{\sum f} - \left(\overline{X}\right)^2}$$

(4.16)

$$\text{Standard Deviation, } SD(X) = \sqrt{\frac{2548.19}{98} - \left(5.0826\right)^2} = 0.41 \text{ mm}$$

✳ **Interpretation**   Average nail length is 5.08 mm with a standard deviation of 0.41 mm.

(c) Mode

The mode can be calculated from equation (4.4):

$$\text{Mode} = L + \frac{\left(f_1 - f_0\right)}{\left(2f_1 - f_0 - f_2\right)} C$$

Where: L = lower class boundary of the modal class, f_0 = frequency of the class below the modal class, f_1 = frequency of the modal class, f_2 = frequency of the class above the modal class, C = modal class width. From the data set we find: L = 5.15, f_0 = 20, f_1 = 34, f_2 = 18, and C = 0.3.

$$\text{Mode} = 5.15 + \frac{(34-20)}{(2(34) - 20 - 18)} 0.3 = 5.29$$

Therefore, modal nail length is 5.29 mm.

> ✳ **Interpretation**   Modal nail length is 5.29 mm.

(d) Median

The median can be calculated from equation (4.5):

$$\text{Median} = L + C\frac{(N+1)/2 - F}{f}$$

Where L = true lower class boundary of the median class, C = median class width, F = cumulative frequency before the median class, f = frequency within the median class, N = total frequency. For Example 4.8 data we can now construct the grouped frequency table and calculate L, C, F, and f.

Length (X)	Frequency (f)	Lower Class Boundary (LCB)	Upper Class Boundary (UCB)	Cumulative Frequency (CF)
4.0–4.2	4	3.95	4.25	4
4.3–4.5	9	4.25	4.55	13
4.6–4.8	13	4.55	4.85	26
4.9–5.1	20	4.85	5.15	46
5.2–5.4	34	5.15	5.45	80
5.5–5.7	18	5.45	5.75	98
	Σf = 98			

Table 4.9 Cumulative frequency table

The position of the median can be estimated from equation (4.2) given that the percentile value for the median is P = 50.

$$\text{Position of Median} = \frac{P}{100}(N+1) = \frac{50}{100}(98+1) = 49.5\text{th item}$$

$$\text{Median Class} = 5.2 - 5.4$$

From Table 4.9 we have L = 5.15, C = 5.45 − 5.15 = 0.3, N = 98, F = 46, f = 34.

$$\text{Median} = 5.15 + 0.3 * \frac{49.5 - 46}{34} = 5.18$$

Median nail length is 5.18 mm.

✵ **interpretation**   Median nail length is 5.18 mm.

(e) Semi interquartile range

The semi interquartile range may now be calculated if we remember that the first and third quartiles are equivalent to the 25th and 75th percentiles; and

$$\text{Percentile Value P} = L + C\frac{(N + 1)P/100 - F}{f}$$

(4.17)

Where L = true lower class boundary of the percentile class, C = percentile class width, F = cumulative frequency before the percentile class, f = frequency within the percentile class, N = total frequency.

3rd quartile, Q_3

Percentile value, P = 75

$$\text{Position of } Q_3 = \frac{P}{100}(N + 1) = \frac{75}{100}(98 + 1) = 74.25\text{th item}$$

Q_3 Class = 5.2 − 5.4

From Table 4.9 we have L = 5.15, C = 5.45 − 5.15 = 0.3, N = 98, F = 46, f = 34.

$$Q_3 = 5.15 + 0.3 * \frac{74.25 - 46}{34} = 5.40$$

Third quartile nail length is 5.40 mm.

✵ **Interpretation**   First quartile nail length is 5.40 mm, i.e. 25% of all the nails are 5.40 mm or less.

1st quartile, Q_1

Percentile value, P = 25

$$\text{Position of } Q_1 = \frac{P}{100}(N + 1) = \frac{25}{100}(98 + 1) = 24.75\text{th item}$$

Q_1 Class = 4.6 − 4.8

From Table 4.9 we have L = 4.55, C = 4.85 – 4.55 = 0.3, N = 98, F = 13, f = 13.

$$Q_1 = 4.55 + 0.3 * \frac{24.75 - 13}{13} = 4.82$$

First quartile nail length is 4.82 mm.

✳ **Interpretation**   Third quartile nail length is 4.82 mm, i.e. 75% of all the nails are 4.82 mm or less.

The semi interquartile range is calculated from equation (4.11):

$$\text{Semi interquartile range} = \frac{(Q_3 - Q_1)}{2} = 0.3 \text{ (to 1 decimal place)}$$

✳ **Interpretation**   Semi interquartile range nail length is 4.82 mm.

Note
1. Using the alternative form of the formula makes calculations quicker and less prone to mistakes.
2. Because of the high frequency of large values the mean value is 'dragged' toward those values, which is reflected in the standard deviation.
3. This form of layout transforms very easily to a spreadsheet.

4.2.4 The coefficient of variation

The coefficient of variation represents the ratio of the standard deviation to the mean, and it is a useful statistic for comparing the degree of variation from one data series to another. Standard deviations vary according to the size of values in the distribution and may not even be in the same unit of measurement. For example, the value of the standard deviation of a set of weights will be different, depending on whether they are measured in pounds or kilograms. The coefficient of variation, however, will be the same in both cases as it does not depend on the unit of measurement. The **coefficient of variation**, V, is calculated as:

$$V = \frac{\text{Standard Deviation}}{\text{Mean}} * 100\% \qquad (4.18)$$

For example, if the coefficient of variation is 10% then this means that the standard deviation is equal to 10% of the average. For some measures, the standard deviation changes as the average changes. In this case, the coefficient of variation is the best way to summarize the variation.

X
Coefficient of variation
The coefficient of variation measures the spread of a set of data as a proportion of its mean.

Example 4.9

Consider the following problem that compares the UK and USA average earnings:
- Mean earnings in the UK are £125 per week with a Standard Deviation of £25.
- Mean earnings in the USA are $1,005 per week with a Standard Deviation of $170.

$$\text{For UK} \quad V = \frac{25}{125} * 100\% = 20\%$$

$$\text{For USA} \quad V = \frac{170}{1005} * 100\% = 16.9\%$$

✴ **Interpretation** The spread of earnings in the UK is greater than the spread in earnings in the USA in this example.

4.2.5 Measures of skewness and kurtosis

A fundamental task in many statistical analyses is to characterize the location and variability of a data set. A further characterization of the data includes *skewness* and *kurtosis*. *Skewness* is a measure of the degree of asymmetry of a distribution and *kurtosis* is a measure of whether the data are peaked or flat relative to a normal distribution. The histogram is an effective graphical technique for showing both the skewness and kurtosis for a data set. Consider the following three distributions A, B, and C as illustrated in Figure 4.24 below.

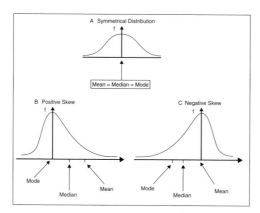

Figure 4.24

Distribution A is said to be symmetrical, the mean, median, and mode have the same value and thus coincide at the same point of the distribution. *Distribution B* has a high frequency of relatively low values and a low frequency of relatively high values. Consequently the mean is 'dragged' toward the right (the high values) of the distribution. It is known as a right or positively skewed distribution. *Distribution C* has a high frequency of relatively high values and a low frequency of relatively low values. Consequently the mean is 'dragged' toward the left (the low values) of the distribution. It is known as a left or negatively skewed distribution. The *skewness* of a frequency distribution can be an important consideration. For example, if your data set is salary, you would prefer a situation that led to a positively skewed distribution of salary to one that is negatively skewed. Positive skewness is more common than negative.

One measure of skewness is *Pearson's coefficient of skewness* defined as,

$$PCS = \frac{3(\text{Mean} - \text{Median})}{\text{Standard Deviation}}$$ (4.19)

> ### Note
> 1. With skewed data, the mean is not a good measure of central tendency because it is sensitive to extreme values. In this case the median would be used to provide the measure of central tendency.
> 2. For symmetric distributions (mean = median), the value for skewness is zero.
> 3. If mean < median, then PCS is negative and the distribution is said to be negatively skewed.
> 4. If mean > median, then PCS is positive and the distribution is said to be positively skewed.
> 5. Pearson's coefficient of skewness is independent of the units being measured.

Example 4.10

Consider the marks obtained in the statistics examination (Example 4.1)

24	27	36	48	52	52	53	53	59	60	85	90	95

Excel spreadsheet solution for Example 4.10

Figure 4.25 illustrates the Excel solution to Example 4.10.

	A	B	C	D	E	F	G
1		MEASURES OF DISPERSION					
2							
3		Set of Numbers			Formula Method		
4					n =	13	=COUNT(B7:B19)
5		Statistics			sum x =	734	=SUM(B7:B19)
6		Marks x	x^2		sum x^2 =	47362	=SUM(C7:C19)
7		24	576		mean =	56.4615	=F5/F4
8		27	729		variance =	455.3254	=F6/F4-F7^2
9		36	1296		standard deviation =	21.3384	=F8^0.5
10		48	2304		Pearson's skew =	0.4867	=3*(F19-F15)/F21
11		52	2704				
12		52	2704		Excel Function Method		
13		53	2809		Range =	71	=MAX(B7:B19)-MIN(B7:B19)
14		53	2809		Q1 =	48.0000	=QUARTILE(B7:B19,1)
15		59	3481		Median =	53.0000	=MEDIAN(B7:B19)
16		60	3600		Q3 =	60.0000	=QUARTILE(B7:B19,3)
17		85	7225		QR =	12.0000	=F16-F14
18		90	8100		SIQR =	6.0000	=(F16-F14)/2
19		95	9025		Mean =	56.4615	=AVERAGE(B7:B19)
20					varp =	455.3254	=VARP(B7:B19)
21					sdp =	21.3384	=STDEVP(B7:B19)
22					Fisher's skew =	0.4410	=SKEW(B7:B19)
23					Fisher's kurtosis =	-0.4253	=KURT(B7:B19)

Figure 4.25

The explanation for the Excel spreadsheet solution is as follows:

> **→ Excel Function Method**
>
> Pearson's skew = Cell F10   Formula: =3*(F19–F15)/F21

The descriptive statistics for mean, median, and standard deviation can be calculated to be: mean $\bar{X} = 56.4615$, standard deviation s = 21.3384, and median = 53. Pearson's correlation coefficient can now be calculated:

$$\text{PCS} = \frac{3*(56.4615-53)}{21.3384} = 0.4867$$

> **❋ Interpretation**   The marks obtained in the statistics examination show positive skewness with a Pearson coefficient of skewness of 0.4867.

If we use the Excel Function Method the results will be somewhat different. Excel uses an alternative measure of skewness based upon *Fisher's skewness coefficient*.

$$\text{Fisher's skewness} = \frac{n}{(n-1)(n-2)}\Sigma\left((X-\bar{X})/s\right)^3 \tag{4.20}$$

Where the sample standard deviation (s) is given by the Excel function STDEV.

> **→ Excel Function Method**
>
> Fisher's skew = Cell F22   Formula: =SKEW(B7:B19)

> **❋ Interpretation**   For Example 4.1 the value of skewness is calculated to be 0.4410 which is positively skewed.

> **Note**   Skewness values greater than $\pm 2\sqrt{\frac{6}{N}}$ (where N is the sample size) would indicate severe skewness. In Example 4.10 we have N = 13 and error measurement $\pm 2\sqrt{\frac{6}{13}} = \pm 1.36$. The measured value of skewness 0.4867 lies within the region ± 1.36 and not outside. We conclude that the distribution is not significantly skewed.

Kurtosis measures how 'peaked' the data is within the distribution. A standard normal distribution has a kurtosis of zero. Positive kurtosis indicates a 'peaked' distribution and negative kurtosis indicates a 'flat' distribution. Consider the two distributions in Figure 4.26. We can see from the two distributions that distribution A is more peaked than distribution B but the means and standard deviations are approximately the same.

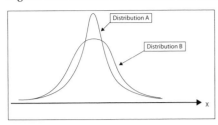

A measure of whether the curve of a distribution is Bell-shaped (Mesokurtic), peaked (Leptokurtic), and flat (Platykurtic) is provided by Fisher's measure of kurtosis given by the equation:

Figure 4.26

$$\text{Kurtosis} = \frac{n(n+1)}{(n-1)(n-2)(n-3)}\Sigma\left((X-\bar{X})/s\right)^4 - \frac{3(n-1)^2}{(n-2)(n-3)} \tag{4.21}$$

This equation is used by Excel to provide an estimate of kurtosis.

➡ **Excel Function Method**

Fisher's Kurtosis = Cell F23   Formula: =KURT(B7:B19)

✳ **Interpretation**   In Example 4.10 the value of kurtosis is calculated to be –0.4253 which illustrates a flat distribution.

Note   Kurtosis values greater than $\pm 2\sqrt{\dfrac{24}{N}}$ (where N is the sample size) would indicate severe kurtosis. For Example 4.10 we have N = 13 and error measurement $\pm 2\sqrt{\dfrac{24}{13}} = \pm 2.72$.

We can see that the measured value of kurtosis –0.4253 lies within the region ± 2.72 and not outside. We conclude that the distribution does not have a significant kurtosis problem.

🖰 **Student Exercises**

X4.10 Over a one month period the number of vacant beds in a West Yorkshire hospital was surveyed. The following frequency distribution resulted:

Beds Vacant	0	2	3	5	6	8
Frequency	4	8	12	4	2	1

Determine the mean and standard deviation.

X4.11 In a number of towns the distance of a sample of 122 supermarkets from the
towns' high street was measured to the nearest metre

Distance	57–59	60–62	63–65	66–68	69–71	72–74	75–77
Frequency	9	10	18	42	27	11	5

Determine the Range, Mean, and Standard Deviation.

X4.12 In a debate on the alteration of a traffic system in the city centre, measurements of the
number of cars per minute were taken at two junctions, the results were as follows:

Number of Cars per minute	Junction A	Junction B
10–14	0	5
15–19	3	8
20–24	13	10
25–29	24	12
30–34	17	14
35–39	3	5
40–44	0	3
45–49	0	3
Totals	60	60

Compare the two distributions by plotting out their frequency polygons and determine the
means and standard deviations.

X4.13 Greendelivery.com has recently decided to review the weekly mileage of its delivery
vehicles that are used to deliver shopping purchased online to customer homes from
a central parcel depot. The sample data collected is part of the first stage in analysing
the economic benefit of potentially moving all vehicles to bio fuels from diesel:

80	165	159	143	140
136	138	118	120	124
159	131	93	145	109
163	136	163	142	80
106	111	123	161	179
144	145	91	112	146
170	105	131	141	122
137	152	109	122	126
114	155	92	143	165

(a) Use Excel to construct a frequency distribution and plot the histogram with
class intervals of 10 and classes 75–84, 85–94, …, 175–184. Comment on the
pattern in mileage travelled by the company vehicles.

(b) Use the raw data to determine the mean, median, standard deviation, and
semi interquartile range.

(c) Comment on which measure you would use to describe the average and measure of dispersion. Explain using your answers to (a) and (b).

(d) Calculate the measure of skewness and kurtosis and comment on the distribution shape.

4.3 Exploratory Data Analysis

In the previous sections we explored methods to describe a data set by computing measures of average, spread, and shape. In this section we will explore exploratory data analysis techniques, including: **five-number summary**, box plots, and using the Excel ToolPak add-in to calculate descriptive statistics.

4.3.1 Five-number summary

The five-number summary is a simple method that provides measures of average and spread; with the added bonus of giving us an idea of the shape of the distribution. This five-number summary consists of the following numbers in the data set: smallest value, first quartile, median, third quartile, and largest value. For symmetrical distributions the following rule would hold:

- Q_3 – Median = Median – Q_1
- Largest value – Q_3 = Q_1 – Smallest value
- Median = Midhinge = Midrange

The midrange is the average of the largest and smallest data values and the midhinge is the average of the first and third quartiles. For non-symmetry the following rule would hold:

- Right-skewed distributions: Largest value – Q_3 greatly exceeds Q_1 – Smallest value
- Left-skewed distributions: Q_1 – Smallest value greatly exceeds Largest value – Q_3

▷ Example 4.11

In this particular case we will assume that the values are as follows: first quartile Q_1 = 15, minimum = 8, median = 33, maximum = 88 and third quartile Q_3 = 62.

Input your data into Excel as illustrated in Figure 4.27.

	A	B	C
1			
2		Statistic	Value
3		Q1	15
4		Minimum	8
5		Median	33
6		Maximum	88
7		Q3	62

Figure 4.27

X

Five-number summary
A five-number summary is especially useful when we have so many data that it is sufficient to present a summary of the data rather than the whole data set.

We can see from the summary statistics that the data distribution is not symmetrical:

- The distance from Q_3 to the median $(62 - 33 = 29)$ is not the same as between Q_1 and the median $(33 - 15 = 18)$.
- The distance from Q_3 and the largest value $(88 - 62 = 26)$ is not the same as the distance between Q_1 and the smallest value $(15 - 8 = 7)$.
- The median (33), the midhinge $((62 + 15)/2 = 38.5$ and the midrange $((88 + 8)/2 = 48)$ are not equal.

The summary numbers indicates right skewness because the distance between Q_3 and the largest number $(88 - 62 = 26)$ is longer than the distance between Q_1 and the smallest value $(15 - 8 = 7)$. The minimum and maximum points are identified and enable identification of any extreme values (or outliers). A simple rule to identify an outlier (or suspected outlier) is that the largest value – smallest value $(88 - 8 = 80)$ should be no longer than three times the length of the box $(Q_3 - Q_1 = 62 - 15 = 47)$. In this case the value of maximum – minimum is 80 and $Q_3 - Q_1$ is 47 and therefore no extreme values are present in the data set.

4.3.2 Box plots

We have already discussed techniques for visually representing data (see histograms and frequency polygons). In this section we present another important method, called box plots. A **box plot** (or **box-and-whisker plot**) is a graphical method of displaying the symmetry or skewness in a data set. It shows a measure of central location (the median),

> ### ⟲ Example 4.12
>
> In this particular case we will assume that the values are the same as in Example 4.11: first quartile $Q_1 = 15$, minimum $= 8$, median $= 33$, maximum $= 88$, and third quartile $Q_3 = 62$. Input your data into Excel as illustrated in Figure 4.27. The box plot is then constructed.
>
>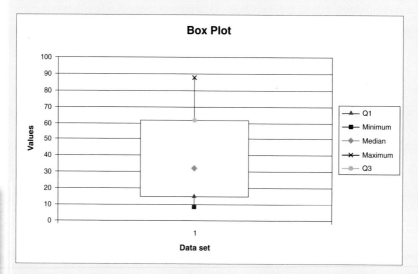
>
> Figure 4.28

two measures of dispersion (the range and interquartile range), the skewness (from the orientation of the median relative to the quartiles), and potential outliers.

The box plot in Example 4.12 is interpreted as follows:

- If the median within the box is not equidistant from the whisker (or hinge), then the data is skewed. The box plot indicates right skewness because the distance between the median and the highest value is greater than the distance between the median and the lowest value. Furthermore, the top whisker (distance between Q_3 and maximum) is longer than the lower whisker (distance between Q_1 and minimum).

- The minimum and maximum points (or whiskers) are identified and enable identification of any extreme values (or outliers). To identify an outlier (or suspected outlier) is that the whisker (maximum value – minimum value) should be no longer than three times the length of the box ($Q_3 - Q_1$). As we know, in this case the value of maximum – minimum is 80 and $Q_3 - Q_1$ is 47 and no extreme values are present in the data set.

Excel Spreadsheet Solution for Example 4.11

Unfortunately, Microsoft Excel does not have a built in box plot chart type. You can create your own charts using stacked bar or column charts and error bars in combination with line or XY scatter chart series to show additional data. For your data set calculate: first quartile, minimum, median, maximum, and third quartile.

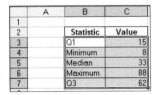

Input your data into Excel as illustrated in Figure 4.29. Highlight Cells B3:C7 and click on Chart Wizard.

Figure 4.29

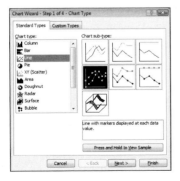

Figure 4.30

Chart Wizard — Step 1 of 4 — Chart Type
Select a Line Chart.
Click **N**ext.

Chart Wizard — Step 2 of 4 — Chart Source Data

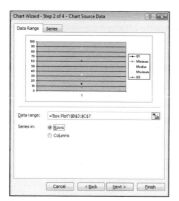

At Step 2 change 'Series in' to Rows
Click <u>N</u>ext.

Figure 4.31

Chart Wizard — Step 3 of 4 — Chart Options

Chart title: Box Plot.
Category (X): Data Set.
Value (Y): Value.
Click <u>N</u>ext.

Figure 4.32

Chart Wizard — Step 4 of 4 — Chart Location

Click <u>F</u>inish.

Figure 4.33

Excel box plot is as illustrated in Figure 4.34.

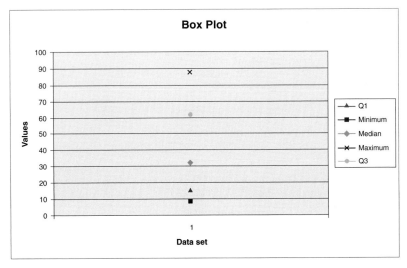

Figure 4.34

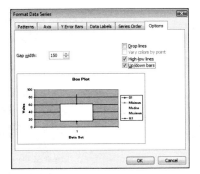

Figure 4.35

Right click on the data series and choose Format Data Series. Select the Options tab and switch on the checkboxes for High-low lines and Up/down bars.

If required, format the data points to increase data point size in the box plot.

4.3.3 Using the Excel ToolPak add-in

You can use the *Descriptive Statistics procedure in the Excel ToolPak add-in* to provide a set of summary statistics, including: mean, median, mode, standard deviation, sample variance, kurtosis, skewness, range, minimum, maximum, sum, count, largest, and smallest number. The skewness and kurtosis values can be used to provide information about the shape of the distribution.

Example 4.13

If we consider Example 4.1 data then the Descriptive Statistics procedure in the Excel ToolPak add-in would give the following results.

Select Tools > Select Data Analysis

Figure 4.36

Select Descriptive Statistics.
Click OK.

Figure 4.37

Input Range: A5:A17
Output Range: D3
Click Summary statistics.
Click OK.

	A	B	C	D	E
1	MEASURES OF DISPERSION				
2					
3	Statistics			*Column1*	
4	Marks x				
5	24			Mean	56.46153846
6	27			Standard Error	6.159852838
7	36			Median	53
8	48			Mode	52
9	52			Standard Deviation	22.20966526
10	52			Sample Variance	493.2692308
11	53			Kurtosis	-0.425319242
12	53			Skewness	0.440986666
13	59			Range	71
14	60			Minimum	24
15	85			Maximum	95
16	90			Sum	734
17	95			Count	13

Figure 4.38

The Excel results would then be calculated and printed out in the Excel worksheet as shown.

We already stated that a skewness value of zero would indicate a symmetrical distribution. In our example in Figure 4.38 we can see the skewness value of 0.44. This implies that the data set is skewed to the right, but only slightly.

We know that kurtosis measures the concentration of data values at the centre of the distribution. A positive value indicates a distribution with a sharp peak compared to a bell shaped curve, whereas a negative value would indicate a distribution with a flatter shape than a bell shaped curve. The result of –0.425 for kurtosis in Figure 4.38 indicates that our dataset follows a flat distribution.

Student Exercises

X4.14 The manager at BIG JIMS restaurant is concerned at the time it takes to process credit card payments at the counter by counter staff. The manager has collected the following processing time data (time in minutes) and requested that summary statistics are calculated.

(a) Calculate a five-number summary for this data set.

(b) Do we have any evidence for a symmetric distribution?

(c) Use the Excel Analysis-ToolPak to calculate descriptive statistics.

(d) Which measures would you use to provide a measure of average and spread?

Processing credit cards (n = 40)				
1.57	1.38	1.97	1.52	1.39
1.09	1.29	1.26	1.07	1.76
1.13	1.59	0.27	0.92	0.71
1.49	1.73	0.79	1.38	2.46
0.98	2.31	1.23	1.56	0.89
0.76	1.23	1.56	1.98	2.01
1.40	1.89	0.89	1.34	3.21
0.76	1.54	1.78	4.89	1.98

X4.15 The local regional development agency is conducting a major review of the economic development of a local community. One economic measure to be collected is the local house prices that reflect on the economic well being of this community. The development agency has collected the following house price data (£'s).

(a) Calculate a five-number summary

(b) Do we have any evidence for a symmetric distribution?

(c) Use the Excel Analysis-ToolPak to calculate descriptive statistics.

(d) Which measures would you use to provide a measure of average and spread?

Local house price values (£'s, n = 50)				
162726	162726	162726	162726	162726
188656	188656	188656	188656	188656
165547	165547	165547	165547	165547
175806	175806	175806	175806	175806
190670	190670	190670	190670	190670
145810	145810	145810	145810	145810
169682	169682	169682	169682	169682
155044	155044	155044	155044	155044
149304	149304	149304	149304	149304
197847	197847	197847	197847	197847

■ Techniques in Practice

1. Coco S.A. supplies a range of computer hardware and software to 2000 schools within a large municipal region of Spain. When Coco S.A. won the contract the issue of customer service was considered to be central to the company being successful at the final bidding stage. The company has now requested that its customer service director creates a series of graphical representations of the data to illustrate customer satisfaction with the service. The following data has been collected during the last six months and measures the time to respond to the received complaint (days).

5	24	34	6	61	56	38	32
87	78	34	9	67	4	54	23
56	32	86	12	81	32	52	53
34	45	21	31	42	12	53	21
43	76	62	12	73	3	67	12
78	89	26	10	74	78	23	32
26	21	56	78	91	85	15	12
15	56	45	21	45	26	21	34
28	12	67	23	24	43	25	65
23	8	87	21	78	54	76	79

The customer service director has analysed this data to create a grouped frequency table and plotted the histogram. From this he made a series of observations regarding the time to respond to customer complaints. He now wishes to extend the analysis to use numerical methods to describe this data.

(a) From the data set calculate the mean and median.

(b) Repeat the analysis to calculate the standard deviation, quartiles (Q_1, Q_2, and Q_3), quartile range, and semi interquartile range.

(c) Describe the shape of the distribution. Do the results suggest that there is a great deal of variation in time to respond to customer complaints?

(d) Which measures would you recommend the customer service manager uses to describe the variation in time to respond to customer complaints?

(e) What conclusions can you draw from these results?

2. Bakers Ltd runs a chain of bakery shops and is famous for the quality of its pies. The management of the company are concerned at the number of complaints from customers who complain it takes too long to serve customers at a particular branch. The motto of the company is 'Have your pies in 2 minutes'. The manager of the branch concerned has been told to provide data on the time it takes for customers to enter the shop and be served by the shop staff.

0.70	0.70	0.70	0.70	0.70	0.70	0.70	0.70	0.70	0.70
0.99	0.99	0.99	0.99	0.99	0.99	0.99	0.99	0.99	0.99
0.12	0.12	0.12	0.12	0.12	0.12	0.12	0.12	0.12	0.12
0.70	0.70	0.70	0.70	0.70	0.70	0.70	0.70	0.70	0.70
1.88	1.88	1.88	1.88	1.88	1.88	1.88	1.88	1.88	1.88
0.55	0.55	0.55	0.55	0.55	0.55	0.55	0.55	0.55	0.55
1.38	1.38	1.38	1.38	1.38	1.38	1.38	1.38	1.38	1.38
0.80	0.80	0.80	0.80	0.80	0.80	0.80	0.80	0.80	0.80
1.25	1.25	1.25	1.25	1.25	1.25	1.25	1.25	1.25	1.25
1.48	1.48	1.48	1.48	1.48	1.48	1.48	1.48	1.48	1.48

(a) From the data set calculate the mean and median.

(b) Repeat the analysis to calculate the standard deviation, quartiles (Q_1, Q_2, and Q_3), quartile range, and semi interquartile range.

(c) Describe the shape of the distribution. Do the results suggest that there is a great deal of variation in time to serve customers?

(d) Which measures would you recommend the shop manager uses to describe the variation in time to serve customers?

(e) What conclusions can you draw from these results?

3. Skodel Ltd is a small brewery which is undergoing a major expansion after a take-over by a large European brewery chain. Skodel Ltd produces a range of beers and lagers and is renowned for the quality of its beers; winning a number of prizes at trade fairs throughout the European Union. The new parent company are reviewing the quality control mechanisms being operated by Skodel Ltd and are concerned at the quantity of lager in its premium lager brand which should contain a mean of 330 ml and a standard deviation of 15 ml. The bottling plant manager provided the parent company with quantity measurements from 100 bottles for analysis.

326	326	326	326	326	326	326	326	326	326
344	344	344	344	344	344	344	344	344	344
333	333	333	333	333	333	333	333	333	333
346	346	346	346	346	346	346	346	346	346
339	339	339	339	339	339	339	339	339	339
353	353	353	353	353	353	353	353	353	353
310	310	310	310	310	310	310	310	310	310
351	351	351	351	351	351	351	351	351	351
350	350	350	350	350	350	350	350	350	350
348	348	348	348	348	348	348	348	348	348

(a) From the data set calculate the mean and median.

(b) Repeat the analysis to calculate the standard deviation, quartiles (Q_1, Q_2, and Q_3), quartile range, and semi interquartile range.

(c) Describe the shape of the distribution. Do the results suggest that there is a great deal of variation in quantity within the bottle measurements? Compare the assumed bottle average and spread with the measured average and spread.

(d) What conclusions can you draw from these results?

■ Summary

This chapter extends your knowledge from using tables and charts to summarizing data using measures of average and dispersion. The mean is the most commonly calculated average to represent the measure of central tendency but this measurement uses all the data within the calculation and therefore outliers will affect the value of the mean. This can imply that the value of the mean may not be representative of the underlying data set. If outliers are present in the data set then you can either eliminate these values or use the median to represent the average. The average provides a measure of the central tendency (or middle value) and the next calculation to perform is to provide a measure of the spread of the data within the distribution. The standard deviation is the most common type of measure of dispersion (or spread) but like the mean, the standard deviation is influenced by the presence of outliers within the data set. If outliers are present in the data set then you can either eliminate these values or use the semi interquartile range to represent the degree of dispersion. You can estimate the degree of skewness in the data set by calculating Pearson's coefficient of skewness (or use Fisher's skewness equation) and the degree of 'peakedness' by calculating the kurtosis statistic. Box plots are graph plots that allow you to visualize the degree of symmetry or skewness in the data set.

The chapter explored the calculation process for raw data and frequency distributions and it is very important to note that the graphical method will not be as accurate as the raw data method when calculating the summary statistics. Table 4.10 provides a summary of which statistics measures to use for different types of data.

	Summary statistic to be applied	
Data type	*Average*	*Spread or Dispersion*
Nominal	Mode	NA
Ordinal	Mode	Range
	Median	Range, interquartile range
Ratio or interval	Mode	Range
	Median	Range, interquartile range
	Mean	Variance, Standard deviation, Skewness, Kurtosis

Table 4.10 Which summary statistic to use?

In the next chapter we will look at the concept of probability.

■ Key Terms

Arithmetic mean
Box plot
Box-and-whisker plot
Central tendency
Coefficient of variation
Cumulative frequency
    distribution
Dispersion

Extreme value
Five-number summary
Interquartile range
Kurtosis
Left-skewed
Mean
Median
Mode

Ogive
Outlier
Population mean
Population standard
    deviation
Population variance
Q_1: first quartile
Q_2: second quartile

Q_3: third quartile	Shape	Symmetrical
Quartiles	Skewness	Variance
Range	Standard deviation	Variation
Right-skewed		

Further Reading

Textbook Resources

1. Albright, S. C., Winston, W. L., and Zappe, C. (1999) *Data Analysis and Decision Making with Microsoft Excel*. Dusbury Press, London (Chapter 3).

2. Burton, G., Carrol, G., and Wall, S. (1999) *Quantitative Methods for Business and Economics*. Longman, New York (Chapter 2).

Web Resources

1. StatSoft Electronic Textbook http://www.statsoft.com/textbook/stathome.html (accessed 28/1/2007).

2. HyperStat Online Statistics Textbook http://davidmlane.com/hyperstat/index.html (accessed 28/1/2007).

3. Eurostat—website is updated daily and provides direct access to the latest and most complete statistical information available on the European Union, the EU Member States, the euro-zone and other countries http://epp.eurostat.ec.europa.eu (accessed 28/1/2007).

4. Economagic—contains international economic data sets (http://www.economagic.com) (accessed 28/1/2007).

5. The ISI glossary of statistical terms provides definitions in a number of different languages http://isi.cbs.nl/glossary/index.htm.

Formula Summary

$$\text{Mean } \bar{X} = \frac{\sum X}{\sum f} \tag{4.1}$$

$$\text{Position of Percentile} = \frac{P}{100}(N+1) \tag{4.2}$$

$$\text{Mean } \bar{X} = \frac{\sum fX}{\sum f} \tag{4.3}$$

$$\text{Mode} = L + \frac{(f_1 - f_0)}{(2f_1 - f_0 - f_2)}C \tag{4.4}$$

$$\text{Median} = L + C\frac{(N+1)/2 - F}{f} \tag{4.5}$$

Percentile Value $P = L + \dfrac{(N+1)P/100 - F}{f}C$

(4.6)

Weighted average $\bar{X} = \dfrac{w_1 X_1 + w_2 X_2 + w_3 X_3}{w_1 + w_2 + w_3} = \dfrac{\sum wX}{\sum w}$

(4.7)

RANGE (ungrouped data) = Highest Extreme Value – Lowest Extreme Value

(4.8)

RANGE (grouped data) = UCB Highest Class – LCB Lowest Class

(4.9)

Interquartile range = $Q_3 - Q_1$

(4.10)

Semi interquartile range = $\dfrac{Q_3 - Q_1}{2}$

(4.11)

Variance, $VAR(X) = \dfrac{\sum(X - \bar{X})^2}{\sum f}$

(4.12)

Standard Deviation, $SD(X) = \sqrt{\dfrac{\sum(X - \bar{X})^2}{\sum f}}$

(4.13)

Variance, $VAR(X) = \dfrac{\sum X^2}{\sum f} - (\bar{X})^2$

(4.14)

Standard Deviation, $SD(X) = \sqrt{\dfrac{\sum X^2}{\sum f} - (\bar{X})^2}$

(4.15)

Standard Deviation, $SD(X) = \sqrt{\dfrac{\sum fX^2}{\sum f} - (\bar{X})^2}$

(4.16)

Percentile Value $P = L + C\dfrac{(N+1)P/100 - F}{f}$

(4.17)

Coefficient of Variability, $V = \dfrac{\text{Standard Deviation}}{\text{Mean}} * 100\%$

(4.18)

$PCS = \dfrac{3(\text{Mean} - \text{Median})}{\text{Standard Deviation}}$

(4.19)

Fisher's Skewness $= \dfrac{n}{(n-1)(n-2)}\sum\left((X - \bar{X})/s\right)^3$

(4.20)

Fisher's Kurtosis $= \dfrac{n(n+1)}{(n-1)(n-2)(n-3)}\sum\left((X - \bar{X})/s\right)^4 - \dfrac{3(n-1)^2}{(n-2)(n-3)}$

(4.21)

Probability Distributions

» Overview «

The concept of probability is an important aspect of the study of statistics and within this chapter we shall introduce the reader to some of the concepts that are relevant to probability distributions. However, the main emphasis of the chapter is to focus on the concepts of discrete and continuous probability distributions and not on the fundamentals of probability theory. We will initially explore the issue of continuous probability distributions (normal) and then introduce the concept of discrete probability distributions (binomial, Poisson). Section 5.1 will provide a very brief introduction to the probability concepts and laws and Sections 5.2 and 5.3 will explore the concept of a probability distribution and introduce two distinct types: (a) continuous and (b) discrete. Table 5.1 summarizes the probability distributions that are applicable to whether the data variables are discrete/continuous and whether the distributions are symmetric/skewed.

Measured characteristic	Variable type			
	Discrete		Continuous	
Shape	Symmetric	Skewed	Symmetric	Skewed
Distribution	Binomial	Poisson	Normal	Exponential

Table 5.1

» Learning Objectives «

On completing this chapter you should be able to:

» Understand the concept of the following terms: experiment, outcome, sample space, relative frequency, and sample probability.

» Understand the concept of events being mutually exclusive and independent.

» Use the basic probability laws to solve simple problems.

» Use tree diagrams (or decision trees) as an aid to the solution process.

X

Probability A probability provides a number value to the likely occurrence of a particular event.

Continuous probability distribution If a random variable is a continuous variable, its probability distribution is called a continuous probability distribution.

Discrete probability distribution If a random variable is a discrete variable, its probability distribution is called a discrete probability distribution.

Sample space The sample space is an exhaustive list of all the possible outcomes of an experiment.

Event An event is any collection of outcomes of an experiment.

» Understand the concept of a probability distribution.

» Calculate using this distribution the expected value and a measure of spread.

» Have an introduction to discrete distributions.

» Understand when to apply the binomial distribution.

» Solve simple problems using both tree diagrams and the binomial formula.

» Understand when to apply the Poisson distribution.

» Solve simple problems using the Poisson formula.

» Have an introduction to continuous distributions.

» Use the normal distribution to calculate the values of a variable that correspond to a particular probability.

» Calculate as one parameter of the normal distribution if the other parameters are known.

» Use the normal distribution to calculate the probability that a variable has a value between specific limits.

» Understand when to apply approximations to simplify the solution process.

» Have an introduction to the uniform distribution.

» Have an introduction to the Student's t distribution.

» Have an introduction to the chi square distribution.

» Have an introduction to the F distribution.

» Solve problems using Microsoft Excel.

5.1 Introduction to Probability

5.1.1 Basic ideas

There are a number of words and phrases that encapsulate the basic concept of probability: chance, probable, odds and so on. In all cases we are faced with a degree of uncertainty and concerned with the likelihood of a particular event happening. Statistically these words and phrases are too vague; we need some measure of likelihood of an event occurring. This measure is termed probability and is measured on a scale ranging between 0 and 1.

From Figure 5.1 we observe that the probability values lie between 0 and 1 with 0 representing no possibility of the event occurring and 1 representing the probability is certain to occur. In reality the value of the probability will lie between 0 and 1.

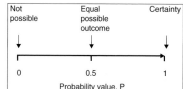

Figure 5.1

Expected value The expected value of a random data variable indicates its population average value.

Normal distribution The normal distribution is a symmetrical, bell-shaped curve, centred at its expected value.

In order to determine a probability of an event occurring, data has to be obtained. This can be achieved through, for example, experience or observation or empirical methods. The procedure or situation that produces a definite result (or outcome) is termed a random experiment. For example tossing a coin, rolling a die, recording the income of a factory worker, determining defective items on an assembly line are all examples of 'experiments'. The characteristics of random experiments are:

- Each experiment is repeatable.
- All possible outcomes can be described.
- Although individual outcomes appear haphazard, continual repeats of the experiment will produce a regular pattern.

The result of an experiment is called an outcome. It is the single possible result of an experiment, e.g. tossing a coin produces 'a head', rolling a die gives a '3'. If we accept the proposition that an experiment can produce a finite number of outcomes then we could in theory define all these outcomes. The set of all possible outcomes is defined as the sample space. For example the experiment of rolling a die could produce the outcomes: 1, 2, 3, 4, 5, and 6; which would thus define the sample space. Another basic notion is the concept of an event and is simply a set of possible outcomes i.e. an event is a subset of the sample space. For example take the experiment of rolling a die, the event of obtaining an even number would be defined as the subset {2, 4, 6}. Furthermore, two events are said to be mutually exclusive if they cannot occur together. Thus in rolling a die, the event 'obtaining a two' is mutually exclusive of the event 'obtaining a three'. The event 'obtaining a two' and the event 'obtaining an even number' are not mutually exclusive since both can occur together i.e. {2} is a subset of {2, 4, 6}.

🖱 Student Exercises

X5.1 Give an appropriate sample space for each of the following experiments:

(a) A card is chosen at random from a pack of cards.

(b) A person is chosen at random from a group containing 5 females and 6 males.

(c) A football team records the results of each of two games as 'win', 'draw', or 'lose'.

X5.2 A dart is thrown at a board and is likely to land on any one of eight squares numbered 1 to 8 inclusive. A represents the event the dart lands in square 5 or 8. B represents the event the dart lands in square 2, 3, or 4. C represents the event the dart lands in square 1, 2, 5, or 6. Which two events are mutually exclusive?

5.1.2 Relative frequency

Suppose we perform the experiment of throwing a die and note the score obtained. We repeat the experiment a large number of times, say 1000, and note the number of times each score was obtained. For each number we could derive the ratio of occurrence that an event A will happen (m) to the total number of experiments ($n = 1000$). This ratio is called the relative frequency. In general, if event A occurs m times, then your estimate of the probability that A will occur is as follows:

$$P(A) = \frac{m}{n}$$

(5.1)

Here m represents the frequency, or the number of times a particular number occurs (an outcome). The result of the die experiment is shown in Table 5.2 below:

Score	1	2	3	4	5	6
Frequency	173	168	167	161	172	159
Relative Frequency	0.173	0.168	0.167	0.161	0.172	0.159

Table 5.2

This notion of relative frequency provides an approach to determine the probability of an event. As the number of experiments increases then the relative frequency stabilizes and approaches the true probability of the event. Thus if we had performed the above experiment 2000 times we might expect 'in the long run' the frequencies of all the scores to approach 0.167, i.e. $P(2) = 0.167$, $P(3) = 0.167$, etc. There are many situations where probabilities are derived through this empirical approach. If a manufacturer indicates that he is 99% certain $(P = 0.99)$ that an electric light bulb will last 200 hours, this figure will have been arrived at from experiments which have tested numerous samples of light bulbs. If we are told that the probability of rain on a June day is 0.42, this will have been determined through studying rainfall records for June over, say, the past 20 years. A number of important issues are assumed when approaching probabilities in general:

- The probability of each event lies between 0 and 1.
- The sum of the probabilities of these events will equal 1.
- If we know the probability of an event, then the probability of it not occurring is P(Event not occurring) $= 1 - $ P(Event occurs).

Student Exercises

X5.3 How would you give an estimate of the probability of a 25 year old passing the driving test at a first attempt?

X5.4 The table below provides information about 200 school leavers and their destination after leaving school.

	Leave school at 16 years	Leave school at a higher age
Full-time education, E	14	18
Full-time job, J	96	44
Other	15	13

Determine the following probabilities that a person selected at random:

(a) Went into full-time education.

(b) Went into a full-time job.

(c) Either went into full-time education or went into a full-time job.

(d) Left school at 16.

(e) Left school at 16 and went into full-time education.

5.1.3 The probability laws

In case we are measuring probabilities for multiple events, very often we would like to be able to calculate what is the probability that either one or the other event will happen, or the probability that both events will happen simultaneously. If this is the case, certain probability laws apply. Let us take a look at the general addition law. In its simplest form the addition law of *mutually exclusive events* states that:

$$P(A \text{ or } B) = P(A) + P(B) \tag{5.2}$$

In other words, a probability that either of the two events will happen is equal to the sum of the two probabilities for every individual event. However, when events are *not* mutually exclusive, i.e. two or more events contain common outcomes within a sample space, then this law does not hold.

⌕ Example 5.1

To illustrate this case consider a sample space consisting of the positive integers from 1 through 10. Let event A represent all odd integers and event B represent all integers less than or equal to 5. These two events within the sample space are displayed in Figure 5.2. While the events A and B overlap (the intersect) common sample points are present and would represent the event {odd integers and integers ≤ 5} or {A and B} or {A ∩ B}.

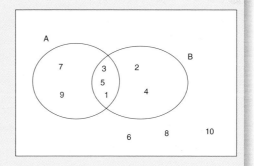

Figure 5.2

The event {A or B} contains the outcomes of either odd integers or integers ≤ 5. A little thought would indicate that the number containing event A or B is given by the equation

$n\{A$ or $B\} = n\{A\} + n\{B\} - n\{A \cap B\}$. Consequently by transforming the events into probabilities the general addition law is as follows:

$$P(A \text{ or } B) = P(A) + P(B) - P(A \cap B) \tag{5.3}$$

Thus if two events are *mutually exclusive*, $P(A \cap B) = 0$.

Example 5.2

A card is chosen from an ordinary pack of cards. Write down the probabilities that the card is: (a) black and an ace, (b) black or an ace, and (c) neither black nor an ace.

Let event A and B represent the events obtaining an ace card and B a black card respectively. The sample space is represented by Figure 5.3.

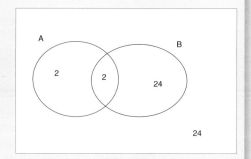

Figure 5.3

(a) $P(B \text{ and } A) = \dfrac{\text{Number of outcomes in } A \cap B}{\text{Total number of outcomes}} = \dfrac{2}{52} = 0.0385$

(b) $P(B \text{ or } A) = P(B) + P(A) - P(B \cap A) = \dfrac{26}{52} + \dfrac{4}{52} - \dfrac{2}{52} = \dfrac{28}{52} = 0.538462$

(c) $P(\text{neither } B \text{ nor } A) = 1 - P(B \text{ or } A) = 1 - 0.5385 = 0.4615$

Let's look at the general multiplication law. We mentioned above mutually exclusive events, i.e. events that cannot occur at the same time, but what about completely **independent events**? An example is rolling a die twice. The fact that we got 6 on the first roll, for example, cannot influence the outcome of the second roll. Similarly take the example of picking a ball from a bag, if it were replaced before another was picked nothing changes; the sample space remains the same. Drawing the first ball and replacing it cannot affect the outcome of the next selection. In these examples we have the notion of independent events. If two (or more) events are independent then the general multiplication law applies:

$$P(A \cap B) = P(A) * P(B) \tag{5.4}$$

Note   The terms independent and mutually exclusive are different and apply to different things. If A and B are events with non-zero probabilities, then we can show that $P(A \cap B)$:

- $P(A \cap B) = 0$, if mutually exclusive. Mutually exclusive events cannot occur at the same time.

- $P(A \cap B) \neq 0$, if independent. Independent events do not influence each other.

Independent events Two events are independent if the occurrence of one of the events has no influence on the occurrence of the other event.

Example 5.3

Suppose a fair die is tossed twice. Let A = Event first die shows an even number and B = Event second die shows a 5 or 6. Events A and B are intuitively unrelated and therefore are independent events. Thus the probability of A occurring is $P(A) = 3/6 = 0.5$ and the probability of event B occurring is $P(B) = 2/6 = 0.3$. Thus, $P(A \text{ and } B) = P(A) * P(B) = 0.5 * 0.3 = 0.16$.

5.1.4 Probability tree diagram

Probability tree diagrams provide a visual aid to help you solve complicated probability problems.

Example 5.4

A bag contains 3 red and 4 white balls. If one ball is taken at random and then replaced and then another ball is taken then, calculate the following probabilities:

(a) P(Red,Red)?

(b) P(just one Red)?

(c) P(2nd Ball White)?

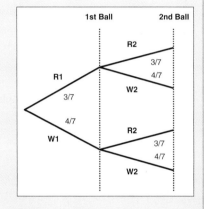

Figure 5.4 displays the experiment in a tree diagram. Each branch of the tree indicates the possible result of a draw and associated probabilities.

Figure 5.4

Multiplying along the branches provides the probability of a final outcome:

(a) $P(R,R) = P(R) * P(R) = 3/7 * 3/7 = 9/49$

(b) $P(\text{Just one Red}) = P(R,W \text{ or } W,R) = P(R) * P(W) + P(W) * P(R) = 3/7 * 4/7 + 4/7 * 3/7 = 24/49$

(c) $P(\text{2nd Ball White}) = P(R,W \text{ or } W,W) = P(R,W) + P(W,W) = 3/7 * 4/7 + 4/7 * 4/7 = 21/49$.

Student Exercises

X5.5 Susan takes examinations in Mathematics, French, and History. The probability that she passes Mathematics is 0.7 and the corresponding probabilities for French and History are 0.8 and 0.6. Given that her performances in each subject are independent, draw a tree diagram to show the possible outcomes. Use this tree diagram to calculate the following probabilities: (a) fails all three examinations, and (b) fails just one examination.

5.1.5 Introduction to probability distributions

We already stated that the concept of relative frequency is one way to interpret probability. Equation (5.1) shows us how to calculate these frequencies. In other words, the relative frequency (or proportion) represents an estimate of the probability of the stated occurrence occurring within the total number of attempts (or experiment sample space). In this respect equation (5.5) provides a *frequency definition of probability* which is known as the *experimental* (or *empirical*) approach.

$$P(X) = \frac{\text{Number of successful outcomes}}{\text{Total number of attempts}} \tag{5.5}$$

▷ Example 5.5

Consider the situation where a financial analyst collects data about the sales of a particular type of fridge freezer. From the data he is interested in the probability that this type of fridge freezer will be sold in a particular region which he will then use to produce sales estimates for the next 12 months. From the data he finds that this region sold 230 out of a national number sold of 1670. From equation (5.1) the relative frequency, or proportion, or probability of this type of fridge being sold is P(X) = 230/1670 = 0.137725 or 13.8%. This can then be used within the sales forecast plan as will be outlined when discussing expectation in Section 5.1.6.

▷ Example 5.6

To illustrate the idea of a probability consider the following frequency distribution representing the mileage travelled by 120 salesmen (Table 5.3). From this table we can calculate the concept of a relative frequency.

Mileage travelled (miles)	Frequency, f
400–420	12
420–440	27
440–460	34
460–480	24
480–500	15
500–520	8

Table 5.3

Note   From Table 5.3 we notice that the class limits are 400–420, 420–440,…, 500–520. We notice that a salesman could have a value of 420 miles and then the question becomes 'which class 400–420 or 420–440'? The answer to this question is to place all values less than 420 in 400–420 and all values equal to or greater than in class 420–440. This rule would then be applied to all data values.

	A	B	C	D	E
1	Probability distributions				
2					
3		Mileage travelled	Frequency, f	Relative frequency	
4		400-420	12	0.100000	=C4/$C$11
5		420-440	27	0.225000	
6		440-460	34	0.283333	
7		460-480	24	0.200000	
8		480-500	15	0.125000	
9		500-520	8	0.066667	=C9/$C$11
10					
11		Total =	120	1.000000	
12			=SUM(C4:C9)	=SUM(D4:D9)	

Figure 5.5

Figure 5.5 illustrates the calculation process.

We observe from Figure 5.5 that the relative frequency for 440–460 miles travelled is 0.283333. This implies that we have a chance or probability of 34/120 that the miles travelled lies within this class.

➡ Excel Solution

Mileage data Cells B4:B9	Values
Frequency, f Cells C4:C9	Values
Relative frequency Cell D4:D9	Formula: =C4/$C$11
	Copy formula from D4:D9
Total f Cell C11	Formula: =SUM(C4:C9)
Total relative frequency Cell D11	Formula: =SUM(D4:D9)

Note   Thus, relative frequencies provide estimates of the probability for that class, or value, to occur. If we were to plot the histogram of relative frequencies we would in fact be plotting out the probabilities for each event e.g. P(400–420 miles) = 0.10, P(420–440 miles) = 0.225.

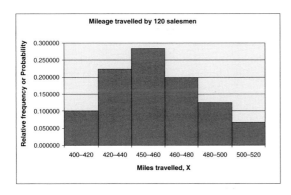

Figure 5.6

The distribution of probabilities given in Table 5.3 and graphically represented in Figure 5.6 are different ways of illustrating the probability distribution.

Whereas for the frequency distribution the area under the histogram is proportional to the total frequency, for the probability distribution the area is proportional to total probability (= 1.0).

Given a particular probability distribution we can determine the probability for any event associated with it. Thus, P(400–460 miles) = P(400 ≤ x ≤ 460) = Area under the distribution from 400 to 460 = P(400–420) + P(420–440) + P(440–460) = 0.10 + 0.225 + 0.283 = 0.608. Thus, we have a probability estimate of 61% for the mileage travelled to lie between 400 and 460 miles.

> **Note**   A point to notice about this type of probability distribution which has been derived from continuous data is that if we decreased the class limits and increased the sample size the associated polygon of the distribution would approximate to a curve—the probability distribution curve.

5.1.6 Expectation and variance for a probability distribution

The value of the mean and standard deviation can be calculated from the frequency distribution by using equations (4.3) and (4.16). By using relative frequencies to determine the mean we have in fact found the mean of the probability distribution. The mean of a probability distribution is called the expected value, E(X), and can be calculated from equation (5.6):

$$E(X) = \sum X \times P(X) \tag{5.6}$$

> **Note**   Some textbooks use the phrases for the expected value and the mean interchangeably.

Further thought along the lines used in developing the notion of expectation would reveal that the variance of the probability distribution, VAR(X), can be determined from equation (5.7):

$$VAR(X) = \sum X^2 \times P(X) - \left[\sum X \times P(X)\right]^2 \tag{5.7}$$

From equation (5.7) the standard deviation can be calculated using the relationship given in equation (5.8):

$$SD(X) = \sqrt{VAR(X)} \tag{5.8}$$

Example 5.7

Returning to the miles travelled by salesmen we can easily calculate the mean number of miles travelled and the corresponding measure of variation as illustrated in Figure 5.7.

	A	B	C	D	E	F	G	H	I	J	K	L
1	**Probability Distributions - Expectation and Variance**											
2												
3												
4	Mileage travelled	Frequency, f	LCB	UCB	Class mid point, X		Relative frequency, P(X = x) = f/N		x * P(X = x)		X^2*P(X = x)	
5												
6	400 - 420	12	400	420	410	=(C6+D6)/2	0.10	=B6/$D$17	41.000	=E6*G6	16810.00	=E6^2*G6
7	420 - 440	27	420	440	430		0.23		96.750		41602.50	
8	440 - 460	34	440	460	450		0.28		127.500		57375.00	
9	460 - 480	24	460	480	470		0.20		94.000		44180.00	
10	480 - 500	15	480	500	490		0.13		61.250		30012.50	
11	500 - 520	8	500	520	510	=(C11+D11)/2	0.07	=B11/$D$17	34.000	=E11*G11	17340.00	=E11^2*G11
12												
13	Summary Statistics											
14												
15		N = Σf =	120.00	=SUM(B6:B11)								
16		ΣXP =	454.50	=SUM(I6:I11)								
17		ΣX^2P =	207320.00	=SUM(K6:K11)								
18		Mean =	454.50	=C16								
19		Variance =	749.75	=C17-C18^2								
20		Standard Deviation =	27.38	=C19^0.5								

Figure 5.7

→ Excel Solution

Mileage travelled Cells A6:A11	Values
Frequency, f Cells B6:B11	Values
LCB Cells C6:C11	Values
UCB Cells D6:D11	Values
Class mid-point Cells E6:E11	Formula: =(C6+D6)/2
	Copy formula from E6:E11
Relative frequency Cells G6:G11	Formula: =B6/$D$17
	Copy formula from G6:G11
X*P(X) Cell I6:I11	Formula: =E6*G6
	Copy formula from I6:I11
X^2*P(X) Cell K6:K11	Formula: =E6^2*G6
	Copy formula from K6:K11
N = Σf = Cell C15	Formula: =SUM(B6:B11)
ΣXP= Cell C16	Formula: =SUM(I6:I11)
ΣX^2P = Cell C17	Formula: =SUM(K6:K11)
Mean = Cell C18	Formula: =C16
Variance = Cell C19	Formula: =C17–C18^2
Standard Deviation = Cell C20	Formula: =C19^0.5

Interpretation From Excel, the expected value is 454.5 miles travelled with a standard deviation of 27.38 miles travelled.

The manual solution to Example 5.7 is illustrated in Figure 5.7 where we have made use of Excel to undertake the calculations:

$$\text{Expected Value, } E(X) = \sum X \times P(X) = 454.5$$

$$\text{Variance } VAR(X) = \sum X^2 \times P(X) - \left[\sum X \times P(X)\right]^2 = 207320 - (454.5)^2 = 749.75$$

$$\text{Standard Deviation } SD(X) = \sqrt{VAR(X)} = 27.38$$

Note Re-arranging equation (4.3) to give the expected value (mean) represented by equation (5.6):

$$E(X) = \frac{\sum fX}{\sum f} = \sum X \times \frac{f}{\sum f} = \sum X \times P(X).$$

The frequency distribution variance equation can be re-arranged to give equation (5.7):

$$VAR(X) = \frac{\sum f(X - \bar{X})^2}{\sum f} = \sum\left[X - E(X)\right]^2 \times P(X) = \sum X^2 \times P(X) - \left[\sum X \times P(X)\right]^2$$

Example 5.8

Consider the problem of a stall at a fete running a game of chance. The game consists of a customer taking turns to choose three balls from a bag that contains 3 white and 17 red balls without replacement. For a customer to win the customer would have to choose 3 white, 2 white, or 1 white with winnings of €5, €2, and €0.50 respectively. On the day of the fete 2000 customers tried the game. How much money might be expected to have been paid out to each customer?

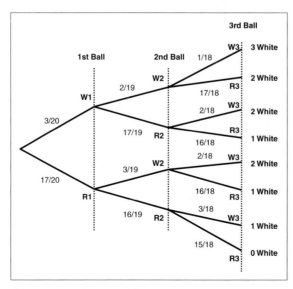

Figure 5.8

To solve this problem we first need to calculate the associated probabilities of choosing 3, 2, 1, and 0 white balls, and a tree diagram (see Figure 5.8) visually enables identification of these probabilities. The final stage consists of calculating the associated expected value given we know what the winnings are for 3, 2, 1, and 0 white balls.

From the tree diagram illustrated in Figure 5.8 we can identify the different routes that we can achieve 3, 2, 1, and 0 white balls. The probability of 3 whites is P(3 White) = P(1st White and 2nd White and 3rd White) = 3/20 * 2/19 * 1/18 = 0.0009.

By a similar process: P(only 2 White) = 0.0447, P(only 1 White) = 0.3579, and P(no white) = 0.5965. The probability distribution for the expected winnings can now be constructed and is illustrated in Figure 5.9.

	A	B	C	D	E	F
1	Example 5.8					
2						
3		Number of white balls	Amount won, X	Probability, P(X)	X*P(X)	
4		0	€ 5.00	0.0009	€ 0.00450	=C4*D4
5		1	€ 2.00	0.0447	€ 0.08940	
6		2	€ 0.50	0.3579	€ 0.17895	
7		3	€ 0.00	0.5965	€ 0.00000	=C7*D7
8						
9				E(X) =	€ 0.27285	=SUM(E4:E7)
10				Total =	€ 545.70	=2000*E9

Figure 5.9

➔ **Excel Solution**

Number of white balls Cells B4:B7   Values
Amount won, X Cells C4:C7   Values
Probability, P(C) Cells D4:D7   Values
X*P(X) Cells E4:E7   Formula: =C4*D4
    Copy formula from E4:E7
E(X) Cell E9   Formula: =SUM(E4:E7)
Total Cell E10   Formula: =2000*E9

✳ **Interpretation** From Excel, we observe that the expected winnings for each game played is E(X) = X * P(X) = 0.27285 (or €0.27 to the nearest cent). Given that we have 2000 players (or games played) then the total winnings is €545.70 (= N * E(X) = 2000 * 0.27285) to the nearest cent.

🔍 **Example 5.9**

A company manufactures and sells product Xbar. The sales price of the product will be €6 per unit, and estimates of sales demand and variable costs of sales are as follows:

Probability	Sales Demand
0.3	5000
0.6	6000
0.1	8000

Table 5.4

Probability	Variable Cost per unit (€)
0.1	3.0
0.3	3.5
0.5	4.0
0.1	4.5

Table 5.5

The unit variable costs are not conditional on the volume of sales demand and fixed costs are estimated to be €10000. What is the expected profit? The expected profit can be calculated if we realize that profit is determined from the following equation: Profit = Sales − Variable Costs − Fixed Costs.

Probability, P	Sales Demand, X	XP
0.3	5000	1500
0.6	6000	3600
0.1	8000	800
	Total =	5900

Table 5.6

The expected sales demand is calculated using equation (5.6) with the probability distribution employed to calculate the column statistics (see Table 5.6). The expected demand is $E(X) = \sum X \times P(X) = 5900$ units.

Probability, P	Variable Cost per unit (€), X	XP
0.1	3	0.30
0.3	3.5	1.05
0.5	4	2.00
0.1	4.5	0.45
	Total =	3.80

Table 5.7

The expected value of the variable cost per unit is calculated using equation (5.7) with the probability distribution employed to calculate the column statistics (see Table 5.7). The expected value per unit is $E(X) = \sum X \times P(X) = €3.80$.

From these calculations we can now calculate the overall value of sales, variable costs, and expected profit as follows: sales = 5900 * €6 = €35400, variable costs = 5900 * €3.80 = €22420, fixed costs = €10000, and expected profit E(profit) = sales − variable costs − fixed costs = €35400 − €22420 − €10000 = €2980. The expected profit is expected to be €2980.

Student Exercises

X5.6 A bag contains 6 white and 4 red counters, 3 of which are drawn at random and without replacement. If X can take on the values of 0, 1, 2, 3 red counters, construct the probability distribution of X. If the experiment was repeated 60 times, how many times would we expect to draw more than one red counter?

X5.7 You are considering putting money into one of two investments A and B. The net profits for identical periods and probabilities of success for investments A and B are given in the following table.

	Probability of Return	
Net profits	A	B
8000	0.0	0.1
9000	0.3	0.2
10000	0.4	0.4
11000	0.3	0.2
12000	0.0	0.1

(a) Which investment yields a higher net profit?

(b) Can you make a decision on which investment is better, given this extra information?

5.2 Continuous Probability Distributions

5.2.1 Introduction

A *random variable* is a variable that provides a measure of the possible values obtainable from an experiment. For example, we may wish to count the number of times that the number 3 appears on the tossing of a fair die or we may wish to measure the weight of people involved in measuring the success of a new diet programme. In the first example, the random variable will consist of the numbers: 1, 2, 3, 4, 5, or 6. If the die was fair then on each toss of the die each possible number (or outcome) will have an equal chance of occurring. The numbers 1, 2, 3, 4, 5, or 6 represent the random variable for this experiment. In the second example, the possible number values will represent the weights of the people participating in the experiment. The random variable in this case would be the values of all possible weights. It is important to note that in the first example the values take whole number answers (1, 2, 3, 4, 5, 6) and this is an example of a discrete random variable. The second example consists of numbers that can take any value with respect to measured accuracy (160.4 lbs, 160.41 lbs, 160.414 lbs, etc) and is an example of a continuous random variable. In this section we shall explore the concept of a continuous probability distribution with the focus on introducing the reader to the concept of a normal probability distribution.

5.2.2 The normal distribution

When a variable is continuous, and its value is affected by a large number of chance factors, none of which predominates, then it will frequently appear as a normal distribution. This distribution does occur frequently and is probably the most widely used statistical distribution. Some of the real-life variables having a normal distribution can be found, for example, in manufacturing (weights of tin cans), or can be associated with the human population (people's heights). The normal distribution is governed by equation (5.9):

$$f(X) = \frac{1}{\sigma\sqrt{2\pi}} \exp^{\left(-\frac{(X-\mu)^2}{2\sigma^2}\right)}$$

(5.9)

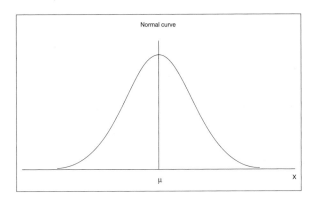

Normal curve

μ   X

Figure 5.10

This equation can be represented by Figure 5.10 and illustrates the symmetrical characteristics of the normal distribution.

For the normal distribution the mean, median, and mode all have the same numerical value.

> **Note**
> 1. The mean and standard deviation are represented by the notation μ and σ respectively.
> 2. If a variable X varies as a normal distribution then we would state that $X \sim N(\mu, \sigma^2)$.
> 3. The total area under the curve represents the total probability of all events occurring which equals 1.0.

To calculate the probability of a particular value of X occurring we would calculate the appropriate area represented in Figure 5.10 and use Excel (or tables) to find the corresponding value of the probability.

Example 5.10

A manufacturing firm quality assures components manufactured and historically the length of a tube is found to be normally distributed with the population mean of 100 cms and a standard deviation of 5 cms. Calculate the probability that a random sample of one tube will have a length of at least 110 cms. From the information provided we define X as the tube length in cms and population mean $\mu = 100$ and standard deviation = 5. This can be represented using the notation $X \sim N(100, 5^2)$. The problem we have to solve is to calculate the probability that 1 tube will have a length of at least 110 cms.

This can be written as $P(X \geq 110)$ and is represented by the shaded area illustrated in Figure 5.11.

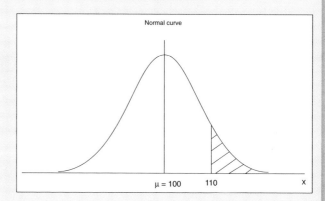

Figure 5.11

This problem can be solved by using the Excel function NORMDIST(X, μ, σ^2, TRUE).

This function calculates the area illustrated in Figure 5.12.

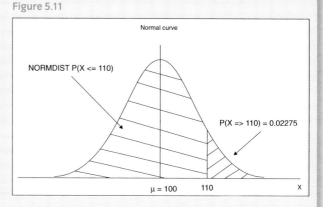

Figure 5.12

Excel solution—Example 5.10

The Excel solution is illustrated in Figure 5.13.

	A	B	C	D
1	Example 5.10 and 5.12			
2				
3		Normal distribution		
4				
5		Mean μ =	100	
6		Standard deviation σ =	5	
7				
8		X =	110	
9				
10		P(X <= 110) =	0.97725	=NORMDIST(C8,C5,C6,TRUE)
11				
12		P(X => 110) =	0.02275	=1-C10

Figure 5.13

➜ **Excel Solution**

Mean = Cell C5   Value

Standard deviation Cell C6   Value

X = Cell C8   Value

P(X <= 110) = Cell C10   Formula: =NORMDIST(C8,C5,C6,TRUE)

P(X => 110) = Cell C12   Formula: =1−C10

From Excel, the NORMDIST() function can be used to calculate P(X ≥ 110) = 0.02275.

✳ **Interpretation**   We observe that the probability that an individual tube length is at least 110 cms is 0.02275 or 2.3%.

⬡ Example 5.11

Calculate the probability that X lies between 85 and 105 cms for the problem outlined in Example 5.10.

In this example we are required to calculate P(85 ≤ X ≤ 105) which represents the area shaded in Figure 5.14.

The value of P(85 ≤ X ≤ 105) can be calculated using Excel's NORMDIST() function.

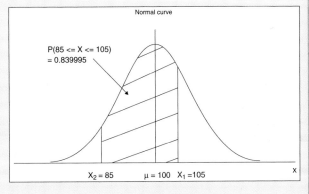

Figure 5.14

Excel solution—Example 5.11

The Excel solution is illustrated in Figure 5.15.

	A	B	C	D
1	Example 5.11 and 5.13			
2				
3		Normal distribution		
4				
5		Mean μ =	100	
6		Standard deviation σ =	5	
7				
8		X_1 =	85	
9		X_2 =	105	
10				
11		P(85 <= X <= 105) = P(X <= 105) - P(X <=85)		
12				
13		P(X <= 85) =	0.00135	=NORMDIST(C8,C5,C6,TRUE)
14		P(X <= 110) =	0.841345	=NORMDIST(C9,C5,C6,TRUE)
15				
16		P(85 <= X <= 105) =	0.839995	=C14-C13

Figure 5.15

→ **Excel Solution**

Mean = Cell C5   Value
Standard deviation = Cell C6   Value
X1 = Cell C8   Value
X2 = Cell C9   Value
P(85 <= X <= 105) = P(X <= 105) − P(X <=85)
P(X <= 85) = Cell C13   Formula: =NORMDIST(C8,C5,C6,TRUE)
P(X <= 110) = Cell C14   Formula: =NORMDIST(C9,C5,C6,TRUE)
P(85 <= X <= 105) = Cell C16   Formula: =C14−C13

From Excel, the NORMDIST() function can be used to calculate $P(85 \leq X \leq 105) = 0.839995$.

✳ **Interpretation**   We observe that the probability that an individual tube length lies between 85 and 105 cms is 0.839995 or 84.0%.

Student Exercises

X5.8 Use NORMDIST to calculate the following probabilities, $X \sim N(100, 25)$: (a) $P(X \leq 95)$, (b) $P(95 \leq X \leq 105)$, (c) $P(105 \leq X \leq 115)$, (d) $P(93 \leq X \leq 99)$. For each probability identify the region to be found by shading the area on the normal probability distribution.

5.2.3 The standard normal distribution (Z distribution)

If we have two different normal populations then it could be difficult to compare them as the units might be different, the means and variances might be different, etc. If this is the case, we would like to be able to standardize these distributions so that we can compare them. This is possible by creating the standard normal distribution. The standard normal distribution is a normal distribution whose mean is always 0 and the standard deviation is always 1. Normal distributions can be transformed to standard normal distributions by equation (5.10):

$$Z = \frac{(X - \mu)}{\sigma}$$

(5.10)

Where X, μ, and σ are the variable score value, population mean, and population standard deviation respectively taken from the original normal distribution. Any distribution can be converted to a standardized distribution using equation (5.10) and the shape of the standardized version will be the same as the original distribution. If the original was symmetric then the Z transformed version would still be symmetric, and if the original was skewed then the Z transformed version would still be skewed.

The advantage of this method is that the Z values are not dependent on the original data units and this allows tables of Z values to be produced with corresponding areas under the curve. This also allows for probabilities to be calculated if the Z value is known, and vice versa, which allows a range of problems to be solved.

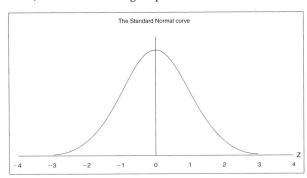

Figure 5.16 illustrate the standard normal distribution (or Z distribution) with Z scores between −4 to +4.

Figure 5.16

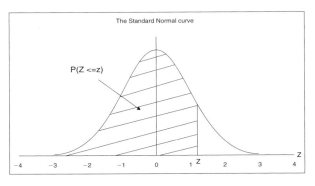

The Excel function NORMSDIST() calculates the probability P (Z ≤ z) as illustrated in Figure 5.17.

Figure 5.17

> **Note** From calculation we can show that the proportion of values between ±1, ±2, and ±3 population standard deviations from the population mean of zero is 68%, 95%, and 99.7% respectively.

▷ Example 5.12

Using the data from Example 5.10, if a variable X varies as a normal distribution with a mean of 100 and a standard deviation of 5, then the value of Z when X = 110 would be equal to $Z = (110 - 100)/5 = +2$. The value of $P(Z \geq 2)$ can be calculated using Excel's NORMSDIST () function. Note the difference between NORMDIST and NORMSDIST.

Excel solution—Example 5.12

The Excel solution is illustrated in Figure 5.18.

	A	B	C	D
1	Example 5.10 and 5.12			
2				
3		Normal distribution		
4				
5		Mean μ =	100	
6		Standard deviation σ =	5	
7				
8		X =	110	
9				
10		P(X <= 110) =	0.97725	=NORMDIST(C8,C5,C6,TRUE)
11				
12		P(X => 110) =	0.02275	=1-C10
13				
14		Z =	2	=(C8-C5)/C6
15		P(Z <= +2) =	0.97725	=NORMSDIST(C14)
16		P(Z => +2) =	0.02275	=1-C15

Figure 5.18

➡ Excel Solution

Mean = Cell C5	Value
Standard deviation Cell C6	Value
X = Cell C8	Value
P(X <= 110) = Cell C10	Formula: =NORMDIST(C8,C5,C6,TRUE)
P(X => 110) = Cell C12	Formula: =1–C10
Z = Cell C14	Formula: =(C8–C5)/C6
P(Z <= +2) = Cell C15	Formula: =NORMSDIST(C14)
P(Z => +2) = Cell C16	Formula: =1–C15

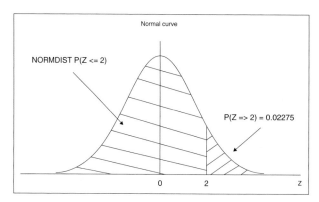

Figure 5.19

This solution can be represented graphically by Figure 5.19.

From Excel, the NORMSDIST() function can be used to calculate $P(Z \geq +2) = 0.02275$.

> **✳ Interpretation**   We observe that the probability that an individual tube length is at least 110 cms is 0.02275 or 2.3% (P(X ≥ 110) = 0.02275).

Note

1. This method is used to solve problems using tables of Z values and associated probabilities.
2. The value of the Z score can be calculated using the Excel function STANDARDIZE().
3. The Excel function NORMDIST() calculates the value of the normal distribution for the specified mean and standard deviation.
4. The Excel function NORMSDIST() calculates the value of the normal distribution for the specified Z score value.

▷ Example 5.13

If we re-consider Example 5.11 and transform the value of X to Z then we find the solution is as follows:

Excel solution—Example 5.13

The Excel solution is illustrated in Figure 5.20.

	A	B	C	D
1	Example 5.11 and 5.13			
2				
3		Normal distribution		
4				
5		Mean μ =	100	
6		Standard deviation σ =	5	
7				
8		X_1 =	85	
9		X_2 =	105	
10				
11		P(85 <= X <= 105) = P(X <= 105) - P(X <=85)		
12				
13		P(X <= 85) =	0.00135	=NORMDIST(C8,C5,C6,TRUE)
14		P(X <= 110) =	0.841345	=NORMDIST(C9,C5,C6,TRUE)
15				
16		P(85 <= X <= 105) =	0.839995	=C14-C13
17				
18		Z_1 =	-3	=(C8-C5)/C6
19		Z_2 =	1	=(C9-C5)/C6
20				
21		P(85 <= X <= 105) = P(Z <= 1) - P(Z <= -3)		
22				
23		P(Z <= -3) =	0.00135	=NORMSDIST(C18)
24		P(Z <= 1) =	0.841345	=NORMSDIST(C19)
25				
26		P(85 <= X <= 105) =	0.839995	=C24-C23

Figure 5.20

Note we can use the Excel function STANDARDIZE to calculate the values of Z (see chapter 6).

➔ Excel Solution

Mean = Cell C5	Value
Standard deviation = Cell C6	Value
X_1 = Cell C8	Value
X_2 = Cell C9	Value
P(85 <= X <= 105) = P(X <= 105) − P(X <= 85)	
~~P(X <= 85)~~ = Cell C13	Formula: =NORMDIST(C8,C5,C6,TRUE)
P(X <= 110) = Cell C14	Formula: =NORMDIST(C9,C5,C6,TRUE)
P(85 <= X <= 105) = Cell C16	Formula: =C14−C13
Z1 = Cell C18	Formula: =(C8−C5)/C6
Z2 = Cell C19	Formula: =(C9−C5)/C6
P(85 <= X <= 105) = P(Z <= 1) − P(Z <= -3)	
P(Z <= −3) = Cell C23	Formula: =NORMSDIST(C18)
P(Z <= 1) = Cell C24	Formula: =NORMSDIST(C19)
P(85 <= X <= 105) = Cell C26	Formula: =C24−C23

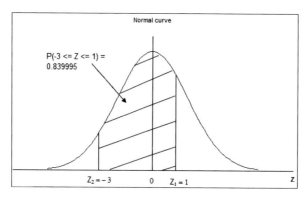

Figure 5.21 illustrates the Excel solution.

From Excel, the NORMSDIST() function can be used to calculate $P(85 \le X \le 105) = P(-3 \le Z \le +1) = 0.839995$.

Figure 5.21

* **Interpretation** We observe that the probability that an individual tube length lies between 85 and 105 cms is 0.839995 or 84.0%.

🖰 Student Exercises

X5.9 Use NORMSDIST to calculate the following probabilities, $X \sim N(100, 25)$: (a) $P(X \le 95)$, (b) $P(95 \le X \le 105)$, (c) $P(105 \le X \le 115)$, (d) $P(93 \le X \le 99)$. In each case convert X to Z. Compare with your answers from Exercise 5.8.

⌕ Example 5.14

A local authority installs 2000 electric lamps. The life of lamps in hours (X) follows a normal distribution, where X~N (1000, 40000). Calculate: (a) what number of lamps might be expected to fail within the first 700 hours, (b) what number of lamps may be expected to fail between 900 and 1300 hours, and (c) after how many hours would we expect 10% of the lamps to fail? From this information we have population mean, μ, of 1000 hours with a variance, σ^2, of 40000 hours². This problem can be solved using either the NORMDIST() or NORMSDIST() Excel functions as follows:

Excel Solution—Example 5.14

(a) The first part of this problem can be split into two parts: (i) calculate the probability that one lamp would fail in the first 700 hours, and (ii) calculate the number of lamps from the 2000 that we would expect to fail in the first 700 hours.

The Excel solution is illustrated in Figure 5.22.

	A	B	C	D
1	Example 5.14			
2				
3		Normal distribution		
4				
5		Mean μ =	1000	
6		Variance σ² =	40000	
7		Standard deviation σ =	200	=SQRT(C6)
8				
9		X =	700	
10				
11		P(X <= 700) =	0.066807	=NORMDIST(C9,C5,C7,TRUE)
12				
13		Z =	-1.5	=(C9-C5)/C7
14		P(Z <= -1.5) =	0.066807	=NORMSDIST(C13)
15				
16		E(X) = N*P(X <= 700) =	133.6144	=2000*C11

Figure 5.22

This solution can be represented graphically by Figure 5.23.

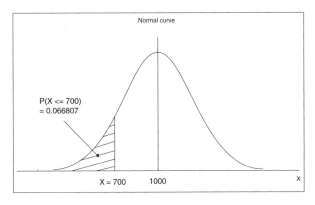

Figure 5.23

→ **Excel Solution**

Mean = Cell C5	Value
Variance = Cell C6	Value
Standard deviation Cell C7	Formula: =SQRT(C6)
X = Cell C9	Value
P(X <= 700) = Cell C11	Formula: =NORMDIST(C9,C5,C7,TRUE)
Z = Cell C13	Formula: =(C9–C5)/C7
P(Z <= –1.5) = Cell C14	Formula: =NORMSDIST(C13)
E(X) = N*P(X <= 700) = Cell C16	Formula: =2000*C11

From Excel, the NORMDIST() or NORMSDIST() function can be used to calculate $P(X \leq 700) = 0.0688$. The number of lamps that are expected to fail out of the 2000 lamps, E(fail) = $2000 * P(X \leq 700) = 133$ lamps.

※ **Interpretation**   This problem consists of solving $P(X \leq 700)$. Using the NORMDIST() function we find that out of the 2000 lamps, 133 lamps are expected to fail within the first 700 hours.

(b)   The second part of the problem requires the calculation of the Probability that X lies between 900 and 1300 hours, and the estimation of the number of lamps from 2000 which will fail between these limits.

The Excel solution is illustrated in Figure 5.24.

	A	B	C	D
1	Example 5.14b			
2				
3		Normal distribution		
4				
5		Mean μ =	1000	
6		Variance σ² =	40000	
7		Standard deviation σ =	200	=SQRT(C6)
8				
9		X_1 =	900	
10		X_2 =	1300	
11				
12		P(X <= 900) =	0.308538	=NORMDIST(C9,C5,C7,TRUE)
13		P(X <= 1300) =	0.933193	=NORMDIST(C10,C5,C7,TRUE)
14		P(900 <= X <= 1300) =	0.624655	=C13-C12
15		E(X) = N*P(900<=X<=1300) =	1249.311	=2000*C14
16				
17				
18		Z_1 =	-0.5	=(C9-C5)/C7
19		Z_2 =	1.5	=(C10-C5)/C7
20				
21		P(Z <= - 0.5) =	0.308538	=NORMSDIST(C18)
22		P(Z <= 1.5) =	0.933193	=NORMSDIST(C19)
23		P(- 0.5 <= Z <= 1.5) =	0.624655	=C22-C21
24		E(X) = N*P(900<=X<=1300) =	1249.311	=2000*C23

Figure 5.24

This solution can be represented graphically by Figure 5.25.

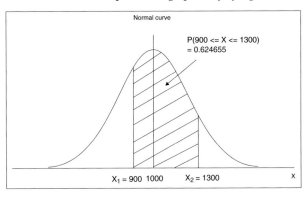

Figure 5.25

→ **Excel Solution**

Mean μ = Cell C5	Value
Variance σ^2 = Cell C6	Value
Standard deviation σ = Cell C7	Formula: =SQRT(C6)
X_1 = Cell C9	Value
X_2 = Cell C10	Value
P(X <= 900) = Cell C12	Formula: =NORMDIST(C9,C5,C7,TRUE)
P(X <= 1300) = Cell C13	Formula: =NORMDIST(C10,C5,C7,TRUE)
P(900 <= X <= 1300) = Cell C14	Formula: =C13–C12
E(X) = N*P(900 <= X <= 1300) = Cell C15	Formula: =2000*C14
Z_1 = Cell C18	Formula: =(C9–C5)/C7
Z_2 = Cell C19	Formula: =(C10–C5)/C7
P(Z <= – 0.5) = Cell C21	Formula: =NORMSDIST(C18)
P(Z <= 1.5) = Cell C22	Formula: =NORMSDIST(C19)
P(–0.5 <= Z <= 1.5) = Cell C23	Formula: =C22–C21
E(X) = N*P(900 <= X <= 1300) = Cell C24	Formula: =2000*C23

From Excel, the NORMDIST() OR NORMSDIST() function can be used to calculate $P(900 \leq X \leq 1300) = 0.624655$. The number of lamps that are expected to fail between 900 and 1300 hours out of the 2000 lamps, E(fail) = 2000 * $P(900 \leq X \leq 1300)$ = 1249 lamps.

✸ **Interpretation** This problem consists of solving $P(900 \leq X \leq 1300)$. Using the NORMDIST() function we find that out of the 2000 lamps, 1249 lamps are expected to fail between 900 and 1300 hours.

(c) The final part of this problem consists of calculating the number of hours for the first 10% to fail. This corresponds to calculating the value of x where $P(X \leq x) = 0.1$.

This problem can be solved using the NORMINV() or NORMSINV() function for standardized distributions, as illustrated in Figure 5.26.

	A	B	C	D
1	Example 5.14c			
2				
3		Normal distribution		
4				
5		Mean μ =	1000	
6		Variance σ² =	40000	
7		Standard deviation σ =	200	=SQRT(C6)
8				
9		P(X = x) =	0.1	
10				
11		X =	743.6897	=NORMINV(C9,C5,C7)
12				
13		Z =	-1.28155	=NORMSINV(C9)
14		X = μ + Z*σ =	743.6897	=C5+C13*C7

Figure 5.26

This solution can be represented graphically by Figure 5.27.

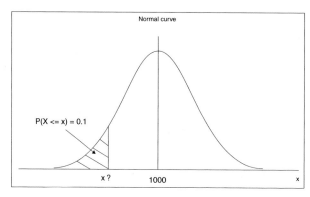

Figure 5.27

> ➜ **Excel Solution**
>
> Mean μ = Cell C5   Value
> Variance σ² = Cell C6   Value
> Standard deviation σ = Cell C7   Formula: =SQRT(C6)
> P(X = x) = Cell C9   Value
> X = Cell C11   Formula: =NORMINV(C9,C5,C7)
> Z = Cell C13   Formula: =NORMSINV(C9)
> X = μ + Z*σ = Cell C14   Formula: =C5+C13*C7

From Excel, the NORMINV() or NORMSINV() function can be used to calculate the expected number of hours for 10% to fail. From Excel, the number of hours obtained for 10% to fail, x = 744 hours.

> ✱ **Interpretation**   The expected number of hours for 10% of the lamps to fail is 744 hours.

Note

1. This problem corresponds to finding the value of x such that $P(X \leq x) = 10\%$ (or 0.1). From Excel, we find that $P(X \leq x) = 0.1$ corresponds to $Z = -1.28$. To find x we would then solve the equation: $-1.28 = (X - 1000)/200$. Re-arranging this equation gives $X = 1000 + (-1.28) * (200) = 744$.

2. The Excel function NORMINV() calculates the value of X from a normal distribution for the specified probability, mean, and standard deviation.

3. The Excel function NORMSINV() calculates the value Z from normal distribution for the specified probability value.

Student Exercises

X5.10 Given that a normal variable has a mean of 10 and a variance of 25, calculate the probability that a member chosen at random is: (a) ≥ 11, (b) ≤ 11, (c) ≤ 5, (d) ≥ 5, (e) between 5 and 11.

X5.11 The lifetimes of certain types of car battery are normally distributed with a mean of 1248 days and standard deviation of 185 days. If the supplier guarantees them for 1080 days, what proportion of batteries will be replaced under guarantee?

X5.12 Electrical resistors have a design resistance of 500 ohms. The resistors are produced by a machine with an output that is normally distributed N(501,9). Resistances below 498 ohms and above 508 ohms are rejected. Find: (a) the proportion that will be rejected, (b) the proportion which would be rejected if the mean was adjusted so as to minimize the proportion of rejects, (c) how much the standard deviation would need to be reduced (leaving the mean at 501 ohms) so that the proportion of rejects below 498 ohms would be halved.

5.2.4 Checking for normality

Normality is a very important concept in business statistics and we shall see that the tests described in Chapters 7–10 require the population distribution to be either normally or approximately normally distributed. The issue of checking whether the population is normally distributed is an important concept and can be achieved by either constructing a *five-number summary* (or *box-and-whisker plot*) described in Section 4.3 and/or by constructing a **normal probability plot** described below. Section 4.3 describes the concept of

X

Normal probability plot Graphical technique to assess whether the data is normally distributed.

a five number summary and corresponding box-and-whisker plot to evaluate whether the distribution is symmetric.

A *normal probability plot* consists of constructing a graph of data values against a corresponding Z value where Z is based upon the ordered value.

▷ Example 5.15

The manager at BIG JIMS restaurant is concerned at the time it takes to process credit card payments at the counter by counter staff.

The manager has collected the following processing time data (time in minutes) and requested that the data be checked to see if it is normally distributed (see Table 5.8).

Processing credit cards (n = 19)				
0.64	0.71	0.85	0.89	0.92
0.96	1.07	0.76	1.09	1.13
1.23	0.76	1.18	0.79	1.26
1.29	1.34	1.38	1.5	

Table 5.8

Excel solution—Example 5.15

Figure 5.28 illustrates the Excel solution to Example 5.15.

	A	B	C	D	E	F	G	H	I	J
1	Example 5.15 - Normal Probability Plot									
2										
3			n =	19	Ordered Value	Area		Z value		Ordered data value
4					1	0.05	=1/(C3+1)	-1.6449	=NORMSINV(F4)	0.64
5					2	0.10	=F4+$F$4	-1.2816		0.71
6					3	0.15		-1.0364		0.76
7					4	0.20		-0.8416		0.76
8					5	0.25		-0.6745		0.79
9					6	0.30		-0.5244		0.85
10					7	0.35		-0.3853		0.89
11					8	0.40		-0.2533		0.92
12					9	0.45		-0.1257		0.96
13					10	0.50		0.0000		1.07
14					11	0.55		0.1257		1.09
15					12	0.60		0.2533		1.13
16					13	0.65		0.3853		1.18
17					14	0.70		0.5244		1.23
18					15	0.75		0.6745		1.26
19					16	0.80		0.8416		1.29
20					17	0.85		1.0364		1.34
21					18	0.90		1.2816		1.38
22					19	0.95	=F21+$F$4	1.6449	=NORMSINV(F22)	1.5

Figure 5.28

→ **Excel Solution**

n = Cell C3	Value
Ordered value Cells E4:E22	Values
Area Cell F4	Formula: =1/(C3+1)
Cell F5	Formula: =F4+$F$4
	Copy formula from F5:F22
Z value Cell H4	Formula: =NORMSINV(F4)
	Copy formula from H5:H22
Ordered data value Cell J4:J22	Values

The method to create the normal probability plot is as follows:

- Order the data values (1, 2, 3, . . . , n) with 1 referring to the smallest data value and n representing the largest data value.

- For the first data value (smallest) calculate the cumulative area using the formula: = 1/(n+1).

- Calculate the value of Z for this cumulative area using the Excel Function: =NORMSINV(Z value).

- Repeat for the other values where the cumulative area is given by the formula: =old area+1/(n+1).

- Input data values with smallest to largest value.

- Plot data value y against Z value for each data point.

Figure 5.29 illustrates the normal probability curve plot for Example 5.15. We observe from the graph that the relationship between the data values and Z is approximately a straight line.

For data that is normally distributed we would expect the relationship to be linear. In this situation we would accept the statement that the data values are approximately normally distributed.

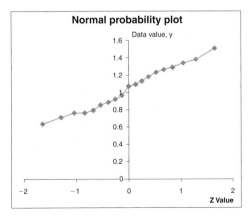

Figure 5.29

✻ **Interpretation** Due to the fact that the normal probability plot shows more or less a straight line, we conclude that the data is approximately normally distributed.

Note From Chapter 4 the decision on the symmetry of a distribution is as follows together with the shape of the normal probability curve:

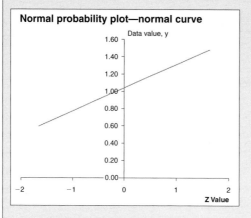

Figure 5.30

(a) Figure 5.30 illustrates a normal distribution where largest value − Q_3 equals Q_1 − smallest value.

In Example 5.15 we have: largest value − Q_3 = 0.18 approximately equal to Q_1 − smallest value = 0.26.

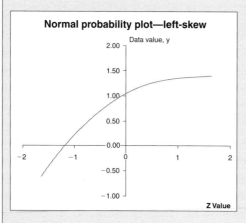

Figure 5.31

(b) Figure 5.31 illustrates a left-skewed distribution where Q_1 − smallest value greatly exceeds largest value − Q_3.

(c) Figure 5.32 illustrates a right-skewed distribution where largest value − Q_3 greatly exceeds Q_1 − smallest value.

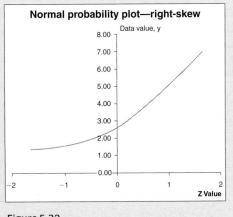

Figure 5.32

5.2.5 Other continuous probability distributions

A number of other continuous probability distributions will be discussed in Chapter 6, including: **Student's t distribution**, **chi square distribution**, and F distribution.

1. **Student's t distribution**

   The *Student's t distribution* is a distribution that is used to estimate a mean value when the population variable is normally distributed but the sample chosen to measure the population value is small and the population standard deviation is unknown. It is the basis of the popular Student's t tests for the statistical significance of the difference between two sample means, and for confidence intervals for the difference between two population means.

2. **Chi square distribution**

   The *chi square distribution* (χ^2 distribution) is a popular distribution that is used to solve statistical inference problems involving contingency tables and assessing the significance of a model to sample data (goodness-of-fit).

3. **F distribution**

   The *F distribution* is a distribution that can be used to test whether the ratios of two variances from normally distributed statistics are statistically different. The test statistic is defined as $F = s_1^2 / s_2^2$, where s_1^2 and s_2^2 are the sample 1 and sample 2 variances respectively. The shape of the distribution depends upon the numerator and denominator degrees of freedom ($df_1 = n_1 - 1$, $df_2 = n_2 - 1$) and the F distribution is written as a function of n_1, n_2 as $F(n_1, n_2)$.

X

Student's t distribution
The t distribution is the sampling distribution of the t statistic.

Chi square distribution
The chi square distribution is a mathematical distribution that is used directly or indirectly in many tests of significance.

> **Note**   The normal, t, and chi square distributions are special cases of the F distribution, as follows:
>
> - Normal distribution = $F(n_1 = 1, n_2 = \text{infinite})$ distribution
> - T distribution = $F(n_1 = 1, n_2)$ distribution
> - Chi square distribution = $F(n_1, n_2 = \text{infinite})$ distribution

Two other continuous probability distributions which are beyond the scope of this text book include the *uniform* and *exponential distribution*. The uniform distribution is used in the generation of random numbers for different probability distributions and the exponential probability distribution is important in the area of queuing theory.

5.3 Discrete Probability Distributions

5.3.1 Introduction

In this section we shall explore probability distributions when dealing with discrete random variables. Two specific distributions we included are: binomial and Poisson probability distributions. We will also explore how to approximate one distribution with another, if appropriate.

5.3.2 Binomial probability distribution

One of the most elementary discrete random variables—*binomial*—is associated with questions that only allow 'Yes' or 'No' type answers, or a classification such as male or female, or recording a component as defective or not defective. If the outcomes are also independent, e.g. the possibility of a defective component does not influence the possibility of finding another defective component then the variable is considered to be a binomial variable. Consider the example of a supermarket that runs a two week television campaign in an attempt to increase the volume of trade at a supermarket. During the campaign all customers are asked if they came to the supermarket because of the television advertising. Each customer response can be classified as either yes or no. At the end of the campaign the proportion of customers that responded yes is determined. For this study the *experiment* is the process of asking customers if they came to the supermarket because of the television advertising. The *random variable*, X, is defined as the number of customers that responded yes. Clearly the random variable can assume only the values 0, 1, 2, 3, . . . , n, where n is the total number of customers. Consequently the random variable is *discrete*. Consider the characteristics that define this experiment:

- The experiment consists of n identical trials.

- Each trial results in one of two outcomes which for convenience we can define as either a *success* or a *failure*.

- The outcomes from trial to trial are *independent.*
- The probability of *success (p)* is the same for each trial.
- The probability of *failure (q)*, where q = 1 − p.
- The *random variable* equals the number of successes in the n trials and can take the value from 0 to n.

These five characteristics define the *binomial experiment* and are applicable for situations of sampling from *finite* populations with replacement or for *infinite* populations with or without replacement.

⬡ Example 5.16

A marksman shoots 3 rounds at a target. His probability of getting a 'bull' is 0.3. Develop the probability distribution for getting: 0, 1, 2, 3, 'bulls'. This experiment can be modelled by a binomial distribution since:

- 3 identical trials (n = 3).
- Each trial can result in either a bull (success) or not a 'bull' (failure).
- The outcome of each trial is independent.
- The probability of a success (P(a bull) = p = 0.3) is the same for each trial.
- The random variable is discrete.

Figure 5.33 illustrates the tree diagram that represents the described experiment.

Let B represent the event that the marksmen hits the bull and B' represents the event that the marksmen misses the bull.

The corresponding individual event probabilities are: P(B) = 0.3 and P(B') = 1 − P(B) = 1 − 0.3 = 0.7.

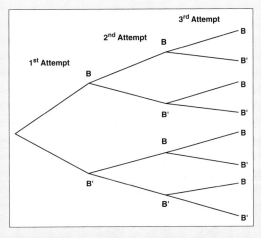

Figure 5.33

From this tree diagram we can identify the possible routes for 0, 1, 2, 3 bull hits, as follows: P(no bull hit) = P(X = 0 success) = P(B'B'B') = 0.7 * 0.7 * 0.7 = (0.7)³ = 0.343. The important lesson is to note the method of how we can use the tree diagram to undertake a calculation of an individual probability but also note the pattern identified in the relationship between the probability, P, and the individual event probability of success, p, or failure, q. We observe that the P (no bull hit) $= (0.7)^3 = q^3$. If we continue the calculation procedure we find:

P(1 bull hit) = P(X = 1 success) = P(BB′B′ or B′BB′ or B′B′B) = 0.3 * 0.7 * 0.7 + 0.7 * 0.3 * 0.7 + 0.7 * 0.7 * 0.3 = 0.3 * (0.7)² + 0.3 * (0.7)² + 0.3 * (0.7)² = 3 * 0.3 * (0.7)² = 0.441

Therefore, P(1 bull hit) $= 3pq^2$

P(2 bull hits) = P(X = 2 successes) = P(BBB′ or BB′B or B′BB) = 0.3 * 0.3 * 0.7 + 0.3 * 0.7 * 0.3 + 0.7 * 0.3 * 0.3 = (0.3)² * 0.7 + (0.3)² * 0.7 + (0.3)² * 0.7 = 3 * (0.3)² * 0.7 = 0.189

Therefore, P(2 bull hits) $= 3p^2q$

P(3 bull hits) = P(X = 3 successes) = P(BBB) = 0.3 * 0.3 * 0.3 = (0.3)³ = 0.027

Therefore, P(3 bull hits) $= p^3$

From these calculations we can now note the probability distribution for this experiment (see Table 5.9).

X	P(X)
0	0.343
1	0.441
2	0.189
3	0.027
Total =	1.000

Table 5.9

This probability distribution is illustrated in Figure 5.34.

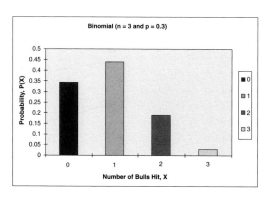

Figure 5.34

Note   From the probability distribution we observe that the total probability equals one. This is expected since the total probability would represent the total experiment.

$$\text{Total Probability} = \sum P(X = r) = 1 \tag{5.11}$$

If we increase the size of the experiment then it becomes quite difficult to calculate the event probabilities. We really need to develop a formula for calculating binomial probabilities. Using the ideas generated earlier, we have:

Total probability = $P\{X = 0 \text{ or } X = 1 \text{ or } X = 2 \text{ or } X = 3\}$

Total probability = $P(X = 0) + P(X = 1) + P(X = 2) + P(X = 3)$

Total probability = $(0.7)^3 + 3 * (0.3) * (0.7)^2 + 3 * (0.3)^2 * (0.7) + (0.3)^3$

Total probability = $q^3 + 3pq^2 + 3p^2q + p^3$, or,

Total probability = $p^3 + 3p^2q + 3pq^2 + q^3$

Repeating this experiment for increasing values of 'n' would enable the identification of a pattern that can be used to develop an equation (equation (5.12)) to calculate the probability of 'r' successes given 'n' attempts of the experiment:

$$P(X = r) = \binom{n}{r} p^r q^{n-r} \tag{5.12}$$

The term $\binom{n}{r}$ calculates the binomial coefficients which are the numbers in front of the letter terms in the binomial expansion. For example, in the previous example we found that the total probability = $p^3 + 3p^2q + 3pq^2 + q^3$ with the numbers in front of the letters of 1, 3, 3, and 1. These numbers are called the binomial coefficients and are calculated using equation (5.13):

$$\binom{n}{r} = \frac{n!}{r!(n-r)!} \tag{5.13}$$

Where n! (n factorial) is defined by equation (5.14):

$$n! = n * (n - 1) * (n - 2) * (n - 3)\ldots\ldots\ldots3 * 2 * 1 \tag{5.14}$$

Note

1. $\binom{n}{r}$ is equivalent to the equation to calculate the number of combinations of obtaining 'r' successes from 'n' attempts of the experiment. This term can be re-written using alternative notation as ^nC_r.

2. It is important to note that $3! = 3 * 2 * 1 = 6$, $2! = 2 * 1 = 2$, $1! = 1$, $0! = 1$.

It can be shown that the mean and variance for a binomial distribution is given by equations (5.15) and (5.16) as follows:

Mean of Binomial Distribution, $E(X) = np$ $\hspace{2cm}$ (5.15)

Variance of Binomial Distribution, $VAR(X) = npq$ $\hspace{2cm}$ (5.16)

Reconsidering Example 5.16 we note that $n = 3$, $p = 0.3$, and $q = 1 - p = 0.7$. Substituting these values into equation (5.12) gives: $P(\text{no bulls}) = P(X = 0) = {}^3C_0 (0.3)^0 (0.7)^3$. Inspecting this equation we note that the problem consists of three terms that are multiplied together to provide the probability of no bulls hit. The terms are: (a) ${}^3C_0$, (b) $(0.3)^0$, and

(c) $(0.7)^3$. Parts (b) and (c) are straightforward to calculate, and part (a) can be calculated from equation (5.12) as follows:

$$^3C_0 = \frac{3!}{0!(3-0)!} = \frac{3!}{0!3!} = \frac{3 \times 2 \times 1}{1 \times 3 \times 2 \times 1} = 1$$

Therefore, substituting these values into the problem solution gives:

$$P(\text{no bulls}) = P(X = 0) = {}^3C_0 (0.3)^0 (0.7)^3 = 1 \times 1 \times (0.7)^3 = 0.343$$

Excel solution—Example 5.16

Figure 5.35 illustrates the Excel solution for Example 5.16:

	A	B	C	D	E	F
1	Binomial distribution					
2	Example 5.16					
3			Number of trials n =	3		
4			Probability of hitting the bull p =	0.3		
5			Probability of missing the bull q =	0.7	=1-D4	
6						
7			Let X represent the number of bulls hit (r) out of 3 attempts (n)			
8						
9			Probability Distribution	r	P(X = r)	
10				0	0.343	=BINOMDIST(D10,$D$3,$D$4,FALSE)
11				1	0.441	
12				2	0.189	
13				3	0.027	=BINOMDIST(D13,$D$3,$D$4,FALSE)
14				Total =	1	=SUM(E10:E13)
15						
16			Number of combinations	r	nCr	
17				0	1	=COMBIN($D$3,D17)
18				1	3	
19				2	3	
20				3	1	=COMBIN($D$3,D20)
21						
22			Factorials	r	r!	
23				0	1	=FACT(D23)
24				1	1	
25				2	2	
26				3	6	=FACT(D26)

Figure 5.35

- Binomial probability of 'r' successes from 'n' attempts using BINOMDIST().
- Binomial coefficients using COMBIN().
- Factorial values using FACT().

→ **Excel Solution**

Number of trials Cell D3 — Value
Probability of hitting bull, p Cell D4 — Value
Probability of missing bull, q Cell D5 — Formula: =1−D4
Probability distribution
r Cells D10:D13 — Values
P(X = r) Cells E10:E13 — Formula: =BINOMDIST(D10,$D$3,$D$4,FALSE)
Copy formula from E10:E13
Total Cell E14 — Formula: =SUM(E10:E13)
Number of combinations
r Cells D17:D20 — Values
nCr Cells E17:E20 — Formula: =COMBIN($D$3,D17)
Copy formula from E17:E20

Factorials

r! Cells E23:E26

Values

Formula: =FACT(D23)

Copy formula from E23:E26

Note   Total probability for the experiment $\sum P(X=r)=1$.

Example 5.17

A local authority surveyed the travel preferences of people who travelled to work by train or bus. The initial analysis suggested that 1 in 5 people travelled by train to work. If 5 people are interviewed what is the probability that: (a) exactly 3 prefer travelling by train, P(X = 3), (b) 3 or more prefer travelling by train, P(X ≥ 3), and (c) less than 3 prefer travelling by train, P(X < 3). This experiment can be modelled by a binomial distribution since:

- 5 identical trials (n = 5).
- Each trial can result in either a person travels by train (success) or does not travel by train (failure).
- The outcome of each trial is independent.
- The probability of a success (P(travels by train) = p = 1/5 = 0.2) is the same for each trial.
- The random variable is discrete.

The random variable, X, represents the number of people travelling by train out of the 5 people interviewed. From the information provided we note that P(success) = P(prefer train) = p = 1/5 = 0.2, P(failure) = 1 − p = q = 0.8, and number of identical trails n = 5.

Excel solution—Example 5.17

The Excel solution is illustrated in Figure 5.36.

	A	B	C	D	E	F
1	Binomial distribution					
2	Example 5.17					
3			Number of trials n =	5		
4			Probability of hitting the Bull p =	0.2		
5			Probability of missing the Bull q =	0.8	=1-D4	
6						
7			Let X represent the number of bulls (r) hit out of 5 attempts (n)			
8						
9			Probability distribution	r	P(X = r)	
10				0	0.32768	=BINOMDIST(D10,$D$3,$D$4,FALSE)
11				1	0.40960	
12				2	0.20480	
13				3	0.05120	
14				4	0.00640	
15				5	0.00032	=BINOMDIST(D15,$D$3,$D$4,FALSE)
16						
17				Total =	1	=SUM(E10:E15)
18						
19				r	P(X = r)	
20			(a) P(X = 3) = 0.0512	3	0.0512	=BINOMDIST(D20,$D$3,$D$4,FALSE)
21			(b) P(X => 3) = 0.05792	2	0.05792	=1-BINOMDIST(D21,$D$3,$D$4,TRUE)
22			(c) P(X < 3) = P(X <= 2) = 0.94208	2	0.94208	=BINOMDIST(D22,$D$3,$D$4,TRUE)

Figure 5.36

➜ **Excel Solution**

Number of trails n = Cell D3	Value
Probability of hitting bull, p = Cell D4	Value
Probability of missing bull, q = Cell D5	Formula: =1−D4
r Cells D10: C15	Values
P(X = r) Cells E10:E15	Formula: =BINOMDIST(D10,$D$3,$D$4,FALSE)
	Copy formula from E10:E15
Total Cell E17	Formula: =SUM(E10:E15)
r Cells D20:D22	Values
(a) P(X = 3) = 0.0512	
P(X = r) Cell E20	Formula: =BINOMDIST(D20,$D$3,$D$4,FALSE)
(b) P(X => 3) = 0.05792	
P(X = r) Cell E21	Formula: =1−BINOMDIST(D21,$D$3,$D$4,TRUE)
(c) P(X < 3) = P(X <= 2) = 0.94208	
P(X = r) Cell E22	Formula: =BINOMDIST(D22,$D$3,$D$4,TRUE)

✳ **Interpretation**

(a) P(exactly 3 prefer train) = P(X = 3) = 0.0512

(b) P(3 or more prefer train) = P(X ≥ 3) = P(X = 3) + P(X = 4) + P(X = 5) = 0.05792

(c) P(less than 3 prefer train) = P(X < 3) = 1 − P(X ≥ 3) = 0.9421

Note Total probability for the experiment is 1 (0.32768 + 0.40960 + . . . +0.0032).

↘ Example 5.18

A manufacturing company regularly conducts quality control checks at specified periods on all products manufactured by the company. A new order for 2000 light bulbs is due to be delivered to a national DIY store. Historically the manufacturing record has a failure rate of 15% and the sample to be tested consists of 4 randomly selected light bulbs. From this information estimate the following probabilities: (a) find the probability distribution for 0, 1, 2, 3, 4 defective light bulbs, (b) calculate the probability that at least three will be defective, and (c) determine the mean and variance of the distribution. This example highlights the case of selecting without replacement from a large population. The effect on the sample space can be considered negligible and therefore we can consider the events as independent. Let the random variable, X, represent the number of defective light bulbs from the random sample. This value of X can take the values: 0 defective from 4 bulbs or 1 defective from 4 bulbs, or

2 defective from 4 bulbs, or 3 defective from 4 bulbs, or all 4 bulbs defective. This can be written as X = 0, 1, 2, 3, 4. For this example we have p = P(success) = P(defective bulb) = 0.15, q = P(failure) = 1 − p = 0.85, and n = 4. The Excel solution is illustrated in Figure 5.37 below:

	A	B	C	D	E	F	G	H	I
1	Binomial distribution								
2	Example 5.18								
3			Number of trials n =	4					
4			Probability of hitting the Bull p =	0.15					
5			Probability of missing the Bull q =	0.85	=1-D4				
6									
7			Let X represent the number of bulls' hit out of 3 attempts						
8									
9			(a) Probability distribution	r	P(X = r)				
10				0	0.52201	=BINOMDIST(D10,$D$3,$D$4,FALSE)			
11				1	0.36848				
12				2	0.09754				
13				3	0.01148				
14				4	0.00051	=BINOMDIST(D14,$D$3,$D$4,FALSE)			
15									
16				Total =	1.00000	=SUM(E10:E14)			
17									
18			(b) P(X => 3) = 0.0119813	r	P(X = r)				
19				2	0.0119813	=1-BINOMDIST(D19,$D$3,$D$4,TRUE)			
20									
21			(c) Mean and Variance	r	P(X = r)	r * P(X=r)		r^2 * P(X=r)	
22				0	0.52201	0	=D22*E22	0.000000	=D22*F22
23				1	0.36848	0.368475		0.368475	
24				2	0.09754	0.195075		0.390150	
25				3	0.01148	0.034425		0.103275	
26				4	0.00051	0.002025	=D26*E26	0.008100	=D26*F26
27									
28				E(X) =	0.6	=SUM(F22:F26)			
29				VAR(X) =	0.51	=SUM(H22:H26)-E28^2			
30				np =	0.6	=D3*D4			
31				npq =	0.51	=D3*D4*D5			

Figure 5.37

Excel solution—Example 5.18

→ Excel Solution

Number of trials n = Cell D3	Value
Probability of hitting bull, p = Cell D4	Value
Probability of missing bull, q = Cell D5	Formula: =1−D4
(a) Probability distribution	
r Cells D10:D14	Values
P(X = r) Cells E10:E14	Formula: =BINOMDIST(D10,$D$3,$D$4,FALSE)
	Copy formula from E10:E14
Total Cell E16	Formula: =SUM(E10:E14)
(b) P(X => 3) = P(X = 3) + P(X = 4) = 1 − P(X < 3) = 1 − P(X <= 2) = 0.0119813	
r Cell D19	Value
P(X = r) Cell E19	Formula: =1−BINOMDIST(D19,$D$3,$D$4,TRUE)
(c) Mean and Variance	
r Cells D22:D26	Values
P(X = r) Cells E22:E26	Formula: =BINOMDIST(D22,$D$3,$D$4,FALSE)
	Copy formula from E22:E26
r*P(X = r) Cells F22:F26	Formula: =D22*E22
	Copy formula from F22:F26

$r^2*P(X = r)$ Cells H22:H26

Formula: =D22*F22

Copy formula from H22:H26

E(x) = Cell E28

Formula: =SUM(F22:F26)

VAR(X) = Cell E29

Formula: =SUM(H22:H26)−E28^2

np = Cell E30

Formula: =D3*D4

npq = Cell E31

Formula: =D3*D4*D5

❄ Interpretation

(a) The probability distribution is as follows:

R	P(X = r)
0	0.52201
1	0.36848
2	0.09754
3	0.01148
4	0.00051

(b) Probability of at least 3 defective bulbs from the sample of 4 light bulbs is 0.0119813.

(c) Mean and variance for the probability distribution is mean = 0.6 and variance = 0.51.

For the example, we have n = 4, p = 0.15, and q = 0.85. From equations (5.15) and (5.16) we find E(X) = np = 4 * 0.15 = 0.6 and VAR(X) = n p q = 4 * 0.15 * 0.85 = 0.51. These answers agree with the first method.

Note   Total probability for the experiment = 1.

🖱 Student Exercises

X5.13 Evaluate the following: (a) $^3C_1$, (b) $^{10}C_3$, (c) $^2C_0$.

X5.14 A binomial model has n = 4 and p = 0.6.

(a) Find the probabilities of each of the five possible outcomes (i.e. P(0), P(1),..., P(4)).

(b) Construct a histogram of this data.

X5.15 Attendance at a cinema has been analysed and shows that audiences consist of 60% men and 40% women for a particular film. If a random sample of six people were selected from the audience during a performance, find the following probabilities:

   (a) All women are selected.

   (b) Three men are selected.

   (c) Less than three women are selected.

X5.16 A quality control system selects a sample of three items from a production line. If one or more is defective, a second sample is taken (also of size three), and if one or more of these are defective then the whole production line is stopped. Given that the probability of a defective item is 0.05, what is the probability that the second sample is taken? What is the probability that the production line is stopped?

X5.17 Five people in seven voted in an election. If four of those on the roll are interviewed what is the probability that at least three voted.

X5.18 A small tourist resort has a weekend traffic problem and is considering whether to provide emergency services to help mitigate the congestion that results from an accident or breakdown. Past records show that the probability of a breakdown or an accident on any given day of a four day weekend is 0.25. The cost to the community caused by congestion resulting from an accident or breakdown is as follows:

   •   a weekend with 1 accident day costs £20000

   •   a weekend with 2 accident days costs £30000

   •   a weekend with 3 accident days costs £60000

   •   a weekend with 4 accident days costs £125000

As part of its contingency planning, the resort needs to know:

   (a) The probability that a weekend will have no accidents.

   (b) The probability that a weekend will have at least two accidents.

   (c) The expected cost that the community will have to bear for an average weekend period.

   (d) Whether or not to accept a tender from a private firm for emergency services of £20000 for each weekend during the season.

5.3.3 Poisson probability distribution

In the previous section we explored the concept of a binomial distribution which represents a discrete probability distribution that enables the probability of achieving 'r' successes from 'n' independent experiments to be calculated. Each experiment (or event) has two possible outcomes ('success' or 'failure') and the probability of 'success' (p) is known. The *Poisson distribution* developed by Simeon Poisson (1781–1840) is a discrete probability distribution that enables the probability of 'r' events to occur during a specified interval (time, distance, area, and volume) if the average occurrence is known and the events are independent of the specified interval since the last event occurred. It has been usefully employed to describe probability functions of phenomena such as product demand, demands for service, numbers of accidents, numbers of traffic arrivals, and numbers of defects in various types of lengths or objects. Like the binomial it is used to describe a discrete random variable. With the binomial distribution we have a sample of definite size and we know the number of 'successes' and 'failures'. There are situations, however, when to ask how many 'failures' would not make sense and/or the sample size is indeterminate. For example if we watch a football match we can report the number of goals scored but we cannot say how many were not scored. In such cases we are dealing with isolated cases in a continuum of space and time, where the number of experiments (n), probability of success (p) and failure (q) cannot be defined. What we can do is divide the interval (time, distance, area, volume) into very small sections and calculate the mean number of occurrences in the interval. This gives rise to the Poisson distribution defined by equation (5.17):

$$P(X=r)\frac{\lambda^r e^{-\lambda}}{r!}$$

(5.17)

Where:

- $P(X=r)$ is the probability of event 'r' occurring.

- The symbol 'r' represents the number of occurrences of an event and can take the value $0 \rightarrow \infty$ (infinity).

- r! is the factorial of 'r' calculated using the Excel function: FACT().

- λ is a positive real number that represents the expected number of occurrences for a given interval. For example, if we found that we had an average of 4 stitching errors in a 1 metre length of cloth, then for 2 metres of cloth we would expect the average number of errors to be $\lambda = 4 * 2 = 8$.

- The symbol 'e' represents the base of the natural logarithm (e = 2.71828...).

Unlike other distributions, the Poisson distribution mean and variance are identical, or very close in practice.

▷ Example 5.19

The following data, derived from the past 100 years, concerns the number of times a river floods in a wet season. Check if the distribution may be modelled using the Poisson distribution and determine the expected frequencies for a 100 year period (see Table 5.10).

Number of Floods (X)	Number of Years with 'X' Floods (f)
0	24
1	35
2	24
3	12
4	4
5	1
Total =	100

Table 5.10

Excel solution is provided in Figures 5.38 and 5.39 below.

	A	B	C	D	E	F	G	H	I
1	POISSON PROBABILITY DISTRIBUTION EXAMPLE								
2	Example 5.19								
3		(a) Calculate frequency distribution mean and variance							
4									
5		Number of Floods	Number of Years with X Floods						
6		X	f	Xf		X^2		$f X^2$	
7		0	24	0	=B7*C7	0	=B7^2	0	=C7*F7
8		1	35	35		1		35	
9		2	24	48		4		96	
10		3	12	36		9		108	
11		4	4	16		16		64	
12		5	1	5	=B12*C12	25	=B12^2	25	=C12*F12
13		Totals =	100	140				328	
14			=SUM(C7:C12)	=SUM(D7:D12)				=SUM(H7:H12)	
15									
16		mean =	1.4	=D13/C13					
17		variance =	1.32	=H13/C13-C16^2					

Figure 5.38

	J	K	L	M	N
2	Example 5.19				
3	(b) Calculate the Poisson probabilities and fit probability model to data set				
4					
5				Expected Frequencies	
6	r	P(X = r)		EF	
7	0	0.2466	=POISSON(J7,$C$16,FALSE)	24.66	=$C$13*K7
8	1	0.3452		34.52	
9	2	0.2417		24.17	
10	3	0.1128		11.28	
11	4	0.0395		3.95	
12	5	0.0111	=POISSON(J12,$C$16,FALSE)	1.11	=$C$13*K12
13					
14	Total =	0.9968		99.68	
15		=SUM(K7:K12)		=SUM(M7:M12)	

Figure 5.39

Excel solution—Example 5.19a

The first stage is to estimate the average number of floods per year, λ, based upon the sample data. Figure 5.38 above illustrates the Excel solution.

→ **Excel Solution**

(a) Calculate frequency distribution mean and variance

Number of floods X Cells B7:B12   Values

Number of years with X floods, f Cells C7:C12   Values

xf Cells D7:D12   Formula: =B7*C7
                                             Copy formula from D7:D12

Totals

ΣX = Cell C13   Formula: =SUM(C7:C12)

ΣXf = Cell D13   Formula: =SUM(D7:D12)

X^2 Cells F7:F12   Formula: =B7^2
                                             Copy formula from F7:F12

fX^2 Cells H7:H12   Formula: =C7*F7
                                             Copy formula from H7:H12

Mean = Cell D16   Formula: =D13/C13

Variance = Cell D17   Formula: =H13/C13–C16^2

The average number of floods per year, λ, and variance is calculated from this frequency distribution: Mean $\lambda = \dfrac{\Sigma fx}{\Sigma f} = \dfrac{140}{100} = 1.4$ floods per year and Variance $VAR(X) = \dfrac{\Sigma fX^2}{\Sigma f} - (mean)^2 = 1.32$.

> ❋ **Interpretation**   The average number of floods, i.e. the mean, is 1.4 floods per year with a variance of 1.32. They seem to be in close agreement (only 5.7% difference), which is one of the characteristics of the Poisson distribution. The mean and variance of the Poisson distribution have the same numerical value and given the closeness of the two values in this numerical example we would conclude that the Poisson distribution should be a good model for the sample data.

The chi square goodness-of-fit test is used to test if the Poisson model is a significant fit to the sample data, but this is beyond the scope of this book.

Excel solution—Example 5.19b

Thus, we can now determine the probability distribution using equation (5.16) as illustrated in Figure 5.39 above.

> ➡ **Excel Solution**
>
> (b)   Calculate the Poisson probabilities and fit probability model to data set
>
> r Cells J7:J12   Values
> P(X = r) Cells K7:K12   Formula: =POISSON(J7,$C$16,FALSE)
> Total = Cell K14   Formula: =SUM(K7:K12)
> Expected frequencies Cells M7:M12   Formula: =$C$13*K7
>   Copy formula from M7:M13
> Total = Cell M14   Formula: =SUM(M7:M12)

> ❋ **Interpretation**
>   (a) The probability distribution is given in Table 5.11 as follows:
>
> | r | P(X = r) |
> |---|----------|
> | 0 | 0.2466 |
> | 1 | 0.3452 |
> | 2 | 0.2417 |
> | 3 | 0.1128 |
> | 4 | 0.0395 |
> | 5 | 0.0111 |
>
> Table 5.11

(b) To check how well the Poisson probability distribution fits the data set we note that the observed frequencies are given in the original table and that the expected frequencies can be calculated from the Poisson probability fit using the equation EF = $(\sum f) \times P(X = r)$. The manual solution is now presented in Table 5.12 as follows:

r	P(X = r)	Observed frequency	Expected frequency
0	0.2466	24	24.66
1	0.3452	35	34.52
2	0.2417	24	24.17
3	0.1128	12	11.28
4	0.0395	4	3.95
5	0.0111	1	1.11
	Totals =	100	99.68

Table 5.12

We note that the expected frequencies are approximately equal to the observed frequency values.

Table 5.13 illustrates the calculation of the Poisson probability values for $\lambda = 1.4$ by applying equation (5.17) as follows:

r	Poisson Value	Excel
0	$P(X = 0) = \dfrac{1.4^0 e^{-1.4}}{0!} = 0.2466$	=POISSON(J7,$C$16,FALSE)
1	$P(X = 1) = \dfrac{1.4^1 e^{-1.4}}{1!} = 0.3452$	=POISSON(J8,$C$16,FALSE)
2	$P(X = 2) = \dfrac{1.4^2 e^{-1.4}}{2!} = 0.2417$	=POISSON(J9,$C$16,FALSE)
3	$P(X = 3) = \dfrac{1.4^3 e^{-1.4}}{3!} = 0.1128$	=POISSON(J10,$C$16,FALSE)
4	$P(X = 4) = \dfrac{1.4^4 e^{-1.4}}{4!} = 0.1128$	=POISSON(J11,$C$16,FALSE)
5	$P(X = 5) = \dfrac{1.4^5 e^{-1.4}}{5!} = 0.0111$	=POISSON(J12,$C$16,FALSE)

Table 5.13

Figure 5.40 illustrates a Poisson probability plot for the number of floods example. The skewed nature of the distribution can be clearly seen (left skewed).

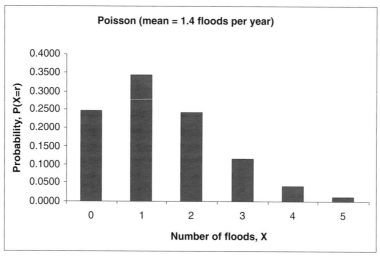

Figure 5.40

If we determine the mean and the variance either using the frequency distribution or the probability distribution we would find.

$$\lambda = VAR(X) = Mean \tag{5.18}$$

For Poisson to be applicable:

- Mean = Variance.
- Events discrete and randomly distributed in time and space.
- Mean number of events in a given interval is constant.
- Events are independent.
- Two or more events cannot occur simultaneously.

Note   Once it has been identified that the mean and variance have the same numerical value, ensure that the other conditions above are satisfied, indicating that the sample data most likely follow the Poisson distribution.

Example 5.20

A company is reviewing the number of telephone lines available for customer support. The average number of calls received per day is 3 calls during a 5 minute period of time. Estimate the proportion of phone calls that cannot be answered during a 5 minute period: (a) if the company installs 4 lines and (b) if the company installs 5 lines?

Excel solution—Example 5.20

The Excel solution is illustrated in Figure 5.41.

	A	B	C	D
1	Example 5.20			
2				
3			$\lambda = 3$	
4				
5		r	P(X=r)	
6		0	0.049787068	=POISSON(B6,$C$3,FALSE)
7		1	0.149361205	
8		2	0.224041808	
9		3	0.224041808	
10		4	0.168031356	=POISSON(B10,$C$3,FALSE)
11				
12		P(X <= 4) =	0.815263245	=POISSON(B10,C3,TRUE)
13		P(X <= 4) =	0.815263245	=SUM(C6:C10)
14				
15		P(X > 4) =	0.184736755	=1-C12
16				
17		P(X > 5) =	0.083917942	=1-POISSON(5,C3,TRUE)

Figure 5.41

→ **Excel Solution**

λ = Cell C3   Value

r Cells B6:B10   Values

P(X = r) Cells C6:C10   Formula: =POISSON(B6,$C$3,FALSE)

P(X <= 4) = Cell C12   Formula: =POISSON(B10,C3,TRUE)

P(X <= 4) = Cell C13   Formula: =SUM(C6:C10)

P(X > 4) = Cell C15   Formula: =1−C12

P(X > 5) = Cell C17   Formula: =1−POISSON(5,C3,TRUE)

❇ **Interpretation**

(a) If the company has 4 lines then the probability that a call cannot be answered
P (call not answered) = 1 − P(X ≤ 4) = 1 − P(X = 0 or X = 1 or X = 2 or X = 3 or X = 4).
From Excel, P(call not answered) = 0.185263245 or 18.5%. Probability that callers
cannot connect is 18.5% of the time.

(b) Should another line be installed? The corresponding calculation shows that if n = 5
then the P(call not answered) = 1 − P(X ≤ 5) = 1 − P(X = 0 or X = 1 or X = 2 or X = 3 or
X = 4 or X = 5). From Excel, P(call not answered) = 0.083917942 or 8.4%. The probability that the switchboard could not handle all calls has been reduced to 8.4%.
Whether or not this was worthwhile depends upon the likely profits that this would
create against the cost of installation and running an extra telephone line.

The probability that a call cannot be answered P(call not answered) = 1 − P(X ≤ 4). Table
5.14 illustrates the calculation of the Poisson probability values for $\lambda = 3$ by applying equation (5.17) as follows:

r	Poisson Value	Excel
0	$P(X=0)=\dfrac{3^0 e^{-3}}{0!}=0.0498$	=POISSON(B6,$C$3,FALSE)
1	$P(X=1)=\dfrac{3^1 e^{-3}}{1!}=0.1494$	=POISSON(B7,$C$3,FALSE)
2	$P(X=2)=\dfrac{3^2 e^{-3}}{2!}=0.2241$	=POISSON(B8,$C$3,FALSE)
3	$P(X=3)=\dfrac{3^3 e^{-3}}{3!}=0.2241$	=POISSON(B9,$C$3,FALSE)
4	$P(X=4)=\dfrac{3^4 e^{-3}}{4!}=0.1681$	=POISSON(B10,$C$3,FALSE)

Table 5.14

Student Exercises

X5.19 Calculate P(0), P(1), P(2), P(3), P(4), P(5), P(6), and P(>6) for a Poisson variable with a mean of 1.2. Using this probability distribution determine the mean and variance.

X5.20 In a machine shop the average number of machines out of operation is 2. Assuming a Poisson distribution for machines out of operation, calculate the probability that at any one time there will be:

(a) Exactly one machine out of operation.

(b) More than one machine out of operation.

X5.21 A factory estimates that 0.25% of its production of small components is defective. These are sold in packets of 200. Calculate the percentage of the packets containing one or more defectives.

X5.22 The average number of faults in a metre of cloth produced by a particular machine is 0.1. (a) What is the probability that a length of 4 metres is free from faults? (b) How long would a piece have to be before the probability that it contains no flaws is less than 0.95?

X5.23 A garage has three cars available for daily hire. Calculate the following probabilities if the variable is a Poisson variable with a mean of 2: (a) Find the probability that on a given day that exactly none, one, two, and three cars will be hired and determine the mean number of cars hired per day. (b) The charge of hire of a car is £25 per day and the total outgoings per car, irrespective of whether or not it is hired, are £5 per day. Determine the expected daily profit from hiring these three cars.

X5.24 Accidents occur in a factory randomly and on average at the rate of 2.6 per month. What is the probability that in a given month: (a) no accidents will occur, and (b) more than one accident will occur?

5.3.4 Poisson approximation to the binomial distribution

When the number of trials in a binomial situation is very large and when p is small then it can be shown that the binomial probability function can be approximated by the Poisson probability function with $\lambda = np$. The larger the n and the smaller the p, the better is the approximation. The following equation for the Poisson probability is used to approximate the true (binomial) result:

$$P\left(X = r\right) \cong \frac{(np)^r \, e^{-np}}{r!} \qquad (5.19)$$

The Poisson random variable theoretically ranges from $0 \to \infty$. However, when used as an approximation to the binomial distribution, the Poisson random variable—the number of successes out of n observations—cannot be greater than the sample size n. With large n and small p, equation (5.19) implies that the probability of observing a large number of successes becomes small and approaches zero quite rapidly. For small values of p (< 0.1), and large values of n, the Poisson distribution will approximate the binomial distribution with $\lambda = np$. For the binomial distribution with p small (< 0.1) the mean (or expected) value $= np$ and the variance $= npq = np(1 - p) \approx np$. This implies that for small p the expected value and variance for the binomial distribution is approximated by the mean and variance of the Poisson distribution ($\lambda = np$, $VAR(X) = np$).

⬡ Example 5.21

In a large consignment of apples 3% are rotten. What is the probability that a carton of 60 apples will contain less than 2 rotten apples? We have here a binomial experiment and therefore could easily apply the binomial distribution with p = 0.03, q = 0.97, and n = 60. We can also apply the Poisson distribution.

Excel solution—Example 5.21

The Excel solution is illustrated in Figure 5.42.

	A	B	C	D	E
1	Example 5.21				
2					
3		n =	60		
4		p =	0.03		
5		np =	1.8	=C3*C4	
6					
7			Binomial: P(X < 2) =	0.459210797	=BINOMDIST(1,C3,C4,TRUE)
8			Poisson: P(X < 2) =	0.462836887	=POISSON(1,C5,TRUE)

Figure 5.42

➜ **Excel Solution**

n = Cell C3   Value
p = Cell C4   Value
np = Cell C5   Formula: =C3*C4
Binomial: P(X < 2) = Cell D7   Formula: =BINOMDIST(1,C3,C4,TRUE)
Poisson: P(X < 2) = Cell D8   Formula: =POISSON(1,C5,TRUE)

> ✳ **Interpretation**   We can see from Excel that the binomial and Poisson distributions provide approximately equal results, 45.92% and 46.28% respectively.

The degree of agreement between the binomial and Poisson probability distributions for this problem can be observed in Figure 5.43. They virtually overlap.

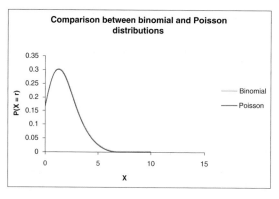

Figure 5.43

Note   The solution process is as follows:

1. Binomial Solution: P(less than 2 rotten) = P(X < 2) = P(X = 0) + P(X = 1).

$$P(X<2) = {}^{60}C_0 p^0 q^{60-0} + {}^{60}C_1 p^1 q^{60-1} \quad = {}^{60}C_0 (0.3)^0 (0.97)^{60} + {}^{60}C_1 (0.3)^1 (0.97)^{59}$$

$$P(X<2) = 0.1608 + 0.2984 = 0.4592$$

2. Poisson Solution: P(less than 2 rotten) = P(X < 2) = P(X = 0) + P(X = 1). Since n is large and p is small we can use the Poisson distribution. To check we will see if the mean and the variance of the distribution are equal: Mean = np = 60 * 0.03 = 1.8, Variance = npq = 60 * 0.03 * 0.97 = 1.746. Comparing the two values we see that they are approximately equal and the binomial distribution can be approximated using the Poisson distribution:

$$P(X<2) = \frac{1.8^0 e^{-1.8}}{0!} + \frac{1.8^1 e^{-1.8}}{1!} = 0.1652 + 0.2975 = 0.4627$$

Table 5.15 compares the two solutions:

Problem	Binomial	Poisson
P(X < 2)	0.4592	0.4627

Table 5.15

Student Exercises

X5.25 A new telephone directory is to be published. Before publication entries are proof-read for errors and any corrections made. Experience suggests that, on average, 0.1% of the entries require correction and that entries requiring correction are randomly distributed. The directory contains 800 pages with 300 entries per page. Two methods for making corrections are proposed: Method A (costs 50p per page containing one correction and £1.50 per page containing two or more corrections), and Method B (costs £1 per page containing one or more corrections). Which method based on cost should be used?

5.3.5 Normal approximation to the binomial distribution

Computing binomial probabilities using the binomial probability distribution can be difficult for large values of n. If we were undertaking the calculation using tables then usually tables are supplied up to a value of n of 50 and for particular values of the probability of success, p. We have seen that the Poisson distribution can be used to approximate the binomial distribution when n > 20 and p < 0.1. Substituting equations (5.15) and (5.16) into (5.10) gives equation (5.20):

$$Z = \frac{(X - np)}{\sqrt{npq}}$$

(5.20)

The normal distribution can be used to approximate a binomial distribution, when n large and p close to 0.5 (np > 5).

Example 5.22

Assume you have a fair coin and wish to know the probability that you would get 8 heads out of 10 flips. The binomial distribution has a mean of $\mu = np = 10 * 0.5 = 5$ and a variance of $\sigma^2 = npq = 10 * 0.5 * 0.5 = 2.5$. The standard deviation is therefore 1.5811. A total of 8 heads is 1.8973 standard deviations above the mean of the distribution [(8 − 5)/1.5811]. The question then is, 'what is the probability of getting a value exactly 1.8973 standard deviations above the mean?' The answer to this question is to remember that the probability of a particular event for a normal distribution is zero given that a particular event (or value of X) will not have an actual area within the normal distribution. The problem is that the binomial distribution is a discrete probability distribution whereas the normal distribution is a continuous distribution. The solution is to round off and consider any value from 7.5 to 8.5 to represent an outcome of 8 heads. Using this approach, we can solve discrete binomial problems with a normal approximation if we transform X = 8 for the binomial to the region 7.5–8.5 for the normal distribution.

The area shaded in Figure 5.44 is an approximation of the probability of obtaining 8 heads. We can see that the binomial probability distribution solution, $P(X = 8)_{Binomial} \approx P (7.5 \le X \le 8.5)_{Normal}$.

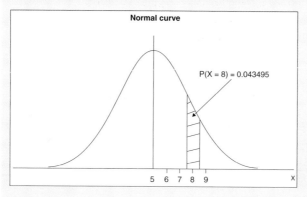

Figure 5.44

Excel solution—Example 5.22

The Excel solution to this problem is illustrated in Figure 5.45 below.

	A	B	C	D	E
1	Normal approximation to Binomial				
2	Example 5.22				
3		Binomial			
4					
5			n =	10	
6			p =	0.5	
7			mean μ =	5	=D5*D6
8			Variance σ² =	2.5	=D5*D6*(1-D6)
9			SD σ =	1.581139	=SQRT(D8)
10			Number of heads X =	8	
11			P(X=8) =	0.043945	=BINOMDIST(D10,D5,D6,FALSE)
12					
13		Normal	Lower X₁ =	7.5	=D10-0.5
14			Upper X₂ =	8.5	=D10+0.5
15			P(X₁ <=7.5) =	0.943077	=NORMDIST(D13,D7,D9,TRUE)
16			P(X₂ <=8.5) =	0.986572	=NORMDIST(D14,D7,D9,TRUE)
17					
18			P(7.5 <= X <= 8.5) =	0.043495	=D16-D15

Figure 5.45

→ **Excel Solution**

Binomial
n = Cell D5   Value
p = Cell D6   Value
Mean μ = Cell D7   Formula: =D5*D6
Variance σ² = Cell D8   Formula: =D5*D6*(1–D6)
SD σ = Cell D9   Formula: =SQRT(D8)
Number of heads X = Cell D10   Value
P(X = 8) = Cell D11   Formula: =BINOMDIST(D10,D5,D6,FALSE)

Normal

Lower X_1 = Cell D13	Formula: =D10–0.5
Upper X_2 = Cell D14	Formula: =D10+0.5
P(X1 <= 7.5) = Cell D15	Formula: =NORMDIST(D13,D7,D9,TRUE)
P(X2 <= 8.5) = Cell D16	Formula: =NORMDIST(D14,D7,D9,TRUE)
P(7.5 <= X <= 8.5) = Cell D18	Formula: =D16–D15

We can see from Excel that the two probabilities agree with one another. The binomial probability of obtaining 8 heads from 10 flips is 0.043945 and the normal approximation probability of containing 8 heads is 0.043495.

✳ **Interpretation**   The probability of obtaining 8 heads from 10 flips of a fair coin is approximately 4.3%.

◈ Example 5.23

Enquiries at a travel agent lead only sometimes to a holiday booking being made. The agent needs to take 35 bookings per week to break even. If during a week there are 100 enquiries and the probability of a booking in each case is 0.4, find the probability that the agent will at least break even in this particular week? To solve this problem let X represent the number of bookings per week, p represents the probability that a booking will be made p = 0.4, and n represents the number of possible bookings over the week, n = 100.

The area shaded in Figure 5.46 is an approximation of the probability of obtaining at least 35 bookings.

We can see that the binomial probability distribution solution, $P(X \geq 35)_{Binomial} \approx 1 - P(X \leq 34.5)_{Normal}$.

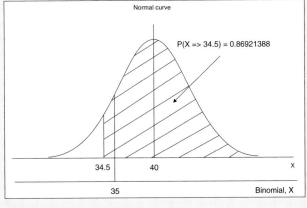

Figure 5.46

Excel solution—Example 5.23

The Excel solution to this problem is illustrated in Figure 5.47.

	A	B	C	D	E
1	Normal approximation to Binomial distribution				
2	Example 5.23				
3			n =	100	
4			p =	0.4	
5			mean μ =	40	=D3*D4
6			Variance σ² =	24	=D3*D4*(1-D4)
7			SD σ =	4.89897949	=SQRT(D6)
8					
9		Binomial			
10			P(X =>35) = 1 - P(X<=34)?		
11					
12			Binomial X =	34	
13			P(X =>35) = 1 - P(X<=34) =	0.86966347	=1-BINOMDIST(D12,D3,D4,TRUE)
14					
15		Normal			
16			P(X => 34.5)?		
17					
18			Normal X =	34.5	
19			P(X => 34.5) =	0.86921388	=1-NORMDIST(D18,D5,D7,TRUE)
20					
21			Z =	-1.1226828	=(D18-D5)/D7
22			P(X => 34.5) =	0.86921388	=1-NORMSDIST(D21)

Figure 5.47

→ **Excel Solution**

n = Cell D3	Value
p = Cell D4	Value
Mean μ = Cell D5	Formula: =D3*D4
Variance σ² = Cell D6	Formula: =D3*D4*(1−D4)
SD σ = Cell D7	Formula: =SQRT(D6)
Binomial	
P(X => 35) = 1 − P(X <= 34)?	
Binomial X = Cell D12	Value
P(X => 35) = 1 − P(X <= 34) = Cell D13	Formula: =1−BINOMDIST(D12,D3,D4,TRUE)
Normal	
P(X => 34.5)?	
Normal X = Cell D18	Value
P(X => 34.5) = Cell D19	Formula: =1−NORMDIST(D18,D5,D7,TRUE)
Z = Cell D21	Formula: =(D18−D5)/D7
P(X => 34.5) = Cell D22	Formula: =1−NORMSDIST(D21)

We can see from Excel that the two probabilities agree with one another. The binomial probability of obtaining at least 35 heads is 0.86966347 and the normal approximation probability of obtaining at least 35 bookings is 0.86921388.

❊ **Interpretation**   The probability of obtaining at least 35 bookings is 87.0%.

Note

(a) Binomial solution

P(X = 35 or more) = P(X ≥ 35) = P(X = 35 or 36 or 37 ... or 100)

This would be quite difficult to solve manually. From Excel we find that this probability value is P(X ≥ 35) = 0.8697.

(b) Normal approximation solution (n = 100, p = 0.4)

$\mu = np = 0.4 * 100 = 40$, $\sigma = \sqrt{npq} = 4.899$.

P(X ≥ 35 for Binomial) ≈ P(X ≥ 34.5 for Normal)

$$P(X \geq 35 \text{ for Binomial}) \approx P\left(Z \geq \frac{34.5 - 40}{4.899}\right) = P(Z \geq -1.12) = 0.8692$$

Comparing the two answers we can see that good agreement has been reached.

Student Exercises

X5.26 Given X is a discrete binomial random variable with p = 0.3 and n = 20: (a) can we use the normal approximation to estimate the binomial probability, (b) what if n is changed to 15, and (c) if n = 40 and p = 0.1 is the normal approximation appropriate?

5.3.6 Normal approximation to the Poisson distribution

The normal distribution can also be used to approximate the Poisson distribution whenever the parameter λ, the expected number of successes, equals or exceeds 5. Since the value of the mean and the variance of a Poisson distribution are the same ($\mu = \lambda = \sigma^2$ then $\sigma = \sqrt{\lambda}$. Substituting these terms into equation (5.10) gives equation (5.21):

$$Z = \frac{(X - \lambda)}{\sqrt{\lambda}}$$

(5.21)

The approximation improves as the value of the mean (λ) grows larger and at a particular value we can assume that the Z variable is normally distributed.

Example 5.24

The average number of broken eggs per lorry is known to be 50. What is the probability that there will be more than 70 broken eggs on a particular lorry load? We may use the Normal approximation to the Poisson distribution, where the mean and variance are calculated as follows: mean ($\mu_{Normal} \approx \mu_{Poisson} = \lambda = 50$) and variance ($\sigma^2_{Normal} \approx \sigma^2_{Poisson} = \lambda = 50$). Require P(X > 70 for Poisson) ≈ P(X ≥ 70.5 for Normal).

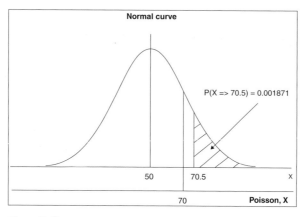

The area shaded in Figure 5.48 is an approximation of the probability of obtaining more than 70 broken eggs.

We can see that the Poisson probability distribution solution, $P(X > 70)_{Poisson} \approx P(X \geq 70.5)_{Normal}$.

Figure 5.48

Excel solution—Example 5.24

The Excel solution to this problem is illustrated in Figure 5.49.

	C	D	E
1	Normal approximation to the Poisson distribution		
2	Example 5.24		
3	mean λ =	50	
4	Variance σ² =	50	
5	SD σ =	7.071068	=SQRT(D4)
6			
7			
8	P(X >70) = 1 - P(X<=70)?		
9			
10	Poisson X =	70	
11	P(X >70) = 1 - P(X<=70) =	0.002971	=1-POISSON(D10,D3,TRUE)
12			
13			
14	P(X => 70.5)?		
15			
16	Normal X =	70.5	
17	P(X => 70.5) =	0.001871	=1-NORMDIST(D16,D3,D5,TRUE)
18			
19	Z =	2.899138	=(D16-D3)/D5
20	P(X => 70.5) =	0.001871	=1-NORMSDIST(D19)

Figure 5.49

→ **Excel Solution**

Mean λ = Cell D3   Value
Variance σ² = Cell D4   Value
SD σ = Cell D5   Formula: =SQRT(D4)
Poisson
$P(X > 70) = 1 - P(X \leq 70)$?
Poisson X = Cell D10   Value
$P(X > 70) = 1 - P(X \leq 70)$ = Cell D11   Formula: =1−POISSON(D10,D3,TRUE)
Normal
$P(X \geq 70.5)$?

Normal X = Cell D16	Value
P(X ≥ 70.5) = Cell D17	Formula: =1−NORMDIST(D16,D3,D5,TRUE)
Z = Cell D18	Formula: =(D16−D3)/D5
P(X ≥ 70.5) = Cell D19	Formula: =1−NORMSDIST(D19)

We can see from Excel that the two probabilities agree with one another. The Poisson probability of obtaining at least 70 broken eggs is 0.002971 and the normal approximation probability of obtaining at least 70 broken eggs is 0.001871.

✳ **Interpretation**   The probability of obtaining at least 70 broken eggs is 0.2%.

Note

(a) Poisson solution

$P(X > 70) = P(X = 71 \text{ or } 72 \ldots)$

This would be quite difficult to solve manually. From Excel we find that this probability value is $P(X > 70) = 0.002971$.

(b) Normal approximation solution (mean = 50)

$\mu = \lambda = 50$ and $\sigma = \sqrt{\lambda} = 7.071068$.

$P(X > 70 \text{ for Poisson}) \approx P(X \geq 70.5 \text{ for Normal})$

$P(X > 70 \text{ for Poisson}) \approx P\left(Z \geq \dfrac{70.5 - 50}{7.071068}\right) = P(Z \geq 2.899138) = 0.001871$.

Comparing the two answers we can see that good agreement has been reached.

Student Exercises

X5.27 A local maternity hospital has an average of 36 births per week. Use this information to calculate the following probabilities: (a) find the probability that there are fewer than 30 births in a given week, (b) find the probability that there will be more than 40 births in a given week, and (c) find the probability that there will be between 30 and 40 births in a given week.

5.3.7 Other discrete probability distributions

Other types of discrete probability distributions include the *hypergeometric* discrete probability distribution which measures, like the binomial distribution, the number of successes from n observations of the experiment. Unlike the binomial which involves replacement and therefore the probability of success (p) is constant. The hypergeometric distribution involves sampling without replacement. In this case the probability of success (p) is dependent upon the outcome of the previous run of the experiment. This topic is beyond the scope of this text book.

■ Techniques in Practice

1. CoCo S.A. is concerned at the time to react to customer complaints and has implemented a new set of procedures for its support centre staff (see Chapter 4 TP1). The customer service director plans to reduce the mean time for responding to customer complaints to 28 days and has collected the following sample data after implementation of the new procedures to assess the time to react to complaints (days):

20	33	33	29	24	30
40	33	20	39	32	37
32	50	36	31	38	29
15	33	27	29	43	33
31	35	19	39	22	21
28	22	26	42	30	17
32	34	39	39	32	38

(a) Estimate the mean time to react to customer complaints.

(b) Calculate the probability that the mean time to react is not greater than 28 days.

2. Bakers Ltd is currently in the process of reviewing the credit line available to supermarkets who are defined as 'good' and 'bad' risk. Based upon €100000 credit line the profit is estimated to be €25000. If the company accepts a 'bad risk' credit request it will lose €8000. If it rejects a 'good risk' it will lose €5000 in good will but if it rejects a 'bad risk' nothing is gained or lost.

(a) Complete the following profit and loss table for this situation.

		DECISION	
		Accept	Reject
Type of Risk	Good		
	Bad		

(b) The credit manager assesses the probability that a particular applicant is a 'good risk' is 4/10 and a 'bad risk' is 6/10. What would be the expected profits for each of the two decisions; consequently what decision should be taken for the applicant?

3. Skodel Ltd is developing a low calorie lager for the European market with a mean designed calorie count of 43 calories per 100 ml. The new product development team are

having problems with the production process and have collected an independent random sample to assess whether the target calorie count is being met.

49.7	45.2	37.7	31.9	34.8	39.8
45.9	40.5	40.6	41.9	51.4	54.0
34.3	47.8	63.1	26.3	41.2	31.7
41.4	45.1	41.1	47.9		

(a) Estimate the mean and variance based upon the sample data.

(b) State the value of calorie count if the production manager would like this value to be $43 \pm 5\%$.

(c) Estimate the probability that the calorie count lies between $43 \pm 5\%$ (assume that your answers to question (a) represent the population values).

Summary

In this chapter we have provided an overview of the concept of probability and its associated rules of addition and multiplication to solve a range of probabilistic problems. To aid the solution of these problems we introduced the idea of using a visual display (tree diagram) to enable the events contributing to the solution to be identified. The concept of relative frequency was applied to enable the concept of a probability distribution and expectation to be introduced to the reader. The notion of a discrete and continuous probability distribution was then introduced and examples provided to illustrate the different types of discrete (binomial, Poisson) and continuous (normal) distributions. In Chapter 6 we shall explore the concept of data sampling from normal and non-normal population distributions and introduce the reader to the central limit theorem. Furthermore, we will introduce a range of continuous probability distributions (Student's t distribution, F distribution, chi square distribution) which will be used in later chapters to solve a range of problems that require statistical inference tests to be applied. Chapter 6 will apply the central limit theorem to provide point and interval estimates to certain population parameters (mean, variance, proportion) based upon sample parameters (sample mean, sample variance, sample proportion).

Key Terms

Binomial distribution	Event	Independent events
Combinations	Expected value	Mean of the Binomial
Continuous probability	Expected value of a	distribution
distribution	discrete variable	Mean of the Normal
Decision tree	General addition rule	distribution
Discrete probability	General multiplication rule	Mean of the Poisson
distribution	Hypergeometric distribution	distribution

Mutually exclusive

Normal distribution

Normal probability plot

Poisson distribution

Probability

Sample space

Standard deviation of a discrete variable

Standard deviation of a normal variable

Standardized normal distribution

Statistical independence

Student's t distribution

Uniform distribution

■ Further Reading

Textbook Resources

1. Whigham, D. (2007). *Business Data Analysis using Excel*. Oxford University Press. ISBN: 9780199296286.

2. Lindsey, J. K. (2003) *Introduction to Applied Statistics: A Modelling Approach* (2nd Edition). Oxford University Press. ISBN: 978-0-19-852895-1.

Web Resources

1. StatSoft Electronic Textbook http://www.statsoft.com/textbook/stathome.html (accessed 28/1/2007).

2. HyperStat Online Statistics Textbook http://davidmlane.com/hyperstat/index.html (accessed 28/1/2007).

3. Eurostat—website is updated daily and provides direct access to the latest and most complete statistical information available on the European Union, the EU Member States, the euro-zone and other countries http://epp.eurostat.ec.europa.eu (accessed 28/1/2007).

4. Economagic—contains international economic data sets (http://www.economagic.com) (accessed 28/1/2007).

5. The ISI glossary of statistical terms provides definitions in a number of different languages http://isi.cbs.nl/glossary/index.htm.

■ Formula Summary

$$P\left(A\right)=\frac{m}{n} \tag{5.1}$$

$$P(A \text{ or } B) = P(A) + P(B) \tag{5.2}$$

$$P(A \text{ or } B) = P(A) + P(B) - P(A \cap B) \tag{5.3}$$

$$P(A \cap B) = P(A) * P(B) \tag{5.4}$$

$$P\left(X\right)=\frac{\text{Number of successful outcomes}}{\text{Total number of attempts}} \tag{5.5}$$

$$E(X) = \sum X \times P\left(X\right) \tag{5.6}$$

$$VAR(X) = \sum X^2 \times P(X) - \left[\sum X \times P\left(X\right)\right]^2 \tag{5.7}$$

$$SD(X) = \sqrt{VAR(X)} \tag{5.8}$$

$$f(X) = \frac{1}{\sigma\sqrt{2\pi}} \exp^{\left(-\frac{(X-\mu)^2}{2\sigma^2}\right)} \tag{5.9}$$

$$Z = \frac{(X-\mu)}{\sigma} \tag{5.10}$$

Total Probability $= \sum P(X=r) = 1$ \hfill (5.11)

$$P(X=r) = \binom{n}{r} p^r q^{n-r} \tag{5.12}$$

$$\binom{n}{r} = \frac{n!}{r!(n-r)!} \tag{5.13}$$

$$n! = n * (n-1) * (n-2) * (n-3)\ldots\ldots\ldots 3 * 2 * 1 \tag{5.14}$$

$$E(X) = n\,p \tag{5.15}$$

$$VAR(X) = n\,p\,q \tag{5.16}$$

$$P(X=r)\frac{\lambda^r e^{-\lambda}}{r!} \tag{5.17}$$

$$\lambda = VAR(X) = \text{Mean} \tag{5.18}$$

$$P(X=r)\frac{(np)^r e^{-np}}{r!} \tag{5.19}$$

$$Z = \frac{(X-np)}{\sqrt{npq}} \tag{5.20}$$

$$Z = \frac{(X-\lambda)}{\sqrt{\lambda}} \tag{5.21}$$

6 Sampling Distributions and Estimating

» Overview «

In Chapter 5 we introduced the concept of a probability distribution via the idea of relative frequency and introduced two distinct types: discrete and continuous. In this chapter we will explore the concept of taking a sample from a population, and use this sample to provide population estimates for the mean, standard deviation, and proportion. The types of statistics that we explored within earlier chapters are statistics that provide an answer to a particular question, where we assume that the data collected is from the complete population. In many situations this is not the case, and the data collected represents a sample from a population being measured. In this case the statistics calculated from the sample (mean, standard deviation, and proportion) represent estimates of the true value that could be calculated if you had access to the complete population of data values. These estimates provide point estimates of the population values with the disagreement between the sample and population value representing the margin of error. The margin of error can be represented by the concept of a confidence interval for the population parameter value estimated from the sample. This interval can be estimated if we assume that the sampling distribution of the mean is normally distributed. We will show that the Central Limit Theorem allows a normal distribution approximation for the sampling distribution of the mean to be assumed even if the population is not normally distributed. This result will allow the methods described in this chapter to be employed to solve a range of statistical hypothesis tests where we test whether the population mean has a particular value based upon the collected sample data.

» Learning Objectives «

On completing this chapter you should be able to:

» Distinguish between the concept of a population and sample.

» Recognize different types of sampling—probability (simple, systematic, stratified, cluster) and non-probability (purposive, quota, snowball, convenience).

X

Sampling distribution
The sampling distribution describes probabilities associated with a statistic when a random sample is drawn from a population.

>> Recognize reasons for sampling error—coverage error, non response error, sampling error, measurement error.

>> Understand the concept of a sampling distribution: mean and proportion.

>> Understand sampling from a normal population.

>> Understand sampling from non-normal population—Central Limit Theorem.

>> Calculate point estimates for one and two samples.

>> Calculate the probabilities for $\bar{x}$ for large samples.

>> Calculate sampling errors and confidence intervals when the population standard deviation is known and unknown (z and t tests).

>> Calculate and plot the sampling distribution of proportions for large n.

>> Calculate confidence intervals for one and two samples.

>> Determine sample sizes.

>> Solve problems using Microsoft Excel.

6.1 Introduction to the Concept of a Sample

There are many research questions we would like to answer that involve populations that are too large to measure every member of the population. How have wages of German car workers changed over the past ten years? What are the management practices of foreign exchange bankers working in Paris? How many voters are planning to vote for a political party at a local election? These questions are all valid and require researchers to design methods to collect the relevant data, which when pooled together, gives the researcher potential answers to the questions identified. In many cases the size of the population is such that it is impractical to measure the wages of all German car workers or all voters who are entitled to vote at a local election. In this situation a proportion of the population would be selected from the population of interest to the researcher. This proportion is achieved by *sampling* from the population and the proportion selected is called the *sample*.

6.1.1 Why sample?

Sampling is usually collected via survey instruments, but could also be achieved by observation, archival record, or other method. What is important to realize is that no matter what method is used to collect the data values, the purpose is to determine how much and how well the data set can be used to generalize the findings from the sample to the population. It is important to avoid data collection methods that maximize the associated errors and a bad sample may well render findings meaningless. Sampling in conjunction with survey research is not only one of the most popular approaches to data collection in business research with the concept of random sampling providing the foundation assumption that allows statistical hypothesis testing to be valid. It is also

X

Population standard deviation The population standard deviation is the standard deviation of all possible values.

important to note that we all tend to perform sampling from populations without realizing that we are doing so. For example, we browse through the television channels to find a programme we may wish to watch and then make a decision based upon this sampling process. From the sampling undertaken we may also make conclusions on the overall quality of television programmes based upon the sample of programmes observed. This concept is called making an inference on the population based upon the sample observations.

The primary aim of sampling is to select a sample from the population that shares the same characteristics as the population. For example, if the population average height of grown men between the ages of 20–50 is 176 cms, then the sample average height would also be expected to be 176 cm, unless we have the problem of sampling error. This concept of sampling error can be measured and will be discussed within this chapter. The concept of sample and population values being in agreement allows us to state that we expect the sample to be representative of the population values being measured. Questions we should answer are:

- How well does the sample represent the larger population from which it was drawn?
- How closely do the features of the sample resemble those of the larger population?

Before we describe the main sampling methods we need to define the terminology we will use in this and later chapters.

6.1.2 Sampling terminology

A few statements hold true in general when dealing with sampling:

- Samples are always drawn from a population.
- The population to be sampled should coincide with the population about which information is wanted (the target population). Sometimes, for reasons of practicality or convenience, the sampled population is more restricted than the target population. In such cases, precautions must be taken to secure that the conclusions only refer to the sampled population.
- Before selecting the sample, the population must be divided into parts that are called sampling units. These units must cover the whole of the population and they must not overlap, in the sense that every element in the population belongs to one and only one unit. For example, in sampling the supermarket spending habits of people living in a town the unit may be an individual or family or a group of individuals living in a particular post code.
- The development of this list of sampling units, called a *frame*, is often one of the major practical problems. The frame is a list that contains the population list of values that you would like to measure. For example, market research firms will access local authority census data to create a sample. The list of registered students may be the *sampling frame* for a survey of the student body at a university. Problems can arise in sampling frame bias. Telephone directories are often used as sampling frames, for instance, but tend to under-represent the poor (who have fewer or no phones) and the wealthy (who have unlisted numbers).
- The final stage is to collect the sample using either probability or non-probability sampling described below.

6.1.3 Types of samples

We may consider different types of probability samples. Although there are a number of different methods that might be used to create a sample, they generally can be grouped into one of two categories: probability samples or non-probability samples.

6.1.3.1 Probability sampling

The idea behind this type of probability sampling is random selection. More specifically, each sample from the population of interest has a known probability of selection under a given sampling scheme.

There are four categories of probability samples as illustrated in Figure 6.1.

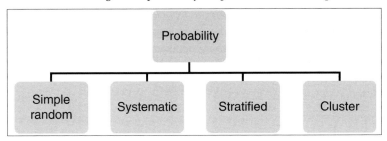

Figure 6.1

(a)   Simple random sampling

The most widely known type of a **random sample** is the *simple random sample*. This is characterized by the fact that the probability of selection is the same for every case in the population. Simple random sampling is a method of selecting 'n' samples from a population of size 'N' such that every possible sample of size 'n' has equal chance of being drawn.

> ### ⌕ Example 6.1
>
> Consider the situation that a marketing researcher will experience when selecting a random sample of 200 shoppers who shop at a supermarket during a particular time period. The researcher notes that the supermarket would like to seek the views of its customers on a proposed re-development of the store. The total footfall (the number of people visiting a shop or a chain of shops in a period of time is called its footfall) within this time period is 10000. With a footfall (or population) of this size we could employ a number of ways of selecting an appropriate sample of 200 from the potential 10000. For example, we could place 10000 consecutively numbered pieces of paper (1–10000) in a box, draw a number at random from the box, shake and select another number to maximize the chances of the second pick being random, shake and continue the process until all 200 numbers are selected. These would then be used to select a customer entering the store with the customer chosen based upon the number selected from the random process. To maximize the chances that customers selected would agree to complete the survey we could enter them into a prize draw. These 200 customers will form our sample with each number in the

Random sample A random sample is a sampling technique where we select a sample from a population of values.

selection having the same probability of being chosen. When undertaking the collection of data via random sampling we generally find it difficult to devise a selection scheme to guarantee that we have a random sample. For example, the selection from a population might not be the total population that you wish to measure, or during the time period when the survey is conducted we may find that the customers sampled may be unrepresentative of the population due to unforeseen circumstances.

(b) Systematic random sampling

With **systematic random sampling**, we create a list of every member of the population. From the list, we randomly select the first sample element from the first n number values on the population list. Thereafter, we select every nth number value on the list. This method involves choosing the nth element from a population list as follows:

- Divide the number of cases in the population by the desired sample size.
- Select a random number between one and the value attained in step 1. For example, we could pick the number 28.
- Starting with case number chosen in step 2, take every 28th record, as per this example.

The advantages of systematic sampling compared to simple random sampling, is that the sample is easier to draw from the population. The disadvantages are that the sample points are not equally likely.

(c) Stratified random sampling

With *stratified random sampling*, the population is divided into two or more mutually exclusive groups, where each group is dependent upon the research area of interest. The sampling procedure is to organize the population into homogenous subsets before sampling, then draw a random sample from each group. With stratified random sampling the population is divided into non-overlapping groups (subpopulations or strata) where all the groups together would comprise the entire population. As an example, suppose we conduct a national survey in Holland. We might divide the population into groups (or strata) based on the regions of Holland. Then we would randomly select from each group (or strata). The advantage of this method is to guarantee that every group within the population is selected and provides an opportunity to undertake group comparisons.

⌕ Example 6.2

To illustrate, consider the situation where we wish to sample the views of graduate job applicants to a major financial institution. The nature of this survey is to collect data on the application process from the applicants' perspective. The survey will therefore have to collect the views from the different specified groups within the identified population. For example, this could be based on gender, race, type of employment requested full or part time, or whether an applicant is classified as disabled. If we use simple random sampling it is possible that we may miss a representative sample from one of these groups due, for example, to the relative size of the group relative to the population. In this case, we would employ stratified random sampling to ensure that appropriate numbers of sample values are drawn from each group in proportion to the percentage of the population as a whole. Stratified sampling offers several advantages over simple random sampling: (a) guards against an unrepresentative sample (e.g. all male from a predominately female population), (b) provides sufficient group data for separate group analysis, (c) requires a smaller sample, and (d) greater precision is achievable compared to simple random sampling for a sample of the same size. Stratified random sampling nearly always results in a smaller variance for the estimated mean or other population parameters of interest. The main disadvantage of a stratified sample is that it may be more costly to collect and process the data compared to a simple random sample. Two different categories of stratified random sampling are available, as follows:

- *Proportionate stratification*. With proportionate stratification, the sample size of each stratum is proportionate to the population size of the stratum (same sampling fraction). Method provides greater precision than for simple random sampling with the same sample size, and this precision is better when dealing with characteristics that are the same (homogeneous) strata.

- *Disproportionate stratification*. With disproportionate stratification, the sampling fraction may vary from one stratum to the next. If differences are explored in the characteristics being measured across strata then disproportionate stratification can provide better precision than proportionate stratification, when the sample points are correctly allocated to strata. In general, given similar costs you would always choose proportionate stratification.

(d)   Cluster sampling

Cluster sampling is a sampling technique in which the entire population of interest is divided into groups, or clusters, and a random sample of these clusters is selected. Each cluster must be mutually exclusive, and together the clusters must include the entire population. After clusters are selected, then all data points within the clusters are selected. No data points from non-selected clusters are included in the sample. This differs from stratified sampling, in which some data values are selected from each group. When all the data values within a cluster are selected, the technique is referred to as one-stage cluster sampling. If a subset of units is selected randomly from each selected cluster, it is called two-stage cluster sampling. Cluster sampling can also be made in three or more stages: it is then referred to as multistage cluster sampling. The main reason for using cluster sampling is that it is usually much cheaper and more convenient to sample the population in clusters rather than randomly. In some cases, constructing a sampling frame that identifies every population element is too expensive or impossible. Cluster sampling can also reduce cost when the population elements are scattered over a wide area.

(e)   Multistage sampling

With *multistage sampling*, we select a sample by using combinations of different sampling methods. For example, in stage 1, we might use cluster sampling to choose clusters from a population. Then, in stage 2, we might use simple random sampling to select a subset of elements from each chosen cluster for the final sample.

6.1.3.2 Non-probability sampling

In many situations it is not possible to select the kinds of probability samples used in large-scale surveys. For example, we may be required to seek the views of local family run businesses that are experiencing financial difficulties during the bank credit crunch of 2007–2009. In this situation there are no easily accessible lists of businesses experiencing difficulties, or there may never be a list created or available. The question of obtaining a sample in this situation is achievable by using *non-probability sampling* methods to collect the required sample data.

Figure 6.2 illustrates the four primary types of non-probability sampling methods.

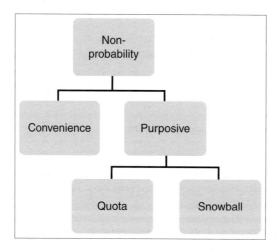

Figure 6.2

We can divide non-probability sampling methods into two broad types: convenience or purposive:

(a) Convenience sampling

Convenience (or availability) sampling is a method of choosing subjects who are available or easy to find. This method is also sometimes referred to as haphazard, accidental, or availability sampling. The primary advantage of the method is that it is very easy to carry out, relative to other methods. Problems can occur with this survey method in that you can never guarantee that the sample is representative of the population. Convenience sampling is a popular method with researchers and provides some data that can be analysed, but the type of statistics that can be applied to the data is compromised by uncertainties over the nature of the population that the survey data represents.

(b) Purposive sampling

Purposive sampling is a sampling method in which elements are chosen based on the purpose of the study. Purposive sampling may involve studying the entire population of some limited group (accounts department at a local engineering firm) or a subset of a population (chartered accountants). As with other non-probability sampling methods, purposive sampling does not produce a sample that is representative of a larger population, but it can be exactly what is needed in some cases—study of organization, community, or some other clearly defined and relatively limited group. Examples of two popular purposive sampling methods include: quota sampling and snowball sampling.

- **Quota sampling**

  Quota sampling is designed to overcome the most obvious flaw of availability sampling. Rather than taking just anyone, you set quotas to ensure that the sample you get represents certain characteristics in proportion to their prevalence in the population. Note that for this method, you have to know something about the characteristics of the population ahead of time. There are two types of quota sampling: proportional and non proportional.

  - In *proportional quota sampling* you want to represent the major characteristics of the population by sampling a proportional amount of each. For instance, if you know the population has 25% women and 75% men, and that you want a total sample size of 400, you will continue sampling until you get those percentages and then you will stop. So, if you've already got the 100 women for your sample, but not the 300 men, you will continue to sample men even if legitimate women respondents come along, you will not sample them because you have already 'met your quota'. The primary problem with this form of sampling is that even when we know that a quota sample is representative of the particular characteristics for which quotas have been set, we have no way of knowing if the sample is representative in terms of any other characteristics. If we set quotas for age, we are likely to attain a sample with good representativeness on age, but one that may not be very representative in terms of gender, education, or other pertinent factors.

  - In *non-proportional quota sampling* you specify the minimum number of sampled data points you want in each category. In this case you are not concerned with having the correct proportions but with achieving the numbers in each category. This method is the non-probabilistic analogue of stratified random sampling in that it is typically used to assure that smaller groups are adequately represented in your sample.

  Finally, researchers often introduce bias when allowed to self-select respondents, which is usually the case in this form of survey research. In choosing males, interviewers are more likely to choose those that are better-dressed, seem more approachable or less threatening. That may be understandable from a practical point of view, but it introduces bias into research findings.

- **Snowball sampling**

  In *snowball sampling*, you begin by identifying someone who meets the criteria for inclusion in your study. You then ask them to recommend others who they may know who also meet the criteria. Thus the sample group appears to grow like a rolling snowball. This sampling technique is often used in hidden populations which are difficult for researchers to access, including: firms with financial difficulties, or students struggling with their studies. The method creates a sample with questionable representativeness, and it can be difficult to judge how a sample compares to a larger population. Furthermore, an issue arises in who the respondents refer you to, for example, friends will refer you to friends but are less likely to refer to ones they don't consider as friends, for whatever reason. This creates a further bias within the sample that makes it difficult to say anything about the population.

> **Note** The primary difference between probability methods of sampling and non-probability methods is that in the latter you do not know the likelihood that any element of a population will be selected for study.

6.1.4 Types of error

In this text book we will be concerned with sampling from populations using probability sampling methods which are the prerequisite for the application of the statistical tests. If we base our decisions on a sample, rather than the whole population, by definition we are going to make some errors. The concept of sampling implies that we'll also have to deal with a number of types of errors, including: sampling error, coverage error, measurement error, and non-response error.

(a) What is sampling error?

Sampling error is the calculated statistical imprecision due to surveying a random sample instead of the entire population. The margin of error provides an estimate of how much the results of the sample may differ due to chance when compared to what would have been found if the entire population were interviewed.

(b) Coverage error

Coverage error is associated with the inability to contact portions of the population. Telephone surveys usually exclude people who do not have access to a landline telephone in their homes. This will exclude people who are not at home or unavailable for a number of reasons: at work, in prison, on holiday, or unavailable at the times when the telephone calls are made.

(c) Measurement error

Measurement error is error, or bias, that occurs when surveys do not survey what they intended to measure. This type of error results from flaws in the measuring instrument, e.g. question wording, question order, interviewer error, timing, and question response options. This is the most common type of error faced by the polling industry.

(d) Non-response error

Non-response error results from not being able to interview people who would be eligible to take the survey. Many households now have answering machines and caller identification that prevent easy contact, or people may simply not want to respond to calls. Non-response bias is the difference in responses of those people who complete the survey against those who refuse to for any reason. While the error itself cannot be calculated, response rates can be calculated and there are countless ways to do so.

The rest of this text will focus on samples that have been randomly selected and the associated statistical techniques that can be applied to a randomly selected data set.

X
Sampling error Sampling error refers to the error that results from taking one sample rather than taking a census of the entire population.

6.2 Sampling from a Population

6.2.1 Introduction

When we wish to know something about a particular population it is usually impractical, especially when considering large populations, to collect data from every unit of that population. It is more efficient to collect data from a sample of the population under study and from the sample make estimates of the population parameters. Essentially, based on a sample, we make generalizations about a population.

6.2.2 Population vs. sample

To describe the difference between a population and a sample, we can say as follows:

- *Population*—a complete set of counts or measurements derived from all objects possessing one or more common characteristic, such as height, age, sales, income, etc. Measures such as means and standard deviations derived from the population data are known as population parameters.
- *Sample*—a proportion of a population under study derived from sample data. Measures such as means and standard deviations are known as sample statistics or estimators.

Parameter	Population	Sample
Size	N	n
Mean	μ	$\bar{x}$
Standard deviation	σ	S
Proportion	π	ρ

The method of using samples to estimate population parameters is known as *statistical inference*. Statistical inference draws upon the probability results discussed in previous chapters, especially the normal distribution. To distinguish between population and sample parameters the following symbols are used.

6.2.3 Sampling distributions

The main issue that we shall shortly explore is that we wish to collect a sample (or samples) from a population and use this sample to provide an estimate of the population parameters (mean, standard deviation, proportion) by using the sample parameter value (sample mean, sample proportion, and sample standard deviation). For example, you may wish to check the quantity of muesli per bag produced by the manufacturing process. To answer this type of question we need to know how the parameter being measured varies. This is called the sampling distribution and we will now explore the sampling distribution of the mean.

6.2.4 Sampling distribution of the mean

In this section we will explore what we mean by the *sampling distribution of the mean*. Let's assume that a sample of size 200 is taken and that the average weight is 135.5 kgs. Another sample is taken and the mean weight is 132.5 kgs. A large number of samples might be taken and the sample means calculated. Obviously, these means are unlikely to be equal and they can be plotted as a frequency distribution of the mean. *What is really important here is that the mean of all the sample means has some interesting properties.* It is identical to the overall population mean.

> **Note** A *sample mean* is unbiased since the mean of all sample means of size n selected from the population is equal to the population mean, μ.

▷ Example 6.3

To illustrate this property consider the problem of tossing a fair die. The die has 6 numbers (1, 2, 3, 4, 5, and 6) with each number likely to have the same frequency of occurrence. If we then take all possible samples of size 2 from this population then we will be able to illustrate two important results of the sampling distribution of the sample means.

Excel solution—Example 6.3

Figure 6.3 illustrates the Excel solution.

	A	B	C	D
1	Sampling distribution of the mean			
2	Example 6.3			
3				
4		Population:		
5				
6				
7		Die value, X	X^2	
8		1	1	=B6^2
9		2	4	
10		3	9	
11		4	16	
12		5	25	
13		6	36	=B11^2
14				
15		N = 6		=COUNT(B8:B13)
16		ΣX = 21		=SUM(B8:B13)
17		ΣX^2 = 91		=SUM(C8:C13)
18		Mean = 3.5		=C16/C15
19		Mean = 3.5		=AVERAGE(B8:B13)
20		Population SDev = 1.7078		=SQRT(C17/C15-C18^2)
21		Population SDev = 1.7078		=STDEVP(B8:B13)

Figure 6.3

Unbiased When the mean of the sampling distribution of a statistic is equal to a population parameter, that statistic is said to be an unbiased estimator of the parameter.

→ **Excel Solution**

X Cells B8:B13	Values
X² Cells C8:C13	Formula: =B8^2, copy formula C8:C13
N = Cell C15	Formula: =COUNT(B8:B13)
ΣX = Cell C16	Formula: =SUM(B8:B13)
ΣX² = Cell C17	Formula: =SUM(C8:C13)
Mean = Cell C18	Formula: =C16/C15
Mean = Cell C19	Formula: =AVERAGE(B8:B13)
Pop Sd = Cell C20	Formula: =SQRT(C17/C15–C18^2)
Pop Sd = Cell C21	Formula: =STDEVP(B8:B13)

The Excel function STDEVP calculates the standard deviation assuming data represents the population values. From the population data values (1, 2, 3, 4, 5, and 6) we can calculate the population mean and standard deviation using equations (4.1) and (4.3):

$$\text{Population mean}, \mu = \frac{\sum X}{N} = \frac{21}{6} = 3.5$$

$$\text{Population standard deviation}, \sigma = \sqrt{\frac{\sum X^2}{N} - (\mu)^2} = \sqrt{\frac{91}{6} - (3.5)^2} = 1.7078$$

If we now sample all possible samples of size 2 (n = 2) from the population then we would have the following sampling distribution of size 2. We can calculate the sample mean mean and corresponding standard deviation of the sample means as illustrated in Figure 6.4 below:

	E	F	G	H	I	J	K	L	M	N
4		Samples:								
5										
6			Sample pairs							
7		Value 1	Value 2	Value mean, Xbar		f	f * Xbar		f * Xbar²	
8		1	1	1	=(F8+G8)/2	1	1	=J8*H8	1	=K8*H8
9		1	2	1.5		2	3		4.5	
10		1	3	2		2	4		8	
11		1	4	2.5		2	5		12.5	
12		1	5	3		2	6		18	
13		1	6	3.5		2	7		24.5	
14		2	2	2		1	2		4	
15		2	3	2.5		2	5		12.5	
16		2	4	3		2	6		18	
17		2	5	3.5		2	7		24.5	
18		2	6	4		2	8		32	
19		3	3	3		1	3		9	
20		3	4	3.5		2	7		24.5	
21		3	5	4		2	8		32	
22		3	6	4.5		2	9		40.5	
23		4	4	4		1	4		16	
24		4	5	4.5		2	9		40.5	
25		4	6	5		2	10		50	
26		5	5	5		1	5		25	
27		5	6	5.5		2	11		60.5	
28		6	6	6	=(F28+G28)/2	1	6	=J28*H28	36	=K28*H28
29										
30		Σf =	36	=SUM(J8:J28)						
31		ΣfX =	126	=SUM(K8:K28)						
32		ΣfX² =	493.5	=SUM(M8:M28)						
33		Mean =	3.5	=G31/G30						
34		SD =	1.20761473	=SQRT(G32/G30-G33^2)						

Figure 6.4

→ **Excel Solution**

Sample pairs
Value 1 Cells F8:F28   Values
Value 2 Cells G8:G28   Values
Value mean Cell H8   Formula: =(F8+G8)/2
                              Copy formula from H8:H28
f Cells J8:J28   Values
f * Xbar Cell K8   Formula: =J8*H8
                             Copy formula from K8:K28
f * Xbar² Cell M8   Formula: =K8*H8
                             Copy formula from M8:M28
Σf = Cell G30   Formula: =SUM(J8:J28)
Σfx = Cell G31   Formula: =SUM(K8:K28)
Σfx² = Cell G32   Formula: =SUM(M8:M28)
Mean = Cell G33   Formula: =G31/G30
SD = Cell G34   Formula: =−SQRT(G32/G30−G33^2)

The sample mean ($\bar{X}$) is calculated using equation (6.1) as follows:

$$\bar{X} = \frac{\sum X}{n}$$

(6.1)

For sample pair (2, 6) the sample mean is equal to 4. For each sample pair we would have a different sample mean as can be observed in Figure 6.4 (column H). From this list of sample means we can calculate the overall mean of the sample means using equation (6.2):

$$\bar{\bar{X}} = \frac{\sum \bar{X}}{\sum f}$$

(6.2)

From Excel, the mean of the sample means ($\bar{\bar{X}}$) is equal to 3.5. From the die experiment we observe $\bar{\bar{X}} = \mu = 3.5$. Furthermore the mean of the sample means is an *unbiased estimator of the population mean*:

$$\bar{\bar{X}} = \mu$$

(6.3)

The standard error of the sample means measures the standard deviation of all sample means from the overall mean. We know the population data ranges from 1–6 with a population standard deviation of 1.7078. We can repeat this exercise to calculate the standard deviation for the samples means using equation (6.4):

$$\sigma_{\bar{x}} = \sqrt{\frac{\sum f\bar{X}^2}{\sum f} - \left(\bar{\bar{X}}\right)^2}$$

(6.4)

From Excel, the standard deviation of the sample means ($\sigma_{\bar{x}}$) is equal to 1.2076. From this we conclude a difference exists between the two values. Why? Observe that in the sampling example we calculate a series of sample means of size 2 and then calculated the overall mean of the sample means. When averaging you replace the data set with a single number that measures the middle value of the data set. The mean will be influenced by any extreme data points in the sample but by repeating the experiment to calculate a series of means we should find that the range between the largest and smallest means is less than the range within the original data sets. In other words, averages have smaller variability than single observations. The *standard deviation of the sampling mean distribution* is not equal to the population standard deviation ($\sigma_{\bar{x}} < \sigma$). In fact, the standard deviation of the sample means is a *biased estimate* of the population standard deviation.

> **Note** The standard deviation of the sample means is a *biased estimate* of the population standard deviation because it is not necessarily the same as the population standard deviation.

It can be shown that the relationship between sample and population is represented by equation (6.5):

$$\sigma_{\bar{x}} = \frac{\sigma}{\sqrt{n}}$$

(6.5)

> **Note** The standard deviation of the sample means is also called the standard error of the sample means.

From equation (6.5) we observe that as n increases, the value of the standard deviation of the sampling mean approaches zero ($\sigma_{\bar{x}} \to 0$). In other words, as n increases the spread of the sample mean decreases to zero. In this situation the measured random variable would have to be constant to produce this result.

> **Note** The *law of large numbers* implies that the sample mean ($\bar{X}$) will approach the population mean (μ) as n increases in value.

Using the numbers from our example, the values of the mean and standard deviation of the sampling means is calculated as follows:

$$\bar{\bar{X}} = \frac{\sum \bar{X}}{\sum f} = \frac{126}{36} = 3.5$$

$$\sigma_{\bar{x}} = \sqrt{\frac{\sum f \bar{X}^2}{\sum f} - \left(\bar{\bar{X}}\right)^2} = \sqrt{\frac{493.6}{36} - (3.5)^2} = 1.2076$$

6.2.5 Sampling from a normal population

If we select a random variable X from a population that is normally distributed with population mean μ and standard deviation σ then we can state this relationship using the notation
$X \sim N(\mu, \sigma^2)$.

Figure 6.5 illustrates the relationship between the variable and the distribution.

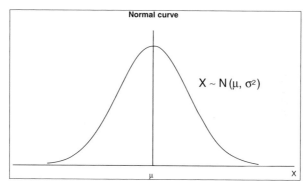

Figure 6.5

If we choose a sample from a normal population then we can show that the sample
means are also normally distributed with a mean of μ and a standard deviation of the
sampling mean given by equation (6.5), where n is the sample size on which the sampling
distribution was based. Figure 6.6 illustrates the relationship between the sampling mean
and the normal distribution.

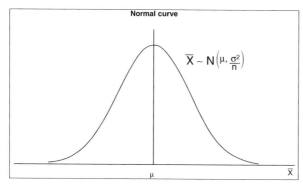

Figure 6.6

▷ Example 6.4

Consider the problem of selecting 1000 random samples from a population that is
assumed to be normally distributed with mean £45000 and standard deviation of
£10000. The population values are based on 40000 data points and the sampling distribution is illustrated in Figure 6.7. We observe from Figure 6.7 that the population data is
approximately normal.

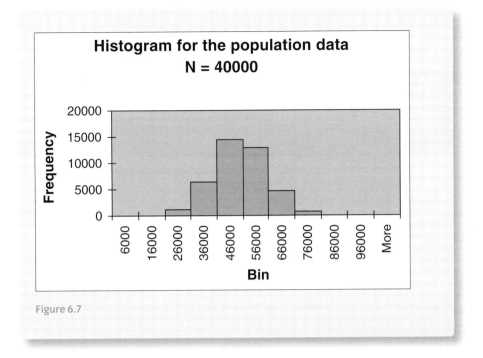

Figure 6.7

If we now sample 1000 data points from this population where each sample is of size n then we observe from Figure 6.8 that the sampling distributions of the mean is approximately normal for sample distributions of size n = 2, 5, 10, and 40. From the histograms we observe that the sample means are less spread out about the mean as the sample sizes increase.

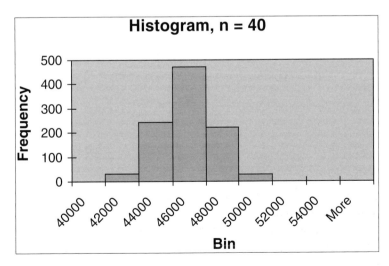

Figure 6.8 (a)

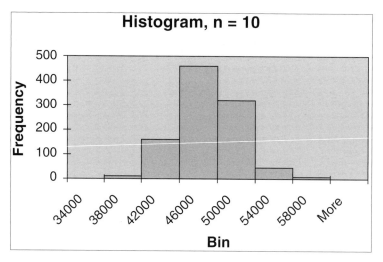

Figure 6.8 (b)

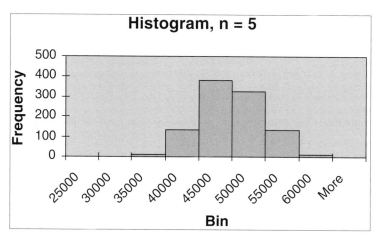

Figure 6.8 (c)

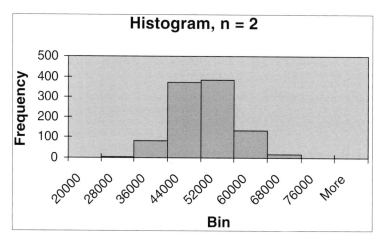

Figure 6.8 (d)

> **Note** From these observations we conclude that if we sample from population that is normally distributed with mean μ and standard deviation σ (X ~ N(μ, σ²)), then the *sampling mean is normally distributed* with mean μ and standard deviation of the sample means of $\sigma_{\bar{x}} = \sigma/\sqrt{n}$.

This relationship is represented by equation (6.6) as follows:

$$\bar{X} \sim N\left(\mu, \frac{\sigma^2}{n}\right)$$

(6.6)

Given that we now know that the sample mean is normally distributed then we can solve a range of problems using the methods to be described in Chapter 6. The standardized sample mean Z value is given by equation (6.7) as follows:

$$Z = \frac{\bar{X} - \mu}{\sigma/\sqrt{n}}$$

(6.7)

▷ Example 6.5

Diet X runs a number of weight reduction centres within a large town in the north east of England. From the historical data it is found that the weight of participants is normally distributed with a mean of 150 lbs and a standard deviation of 25 lbs. This can be written in mathematical notation as X ~ N (150, 25²). Calculate the probability that the average sample weight is greater than 160 lbs when 25 participants are randomly selected for the sample?

Excel solution—Example 6.5

Figure 6.9 illustrates the Excel solution.

	A	B	C	D	E
1	**Sampling Distribution - Example 6.5**				
2					
3			$P(\bar{X} > 160)$		
4					
5			Population: X ~ N (150, 25²)		
6					
7			Mean μ =	150	
8			Standard Deviation σ =	25	
9					
10		Sample:			
11			n =	25	
12			$\bar{X}$ =	160	
13			$\sigma_{\bar{X}}$ =	5	=D8/D11^0.5
14					
15			Z =	2	=(D12-D7)/D13
16			Z =	2	=STANDARDIZE(D12,D7,D13)
17					
18			$P(\bar{X} > 160)$ =	0.022750132	=1-NORMDIST(D12,D7,D13,TRUE)
19			$P(\bar{X} > 160)$ =	0.022750132	=1-NORMSDIST(D16)

Figure 6.9

→ **Excel Solution**

Population mean = Cell D7	Value
Population standard deviation = Cell D8	Value
Sample size n = Cell D11	Value
Sample mean = Cell D12	Value
Standard error of mean = Cell D13	Formula: =D8/D11^0.5
Z = Cell D15	Formula: =(D12–D7)/D13
Z = Cell D16	Formula: =STANDARDIZE(D12,D7,D13)
P = Cell D18	Formula: =1–NORMDIST(D12,D7,D13,TRUE)
P = Cell D19	Formula: =1–NORMSDIST(D16)

The problem requires the solution to the problem $P(\overline{X} > 160)$. Figure 6.10 illustrates the region to be found that represents this probability. Excel can be used to solve this problem by either using the NORMDIST() or NORMSDIST() functions.

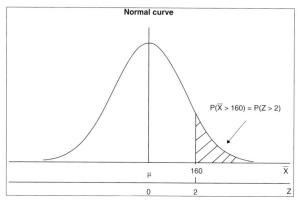

Normal curve

$P(\overline{X} > 160) = P(Z > 2)$

μ   160 $\overline{X}$

0   2   Z   Figure 6.10

📎 **Note**   We already described both Excel functions NORMDIST() and NORMSDIST(). In this example they result with the same value, but ensure you do not confuse them.

Given the population mean ($\mu = 150$), population standard deviation ($\sigma = 25$), sample size ($n = 25$), and standard error ($\sigma_{\bar{x}} = \sigma/\sqrt{n} = 25/\sqrt{25} = 5$).

Method 1—NORMDIST() function: =NORMDIST($\overline{X}$, μ, $\sigma_{\bar{x}}$, TRUE)

From Excel, $P(\overline{X} > 160) = 1 - \text{NORMDIST}(\overline{X}, \mu, \sigma_{\bar{x}}, \text{TRUE}) = 0.022750132$.

Method 2—NORMSDIST() function: =NORMSDIST(Z)

From equation (6.7) we have:

$$Z = \frac{\bar{X} - \mu}{\sigma/\sqrt{n}} = \frac{160 - 150}{25/\sqrt{25}} = \frac{10}{5} = 2$$

From Excel, $P(\bar{X} > 160) = P(Z > 2) = 1 - \text{NORMSDIST}(Z) = 0.022750132$.

As expected, both methods provided the same answer to the problem of calculating the required probability.

> ❋ **Interpretation**   Based upon a random sample the probability that the sample mean is greater than 160 lbs is 0.0228 or 2.28%.

↳ Example 6.6

Calculate the probability that the sample mean lies between 146 lbs and 158 lbs for the population distribution described in Example 6.5.

Excel solution—Example 6.6

Figure 6.11 illustrates the Excel solution.

	A	B	C	D	E
1	Sampling Distribution - Example 6.6				
2					
3		$P(140 < \bar{X} < 160)$?			
4					
5		Population: $X \sim N(150, 25^2)$	$\mu =$	150	
6			$\sigma =$	25	
7					
8		Sample:	$n =$	25	
9			$\sigma_{\bar{X}} =$	5	=D6/D8^0.5
10			$\bar{X}_1 =$	140	
11			$\bar{X}_2 =$	158	
12			$Z_1 =$	-2	=(D10-D5)/D9
13			$Z_2 =$	1.6	=(D11-D5)/D9
14					
15			$P(140 < \bar{X} < 158) =$	0.922450576	=NORMDIST(D11,D5,D9,TRUE)-NORMDIST(D10,D5,D9,TRUE)
16			$P(-2 < Z < 1.6) =$	0.922450576	=NORMSDIST(D13)-NORMSDIST(D12)

Figure 6.11

> ➔ **Excel Solution**
>
> Population mean = Cell D5   Value
> Population standard deviation = Cell D6   Value

Sample size n = Cell D8	Value
Standard error = Cell D9	Formula: =D6/D8^0.5
Sample 1 mean = Cell D10	Value
Sample 2 mean = Cell D11	Value
Z_1 = Cell D12	Formula: =(D10–D5)/D9
Z_2 = Cell D13	Formula: =(D11–D5)/D9
P = Cell D15	Formula: =NORMDIST(D11,D5,D9, TRUE)–NORMDIST(D10,D5,D9,TRUE)
P = Cell D16	Formula: =NORMSDIST(D13)– NORMSDIST(D12)

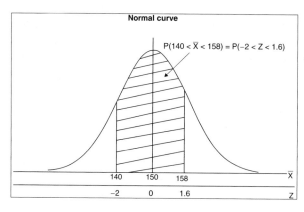

Figure 6.12

The problem requires the solution to the problem $P(140 < \bar{X} < 158)$.

Figure 6.12 illustrates the region to be found that represents this probability. Again, Excel can be used to solve this problem by either using the NORMDIST() or NORMSDIST() functions.

Given the population mean ($\mu = 150$), population standard deviation ($\sigma = 25$), sample size ($n = 25$), and standard error ($\sigma_{\bar{x}} = \sigma/\sqrt{n} = 25/\sqrt{25} = 5$).

Method 1—NORMDIST() function: =NORMDIST($\bar{X}$, μ, $\sigma_{\bar{x}}$, TRUE)

From Excel, $P(140 < \bar{X} < 158)$ = NORMDIST($\bar{X}_2$, μ, $\sigma_{\bar{x}}$, TRUE) – NORMDIST($\bar{X}_1$, μ, $\sigma_{\bar{x}}$, TRUE) = 0.922450576.

Method 2—NORMSDIST() function: =NORMSDIST(Z)

From equation (6.6) we have:

$$Z_1 = \frac{\bar{X}_1 - \mu}{\sigma/\sqrt{n}} = \frac{140 - 150}{25/\sqrt{25}} = \frac{-10}{5} = -2$$

$$Z_2 = \frac{\bar{X}_2 - \mu}{\sigma/\sqrt{n}} = \frac{158 - 150}{25/\sqrt{25}} = \frac{8}{5} = 1.6$$

From Excel, $P(140 < \bar{X} < 158)$ = $P(-2 < Z < 1.6)$ = NORMSDIST(Z_2) – NORMSDIST(Z_1) = 0.922450576.

Both methods provided the same answer to the problem of calculating the required probability.

> ✳ **Interpretation**   Based upon a random sample the probability that the sample mean is between 140 and 158 lbs is 0.9224 or 92.24%.

6.2.6 Sampling from a non-normal population

In Section 6.2.5 we sampled from a population which is normally distributed and we stated that the sample means will be normally distributed with mean μ and standard deviation $\sigma_{\bar{x}}$. What if the data does not come from the normal distribution? It can be shown that if we select a random sample from a non-normal distribution then the *sampling mean will be approximately normal* with mean μ and standard deviation $\sigma_{\bar{x}}$ if the sample size is sufficiently large. In most cases the value of n should be at least 30 for non-symmetric distributions and at least 20 for symmetric distributions, before we apply this approximation. This relationship is already represented by equation (6.6).

This leads to an important concept in statistics and is known as the **Central Limit Theorem**. The Central Limit Theorem provides us with a shortcut to the information required for constructing a sampling distribution. By applying the Central Limit Theorem we can obtain the descriptive values for a sampling distribution (usually the mean and the standard error, which is computed from the sampling variance) and we can also obtain probabilities associated with any of the sample means in the sampling distribution.

> **Note**   The Central Limit Theorem states that no matter what the shape of the population distribution, the sampling distribution of the means will be approximately normal with increasing sample sizes providing better approximations to the normal distribution.

If the mean is approximately normally distributed then we can solve a range of problems using the methods described in Chapter 6. The standardized sample mean Z value is already given by equation (6.7).

> ▷ **Example 6.7**
>
> Consider the sampling of 50 electrical components from a production run where historically the components' average lifetime was found to be 950 hours with a standard deviation of 25 hours. The population data is right-skewed and therefore cannot be considered to be normally distributed. Calculate the probability that the sample mean is less than 958 hours?

X

Central Limit Theorem
The Central Limit Theorem states that whenever a random sample is taken from any distribution (μ, σ^2), then the sample mean will be approximately normally distributed with mean μ and variance σ^2/n.

Excel solution—Example 6.7

Figure 6.13 illustrates the Excel solution.

	A	B	C	D	E
1	Sampling Distribution - Example 6.7				
2					
3		Population:	$\mu =$	950	
4			$\sigma =$	25	
5					
6		Sample:	$n =$	50	
7			$\sigma_{\bar{X}} =$	3.5355339	=D4/D6^0.5
8			$\bar{X} =$	958	
9			$Z =$	2.2627417	=(D8-D3)/D7
10					
11			$P(\bar{X} < 702) =$	0.9881742	=NORMDIST(D8,D3,D7,TRUE)
12			$P(Z < 1) =$	0.9881742	=NORMSDIST(D9)

Figure 6.13

> ➡ **Excel Solution**
>
> Population mean = Cell D3 — Value
> Population standard deviation = Cell D4 — Value
> Sample size n = Cell D6 — Value
> Standard error = Cell D7 — Formula: =D4/D6^0.5
> Sample mean = Cell D8 — Value
> Z = Cell D9 — Formula: =(D8–D3)/D7
> P = Cell D11 — Formula: =NORMDIST(D8,D3,D7,TRUE)
> P = Cell D12 — Formula: =NORMSDIST(D9)

Since the sample size is reasonably large, we will apply the Central Limit Theorem to the problem and assume that the sampling mean distribution is approximately normally distributed. From equation (6.6) we have $\bar{X} \sim N(\mu, \sigma^2/n) = N(950, 25^2/50)$.

The problem requires the solution to the problem $P(\bar{X} < 958)$. Figure 6.14 illustrates the region to be found that represents this probability. Excel can be used to solve this problem by either using the NORMDIST () or NORMSDIST () functions.

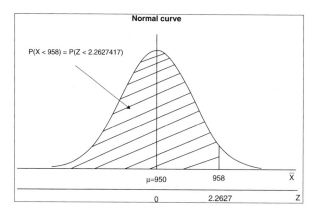

Figure 6.14

Given the population mean ($\mu = 950$), population standard deviation ($\sigma = 25$), sample size ($n = 50$), and standard error ($\sigma_{\bar{x}} = \sigma/\sqrt{n} = 25/\sqrt{50} = 3.535533906$).

Method 1—NORMDIST() function: =NORMDIST($\bar{X}$, μ, $\sigma_{\bar{x}}$, TRUE)

From Excel, $P(\bar{X} < 958) = $ NORMDIST($\bar{X}$, μ, $\sigma_{\bar{x}}$, TRUE) = 0.988174192.

Method 2—NORMSDIST() function: =NORMSDIST(Z)

From equation (6.7) we have:

$$Z = \frac{\bar{X} - \mu}{\sigma/\sqrt{n}} = \frac{958 - 950}{25/\sqrt{50}} = \frac{8}{3.535533906} = 2.2627417$$

From Excel, $P(\bar{X} < 958) = P(Z < 2.2627417) = $ NORMSDIST(Z) = 0.988174192.

Both methods provided the same answer to the problem of calculating the required probability.

> ❋ **Interpretation**　Based upon a random sample the probability that the sample mean is less than 958 hours is 0.988174192 or 98.82%.

In the previous cases we assumed that sampling will have taken place with replacement (very large or infinite population). If no replacement is undertaken then equation (6.5) is modified by a correction factor to give equation (6.8) as follows:

$$\sigma_{\bar{x}} = \frac{\sigma}{\sqrt{n}} \times \sqrt{\frac{N - n}{N - 1}} \tag{6.8}$$

Where N = size of population and n = size of sample.

▷ Example 6.8

A random sample of 30 part-time employees is chosen without replacement from a firm employing 200 part-time workers. The mean hours worked per month is 60 hours with a standard deviation of 5 hours. Determine the probability that the sample mean: (a) will be greater than 60 but less than 62 hours and (b) be over 63 hours. In this example we have a finite population of size N (= 200) and a sample size of 30 (n = 30). From equation (6.8) we can calculate the standard deviation of the sampling mean and then use Excel to calculate the two probability values.

Excel solution—Example 6.8

Figure 6.15 illustrates the Excel solution.

	A	B	C	D	E
1	Sampling Distribution - Example 6.8				
2					
3		Population: X ~ N (150, 252)	$\mu =$	60	
4			$\sigma =$	5	
5					
6		Sample:	N =	200	
7			n =	30	
8					
9			$\sigma_{\bar{X}} =$	0.843737398	=(D4/D7^0.5)*SQRT((D6-D7)/(D6-1))
10					
11			$(a) P(60 < \bar{X} < 62)$		
12			$X_1 =$	60	
13			$X_2 =$	62	
14			$P(60 < \bar{X} < 62) =$	0.491115714	=NORMDIST(D13,D3,D9,TRUE)-NORMDIST(D12,D3,D9,TRUE)
15			$Z_1 =$	0	=(D12-D3)/D9
16			$Z_2 =$	2.370405773	=(D13-D3)/D9
17			$P(0 < Z < 2.37) =$	0.491115714	=NORMSDIST(D16)-NORMSDIST(D15)
18					
19			$(b) P(\bar{X} > 63)$		
20			X =	63	
21			Z =	3.55560866	=(D20-D3)/D9
22			$P(\bar{X} > 63) =$	0.000188553	=1-NORMDIST(D20,D3,D9,TRUE)

Figure 6.15

➜ **Excel Solution**

Population mean = Cell D3   Value

Population standard deviation = Cell D4   Value

Population size N = Cell D6   Value

Sample size n = Cell D7   Value

Standard error = Cell D9   Formula: =(D4/D7^0.5)*
                                                 SQRT((D6–D7)/(D6–1))

(a)

Sample 1 mean = Cell D12   Value

Sample 2 mean = Cell D13   Value

P = Cell D14   Formula: =NORMDIST(D13,D3,D9,TRUE)–
                                                 NORMDIST(D12,D3,D9,TRUE)

Z_1 = Cell D15   Formula: =(D12–D3)/D9

Z_2 = Cell D16   Formula: =(D13–D3)/D9

P = Cell D17   Formula: =NORMSDIST(D16)–
                                                 NORMSDIST(D15)

(b)

Sample mean = Cell D20   Value

Z = Cell D21   Formula: =(D20–D3)/D9

P = Cell D22   Formula: =1–NORMDIST(D20,D3,D9,TRUE)

Since the sample size is relatively large for the population, we will apply the Central Limit Theorem to the problem and assume that the sampling mean distribution is approximately normally distributed. From equation (6.6) we have $\bar{X} \sim N(\mu, \sigma^2/n)$.

(a) The problem requires the solution to the problem $P(60 < \overline{X} < 62)$.

Figure 6.16 illustrates the region to be found that represents this probability.

Excel can be used to solve this problem by either using the NORMDIST() or NORMS-DIST() functions. Given population mean ($\mu = 60$), population standard deviation ($\sigma = 5$), sample size ($n = 30$), population size ($N = 200$), and standard error of the mean ($\sigma_{\overline{x}} = 0.84373$).

Calculate $P(60 < \overline{X} < 62)$.

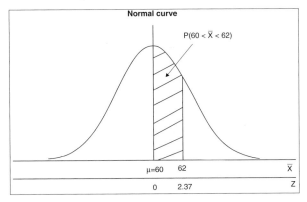

Normal curve

$P(60 < \overline{X} < 62)$

μ=60   62 $\overline{X}$

0   2.37   Z

Figure 6.16

Method 1—NORMDIST() function: =NORMDIST($\overline{X}$, μ, $\sigma_{\overline{x}}$, TRUE)

From Excel, $P(60 < \overline{X} < 62)$ = NORMDIST(D13, D3, D9, TRUE) – NORMDIST(D12, D3, D9, TRUE) = 0.491115714.

Method 2—NORMSDIST() function: =NORMSDIST(Z)

From equation (6.8) we have:

$$Z_1 = \frac{\overline{X}_1 - \mu}{\sigma_{\overline{x}}} = \frac{60 - 60}{0.84373} = 0$$

$$Z_2 = \frac{\overline{X}_2 - \mu}{\sigma_{\overline{x}}} = \frac{62 - 60}{0.84373} = 2.3704$$

From Excel, $P(60 < \overline{X} < 62)$ = $P(0 < Z < 2.3704)$ = NORMSDIST(Z_2) – NORMSDIST(Z_1) = 0.491115714.

Both methods provided the same answer to the problem of calculating the required probability.

✳ **Interpretation**   Based upon a random sample the probability that the sample mean is lies between 60 and 62 is 0.491115714 or 49.11%.

(b) The problem requires the solution to the problem $P(\overline{X} > 63)$.

Figure 6.17 illustrates the region to be found that represents this probability.

Excel can be used to solve this problem by either using the NORMDIST() or NORMSDIST() functions. Given population mean ($\mu = 60$), population standard deviation ($\sigma = 5$), sample size ($n = 30$), population size ($N = 200$), and standard error of the mean ($\sigma_{\bar{x}} = 0.84373$).

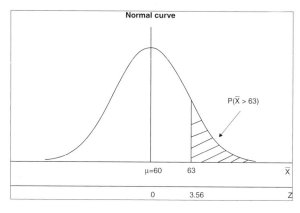

Figure 6.17

Calculate $P\left(\bar{X} > 63\right)$.

Method 1—NORMDIST() function: =NORMDIST($\bar{X}$, μ, $\sigma_{\bar{x}}$, TRUE)

From Excel, $P\left(\bar{X} > 63\right) = 1-$NORMDIST($\bar{X}$, μ, $\sigma_{\bar{x}}$, TRUE) $= 0.000188553$.

Method 2—NORMSDIST() function: =NORMSDIST(Z)

From equation (6.8) we have:

$$Z = \frac{\bar{X}-\mu}{\sigma_{\bar{x}}} = \frac{63 - 60}{0.84373} = 3.55560866$$

From Excel, $P\left(\bar{X} > 63\right) = P\left(Z > 3.55560866\right) = 1-$NORMSDIST(Z) $= 0.000188553$.

Both methods provided the same answer to the problem of calculating the required probability.

> ✳ **Interpretation**   Based upon a random sample the probability that the sample mean is greater than 63 is 0.000188553 or 0.02%.

6.2.7 Sampling distribution of the proportion

Consider the case where a variable has two possible values 'yes' or 'no', and we are interested in the proportion that choose 'yes' or 'no' in some survey, that measured the response of shoppers in deciding whether to purchase a particular product A. From the historical data it is found that 40% of people surveyed preferred product A and we would define this as the estimated population proportion, π, who prefers product A. If we then took a random sample from this population, it would be unlikely that exactly 40% would choose product A, but given sampling error it is likely that this proportion could be slightly less or slightly more than 40%. If we continued to sample proportions from this population, then each sample would have an individual sample proportion value, which when placed together, would form the sampling distribution of the sample proportion that choose product A.

The sampling distribution for the proportion is approximated using the binomial distribution, given that the binomial distribution represents the distribution of 'r' successes (choosing product A) from 'n' trials (or selections). The binomial distribution is the distribution of the total number of successes, whereas the distribution of the population proportion is the distribution of the mean number of successes. Given that the mean is the total divided by the sample size, n, then the sampling distribution of the proportions and the binomial distribution differ in that the sample proportion is the mean of the scores and the binomial distribution is dealing with the total number of successes. We know from equation (5.15) that the mean of a binomial distribution is given by the equation $\mu = n\pi$, where π *represents the population proportion*. If we divide through by 'n', then this equation gives equation (6.9) which represents the unbiased estimator of the *mean of the sampling distribution for the proportions*:

$$\mu_p = \pi \tag{6.9}$$

Equation (5.16) represents the variance of the binomial distribution which when divided by 'n' gives equation (6.10), the standard deviation of the sampling proportion σ_p (or standard error of the proportions), where π represents the population proportion:

$$\sigma_p = \sqrt{\frac{\pi(1-\pi)}{n}} \tag{6.10}$$

From equations (6.9) and (6.10) the sampling distribution of the proportion is approximated by a binomial distribution with mean (μ_p) and standard deviation (σ_p). Furthermore, the sampling distribution of the sample proportion (p) can be approximated with a normal distribution when the probability of success is approximately 0.5, and $n\pi$ and $n(1-\pi)$ are at least 5:

$$p \sim N\left(\pi, \frac{\pi(1-\pi)}{n}\right) \tag{6.11}$$

The standardized sample mean Z value is given by modifying equation (6.7) to give equation (6.12) as follows:

$$Z = \frac{p - \pi}{\sqrt{\frac{\pi(1-\pi)}{n}}} \tag{6.12}$$

▷ Example 6.9

It is known that 25% of workers in a factory own a personal computer. Find the probability that at least 26% of a random sample of 80 workers will own a personal computer. In this example, we have the population proportion $\pi = 0.25$ and sample size $n = 80$. The problem requires the calculation of $P(p \geq 0.26)$.

Excel solution—Example 6.9

Figure 6.18 illustrates the Excel solution.

	A	B	C	D	E
1	Sampling Distribution - Example 6.9				
2					
3		Population: $\rho \sim N\,[\Pi,\,n\Pi(1-\Pi)]$	$\Pi =$	0.25	
4					
5		Sample:	$\rho =$	0.26	
6			$n =$	80	
7					
8			$\sigma_{\bar{x}} =$	0.0484123	=SQRT(D3*(1-D3)/D6)
9					
10			$Z =$	0.206559	=(D5-D3)/D8
11					
12			$P(\rho => 0.26) =$	0.418177	=1-NORMDIST(D5,D3,D8,TRUE)
13					
14			$P(\rho => 0.26) =$	0.418177	=1-NORMSDIST(D10)

Figure 6.18

> ➜ **Excel Solution**
>
> Population proportion = Cell D3   Value
> Sample proportion = Cell D5   Value
> Sample size n = Cell D6   Value
> Standard error = Cell D8   Formula: =SQRT(D3*(1−D3)/D6)
> Z = Cell D10   Formula: =(D5−D3)/D8
> P = Cell D12   Formula: =1−NORMDIST(D5,D3,D8,TRUE)
> P = Cell D14   Formula: =1−NORMSDIST(D10)

From equation (6.10) the standard error for the sampling distribution of the proportion is:

$$\sigma_\rho = \sqrt{\frac{\pi(1-\pi)}{n}} = \sqrt{\frac{0.25(1-0.25)}{80}} = 0.04841$$

Substituting this value into equation (6.12) gives the standardized Z value:

$$Z = \frac{\rho - \pi}{\sqrt{\dfrac{\pi(1-\pi)}{n}}} = \frac{0.26 - 0.25}{0.04841} = 0.206559$$

From Excel, $P(\rho \geq 0.26) = P(Z \geq 0.206559) = 0.418177$.

> ✳ **Interpretation**   Probability that at least 26% of the workers own a computer is 41.82%.

6.2.8 Using Excel to generate a sample from a sampling distribution

Excel can be used to generate random samples from a range of probability distributions, including: uniform, normal, binomial, and Poisson distributions. To generate a random sample select Tools > Data Analysis as illustrated in Figures 6.19 and 6.20:

Figure 6.19 Excel Data Analysis add-in

Figure 6.19

Figure 6.20

Select Random Number Generation and click OK

Figure 6.20 Excel Random Number Generation

- Input number of variables (or samples)
- Input number of data values in each sample
- Select the distribution
- Input distribution parameters e.g. for normal: μ, σ.
- Decide on where the results should appear (Output range)
- Click OK

▷ Example 6.10

Consider the problem of sampling from a population which consists of the salaries for public sector employees employed by a national government. The historical data suggests that the population data is normally distributed with mean of €45000 and standard deviation of €10000. We can use Excel to generate 'N' random samples with each sample containing 'n' data values.

(a) Create 10 random samples each with 1000 data points.

(b) Calculate the mean for each random sample.

(c) Plot the histogram representing the sampling distribution for the sample mean.

(a)   Generate 'n' samples with 'N' data values (n = 10, N = 1000) as illustrated in Figure 6.21 below

From Excel, Select Tools > Data Analysis > Random Number Generation

n = 10

N = 1000

Normal distribution

Mean = 45000

SD = 1000

Output range: Cell B5. Click OK

Figure 6.21

The 'n' samples are located in the rows of the table of values, e.g. sample 1: B5:K5, sample 2: B6:K6, and sample 1000: B1006:K1006.

(b)   Calculate 'n' sample means

Calculate the sample mean using Excel function AVERAGE(), e.g. from sample 1: mean = average(B5:K5), sample 2: mean = average(B6:K6), and sample 1000: mean = average (B1006:K1006).

Figure 6.22 illustrates the first three samples and sample means.

	A	B	C	D	E	F	G	H	I	J	K	L
1	Sampling Distribution - Example 6.10											
2												
3		Population: X ~ N (45000, 10000²)										
4												Sample means
5	Sample 1	46379.9308	45967.32	45723.1	44073.99	43314.97	44850.85	45862.23	46320.37	47214.49	44114.46	45382.17138
6	Sample 2	47410.4884	45411.45	42393.82	45423.63	46222.22	44305.03	45442.45	45463.47	42270.72	45986.3	45032.95861
7		46051.2122	46324.22	46829.09	43481.1	45341.47	45734.17	43207.17	43784.54	43386.76	45867.79	45000.75295
8		43509.1108	44880.19	43706.06	44670.34	45274.96	44051.08	45920.27	46070.55	44414.09	44884.42	44738.10679

Figure 6.22

(c)   Create histogram bins and plot histogram of sample means

	L	M	N	O
5	45382.17138	=AVERAGE(B5:K5)		
6	45032.95861		Min =	44014.28
7	45000.75295		Max =	46197.74
8	44738.10679			
9	44690.48861		BIN	
10	45042.01729		44000	
11	45063.33664		44500	
12	44799.90491		45000	
13	44710.24397		45500	
14	45151.71213		46000	
15	44878.03142		46500	

Figure 6.23

We note that from the spreadsheet the smallest and largest sample means is 44014.28 and 46197.74 respectively. Based upon these two values we then determine the histogram bin size as: 44000 with step size of 500 (44000, 44500, ... , 46500) illustrated in Figure 6.23.

Figure 6.24

To create the histogram select Tools > Data Analysis > Histogram and select values as illustrated in Figure 6.24.

Input Range: L5:L1004
Bin Range: N10:N15
Output Range: P9
Click OK

Figures 6.25 and 6.26 illustrate the frequency distribution and corresponding histogram.

	N	O	P	Q
6	Min =	44014.28		
7	Max =	46197.74		
8				
9	BIN		Bin	Frequency
10	44000		44000	0
11	44500		44500	58
12	45000		45000	454
13	45500		45500	434
14	46000		46000	53
15	46500		46500	1
16			More	0

Figure 6.25

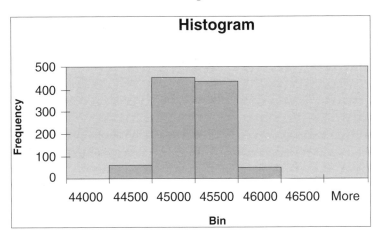

Figure 6.26

From the histogram we note that the histogram values are centred about the population mean value of €45000. If we repeated this exercise from different values of sample size 'n' we would find that the range would reduce as the sample sizes increase.

Student Exercises

X6.1 The following five people have all made claims for the amounts shown:

Person	1	2	3	4	5
Insurance claim (€)	500	400	900	1000	1200

A sample of two people is to be taken at random, with replacement, from the five. Derive the sampling distribution of the mean and prove: (a) $\bar{\bar{X}} = \mu$, and (b) $\sigma_{\bar{x}} = \sigma/\sqrt{n}$.

X6.2 If X is a normal random variable with mean 10 and standard deviation 2, i.e. $X \sim N$ (10, 4). Define and compare the sampling distribution for samples of size: (a) 2, (b) 4, (c) 16.

X6.3 If X is any random variable with mean = 63 and standard deviation = 10. Define and compare the sampling distribution for samples of size: (a) 40, (b) 60, and (c) 100.

X6.4 Use the Excel spreadsheet to generate a random sample of 100 observations from a normal distribution with a mean of 10 and a standard deviation of 4. Calculate the sample mean and standard deviation. Why are these values different from the population values?

X6.5 Assuming that the weights of 10000 items are normally distributed and that the distribution has a mean of 115 Kg and a standard deviation of 3 Kg: (a) estimate how many items have weights between 115–118 Kgs, (b) if you have to pick one item at random from the whole 10000 items, how confident would you be in predicting that its value would lie between 112 and 115 Kg, and (c) if a sample of 10 items were drawn from the 10000 items what would be the standard error of the sample mean? What would be the standard error if the sample consisted of 40 items?

X6.6 By treating the following as finite and infinite samples comment on the standard errors: (a) find the sample mean and standard error for random samples of 1000 accounts if bank A has 5024 saving accounts with an average in each account of £512 and a standard deviation of £150, and (b) find the sample mean and standard error for random samples of 1000 accounts if bank A has 10244 saving accounts with an average in each account of £564 and a standard deviation of £150.

X6.7 A sample of 100 was taken from a population with $\pi = 0.5$. Find the probability that the sample proportion will lie between: (a) 0.4 and 0.6, (b) 0.35 and 0.65, and (c) 0.5 and 0.65.

X6.8 From a parliamentary constituency a sample of 100 were asked whether they would vote Labour or Conservative. It is thought that 40% of the constituency will favour Labour. Find the approximate probability that in an election that Labour will win (assume only a two party vote).

X6.9 The annual income of doctors constitutes a highly positive skewed distribution. Suppose the population has an unknown mean and a standard deviation of £10000. An estimate of the population mean is to be made using the sample mean. This estimate must be within £1000 either side of the true mean: (a) if n = 100, find the probability that the estimate will meet the desired accuracy, and (b) if n = 625, find the probability that the estimate will meet the desired accuracy.

X6.10 The average number of Xerox copies made in a working day in a certain office is 356 with a standard deviation of 55. It costs the firm 3 pence per copy. During a working period of 121 days what is the probability that the average cost per day is more than £11.10?

6.3 Population Point Estimates

6.3.1 Introduction

In the previous section we explored the sampling distribution of the mean and proportion and stated that these distributions can be considered to be normal with particular population parameters (μ, σ^2). For many populations, it is likely that we do not know the value of the population mean (or proportion). Fortunately, we can use the sample mean (or proportion) to provide an estimate of the population value. The objective of estimation is to determine the approximate value of a population parameter on the basis of a sample statistic. The method described in this section is dependent upon the sampling distribution being normally distributed (or approximately) and we can provide two estimates of the population value: point and confidence interval estimate. Figure 6.27 illustrates the relationship between population mean, point and interval estimates.

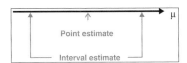

Figure 6.27

Suppose that you want to find the mean weight of all football players who play in a local football league. Due to practical constraints you are unable to measure all the players but you are able to select a sample of 25 players at random and weigh them to provide a sample mean. From Section 6.2 we know that the sampling distribution of the mean is approximately normally distributed for large sample size and that the sample mean can be considered to be an unbiased estimator of the population mean. After the sampling, we establish that the mean weight of the sample of players is 188 lbs. This number becomes the point estimate of the population mean. If we know, or can estimate the population standard deviation (σ), then we can apply equation (6.7) to provide an interval estimate for the population mean based upon some degree of error between the sample and population means. This interval estimate is called the confidence interval for the population mean (or confidence interval for the population proportion, if we are measuring proportions). In this section we shall consider the following topics:

- Types of estimates.

- Criteria of a good estimator.

- Point estimate of the population mean, μ.

- Point estimate of the population proportion, π.

- Point estimate of the population variance, σ^2.

In Section 6.4 we shall consider the following topics:

- Confidence interval estimate of the population mean (μ) and proportion (π), σ known.

- Confidence interval estimate of the population mean (μ) and proportion (π), σ unknown, $n \geq 30$.

- Confidence interval estimate of the population mean (μ) and proportion (π), σ unknown, $n < 30$.

X

Estimate An estimate is an indication of the value of an unknown quantity based on observed data.

Point estimate A point estimate (or estimator) is any quantity calculated from the sample data which is used to provide information about the population.

Confidence interval $(1 - \infty)$ A confidence interval gives an estimated range of values which is likely to include an unknown population parameter.

Population variance The population variance is the variance of all possible values.

6.3.2 Types of estimate

To recap: A *point estimate* is a sample statistic that is used to estimate an unknown population parameter. An *interval estimate* is a range of values used to estimate a population parameter. It indicates error by the extent of its range and by the probability of the true population parameter lying within that range.

6.3.3 Criteria of a good estimator

Qualities desirable in estimators include: unbiased, consistency, and efficiency:

1. An *unbiased estimator* of a population parameter is an estimator whose expected value is equal to that parameter. As we already know, the sample mean $\bar{X}$ is an unbiased estimator of the population mean, μ. This can also be written as the expected value of the sample mean equals the population mean as given by equation (6.13):

$$E(\bar{X}) = \mu \tag{6.13}$$

2. An unbiased estimator is said to be *consistent* if the difference between the estimator and the parameter grows smaller as the sample size grows larger. The sample mean $\bar{X}$ is a consistent estimator of the population mean, μ, with the variance given by equation (6.14), which is the re-statement of equation (6.5):

$$VAR(\bar{X}) = \sigma/\sqrt{n} \tag{6.14}$$

If n grows larger, then the value of the variance of the sample mean grows smaller.

3. If there are two unbiased estimators of a parameter, the one whose variance is smaller is said to be *efficient*. For example, both the sample mean and median are unbiased estimators of the population mean. Which one should we use? The sample median has a greater variance than the sample mean, so we choose the sample mean since it is *relatively efficient* when compared to the sample median.

6.3.4 Point estimate of the population mean and variance

A *point estimator* draws inferences about a population by estimating the value of an unknown parameter using a single point or data value. The sample mean is the best estimator of the population mean. It is unbiased, consistent, and the most efficient estimator as long as the sample was either

(a) Drawn from a normal population, or

(b) If the population was not normal, the sample was sufficiently large so that the sampling distribution can be approximated by the normal distribution.

Thus a point estimate of the population mean, $\hat{\mu}$, is given by equation (6.15):

$$\hat{\mu} = \bar{X} \tag{6.15}$$

In Chapter 5 we noted that the point probabilities in continuous distributions were zero and in Chapter 6 we are stating we would expect the point estimator to get closer and closer to the true population value as the sample size increases. The degree of error is not reflected by the point estimator but we can employ the concept of the interval estimator to put a probability to the value of the population parameter lying between two values, with the middle value being represented by the point estimator. Section 6.4 will discuss the concept of an interval estimate or confidence interval. The most frequently used estimate of the population standard deviation, σ, is the sample standard deviation (s). However, as seen in Section 6.2, $\sigma \neq s$. Therefore, the sample standard deviation s (let us call this s_b), is a *biased estimator* of the population standard deviation, σ. It can be shown that an unbiased estimator of the population standard deviation, $\hat{\sigma}$, is given by equation (6.16):

$$\hat{\sigma} = s_b \times \sqrt{\frac{n}{n-1}} \tag{6.16}$$

Where s_b is given by equation (4.13). The value of s_b is given by the Excel function STDEVP().

To calculate the standard deviation of the sample mean, or the *standard error* of the mean, equation (6.5) is converted to equation (6.17):

$$\hat{\sigma}_{\bar{x}} = \frac{\hat{\sigma}}{\sqrt{n}} = \frac{s_b}{\sqrt{n-1}} \tag{6.17}$$

Alternatively, we can use equation (6.18) which is the unbiased estimator of the population standard deviation, $\hat{\sigma}$:

$$\hat{\sigma} = s = \sqrt{\frac{\sum(X-\bar{X})^2}{n-1}} \tag{6.18}$$

$$\hat{\sigma}_{\bar{x}} = \frac{\hat{\sigma}}{\sqrt{n}} = \frac{s}{\sqrt{n}} \tag{6.19}$$

Where the unbiased estimator is given by the Excel function STDEV().

Note When n is large then $\hat{\sigma} = s = s_b$.

Example 6.11

An experiment was performed five times on the measurement of the length of rods with the following results: 1.010, 1.012, 1.008, 1.013, and 1.011. Calculate the unbiased estimates of the mean and variance of possible measurements and give an estimate for the standard error of your estimate of the mean?

Excel solution—Example 6.11

Figure 6.28 illustrates the Excel solution.

	A	B	C	D	E	F	G	H
1	Point Estimates, Example 6.11							
2								
3		Sample Data				Summary Statistics		
4		X	(X-Xbar)^2			n =	5	=COUNT(B5:B9)
5		1.010	0.000001	=(B5-$G$9)^2		ΣX =	5.054	=SUM(B5:B9)
6		1.012	0.000001			Σ(X-Xbar)^2 =	0.000015	=SUM(C5:C9)
7		1.008	0.000008					
8		1.013	0.000005			Formula Solution		
9		1.011	0.000000	=(B9-$G$9)^2		Sample mean =	1.0108	=G5/G4
10						Sample variance =	3.7E-06	=G6/(G4-1)
11						Sample standard deviation =	0.0019235	=G10^0.5
12						Estimate of population mean =	1.0108	=G9
13						Estimate of population standard deviation =	0.0019235	=G11
14						Estimate of the standard error of the mean =	0.0008602	=G13/G4^0.5
15								
16						Function Solution		
17						mean x =	1.011	=AVERAGE(B5:B9)
18						Sample variance =	3.7E-06	=VAR(B5:B9)
19						Sample standard deviation =	0.0019235	=STDEV(B5:B9)
20						Estimate of population mean =	1.0108	=G17
21						Estimate of population standard deviation =	0.0019235	=G19
22						Estimate of the standard error of the mean =	0.0008602	=G21/G4^0.5

$$S = \sqrt{\frac{\Sigma \left(X - \overline{X}\right)^2}{n - 1}}$$

Figure 6.28

→ **Excel Solution**

X Cells B5:B9   Values

$(X-X_{bar})^2$ Cell C5   Formula: = $(B5-\$G\$9)^2$

     Copy formula C5:C9

n = Cell G4   Formula: =COUNT(B5:B9)

ΣX = Cell G5   Formula: =SUM(B5:B9)

$\Sigma(X-X_{bar})^2$ = Cell G6   Formula: =SUM(C5:C9)

Formula Solution

Sample mean = Cell G9   Formula: =G5/G4

Sample variance = Cell G10   Formula: =G6/(G4−1)

Sample standard deviation = Cell G11   Formula: =G10^0.5

Estimate of population mean = Cell G12   Formula: =G9

Estimate of population standard deviation = Cell G13   Formula: =G11

Estimate of the standard error of the mean = Cell G14   Formula: =G13/G4^0.5

Function Solution

mean x = Cell G17   Formula: =AVERAGE(B5:B9)

Sample variance = Cell G18   Formula: =VAR(B5:B9)

Sample standard deviation = Cell G19   Formula: =STDEV(B5:B9)

Estimate of population mean = Cell G20   Formula: =G17

Estimate of population standard deviation = Cell G21   Formula: =G19

Estimate of the standard error of the mean = Cell G22   Formula: =G21/G4^0.5

The value of the unbiased estimates of the population mean, variance, and standard error of the mean are provided by solving equations (6.15), (6.18), and (6.19). From Excel:

(a) *Sample values*

Sample size n = 5

Sample mean, $\bar{X} = \dfrac{1.010 + 1.012 + 1.008 + 1.013 + 1.011}{5} = 1.0108$

Unbiased sample standard deviation, $s = \sqrt{\dfrac{\sum(X-\bar{X})^2}{n-1}} = 0.0019235$

(b) *Population estimates*

Estimate of population mean $\hat{\mu} = \bar{X} = 1.0108$

Estimate of population standard deviation $\hat{\sigma} = s = 0.0019235$

Estimate of population standard error $\hat{\sigma}_{\bar{x}} = \dfrac{\hat{\sigma}}{\sqrt{n}} = \dfrac{s}{\sqrt{n}} = 0.0008602$

✳ **Interpretation**   The value of the unbiased estimates of the mean, variance, and standard error are 1.011, 0.0019, and 0.0009 respectively.

6.3.5 Point estimate for the population proportion and variance

In the previous section we provided the equations to calculate the point estimate for the population mean based upon the sample data. Instead of solving problems involving the mean we can use the sample proportion to provide point estimates of the population proportion. Equations (6.20) and (6.21) provide unbiased estimates of the population proportion and standard error of the proportion:

Estimate of Population Proportion, $\hat{\pi} = p$ 　　　　　　　　　　　　　　(6.20)

Estimate of Standard Error, $\hat{\sigma}_p = \sqrt{\dfrac{\hat{\pi}(1-\hat{\pi})}{n}}$ 　　　　　　　　(6.21)

▷ **Example 6.12**

In a sample of 400 textile workers, 184 expressed dissatisfaction regarding a prospective plan to modify working conditions. Provide a point estimate of the population proportion of total workers who would be dissatisfied and give an estimate for the standard error of your estimate?

Excel solution—Example 6.12

Figure 6.29 illustrates the Excel solution.

	A	B	C	D
1	Point Estimates, Example 6.12			
2				
3		Sample Data		
4				
5		Total in sample n =	400	
6		Number dissatisfied X =	184	
7				
8		Sample proportion r =	0.460000	=C6/C5
9				
10		Population		
11				
12		Estimate population proportion =	0.460000	=C8
13		Estimate population proportion standard error =	0.02491987	=SQRT(C12*(1-C12)/C5)

Figure 6.29

➡ **Excel Solution**

Total in sample n = Cell C5   Value

X Cell C6   Value

Sample proportion = Cell C8   Formula: =C6/C5

Estimate population proportion = Cell C12   Formula: =C8

Estimate population standard error = Cell C13   Formula: =SQRT(C12*(1−C12)/C5)

Point Estimate of the population proportion, $\hat{\pi} = \rho = 184/400 = 0.46$

$$\text{Standard error, } \hat{\sigma}_\rho = \sqrt{\hat{\pi}\left(1 - \hat{\pi}\right)/n} = \sqrt{0.46 \times \left(1 - 0.46\right)/400} = 0.025$$

The value of the unbiased estimates of the population mean, and standard error of the mean are provided by solving equations (6.20) and (6.21). From Excel:

(a) Sample values

Sample size n = 400

Number of successes X = 184

Sample proportion, $\rho = X/n = 184/400 = 0.46$

(b) Population estimates

Estimate of population proportion $\hat{\pi} = \rho = 0.46$

$$\text{Estimate of population standard error } \hat{\sigma}_\rho = \sqrt{\frac{\hat{\pi}\left(1 - \hat{\pi}\right)}{n}} = \sqrt{\frac{0.46\left(1 - 0.46\right)}{400}}$$

$$= 0.0249$$

✳ **Interpretation**   The value of the unbiased estimates of the proportion and standard error are 0.46 and 0.0249 respectively.

6.3.6 Pooled estimates

If more than one sample is taken from a population then the resulting sample statistics can be combined to provide *pooled estimates* for the population mean, variance, and proportion.

Estimate of the population mean is provided by the pooled sample mean

$$\bar{X} = \frac{n_1 \bar{X}_1 + n_2 \bar{X}_2}{n_1 + n_2} \tag{6.22}$$

Estimate of the population variance is provided by the pooled sample variance

$$\hat{\sigma}^2 = \frac{n_1 s_1^2 + n_2 s_2^2}{n_1 + n_2 - 2} \tag{6.23}$$

Estimate of the population proportion is provided by the pooled sample proportion

$$\hat{\pi} = \frac{n_1 \hat{\pi}_1 + n_2 \hat{\pi}_2}{n_1 + n_2} = \frac{n_1 P_1 + n_2 P_2}{n_1 + n_2} \tag{6.24}$$

Student Exercises

X6.11 A random sample of five values was taken from a population: 8.1, 6.5, 4.9, 7.3, and 5.9. Estimate the population mean and standard deviation, and the standard error of the estimate for the population mean.

X6.12 The mean of 10 readings of a variable was 8.7 with standard deviation 0.3. A further 5 readings were taken: 8.6, 8.5, 8.8, 8.7, and 8.9. Estimate the mean and standard deviation of the set of possible readings using all the data available.

X6.13 Two samples are drawn from the same population as follows: sample 1 (0.4, 0.2, 0.2, 0.4, 0.3, and 0.3) and sample 2 (0.2, 0.2, 0.1, 0.4, 0.2, 0.3, and 0.1). Determine the best unbiased estimates of the population mean and variance.

X6.14 A random sample of 100 rods from a population line were measured and found to have a mean length of 12.132 with standard deviation 0.11. A further sample of 50 is taken, find the probability that the mean of this sample will be between 12.12 and 12.14.

X6.15 A random sample of 20 children in a large school were asked a question and 12 answered correctly. Estimate the proportion of children in the school who answered correctly and the standard error of this estimate.

X6.16 A random sample of 500 fish is taken from a lake and marked. After a suitable interval a second sample of 500 is taken and 25 of these are found to be marked. By considering the second sample estimate the number of fish in the lake.

6.4 Population Confidence Intervals

6.4.1 Introduction

If we take just one sample from a population we can estimate a population parameter. Our knowledge of sampling error would indicate that the standard error provides an evaluation of the likely error associated with a particular estimate. If we assume that the sampling distribution of the sample means are normally distributed then we can provide a measure of this error in terms of a probability value that the value of the population mean will lie within a specified interval. This interval is called an *interval estimate* (or *confidence interval*) where the interval is centred at the point estimate for the population mean. Assuming that the sampling distribution of the mean follows a normal distribution then we can allocate probability values to these interval estimates. From equation (6.7) we can restructure into equation (6.25):

$$\mu = \bar{X} - Z \times \frac{\sigma}{\sqrt{n}}$$

(6.25)

From our knowledge of the normal distribution we know that 95% of the distribution lies within ± 1.96 standard deviations of the mean. Thus for the distribution of sample means, 95% of these sample means will lie in the interval defined by equation (6.25):

$$\mu = \bar{X} \pm 1.96 \times \sigma/\sqrt{n}.$$

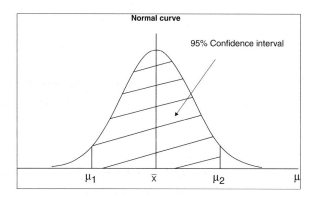

Therefore, this equation tells us that an interval estimate (or confidence interval) is centred at $\bar{X}$ with a lower value of $\mu_1 = \bar{X} - 1.96 \times \sigma/\sqrt{n}$ and upper value of $\mu_2 = \bar{X} + 1.96 \times \sigma/\sqrt{n}$ as illustrated in Figure 6.30. We will now look at how interval estimates and associated levels of confidence can be calculated.

Figure 6.30

6.4.2 Confidence interval estimate of the population mean, μ (σ known)

If a random sample of size 'n' is taken from a normal population $N(\mu, \sigma^2)$ then the sampling distribution of the sample means will be normal, $\bar{X} \sim N(\mu, \sigma^2/n)$, and the confidence interval of the population mean is given by equation (6.26):

$$\bar{X} - Z \times \frac{\sigma}{\sqrt{n}} \leq \mu \leq \bar{X} + Z \times \frac{\sigma}{\sqrt{n}}$$

(6.26)

Example 6.13

8 samples measuring the length of cloth are sampled from a population where the length is normally distributed with population standard deviation 0.2. Calculate a 95% confidence interval for the population mean based on a sample of 8 observations: 4.9, 4.7, 5.1, 5.4, 4.7, 5.2, 4.8, and 5.1.

Excel solution—Example 6.13

Figure 6.31 illustrates the Excel solution.

	A	B	C	D	E	F	G
1		Confidence interval for μ - population standard deviation known					
2		Example 6.13					
3							
4		Sample Data			Population standard deviation σ =	0.2	Known
5		X	X^2		2 tails, 95% confidence interval =	0.05	Chosen 5%
6		4.9	24.01	=B6^2	CDF =	0.975	=1-F5/2
7		4.7	22.09		Z_{cri} =	1.959964	=NORMSINV(F6)
8		5.1	26.01		Formula Solution		
9		5.4	29.16		Sample mean =	4.9875	=C18/C17
10		4.7	22.09		Estimate of population mean =	4.9875	=F9
11		5.2	27.04		Standard error of the mean =	0.0707107	=F4/C17^0.5
12		4.8	23.04		μ_1 =	4.8489096	=F9-F7*F11
13		5.1	26.01	=B13^2	μ_2 =	5.1260904	=F9+F7*F11
14							
15		Summary Statistics			Function Solution		
16					Sample mean x =	4.9875	=AVERAGE(B6:B13)
17		n =	8	=COUNT(B6:B13)	Estimate of population mean =	4.9875	=F16
18		ΣX =	39.900	=SUM(B6:B13)	Standard error of the mean =	0.0707107	=F4/C17^0.5
19		ΣX^2 =	199.45	=SUM(C6:C13)	μ_1 =	4.8489096	=F16-CONFIDENCE(F5,F4,C17)
20					μ_2 =	5.1260904	=F16+CONFIDENCE(F5,F4,C17)

Figure 6.31

→ **Excel Solution**

X: Cell B6:B13   Values
X^2: Cell C6:C13   Formula: =B6^2
                                                    Copy Formula from C6:C13
n = Cell C17   Formula: =COUNT(B6:B13)
ΣX = Cell C18   Formula: =SUM(B6:B13)
ΣX^2 = Cell C19   Formula: =SUM(C6:C13)
Population standard deviation σ = Cell F4   Value
2 tails, 95% confidence interval = Cell F5   Value
CDF = Cell F6   Formula: =1–F5/2
Z_{cri} = Cell F7   Formula: =NORMSINV(F6)

Formula Solution

Sample mean = Cell F9   Formula: =C18/C17
Estimate of population mean = Cell F10   Formula: =F9
Standard error of the mean = Cell F11   Formula: =F4/C17^0.5
μ_1 = Cell F12   Formula: =F9–F7*F11
μ_2 = Cell F13   Formula: =F9+F7*F11

Function Solution

Sample mean x = Cell F16	Formula: =AVERAGE(B6:B13)
Estimate of population mean = Cell F17	Formula: =F16
Standard error of the mean = Cell F18	Formula: =F4/C17^0.5
μ_1 = Cell F19	Formula: =F16–CONFIDENCE(F5,F4,C17)
μ_2 = Cell F20	Formula: =F16+CONFIDENCE(F5,F4,C17)

The value of the lower and upper confidence interval is given by equation (6.26). From Excel: population standard deviation σ = 0.2 (known), sample mean $\bar{X}$ = 4.9875, sample size = 8, and value of Z for 95% confidence = ±1.96. Substituting values into equation (6.27) gives:

$$\text{Standard error } \sigma_{\bar{x}} = \frac{\sigma}{\sqrt{n}} = \frac{0.2}{\sqrt{8}} = 0.0707$$

$$\mu_1 = \bar{X} - Z \times \frac{\sigma}{\sqrt{n}} = 4.9875 - 1.96 \times 0.0707 = 4.8489$$

$$\mu_2 = \bar{X} + Z \times \frac{\sigma}{\sqrt{n}} = 4.9875 + 1.96 \times 0.0707 = 5.1261$$

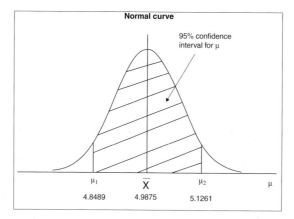

Figure 6.32 illustrates the 95% confidence interval for the population mean.

Thus, the 95% confidence interval for μ is = 4.9875 ± 1.96 * 0.0707 = 4.9875 ± 0.1386 = 4.8489 → 5.1261.

Figure 6.32

※ **Interpretation**   We are 95% confident that on the basis of this sample the true mean is between 4.8489 and 5.1261.

6.4.3 Confidence interval estimate of the population mean, μ (σ unknown, n < 30)

In the previous example we calculated the point and interval estimates when the population was normally distributed but the population standard deviation was known. In most cases the population standard deviation would be an unknown value and we would have to use the sample value to estimate the population value with associated errors. The population mean estimate is still given by the value of the sample mean but what about the confidence interval? In the previous example the sample mean and size were used to provide this interval but in the new case we have an extra unknown, that has to be estimated from the sample data, to find this confidence interval.

> **Note**   This is often the case in many student research projects. They handle small sizes and the population standard deviation is unknown.

If we have more information about the population then we would expect the probability of the population mean lying within 1.96 standard errors of the mean will be smaller when the population standard deviation is known compared to being unknown. The question then becomes can we measure how much smaller will this probability be? This question was answered by W. S. Gossett who determined the distribution of the mean when divided by an estimate of the standard error. The resultant distribution is called the *Student's t distribution* defined by equation (6.27):

$$t_{df} = \frac{\overline{X} - \mu}{s/\sqrt{n}}$$

(6.27)

This distribution is similar to the normal probability distribution when the estimate of the variance is based on many **degrees of freedom** ($df = n - 1$) but the left and right tails have more values in compared to the normal distribution.

> **Note**   The t distribution is very similar to the normal distribution when the estimate of variance is based on many degrees of freedom but has relatively more scores in its tails when there are fewer degrees of freedom. The t distribution is symmetric, like the normal distribution, but flatter.

Figure 6.33 shows the t distribution with 5 degrees of freedom and the standard normal distribution. The t distribution is flatter than the normal distribution (leptokurtic).

Since the t distribution is leptokurtic, the percentage of the distribution within 1.96 standard deviations of the mean is less than the 95% for the normal distribution.

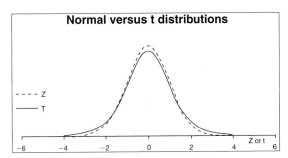

Figure 6.33

X

Degrees of freedom
Refers to the number of independent observations in a sample minus the number of population parameters that must be estimated from sample data.

However, if the number of degrees of freedom (df) is large (df = n − 1 ≥ 30) then there is very little difference between the two probability distributions. The sampling error for the t distribution is given by the unbiased sample standard deviation (s) and sample size (n), as follows defined by equation (6.28):

$$\sigma_{\bar{X}} = \frac{\hat{\sigma}}{\sqrt{n}} = \frac{s}{\sqrt{n}}$$

(6.28)

With the degrees of freedom and confidence interval given by equations (6.29) and (6.30) respectively:

$$df = n - 1$$

(6.29)

$$\bar{X} - t_{df} \times \frac{s}{\sqrt{n}} \leq \mu \leq \bar{X} + t_{df} \times \frac{s}{\sqrt{n}}$$

(6.30)

Example 6.14

For the following sample of 8 observations from an infinite Normal population find the sample mean and standard deviation and hence determine the standard error, the population standard deviation and a 95% confidence interval for the mean: 10.3, 12.4, 11.6, 11.8, 12.6, 10.9, 11.2, and 10.3.

Excel solution—Example 6.14

Figure 6.34 illustrates the Excel solution.

	A	B	C	D	E	F	G	H
1	Confidence interval for μ - population standard deviation unknown, n small							
2	Example 6.14							
3								
4		Sample Data				2 tails, 95% confidence interval =	0.05	
5		X	(X-Xbar^2			df = n - 1 =	7	=C18-1
6		10.3	1.1826563	=(B6-$G$9)^2		t_cri =	2.3646243	=TINV(G4,G5)
7		12.4	1.0251563					
8		11.6	0.0451562			Formula Solution		
9		11.8	0.1701563			Sample mean =	11.3875	=C19/C18
10		12.6	1.4701563			Sample variance =	0.7641071	=C20/(C18-1)
11		10.9	0.2376563			Sample standard deviation =	0.8741322	=G10^0.5
12		11.2	0.0351563			Estimate of population mean =	11.388	=G9
13		10.3	1.1826563	=(B13-$G$9)^2		Standard error of the mean =	0.3090524	=G11/C18^0.5
14						Confidence Interval for μ₁ =	10.656707	=G9-G6*G13
15						Confidence Interval for μ₂ =	12.118293	=G9+G6*G13
16		Summary Statistics						
17								
18		n =	8	=COUNT(B6:B13)		Function Solution		
19		ΣX =	91.100	=SUM(B6:B13)		Sample mean =	11.388	=AVERAGE(B6:B13)
20		Σ(X-Xbar)2 =	5.34875	=SUM(C6:C13)		Sample variance =	0.7641071	=VAR(B6:B13)
21						Sample standard deviation =	0.8741322	=STDEV(B6:B13)
22						Estimate of population mean =	11.388	=G19
23		$$S = \sqrt{\frac{\Sigma (X - \bar{X})^2}{n - 1}}$$				Standard error of the mean =	0.3090524	=G21/C18^0.5
24						Confidence Interval for μ₁ =	10.656707	=G19-G6*G23
25						Confidence Interval for μ₂ =	12.118293	=G19+G6*G23
26								

Figure 6.34

→ Excel Solution

X: Cell B6:B13	Values
$(X - X_{bar})^{\wedge}2$ Cell C6	Formula: =(B6–$G$9)^2
	Copy Formula from C6:C13
n = Cell C18	Formula: =COUNT(B6:B13)
$\sum X$ = Cell C19	Formula: =SUM(B6:B13)
$\sum(X - X_{bar})^{\wedge}2$ = Cell C20	Formula: =SUM(C6:C13)
2 tails, 95% confidence interval = Cell G4	Value
Df = n – 1 = Cell G5	Formula: =C18–1
t_{cri} = Cell G6	Formula: =TINV(G4,G5)

Formula Solution

Sample mean = Cell G9	Formula: =C19/C18
Sample Variance Cell G10	Formula: =C20/(C18–1)
Sample standard deviation = Cell G11	Formula: =G10^0.5
Estimate of population mean = Cell G12	Formula: =G9
Standard error of the mean = Cell G13	Formula: =G11/C18^0.5
μ_1 = Cell G14	Formula: =G9–G6*G13
μ_2 = Cell G15	Formula: =G9+G6*G13

Function Solution

Sample mean = Cell G19	Formula: =AVERAGE(B6:B13)
Sample Variance Cell G20	Formula: =VAR(B6:B13)
Sample standard deviation = Cell G21	Formula: =STDEV(B6:B13)
Estimate of population mean = Cell G22	Formula: =G19
Standard error of the mean = Cell G23	Formula: =G21/C18^0.5
μ_1 = Cell G24	Formula: =G19–G6*G23
μ_2 = Cell G25	Formula: =G19+G6*G23

The value of the lower and upper confidence interval is given by equation (6.30). From Excel: sample mean, $\overline{X}$ = 11.3875, sample size = 8, unbiased sample variance = 0.7641071, unbiased sample standard deviation = 0.8741322, and value of t_8 for 95% confidence = ±2.3646243. Substituting values into equation (6.30) gives:

$$\text{Standard error } \sigma_{\bar{x}} = \frac{s}{\sqrt{n}} = \frac{0.8741322}{\sqrt{8}} = 0.3090524$$

$$\mu_1 = \overline{X} - t_8 \times \frac{s}{\sqrt{n}} = 11.3875 - 2.3646243 \times 0.3090524 = 10.656707$$

$$\mu_2 = \overline{X} - t_8 \times \frac{s}{\sqrt{n}} = 11.3875 + 2.3646243 \times 0.3090524 = 12.118293$$

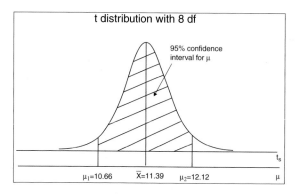

Figure 6.35

Figure 6.35 illustrates the 95% confidence interval for the population mean.

Thus, the 95% confidence interval for μ is = 11.3875 ± 2.3646243 * 0.3090524 = 10.6567 → 12.1183.

> ❋ **Interpretation**   We are 95% confident that, on the basis of the sample, the true population mean is between 10.6567 and 12.1183.

6.4.4 Confidence interval estimate of the population mean, μ (σ unknown, n ≥ 30)

In the next two sections we relax the assumption that the population variance, σ^2, is known. Certainly it is important that we drop this assumption, since it is rare in practice for it to hold. For large samples (n ≥ 30), we find that the sampling distribution of the mean is approximately normal with the population variance being estimated from the sample variance ($\sigma^2 \approx s^2$). Substituting this approximation into equation (6.7) gives equations (6.31) and (6.32):

$$Z = \frac{\bar{X} - \mu}{s/\sqrt{n}}$$

(6.31)

$$\bar{X} - Z \times \frac{s}{\sqrt{n}} \leq \mu \leq \bar{X} + Z \times \frac{s}{\sqrt{n}}$$

(6.32)

⌕ Example 6.15

8 samples measuring the length of cloth are sampled from a population where the length is normally distributed with population standard deviation unknown. Calculate a 95% confidence interval for the population mean based on a sample of 8 observations: 4.9, 4.7, 5.1, 5.4, 4.7, 5.2, 4.8, and 5.1.

Please note we are using a small sample to illustrate the application of the method. When n < 30 (σ unknown), we would use the t distribution to fit a confidence interval.

Excel Solution—Example 6.15

Figure 6.36 illustrates the Excel solution.

	A	B	C	D	E	F	G
1	Confidence interval for μ - population standard deviation unknown, n large						
2	Example 6.15						
3							
4		Sample Data					
5		X	(X-Xbar)^2		2 tails, 95% confidence interval =	0.05	Chosen 5%
6		4.9	0.00765625	=(B6-$F$9)^2	CDF =	0.975	=1-F5/2
7		4.7	0.08265625		Z_cri =	1.959963985	=NORMSINV(F6)
8		5.1	0.01265625		Formula Solution		
9		5.4	0.17015625		Sample mean =	4.9875	=C18/C17
10		4.7	0.08265625		Estimate of population mean =	4.9875	=F9
11		5.2	0.04515625		Sample variance =	0.064107143	=C19/(C17-1)
12		4.8	0.03515625		Sample standard deviation =	0.253193884	=F11^0.5
13		5.1	0.01265625	=(B13-$F$9)^2	Standard error of the mean =	0.089517556	=F12/C17^0.5
14					μ₁ =	4.812048814	=F9-F7*F13
15		Summary Statistics			μ₂ =	5.162951186	=F9+F7*F13
16							
17		n =	8	=COUNT(B6:B13)	Function Solution		
18		ΣX =	39.900	=SUM(B6:B13)	Sample mean x =	4.9875	=AVERAGE(B6:B13)
19		Σ(X-Xbar)^2 =	0.44875	=SUM(C6:C13)	Estimate of population mean =	4.9875	=F18
20					Sample variance =	0.064107143	=VAR(B6:B13)
21					Sample standard deviation =	0.253193884	=STDEV(B6:B13)
22			$S = \sqrt{\dfrac{\sum (X - \bar{X})^2}{n-1}}$		Standard error of the mean =	0.089517556	=F21/C17^0.5
23					μ₁ =	4.8120488	=F18-CONFIDENCE(F5,F21,C17)
24					μ₂ =	5.1629512	=F18+CONFIDENCE(F5,F21,C17)

Figure 6.36

→ **Excel Solution**

X: Cell B6:B13

$(X - X_{bar})^2$: Cell C6 — Formula: =(B6–$F$9)^2
Copy Formula from C6:C13

n = Cell C17 — Formula: =COUNT(B6:B13)

$\sum X$ = Cell C18 — Formula: =SUM(B6:B13)

$\sum(X - \bar{X})^2$ = Cell C19 — Formula: =SUM(C6:C13)

2 tails, 95% confidence interval = Cell F5 — Value

CDF = Cell F6 — Formula: =1–F5/2

Z_{cri} = Cell F7 — Formula: =NORMSINV(F6)

Formula Solution

Sample mean = Cell F9 — Formula: =C18/C17

Estimate of population mean = Cell F10 — Formula: =F9

Sample Variance Cell F11 — Formula: =C19(C17–1)

Sample standard deviation = Cell F12 — Formula: =F11^0.5

Standard error of the mean = Cell F13 — Formula: =F12/C17^0.5

μ_1 = Cell F14 — Formula: =F9–F7*F13

μ_2 = Cell F15 — Formula: =F9+F7*F13

Function Solution

Sample mean = Cell F18 — Formula: =AVERAGE(B6:B13)

Estimate of population mean = Cell F19 — Formula: =F18

Sample Variance Cell F20 — Formula: =VAR(B6:B13)

Sample standard deviation = Cell F21 — Formula: =STDEV(B6:B13)

Standard error of the mean = Cell F22 — Formula: =F21/C17^0.5

μ_1 = Cell F23 — Formula: =F18–CONFIDENCE(F5,F21,C17)

μ_2 = Cell F24 — Formula: =F18+CONFIDENCE(F5,F21,C17)

The value of the lower and upper confidence interval is given by equation (6.32). From Excel: sample mean, $\bar{X} = 4.9875$, sample size = 8, unbiased sample variance = 0.064107143, unbiased sample standard deviation = 0.253193884, and value of Z for 95% confidence = ±1.96. Substituting values into equation (6.32) gives:

$$\text{Standard error } \sigma_{\bar{X}} = \frac{s}{\sqrt{n}} = \frac{0.253193884}{\sqrt{8}} = 0.089517556$$

$$\mu_1 = \bar{X} - Z \times \frac{\sigma}{\sqrt{n}} = 4.9875 - 1.96 \times 0.089517556 = 4.8120488$$

$$\mu_2 = \bar{X} + Z \times \frac{\sigma}{\sqrt{n}} = 4.9875 + 1.96 \times 0.089517556 = 5.1629512$$

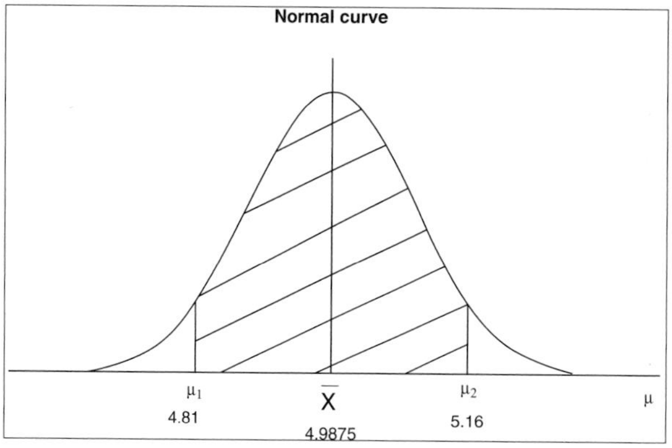

Figure 6.37

Figure 6.37 illustrates the 95% confidence interval for the population mean.

Thus, the 95% confidence interval for μ is = 4.9875 ± 1.96 * 0.089517556 = 4.8120 → 5.1630.

> ❊ **Interpretation** The 95% confidence interval for the population mean is 4.8120 to 5.1630.

6.4.5 Confidence interval estimate of a population proportion

If the population is normally distributed or the sample size is large (Central Limit Theorem, $n \geq 30$) then the confidence interval for a proportion is given by transforming equation (6.12) to give equation (6.33), where the population proportion, π, is estimated from the sample proportion, ρ:

$$\rho - Z \times \sqrt{\frac{\rho(1-\rho)}{n}} \leq \pi \leq \rho + Z \times \sqrt{\frac{\rho(1-\rho)}{n}} \quad (6.33)$$

👆 Example 6.16

In Example 6.9 we stated that 25% of workers in a factory own a personal computer. If this was not known we can use the idea of a confidence interval to put a level of confidence on the population proportion based upon the sample data collected. The sample data resulted in a sample proportion = 0.26 with a sample size = 80.

Excel solution—Example 6.16

Figure 6.38 illustrates the Excel solution.

	A	B	C	D
1	Confidence interval for the population proportion, n large			
2	Example 6.16			
3				
4				
5		Sample proportion ρ =	0.26	
6		Sample size n =	80	
7				
8		Point estimate of population proportion Π =	0.26	
9				
10		2 tails, 95% confidence interval =	0.05	
11		Proportion in right and left tails =	0.025	=C10/2
12		Upper Z$_{cri}$ =	1.959964	=NORMSINV(1-C11)
13				
14		Estimate of standard error =	0.0490408	=SQRT(C5*(1-C5)/C6)
15				
16		Lower population proportion estimate ρ$_1$ =	0.1638818	=C5-C12*C14
17		Lower population proportion estimate ρ$_2$ =	0.3561182	=C5+C12*C14

Figure 6.38

➜ Excel Solution

Sample proportion = Cell C5	Value
Sample size n = Cell C6	Value
Point estimate of population mean = Cell C8	Value
2 tails, 95% confidence interval = Cell C10	Value
Proportion in right and left tails = Cell C11	Formula: =C10/2
Upper Z$_{cri}$ = Cell C12	Formula: =NORMSINV(1–C11)
Estimate of standard error = Cell C14	Formula: =SQRT(C5*(1–C5)/C6)
Lower population proportion estimate = Cell C16	Formula: =C5–C12*C14
Upper population proportion estimate = Cell C17	Formula: =C5+C12*C14

The value of the lower and upper confidence interval is given by equation (6.33). From Excel: sample proportion, $\rho = 0.26$, and sample size = 80, and value of Z for 95% confidence = ±1.96. Substituting values into equation (6.33) gives:

$$\text{Standard error } \sigma_\rho = \sqrt{\frac{\rho(1-\rho)}{n}} = \sqrt{\frac{0.26(1-0.26)}{80}} = 0.0490408$$

$$\mu_1 = \rho - Z \times \sqrt{\frac{\rho(1-\rho)}{n}} = 0.26 - 1.96 \times 0.0490408 = 0.1638818$$

$$\mu_2 = \rho + Z \times \sqrt{\frac{\rho(1-\rho)}{n}} = 0.26 + 1.96 \times 0.0490408 = 0.3561182$$

Level of confidence The confidence level is the probability value (1–α) associated with a confidence level.

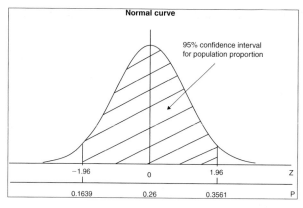

Figure 6.39

Figure 6.39 illustrates the 95% confidence interval for the population proportion.

Thus, the 95% confidence interval for ρ is
= 0.26 ± 1.96 * 0.0490408
= 0.1639 → 0.3561.

❋ **Interpretation**   The 95% confidence interval for the proportion of people who own the PC in the whole population is between 16.3% and 35.6%.

Student Exercises

X6.17 The standard deviation for a method of measuring the concentration of nitrate ions in water is known to be 0.05 ppm. If 100 measurements give a mean of 1.13 ppm, calculate the 90% confidence limits for the true mean.

X6.18 In trying to determine the sphere of influence of a sports centre a random sample of 100 visitors was taken. This indicated a mean travel distance (d) of 10 miles with a standard deviation of 3 miles: (a) what are the 90% confidence limits for the population mean travel distance (D), and (b) what sample size would be required to ensure that the confidence interval for D was 0.5 miles at the 95% level?

X6.19 The masses, in grams, of thirteen ball bearings taken at random from a batch are: 21.4, 23.1, 25.9, 24.7, 23.4, 24.5, 25.0, 22.5, 26.9, 26.4, 25.8, 23.2, 21.9. Calculate a 95% confidence interval for the mean mass of the population, supposed normal, from which these masses were drawn.

6.5 Calculating Sample Sizes

We can control the width of the confidence interval by determining the *sample size* necessary to produce narrow intervals. For example, if we assume that we are sampling a mean from a population that is normally distributed then we can use equation (6.25) to calculate an appropriate sample size for a stated interval, as per equation (6.34):

$$\text{Interval} = 2 \times Z \times \frac{\sigma}{\sqrt{n}}$$

(6.34)

Re-arranging equation (6.34) will enable the calculation of the size via equation (6.35):

$$n = \left(\frac{2 \times Z \times \sigma}{\text{Interval}} \right)^2 \tag{6.35}$$

Where interval $= 2 \times$ margin of error (e) $= \mu_2 - \mu_1$.

▷ Example 6.17

A researcher determines that a margin of error (or sampling error, e) of no more than ± 0.05 units is desired, along with a 98% confidence interval. Calculate the sample size, n.

Excel solution—Example 6.17

Figure 6.40 illustrates the Excel solution.

	A	B	C	D
1	Calculating sample size			
2				
3				
4		Specified interval =	0.1	
5		Population standard deviation σ =	0.2	
6				
7		2 tails, 98% confidence interval =	0.02	
8		Proportion in right and left hand tails =	0.01	=C7/2
9		Upper Z_cri =	2.326347874	=NORMSINV(1-C8)
10				
11		Sample size n =	86.5903109	=(2*C9*C5/C4)^2

Figure 6.40

→ Excel Solution

Specified interval = Cell C4   Value
Population standard deviation = Cell C5   Value
2 tails, 98% confidence interval = Cell C7   Value
Proportion in right and left hand tails = Cell C8   Formula: =C7/2
Upper Z_{cri} = Cell C9   Formula: =NORMSINV(1−C8)
Sample size n = Cell C11   Formula: =(2*C9*C5/C4)^2

From Excel: interval = 0.1, population standard deviation = 0.2, Z_{cri} for 98% = ±2.326347874 and the sample size is calculated from equation (6.35):

$$n = \left(\frac{2 \times Z \times \sigma}{\text{Interval}} \right)^2 = \left(\frac{2 \times 2.326347874 \times 0.2}{0.1} \right)^2 = 86.59$$

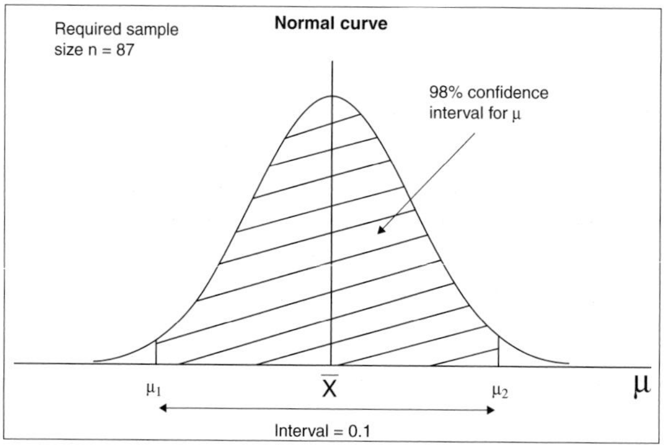

Figure 6.41

Figure 6.41 illustrates the relationship between interval, confidence interval, and size of sample.

Interpretation Thus, to produce a 98% confidence interval estimate of the mean, we need a sample size of 87.

Note To see what impact the selection of the error of margin and confidence interval has on the sample size, we'll run a small simulation. We'll keep all the data from the previous example.

Margin error	10%	10%	10%	10%
Conf. interval	90%	95%	98%	99%
Sample size	43	61	87	106

By keeping the same margin of error, but changing the confidence interval, we can see how the sample size changes. Effectively, in this example, we need to increase the sample size almost two and a half times if we wanted our confidence interval to increase from 90% to 99%. Let's now keep the confidence interval constant, at 90%, but let's change the margin of error.

Margin error	10%	5%	3%	1%
Conf. interval	90%	90%	90%	90%
Sample size	43	173	481	4329

As we can see the margin of error has a tremendous impact on the sample size. This explains why political polls are often conducted with 3% error margin. To increase the accuracy, in this case we would have to increase the sample size by tenfold, which is clearly too expensive.

It is particularly important to emphasize here that the margin of error depends very little on the size of the population from which we are sampling, as long as the sampling fraction is less than 5% of the total population. For very large populations, the impact is almost negligible.

Student Exercises

X6.20 A business analyst has been requested by the managing director of a national supermarket chain to undertake a business review of the company. One of the key objectives is to assess the level of spending of shoppers who historically have weekly mean levels of spending of €168 with a standard deviation of €15.65. Calculate the size of a random sample to produce a 98% confidence interval for the population mean spend, given that the interval is €30. Is the sample size appropriate given the practical factors?

■ Techniques in Practice

1. CoCo S.A. is concerned at the time to react to customer complaints and has implemented a new set of procedures for its support centre staff (see Chapter 4 TP1). The customer service director has directed that a suitable test is applied to a new sample to assess whether the new target mean time for responding to customer complaints is 28 days:

20	33	33	29	24	30
40	33	20	39	32	37
32	50	36	31	38	29
15	33	27	29	43	33
31	35	19	39	22	21
28	22	26	42	30	17
32	34	39	39	32	38

(a) Construct a point estimate for the mean time to respond.

(b) What are the model assumptions for part (a)?

(c) Construct a 95% confidence interval for the mean time.

(d) Is there any evidence to suggest that the mean time to respond to complaints is greater than 28 days?

2. Bakers Ltd is currently undertaking a review of the delivery vans used to deliver products to customers. The company runs two types of delivery van (type A—recently purchased and type B—at least 3 years old) which are supposed to be capable of achieving 20 km per litre of petrol. A new sample has now been collected as follows:

A	B	A	B
17.68	15.8	26.42	34.8
18.72	36.1	25.22	16.8
26.49	6.3	13.52	15.0
26.64	12.3	14.01	28.9
9.31	15.5		33.9
22.38	40.1		27.1

20.23	20.4	16.8
28.80	3.7	23.6
17.57	13.6	29.7
9.13	35.1	28.2
20.98	33.3	

(a) Construct a point estimate for the mean times.

(b) What are the model assumptions for part (a)?

(c) Construct a 95% confidence interval for the mean times.

(d) Assuming that the population distance travelled varies as a normal distribution do we have any evidence to suggest that the two types of delivery vans differ in their mean distance travelled?

(e) Based upon your analysis do we have any evidence that the new delivery vans meet the mean average of 20 km per litre?

3. Skodel Ltd is developing a low calorie lager for the European market with a mean designed calorie count of 43 calories per 100 ml. The new product development team are having problems with the production process and have collected two independent random samples to assess whether the target calorie count is being met (assume the population variables are normally distributed):

A	B	A	B
49.7	39.4	45.2	34.5
45.9	46.5	40.5	43.5
37.7	36.2	31.9	37.8
40.6	46.7	41.9	39.7
34.8	36.5	39.8	41.1
51.4	45.4	54.0	33.6
34.3	38.2	47.8	35.8
63.1	44.1	26.3	44.6
41.2	58.7	31.7	38.4
41.4	47.1	45.1	26.1
41.1	59.7	47.9	30.7

(a) Construct a point estimate for the calorie count.

(b) What are the model assumptions for part (a)?

(c) Construct a 95% confidence interval for the calorie count.

(d) Is it likely that the target average number of calories is being achieved?

■ Summary

In this chapter we have provided an introduction to the important statistical concept of sampling and explored methods that can be used to provide point and confidence intervals. We have shown that the Central Limit Theorem is a very important theorem that allows the application of a range of statistical tests to be performed:

1. We have shown how the Central Limit Theorem can eliminate the need to construct a sampling distribution by examining all possible samples that might be drawn from a population. The Central Limit Theorem allows us to determine the sampling distribution by using the population mean and variance values or estimates of these obtained from a sample.

2. Furthermore, an unbiased estimate of the population mean is provided by the sample mean, and the sample variance (or standard deviation) is a biased estimate of the population variance (or standard deviation).

3. From the Central Limit Theorem we know that the sampling distribution can be approximated by the normal distribution.

We have shown that, as the sample size increases, the standard error decreases but be aware that any advantage quickly vanishes as any improvements in standard error tends to be smaller as the sample size gets larger and larger. The next chapter will use these results to introduce the concept of statistical hypothesis testing. In this chapter we shall explore testing a statement about the value of a population parameter given information about one or two samples.

■ Key Terms

Central limit theorem
Confidence interval
Critical value
Degrees of freedom
Estimate
Level of confidence
Point estimate
Point estimate for
  the mean
Point estimate for the
  proportion

Point estimate for the
  variance
Random sample
Sampling distribution
Sampling distribution of
  the mean
Sampling distribution of
  the proportion
Sampling distribution of
  the variance
Sampling error

Sampling frame
Sampling with
  replacement
Sampling without
  replacement
Standard error of
  the mean
Standard error of the
  proportion
Student's t distribution
Unbiased

■ Further Reading

Textbook Resources

1. Whigham, D. (2007) *Business Data Analysis using Excel*. Oxford University Press. ISBN: 9780199296286.

2. Lindsey, J. K. (2003) *Introduction to Applied Statistics: A Modelling Approach* (2nd Edition). Oxford University Press. ISBN: 978-0-19-852895-1.

Web Resources

1. StatSoft Electronic Textbook http://www.statsoft.com/textbook/stathome.html (accessed 28/1/2007).

2. HyperStat Online Statistics Textbook http://www.davidmlane.com/hyperstat/index.html (accessed 28/1/2007).

3. Eurostat—website is updated daily and provides direct access to the latest and most complete statistical information available on the European Union, the EU Member States, the euro-zone and other countries http://www.epp.eurostat.ec.europa.eu (accessed 28/1/2007).

4. Economagic—contains international economic data sets (http://www.economagic.com) (accessed 28/1/2007).

5. The ISI glossary of statistical terms provides definitions in a number of different languages http://www.isi.cbs.nl/glossary/index.htm.

■ Formula Summary

$$\bar{X} = \frac{\sum X}{n} \tag{6.1}$$

$$\bar{\bar{X}} = \frac{\sum \bar{X}}{\sum f} \tag{6.2}$$

$$\bar{\bar{X}} = \mu \tag{6.3}$$

$$\sigma_{\bar{x}} = \sqrt{\frac{\sum f\bar{X}^2}{\sum f} - \left(\bar{\bar{X}}\right)^2} \tag{6.4}$$

$$\sigma_{\bar{x}} = \frac{\sigma}{\sqrt{n}} \tag{6.5}$$

$$\bar{X} \sim N\left(\mu, \frac{\sigma^2}{n}\right) \tag{6.6}$$

$$Z = \frac{\bar{X} - \mu}{\sigma/\sqrt{n}} \tag{6.7}$$

$$\sigma_{\bar{x}} = \frac{\sigma}{\sqrt{n}} \times \sqrt{\frac{N-n}{N-1}} \tag{6.8}$$

$$\mu_p = \pi \tag{6.9}$$

$$\sigma_p = \sqrt{\frac{\pi(1-\pi)}{n}} \tag{6.10}$$

$$p \sim N\left(\pi, \frac{\pi(1-\pi)}{n}\right)$$ (6.11)

$$Z = \frac{p - \pi}{\sqrt{\dfrac{\pi(1-\pi)}{n}}}$$ (6.12)

$$E(\bar{X}) = \mu$$ (6.13)

$$VAR(\bar{X}) = \sigma/\sqrt{n}$$ (6.14)

$$\hat{\mu} = \bar{X}$$ (6.15)

$$\hat{\sigma} = s_b \times \sqrt{\frac{n}{n-1}}$$ (6.16)

$$\hat{\sigma}_{\bar{X}} = \frac{\hat{\sigma}}{\sqrt{n}} = \frac{s_b}{\sqrt{n-1}}$$ (6.17)

$$\hat{\sigma} = s = \sqrt{\frac{\Sigma(X-\bar{X})^2}{n-1}}$$ (6.18)

$$\hat{\sigma}_{\bar{X}} = \frac{\hat{\sigma}}{\sqrt{n}} = \frac{s}{\sqrt{n}}$$ (6.19)

$$\hat{\pi} = p$$ (6.20)

$$\hat{\sigma}_p = \sqrt{\frac{\hat{\pi}(1-\hat{\pi})}{n}}$$ (6.21)

$$\bar{X} = \frac{n_1 \bar{X}_1 + n_2 \bar{X}_2}{n_1 + n_2}$$ (6.22)

$$\hat{\sigma}^2 = \frac{n_1 s_1^2 + n_2 s_2^2}{n_1 + n_2 - 2}$$ (6.23)

$$\hat{\pi} = \frac{n_1 \hat{\pi}_1 + n_2 \hat{\pi}_2}{n_1 + n_2} = \frac{n_1 p_1 + n_2 p_2}{n_1 + n_2}$$ (6.24)

$$\mu = \bar{X} - Z \times \frac{\sigma}{\sqrt{n}}$$ (6.25)

$$\bar{X} - Z \times \frac{\sigma}{\sqrt{n}} \leq \mu \leq \bar{X} + Z \times \frac{\sigma}{\sqrt{n}}$$ (6.26)

$$t_{df} = \frac{\bar{X} - \mu}{s/\sqrt{n}}$$ (6.27)

$$\sigma_{\bar{x}} = \frac{\hat{\sigma}}{\sqrt{n}} = \frac{s}{\sqrt{n}}$$

(6.28)

$$df = n - 1$$

(6.29)

$$\bar{X} - t_{df} \times \frac{s}{\sqrt{n}} \leq \mu \leq \bar{X} + t_{df} \times \frac{s}{\sqrt{n}}$$

(6.30)

$$Z = \frac{\bar{X} - \mu}{s/\sqrt{n}}$$

(6.31)

$$\bar{X} - Z \times \frac{s}{\sqrt{n}} \leq \mu \leq \bar{X} + Z \times \frac{s}{\sqrt{n}}$$

(6.32)

$$p - Z \times \sqrt{\frac{p(1-p)}{n}} \leq \pi \leq p + Z \times \sqrt{\frac{p(1-p)}{n}}$$

(6.33)

$$\text{Interval} = 2 \times Z \times \frac{\sigma}{\sqrt{n}}$$

(6.34)

$$n = \left(\frac{2 \times Z \times \sigma}{\text{Interval}} \right)^2$$

(6.35)

Introduction to Parametric Hypothesis Testing

» Overview «

Experiments, surveys, and pilot projects are often carried out with the objective of testing a theory, or hypothesis, about the nature of the process under investigation. Consider a UK company attempting to enter the German market. They appoint a distributor in Bavaria who reports that on average 2.7 litres of their product is consumed per week per family. Is this number representative and indicative of the whole country? Should they decide to expand the network of distributors? What confidence can be assigned to these numbers? Are these figures from Germany comparable to the UK market? Just how much confidence can be placed on the inference that there is no difference between two populations? In order to provide answers to these questions we set up a statement (a hypothesis) and test its validity by the application of probability theory.

In this chapter we shall explore a range of hypothesis tests for one and two samples where the population is normally distributed. The type of test employed, z or t, depends mainly on the sample size. Even if the population is not normal, the tests will still give an approximate solution if the sample size is suffciently large (Central Limit Theorem). In Chapter 8 we will describe hypothesis tests appropriate for categorical (chi square) and ordinal (non-parametric) data. In Chapter 9 we will extend the range of tests to include an introduction to the analysis of variance (ANOVA) and applying non-parametric procedures to problems involving more than two samples.

» Learning Objectives «

On completing this chapter you should be able to:

- » Understand the concept of null and alternative hypothesis.
- » Understand the difference between one and two samples.
- » Understand the difference between the terms parametric and non-parametric.
- » Identify appropriate one and two sample tests.
- » Explain what is meant by a significance level.
- » Choose an appropriate sampling distribution.

X

Hypothesis test procedure A series of steps to determine whether to accept or reject a null hypothesis, based on sample data.

Significance level, α The significance level of a statistical hypothesis test is a fixed probability of wrongly rejecting the null hypotheses, H_0, if it is in fact true.

» Understand the difference between one and two tail tests.

» Distinguish between type I and II errors.

» Understand the concept of a p-value.

» Understand the concept of a critical test statistic.

» Understand the use of the p-value and critical test statistic in making decisions.

» Identify and apply a step procedure in solving hypothesis related problems.

» Conduct one sample hypothesis tests for the sample mean and proportion.

» Conduct two sample hypothesis tests for the sample mean and proportion.

» Conduct an F Test for two population variances.

» Solve hypothesis test problems using Microsoft Excel.

7.1 Hypothesis Testing Rationale

A hypothesis is a statement of the perceived value of a variable or perceived relationship between two or more variables that can be measured. For example, the 'average salary of accountants is €31000' can be classed as a hypothesis statement which can be measured and assessed. It contains one variable that can be classed as salary. In another example, University of Teesside and Leeds undergraduate business degree students have similar entry qualifications can be written as a hypothesis statement. When dealing with a hypothesis test we have to formulate our initial research hypothesis into *two statements* which can then be evaluated: **null hypothesis** and **alternative hypothesis**.

7.1.1 Hypothesis statements H_0 and H_1

The null hypothesis (H_0) is known as the hypothesis of no difference and is formulated in anticipation of being rejected as false. The alternative hypothesis (H_1) is a positive proposition which states that a significant difference exists. In our first example, the average salary of accountants is €31000 can be stated as: H_0: μ = €31000 and the alternative hypothesis H_1: $\mu \neq$ €31000. In our second example, we state that there is no difference between the mean Teesside and Leeds entry scores, can be stated as H_0: Teesside mean = Leeds mean and the alternative hypothesis H_1: Teesside mean ≠ Leeds mean.

> **Note** The rejection of the null hypothesis in favour of the alternative hypothesis cannot be taken as conclusive proof that the alternative hypothesis is true, but rather as a piece of evidence that increases one's belief in the truth of the alternative hypothesis.

P-value The p-value is the probability of getting a value of the test statistic as extreme as or more extreme than that observed by chance alone, if the null hypothesis is true.

Critical test statistic The critical value for a hypothesis test is a limit at which the value of the sample test statistic is judged to be such that the null hypothesis may be rejected.

Test statistic A test statistic is a quantity calculated from our sample of data.

F test for variances Tests whether two population variances are the same based upon sample values.

Null hypothesis (H_0) The null hypothesis, H_0, represents a theory that has been put forward but has not been proved.

Alternative hypothesis (H_1) The alternative hypothesis, H_1, is a statement of what a statistical hypothesis test is set up to establish.

Example 7.1

The historical output by employees is a mean rate of 100 units per hour with a standard deviation of 20 units per hour. A new employee is tested on 36 separate random occasions and found to have an output of 90 units per hour. Does this indicate that the new employee's output is significantly different from the population mean output? Figure 7.1 illustrates the Excel solution to solve the problem outlined in Example 7.1. As we can see, we have used several built in Excel functions, which we will explain shortly, to help us make a decision. What is our decision? In this example we would reject H_0 in favour of H_1 and conclude that there is a significant difference between new employee output and the firm's existing employee output. In fact, this test gives us power to state that we are 95% certain of our decision. How did we do this? Hypothesis testing requires only a few strict steps and they are as follows:

(1) State hypothesis.

(2) Select the test.

(3) Set the level of significance.

(4) Extract relevant statistic.

(5) Make a decision.

Figure 7.1 illustrates the Excel solution.

	A	B	C	D	E	F
1	Hypothesis Testing Example - One Sample Z Test of the Population Mean					
2						
3			State Hypothesis			
4				H_0 : population mean $\mu = 100$	①	
5				H_1 : population mean μ not equal to 100		
6				Two tail test		
7			Select Test	One Sample Z Test for Mean	②	
8				Population distribution unknown but large n		
9				Population standard deviation known σ		
10			Set level of significance	Significance Level =	0.05	③
11						
12			Extract relevant statistic	Population		
13				Mean μ =	100	
14				Standard Deviation σ =	20	
15				Sample		
16				n =	36	
17				Xavg =	90	
18				Standard Error =	3.33333333	=E14/E16^0.5
19			④	Z_{cal} =	-3	=STANDARDIZE(E17,E13,E18)
20						
21				P-value and Critical Z		
22				Two tail p-value =	0.0026998	=2*(1-NORMSDIST(ABS(E19)))
23				Lower Z_{cri} =	-1.95996	=NORMSINV(E10/2)
24				Upper Z_{cri} =	1.95996	=NORMSINV(1-E10/2)
25					⑤	
26			Decision:	Since Z_{cal} < Lower Z_{cri}, Accept H_1		

Figure 7.1

As we already introduced how to state the hypothesis, let's explain the remaining four steps.

7.1.2 Parametric vs. non-parametric tests of difference

Tests of hypothesis are usually classified into two methods: parametric and non-parametric. Parametric methods make assumptions about the underlying distribution from which sample populations are selected. Non-parametric methods make no assumptions about the sample populations distribution. Parametric statistical tests assume that your data is approximately normally distributed (follows a classic bell-shaped curve) and that the data is at the interval/ratio level of measurement. This chapter is concerned with the type of hypothesis tests where the population is at the interval/ratio level of measurement and is either normally distributed or can be considered to be approximately normally distributed. This chapter will look at two types of parametric test: z, and Student's t test for one and two samples. If you have more than two samples then we can use a technique called analysis of variance (ANOVA) to undertake the hypothesis test (see Chapter 9).

Non-parametric methods do not make any assumptions about the sample population distribution and are often based upon data that has ben ranked, rather than actual measurement data. In many cases it is possible to replace a parametric test with a corresponding non-parametric test and Chapters 8 and 9 will explore a range of non-parametric tests, such as: sign test, Wilcoxon rank sum test (or Mann-Whitney U test), Wilcoxon matched pairs test, Kruskal-Wallis test, and Friedman's test.

7.1.3 One and two sample tests

In this chapter we will explore hypothesis tests involving both one and two samples. A *one sample test* involves testing a sample parameter (e.g. mean value) against a perceived population value (e.g. accountant salary €31000) to ascertain whether there is not a significant difference between a sample statistic and a population parameter (e.g. H_0: μ = €31000). For *two sample tests* we test a sample against another sample to ascertain whether or not there is a significant difference between two samples and, consequently, whether or not the two samples represent different populations. In both cases we shall use tests that utilize the normal probability distribution and will be testing for differences between means and proportions. The hypothesis tests that we will explore include: one sample z test for the population mean, one sample t test for the population mean, two sample z test for the population mean, two sample z test for the population proportion, two sample t test for population mean (independent samples), two sample t test for population mean (dependent samples), F test for two population variances (variance ratio test).

7.1.4 Choosing an appropriate test

Figure 7.2 provides a diagrammatic representation of the decisions required to decide on which one or two sample parametric test to use to undertake the correct hypothesis test. The key questions are as follows:

1. What are you testing: difference or association? For parametric tests we are measuring the difference between data values.

2. What is the type of data being measured? For parametric tests we are dealing with interval/ratio data.

3. Can we assume that the population is normally distributed? For parametric tests we expect the variable(s) being measured to be normally distributed or approximately normally distributed.

4. How many samples? In Figure 7.2 we are dealing with one and two sample parametric tests. If we have more then two samples then we would be dealing with an advanced statistical hypothesis concept called **analysis of variance (ANOVA)**.

5. From Figure 7.2 we can then choose the appropriate test by answering extra questions regarding whether we are dealing with means, proportions, or whether two samples are related or independent of one another.

> **Note** It is important to note that we have a range of other hypothesis tests to measure association (see Chapter 8 and Sections 10.1.3 and 10.1.5), and dealing with distribution free tests (see Chapters 8 and 9).

How to decide which parametric test to use?

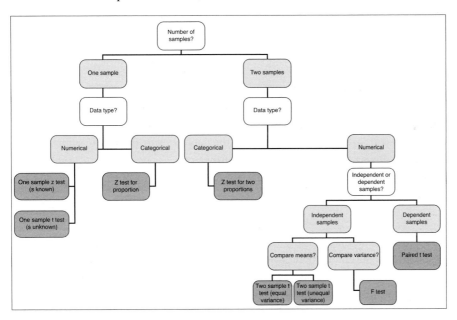

Figure 7.2

7.1.5 Significance level

The *level of significance* represents the amount of risk that an analyst will accept when making a decision. Whenever research is undertaken we will always have the possibility that the data values are subject to chance. The use of the significance level

X

Analysis of variance (ANOVA) Analysis of variance is a method for testing hypotheses about means.

is to seek to put beyond reasonable doubt the notion that the findings are due to chance. The level of significance is usually denoted by the Greek letter **alpha** (α) and represents the amount of error associated with rejecting the null hypothesis when it is true. The value of α is normally 5% (0.05) or 1% but the value of α depends upon how sure you want to be that your decisions are an accurate reflection of the true population relationship.

> ❊ **Interpretation**   If an analyst states that the results are significant at the 5% level then what they are saying is that there is a 5% probability that the sample data values collected have occurred by chance. An alternative view is to use the concept of a confidence interval. In this case we can observe that we are 95% confident that the results have not occurred by chance.

> **Note**   Most of the examples in this chapter use 0.05 for the level of significance. In practice you will notice that sometimes certain hypotheses can be accepted at that level of significance but would have to be rejected if we used 0.01 as the level of significance. What do we do in such situations? Read further on and Section 7.1.9 on types of errors might offer some resolution.

7.1.6 Sampling distributions

In Chapter 6 we explored the concept of sampling data from both a *normally distributed population* and explored the application of the *Central Limit Theorem* in sampling data from populations which are not normally distributed:

1. If we sampled from a population data set that is normally distributed then the sampling distribution for the sample mean $\bar{X}$ will be normally distributed with sample mean $\mu_{\bar{x}}$ = population mean μ, and sampling error $\sigma_{\bar{x}} = \sigma/\sqrt{n}$.

2. For populations that are not normally distributed we can make use of the Central Limit Theorem. The Theorem states that as the sample size increases then the sampling distribution of the mean approximates to a normal distribution. In general this is the case if the sample size is larger than 30 ($n \geq 30$).

3. For small sample size we will employ the Student's t distribution which states that if a population is normally distributed then the sample mean is normally distributed with sample mean $\mu_{\bar{x}}$ = population mean μ, and sampling error $\sigma_{\bar{x}} = s/\sqrt{n}$.

X

Alpha, α Alpha refers to the probability that the true population parameter lies outside the confidence interval. Not to be confused with the symbol alpha in a time series context i.e. exponential smoothing, where alpha is the smoothing constant.

Figure 7.3 illustrates a comparison between the normal and t distribution where the number of degrees of freedom increases from 8 to 30. We observe that the error between the normal and t distributions decreases as the number of degrees of freedom increases and that very little numerical difference exists between the normal and the t distribution when we have 30 degrees of freedom.

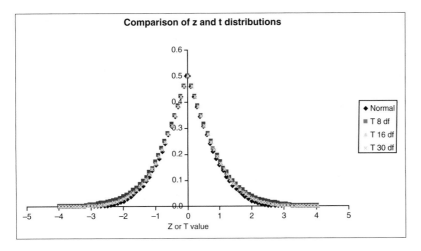

Figure 7.3

From this concept we can calculate the corresponding test statistic and calculate the critical test statistic value given a significance level.

> **Note**
>
> 1. The Central Limit Theorem states that regardless what the distribution of individual samples, if the number of samples is large enough, then their means will follow a normal distribution.
>
> 2. The Student's t test assumes that the sample standard deviation (s) provides an approximation to the population standard deviation (σ).

7.1.7 One and two tail tests

In Section 7.1.1 we stated that the alternative hypotheses were of the form $H_1: \mu \neq \text{€}31000$ or $H_1: \mu_T \neq \mu_L$. The $\neq$ sign tells us that we are not sure what the direction of the difference will be (< or >) but that a difference exists. In this case we have a **two tailed test**. It is possible that we are assessing that the average accountant salary is greater than €31000 (implying $H_1: \mu > \text{€}31000$) or is smaller than €31000 (implying $H_1: \mu < \text{€}31000$). In both cases the **direction** is known and these are known as **one tail tests**.

> **Note** The hypothesis test set up (H_0 and H_1) will automatically tell you whether you have a one or two tailed test.

The **region of rejection** is located in the tail(s) of the distribution. The exact location is affected by the way H_1 is expressed.

X

Two tail test A two tail test is a statistical hypothesis test in which the values for which we can reject the null hypothesis, H_0, are located in both tails of the probability distribution.

Directional test Implies a direction for the implied hypothesis (one tailed test).

One tail test A one tail test is a statistical hypothesis test in which the values for which we can reject the null hypothesis, H_0, are located entirely in one tail of the probability distribution.

Region of rejection The range of values that leads to rejection of the null hypothesis.

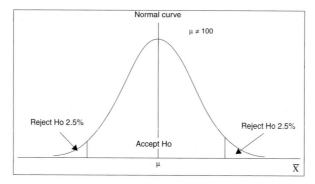

Figure 7.4

If H_1 simply states that there is a difference, e.g. $H_1: \mu \neq 100$ then the region of rejection is located in both tails of the sampling distribution with areas equal to $\alpha/2$, e.g. if α is set at 0.05 then the area in both tails will be 0.025 (see Figure 7.4).

This is known as a *two tail test*. If H_1 states that there is a direction of difference e.g. $\mu < 100$ or $\mu > 100$, then the region of rejection is located in one tail of the sampling distribution, the tail being defined by the direction of the difference.

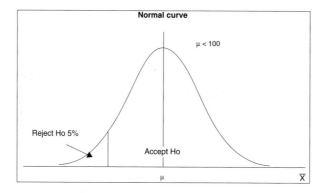

Figure 7.5

Hence for a less than direction the left hand tail would be used (see Figure 7.5).

This is known as a *lower one tail test*.

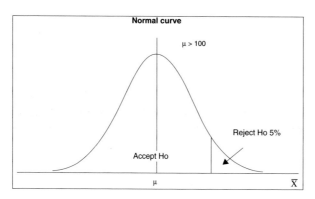

Figure 7.6

Hence for a greater than direction the right hand tail would be used (see Figure 7.6). This is known as an *upper one tail test*.

The actual location of this critical region will be determined by whether the variable being measured varies as a normal or Student's t distribution.

7.1.8 Check t test model assumptions

To undertake a Student's t test we assume that the population being measured varies as a normal distribution. To test this assumption we can use the exploratory data analysis techniques described in Section 4.3. What is important is that the mean and median are approximately equivalent, and that the distribution is approximately symmetrical. The t test is called a *robust* test in the sense that the accuracy of the technique is not unduly influenced by moving away from symmetry for increasing values of the sample size (see Section 6.2.6—Central Limit Theorem).

> **Note** Care should be taken for small samples if the population distribution is unknown. In this case you should consider using non-parametric tests (see Chapters 8 and 9) that do not make the assumption that the population of the variable being measured varies as a normal distribution.

7.1.9 Types of error

When making a decision, in hypothesis testing we can distinguish between two types of possible errors: type I and type II. A type I error is committed when we reject a null hypothesis when it is true whilst a type II error occurs when we accept a null hypothesis when it is not true.

		Truth	
		H_0 **true**	H_1 **true**
Decision	Reject H_0	Type I error	Correct
	Do not reject H_0	Correct	Type II error

Table 7.1 Types of error

Type I error

From Table 7.1 we observe that it is the rejection of a true null hypothesis that is a type I error. This probability is represented by the level of significance (Greek letter Alpha α) and the significance value chosen represents the maximum probability of making a type I error (α is normally 0.05).

Type II error

A type II error (denoted by Greek letter **Beta** β) is only an error in the sense that an opportunity to reject the null hypothesis correctly was lost. It is not an error in the sense that an

Type I error, α A type I error occurs when the null hypothesis is rejected when it is in fact true.

Type II error, β A type II error occurs when the null hypothesis, H_0, is not rejected when it is in fact false.

Beta, β Beta refers to the probability that a false population parameter lies inside the confidence interval.

incorrect conclusion was drawn since no conclusion is drawn when the null hypothesis is not rejected.

> **Note**   Which of the errors is more serious? The answer to this question depends on the damage that is related to it. Type I and type II errors are related to each other and increasing the type I error will decrease the type II error and vice versa.

Power

The power of the test is the probability of accepting the true alternative hypothesis or the probability of rejecting a false null hypothesis.

7.1.10 P-values

Unlike the classical approach using the critical test statistic we can use the p-value to decide on accepting or rejecting H_0. The p-value represents the probability of the calculated random sample test statistic being this extreme if the null hypothesis is true. This p-value can then be compared to the chosen significance level (α) to make a decision between accepting or rejecting the null hypothesis H_0.

> ✳ **Interpretation**   If $p < \alpha$ then we would reject the null hypothesis H_0 and accept the alternative hypothesis H_1.

Microsoft Excel can be used to calculate a p-value depending upon whether the variable being measured varies as a normal or Student's t distribution.

> **Note**   The Excel screenshots will identify each of these stages in the solution process.

The p-value will automatically be generated by Excel when using the Analysis ToolPak solution method.

7.1.11 Critical test statistic

A different approach to using the p-value is to calculate the test statistic and compare the value with a *critical test statistic* estimate from an appropriate table or via Excel. The value of the critical test statistic will depend upon the following factors: (i) significance level for z test problems, and (ii) the significance level and number of degrees of freedom for t test problems. This critical test statistic can then be compared to the calculated test statistic to make a decision between accepting or rejecting the null hypothesis H_0.

> ✳ **Interpretation**   If test statistic > critical test statistic then we would reject the null hypothesis H_0 and accept the alternative hypothesis H_1.

Microsoft Excel can also be used to calculate the critical test statistic values depending upon whether the variable being measured varies as a normal or Student's t distribution.

> 📎 **Note**   The Excel screenshots will identify each of these stages in the solution process.

These values will automatically be generated by Excel when using the Analysis ToolPak solution method.

> 🖱 **Student Exercises**
>
> X7.1   A supermarket is supplied by a consortium of milk producers. Recently a quality assurance check suggests that the amount of milk supplied is significantly different from the quantity stated within the contract: (i) Define what we mean by significantly different, (ii) state the null and alternative hypothesis statements, and (iii) for the alternative hypothesis do we have a two tail, lower one tail, or upper one tail test?
>
> X7.2   A business analyst is attempting to understand visually the meaning of the critical test statistic and the p-value. For a z value of 2.5 and significance level of 5% provide a sketch of the normal probabilty distribution and use the sketch to illustrate the location of the following statistics: test statistic, critical test statistic, significance value, and p-value (you do not need to calculate the values of z_{cri} or the p-value).

7.2 One Sample Z Test for the Population Mean

The first test we will explore is the one sample z test for the population mean that assumes that the sample data is randomly collected from a population that is normally distributed. In this particular case we know the value of the population standard deviation.

> ▷ **Example 7.2**
>
> Employees of a firm produce units at a rate of 100 per hour with a standard deviation of 20 units. A new employee is tested on 36 separate random occasions and found to have an output of 90 units per hour. Does this indicate that the new employee's output is significantly different from the average output?

Figure 7.7 illustrates the Excel solution.

	A	B	C	D	E	F
1	Hypothesis Testing Example - One Sample Z Test of the Population Mean					
2						
3			State Hypothesis			
4				H_0 : population mean μ = 100		
5				H_1 : population mean μ not equal to 100		
6				Two tail test		
7			Select Test	One Sample Z Test for Mean		
8				Population distribution unknown but large n		
9				Population standard deviation known σ		
10			Set level of significance	Significance Level =	0.05	
11						
12			Extract relevant statistic	Population		
13				Mean μ =	100	
14				Standard Deviation σ =	20	
15				Sample		
16				n =	36	
17				Xavg =	90	
18				Standard Error =	3.33333333	=E14/E16^0.5
19				Z_{cal} =	-3	=STANDARDIZE(E17,E13,E18)
20						
21				P-value and Critical Z		
22				Two tail p-value =	0.0026998	=2*(1-NORMSDIST(ABS(E19)))
23				Lower Z_{cri} =	-1.95996	=NORMSINV(E10/2)
24				Upper Z_{cri} =	1.95996	=NORMSINV(1-E10/2)
25						
26			Decision:	Since Z_{cal} < Lower Z_{cri}, Accept H_1		

Figure 7.7

→ **Excel Solution**

Significance level Cell E10   Value = 0.05
Population mean Cell E13   Value = 100
Population standard deviation Cell E14   Value = 20
Sample size n Cell E16   Value = 36
Sample mean Xavg Cell E17   Value = 90
Sample standard error Cell E18   Formula: =E14/E16^0.5
Z_{cal} Cell E19   Formula: =STANDARDIZE(E17,E13,E18)
Two tail p-value Cell E22   Formula: =2*(1−NORMSDIST(ABS(E19)))
Lower Z_{cri} = Cell E23   Formula: =NORMSINV(E10/2)
Upper Z_{cri} = Cell E24   Formula: =NORMSINV(1−E10/2)

Excel solution using the p-value

To use the p-value statistic method to make a decision:

(1) State hypothesis

Null hypothesis H_0: $\mu = 100$ (population mean is equal to 100 units per hour)
Alternative hypothesis H_1: $\mu \neq 100$ (population mean is not 100 units per hour)
The $\neq$ sign implies a two tail test.

(2) Select test

We now need to choose an appropriate statistical test for testing H_0. From the information provided we note:

- Number of samples—one sample.
- The statistic we are testing—testing for a difference between a sample mean ($\bar{x} = 90$) and population mean ($\mu = 100$). Population standard deviation is known ($\sigma = 20$).
- Size of the sample—large ($n = 36$).
- Nature of population from which sample drawn—population distribution is not known but sample size is large. For large n, the Central Limit Theorem states that the sample mean is distributed approximately as a normal distribution.

One sample z test of the mean is therefore selected.

(3) Set the level of significance (α) = 0.05 (see Cell E10)

(4) Extract relevant statistic

When dealing with a normal sampling distribution we calculate the z statistic using equation (7.1):

$$Z_{cal} = \frac{(\bar{x} - \mu)}{\sigma / \sqrt{n}}$$

(7.1)

From Excel, population mean = 100 (see Cell E13), population standard deviation = 20 (see Cell E14), sample size n = 36 (see Cell E16), sample mean $\bar{x} = 90$ (see Cell E17), standard error of the mean $\sigma_{\bar{x}} = 3.33333'$ (see Cell E18):

$$Z_{cal} = \frac{\bar{X} - \mu}{\sigma / \sqrt{n}} = \frac{90 - 100}{20 / \sqrt{36}} = -3 \text{ (see Cell E19)}$$

In order to identify region of rejection, in this case, we need to find the p-value. The p-value can be found from Excel by using the NORMSDIST() function. In the example $H_1: \mu \neq 100$ units/hour. From Excel, the two tail p-value = 0.0026998 (see Cell E22).

> **Note**   For *two tail tests the p-value* is given by the Excel formula:
> =2*(1−NORMSDIST(ABS(z value or cell reference)))
> For *one tail tests the p-value* would be given by the Excel formula:
> =NORMSDIST(z value or cell reference) for *lower tail p-value*, where z has a negative value
> =1−NORMSDIST(z value or cell reference) for *upper tail p-value*, where z has a positive value

(5) Make a decision

Does the test statistic lie within the region of rejection? Compare the chosen significance level (α) of 5% (or 0.05) with the calculated two-tail p-value of 0.0026998. We can observe that the p-value < α and we conclude that given two tail p-value (0.0026998) < (α) (0.05) we reject H_0 and accept H_1.

✻ **Interpretation**   Conclude that there is a significant difference, at the 0.05 level, between new employee output and the firm's existing employee output. In other words, the sample mean value (90 units per hour) is not close enough to the population mean value (100 units per hour) to allow us to assume that the sample comes from that population.

Note   Figure 7.8 illustrates the relationship between the p-value and test statistic.

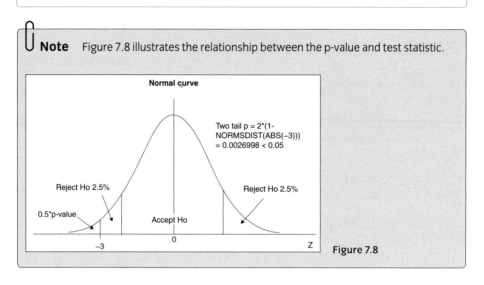

Figure 7.8

Excel solution using the critical test statistic, Z_{cri}

The solution procedure is exactly the same as for the p-value except that we use the critical test statistic value to make a decision:

(1) State hypothesis

(2) Select test

(3) Set the level of significance ($\alpha = 0.05$)

(4) Extract relevant statistic
     The calculated test statistic $Z_{cal} = -3.0$ (see Cell E19). We need to compare it with the critical test statistic, Z_{cri}. In the example $H_1: \mu \neq 100$ units/hour. The critical z values can be found from Excel by using the NORMSINV() function, two tail $Z_{cri} = \pm 1.96$ (see Cells E23 and E24).

Note   We can calculate the *critical two tail value of z* as follows:
=NORMSINV(significance level/2) for lower critical z value
=NORMSINV(1−significance level/2) for upper critical z value
The corresponding *one tail critical z values* are given as follows:
=NORMSINV(significance level) for lower tail
=NORMSINV(1−significance level) for upper tail

(5) Make decision

Does the test statistic lie within the region of rejection? Compare the calculated and critical z values to determine which hypothesis statement (H_0 or H_1) to accept. In Figure 7.9 we observe that Z_{cal} lies in the lower rejection zone ($-3 < -1.96$). Given Z_{cal} (-3) < lower two tail Z_{cri} (-1.96), we will reject H_0 and accept H_1.

Interpretation Conclude that there is a significant difference, at the 0.05 level, between new employee output and the firm's existing employee output. In other words, the sample mean value (90 units per hour) is not close enough to the population mean value (100 units per hour) to allow us to assume that the sample comes from that population.

Note Figure 7.9 illustrates the relationship between the critical z value and test statistic.

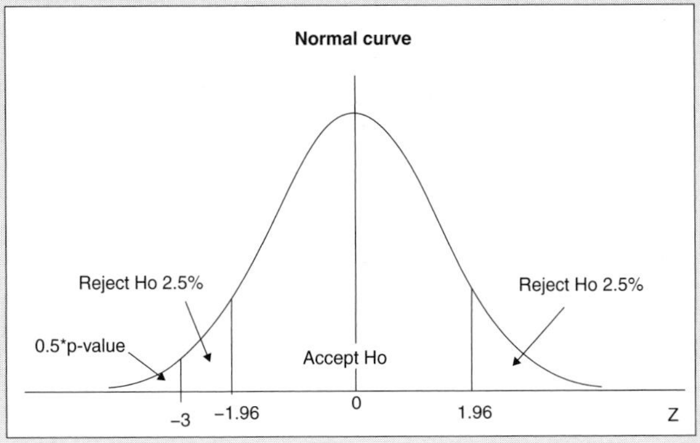

Figure 7.9

Student Exercises

X7.3 What are the critical z values for a significance level of 2%: (i) two tail, (ii) lower one tail, and (iii) upper one tail?

X7.4 A marketing manager has undertaken an hypothesis test to test for the difference between accessories purchased for two different products. The initial analysis has been performed and a upper one tail z test chosen. Given that the z value was calculated to be 3.45 find the corresponding p-value. From this result what would you conclude?

X7.5 A mobile phone company are concerned at the life time of phone batteries supplied by a new supplier. Based upon historical data this type of battery should last for 900 days with a standard deviation of 150 days. A recent randomly selected sample of 40 batteries was selected and the sample battery life was found to be 942 days. Is the population battery life significantly different from 900 days (significance level 5%)?

X7.6 A local Indian restaurant advertises home delivery times of 30 minutes. To monitor the effectiveness of this promise the restaurant manager monitors the time that the order was received and the time of delivery. Based upon historical data the average time for delivery is 30 minutes with a standard deviation of 5 minutes. After a series of complaints from customers regarding this promise the manager decided to analyse the last 50 data orders which resulted in an average time of 32 minutes. Conduct an appropriate test at a significance level of 5%. Should the manager be concerned?

Note As emphasized, the use of the p-value or comparison of z-calculated vs. z-critical value is a matter of preference. Both methods yield identical results. In conventional statistics textbooks z-critical values are given in special tables usually found in the textbook appendices. In this textbook we rely on Excel to calculate these values and no tables were used.

7.3 One Sample T Test for the Population Mean

If the population standard deviation is not known then we may use a one sample t test if the population distribution is normal. The t test uses the sample standard deviation, s, as an estimate of the population standard deviation, σ.

Example 7.3

A local car dealer wants to know if the purchasing habits of a buyer buying extras have changed. He is particularly interested in male buyers. Based upon collected data he has estimated that the distribution of extras purchased is approximately normally distributed with an average of £2000 per customer. To test this hypothesis he has collected the extras purchased by the last seven male customers (£): 2300, 2386, 1920, 1578, 3065, 2312 and 1790. Test whether the extras purchased on average has changed. Figure 7.10 illustrates the Excel solution.

	B	C	D	E	F
1	Testing Example - One Sample T Test of the Population Mean				
2					
3					
4		Hypothesis Test			
5			H_0 : population mean μ = 2000		
6			H_1 : population mean not equal to 2000 ①		
7			Two tail test		
8					
9		Select Test	One Sample T Test for Means ②		
10			Population distribution normal		
11			Population standard deviation unknown		
12					
13		Set level of significance	Significance Level =	0.05 ③	
14					
15		Extract relevant statistic	Population		
16			Population mean μ =	2000	
17			Sample	X (£'s)	
18				2300	
19				2386	
20				1920	
21				1578	
22				3065	
23				2312	
24				1790	
25					
26			Sample size n =	7	=COUNT(E18:E24)
27			Sample mean Xavg =	2193	=AVERAGE(E18:E24)
28			Sample standard deviation s =	489.6267286	=STDEV(E18:E24)
29			Standard Error =	185.0615084	=E28/E26^0.5
30		④	t_{cal} =	1.042896503	=(E27-E16)/E29
31					
32			P-value or Critical t		
33			Number of Degrees of freedom u =	6	=E26-1
34			Two tail p-value =	0.337182452	=TDIST(ABS(E30),E33,2)
35			Upper tcri =	2.446911846	=TINV(E13,E33)
36			Lower tcri =	-2.446911846	=-TINV(E13,E33)
37					
38		Decision:			
39		Since t_{cal} > Lower t_{cri} and < Upper t_{cri}, Accept H_0 ⑤			

Figure 7.10

→ **Excel Solution**

Significance level = Cell E13	Value = 0.05
Population mean = Cell E16	Value = 2000
Sample Data: Cells E18:E24	Values
Sample size = Cell E26	Formula: =COUNT(E18:E24)
Sample mean Xavg = Cell E27	Formula: =AVERAGE(E18:E24)
Sample standard deviation s = Cell E28	Formula: =STDEV(E18:E24)
Standard Error = Cell E29	Formula: =E28/E26^0.5
t = Cell E30	Formula: =(E27−E16)/E29
No of degrees of freedom = Cell E33	Formula: =E26−1
Two tail p-value = Cell E34	Formula: =TDIST(ABS(E30),E33,2)
Upper t_{cri} = Cell E35	Formula: =TINV(E13,E33)
Lower t_{cri} = Cell E36	Formula: =−TINV(E13,E33)

Excel solution using the p-value

To use the p-value statistic method to make a decision:

(1) State hypothesis

Null hypothesis H_0: $\mu = 2000$ (population mean spend on extras is equal to £2000).
Alternative Hypothesis H_1: $\mu \neq 2000$ (population mean is not equal to £2000).
The sign implies a two tail test.

(2) Select test

We now need to choose an appropriate statistical test for testing H_0. From the information provided we note:

- Number of samples—one sample.
- The statistic we are testing—testing for a difference between a sample mean and population mean ($\mu = 2000$). Two tail test. Population standard deviation is not known.
- Size of the sample—small ($n = 7$).
- Nature of population from which sample drawn—population distribution is normal, sample size is small, and population standard deviation is unknown. The sample standard deviation will be used as an estimate of the population standard deviation and the sampling distribution of the mean is a t distribution with $n - 1$ degrees of freedom.

We conclude that one sample t test of the mean is appropriate.

(3) Set the level of significance (α) = 0.05 (see Cell E13)

(4) Extract relevant statistic

The required distribution is a t distribution given by equation (7.2):

$$t_{cal} = \frac{(\bar{x} - \mu)}{s/\sqrt{n}}$$

(7.2)

From Excel, population mean = 2000 (see Cell E16), sample size $n = 7$ (see Cell E26), sample mean $\bar{x} = 2193$ (see Cell E27), sample standard deviation $s = 489.62673$ (see Cell E28), standard error of the mean $\sigma_{\bar{x}} = 185.0615084$ (see Cell E29):

$$t_{cal} = \frac{(\bar{x} - \mu)}{s/\sqrt{n}} = \frac{2193 - 2000}{489.62673/\sqrt{7}} = 1.0429 \text{ (see Cell E30)}$$

Identify region of rejection using the p-value method—the p-value can be found from Excel by using the TDIST() function. In the example H_1: $\mu \neq$ £2000. From Excel, the two tail p-value = 0.337182452 (see Cell E34).

> **Note**   We can calculate the *one and two tail p-value* using the Excel function:
> =TDIST(ABS(t value or cell reference), degrees of freedom, number of tails: 2 = 2 tail and 1 = one tail)

(5) Make a decision

Does the test statistic lie in the region of rejection? Compare the chosen significance level (α) of 5% (or 0.05) with the calculated two tail p-value of 0.337182452. We can observe that the p-value > α and we decided that we accept H_0. Given two tail p-value (0.337182452) > (α) (0.05), we will accept H_0 and reject H_1.

❈ **Interpretation**   Conclude that there is no significant difference, at the 0.05 level, between the extras purchases by the sample and the historical extras purchased of £2000.

Note   Figure 7.11 illustrates the relationship between the p-value and test statistic.

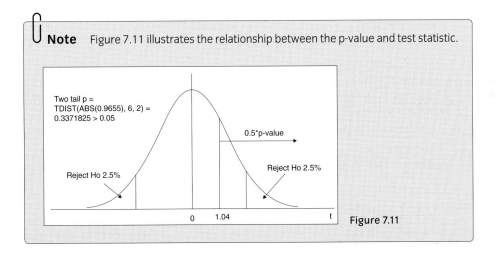

Figure 7.11

Excel solution using the critical test statistic, t_{cri}

The solution procedure is exactly the same as for the p-value except that we use the critical test statistic value to make a decision:

(1) State hypothesis

(2) Select test

(3) Set level of significance (α) of 5%

(4) Extract relevant statistic

The calculated test statistic t_{cal} = 1.0429 (see Cell E30). Calculate the critical test statistic, t_{cri}. In the example H_1: $\mu \neq$ £2000. The critical t values can be found from Excel by using the TINV() function, two tail t_{cri} = ±2.447 (see Cells E35–E36).

(5) Make decision

Note We can calculate the *critical two tail value of t* as follows:
=TINV(significance level, degrees of freedom) for upper critical t value
=–TINV(significance level, degrees of freedom) for lower critical t value
The corresponding *one tail critical value t* value are given as follows:
=TINV(2*significance level, degrees of freedom) for upper tail
=–TINV(2*significance level, degrees of freedom) for lower tail

Does the test statistic lie within the region of rejection? Compare the calculated and critical t values to determine which hypothesis statement (H_0 or H_1) to accept. Since t_{cal} (1.0429) lies between the two critical values (–2.447 → +2.447) we would accept H_0.

Interpretation Conclude that there is no significant difference, at the 0.05 level, between the extras purchases by the sample and the historical extras purchased of £2000.

Note Figure 7.12 illustrates the relationship between the critical t value and test statistic.

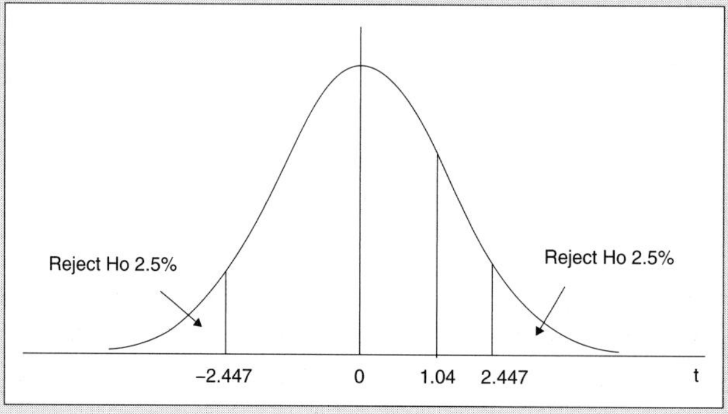

Figure 7.12

🖰 Student Exercises

X7.7 Calculate the critical t values for a significance level of 1% and 12 degrees of freedom: (i) two tail, (ii) lower one tail, and (iii) upper one tail.

X7.8 After further data collection the marketing manager (Exercise X7.4) decides to revisit the data analysis and changes the type of test to a t test. (i) Explain under what conditions a t test could be used rather than the z test, and (ii) calculate the corresponding p-value if the sample size was 13 and the test statistic equal to 2.03. From this result what would you conclude?

X7.9 A tyre manufacturer conducts quality assurance checks on the tyres that it manufactures. One of the tests consists of undertaking a test on their medium quality tyres with an independent random sample of 12 tyres providing a sample mean and standard deviation of 14500 kms and 800 kms respectively. Given that the historical average is 15000 kms and that the population is normally distributed test whether the sample would raise a cause for concern.

X7.10 A new low fat fudge bar is advertised with 120 calories. The manufacturing company conducts regular checks by selecting independent random samples and testing the sample average against the advertised average. Historically the population varies as a normal distribution and the most recent sample consists of the numbers: 99, 132, 125, 92, 108, 127, 105, 112, 102, 112, 129, 112, 111, 102, and 122. Is the population value significantly different from 120 calories (significance level 5%)?

7.4 Two Sample Z Test for the Population Mean

▷ Example 7.4

A large organization produces electric light bulbs in each of its two factories (A and B). It is suspected that the quality of production from factory A is better than from factory B. To test this assertion the organization collects samples from factory A and B and measures how long each light bulb works (in hours) before the light bulb fails. Both population variances are known ($\sigma_A^2 = 52783$, $\sigma_B^2 = 61650$). Conduct an appropriate test to test this hypothesis.

Figure 7.13 illustrates the Excel solution.

	A	B	C	D	E	F	G	H
1	Two Sample Z-Test for the Population Mean							
2								
3		A	B		Hypothesis Test			
4		900	1052			$H_0: \mu_A <= \mu_B$		
5		1276	947			$H_1: \mu_A > \mu_B$		
6		1421	886			One tail upper		
7		1014	788					
8		1246	1188		Select Test	Two Sample Z Test		
9		1507	928			Comparing two means with population distribution unknown		
10		975	983			Given large sample sizes we can assume normal distribution appropriate (CLT)		
11		1177	970			Population standard deviations unknown but since n large use sample to provide estimate		
12		1246	766					
13		875	1369		Set level of significance	Significance Level =	0.05	
14		816	737					
15		983	1114		Extract relevant statistic			
16		1119	354			Factory A:		
17		988	1347			$n_A =$	30	=COUNT(B4:B33)
18		1137	1062			Average A =	1135.333333	=AVERAGE(B4:B33)
19		1227	756			Population variance known $\sigma^2_A =$	52783.00	
20		858	1052					
21		941	754			Factory B:		
22		1299	990			$n_B =$	32	=COUNT(C4:C35)
23		1110	950			Average B =	894.21875	=AVERAGE(C4:C35)
24		929	783			Population variance known $\sigma^2_B =$	61560.000	
25		843	816					
26		1156	658			$Z_{cal} =$	3.972938206	=(G18-G23)/SQRT((G19/G17)+(G24/G22))
27		867	504					
28		1454	1076			P-value or Critical Z		
29		1403	500					
30		1165	1025			One tail upper p-value =	3.54957E-05	=1-NORMSDIST(G26)
31		1653	649			Upper Zcri =	1.644853627	=NORMSINV(1-G13)
32		1288	1166					
33		1187	498		Decision:			
34			945		Since $Z_{cal} >$ Upper Z_{cri}, Accept H_1			
35			1002					

Figure 7.13

→ **Excel Solution**

A: Cells B4:B33   Values
B: Cells C4:C35   Values
Significance level = Cell G13   0.05
n_A = Cell G17   Formula: =COUNT(B4:B33)
Sample average = Cell G18   Formula: =AVERAGE(B4:B33)
Population variance
known σ^2_A = Cell G19   Value
n_B = Cell G22   Formula: =COUNT(C4:C35)
Sample average = Cell G23   Formula: =AVERAGE(C4:C35)
Population variance
known σ^2_B = Cell G24   Value
Z_{cal} = Cell G26   Formula: =(G18–G23)/SQRT((G19/G17)+(G24/G22))
One tail upper
p-value = Cell G30   Formula: =1–NORMSDIST(G26)
Upper Z_{cri} = Cell G31   Formula: =NORMSINV(1–G13)

Excel solution using the p-value

To use the p-value statistic method to make a decision:

1. State hypothesis

   Null hypothesis $H_0: \mu_A \le \mu_B$

Alternative hypothesis H_1: $\mu_A > \mu_B$

The > sign implies an upper one tail test.

(2) Select test

We now need to choose an appropriate statistical test for testing H_0. From the information provided we note:

- Number of samples—two samples.
- The statistic we are testing—testing that the lifetime of light bulbs from factory A last longer than for factory B. Both population standard deviations are known ($\sigma_A = 52783$ and $\sigma_B = 61560$).
- Size of both samples large ($n_A = 30$ and $n_B = 32$).
- Nature of population from which samples drawn—population distribution is not known but sample size large. For large n, the Central Limit Theorem states that the sample means are approximately normally distributed.

Two sample z test of the mean.

(3) Specify a significance level ($\alpha = 0.05$) (see Cell G13)

(4) Extract relevant statistic

When dealing with a normal sampling distribution we calculate the z statistic using equation (7.3):

$$Z_{cal} = \frac{(\bar{X}_A - \bar{X}_B) - (\mu_A - \mu_B)}{\sqrt{\left[\dfrac{\sigma_A^2}{n_A} + \dfrac{\sigma_B^2}{n_B}\right]}}$$

(7.3)

From Excel: $n_A = 30$ (see Cell G17), $\bar{X}_A = 1135.33'$ (see Cell G18), $\sigma_A^2 = 52783$ (see Cell G19), $n_b = 32$ (see Cell G22), $\bar{X}_B = 894.21575$ (see Cell G23), $\sigma_B^2 = 61560$ (see Cell G24). If H_0 is true ($\mu_A - \mu_B = 0$) then equation (7.3) simplifies to:

$$Z_{cal} = \frac{\bar{X}_A - \bar{X}_B}{\sqrt{\left[\dfrac{\sigma_A^2}{n_A} + \dfrac{\sigma_B^2}{n_B}\right]}} = 3.9729 \text{ (see Cell G26)}$$

Identify region of rejection using the p-value method—the p-value can be found from Excel by using the NORMSDIST() function. In the example H_1: $\mu_A > \mu_B$. From Excel, the upper one tail p-value = 0.0000354957 (see Cell G30).

(5) Make a decision

Does the test statistic lie within the region of rejection? Compare the chosen significance level (α) of 5% (or 0.05) with the calculated upper one tail p value of 0.0000354957. We can observe that the p value < α and we conclude that we reject H_0 and accept H_1. Given upper one tail p-value (0.0000354957) < (0.05), we will reject H_0 and accept H_1.

✳ **Interpretation**   Conclude that at the 5% level of significance the light bulbs from factory A have significantly longer life times than the light bulbs from factory B.

Note   Figure 7.14 illustrates the relationship between the p-value and test statistic.

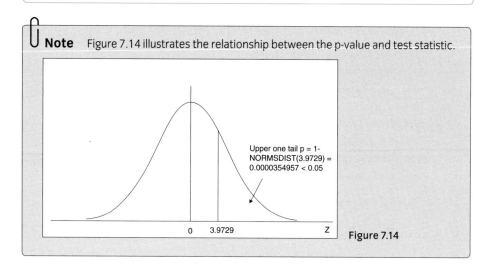

Upper one tail p = 1-
NORMSDIST(3.9729) =
0.0000354957 < 0.05

0   3.9729   Z   **Figure 7.14**

Excel solution using the critical test statistic, Z_{cri}

The solution procedure is exactly the same as for the p-value except that we use the critical test statistic value to make a decision (see Section 7.1.11). For Example 7.4 we find $Z = 3.9729$ and $Z_{cri} = +1.64$ (see Cell G31). Does the test statistic lie within the region of rejection? The calculation of Z yields a value of 3.9729 and therefore lies in the region of rejection for H_0. Given Z_{cal} (3.9729) > upper Z_{cri} (1.64) we will reject H_0 and accept H_1.

✳ **Interpretation**   Conclude that at the 0.05 level light bulbs from factory A have significantly longer life times that the light bulbs from factory B. We can express our decision in an alternative way: we can conclude with 95% confidence that light bulbs from factory A have significantly larger life time than bulbs from factory B.

Excel Analysis ToolPak solution

As an alternative to either of the two previous methods, we can use a method embedded in Excel Analysis Toolpak. Figure 7.15 screenshot illustrates the application of the Analysis ToolPak: Z test: Two Sample for Means (Select Tools > Data Analysis > Z Test: Two Sample for Means).

We observe from Figure 7.15 that the relevant results agree with the p-value and critical test methods described.

	A	B	C	D	E	F	G
1	Two Sample Z-Test for the Population Mean						
2							
3		A	B		z-Test: Two Sample for Means		
4		900	1052				
5		1276	947			Variable 1	Variable 2
6		1421	886		Mean	1135.333333	894.21875
7		1014	788		Known Variance	52783	61560
8		1246	1188		Observations	30	32
9		1507	928		Hypothesized Mean Difference	0	
10		975	983		z	3.972938206	
11		1177	970		P(Z<=z) one-tail	3.54957E-05	
12		1246	766		z Critical one-tail	1.644853627	
13		875	1369		P(Z<=z) two-tail	7.09915E-05	
14		816	737		z Critical two-tail	1.959963985	
15		983	1114				
16		1119	354		z-Test: Two Sample for Means		
17		988	1347		Input		
18		1137	1062		Variable 1 Range: $B$4:$B$33	OK	
19		1227	756		Variable 2 Range: $C$4:$C$35	Cancel	
20		858	1052		Hypothesized Mean Difference: 0	Help	
21		941	754				
22		1299	990		Variable 1 Variance (known): 52783		
23		1110	950		Variable 2 Variance (known): 61560		
24		929	783				
25		843	816		Labels		
26		1156	658		Alpha: 0.05		
27		867	504		Output options		
28		1454	1076		Output Range: $E$3		
29		1403	500		New Worksheet Ply:		
30		1165	1025		New Workbook		
31		1653	649				
32		1288	1166				
33		1187	498				
34			945				
35			1002				

Figure 7.15

✳ **Interpretation**   Conclude that at the 0.05 level light bulbs from factory A have significantly longer life times that the light bulbs from factory B.

🖱 **Student Exercises**

X7.11   A battery manufacturer supplies a range of car batteries to car manufacturers. The 40 amp-hour battery is manufactured at two manufacturing plants with a stated mean time between charges of 8.3 days and a variance of 1.25 days. The company regularly selects an independent random sample from the two plants with the following results:

Plant A				Plant B			
6.72	10.13	9.31	7.83	9.93	8.10	6.27	8.54
9.83	7.38	9.36	9.23	10.36	7.81	9.69	8.51
7.15	6.93	7.23	8.70	9.06	7.58	8.01	9.54
7.72	9.32	8.32	10.65	8.08	8.35	7.78	9.08
9.20	8.70	9.32	8.09	9.82	6.51	8.33	7.01
11.36	8.50	8.86	10.06	9.56	7.98	8.94	7.06
6.38	7.99	9.34	6.62	7.81	6.62	9.82	9.26
9.57	7.23	8.91	10.74	7.27	8.14	9.45	10.26

(a) For the given samples conduct an appropriate hypothesis test to test that the sample mean values are not different at the 5% level of significance.

(b) If the sample means are not significantly different test whether the population mean is 8.3 days (choose sample A to undertake the test).

X7.12 The Indian restaurant manager has employed two new delivery drivers and wishes to assess their performance. The following data represents the delivery times for person A and B undertaken on the same day:

Person A					Person B				
32.9	25.6	36.2	34.6	30.3	31.6	25.5	36.5	36.0	36.3
29.4	33.5	32.5	40.7	32.7	25.5	28.1	38.8	32.4	32.8
41.2	35.6	40.8	32.4	35.3	34.2	37.5	33.3	25.9	37.7
40.3	34.6	30.2	37.1		31.0	33.4	32.3	33.2	
39.3	36.5	35.0	32.7		35.5	32.6	31.9	36.8	
30.3	35.7	40.2	34.2		36.5	34.0	35.9	25.1	
37.5	38.0	33.4	33.2		36.1	41.4	29.0	37.6	
45.0	30.7	37.8	37.7		28.9	29.8	34.3	34.4	

Based upon your analysis of the two samples is there any evidence that the delivery times are different (test at 5%)?

7.5 Two Sample Z Test for the Population Proportion

▷ Example 7.5

A local police authority concerned at the number of passengers wearing rear seat belts in cars decided to undertake a series of surveys based upon two large cities. The survey consisted of two independent random samples collected from city A and B and the police authority would like to know if the proportions of passengers wearing seat belts between city A and B are different. Conduct an appropriate test to test this hypothesis?

Figure 7.16 illustrates the Excel solution.

	A	B	C	D	E
1	Two Sample Z Test for Proportion				
2					
3			City A	City B	
4		Number interviewed, N	250	190	
5		Number wearing rear seat belts, n	135	80	
6					
7		Hypothesis Test			
8			$H_0: \pi_A = \pi_B$	①	
9			$H_1: \pi_A \neq \pi_B$		
10			Two tail test		
11		Select Test	Two sample Z test for proportions	②	
12					
13			Population distribution unknown but sample size large		
14					
15		Set level of significance	Significance level =	0.05	③
16					
17		Extract relevant statistic	$N_A =$	250	=C4
18			$N_B =$	190	=D4
19			$n_A =$	135	=C5
20			$n_B =$	80	=D5
21			$p_A =$	0.54	=D19/D17
22			$p_B =$	0.421052632	=D20/D18
23					
24					
25		④	$Z_{cal} =$	2.492945713	=(D21-D22)/SQRT((D21*(1-D21)/D17+D22*(1-D22)/D18))
26					
27			P-value and critical Z		
28					
29			Two tail p-value =	0.013	=2*(1-NORMSDIST(ABS(D25)))
30			Lower z_{cri} =	-1.959963985	=NORMSINV(D15/2)
31			Upper Z_{cri} =	1.959963985	=NORMSINV(1-D15/2)
32					
33		Decision:			
34		Since $Z_{cal} >$ Upper Z_{cri}, Accept H_1	⑤		

Figure 7.16

→ Excel Solution

N_A = Cell C4	Value
N_B = Cell D4	Value
n_A = Cell C5	Value
n_B = Cell D5	Value
Significance level = Cell D15	Value = 0.05
N_A = Cell D17	Formula: =C4
N_B = Cell D18	Formula: =D4
n_A = Cell D19	Formula: =C5
n_B = Cell D20	Formula: =D5
α_A = Cell D21	Formula: =D19/D17
α_B = Cell D22	Formula: =D20/D18
Z = Cell D25	Formula: =(D21−D22)/SQRT((D21*(1−D21)/D17+D22*(1−D22)/D18))
Two tail p-value = Cell D29	Formula: =2*(1−NORMSDIST(ABS(D25)))
Lower Z_{cri} = Cell D30	Formula: =NORMSINV(D15/2)
Upper Z_{cri} = Cell D31	Formula: =NORMSINV(1−D15/2)

Excel solution using the p-value

To use the p-value statistic method to make a decision:

(1) State hypothesis

Null hypothesis $H_0: \pi_A = \pi_B$

Alternative hypothesis $H_1: \pi_A \neq \pi_B$

The $\neq$ sign implies a two tail test.

(2) Select test

We now need to choose an appropriate statistical test for testing H_0. From the information provided we note:

- Number of samples—two samples.
- The statistic we are testing—testing that the proportions wearing seatbelts is different between the two cities. Both population standard deviations are unknown.
- Size of both samples large ($n_A = 250$ and $n_B = 190$).
- Nature of population from which sample drawn—population distribution is not known but sample size large. For large n, the Central Limit Theorem states that the sample proportions are approximately normal distributed.

From this information we will undertake a two sample Z test for proportions.

(3) Set the level of significance (α) = 0.05 (see Cell D15)

(4) Extract the relevant statistic

When dealing with a normal sampling distribution we calculate the Z statistic using equation (7.4):

$$Z_{cal} = \frac{(p_A - p_B) - (\pi_A - \pi_B)}{\sqrt{\dfrac{\pi_A(1 - \pi_A)}{n_A} + \dfrac{\pi_B(1 - \pi_B)}{n_B}}} \qquad (7.4)$$

Where, p_A and p_B are proportions for sample A and B and π_A and π_B are the population proportions ($\pi_A \sim p_A$, $\pi_B \sim p_B$). From Excel: $N_A = 250$ (see Cell D17), $N_B = 190$ (see Cell D18), $n_A = 135$ (see Cell D19), $n_B = 80$ (see Cell D20), $p_A = 0.54$ (see Cell D21), $p_B = 0.42$ (see Cell D22). If H_0 is true ($\pi_A - \pi_B = 0$) then equation (7.4) simplifies to:

$$Z_{cal} = \frac{p_A - p_B}{\sqrt{\dfrac{p_A(1 - p_A)}{n_A} + \dfrac{p_B(1 - p_B)}{n_B}}} = 2.49 \text{ (see Cell D25)}$$

Identify region of rejection using the p-value method—the p-value can be found from Excel by using the NORMSDIST() function. In the example $H_1: \pi_A \neq \pi_B$. From Excel, the two tail p-value = 0.013 (see Cell D29).

(5) Make a decision

Is the test statistic within the region of rejection? Compare the chosen significance level (α) of 5% (or 0.05) with the calculated two tail p-value of 0.013. We can observe that the p value < α and we conclude that we reject H_0 and accept H_1. Given two tail p-value (0.013) < α (0.05) we will reject H_0 and accept H_1.

❋ **Interpretation**   We conclude that a significant difference exists between the proportions of rear passengers wearing seat belts between city A and B. Furthermore, the evidence suggests that the proportion wearing seat belts is higher for city A. To test this we could undertake an upper one tail test to test whether the proportion for city A is significantly larger than for city B. It should be noted that the decision will change if you choose a 1% level of significance.

Note   Figure 7.17 illustrates the relationship between the p-value and test statistic.

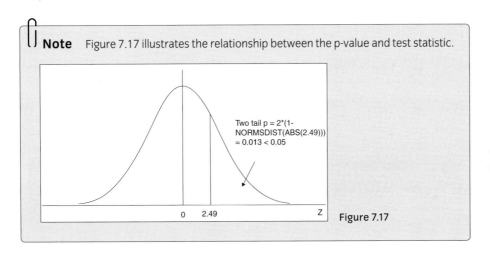

Figure 7.17

Excel solution using the critical test statistic, Z_{cri}

The solution procedure is exactly the same as for the p-value except that we use the critical test statistic value to make a decision. For Example 7.5 we find $Z = 2.49$ and $Z_{cri} = \pm 1.96$ (see Cells D30 and D31). Does the test statistic lie within the region of rejection? The calculation of Z yields a value of 2.49 and therefore lies in the region of rejection for H_0. Given Z_{cal} (2.49) > upper two tail Z_{cri} (+1.96) we will reject H_0 and accept H_1.

❋ **Interpretation**   We conclude that a significant difference exists between the proportions of rear passengers wearing seat belts between cities A and B.

🖱 **Student Exercises**

X7.13 During a national election a national newspaper wanted to assess whether there was a similar voting pattern for a particular party between two towns in the North East of England. The sample results were as follows:

	Town A	Town B
Number interviewed, N	456	345
Intention to vote for party, n	243	212

Assess whether there is a significant difference in voting intentions between town A and town B (test at 5%).

X7.14 A national airline keeps a record of luggage misplaced at two European airports during one week in the summer of 2009. A summary table representing the sample data is as follows:

	Airport A	Airport B
Total number of items processed, N	15596	25789
Number of items of luggage misplaced, n	123	167

Assess whether there is a significant difference in misplaced luggage between the two airports (test at 5%).

7.6 Two Sample T Test for Population Mean (Independent Samples, Equal Variances)

Example 7.6

A certain product of organic beans are packed in tins and sold by two local shops. The local authority have received complaints from customers that the amount of beans within the tins sold by the shop are different. To test this statistically two small random samples were collected from both shops.

Figure 7.18 illustrates the Excel solution.

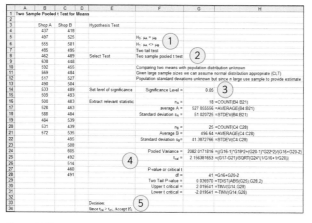

Figure 7.18

→ Excel Solution

A: Cells B4:B21	Values
B: Cells C4:C28	Values
Significance level = Cell G14	Value = 0.05
n_A = Cell G16	Formula:=COUNT(B4:B21)
average$_A$ = Cell G17	Formula: =AVERAGE(B4:B21)
s_A = Cell G18	Formula: =STDEV(B4:B21)
n_B = Cell G20	Formula: =COUNT(C4:C28)
average$_B$ = Cell G21	Formula: =AVERAGE(C4:C28)
s_B = Cell G22	Formula: =STDEV(C4:C28)
Pooled variance = Cell G24	Formula: =((G16–1)*G18^2+(G20–1)*G22^2)/(G16+G20–2)
t_{cal} = Cell G25	Formula: =(G17–G21)/SQRT(G24*(1/G16+1/G20))
df = Cell G28	Formula: =G16+G20–2
Two tail p-value = Cell G29	Formula: =TDIST(ABS(G25),G28,2)
Upper t critical = Cell G30	Formula: =TINV(G14,G28)
Lower t critical = Cell G31	Formula: =–TINV(G14,G28)

Excel solution using the p-value

To use the p-value statistic method to make a decision:

(1) State hypothesis

Null hypothesis H_0: $\mu_A = \mu_B$

Alternative hypothesis H_1: $\mu_A \neq \mu_B$

The $\neq$ sign implies a two tail test.

(2) Select test

We now need to choose an appropriate statistical test for testing H_0. From the information provided we note:

- Number of samples—two samples.
- The statistic we are testing—testing that the amount of beans in a tin sold by both shops are the same. Both population standard deviations are unknown.
- Size of both samples small $(n_A = 18$ and $n_B = 25)$.
- Nature of population from which sample drawn—population distribution is not known but we will assume that the population is approximately normal given sample size is close to 30. The t test is quite robust to departures from normality, even for small samples.

We will assume that the population variances are equal and conduct a *Two Sample t test: Assuming Equal Variances* (also called *pooled-variance t test*).

(3) Set level of significance (α) = 0.05 (see Cell G14)

(4) Extract relevant statistic

When dealing with a normal sampling distribution we calculate the t test statistic using equation (7.5), population standard deviation estimate from equation (7.6), and the number of degrees of freedom from equation (7.7):

$$t_{cal} = \frac{(\overline{X}_A - \overline{X}_B) - (\mu_A - \mu_B)}{(\hat{\sigma}_{A+B}) \times \sqrt{\left[\frac{1}{n_A} + \frac{1}{n_B}\right]}} \tag{7.5}$$

$$\hat{\sigma}_{A+B} = \sqrt{\frac{\left[(n_A - 1) s_A^2 + (n_B - 1) s_B^2\right]}{n_A + n_B - 2}} \tag{7.6}$$

$$df = n_A + n_B - 2 \tag{7.7}$$

From Excel: $n_A = 18$ (see Cell G16), $\overline{X}_A = 572.055'$ (see Cell G17), $n_B = 25$ (see Cell G20), $\overline{X}_B = 496.64$ (see Cell G21), and sample standard deviations $S_A = 51.02$ (see Cell G18), and $S_B = 41.38$ (see Cell G22).

$$\hat{\sigma}_{A+B} = \sqrt{\frac{\left[(n_A - 1) s_A^2 + (n_B - 1) s_B^2\right]}{n_A + n_B - 2}} = 2082.0171816 \text{ (see Cell G24)}.$$

If H_0 is true $(\mu_A - \mu_B = 0)$ then equation (7.5) simplifies to:

$$t_{cal} = \frac{(X_A - X_B)}{(\hat{\sigma}_{A+B}) \times \sqrt{\left[\frac{1}{n_A} + \frac{1}{n_B}\right]}} = 2.156 \text{ (see Cell G25)}$$

$$df = n_A + n_B - 2 = 41 \text{ (see Cell G28)}$$

Identify region of rejection using the p-value method—the p-value can be found from Excel by using the TDIST() function. In the example $H_1: \mu_A \neq \mu_B$. From Excel, two tail p-value = 0.036970 (see Cell G29).

⑤ Make a decision

Does the test statistic lie within the region of rejection? Compare the chosen significance level (α) of 5% (or 0.05) with the calculated two tail p value of 0.036970. We can observe that the p value < α and we conclude that we reject H_0 and accept H_1. Given the two tail p-value (0.036970) < α (0.05) we will reject H_0 and accept H_1.

❄ **Interpretation** We conclude that based upon the sample data collected that we have evidence that the quantity of beans sold by shops A and B are significantly different at the 5% level of significance. It should be noted that the decision will change if you choose a 1% level of significance.

Note   Figure 7.19 illustrates the relationship between the p-value and test statistic.

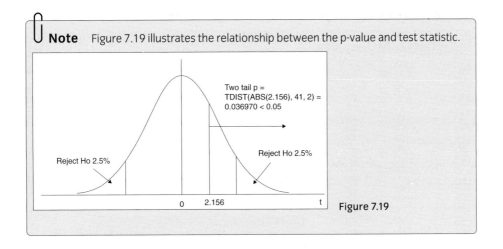

Two tail p =
TDIST(ABS(2.156), 41, 2) =
0.036970 < 0.05

Reject Ho 2.5%

Reject Ho 2.5%

0   2.156   t

Figure 7.19

Excel solution using the critical test statistic, t_{cri}

The solution procedure is exactly the same as for the p-value except that we use the critical test statistic value to make a decision. For Example 7.6 we find $t = 2.156$ and $t_{cri} = \pm 2.019541$ (see Cells G30 and G31). Does the test statistic lie within the region of rejection? The calculation of t yields a value of 2.156 and therefore lies in the region of rejection for H_0. Given the t_{cal} (2.156) > upper two tail t_{cri} (2.019541) we will reject H_0 and accept H_1.

✳ **Interpretation**   We conclude that based upon the sample data collected that we have evidence that the quantity of beans sold by shops A and B are significantly different at the 5% level of significance.

Excel Analysis ToolPak solution

As an alternative to either of the two previous methods, we can use a method embedded in Excel Analysis Toolpak. Figure 7.20 screenshot illustrates the application of the Analysis ToolPak: Two Sample Assuming Equal Variance Test (Select Tools > Data Analysis > t Test: Two Sample Assuming Equal Variances). We observe from Figure 7.20 that the relevant results agree with the p-value and critical test methods described.

	A	B	C	D	E	F	G
1	Two Sample Pooled t Test for Means						
2							
3		Shop A	Shop B		t-Test: Two-Sample Assuming Equal Variances		
4		437	418				
5		497	525			Variable 1	Variable 2
6		555	581		Mean	527.0555556	496.64
7		485	495		Variance	2603.114379	1712.906667
8		462	489		Observations	18	25
9		638	448		Pooled Variance	2082.017182	
10		592	455		Hypothesized Mean Difference	0	
11		569	484		df	41	
12		517	527		t Stat	2.156381653	
13		490	504		P(T<=t) one-tail	0.018485215	
14		533	489		t Critical one-tail	1.682878003	
15		509	493		P(T<=t) two-tail	0.03697043	
16		500	483		t Critical two-tail	2.019540948	
17		528	463				
18		588	484		t-Test: Two-Sample Assuming Equal Variances		
19		484	539		Input		
20		531	439		Variable 1 Range: $B$4:$B$21		OK
21		572	535		Variable 2 Range: $C$4:$C$28		Cancel
22			495				
23			508		Hypothesized Mean Difference: 0		Help
24			605		□ Labels		
25			492		Alpha: 0.05		
26			514				
27			460		Output options		
28			491		⊙ Output Range: $E$3		
29					○ New Worksheet Ply:		
30					○ New Workbook		
31							

Figure 7.20

✳ **Interpretation** We conclude that based upon the sample data collected that we have evidence that the quantity of beans sold by shops A and B are significantly different at the 5% level of significance.

🖰 Student Exercises

X7.15 During an examination board concerns were raised concerning the marks obtained by students sitting the final year advanced economics (AE) and e-Marketing (EM) papers:

AE	AE	EM	EM	EM
51	63	71	68	61
66	35	69	53	59
50	9	63	65	55
48	39	66	48	66
54	35	43	63	61
83	44	34	48	58
68	68	57	47	77
48	36	58	53	73
45		68	64	54

Historically the sample data varies as a normal distribution and the population standard deviations are approximately equal. Assess whether there is a significant difference between the two sets of results (test at 5%).

X7.16 A university finance department would like to compare the travel expenses claimed by staff attending conferences. After initial data analysis the finance director has identified two departments who seem to have very different levels of claims. Based upon the data provided undertake a suitable test to assess whether the level of claims from department A is significantly greater than from department B. You can assume that the population expenses data is normally distributed and that the population standard deviations are approximately equal.

Department A				Department B		
156.67	146.81	147.28	140.67	108.21	109.10	127.16
169.81	143.69	157.58	154.78	142.68	110.93	101.85
130.74	155.38	179.89	154.86	135.92	132.91	124.94
158.86	170.74					

7.7 Two Sample Tests for Population Mean (Independent Samples, Unequal Variances)

7.7.1 Two sample t test for independent samples (unequal variances)

In Example 7.6 we assumed that the variances were equal for the two samples and conducted a two sample pooled t test. In this test we assume that the population variances are equal and the sample variances are combined together to give a pooled estimate of $\hat{\sigma}_{A+B}$ given by equation (7.6). If we are concerned that the assumption of equal variances is unsound then we can conduct a two sample t test using equations (7.8) and (7.9).

Example 7.7

A certain product of organic beans are packed in tins and sold by two local shops. The local authority have received complaints from customers that the amount of beans within the tins sold by the shop are different. To test this statistically two small random samples were collected from both shops.

Figure 7.21 illustrates the Excel solution.

	A	B	C	D	E	F	G	H
1	Two Sample t Test for Means assuming unequal variances							
2								
3		Shop A	Shop B		Hypothesis Test			
4		437	418			H_0: $\mu_A = \mu_B$ ①		
5		497	525			H_1: $\mu_A <> \mu_B$		
6		555	581			Two tail test		
7		485	495					
8		462	489		Select Test	Two Sample t test assuming unequal variances ②		
9		638	448			Comparing two means with population distribution unknown		
10		592	455			Given large sample sizes we can assume normal distribution appropriate (CLT)		
11		569	484			Population standard deviations unknown but since n large use sample to provide estimate		
12		517	527					
13		490	504		Set level of significance	Significance Level =	0.05 ③	
14		533	489					
15		509	493		Extract relevant statistic	n_A =	18	=COUNT(B4:B21)
16		500	483			average A =	527.055556	=AVERAGE(B4:B21)
17		528	463			Standard deviation s_A =	51.020725	=STDEV(B4:B21)
18		588	484					
19		484	539			n_B =	25	=COUNT(C4:C28)
20		531	439			Average B =	496.64	=AVERAGE(C4:C28)
21		572	535			Standard deviation s_B =	41.3872766	=STDEV(C4:C28)
22			495					
23			508			t_{cal} = ④	2.083385602	=(G16-G20)/(G17^2/(G15)+G21^2/(G19))^0.5
24			605					
25			492			P-value or critical t		
26			514			df num =	45425.98779	=(G17^2/G15+G21^2/G19)^2
27			460			df denom =	1425.851008	=((G17^2/G15)^2/(G15-1)+(G21^2/G19)^2/(G19-1))
28			491			df =	32	=IF((G26/G27-INT(G26/G27)<0.5),INT(G26/G27),INT(G26/G27)+1)
29								
30						Two Tail P-value =	0.045288	=TDIST(ABS(G23),G28,2)
31						Upper t critical =	2.036933	=TINV(G13,G28)
32						Lowr t critical =	-2.036933	=-TINV(G13,G28)
33								
34					Decision:			
35					Since $t_{cal} > t_{cri}$, Accept H_1 [Borderline decision] ⑤			

Figure 7.21

→ **Excel Solution**

A: Cells B4:B21   Values
B: Cells C4:C28   Values
Significance level = Cell G13   Value = 0.05
n_A = Cell G15   Formula: =COUNT(B4:B21)
$average_A$ = Cell G16   Formula: =AVERAGE(B4:B21)
s_A = Cell G17   Formula: =STDEV(B4:B21)
n_B = Cell G19   Formula: =COUNT(C4:C28)
$average_B$ = Cell G20   Formula: =AVERAGE(C4:C28)
s_B = Cell G21   Formula: =STDEV(C4:C28)
t_{cal} = Cell G23   Formula: =(G16−G20)/(G17^2/(G15)+G21^2/(G19))^0.5
df num = Cell G26   Formula: =(G17^2/G15+G21^2/G19)^2
df denom = Cell G27   Formula: =((G17^2/G15)^2/(G15−1)+(G21^2/G19)^2/(G19−1))
df = Cell G28   Formula: =IF((G26/G27−INT(G26/G27)<0.5), INT(G26/G27),INT(G26/G27)+1)
Two tail p-value = Cell G30   Formula: =TDIST(ABS(G23),G28,2)
Upper t critical = Cell G31   Formula: =TINV(G13,G28)
Lower t critical = Cell G32   Formula: =−TINV(G13,G28)

Excel solution using the p-value

To use the p-value statistic method to make a decision:

① State hypothesis
    Null hypothesis H_0: $\mu_A = \mu_B$
    Alternative hypothesis H_1: $\mu_A \neq \mu_B$
    The $\neq$ sign implies a two tail test.

② Select test

We now need to choose an appropriate statistical test for testing H_0. From the information provided we note:

- Number of samples—two samples.
- The statistic we are testing—testing that the amount of beans in a tin sold by both shops are the same. Both population standard deviations are unknown.
- Size of both samples small ($n_A = 18$ and $n_B = 25$).
- Nature of population from which sample drawn—population distribution is not known but we will assume that the population is approximately normal given sample size is close to 30. The t test is quite robust to departures from normality, even for small samples.

We will assume that the population variances are not equal and conduct a *Two Sample t test: Assuming Unequal Variances* (also called *separate-variance t test*).

③ Set the level of significance (α) = 0.05 (see Cell G13)

④ Extract relevant statistic

When dealing with a normal sampling distribution we calculate the *Satterthwaite's approximate t test statistic* equation (7.8) with the number of degrees of freedom given by equation (7.9):

$$t_{cal} = \frac{(\overline{X}_A - \overline{X}_B) - (\mu_A - \mu_B)}{\sqrt{\left[\dfrac{S_A^2}{n_A} + \dfrac{S_B^2}{n_B}\right]}} \quad (7.8)$$

$$df = \frac{\left(\dfrac{S_A^2}{n_A} + \dfrac{S_B^2}{n_B}\right)^2}{\left(\dfrac{\left(\dfrac{S_A^2}{n_A}\right)^2}{n_A - 1} + \dfrac{\left(\dfrac{S_B^2}{n_B}\right)^2}{n_B - 1}\right)} \quad (7.9)$$

From Excel: $n_A = 18$ (see Cell G15), $\overline{X}_A = 527.055'$ (see Cell G16), $n_B = 25$ (see Cell G19), $\overline{X}_B = 496.64$ (see Cell G20), and sample standard deviations $S_A = 51.02$ (see Cell G17), and $S_B = 41.38$ (see Cell G21). If H_0 is true ($\mu_A - \mu_B = 0$) then equation (7.8) simplifies to:

$$t_{cal} = \frac{\overline{X}_A - \overline{X}_B}{\sqrt{\left[\dfrac{S_A^2}{n_A} + \dfrac{S_B^2}{n_B}\right]}} = 2.083 \quad \text{(see Cell G23)}$$

$$df = \frac{\left(\dfrac{S_A^2}{n_A} + \dfrac{S_B^2}{n_B}\right)^2}{\left(\dfrac{\left(\dfrac{S_A^2}{n_A}\right)^2}{n_A - 1} + \dfrac{\left(\dfrac{S_B^2}{n_B}\right)^2}{n_B - 1}\right)} = 32 \quad \text{(see Cell G28)}$$

Identify region of rejection using the p-value method—the p-value can be found from Excel by using the TDIST() function. In the example $H_1: \mu_A \neq \mu_B$. From Excel, the two tail p-value = 0.045288 (see Cell G30).

(5) Make a decision

Does the test statistic lie within the region of rejection? Compare the chosen significance level (α) of 5% (or 0.05) with the calculated two tail p value of 0.045288. We can observe that the p value < α and we conclude that we reject H_0 and accept H_1. Given the two tail p-value (0.045288) < α (0.05) we will reject H_0 and accept H_1.

✳ **Interpretation**   We conclude that based upon the sample data collected that we have evidence that the quantity of beans sold by shops A and B are significantly different at the 5% level of significance. It should be noted that the result in this case rests at the borderline of accepting either H_0 or H_1. At this stage a recommendation would be to revisit the data collection methods employed and increase the sample sizes.

Note   Figure 7.22 illustrates the relationship between the p-value and test statistic.

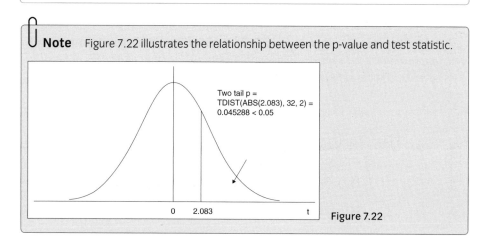

Two tail p = TDIST(ABS(2.083), 32, 2) = 0.045288 < 0.05

Figure 7.22

Excel solution using the critical test statistic, t_{cri}

The solution procedure is exactly the same as for the p-value except that we use the critical test statistic value to make a decision. For Example 7.7 we find t_{cal} = 2.083 and t_{cri} = ±2.036933 (see Cells G31 and G32). Does the test statistic lie within the region of rejection? The calculation of t yields a value of 2.083 and therefore lies within the region of rejection for H_0. Given that t_{cal} (2.083) > upper two tail t_{cri} (2.036933) we will reject H_0 and accept H_1.

✳ **Interpretation**   We conclude that based upon the sample data collected that we have evidence that the quantity of beans sold by shops A and B are significantly different at the 5% level of significance.

Excel Analysis ToolPak solution

As an alternative to either of the two previous methods, we can use a method embedded in Excel Analysis Toolpak. Figure 7.23 screenshot illustrates the application of the Analysis ToolPak: t test: Two Sample Assuming Unequal Variances (Select Tools > Data Analysis > t test: Two Sample Assuming Unequal Variances).

We observe from Figure 7.23 that the relevant results agree with the p-value and critical test methods described.

	A	B	C	D	E	F	G
1	Two Sample t Test for Means assuming unequal variances						
2							
3		Shop A	Shop B		t-Test: Two-Sample Assuming Unequal Variances		
4		437	418				
5		497	525			Variable 1	Variable 2
6		555	581		Mean	527.0555556	496.64
7		485	495		Variance	2603.114379	1712.906667
8		462	489		Observations	18	25
9		638	448		Hypothesized Mean Difference	0	
10		592	455		df	32	
11		569	484		t Stat	2.083385602	
12		517	527		P(T<=t) one-tail	0.022644068	
13		490	504		t Critical one-tail	1.693888703	
14		533	489		P(T<=t) two-tail	0.045288136	
15		509	493		t Critical two-tail	2.036933334	
16		500	483				
17		528	463		t-Test: Two-Sample Assuming Unequal Variances		
18		588	484		Input		
19		484	539		Variable 1 Range: $B$4:$B$21		OK
20		531	439		Variable 2 Range: $C$4:$C$28		Cancel
21		572	535		Hypothesized Mean Difference: 0		Help
22			495				
23			508		Labels		
24			605		Alpha: 0.05		
25			492				
26			514		Output options		
27			460		Output Range: $E$3		
28			491		New Worksheet Ply:		
29					New Workbook		
30							

Figure 7.23

✳ **Interpretation** We conclude that based upon the sample data collected that we have evidence that the quantity of beans sold by shops A and B are significantly different at the 5% level of significance.

7.7.2 Equivalent non-parametric test: Mann-Whitney U test

For two independent samples the non-parametric equivalent test is the Mann-Whitney U test which will be described in Chapter 8. Please note that this is also called the Wilcoxon rank sum test.

🖱 **Student Exercises**

X7.17   Apply a two sample t test to X7.15 but do not assume equal variance. Is there a significant difference (test at 5%)?

X7.18   Apply a two sample t test to X7.16 but do not assume equal variance. Is there a significant difference (test at 5%)?

7.8 Two Sample Tests for Population Mean (Dependent or Paired Samples)

7.8.1 Two sample t test for dependent samples

👆 **Example 7.8**

Suppose that Super Slim is offering a weight reduction programme that they advertise will result in more than a 10 pound weight loss in the first 30 days. Twenty six subjects were independently randomly selected for a study and their weights before and after the weight loss programme were recorded. Super Slim have stated that the historical data shows that the populations are normally distributed. Figure 7.24 contains the raw data and Excel solution.

Figure 7.24 illustrates the Excel solution

	A	B	C	D	E	F	G	H	I	J	K	L	M
1		TWO SAMPLE T TEST ASSUMING PAIRED SAMPLES											
2													
3													
4		Person	Before Weight, B	After Weight, A	d = B - A		d^2						
5		1	170	170	0	=C5-D5	0	=E5^2		Hypothesis			
6		2	159	153	6		36				H_0: Weight loss 10 lbs or le		1
7		3	162	129	33		1089				H_1: Weight loss > 10 lbs		
8		4	153	143	10		100				Upper one tail test		
9		5	177	137	40		1600						
10		6	167	134	33		1089			State Test	Two sample paired t test		2
11		7	158	133	25		625				Populations normally distributed		
12		8	178	128	50		2500						
13		9	141	152	-11		121			Set level of significance	Signicance level	0.05	3
14		10	163	142	21		441						
15		11	154	140	14		196			Extract relevant statistic	n =	26	=COUNT(B5:B30)
16		12	159	154	5		25				Σd =	447	=SUM(E5:E30)
17		13	159	143	16		256				Σd^2 =	12989	=SUM(G5:G30)
18		14	138	147	-9		81				Mean d =	17.1923	=AVERAGE(E5:E30)
19		15	161	142	19		361				sd =	14.5658	=SQRT((L17-L16^2/L15)/(L15-1))
20		16	156	149	7		49			4	t_{cal} =	2.5178	=(L18-10)/(L19/SQRT(L15))
21		17	165	136	29		841						
22		18	158	154	4		16				P-value and critical t		
23		19	151	140	11		121				df =	25	=L15-1
24		20	165	145	20		400				Upper p-value =	0.0093	=TDIST(ABS(L20),L23,1)
25		21	155	125	30		900				Upper t cri =	1.7081	=TINV(2*L13,L23)
26		22	154	140	14		196						
27		23	147	125	22		484			Decision:			
28		24	156	141	15		225			Since t_{cal} > t_{cri}, Accept H_1	5		
29		25	155	146	9		81						
30		26	169	135	34		1156						

Figure 7.24

→ **Excel Solution**

Person Cells B5:B30	Values	
Before weight, B Cells C5:C30	Values	
After weight, A Cells D5:D30	Values	
d =B-A Cell E5	Formula:=C5–D5	
	Copy formula: E5:E30	
d^2 = Cell G5	Formula:=E5^2	
	Copy formula: G5:G30	
Significance level Cell L13	Value = 0.05	
n = Cell L15	Formula: =COUNT(B5:B30)	
Σd = Cell L16	Formula: =SUM(E5:E30)	
Σd^2 = Cell L17	Formula: =SUM(G5:G30)	
Mean d = Cell L18	Formula: =AVERAGE(E5:E30)	
s_d = Cell L19	Formula: =SQRT((L17–L16^2/L15)/(L15–1))	
t_{cal} = Cell L20	Formula: =(L18–10)/(L19/SQRT(L15))	
df = Cell L23	Formula: =L15–1	
Upper p-value = Cell L24	Formula: =TDIST(ABS(L20),L23,1)	
Upper t_{cri} = Cell L25	Formula: =TINV(2*K13,L23)	

Excel solution using the p-value

(1) State hypothesis

The hypothesis statement implies that the population mean weight loss between A and B should be at least 10 pounds. If $d = \mu_A - \mu_B$, then the null and alternative hypotheses would be stated as follows:

Null hypothesis H_0: $d \leq 10$
Alternative hypothesis H_1: $d > 10$ (or $d - 10 > 0$)
The > sign implies an upper one tail test.

(2) Select test

We now need to choose an appropriate statistical test for testing H_0. From the information provided we note:

- Number of samples—two samples.
- The statistic we are testing—testing that the weight reduction programme results in a weight loss. Both population standard deviations are unknown.
- Size of both samples (n_A and $n_B = 26$).
- Nature of population from which sample drawn—population distribution is not known, we will assume that the population is approximately normal given sample size is close to 30. The t test is quite robust to departures from normality, even for small samples.

In this case we have two variables that are related to each other (weight before vs weight after treament) and we will conduct a *Two Sample t test: Paired Sample for Means*.

(3) Set level of significance (α) = 0.05 (see Cell L13)

(4) Extract relevant statistic

The t test statistic is given by equation (7.10) with the number of degrees of freedom given by equation (7.12):

$$t_{cal} = \frac{\bar{d} - d}{\frac{s_d}{\sqrt{n}}} \tag{7.10}$$

$$s_d = \sqrt{\frac{\sum d^2 - (\sum d)^2 / n}{n - 1}} \tag{7.11}$$

$$df = n - 1 \tag{7.12}$$

From Excel: n = 26 (see Cell L15), $\sum d = 447$ (see Cell L16), $\sum d^2 = 12989$ (see Cell L17), $\bar{d} = 17.19231$ (see Cell L18), and d = 10:

$$s_d = \sqrt{\frac{\sum d^2 - (\sum d)^2 / n}{n - 1}} = 14.56577 \quad \text{(see Cell L19)}$$

$$t_{cal} = \frac{\bar{d} - d}{\frac{s_d}{\sqrt{n}}} = 2.517802 \quad \text{(see Cell L20)}$$

$$df = n - 1 = 25 \quad \text{(see Cell L23)}$$

Identify region of rejection using the p-value method—the p-value can be found from Excel by using the TDIST() function. In the example $H_1: D > 10$. From Excel, the upper one tail p-value = 0.0093 (see Cell L24).

(5) Make a decision

Does the test statistic lie within the region of rejection? Compare the chosen significance level (α) of 5% (or 0.05) with the calculated upper one tail p value of 0.0093. We can observe that the p value < α and we conclude that we reject H_0 and accept H_1. Given that the upper one tail p-value (0.0093) < α (0.05) we will reject H_0 and accept H_1.

❋ **Interpretation** Conclude that the average weight loss is more than 10 lbs at a 5% level of significance.

Note Figure 7.25 illustrates the relationship between the p-value and test statistic.

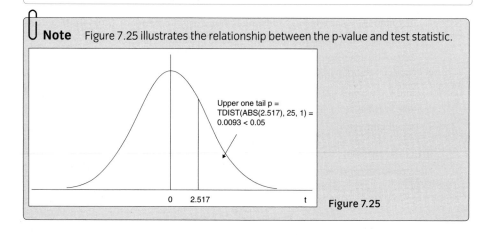

Upper one tail p =
TDIST(ABS(2.517), 25, 1) =
0.0093 < 0.05

0   2.517   t

Figure 7.25

Excel solution using the critical test statistic, t_{cri}

The solution procedure is exactly the same as for the p-value except that we use the critical test statistic value to make a decision. For Example 7.7 we find t_{cal} = 2.5178 and t_{cri} = +1.708141 (see Cell L25). Does the test statistic lie within the region of rejection? The calculation of t yields a value of 2.5178 and therefore lies in the region of rejection for H_0. Given that t_{cal} > upper one tail t_{cri} (1.708141) we will reject H_0 and accept H_1.

✳ **Interpretation**   Conclude that the average weight loss is more than 10 lbs at a 5% level of significance.

Excel Analysis ToolPak solution

As an alternative to either of the two previous methods, we can use a method embedded in Excel Analysis Toolpak. Figure 7.26 screenshot illustrates the application of the Analysis ToolPak: Two Sample Z Test for Paired Means (Select Tools > Data Analysis > T Test: Paired Two Sample for Means).

We observe from Figure 7.26 that the relevant results agree with the p-value and critical test methods described.

	A	B	C	D	E	F	G	H
1	TWO SAMPLE T TEST ASSUMING PAIRED SAMPLES							
2								
3								
4		Person	Before Weight, B	After Weight, A				
5		1	170	170		t-Test: Paired Two Sample for Means		
6		2	159	153				
7		3	162	129			Variable 1	Variable 2
8		4	153	143		Mean	158.8461538	141.6538462
9		5	177	137		Variance	87.25538462	104.0753846
10		6	167	134		Observations	26	26
11		7	158	133		Pearson Correlation	-0.10929623	
12		8	178	128		Hypothesized Mean Difference	10	
13		9	141	152		df	25	
14		10	163	142		t Stat	2.517802176	
15		11	154	140		P(T<=t) one-tail	0.009292088	
16		12	159	154		t Critical one-tail	1.708140745	
17		13	159	143		P(T<=t) two-tail	0.018584176	
18		14	138	147		t Critical two-tail	2.059538536	
19		15	161	142				
20		16	156	149		t-Test: Paired Two Sample for Means		
21		17	165	136		Input		
22		18	158	154		Variable 1 Range: $C$5:$C$30		OK
23		19	151	140		Variable 2 Range: $D$5:$D$30		Cancel
24		20	165	145				
25		21	155	125		Hypothesized Mean Difference: 10		Help
26		22	154	140				
27		23	147	125		☐ Labels		
28		24	156	141		Alpha: 0.05		
29		25	155	146		Output options		
30		26	169	135		◉ Output Range: $F$5		
31						◯ New Worksheet Ply:		
32						◯ New Workbook		
33								

Figure 7.26

> ❊ **Interpretation**   Conclude that the average weight loss is more than 10 lbs at a 5% level of significance.

7.8.2 Equivalent non-parametric test: Wilcoxon matched pairs test

For two dependent (or paired, repeated measures) samples the non-parametric equivalent test is the Wilcoxon matched pairs test which will be described in Chapter 8.

🖰 Student Exercises

X7.19 Choko Ltd provides training to its salespeople to aid the ability of each salesperson to increase the value of their sales. During the last training session 15 salespeople attended and their weekly sales before and sales after are provided below:

Person	Before	After
1	2911.48	2287.22
2	1465.44	3430.54
3	2315.36	2439.93
4	1343.16	3071.55
5	2144.22	3002.40
6	2499.84	2271.37
7	2125.74	2964.65
8	2843.05	3510.43
9	2049.34	2727.41
10	2451.25	2969.99
11	2213.75	2597.71
12	2295.94	2890.20
13	2594.84	2194.37
14	2642.91	2800.56
15	3153.21	2365.75

Assuming that the populations are normally distributed assess whether there is any evidence for the training company's claims (test at 5% and 1%).

X7.20 Concern has been raised at the standard achieved by students completing final year project reports within a university department. One of the factors identified as important is the research methods module mark achieved, which is studied before the students start their project. The department has now collected data for 15 students as follows:

Student	RM	Project
1	38	71
2	50	46
3	51	56
4	75	44
5	58	62
6	42	65
7	54	50
8	39	51
9	48	43
10	14	62
11	38	66
12	47	75
13	58	60
14	53	75
15	66	63

Assuming that the populations are normally distributed is there any evidence that the marks are different (test at 5%)?

7.9 F Test for Two Population Variances (Variance Ratio Test)

In the previous sections we introduced the concept of hypothesis testing to test the difference between interval level variables using both z and t tests. In Example 7.6 we assumed that the population variances were equal for both populations (Shop A and B) and conducted a pooled two sample t test. In Example 7.7 we described the corresponding t test for population variances which are considered to be not equal.

Example 7.9

In this example we will use the F test to check if the two population variances in Example 7.6 can be considered equal with a 95% confidence.

Figure 7.27 illustrates the Excel solution.

	A	B	C	D	E	F	G	H
1	F-Test for Two Population Variances (Variance Ratio Test)							
2								
3		Shop A	Shop B		Hypothesis			
4		437	418			H_0: Variance A = Variance B		
5		497	525			H_1: Variance A not equal to Variance B		1
6		555	581					
7		485	495		State Test	F Test for variances		
8		462	489			Populations normally distributed		2
9		638	448					
10		592	455		Set level of signicance	Significance level =	0.05	3
11		569	484					
12		517	527		Extract relevant statistic	n_A =	18	=COUNT(B4:B21)
13		490	504			n_B =	25	=COUNT(C4:C28)
14		533	489			s_A =	51.020725	=STDEV(B4:B21)
15		509	493			s_B =	41.387277	=STDEV(C4:C28)
16		500	483		4	F_{cal} =	1.5197059	=G14^2/G15^2
17		528	463					
18		588	484			P-value and critical test statistic		
19		484	539			df_A =	17	=G12-1
20		531	439			df_B =	24	=G13-1
21		572	535			Two tail P-value =	0.3393282	=IF(G16>1,2*FDIST(G16,G19,G20),2*(1-FDIST(G16,G19,G20)))
22			495			Upper two tail F_{cri} =	2.3864801	=FINV(G10/2,G19,G20)
23			508			Lower two tail F_{cri} =	0.3906518	=FINV(1-G10/2,G19,G20)
24			605					
25			492		Decision: Since $F_{cal} < F_{cri}$, Accept H_0	5		
26			514					
27			460		For a one tail test:	Upper p-value =	0.1696641	=FDIST(G16,G19,G20)
28			491			Upper F_{cri} =	2.070284	=FINV(G10,G19,G20)
29						Lower p-value =	0.8303359	=1-G27
30						Lower F_{cri} =	0.4566697	=FINV(1-G10,G19,G20)

Figure 7.27

→ Excel Solution

Shop A: Cells B4:B21	Values
Shop B: Cells C4:C28	Values
Significance level Cell G10	Value = 0.05
n_A = Cell G12	Formula: =COUNT(B4:B21)
n_B = Cell G13	Formula: =COUNT(C4:C28)
s_A = Cell G14	Formula: =STDEV(B4:B21)
s_B = Cell G15	Formula: =STDEV(C4:C28)
F_{cal} = Cell G16	Formula: =G14^2/G15^2
df_A = Cell G19	Formula: =G12–1
df_B = Cell G20	Formula: =G13–1
Two tail p-value = Cell G21	Formula: =IF(G16>1,2*FDIST(G16,G19,G20),2*(1–FDIST(G16,G19,G20)))
Upper two tail F_{cri} = Cell G22	Formula: =FINV(G10/2,G19,G20)
Lower two tail F_{cri} = Cell G23	Formula: =FINV(1–G10/2,G19,G20)
One tail test	
Upper p-value = Cell G27	Formula: =FDIST(G16,G19,G20)
Upper F_{cri} = Cell G28	Formula: =FINV(G10,G19,G20)
Lower p-value = Cell G29	Formula: =1–G27
Lower F_{cri} = Cell G30	Formula: =FINV(1–G10,G19,G20)

Excel solution using the p-value

① State hypothesis

The alternative hypothesis statement implies that the population variances are not equal. The null and alternative hypotheses would be stated as follows:

Null hypothesis H_0: $\sigma_A^2 = \sigma_B^2$
Alternative hypothesis H_1: $\sigma_A^2 \neq \sigma_B^2$
The $\neq$ sign implies a two tail test.

② S.tate test

We now need to choose an appropriate statistical test for testing H_0. From the information provided we note:

- Number of samples—two samples.
- The statistic we are testing—testing that the variances are different from each other.
- Size of both samples ($n_A = 18$ and $n_B = 25$).
- Nature of population from which sample drawn—population distribution is not known but we will assume that the population is approximately normal given sample sizes close to 30. The F test is sensitive to the normality assumption. If two samples are not normally distributed, do not use this test.

In this case conduct an *F test for variance*.

③ Set level of significance $\alpha = 0.05$ (see Cell G10)

④ Extract relevant statistic

The difference between two variances can be studied using another sampling distribution called the *F distribution* defined by equation (7.13):

$$F = \frac{s_A^2}{s_B^2}$$

(7.13)

Where s_A^2 and s_B^2 are the sample variances, given by Excel function VAR().

Just as with the previous hypothesis tests we calculate F_{cal} and compare this to a critical test value (F_{cri}) or calculate the corresponding p-value for the F distribution. If the two populations are independent and vary as normal distributions then this ratio will vary as a F distribution with two sets of degrees of freedom (df_A and df_B) given by equations (7.14) and (7.15):

$$df_{numerator} = n_A - 1$$

(7.14)

$$df_{denominator} = n_B - 1$$

(7.15)

With the hypothesis tests considered so far we have been able to write the hypothesis statement as either a one or two tail test. With the F test we have a similar situation but we are dealing with variances rather than mean values.

Note For a one tail test we have:

Upper One Tail Test

Null hypothesis H_0: $\sigma_A{}^2 \leq \sigma_B{}^2$

Alternative hypothesis H_1: $\sigma_A{}^2 > \sigma_B{}^2$

Lower One Tail Test

Null hypothesis H_0: $\sigma_A{}^2 \geq \sigma_B{}^2$

Alternative hypothesis H_1: $\sigma_A{}^2 < \sigma_B{}^2$

From Excel: $n_A = 18$ (see Cell G12), $n_B = 25$ (see Cell G13), and unbiased sample standard deviations $S_A = 51.02$ (see Cell G14), and $S_B = 41.38$ (see Cell G15).

$$F_{cal} = \frac{S_A{}^2}{S_B{}^2} = 1.5197059 \text{ (see Cell G16)}$$

Identify region of rejection using the p-value method—the p-value can be found from Excel by using the FDIST() function. In the example H_1: $\sigma_A{}^2 \neq \sigma_B{}^2$. From Excel, the two tail p-value = 0.3393282 (see Cell G21).

(5) Make a decision

Does the test statistic lie within the region of rejection? Compare the chosen significance level (α) of 5% (or 0.05) with the calculated two tail p-value of 0.3393282. We can observe that the p-value > α and we conclude that we accept H_0 and reject H_1. Given that the two tail p-value (0.3393282) > α (0.05) we will accept H_0 and reject H_1.

✳ **Interpretation** Conclude that the two population variances are not significantly different at the 95% level of confidence.

Note Figure 7.28 illustrates the relationship between the p-value and F test statistic.

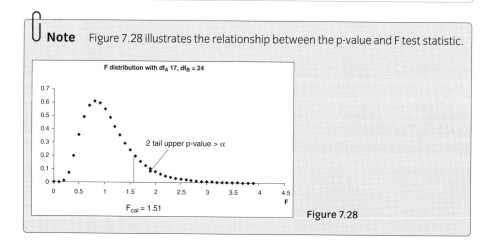

Figure 7.28

Excel solution using the critical test statistic, F_{cri}

The solution procedure is exactly the same as for the p-value except that we use the critical test statistic value to make a decision:

(1) State hypothesis

(2) State test

(3) Set level of significance ($\alpha = 0.05$)

(4) Extract test statistic

The calculated test statistic $F_{cal} = 1.5197$. Calculate the critical test statistic, F_{cri}. In the example H_1: $\sigma_A^2 \neq \sigma_B^2$. The critical F values can be found from Excel by using the FINV() function. Thus direction is not implied and therefore we have a two tail test and our region of rejection is as shown in Figure 7.29. From Excel the critical F values are upper critical value $F_U = +2.3864801$ (see Cell G22) and lower critical value $F_L = 0.3906518$ (see Cell G23).

(5) Make decision

Does the test statistic lie within the region of rejection? Compare the calculated and critical F values to determine which hypothesis statement (H_0 or H_1) to accept. The calculation of F_{cal} yields a value of 1.5197 and therefore lies in the region of rejection for H_1. Given that the F_{cal} (1.5197) lies between the lower critical value F_L (0.3906518) and upper critical value F_U (2.3864801) we will accept H_0 and reject H_1.

⁂ **Interpretation**   We conclude that based upon the sample data collected that we have evidence that the population variances are not significantly different at the 95% level of confidence. In this case we would be reasonably happy to conduct the 2 sample pooled t test.

Note   Figure 7.29 illustrates the relationship between the critical F value and test statistic.

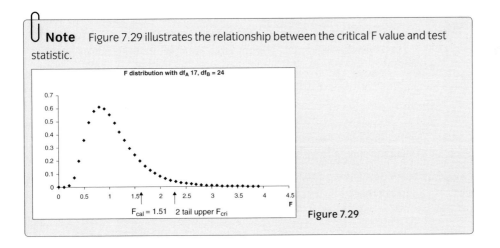

Figure 7.29

Excel Analysis ToolPak solution

As an alternative to either of the two previous methods, we can use a method embedded in Excel Analysis Toolpak. Figure 7.30 screenshot illustrates the application of the Excel Analysis ToolPak: F Test: Two Sample for Variances (Select Tools > Data Analysis > F Test: Two Sample for Variances).

We observe from Figure 7.30 that the relevant results agree with the p-value and critical test methods described.

	A	B	C	D	E	F	G	H
1	F-Test for Two Population Variances (Variance Ratio Test)							
2								
3		Shop A	Shop B					
4		437	418		F-Test Two-Sample for Variances			
5		497	525					
6		555	581			Variable 1	Variable 2	
7		485	495		Mean	527.0555556	496.64	
8		462	489		Variance	2603.114379	1712.906667	
9		638	448		Observations	18	25	
10		592	455		df	17	24	
11		569	484		F	1.519705907		
12		517	527		P(F<=f) one-tail	0.169664107		
13		490	504		F Critical one-tail	2.070283955		
14		533	489					
15		509	493		F-Test Two-Sample for Variances			
16		500	483		Input			
17		528	463		Variable 1 Range:	$B$4:$B$21		OK
18		588	484		Variable 2 Range:	$C$4:$C$28		Cancel
19		484	539					
20		531	439		Labels			Help
21		572	535		Alpha: 0.05			
22			495					
23			508		Output options			
24			605		Output Range: $E$4			
25			492		New Worksheet Ply:			
26			514		New Workbook			
27			460					
28			491					

Figure 7.30

✳ **Interpretation**   We conclude that based upon the sample data collected that we have evidence that the population variances are not significantly different at the 5% level of confidence. In this case we would be reasonably happy to conduct the 2 sample pooled t test.

🖰 **Student Exercises**

X7.21   In Exercise X7.15 we assumed that the two population variances are equal. Conduct an appropriate test to check if the variances are equal (test at 5% and 1%).

X7.22   In Exercise X7.16 we assumed that the two population variances are equal. Conduct an appropriate test to check if the variances are equal (test at 5%).

■ Techniques in Practice

1. CoCo S.A. is concerned at the time to react to customer complaints and has implemented a new set of procedures for its support centre staff (see Chapter 4 TP1). The customer service director has directed that a suitable test is applied to a new sample to assess whether the new target mean time for responding to customer complaints is 28 days. The recent sample of the number of days needed to respond to customer complaints is as follows:

20	33	33	29	24	30
40	33	20	39	32	37
32	50	36	31	38	29
15	33	27	29	43	33
31	35	19	39	22	21
28	22	26	42	30	17
32	34	39	39	32	38

(a) Describe the test to be applied with stated assumptions.

(b) Conduct the required test to assess whether evidence exists for the mean time to respond to complaints to be greater than 28 days.

(c) What would happen to your results if the population mean time to react to customer complaints changes to 30 days?

2. Bakers Ltd is currently undertaking a review of the delivery vans used to deliver products to customers. The company runs two types of delivery van (type A—recently purchased and type B—at least 3 years old) which are supposed to be capable of achieving 20 km per litre of petrol. A new sample has now been collected as follows:

A	B	A	B
17.68	15.8	26.42	34.8
18.72	36.1	25.22	16.8
26.49	6.3	13.52	15.0
26.64	12.3	14.01	28.9
9.31	15.5		33.9
22.38	40.1		27.1
20.23	20.4		16.8
28.80	3.7		23.6
17.57	13.6		29.7
9.13	35.1		28.2
20.98	33.3		

(a) Assuming that the population distance travelled varies as a normal distribution do we have any evidence to suggest that the two types of delivery vans differ in their mean distance travelled?

(b) Based upon your analysis do we have any evidence that the new delivery vans meet the mean average of 20 km per litre?

3. Skodel Ltd is developing a low calorie lager for the European market with a mean designed calorie count of 43 calories per 100 ml. The new product development team are having problems with the production process and have collected two independent random samples to assess whether the target calorie count is being met (assume the population variables are normally distributed):

A	B	A	B
49.7	39.4	45.2	34.5
45.9	46.5	40.5	43.5
37.7	36.2	31.9	37.8
40.6	46.7	41.9	39.7
34.8	36.5	39.8	41.1
51.4	45.4	54.0	33.6
34.3	38.2	47.8	35.8
63.1	44.1	26.3	44.6
41.2	58.7	31.7	38.4
41.4	47.1	45.1	26.1
41.1	59.7	47.9	30.7

(a) Describe the test to be applied with stated assumptions.
(b) Is the production process achieving a similar mean number of calories?
(c) Is it likely that the target average number of calories is being achieved?

■ Summary

In this chapter we have provided an introduction to the important statistical concept of parametric hypothesis testing for one and two samples. What is important in hypothesis testing is that you are able to recognize the nature of the problem and should be able to convert this into two appropriate hypothesis statements (H_0 and H_1) that can be measured. If you are comparing more than two samples then you would need to employ advanced statistical parametric hypothesis tests. These tests are called analysis of variance (ANOVA) and are described in Chapeter 9. In this chapter we have described a simple five step procedure to aid your solution process and have focused on the application of Excel to solve the data problems. The main emphasis is placed on the use of the p-value which provides a number to the probability of the null hypothesis (H_0) being rejected. Thus, if the measured p-value $> \alpha$ (alpha) then we would accept H_0 to be statistically significant. Remember the value of the p-value will depend on whether we are dealing with a two or one tail test. So take extra care with this concept since this is where most students slip up.

The focus of parametric tests is that the underlying variables are at the interval/ratio level of measurement and the population being measured is distributed as a normal or approximately normal distribution. In the next chapter we shall explore how we undertake hypothesis testing for variables that are at the nominal or ordinal level of measurement by exploring the concept of the chi square and distribution free (or non-parametric) tests.

■ Key Terms

α Alpha

Alternative hypothesis (H_1)

Analysis of variance (ANOVA)

β Beta

Central Limit Theorem

Confidence interval ($1 - \alpha$)

Critical test statistic

Directional test

F distribution

F test for variances

Hypothesis test procedure

Non-parametric

Normally distributed

Null hypothesis (H_0)

One sample t test for mean

One sample z test for
population mean

One tail test

Parametric

Power of test

P-value

Randomization

Region of rejection

Repeated measures

Robust

Sampling distributions

Significance level (α)

T test model asssumptions

Test statistic

Two sample pooled t test
for means

Two sample t test for
dependent (or paired,
repeated) samples

Two sample t test for
independent samples
(equal variances)

Two sample t test for
independent samples
(unequal variances)

Two sample z test for
population means

Two sample z test for
proportions

Two tail test

Type I error (α)

Type II error (β)

Types of error

■ Further Reading

Textbook Resources

1. Whigham, D. (2007) *Business Data Analysis using Excel*. Oxford University Press. ISBN: 9780199296286.

2. Lindsey, J., K. (2003) *Introduction to Applied Statistics: A Modelling Approach* (2nd Edition). Oxford University Press. ISBN: 978-0-19-852895-1.

Web Resources

1. StatSoft Electronic Textbook http://www.statsoft.com/textbook/statsoft.com/textbook/stathome.html (accessed 28/1/2007).

2. HyperStat Online Statistics Textbook http://davidmlane.com/hyperstat/index.html (accessed 28/1/2007).

3. Eurostat—website is updated daily and provides direct access to the latest and most complete statistical information available on the European Union, the EU Member States, the euro-zone and other countries http://epp.eurostat.ec.europa.eu (accessed 28/1/2007).

4. Economagic—contains international economic data sets (http://www.economagic.com) (accessed 28/1/2007).

5. The ISI glossary of statistical terms provides definitions in a number of different languages http://isi.cbs.nl/glossary/index.htm.

■ Formula Summary

$$Z_{cal} = \frac{\left(\bar{x} - \mu\right)}{\sigma / \sqrt{n}} \tag{7.1}$$

$$t_{cal} = \frac{\left(\bar{x} - \mu\right)}{s / \sqrt{n}} \tag{7.2}$$

$$Z_{cal} = \frac{\left(\bar{X}_A - \bar{X}_B\right) - \left(\mu_A - \mu_B\right)}{\sqrt{\left[\dfrac{\sigma_A^{\,2}}{n_A} + \dfrac{\sigma_B^{\,2}}{n_B}\right]}} \tag{7.3}$$

$$Z_{cal} = \frac{\left(P_A - P_B\right) - \left(\pi_A - \pi_B\right)}{\sqrt{\dfrac{\pi_A\left(1 - \pi_A\right)}{n_A} + \dfrac{\pi_B\left(1 - \pi_B\right)}{n_B}}} \tag{7.4}$$

$$t_{cal} = \frac{\left(\bar{X}_A - \bar{X}_B\right) - \left(\mu_A - \mu_B\right)}{\left(\hat{\sigma}_{A+B}\right) \times \sqrt{\left[\dfrac{1}{n_A} + \dfrac{1}{n_B}\right]}} \tag{7.5}$$

$$\hat{\sigma}_{A+B} = \sqrt{\frac{\left[\left(n_A - 1\right)s_A^{\,2} + \left(n_B - 1\right)s_B^{\,2}\right]}{n_A + n_B - 2}} \tag{7.6}$$

$$df = n_A + n_B - 2 \tag{7.7}$$

$$t_{cal} = \frac{\left(\bar{X}_A - \bar{X}_B\right) - \left(\mu_A - \mu_B\right)}{\sqrt{\left[\dfrac{s_A^{\,2}}{n_A} + \dfrac{s_B^{\,2}}{n_B}\right]}} \tag{7.8}$$

$$df = \frac{\left(\dfrac{s_A^{\,2}}{n_A} + \dfrac{s_B^{\,2}}{n_B}\right)^2}{\left(\dfrac{\left(\dfrac{s_A^{\,2}}{n_A}\right)^2}{n_A - 1} + \dfrac{\left(\dfrac{s_B^{\,2}}{n_B}\right)^2}{n_B - 1}\right)} \tag{7.9}$$

$$t_{cal} = \frac{\bar{d} - d}{\dfrac{s_d}{\sqrt{n}}} \tag{7.10}$$

$$s_d = \sqrt{\frac{\sum d^2 - \left(\sum d\right)^2 / n}{n-1}}$$

(7.11)

$$df = n - 1$$

(7.12)

$$F_{cal} = \frac{s_A^2}{s_B^2}$$

(7.13)

$$df_{numerator} = n_A - 1$$

(7.14)

$$df_{denominator} = n_B - 1$$

(7.15)

8 Chi-Squared and Non-Parametric Hypothesis Testing

» Overview «

In Chapter 7 we explored a series of parametric tests to assess whether the differences between means (or variances) are statistically significant. Within parametric tests we sample from a distribution with a known parameter value e.g. population mean (μ), variance (σ^2), or proportion (ρ). The techniques described were defined by three assumptions: (i) the underlying population being measured varies as a normal distribution, (ii) the level of measurement is of equal interval or ratio scaling, and (iii) the population variances are equal. Unfortunately, we will come across data that does not fit these assumptions. How do we measure the difference between the attitudes of people surveyed in assessing their favourite car, when the response by each person is of the form: 1, 2, 3…, n. In this situation we have ordinal data in which taking differences between the numbers (or ranks) is meaningless. Furthermore, if we are asking for opinions where the opinion is of a categorical form (e.g. strongly agree, agree, do not agree) then the concept of difference is again meaningless. The responses are words not numbers, but you can, if you so wish, solve this problem by allocating a number to each response, with 1 for strongly agree, 2 for agree, and so on. This gives you a rating scale of responses but remember that the opinions of people are not quite the same as measuring time or measuring the difference between two times. Can we say that the difference between strongly agree and agree is the same as the difference between agree and disagree? Another way of looking at this problem is to ask the question: can we say that a rank of 5 is five times stronger than a rank of 1?

This chapter will provide an overview to the chi square distribution (χ^2) and non-parametric tests that can be used when parametric methods are not appropriate.

X

Ranks List data in order of size.

Test of association The chi square test of association allows the comparison of two attributes in a sample of data to determine if there is any relationship between them.

Sign test The sign test is designed to test a hypothesis about the location of a population distribution.

» Learning Objectives «

On completing this chapter you should be able to:

» Apply the chi square test to measure the difference between two proportions from two samples.

» Apply the chi square test to test for association between categorical variables.

» Apply the sign test to one sample.

» Apply the Wilcoxon signed rank t test to two paired samples.

» Apply the Mann-Whitney U test to two independent samples.

» Solve problems using Microsoft Excel.

To remind the reader we summarize the hypothesis test procedure we will follow:

(1) State hypothesis.

(2) Select the test.

(3) Set the level of significance.

(4) Extract relevant statistic.

(5) Make a decision.

8.1 Chi Square Tests

This test is a versatile and widely used test that is applicable to dealing with data that is categorical (or nominal or qualitative) in nature and cannot be stated as number, e.g. responses such as 'Yes', 'No', 'Red', and 'No agreement'. In Chapter 3 we explored tabulating such data and charting via bar and pie charts, where we were dealing with proportions that fall into each of the categories being measured which form a sample from a proportion of all possible responses. In Chapter 7 we explored the situation of comparing two proportions where we assumed that the underlying population distribution is normal or approximately normal. In many cases the variable is descriptive and in these cases the chi square test can be used.

To illustrate how this test can be used imagine you are doing a small survey for your dissertation. Part of your overall research project is to establish if students' attitudes towards work ethics change as they progress through their studies. To establish this, you interview a group of first year students and a group of the final year students and ask them certain questions to illuminate this problem The results are tabulated in a simple table, where the rows represent first year and last year students and the columns represent their attitudes (a scale such as: strongly agree, agree, disagree, etc.). Once you have such a table constructed, you can establish if the maturity of students is in some way linked with their views on work ethics. The chi square test can be used to test this claim of an association between their views on work ethics. Within this chapter we will explore a series of methods that make use of the chi square distribution to make inferences about two and more proportions. For the chi square test we require the independent observations are capable of being classified into a number of separate categories and that the probability of lying in this category can be calculated when the appropriate null hypothesis is assumed to be true. This section will explore two particular applications of the chi square test:

1. Comparing two or more sample proportions where we have categorical data.

2. Undertake a chi square test of association that is popular with students in analysing survey data.

X

Wilcoxon signed rank t test The Wilcoxon signed ranks test is designed to test a hypothesis about the location of the population median (one or two matched pairs).

Mann-Whitney U test The Mann-Whitney U test is used to test the null hypothesis that two populations have identical distribution functions against the alternative hypothesis that the two distribution functions differ only with respect to location (median), if at all.

8.1.1 Tests of association

The chi square test of association is a hypothesis test used to determine whether the frequency occurrence for two category variables (or more) is significantly related (or associated) to each other. The null hypothesis states that the row and column variables (the student maturity and their attitudes) are not associated. It can be shown that if the null hypothesis is true then the expected frequencies (E) can be calculated using the following equation (8.1):

$$E = \frac{\text{Row Total * Column Total}}{\text{Total Sample Size}} \tag{8.1}$$

To test the null hypothesis we would compare the expected cell frequencies with the observed cell frequencies and calculate the chi square test statistic given by equation (8.2):

$$\chi^2_{cal} = \Sigma \frac{(O-E)^2}{E} \tag{8.2}$$

The chi square test statistic enables a comparison to be made between the observed (O) frequencies and expected (E) frequencies calculated via equation (8.1). Remember equation (8.1) tells us what the expected frequencies would be if there was no association between the two categorical variables: student maturity and attitude. If the values are close to one another then this provides evidence that there is no association and conversely if we find large differences between the observed and expected frequencies then we have evidence to suggest an association does exist between the two categorical variables: student maturity and attitude. Statistical hypothesis testing allows us to confirm whether the differences are likely to be statistically significant. The chi square distribution varies in shape with the number of degrees of freedom and thus we need to find this value before we can look up the appropriate critical values. The number of degrees of freedom (df) is given by equation (8.3):

$$df = (r-1) * (c-1) \tag{8.3}$$

Where r = number of rows and c = number of columns. The region of rejection will be identified using either the p-value method or calculate the critical test statistic, as in all previous tests.

Example 8.1

Suppose a university sampled 485 of its students to determine whether males and females differed in preference for five courses offered. The question we would like to answer is to confirm whether or not we have an association between the courses chosen and the person's gender. In this case we have two attributes, gender and course, both of which have been divided into categories: 2 for gender and 5 for course. The resulting table is called a 5 * 2 contingency table because it consists of 5 rows and 2 columns. To determine whether gender and course preference are associated (or independent) we conduct a chi square test of association on the contingency table.

Contingency table A contingency table is a table of frequencies classified according to the values of the variables in question.

Figure 8.1 illustrates the Excel solution.

Figure 8.1

→ Excel Solution

Original data Cells D4:E8	Values	
Number of males Cell D9	Formula: =SUM(D4:D8)	
Number of females Cell E9	Formula: =SUM(E4:E8)	
Number A101 Cell F4	Formula: =SUM(D4:E4)	
Number D102 Cell F5	Formula: =SUM(D5:E5)	
Number M101 Cell F6	Formula: =SUM(D6:E6)	
Number S101 Cell F7	Formula: =SUM(D7:E7)	
Number T101 Cell F8	Formula: =SUM(D8:E8)	
Grand Total Cell F9	Formula: =SUM(D9:E9)	

Rearranged table:

O Cells C15:C24	Values	
E Cell D15	Formula: =F4*$D$9/$F$9	
Cell D16	Formula: =F5*$D$9/$F$9	
Cell D19	Formula: =F8*$D$9/$F$9	
Cell D20	Formula: =F4*$E$9/$F$9	
Cell D21	Formula: =F5*$E$9/$F$9	
Cell D22	Formula: =F8*$E$9/$F$9	
$(O-E)^2/E$ Cell F15	Formula: =(C15–D15)^2/D15	
	Copy formula F15:F24	
Significance level= Cell K12	Value	
χ^2_{cal} = Cell K15	Formula: =SUM(F15:F24)	
r= Cell K18	Formula: =COUNT(D5:D9)	
c= Cell K19	Formula: =COUNT(D5:E5)	
df= Cell K20	Formula: =(K18–1)*(K19–1)	
Critical χ^2 = Cell K21	Formula: =CHIINV(K12,K20)	
P-value= Cell K22	Formula: =CHIDIST(K15,K20)	

Excel solution using the p-value

(1) State hypothesis

H_0: Gender and course preference are not associated (or independent)

H_1: There is an association between sex and course preference (or dependent)

(2) Select test

- Number of samples—two category data variables (gender and course). The sample data are randomly selected and are represented as frequency counts within the contingency table.
- The statistic we are testing—testing for an association between the two category data variables.

Apply a chi square test of association to the sample data.

(3) Set the level of significance (α) = 0.05 (Cell K12)

(4) Extract relevant statistic

Expected frequencies: from equation (8.1) we can calculate the expected frequencies (see Cells D15:D24).

Calculate test statistic: from Excel, the ratio in equation (8.2) is calculated and displayed in Cells F15:F24, with the sum χ^2_{cal} = 63.2 (see Cell K15).

Calculate the number of degrees of freedom: the number of degrees of freedom (df) is given by equation (8.3): df = (r − 1) * (c − 1) = 4 * 1 = 4 (see Cell K20).

Identify rejection region: indentify a region of rejection using the p-value method— The p-value can be found from Excel by using the CHIDIST() function. From Excel, the p-value = 5.7E-13 (see Cell K22). Does the test statistic lie within the region of rejection? Compare the chosen significance level (α) of 5% (or 0.05) with the calculated p-value of 5.7E-13.

> **Note**   The p-value is given by the Excel function:
> =CHIDIST(test statistic, df)

(5) Make a decision

In Figure 8.2 we observe that the p value < α (5.7E-13 < 0.05), and conclude that we reject H_0 and accept H_1.

❋ **Interpretation**   There is a significant relationship or association between the category variables gender and course preference. The chi square table indicates that the main contributors to the chi square values are A101 and T101, whereas S101 has very little contribution. This table would indicate: (i) Fewer men opt for A101 whereas fewer women opt for T101, and (ii) Men tend towards M101 and T101 whereas women prefer A101 and D102.

Note   Figure 8.2 illustrates the relationship between the p-value and test statistic.

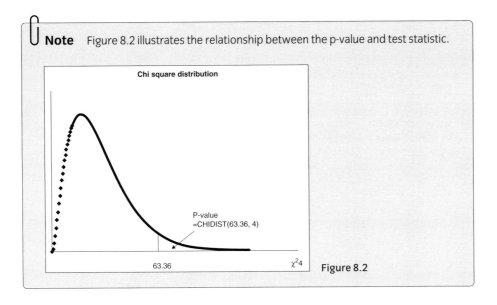

Figure 8.2

Note

1. For the chi square test to give meaningful results the expected frequency for each cell is required to be at least 5. Cochran suggests that if degrees of freedom are greater than 1, then tolerable accuracy can be obtained provided 80% of expected frequencies ≥ 5 and no cell has expected frequency < 1. If this criteria cannot be met then increase the sample size or/and combine classes to eliminate frequencies that are too small.

2. In the example you may have noticed that the frequency counts are discrete variables which are mapped onto the continuous χ^2 distribution. In case we have expected frequency for each cell ≤ 5, we need to apply the Yates' correction for continuity given by equation (8.4):

$$\chi^2_{cal} = \Sigma \frac{\left(\left|O-E\right|-0.5\right)^2}{E} \tag{8.4}$$

Excel solution using the critical test statistic

The solution procedure is exactly the same as for the p-value except that we use the critical test statistic value to make a decision. The calculated test statistic $\chi^2_{cal} = 63.3562$ (see Cell K15). Calculate the critical test statistic, χ^2_{cri}. The critical value can be found from Excel by using the CHIINV() function, $\chi^2_{cri} = 9.4877$ (see Cell K21). Does the test statistic lie within the region of rejection? Compare the calculated and critical χ^2 values to determine which hypothesis statement (H_0 or H_1) to accept. In this case $\chi^2_{cal}(63.3562)$ > $\chi_{cri}(9.49)$, so we reject H_0 and accept the alternative hypothesis H_1.

Expected frequency
In a contingency table the expected frequencies are the frequencies that you would predict in each cell of the table, if you knew only the row and column totals, and if you assumed that the variables under comparison were independent.

> **Note**   The χ^2_{cri} is given by the Excel function:
> =CHIINV(significance level, df)

> ✳ **Interpretation**   There is a significant relationship (or association) between the category variables gender and course preference.

🖱 Student Exercises

X8.1   A business consultant requests that you perform some preliminary calculations before analysing a data set using Excel:

    i.   Calculate the number of degrees of freedom for a contingency table with 3 rows and 4 columns.

    ii.   Find the critical χ^2 value with a significance level of 5% and 1%. What Excel function would you use to find this value?

    iii.   Describe how you would use Excel to calculate the test p-value. What does the p-value represent if the calculated chi square test statistic equals 8.92?

X8.2   A trainee risk manager for an investment bank has been told that the level of risk is directly related to the industry type (manufacturing, retail, financial). For the data presented in the contingency table analyse whether or not perceived risk is dependent upon the type of industry identified (assess at 5%). If the two variables are associated then what is the form of the association?

Level of Risk	Industrial Class		
	Manufacturing	Retail	Financial
Low	81	38	16
Moderate	46	42	33
High	22	26	29

X8.3   A manufacturing company is concerned at the number of defects produced by the manufacture of office furniture. The firm operates 3 shifts and has classified the number of defects as low, moderate, high, or very high. Is there any evidence to suggest a relationship between types of defect and shifts (assess at 5%)? If the two variables are associated then what is the form of the association?

Shift	Defect Type			
	Low	Moderate	High	Very high
1	29	40	91	25
2	54	65	63	8
3	70	33	96	38

X8.4 A local trade association is concerned at the level of business activity within the local region. As part of a research project a random sample of business owners were surveyed on how optimistic they were for the coming year. Based upon the contingency table do we have any evidence to suggest different levels of optimism for business activity (assess at 5%)? If the two variables are associated then what is the form of the association?

Optimism level	Type of business			
	Bankers	Manufacturers	Retailers	Farmers
High	38	61	59	96
No change	16	32	27	29
Low	11	26	35	41

X8.5 A group of students at a language school volunteered to sit a test that is to be undertaken to assess the effectiveness of a new method to teach German to English speaking students. To assess the effectiveness students sit two different tests with one test in English and the other test in German. Is there any evidence to suggest that the student test performances in English are replicated by their test performances in German (assess at 5%)? If the two variables are associated then what is the form of the association?

German	English		
	$\geq 60\%$	40%–59%	< 40%
$\geq 60\%$	90	81	8
40%–59%	61	90	8
< 40%	29	39	6

8.1.2 Test differences in proportions for two samples

In Chapter 7 we explored the application of the z test to solve problems involving two proportions. If we are concerned that the parametric assumptions are not valid then we can use the chi square test to test two independent proportions or apply the McNemar χ^2 or z test which uses a normal approximation for two paired (or dependent) samples.

Chi square test for independent samples

In this situation we have two samples consisting of data that involves counting the number of times a categorical choice is chosen. In this situation we can develop a cross tab (or contingency) table to display the frequency that each possible value was chosen.

▷ Example 8.2

To illustrate the concept consider the example of a firm who surveys whether or not employees use the train to travel to work. The firm collects the data and has created a 2 * 2 contingency table (see Table 8.1) to summarize the responses for only the people who work on two days:

	Monday	Wednesday
Take train to work	89	76
Do not take train to work	64	88

Table 8.1 Employee travel intentions

The question is now whether or not we have a significant difference between the Monday and Wednesday employees who travel to work by train. Figure 8.3 illustrates the Excel solution.

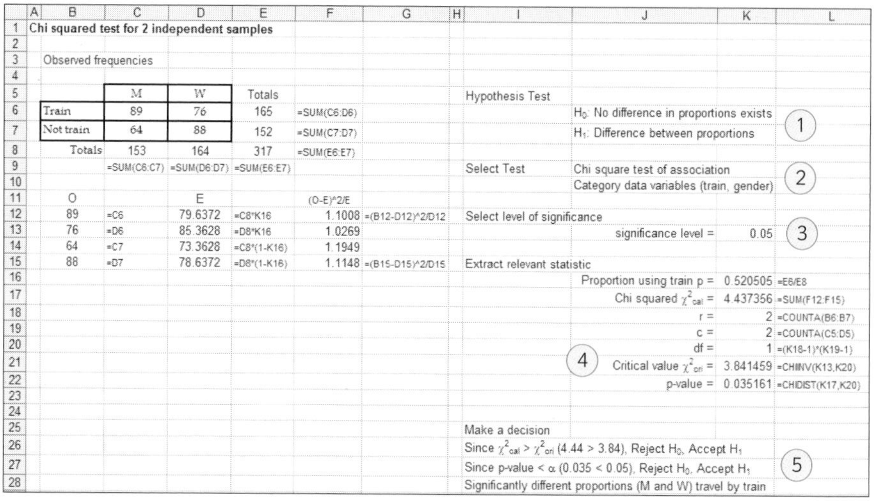

Figure 8.3

➜ Excel Solution

Data series: Cells C6:D7

Sum row 1	Cell E6	Formula: =SUM(C6:D6)
Sum row 2	Cell E7	Formula: =SUM(C7:D7)
Sum column 1	Cell C8	Formula: =SUM(C6:C7)
Sum column 2	Cell D8	Formula: =SUM(D6:D7)

Grand total = Cell E8	Formula: =SUM(E6:E7)
O Cell B12	Formula: =C6
O Cell B13	Formula: =D6
O Cell B14	Formula: =C7
O Cell B15	Formula: =D7
E Cell D12	Formula: =C8*K16
E Cell D13	Formula: =D8*K16
E Cell D14	Formula: =C8*(1−K16)
E Cell D15	Formula: =D8*(1−K16)
(O−E)^2/E Cell F12	Formula: =(B12−D12)^2/D12
(O−E)^2/E Cell F13	Formula: =(B13−D13)^2/D13
(O−E)^2/E Cell F14	Formula: =(B14−D14)^2/D14
(O−E)^2/E Cell F15	Formula: =(B15−D15)^2/D15
level Cell K13	Value
p Cell K16	Formula: =E6/E8
χ^2_{cal} = Cell K17	Formula: =SUM(F12:F15)
r = Cell K18	Formula: =COUNTA(B6:B7)
c = Cell K19	Formula: =COUNTA(C5:D5)
df = Cell K20	Formula: =(K18−1)*(K19−1)
χ^2_{cri} = Cell K21	Formula: =CHIINV(K13,K20)
p-value = Cell K22	Formula: =CHIDIST(K17,K20)

In general the 2 * 2 contingency table can be structured as follows:

		Column variable		
		1	2	Totals
Row variable	1	n_1	n_2	N
	2	$t_1 - n_1$	$t_2 - n_2$	T − N
	Totals	t_1	t_2	T

From this table we can estimate the proportion (or probability) that employees will use the train by calculating the overall proportion (ρ) using equation (8.5):

$$\rho = \frac{n_1 + n_2}{t_1 + t_2} = \frac{N}{T} \tag{8.5}$$

We can now use this estimate to calculate the expected frequency (E) for each cell within the contingency table by multiplying the column total by ρ for the cells linked to travelled by train and $(1-\rho)$ for those cells who did not travel by train.

$$E = \rho * \text{Column Total} \tag{8.6}$$

Calculate the χ^2 test statistic to compare the observed and expected frequencies using equation (8.2):

$$\chi^2_{cal} = \Sigma \frac{(O-E)^2}{E}$$

Where O = **observed frequency**, E = *expected frequency* calculated if the null hypothesis is true, and the number of *degrees of freedom* df = $(r - 1)(c - 1) = 1$. In this case we would expect the proportion of employees taking the train to be exactly the same on each day, and this fact can then be used to calculate the expected frequency. Given the expected frequencies can be calculated we can calculate the chi square test statistic and compare this value with a critical value to make a decision.

Excel solution using the p-value

① State hypothesis

Given that the population proportions are π_1 and π_2 then the null and alternative hypotheses are as follows:

$H_0: \pi_1 = \pi_2$ (proportions travelling by train on the two days is the same)
$H_1: \pi_1 \neq \pi_2$ (proportions different)

② Select the test

Two independent samples
Categorical data
Chi square test for the difference between two proportions

③ Set the level of significance ($\alpha = 0.05$) (see Cell K13)

④ Extract relevant statistic

Proportion travelling by train (ρ)
From Excel, $\rho = 0.52$ (see Cell K16).

Calculate expected frequencies

Calculate the expected frequencies for each cell using equation (8.6), e.g. for train on Monday the expected frequency would be 153 * 0.520505 = 79.6372 (see Cell D12). Repeat this calculation for the other cells within the contingency table (see Cells D13:D15).

Calculate the chi squared test statistic

For each cell we now need to calculate the ratio $(O-E)^2/E$ given in equation (8.2) and sum to give the χ^2 test statistic located in Cells F12:F15:

$$\chi^2_{cal} = \Sigma \frac{(O - E)^2}{E} = 4.437356 \text{ (Cell K17)}$$

Calculate the p-value

Identify region of rejection using the p-value method—the p-value can be found from Excel by using the CHIDIST(test statistic, df) function. From Excel, the p-value = 0.035161 (see Cell K22). Does the test statistic lie within the region of rejection? Compare the chosen significance level (α) of 5% (or 0.05) with the calculated p-value of 0.035161.

⑤ Make a decision

We observe that the p value < α (0.035161 < 0.05), and we conclude that we reject H_0 and accept H_1.

X
Observed frequency
In a contingency table the observed frequencies are the frequencies actually obtained in each cell of the table, from our random sample.

> ✴ **Interpretation** There is a significant difference in the proportions travelling by train on Monday and Wednesday.

> **Note** If you decided that the significance level is 1% (0.01), then we would have a reverse decision given that the two tail p-value > α (0.035161 > 0.01). In this case we would accept H_0 and reject H_1. This is an example of modifying your decision based upon how confident you would like to be with your overall decision.

Excel solution using the critical test statistic

The solution procedure is exactly the same as for the p-value except that we use the critical test statistic value to make a decision. The calculated test statistic $\chi^2_{cal} = 4.437356$ (see Cell K17). Calculate the critical test statistic, χ^2_{cri}. The critical value can be found from Excel by using the CHIINV(significance level, df) function, $\chi^2_{cri} = 3.841459$ (see Cell K21). Does the test statistic lie within the region of rejection? Compare the calculated and critical χ^2 values to determine which hypothesis statement (H_0 or H_1) to accept. We observe that χ^2_{cal} lies in the region of rejection (4.437356 > 3.841459) and we reject H_0 and accept H_1.

> ✴ **Interpretation** There is a significant difference in the proportions travelling by train on Monday and Wednesday.

> **Note**
>
> 1. For the chi squared test to give meaningful results the expected frequency for each cell in the 2 * 2 contingency table is required to be at least 5. If this is not the case then the χ^2 distribution is not a good approximation to the ratio $(O-E)^2/E$. In this situation, we can use *Fisher's test* which provides an exact p-value.
> 2. In the example you may have noticed that the frequency counts are discrete variables which are mapped onto the continuous χ^2 distribution. In this case we need to apply the Yates' correction for continuity given by equation (8.4).
> 3. In Section 7.5 we compared two sample proportions using a normal approximation. When we have 1 degree of freedom we can show that there is a simple relationship between the value of χ^2_{cal} and the corresponding value of Z is given by the relationship $\chi^2_{cal} = \left(Z_{cal}\right)^2$.
> 4. If we are interested in testing for direction in the alternative hypothesis (e.g. $H_1: \pi_1 > \pi_2$) then you cannot use a χ^2 test but will have to undertake a normal distribution Z test to test for direction.

The two proportion solution can be extended to more than two proportions but this is beyond the scope of this text.

McNemar's test for matched pairs

The previous test explored the application of the χ^2 test to compare two proportions taken from random independent samples. If you have paired samples then we can use the McNemar test to compare two proportions.

⌕ Example 8.3

Consider the problem of estimating the effectiveness of a political campaign on the voting patterns of a group of voters. Two groups of voters are selected at random and their voting intentions (Drop CO2, Tax) for a local election recorded. Both groups are then subjected to the same campaign and their voting intentions recorded. The question that arises is whether or not the campaign was effective on the voting intentions of the voters. In this case we have two groups who are recorded before and after and we recognize that we are dealing with paired samples. To solve this problem we can use the McNemar test for two sets of nominal data that are randomly selected. Table 8.2 contains the outcome of the voting intentions before and after the campaign:

Before	After	
	Drop CO2	Tax
Drop CO2	287	89
Tax	45	200

Table 8.2

The question is whether the political campaign has been successful on Drop CO2 voters and Tax voters who both received the same marketing campaign. To simplify the problem we shall look at whether or not the proportion voting Drop CO2 has significantly changed:

H_0: Proportion voting for Drop CO2 not changed
H_1: Proportion voting for Drop CO2 changed

In terms of notation this can be written as: $H_0: \pi_1 = \pi_2$, $H_1: \pi_1 \neq \pi_2$, where π_1 = population proportion voting Drop CO2 before campaign and π_2 = population proportion voting Drop CO2 after campaign.

> ⌔ **Note**   Remember that the other hypothesis is whether or not the proportions voting for the Tax party are the same before and after the campaign.

In general the 2 * 2 contingency table can be structured as follows:

		Column variable		
		Drop CO2	Tax	Totals
Row variable	Drop CO2	a	b	a + b
	Tax	c	d	c + d
	Totals	a + c	b + d	N

From this table we observe that the sample proportions are given by equations (8.7) and (8.8):

$$p_1 = \frac{a + b}{N} \tag{8.7}$$

$$p_2 = \frac{a + c}{N} \tag{8.8}$$

This problem can be solved using either a z or chi square test to test the difference between the two proportions. **It is important to note that the χ^2 test cannot be used for one tail tests.** In this situation you will have to use a z test.

1. McNemar z test

    To test the null hypothesis we can use the McNemar z test statistic defined by equation (8.9) which is normally approximated:

$$Z_{cal} = \frac{b - c}{\sqrt{b + c}} \tag{8.9}$$

2. McNemar χ^2 test

    To test the null hypothesis we can use the McNemar χ^2 test statistic defined by equation (8.10):

$$\chi^2_{cal} = \frac{(b - c)^2}{b + c} \tag{8.10}$$

For 1 degree of freedom the relationship between χ^2 and Z is given by the relationship $\chi^2_{cal} = (Z_{cal})^2$.

Figure 8.4 illustrates the Excel solution for the McNemar Z and χ^2 tests.

	A	B	C	D	E	F	G	H	I	J	K
1		McNemar's test for 2 paired samples									
2											
3											
4				After							
5				Drop CO2	Tax	Totals		Hypothesis Test			
6		Before	Drop CO2	287	89	376			H₀: Proportion voting yes not changed		
7			Tax	45	200	245			H₁: Proportion changed	①	
8			Totals	332	289	621					
9								Select Test	McNemar test	②	
10									Category data variables (vote before, vote after)		
11											
12								Select level of significance			
13									significance level =	0.05	③
14											
15								Extract relevant statistic			
16									p₁ =	0.605475	=(D6+E6)/F8
17									p₂ =	0.534622	=(D6+D7)/F8
18									Z_cal =	3.801021	=(E6-D7)/SQRT(E6+D7)
19								④			
20									Lower two tail Z_cri =	-1.9600	=NORMSINV(J13/2)
21									Upper two tail Z_cri =	1.9600	=NORMSINV(1-J13/2)
22									two tail p-value =	0.00014	=2*(1-NORMSDIST(ABS(J18)))
23											
24									χ²_cal =	14.44776	=(E6-D7)^2/(E6+D7)
25									(Z_cal)² =	14.44776	=J18^2
26									χ² p-value =	0.00014	=CHIDIST(J24,1)
27											
28								Make a decision		⑤	
29								Since Z_cal > Z_cri (3.8 > 1.96), Reject H₀, Accept H₁			
30								Since p-value < α (0.000144 < 0.05), Reject H₀, Accept H₁			
31								Significantly difference in proportions			

Figure 8.4

→ **Excel Solution**

Data series: Cells D6:E7

Sum row 1 Cell F6	Formula: =SUM(D6:E6)
Sum row 2 Cell F7	Formula: =SUM(D7:E7)
Sum column 1 Cell D8	Formula: =SUM(D6:D7)
Sum column 2 Cell E8	Formula: =SUM(E6:E7)
Grand total = Cell F8	Formula: =SUM(F6:F7)
level Cell J13	Value
p_1 = Cell J16	Formula: =(D6+E6)/E6
p_2 = Cell J17	Formula: =(D6+D7)/E8
Z_{cal} = Cell J18	Formula: =(E6–D7)/SQRT(E6+D7)
Lower Z_{cri} = Cell J20	Formula: =NORMSINV(J13/2)
Upper Z_{cri} = Cell J21	Formula: =NORMSINV(1–J13/2)
Two tail p-value = Cell J22	Formula: =2*(1–NORMSDIST(ABS(J18)))
χ^2_{cal} = Cell J24	Formula: =(E6–D7)^2/(E6+D7)
$(Z_{cal})^2$ = Cell J25	Formula: =J18^2
χ^2 p-value = Cell J26	Formula: =CHIDIST(J24,1)

Excel solution using the p-value

(1) State hypothesis

Given that the population proportions are π_1 and π_2 then the null and alternative hypothesis are as follows:

$H_0: \pi_1 = \pi_2$

$H_1: \pi_1 \neq \pi_2$

Where π_1 represents the proportion voting Drop CO2 before campaign and π_2 represents the proportion voting CO2 after campaign

(2) Select the test

Two dependent samples

Categorical data

McNemar test

(3) Set the level of significance ($\alpha = 0.05$) (see Cell J13)

(4) Extract relevant statistic

Calculate proportions

From Excel, the proportion voting yes before and after campaign for Drop CO2:

$p_1 = 0.605475$ and $p_2 = 0.534622$ (Cells J16 and J17).

Calculate Z_{cal} from equation (8.9): $Z_{cal} = \dfrac{b - c}{\sqrt{b + c}} = \dfrac{89 - 45}{\sqrt{89 + 45}} = 3.801021$ (Cell J18)

Calculate the p-value

Identify region of rejection using the p-value method—the p-value can be found from Excel by using the NORMSDIST() function. From Excel, the two tail p-value = 0.00014 (see Cell J22). Does the test statistic lie within the region of rejection? Compare the chosen significance level (α) of 5% (or 0.05) with the calculated two tail p-value of 0.00014.

(5) Make a decision

We observe that the two tail p value < α (0.00014 < 0.05), and we conclude that we reject H_0 and accept H_1.

✳ **Interpretation**   There is a significant difference in the voting intentions for Drop CO_2 after the campaign compared with before the campaign.

Excel solution using the critical test statistic

The solution procedure is exactly the same as for the p-value except that we use the critical test statistic value to make a decision. From Excel, the proportion voting yes before and after campaign for Drop CO_2: $p_1 = 0.605475$ and $p_2 = 0.534622$ (Cells J16 and J17). Calculate Z_{cal} from equation (8.9):

$$Z_{cal} = \frac{b - c}{\sqrt{b + c}} = \frac{89 - 45}{\sqrt{89 + 45}} = 3.801021 \text{ (Cell J18)}$$

Identify region of rejection using the critical test statistic—the critical value can be found from Excel by using the NORMSINV() function. From Excel, the two tail $Z_{cri} = \pm 1.96$ (see Cells J20 and J21). Does the test statistic lie within the region of rejection? Compare the calculated and critical value to determine which hypothesis statement (H_0 or H_1) to accept. We observe that Z_{cal} lies in the region of rejection (3.801021 > 1.96) so accept H_1.

✳ **Interpretation**   There is a significant difference in the voting intentions for Drop CO_2 after the campaign compared with before the campaign.

Student Exercises

X8.6   A business analyst requests answers to the following questions:

   i.   What is the value of the p-value when the χ^2 test statistic = 2.89 and we have 1 degree of freedom?

   ii   If you have 1 degree of freedom, what is the value of the z test statistic.

   iii   Find the critical χ^2 value for a significance level of 1% and 5%.

X8.7   The petrol prices during the summer of 2008 have raised concerns with new car sellers that potential customers are taking prices into account when choosing a new car. To provide evidence to test this possibility a group of 5 local car showrooms agree to ask fleet managers and individual customers during August 2008 whether they are or are not influenced by petrol prices. The results are as follows:

Are petrol prices influencing you in purchasing?	Fleet customers	Individual customers
Yes	56	66
No	23	36

At a 5% level of significance is there any evidence for the concerns raised by the car show-room owners? Answer this question using both the critical test statistic and p-value.

X8.8   A business analyst has been asked to confirm the effectiveness of a marketing campaign on people's attitudes to global warming. To confirm that the campaign was effective a group of 500 people were randomly selected from the population and asked the simple question about whether they agree that national governments should be concerned, with an answer of 'Yes' or 'No'. The results are as follows:

Before campaign	After campaign	
	Yes	No
Yes	202	115
No	89	75

At a 5% level of significance is there any evidence that the campaign has increased the number of people requesting that national governments should be concerned that global warming is an issue? Answer this question using both the critical test statistic and p-value.

8.2 Non-Parametric (or Distribution Free) Tests

Many statistical tests require that your data follow a normal distribution. Sometimes this is not the case. In some instances it is possible to transform the data to make them follow a normal distribution; in others this is not possible or the sample size might be so small that it is difficult to ascertain whether or not the data are normally distributed. In such cases it is necessary to use a statistical test that does not require the data to follow a particular distribution. In this section we shall explore three non-parametric tests: sign test, Wilcoxon signed rank test, and Mann-Whitney U test. Table 8.3 compares the non-parametric tests with the parametric tests for one and two samples discussed in Chapter 7.

Test	Parametric test	Non-parametric test
One sample	One sample z test One sample t test	Sign test Wilcoxon signed rank test

Paired samples	Two paired sample t test	Sign test
		Wilcoxon signed rank test
Independent samples	Two independent sample t test	Mann-Whitney U test (Wilcoxon rank sum test)

Table 8.3

8.2.1 The sign test

The sign test is used to test a set of data values against a perceived hypothesis statement, including:

(a) Assessing the validity of a population median value assessed from collected sample data—replaces the one sample t test which assumes a normal population and that a mean value has meaning.

(b) Assessing the validity that the difference between two population medians is zero based upon sample data—replaces the paired t test which assumes a normal population and that a mean value has meaning.

(c) Assessing the validity of proportions where the proportions are estimated from ordered nominal (or categorical) data where a numerical scale is inappropriate but where we can rank the data observations—replaces the sample z test for proportions which assumes a normal population.

If we rank the data then the null hypothesis would result in half the ranks to be less than the median (r_1) and half the ranks would be greater than the median (r_2). In this situation the null hypothesis can be modelled by a binomial distribution with the probability of a data value being less than or greater than the median being equal to $p = 0.5$, with sample size n. The sign test assumptions are: (1) randomly selected samples, and (2) continuous distribution. The sign test measures the number of counts that fall above and below the median value. Given that 50% of all values lie below and 50% of all values lie above then the population proportion (or probability) at the median value is 50% or 0.5. Under the null hypothesis, we would expect the number of counts distribution to be approximately symmetric around the median and the distribution of values below and above to be distributed at random among the ranks. The corresponding hypothesis statements for two tail and one tail tests are as follows:

Two tail test

H_0: sample median = population median
H_1: sample median ≠ population median

Upper one tail test	Lower one tail test
H_0: sample median ≤ population median	H_0: sample median ≥ population median
H_1: sample median > population median	H_1: sample median < population median

In this case the probability distribution is a binomial distribution with the probability (or proportion) of success = 0.5 and the number of trials represented by the number of paired observations (n). In this case we can model the situation using a binomial distribution $X \sim Bin(n, p)$. In this situation the value of the probability $(P(X = r))$, mean (μ), and standard deviation is given by equations (5.12), (5.15), and (5.16): $P(X = r) = {}^nC_r\, p^r\, q^{n-r}$, $\mu = np$, and $\sigma = \sqrt{np(1 - p)}$.

▷ Example 8.4

To illustrate the concept consider the situation where 16 randomly selected people were chosen to measure the effectiveness of a new training programme on the value of sales. For the training programme to be effective we would expect the hypothesis statement to be H_1: the training programme results in the average value in sales to increase. Given that we are told only that we have a random selection and no information is given about the distribution then we will use the sign test to answer the question. Let A = sales after training and B = sales before training.

Figure 8.5 illustrates the Excel solution.

	A	B	C	D	E	F	G	H	I	J	K	L
1	Sign test for matched pairs											
2												
3	Per.	A	B	d=A-B		Sign			Hypothesis Test	H₀: Median difference d = A - B <= zero		①
4	1	3.5	2.0	1.5	=B4-C4	+	=IF(D4<0,"-",IF(D4>0,"+","0"))			H₁: Median difference d = A - B > zero		
5	2	5.7	3.6	2.1		+				Upper one tail test		
6	3	2.9	2.6	0.3		+			Select Test	Sign test for matched pairs		②
7	4	2.4	2.6	-0.2		-						
8	5	9.9	7.3	2.6		+			Select level of significance	Significance level =	0.05	③
9	6	3.3	3.4	-0.1		-						
10	7	16.7	14.9	1.8		+			Extract relevant statistic	median d =	1.5000	=MEDIAN(D4:D19)
11	8	6.0	6.6	-0.6		-				Probability of success p =	0.5	
12	9	3.8	2.3	1.5		+				Total number of trials N =	16	=COUNT(A4:A19)
13	10	4.0	2.0	2.0		+				r₋ =	4	=COUNTIF(F4:F19,"-")
14	11	9.1	6.8	2.3		+				r₊ =	12	=COUNTIF(F4:F19,"+")
15	12	20.9	8.5	12.4		+				r₀ =	0	=COUNTIF(F4:F19,"=0")
16	13	3.5	2.0	1.5		+				x =	12	=MAX(K13,K14)
17	14	5.7	3.6	2.1		+				number of binomial trials n' =	16	=K12-K15
18	15	2.9	2.6	0.3		+				P(X = 12) =	0.0278	=BINOMDIST(12,$K$17,$K$11,FALSE)
19	16	2.4	2.6	-0.2	=B19-C19	-				P(X = 13) =	0.0085	=BINOMDIST(13,$K$17,$K$11,FALSE)
20										P(X = 14) =	0.0018	=BINOMDIST(14,$K$17,$K$11,FALSE)
21										P(X = 15) =	0.0002	=BINOMDIST(15,$K$17,$K$11,FALSE)
22										P(X = 16) =	0.0000	=BINOMDIST(16,$K$17,$K$11,FALSE)
23								④	one sided binomial p-value =	0.0384	=SUM(K18:K22)	
24												
25										mu =	8	=K17*K11
26										sigma =	2.0000	=SQRT(K25*(1-K11))
27										mu - 2*sigma =	4.0000	=K25-2*K26
28										mu + 2*sigma =	12.0000	=K25+2*K26
29										X corrected Xc =	11.5	=K16-0.5
30										Z_cal =	1.7500	=(K29-K25)/K26
31										Upper one tail Z_cri =	1.6449	=NORMSINV(1-K8)
32										Upper one tail p-value =	0.0401	=1-NORMSDIST(K30)
33												
34									Make decision			
35									Since one sided binomial p-value = 0.0384 < 0.05 Accept H₁			⑤
36									Since Z_cal > Z_cri (1.75 > 1.64) Accept H₁ and upper one tail p-value = 0.0401 < 0.05 Accept H₁			
37									[Borderline decision for 5%]			

Figure 8.5

→ **Excel Solution**

A: Cells B4:B19
B: Cells C4:C19
d = Cell D4   Formula: =B4–C4 (copied from D4:D19)
Sign Cell F4   Formula: =IF(D4<0,"–",IF(D4>0,"+","0"))
                                     (copied from F4:F19)

level = Cell K8   Value
Median d = Cell K10   Formula: =MEDIAN(D4:D19)
p = Cell K11   Value
N = Cell K12   Formula: =COUNT(A4:A19)
r_ = Cell K13   Formula: =COUNTIF(F4:F19,"–")

r_+ = Cell K14	Formula: =COUNTIF(F4:F19,"+")
r_0 = Cell K15	Formula: =COUNTIF(F4:F19,"=0")
x = Cell K16	Formula: =MAX(K13,K14)
n = Cell K17	Formula: =K12–K15
P(X=12) = Cell K18	Formula: =BINOMDIST(12,$K$17,$K$11,FALSE)
P(X=13) = Cell K19	Formula: =BINOMDIST(13,$K$17,$K$11,FALSE)
P(X=14) = Cell K20	Formula: =BINOMDIST(14,$K$17,$K$11,FALSE)
P(X=15) = Cell K21	Formula: =BINOMDIST(15,$K$17,$K$11,FALSE)
P(X=16) = Cell K22	Formula: =BINOMDIST(16,$K$17,$K$11,FALSE)
One sided p = Cell K23	Formula: =SUM(K18:K22)
mu = Cell K25	Formula: =K17*K11
sigma = Cell K26	Formula: =SQRT(K25*(1–K11))
mu-2sigma = Cell K27	Formula: =K25–2*K26
mu-2sigma = Cell K28	Formula: =K25+2*K26
X_c = Cell K29	Formula: =K16–0.5
Z_{cal} = Cell K30	Formula: =(K29–K25)/K26
Upper one tail Z_{cri} = Cell K31	Formula: =NORMSINV(1–K8)
Upper one tail p-value = Cell K32	Formula: =1–NORMSDIST(K30)

Excel solution using the p-value

(1) State hypothesis

H_0: The median sales difference is zero

H_1: Median sales after training > Median sales before training

Upper one tail test

(2) Select test

Two dependent samples, both samples consist of ratio data, and no information on the form of the distribution. Signed rank test.

(3) Set the level of significance (α = 0.05) (see Cell K8).

(4) Extract relevant statistic

The solution process can be broken down into a series of steps:

Enter data

Sales values after training A (see Cells B4:B19) and before training B (see Cells C4:C19).

Calculate the differences (d = A – B)

From Excel, we observe that the median difference d = 1.5 (Cell K10) which suggests that the sales are moving in the correct direction (H_1: d > 0). The question now becomes whether this positive difference is significant.

Allocate '+' and '−' depending on whether d > 0 or d < 0

Calculate number of paired values

Total number of trials, N = 16 (see Cell K12)

Number of negative ranks, r_- = 4 (see Cell K13)

Number of positive ranks, r_+ = 12 (see Cell K14)

Number of shared ranks with d = 0, n_0 = 0 (see Cell K15)

Calculate x = MAX(r_-, r_+) = MAX (4, 12) = 12 (see Cell K16)

Adjust n to remove shared ranks with d = 0, n' = 16 (see Cell K17)

Calculate test statistic

Calculate binomial probabilities, $P(X \geq x)$

Given x = 12 (see Cell K16). In this case we wish to solve the problem $p = P(X \geq 12) = P(X = 12, 13, 14, 15, 16) = P(X = 12) + P(X = 13) + P(X = 14) + P(X = 15) + P(X = 16)$. From the Binomial distribution $(P(X = r) = {}^nC_r\ p^r\ q^{n-r})$ we can calculate the probabilities using the BINOMDIST() function. From Excel, the values are as follows: P(X = 12) (Cell K18), P(X = 13) (Cell K19), P(X = 14) (Cell K20), P(X = 15) (Cell K21), and P(X = 16) (Cell K22).

> **Note**   These values given by the binomial equation represent exact p-values.

If n is sufficiently large (n > 25) then we can use a normal approximation with the value of the mean and standard deviation given by equations (5.15)–(5.16). From Excel, μ = 8 (see Cell K25) and σ = 2 (see Cell K26). If μ ± 2σ is contained within the range of the binomial 0 → n', then the normal approximation should be an accurate approximation. The normal approximation Z equation is given by equation (8.11):

$$Z_{cal} = \frac{X_c - \mu}{\sigma}$$

(8.11)

$$Z_{cal} = \frac{X_c - \mu}{\sigma} = \frac{11.5 - 8}{2} = 1.75 \text{ (Cell K30)}$$

Calculate critical values

Identify region of rejection using the p-value method:

(a) For n < 25, the p-value can be found from Excel by summing the individual binomial probabilities, $p = P(X \geq 12) = 0.0384$ (Cell K23). This represents the probability of a value being at this value or more extreme and is an exact p-value. Does the test statistic lie in the region of rejection? Compare the chosen significance level (α) of 5% (or 0.05) with the calculated p value of 0.0384.

(b) For n > 25, the p-value can be found from Excel by using the NORMSDIST() function. From Excel, upper one tail p-value = 0.0401 (see Cell K32) Does the test statistic lie in the region of rejection? Compare the chosen significance level (α) of 5% (or 0.05) with the calculated p value of 0.0401.

Note

1. If your value of n < 25 then you should use the exact binomial method to solve this problem.

2. If n > 25 then a normal approximation will provide appropriate results. From these calculations we note that both methods produce similar results. Note that this result is a marginal decision at 5%.

(5) Make decision

We will reject H_0 and accept H_1 given that the binomial p-value (0.0384) < α (0.05) and normal approximation p-value = 0.0401 < α (0.05).

�֎ **Interpretation**   From the sample data we have sufficient statistical evidence that the after sales is significantly larger than the before sales.

Excel solution using the critical test statistic

The solution procedure is exactly the same as for the p-value except that we use the critical test statistic value to make a decision. From Excel, Z_{cal} = 1.75 (see Cell K30). Calculate the critical test statistic, Z_{cri}. The critical Z values can be found from Excel by using the NORMSINV() function, upper one tail Z_{cri} = 1.6449 (see Cell K31). Does the test statistic lie within the region of rejection? Compare the calculated and critical Z values to determine which hypothesis statement (H_0 or H_1) to accept. We will reject H_0 and accept H_1 given Z_{cal} lies in the upper rejection zone (1.75 > 1.6449).

✖ **Interpretation**   From the sample data we have sufficient statistical evidence that the after sales is significantly larger than the before sales.

Student Exercises

X8.9   A researcher has undertaken a sign test with the following results: sum of positive and negative signs are 15 and 4 respectively with 3 ties. Given that binomial p = 0.5 assess whether there is evidence that the median value is greater than 0.5 (assess at 5%).

X8.10 A teacher of 40 university students studying the application of Excel within a business context is concerned that students are not taking seriously a group work assignment. This is deemed to be important given that the group work element is contributing to the development of personal development skills. To assess whether or not this is a problem the module tutor devised a simple experiment which judged the individual level of cooperation by each individual student within their own group. In the experiment a rating scale was employed to measure the level of cooperation: 1 = limited cooperation, 5 = moderate cooperation, and 10 = complete cooperation. The form of the testing consisted of an initial observation, a two hour lecture on working in groups, and a final observation. Given the raw data below conduct a relevant test to assess whether or not we can observe that cooperation has significantly changed (assess at 5%).

5, 8	4, 6	3, 3	6, 5	8, 9	10, 9	8, 8	4, 8	5, 5	8, 9
3, 5	5, 4	6, 5	4, 4	7, 8	7, 9	9, 9	8, 7	5, 8	5, 6
8, 7	8, 8	3, 4	5, 6	6, 7	4, 8	7, 8	9, 10	10, 10	8, 9
8, 8	4, 6	4, 5	7, 8	5, 7	7, 9	8, 10	3, 6	5, 6	7, 8

X8.11 A leading business training firm advertises in its promotional material that its class sizes at its Paris branch are no greater than 25. Recently the firm has received a number of complaints from disgruntled students who have complained that class sizes are greater than 25 for a majority of its courses in Paris. To assess this claim the company randomly selects 15 classes and measures the class sizes as follows: 32, 19, 26, 25, 28, 21, 29, 22, 27, 28, 26, 23, 26, 28, and 29. Undertake an appropriate test to assess whether there is any justification to the complaints (assess at 5%). What would your decision be if you assessed at 1%?

8.2.2 Wilcoxon signed rank sum (or matched pairs) test

The t test is the standard test for testing that the difference between population means for two paired samples are equal. If the populations are non-normal, particularly for small samples, then the t test may not be valid. The Wilcoxon signed rank sum test is another example of a non-parametric or distribution free test. As for the sign test, the Wilcoxon signed rank sum test is used to test the null hypothesis that the median of a distribution is equal to some value. It can be used: (a) in place of a one sample t test, (b) in place of a paired t test, or (c) for ordered categorical data where a numerical scale is inappropriate but where it is possible to rank the observations. The method considers the differences between 'n' matched pairs as one sample. If the two population distributions are identical, then we can show that the sample statistic has a symmetric null distribution. As with the Mann-Whitney test (Section 8.2.3), where the number of paired observations is small ($n \leq 20$) we need to consult tables; but where the number of paired observations is large ($n > 20$) we can use a test based on the normal distribution. The Wilcoxon signed rank sum test assumptions are:

1. Each matched data pair is randomly distributed.

2. The matched pair differences should be symmetrically distributed.

Although the Wilcoxon test assumes neither normality nor homogeneity of variance, it does assume that the two samples are from populations with the same distribution shape. It is also vulnerable to outliers although not to nearly the same extent as the t test. If we cannot make this assumption about the distribution then we should use a test called the *sign test* for ordinal data. The *McNemar* test is available for nominal paired data relating to dichotomous qualitative variables and is described in Section 8.1.2. In this section we shall solve the Wilcoxon signed rank sum test where we have a large and small number of paired observations. In the case of a large number of paired observations (n > 20) we shall use a normal approximation to provide an answer to the hypothesis statement. Furthermore, for a large number of paired observations we shall use Excel to calculate both the p-value and critical Z value to make a decision. The situation of a small number of paired observations (n ≤ 20) will be described together with an outline of the solution process.

Example 8.5

Suppose that Slim-Gym is offering a weight reduction programme that they advertise will result in more than a 10 lb weight loss in the first 30 days. Twenty subjects were selected for a study and their weights before and after the weight loss programme were recorded. The results are presented in Figure 8.6 with the Excel solution for the Wilcoxon signed rank sum test.

Figure 8.6 illustrates the Excel solution where X and Y represent the weight before and after the weight loss programme. For this problem we should be able to write the null and alternative hypotheses as $H_0: X - Y - 10 \leq 0$, $H_1: X - Y - 10 > 0$.

	A	B	C	D	E	F	G	H	I	J	K	L
1	Wilcoxon test procedure for paired samples											
2												
3	X	Y	d=X-Y-D		ABS(d)		Rank*			Hypothesis Test		
4	132.2	123.7	-1.5	=A4-B4-$K$6	1.5	=ABS(C4)	6	=RANK(E4,$E$4:$E$27,1)		H0: Weight loss at least 10lbs (X - Y - D0 <= 0) (1)		
5	121.6	111.9	-0.3		0.3		1			H1: Weight loss greater then 10 lbs (X - Y - D0 > 0)		
6	156.4	141.1	5.3		5.3		16			Upper one tail test, X - Y - D > 0		
7	167.9	151.4	6.5		6.5		19			Do =	10	
8	141.7	124.6	7.1		7.1		20			Median difference =	4.1	=MEDIAN(C4:C27)
9	183.5	163.8	9.7		9.7		21			Select Test		
10	137.0	126.2	0.8		0.8		3			Wilcoxon signed rank test (2)		
11	153.1	145.1	-2.0		2		7					
12	138.4	125.8	2.6		2.6		9			Select level of significance		
13	145.4	123.9	11.5		11.5		22			Significance level =	0.05	(3)
14	161.0	152.2	-1.2		1.2		4					
15	150.8	137.9	2.9		2.9		10			Extract relevant statistic		
16	132.2	121.7	0.5		0.5		2			n =	24	=COUNT(A4:A27)
17	121.6	112.9	-1.3		1.3		5			n0 =	0	=COUNTIF(E4:E27,"0")
18	156.4	132.7	13.7		13.7		23			n' =	24	=K16-K17
19	170.9	155.8	5.1		5.1		15			T - =	35	=SUMIF(C4:C27,"<0",G4:G27)
20	153.6	141.4	2.2		2.2		8			T + =	265	=SUMIF(C4:C27,">0",G4:G27)
21	183.5	158.7	14.8		14.8		24			n'(n'+1)/2 =	300	=K18*(K18+1)/2
22	137.0	122.8	4.2		4.2		13			T. + T. =	300	=K19+K20
23	153.1	138.4	4.7		4.7		14			Two Tail Test, T =	35	=MIN(K19,K20)
24	138.4	124.5	3.9		3.9		11			Upper one tail T =	265	=K20
25	145.4	129.3	6.1		6.1		18			Lower one tail T =	35	=K19
26	162.1	156.1	-4.0		4		12			mu =	150	=K18*(K18+1)/4
27	153.5	137.9	5.6	=A27-B27-K	5.6		17			sigma =	35.0	=SQRT((K18*(K18+1)*(2*K18+1)/24))
28									(4)	Zcal =	3.2714	=(K24-K26-0.5)/K27
29												
30										Upper one tail Zcrit =	1.6449	=NORMSINV(1-K13)
31										Upper one tail p-value =	0.0005	=1-NORMSDIST(K28)
32												
33										Make a decision		
34										Since Zcal > Zcrit (3.2857 > 1.6449) accept H1 (5)		
35										Since upper one tail p-value (0.0005) < 0.05 Accept H1		

Figure 8.6

➜ Excel Solution

X: Cells A4:A27	
Y: Cells B4:B27	
d = Cell C4	Formula: =A4-B4-$K$6 (copied from C4:C27)
ABS(d) = Cell E4	Formula: =ABS(C4) (copied from E4:E27)
Rank Cell G4	Formula: =RANK(E4,$E$4:$E$27,1) (copied from G4:G27)
D_0 = Cell K7	Value
Median difference = Cell K8	Formula: =MEDIAN(C4:C27)
Significance level = Cell K13	Value
n = Cell K16	Formula: =COUNT(A4:A27)
n_0 = Cell K17	Formula: =COUNTIF(E4:E27,"0")
n' = Cell K18	Formula: =K16–K17
T_- = Cell K19	Formula: =SUMIF(C4:C27,"<0",G4:G27)
T_+ = Cell K20	Formula: =SUMIF(C4:C27,">0",G4:G27)
n'(n'+1)/2 = Cell K21	Formula: =K18*(K18+1)/2
$T_- + T_+$ = Cell K22	Formula: =K19+K20
Two tail test, T = Cell K23	Formula: =MIN(K19,K20)
Upper one tail test, T = Cell K24	Formula: =K20
Lower one tail test, T = Cell K25	Formula: =K19
mu = Cell K26	Formula: =K18*(K18+1)/4
sigma = Cell K27	Formula: =SQRT((K18*(K18+1)*(2*K18+1)/24))
Z = Cell K28	Formula: =(K24–K26–0.5)/K27
Upper one tail Z_{cri} = Cell K30	Formula: =NORMSINV(1–K13)
Upper one tail p-value = Cell K31	Formula: =1–NORMSDIST(K28)

📎 Note

1. The Excel function RANK, will give the lower rank value to tied numbers. For example, consider the numbers: 3, 4, 5, and 4. If you use the Excel RANK() function then Excel will record ranks of 1, 2, 4, and 2. This is contrary to the test procedure which should average the tied ranks to give rank 1, 2.5, 4, and 2.5. This error needs to be kept in mind when calculating the Wilcoxon test statistic. In this example we have no tied ranks.

2. To overcome this problem you may replace the RANK function with the alternative Excel formula that can handle shared ranks: =0.5*(COUNT($E$4:$E$27)+1+RANK(E4,$E$4:$E$27,1)–RANK(E4,$E$4:$E$27,0)). This formula would be placed in Cell G4 and copied from Cells G4:G27.

3. The value of z has been corrected for continuity by subtracting 0.5 ($H_1: > 0$). For the case where we have a lower one tail test ($H_1: < 0$), then add 0.5 to satisfy continuity requirement.

X

Tied ranks Two or more data values share a rank value.

Excel solution using the p-value

① State hypothesis

Under the null hypothesis, we would expect the distribution of the differences to be approximately symmetric around zero and the distribution of positives and negatives to be distributed at random among the ranks.

H_0: the population median weight loss is at least 10lbs $(X - Y \leq 10)$
H_1: the population median weight loss is at least 10 lbs $(X - Y - 10 > 0)$
Upper one tail test

② Select test

Two dependent samples
Both samples consist of ratio data
No information on the form of the distribution
Wilcoxon signed rank test
Median value centred at $D_0 = 10$ (see Cell K7)

The median difference is +4.1 (Cell K8) which supports the alternative hypothesis that $d > 0$. If this was negative, or zero, then you would not conduct the test since there is no evidence from the sample that $d > 0$.

③ Set the level of significance $(\alpha = 0.05)$ (see Cell K13)

④ Extract relevant statistic

The solution process can be broken down into a series of steps:
Calculate the differences $(d = X - Y - D_0)$

From Excel, we observe that the median difference = +4.1 (Cell K8) which suggests that the weight loss is moving in the correct direction $(H_1: d > 0)$. The question now becomes whether this positive differences is significant.

Rank data

The convention is to assign rank 1 to the smallest value and rank n' to the largest value. If you have any shared ranks then the policy is to assign the average rank to each of the shared values. Note that in Excel it will allocate the lowest rank value and not the shared rank value. Input formula =RANK(E4,$E$4:$E$27,1) into Cell G4 and copy formula down from Cell G4:G27.

Calculate number of paired values

Number of paired ranks, n = 24 (see Cell K16)
Number of shared ranks with d = 0, $n_0 = 0$ (see Cell K17)
Adjust n to remove shared ranks with d = 0, n' = 24 (see Cell K18)

Calculate the sum of the ranks, T_- and T_+:

T_- = Sum of –ve ranks = 35 (see Cell K19)
T_+ = Sum of +ve ranks = 265 (see Cell K20)

Check rankings: If you have any shared ranks then these two equations would not agree if you use the basic Excel ranking function to rank the data.

$$T_+ + T_- = \frac{n'(n' + 1)}{2}$$

(8.12)

$$T_+ + T_- = \frac{n'(n' + 1)}{2} = 300 \text{ (Cells K22 and K21)}$$

Find T_{cal}

The value of T_{cal} is determined from the criteria outlined in Table 8.3:

Test	Hypothesis	T_{cal}	Cell
Two Sided Test	H_1: Population locations not centred at 0	T_{cal} = Minimum of T_- and T_+	K23
One Sided Tests	H_1: Population differences are centred at a value > 0	$T_{cal} = T_+$	K24
	H_1: Population differences are centred at a value < 0	$T_{cal} = T_-$	K25

Table 8.4

Given that we have an upper one tail test then $T_{cal} = 265$.

Find Z_{cal}

If the number of pairs is such that n is large enough (> 20) a normal approximation can be used with Z_{cal} given by equation (8.13) and the mean and standard deviation given by equations (8.14) and (8.15) respectively:

$$Z_{cal} = \frac{T_{cal} - \mu_T \pm 0.5}{\sigma_T} \tag{8.13}$$

$$\mu_T = \frac{n'(n' + 1)}{4} \tag{8.14}$$

$$\sigma_T = \sqrt{\frac{n'(n' + 1)(2n' + 1)}{24}} \tag{8.15}$$

The value of Z_{cal} is corrected for continuity by subtracting 0.5 if H_1: > 0 or add 0.5 if H_1: < 0. From Excel: $\mu_T = 150$ (see Cell K26), $\sigma_T = 35.0$ (see Cell K27), and Z_{cal} is given by equation (8.13):

$$Z_{cal} = \frac{T_{cal} - \mu_T - 0.5}{\sigma_T} = \frac{265 - 150 - 0.5}{35.0} = 3.2714 \text{ (Cell K28)}$$

Calculate critical values

Identify region of rejection using the p-value method—the p-value can be found from Excel by using the NORMSDIST() function. From Excel, the upper one tail p-value = 0.0005 (see Cell K31). Does the test statistic lie in the region of rejection? Compare the chosen significance level (α) of 5% (or 0.05) with the calculated upper one tail p value of 0.0005. We can observe that the p-value < α, and we accept H_1.

(5) Make decision

We will reject H_0 and accept H_1 given upper one tail p-value (0.0005) < α (0.05).

> ✽ **Interpretation**   From the sample data we have sufficient statistical evidence to conclude that the weight loss is greater than 10 lbs.

Note   Figure 8.7 illustrates the relationship between the p-value and test statistic.

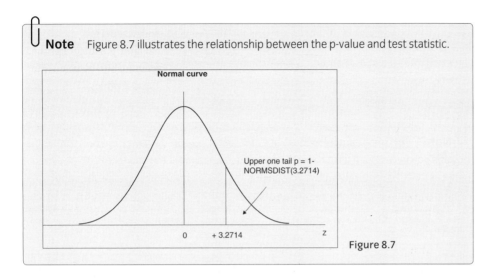

Figure 8.7

Excel solution using the critical test statistic

The solution procedure is exactly the same as for the p-value except that we use the critical test statistic value to make a decision. The calculated test statistic $Z_{cal} = 3.2714$ (see Cell K28). Calculate the critical test statistic, Z_{cri}. The critical Z values can be found from Excel by using the NORMSINV() function, upper one tail $Z_{cri} = +1.6449$ (see Cell K30). Does the test statistic lie within the region of rejection? Compare the calculated and critical Z values to determine which hypothesis statement (H_0 or H_1) to accept. We observe that Z_{cal} lies in the upper rejection zone ($3.2714 > 1.6449$), and we accept H_1.

> ✽ **Interpretation**   From the sample data we have sufficient statistical evidence to conclude that the weight loss is greater than 10 lbs.

Small number of paired observations (n ≤ 20)

If the number of pairs is such that n is ≤ 20 then we calculate T_{cal} and use tables to look up an exact value of the critical test statistic, T_{cri}. The value of T_{cal} is chosen to be $T_{cal} = MIN (T_-, T_+) = MIN (35, 265) = 35$. The decision rule is to reject H_0 if $T_{cal} \leq T_{cri}$ with the exact value of the critical test statistic T_{cri} available from a table representing the critical values of the T statistic for the Wilcoxon signed ranks sum test.

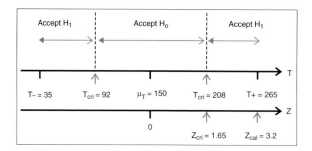

Figure 8.8

If we were to look up such a table we would find $T_{cri} = 92$ for $\alpha = 0.05$ with no tied ranks. We can see that $T_{cal} \leq T_{cri}$ $(35 < 92)$ and therefore we would reject H_0 and accept H_1.

Figure 8.8 illustrates the relationship between the T and Z values.

> **Note** The small sample method uses tables to look up the lower critical value (e.g. 92) and you have to use the smallest T value as T_{cal}. If you want the upper critical value then you can calculate the value if you remember that the distribution is symmetric about the median (remember median = mean for symmetric distributions). From Figure 8.8 μ_T – lower T_{cri} = upper T_{cri} – μ_T.

Dealing with ties

There are two types of tied observations that may arise when using the Wilcoxon signed rank test:

1. Observations in the sample may be exactly equal to zero in the case of paired differences. Ignore such observations and adjust n accordingly. For the previous example we removed any values and used n' instead of n.

2. Two or more observations/differences may be equal. If so, average the ranks across the tied observations and reduce the variance by equation (8.16) for each group of t tied ranks.

$$(t^3 - t)/48 \tag{8.16}$$

> **Note** In the example and exercises we have not modified the solution for tied ranks.

Student Exercises

X8.12 The Wilcoxon paired ranks test is considered to be more powerful than the sign test. Explain why.

X8.13 A company is planning to introduce new packaging for a product that has used the same packaging for over 20 years. Before it makes a decision on the new packaging it decides to ask a panel of 20 participants to rate the current and proposed packaging (using a rating scale of do not change 0–change 100). Is there any evidence that the new packaging is more favourably received compared to the older packaging (assess at 5%)?

Participant	Before	After	Participant	Before	After
1	80	89	11	37	40
2	75	82	12	55	68
3	84	96	13	80	88
4	65	68	14	85	95
5	40	45	15	17	21
6	72	79	16	12	18
7	41	30	17	15	21
8	10	22	18	23	25
9	16	12	19	34	45
10	17	24	20	61	80

X8.14 A local manufacturer is concerned at the number of errors made by machinists in the production of kites for a multinational retail company. To reduce the number of errors being made the company decides to retrain all staff in a new set of procedures to minimize the problem. To assess whether the training worked a random sample of 10 machinists were selected and the number of errors made before and after the training recorded as follows:

Machinist										
	1	2	3	4	5	6	7	8	9	10
Before	49	34	30	46	37	28	48	40	42	45
After	22	23	32	24	23	21	24	29	27	27
	11	12	13	14	15	16	17	18	19	20
Before	29	45	32	44	49	28	44	39	47	41
After	23	29	37	22	33	27	35	32	35	24
	21	22	23	24	25	26	27	28	29	30
Before	33	38	35	35	47	47	48	35	41	35
After	37	37	24	23	23	37	38	30	29	31

Is there any evidence that the training has reduced the number of errors (assess at 5%)?

8.2.3 Mann-Whitney U test for two independent samples

The Mann-Whitney U test is a non-parametric test that can be used in place of an unpaired t test. It is used to test the null hypothesis that two samples come from the same population (i.e. have the same median) or, alternatively, whether observations in one sample tend to be larger than observations in the other. Although it is a non-parametric test it does assume that the two distributions are similar in shape. Where the samples are small we need to use tables of critical values to find whether or not to reject the null hypothesis; but where the sample is large, we can use a test based on the normal distribution. The basic premise of the test is that once all of the values in the two samples are put into a single ordered list, if they come from the same parent population, then the rank at which values from sample 1 and sample 2 appear will be by chance. If the two samples come from different populations, then the rank at which the sample values will appear will not be random and there will be a tendency for values from one of the samples to have lower ranks than values from the other sample. We are thus testing for different locations of the two samples. Whenever n_1 and n_2 is greater than 20, a large sample approximation can be used for the distribution of the Mann-Whitney U statistic. The Mann-Whitney assumptions are as follows: (1) independent random samples are obtained from each population, and (2) the two populations are continuous and have the same shape.

Example 8.6

A local training firm has developed an innovative programme to improve the performance of students on the courses it offers. To assess whether the new programme improves student performance the firm have collected two random samples from the population of students sitting an accountancy examination, where sample 1 students have studied via the traditional method and sample 2 students via the new programme. The firm have analysed previous data and the outcome of the results provides evidence that the distribution is not normally distributed but is skewed to the left. This information provides concerns at the suitability of using a two sample independent t test to undertake the analysis and instead decide to use a suitable distribution free test. In this case the appropriate test is the Mann-Whitney U test.

Figure 8.9 illustrates the Excel Mann-Whitney U test solution.

	A	B	C	D	E	F	G	H	I
1	**Mann-Whitney U test**								
2									
3	Training type	Combined Samples	Rank*			State hypothesis	H_0: No improvement in performancs		
4	1	56	2	=RANK(B4,$B$4:$B$18,1)			H_1: new programme improved performance $M_1 < M_2$		1
5	1	62	4				Lower one tail test		
6	1	55	1						
7	1	75	11			Select test	Mann-Whitney U test	2	
8	1	71	9						
9	1	58	3			Set level of significance			
10	1	66	7				Significance Level =	0.05	3
11	2	82	14						
12	2	86	15			Extract relevant statistic	Median sample 1 =	62	=MEDIAN(B4:B10)
13	2	80	13				Median sample 2 =	75	=MEDIAN(B11:B18)
14	2	78	12				n_1 =	7	=COUNTIF(A4:A18,"=1")
15	2	67	8				n_2 =	8	=COUNTIF(A4:A18,"=2")
16	2	63	5				T_1 =	37	=SUMIF(A4:A18,"=1",C4:C18)
17	2	72	10				T_2 =	83	=SUMIF(A4:A18,"=2",C4:C18)
18	2	65	6	=RANK(B18,$B$4:$B$18,1)			T_1 max =	84	=H14*H15+H14*(H14+1)/2
19							T_2 max =	92	=H14*H15+H15*(H15+1)/2
20							U_1 =	47	=H18-H16
21						4	U_2 =	9	=H19-H17
22							U_1+U_2 =	56	=H20+H21
23							n_1n_2 =	56	=H14*H15
24							U_{cal} =	9	=MIN(H20,H21)
25							mu =	28	=H14*H15/2
26							sigma =	8.6410	=SQRT(H14*H15*(H14+H15+1)/12)
27							Z_{cal} =	-2.1410	=(H24-H25+0.5)/H26
28							Lower one tail Z_{cri} =	-1.6449	=NORMSINV(H10)
29							Lower one tail p-value =	0.0161	=NORMSDIST(H27)
30						Make a decision			
31						Since $Z_{cal} < Z_{cri}$ (-2.24 < -1.65), Accept H_1	5		
32						Since lower one tailed p-value (0.0161) < 0.05, Accept H_1			
33						[Borderline decision - if you change to 1% then your decision may change]			

Figure 8.9

→ **Excel Solution**

Combined sample: Cells A4:A18
Combined samples: Cells B4:B18

Rank Cell C4	Formula: =RANK(B4,\$B\$4:\$B\$18,1) (copied from C4:C18)
Significance level = Cell H10	Value
Median sample 1 = Cell H12	Formula: =MEDIAN(B4:B10)
Median sample 2 = Cell H13	Formula: =MEDIAN(B11:B18)
n_1 = Cell H14	Formula: =COUNTIF(A4:A18,"=1")
n_2 =Cell H15	Formula: =COUNTIF(A4:A18,"=2")
T_1 = Cell H16	Formula: =SUMIF(A4:A18,"=1",C4:C18)
T_2 = Cell H17	Formula: =SUMIF(A4:A18,"=2",C4:C18)
T_{1max} = Cell H18	Formula: =H14*H15+H14*(H14+1)/2
T_{2max} = Cell H19	Formula: =H14*H15+H15*(H15+1)/2
U_1 = Cell H20	Formula: =H18–H16
U_2 = Cell H21	Formula: =H19–H17
$U_1 + U_2$ = Cell H22	Formula: =H20+H21
$n_1 n_2$ = Cell H23	Formula: =H14*H15
U_{cal} = Cell H24	Formula: =MIN(H20,H21)
mu = Cell H25	Formula: =H14*H15/2
sigma = Cell H26	Formula: =SQRT(H14*H15*(H14+H15+1)/12)
Z = Cell H27	Formula: =(H24–H25+0.5)/H26
Lower one tail Z_{cri} = Cell H28	Formula: =NORMSINV(H10)
Lower p-value = Cell H29	Formula: =NORMSDIST(H27)

Excel solution using the p-value

(1) State hypothesis

H_0: no difference in examination performance between the two groups

H_1: new programme improved performance ($M_1 < M_2$)

Lower one tailed test

(2) Select test

Comparing two independent samples

Both samples consist of ratio data

Unknown population distribution

Mann-Whitney U test

(3) Set the level of significance ($\alpha = 0.05$) (see Cell H10)

(4) Extract relevant statistic

The solution process can be broken down into a series of steps:

Input samples into two columns

Combined sample (Cells A4:A18): sample 1 = 1, and sample 2 = 2, etc.

Sample data in cells B4:B18

Median sample 1 $M_1 = 62$ (Cell H12)

Median sample 2 $M_2 = 75$ (Cell H13)

We can observe that the median for sample 2 is larger than for sample 1 (75 > 62). The question now reduces to whether or not the significance is significant.

Rank data

The convention is to assign rank 1 to the smallest value and rank n´ to the largest value. If you have any shared ranks then the policy is to assign the average rank to each of the shared values. Note that in Excel it will allocate the lowest rank value and not the shared rank value. Input formula =RANK(B4,$B$4:$B$18,1) into Cell C4 and copy formula down from Cell C4:C18.

Calculate number of data points in each sample:

Number in sample 1, $n_1 = 7$ (see Cell H14)

Number in sample 2, $n_2 = 8$ (see Cell H15)

Calculate the sum of the ranks, T_1 and T_2:

Input formulae to calculate T_1, T_2

T_1 = Sum of male ranks = 37 (see Cell H16)

T_2 = Sum of female ranks = 83 (see Cell H17)

T_{1MAX} = Maximum sum value of male ranks = 84 (see Cell H18)

T_{2MAX} = Maximum sum value of female ranks = 92 (see Cell H19)

Calculate U_1, U_2 and the test statistic U_{cal}:

The value of U is equal to the difference between the maximum possible values of T for the sample versus the actually observed values of T: $U_1 = T_{1[max]} - T_1$ and $U_2 = T_{2[max]} - T_2$. U_1 and U_2 can be calculated from equations (8.17) and (8.18) respectively as follows:

$$U_1 = n_1 n_2 + \frac{n_1 (n_1 + 1)}{2} - T_1$$

(8.17)

$$U_2 = n_1 n_2 + \frac{n_2 (n_2 + 1)}{2} - T_2$$

(8.18)

Substituting the computed values into equations (8.17) and (8.18) gives $U_1 = 47$ (see Cell H20), $U_2 = 9$ (see Cell H21). Check:

$$U_1 + U_2 = n_1 n_2$$

(8.19)

From Excel, $U_1 + U_2 = 56$ (Cell H22) and $n_1 n_2 = 56$ (Cell H23). The value of U_{cal} can be either U_1 or U_2 and for this example we will choose U_{cal} = Minimum of U_1 and U_2 = MIN (47, 9) = 9 (see Cell H24).

Note   The value of U_{cal} can be either U_1 or U_2.

If the null hypothesis is true then we would expect U_1 and U_2 both to be centred at the mean value μ_U given by equation (8.20):

$$\mu_U = \frac{n_1 n_2}{2} \tag{8.20}$$

From Excel, $\mu_U = 28$ (see Cell H25). Therefore, if there is no difference in performance between the old and new training methods, how likely is it that we could end up, by mere chance, with an observed value of U_1 as large as 47? This is equivalent to asking how likely it is for U_2 to be as small as 9? This problem can be solved exactly but we will use a normal approximation to provide a solution to this problem.

Find Z_{cal}

If the total number of pair wise comparisons $(n_1 n_2 = 7 * 8 = 56 > 20)$ we can approximate the Mann-Whitney distribution with a normal distribution given by equation (8.21):

$$Z = \frac{U_{cal} - \mu_U + 0.5}{\sigma_U} \tag{8.21}$$

Where the standard deviation is given by equation (8.22):

$$\sigma_U = \sqrt{\frac{n_1 n_2 (n_1 + n_2 + 1)}{12}} \tag{8.22}$$

The value of Z_{cal} is corrected for continuity by subtracting 0.5 if $H_1: > 0$ or add 0.5 if $H_1: < 0$. From Excel, $\mu_U = 28$ (see Cell H25), $\sigma_U = 8.6410$ (see Cell H26), and Z_{cal} is given by equation (8.21):

$$Z_{cal} = \frac{U_{cal} - \mu_U + 0.5}{\sigma_U} = \frac{9 - 28 + 0.5}{8.6410} = -2.1410 \text{ (Cell H27)}$$

Calculate critical values

Identify region of rejection using the p-value method—the p-value can be found from Excel by using the NORMSDIST() function. From Excel, the lower one tail p-value = 0.0161 (see Cell H29). Does the test statistic lie in the region of rejection? Compare the chosen significance level (α) of 5% (or 0.05) with the calculated lower one tail p-value of 0.0161. We can observe that the p-value $< \alpha$, and we accept H_1.

(5) Make decision
We will reject H_0 and accept H_1 given the lower one tail p-value $(0.0161) < \alpha$ (0.05).

❋ **Interpretation**　Based upon the data, there is sufficient evidence to indicate at a 5% significance level that the performance has improved. Note that if we modify the level of significance to 1% then the decision would be a borderline decision.

Note Figure 8.10 illustrates the relationship between the p-value and test statistic.

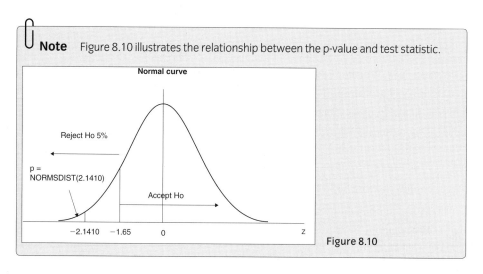

Figure 8.10

Excel solution using the critical test statistic

The solution procedure is exactly the same as for the p-value except that we use the critical test statistic value to make a decision. The calculated test statistic $Z_{cal} = -2.1410$ (see Cell H27). Calculate the critical test statistic, Z_{cri}. The critical Z values can be found from Excel by using the NORMSINV() function, lower one tail $Z_{cri} = -1.65$ (see Cells H28). Does the test statistic lie within the region of rejection? Compare the calculated and critical Z values to determine which hypothesis statement (H_0 or H_1) to accept. We observe that Z_{cal} lies in the lower rejection zone ($-2.1410 < -1.65$), and we accept H_1.

❋ Interpretation Based upon the data, there is sufficient evidence to indicate at a 5% significance level that the performance has improved.

Small number of pair wise comparisons (n ≤ 20)

For a small number of paired comparisons ($n = n_1 n_2 \le 20$) we use tables to calculate an exact value of the critical test value (U_{cri}) or an exact p-value based upon P ($U \le 9$). For a 5% two tail test with $n_1 = 7$, $n_2 = 8$: (i) the lower critical U value, $U_{cri} = 11$. Since $U_{cal} < U_{cri}$ ($9 < 11$), we reject H_0 and accept H_1, and (ii) the lower p-value = 0.014.

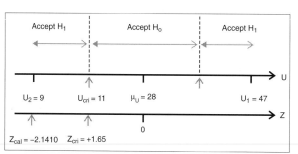

Given that we have a lower one tail test then the lower tail p-value = 0.014 < 0.05, we reject H_0 and accept H_1. The theory suggests that if the null hypothesis is true then the U test statistic will be centred at $\mu_U = 28$ with critical regions identified in Figure 8.11.

Figure 8.11

Dealing with data ties

If we find data with the same number value then we can deal with this problem by allocating the average tie value to each shared data value. In this situation we would then have to use the normal approximation with the standard deviation σ_U adjustment give by equation (8.23):

$$\sigma_U = \sqrt{\frac{n_1 n_2}{(n_1 + n_2)(n_1 + n_2 - 1)} \times \left[\frac{(n_1 + n_2)^3 - (n_1 + n_2)}{12} - \sum_{j=1}^{g} \frac{t_j^3 - t_j}{12} \right]}$$ (8.23)

> **Note**
>
> 1. In the example and exercises we have not modified the solution for tied ranks.
> 2. The Mann-Whitney U test is statistically equivalent to the Wilcoxon rank sum test.

Student Exercises

X8.15 What assumptions need to be made about the type and distribution of the data when the Mann-Whitney test is used?

X8.16 Two groups of randomly selected students are tested on a regular basis as part of professional appraisals that are conducted on a two year cycle by a leading financial services company based in London. The first group has eight students with their sum of the ranks equal to 65 and the second group has nine students. Is there sufficient evidence to suggest that the performance of the second group is higher than the performance of the first group (assess at 5%)?

X8.17 The sale of new homes is closely tied to the level of confidence within the financial markets. A developer builds new homes in two European countries (A and B) and is concerned that there is a direct relationship between the country and the interest rates obtainable to build properties. To provide answers the developer decides to undertake market research to see what interest rates would be obtainable if he decided to borrow €300,000 over 20 years from five financial institutions in country A and eight financial institutions in country B. Based upon the data below do we have any evidence to suggest that the interest rates are significantly different?

A:	10.20	10.97	10.63	10.70	10.50	10.30	10.65
	10.25	10.75	11.00				
B:	10.60	10.80	11.40	10.90	11.10	11.20	10.89
	10.78	11.05	11.15	10.85	11.16	11.18	

■ Techniques in Practice

1. CoCo S.A. is concerned at the time to react to customer complaints and has implemented a new set of procedures for its support centre staff (see Chapter 7 TP1). The customer service director has decided that there is no evidence for the population distribution to be normally distributed and has directed that a suitable test is applied to the sample to assess whether the new target mean time for responding to customer complaints is 28 days.

20	33	33	29	24	30
40	33	20	39	32	37
32	50	36	31	38	29
15	33	27	29	43	33
31	35	19	39	22	21
28	22	26	42	30	17
32	34	39	39	32	38

(a) Describe the test to be applied with stated assumptions.

(b) Conduct the required test to assess whether evidence exists for the mean time to respond to complaints to be greater than 28 days.

(c) What would happen to your results if the population mean time to react to customer complaints changes to 30 days?

2. Bakers Ltd is currently undertaking a review of the delivery vans used to deliver products to customers (see Chapter 7 TP2). The company runs two types of delivery van (type A—recently purchased and type B—at least 3 years old) which are supposed to be capable of achieving 20 km per litre of petrol. A new sample has now been collected as follows:

A	B	A	B
17.68	15.8	26.42	34.8
18.72	36.1	25.22	16.8
26.49	6.3	13.52	15.0
26.64	12.3	14.01	28.9
9.31	15.5		33.9
22.38	40.1		27.1
20.23	20.4		16.8
28.80	3.7		23.6
17.57	13.6		29.7
9.13	35.1		28.2
20.98	33.3		

(a) Assuming that the population distance travelled does not vary as a normal distribution do we have any evidence to suggest that the two types of delivery vans differ in their mean distance travelled?

(b) Based upon your analysis do we have any evidence that the new delivery vans meet the mean average of 20 km per litre?

3. Skodel Ltd is developing a low calorie lager for the European market with a mean designed calorie count of 43 calories per 100 ml (see Chapter 7 TP3). The new product development team are having problems with the production process and have collected two independent random samples to assess whether the target calorie count is being met (do not assume that the population variables are normally distributed):

A	B	A	B
49.7	39.4	45.2	34.5
45.9	46.5	40.5	43.5
37.7	36.2	31.9	37.8
40.6	46.7	41.9	39.7
34.8	36.5	39.8	41.1
51.4	45.4	54.0	33.6
34.3	38.2	47.8	35.8
63.1	44.1	26.3	44.6
41.2	58.7	31.7	38.4
41.4	47.1	45.1	26.1
41.1	59.7	47.9	30.7

(a) Describe the test to be applied with stated assumptions.

(b) Is the production process achieving a similar mean number of calories?

(c) Is it likely that the target average number of calories is being achieved?

■ Summary

In this chapter we have explored the concept of hypothesis testing for data involving category data using the chi square distribution, and extended the parametric tests to the case of non-parametric tests (or so called distribution free tests) which do not require the assumption of the population (or sample) distributions being normal. This chapter adopted the simple five step procedure described in Chapter 7 to aid the solution process and focused on the application of Excel to solve the data problems. The main emphasis is placed on the use of the p-value which provides a number to the probability of the null hypothesis (H_0) being rejected. Thus, if the measured p-value $> \alpha$ (alpha) then we would accept H_0 to be statistically significant. Remember the value of the p-value will depend on whether we are dealing with a two or one tail test. So take extra care with this concept since this is where most students slip up. The second part of the decision making described the use of the critical test statistic in making decisions. This is the traditional text book method which uses published tables to provide estimates of critical values for various test parameter values. In the case of the chi square test we looked at a range of applications, including: testing for differences in proportions, and testing for association. In the case of non-parametric tests we looked at a range of tests, including: sign test for one sample, two paired sample Wilcoxon signed rank test, and two independent samples Mann-Whitney test. In the case where we have more than two samples then we would have to use techniques like Kruskal-Wallis test (or Friedman's test) depending upon whether we are dealing with independent or dependent samples.

Figure 8.12 provides a diagrammatic representation of the decisions required to decide on which test to use to undertake the correct hypothesis test.

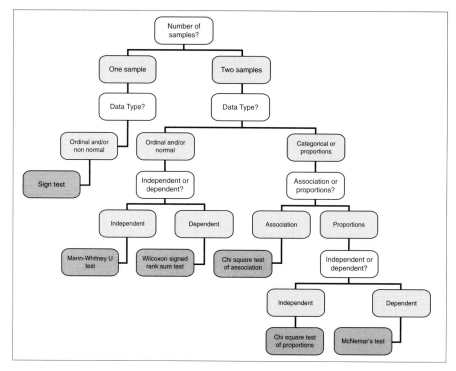

Figure 8.12

The key questions are as follows:

1. What are you testing: difference or association? For non-parametric tests we are dealing with ordinal and/or non-normal distributions; whilst the chi square test will test for association.

2. What is the type of data being measured? For non-parametric tests we are dealing with ordinal data and categorical data for the chi square test of association.

3. Can we assume that the population is normally distributed? For both types of tests we are not assuming that the population distribution is normal.

4. How many samples? In Figure 8.12 we are dealing with one and two sample tests.

> **Note**   It is important to note that we have a range of other hypothesis tests to measure association (see Chapter 10), and dealing with data that is normally distributed (see Chapter 7). Chapter 9 will extend the parametric methods (Chapter 7) and non-parametric methods (Chapter 8) to more than two samples.

■ Key Terms

BINOMDIST function	Chi square distribution	CHIDIST function
Binomial distribution	Chi square test	CHIINV function

Contingency table	Independent tests	Sign test
Critical chi square statistic	Kruskal-Wallis test	Test of association
Critical z statistic	McNemar's test for matched pairs	Test differences in proportions:
Cross tabulation	NORMSDIST function	independent samples
Degrees of freedom	Observed frequency	Tied ranks
Dependent tests	One tail tests	Two tail tests
Expected frequency	P-value	Wilcoxon signed rank
Hypothesis testing	Ranks	sum test

■ Further Reading

Textbook Resources

1. Whigham, D. (2007) *Business Data Analysis using Excel*. Oxford University Press. ISBN: 9780199296286.

2. Lindsey, J., K. (2003) *Introduction to Applied Statistics: A Modelling Approach* (2nd Edition). Oxford University Press. ISBN: 978-0-19-852895-1.

Web Resources

1. StatSoft Electronic Textbook http://www.statsoft.com/textbook/stathome.html (accessed 28/1/2007).

2. HyperStat Online Statistics Textbook http://davidmlane.com/hyperstat/index.html (accessed 28/1/2007).

3. Eurostat—website is updated daily and provides direct access to the latest and most complete statistical information available on the European Union, the EU Member States, the euro-zone and other countries http://epp.eurostat.ec.europa.eu (accessed 28/1/2007).

4. Economagic—contains international economic data sets (http://www.economagic.com) (accessed 28/1/2007).

5. The ISI glossary of statistical terms provides definitions in a number of different languages http://isi.cbs.nl/glossary/index.com.htm.

■ Formula Summary

$$E = \frac{\text{Row Total} * \text{Column Total}}{\text{Total Sample Size}} \tag{8.1}$$

$$\chi^2_{cal} = \Sigma \frac{(O - E)^2}{E} \tag{8.2}$$

$$df = (r - 1) * (c - 1) \tag{8.3}$$

$$\chi^2_{cal} = \Sigma \frac{(|O - E| - 0.5)^2}{E} \tag{8.4}$$

$$\rho = \frac{n_1 + n_2}{t_1 + t_2} = \frac{N}{T}$$

(8.5)

$$E = \rho * \text{Column Total}$$

(8.6)

$$P_1 = \frac{a + b}{N}$$

(8.7)

$$P_2 = \frac{a + c}{N}$$

(8.8)

$$Z_{cal} = \frac{b - c}{\sqrt{b + c}}$$

(8.9)

$$\chi^2_{cal} = \frac{(b - c)^2}{b + c}$$

(8.10)

$$Z_{cal} = \frac{X_c - \mu}{\sigma}$$

(8.11)

$$T_+ + T_- = \frac{n'(n' + 1)}{2}$$

(8.12)

$$Z_{cal} = \frac{T_{cal} - \mu_T \pm 0.5}{\sigma_T}$$

(8.13)

$$\mu_T = \frac{n'(n' + 1)}{4}$$

(8.14)

$$\sigma_T = \sqrt{\frac{n'(n' + 1)(2n' + 1)}{24}}$$

(8.15)

$$(t^3 - t)/48$$

(8.16)

$$U_1 = n_1 n_2 + \frac{n_1(n_1 + 1)}{2} - T_1$$

(8.17)

$$U_2 = n_1 n_2 + \frac{n_2(n_2 + 1)}{2} - T_2$$

(8.18)

$$U_1 + U_2 = n_1 n_2$$

(8.19)

$$\mu_U = \frac{n_1 n_2}{2}$$

(8.20)

$$Z = \frac{U_{cal} - \mu_U \pm 0.5}{\sigma_U}$$

(8.21)

$$\sigma_U = \sqrt{\frac{n_1 n_2 (n_1 + n_2 + 1)}{12}}$$

(8.22)

$$\sigma_U = \sqrt{\frac{n_1 n_2}{(n_1 + n_2)(n_1 + n_2 -)} \times \left[\frac{(n_1 + n_2)^3 - (n_1 + n_2)}{12} - \sum_{j=1}^{g} \frac{t_j^3 - t_j}{12} \right]}$$

(8.23)

Factorial Experiments

9

» Overview «

In Chapters 7 and 8 we were dealing with one or two samples and we either applied parametric tests such as the t test or we applied non-parametric tests such as the Mann-Whitney test to answer the question involving the population mean or median. In this chapter we will extend the testing concepts to other tests, including analysis of variance (ANOVA).

» Learning Objectives «

On completing this chapter you should be able to:

» Identify an appropriate statistical test for data sets with more than 2 groups.

» Solve one-factor experiments using one-factor analysis of variance.

» Solve one-factor experiments using Kruskal-Wallis.

» Solve two-factor experiments with one repeated measure using two-factor analysis of variance.

» Solve two-factor experiments with one repeated measure using Friedman's test.

» Solve two-factor experiments with repeated measure using two-factor analysis of variance.

» Solve problems using Microsoft Excel.

9.1 Introduction

In Chapters 7 and 8 we explored techniques to test whether or not two population means are equal. For example, do people spend equal average amounts at two supermarkets? In this case we can solve this problem using a suitable two sample z or t test. But what if we have more than two population means? In this case we could undertake a series of paired comparisons between each of the sample means representing estimates of the population mean. If we were to do this then we would have to undertake 10 paired comparison tests for five population means ($^5C_2 = 10$). Fortunately, we can use analysis of variance (ANOVA) to test for equality of more than two population means. Analysis of variance is based on the observation that sample means will differ due to sampling error and that sample means will differ even if the sample means do have the same population mean. If the sample means are different due to sampling error then we would expect the sample values to be quite close to each other. Conversely, if they are far apart then we would conclude that the population means are different. Thus, a measure of spread (variance) can be used to test whether or not the differences are close enough for us to say that the population means are the same. Microsoft Excel contains three macros which can be used to undertake analysis of variance:

- Single-factor ANOVA (or one-way ANOVA).
- Two-factor ANOVA without replication (or two-way ANOVA without replication).
- Two-factor ANOVA with replication (or two-way ANOVA with replication).

When the assumptions underlying a standard parametric test (normality, independence, common variance) are not satisfied, we can use an appropriate non-parametric test. We recall that, in the case of two independent samples, the two sample t test could be substituted by the non-parametric Mann-Whitney test based on the rank sums of the samples within the combined data set. The non-parametric test is less powerful (capable of detecting differences) but more widely applicable since it relies only on the relative magnitudes of the observations. Similarly, in the paired comparisons case, the paired samples t test could be replaced by a sign test, or the Wilcoxon signed rank test based on the differences between the pairs of observations. In the case of comparisons of several populations, the ANOVA tests for independent and related samples described also depend on the parametric assumptions of normality, independence, and common variance. In these cases it is again possible to use non-parametric rank-based tests:

- The *Kruskal-Wallis test* is a non-parametric alternative to the one-way ANOVA for independent samples.
- Friedman's test is designed for the case of related samples, e.g. where the same subjects are tested under a variety of experimental conditions. It replaces the two-way ANOVA (i.e. one factor with repeated measures).

9.2 Single-Factor Experiments

Friedman's test for > 2 medians The Friedman rank test is primarily used to test whether c sample groups have been selected from populations having equal medians.

Factor A factor of an experiment is a controlled independent variable; a variable whose levels are set by the experimenter.

☐ Example 9.1

In a research project a human resource manager is concerned at the levels of stress (factor—stress) within three supermarkets identified by analysing the number of sickness days reported.

The human resource manager conducts a survey at the three supermarkets (A, B, C) where 15 randomly selected employees completed a survey to measure overall stress levels (see Figure 9.1). The solution to this problem depends upon the nature of the data set sampled and the properties of the underlying population.

	A	B	C	D
1	One-Way ANOVA			
2	Example 9.1			
3				
4				
5		A	B	C
6		87	45	66
7		55	60	50
8		72	65	55
9		76	50	88
10		48	55	72
11		67	78	65
12		65	68	84
13		58	57	77
14		66	54	48
15		71	80	56
16		68	53	54
17		73	45	72
18		86	68	60
19		78	78	56
20		68	59	53

Figure 9.1

Table 9.1 may help you to choose a particular test when the samples are independent of each other:

Data Type	Statistics Test
Interval or ratio	One-way ANOVA—between or no repeated measures (see Section 9.2.1)
Ordinal	Kruskal-Wallis test (see Section 9.2.2)
Nominal	Chi square test (See Chapter 8)

Table 9.1

9.2.1 Single-factor ANOVA (or one-way ANOVA)

The ANOVA test enables a comparison of more than two sample means by comparing the spread between the group means with the spread of values within each group. If the spread of group means (often described as the between-groups sum of squares) is larger than expected from the spread of the data within the groups (the within-group sum of squares) then this indicates that the means differ. With an ANOVA our research question is 'Do the means of the groups differ?' In general, hypothesis tests procedure may be summarized by the following steps: (i) the population means for all treatment groups are really the same (any differences are due to chance), and (ii) the population means for the treatment groups are different (the mean difference between samples is due to the effect of the treatment group). A general procedure is to create the ANOVA table and make the relevant decisions by applying the five step procedure outlined in Chapters 7 and 8. However, the calculations are a little bit more complicated and we will introduce several subprocedures. Let's explain the rationale first.

The rationale

We said that we are going to compare several samples and try to establish if their means are the same or not. We also said that, among other assumptions, two in particular need to be observed, i.e. the assumption of normality and the assumption of equal variance must

X

Level The number of levels of a factor or independent variable is equal to the number of variations of that factor that were used in the experiment.

hold. What does that mean? Well, it means exactly what we say. To illustrate, consider three different populations we intend to sample. In Figure 9.2, all three populations are normal, they have the same mean, as well as the variance. In Figure 9.3 all three populations are normal and have the same variance, but do not have the same mean. In Figure 9.4 all three populations are approximately normal, they have the same mean, but do not have the same variance. The ANOVA test is all about the second example (Figure 9.3). However, before we conduct the test, we need to ensure that we do not have a problem as described in the third example (Figure 9.4).

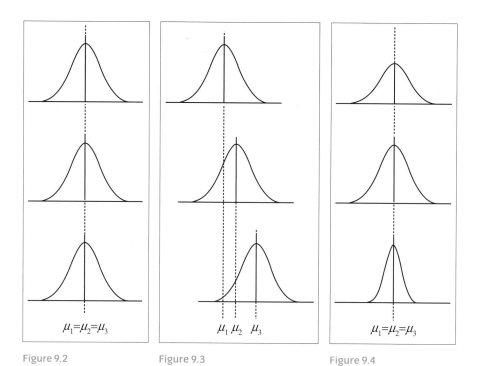

$\mu_1 = \mu_2 = \mu_3$ $\mu_1 \, \mu_2 \ \ \mu_3$ $\mu_1 = \mu_2 = \mu_3$

Figure 9.2   Figure 9.3   Figure 9.4

So, here is what we are going to do. We will first apply the testing steps to verify if the variances are the same:

①   State hypothesis: All Group variances are the same. H_0: $\sigma_1^2 = \sigma_2^2 = \sigma_3^2 = \ldots \sigma_K^2$

②   Select the test

③   Set the level of significance

④   Extract relevant statistic

⑤   Make a decision

Once we've done that, we will embark on the main aim of our analysis, i.e. to establish if the means are the same:

(1) State hypothesis: All Group means are the same. $H_0: \mu_1 = \mu_2 = \mu_3 = \ldots \mu_k$

(2) Select the test

(3) Set the level of significance

(4) Extract relevant statistic

(5) Make a decision

If we find that a significant difference in the groups means is observed then we can conduct an appropriate post hoc test. Post hoc tests are designed to compare all difference combinations of the treatment groups.

(1) State hypothesis

(2) Select the test

(3) Set the level of significance

(4) Extract relevant statistic

(5) Make a decision

The ANOVA formulae

As we said, the null hypothesis in ANOVA is that the means of the groups are equal:

$$H_0: \mu_1 = \mu_2 = \mu_3 = \ldots = \mu_k$$

H_1: At least one mean is different

One-way analysis of variance is an extension of the t test with modelling assumptions as follows:

1. Interval or ratio level of measurement.
2. The samples should be randomly selected from the population.
3. The populations are independent.
4. The population standard deviations (i.e. variances) are equal.
5. The populations are normally distributed.

Assumptions 1, 2, and 3 are design issues whilst assumptions 4 and 5 can be tested using a number of different methods explored in earlier sections. Should the data be unsuitable for ANOVA (as when there is marked heterogeneity of variance or the data are highly skewed), one should consider using non-parametric tests, which require neither homogeneity of variance nor that the data be normally distributed.

X

Homogeneity of variance Population variances are equal.

Example 9.1

Consider a table with k groups and n row values per group as illustrated in Figure 9.5.

In the ANOVA model we are concerned with exploring the differences between the groups and within the groups.

This analysis of the differences between the groups will allow the group means to be evaluated for equality.

	Groups j = 1, k	
A	B	C
87	45	66
55	60	50
72	65	55
76	50	88
48	55	72
67	78	65
65	68	84
58	57	77
66	54	48
71	80	56
68	53	54
73	45	72
86	68	60
78	78	56
68	59	53

Values i = 1, n

Figure 9.5

Step 1 Calculate sample means, $\bar{X}_j$ (where j = 1,......,k)

$$\bar{X}_j = \sum_{i=1}^{n} \frac{X_{\bullet i}}{n_j}$$

(9.1)

In this case we have introduced some new notation $X_{\bullet i}$. This notation tells us that the value of the first group mean ($\bar{X}_1$) is represented by the term $\dfrac{X_{11} + X_{12} + \ldots\ldots\ldots + X_{1n}}{n_1}$.

Therefore, the first group mean represents the first group data values added together divided by the number of data points in the first group. Therefore, $X_{\bullet i}$ represents the value of X for a fixed value of j but with variable i variable. Equation (9.1) can then be used to calculate the other group means ($\bar{X}_2$, $\bar{X}_3$).

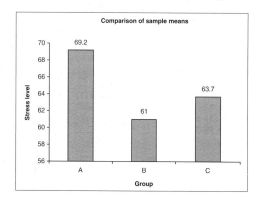

Comparison of sample means

Figure 9.6

Figure 9.6 graphically illustrates the difference in sample mean values for sample groups A–C.

We observe that the sample means are all different and we now wish to know whether or not this difference is statistically significant. To answer this question we apply ANOVA to the data set.

Step 2 Calculate the grand mean, $\bar{\bar{X}}$

$$\bar{\bar{X}} = \frac{\left(\sum_{j=1}^{k} \bar{X}_j\right)}{k}$$

(9.2)

The total variation (SST) is dependent upon the variation due to the difference between groups (SSG) and the variation due to within groups (SSW). This relationship is provided in equation (9.3) as follows:

$$SST = SSG + SSW \qquad (9.3)$$

The value of SST, SSG, and SSW are calculated using equations (9.4)–(9.6) as shown in the steps below:

Step 3 Calculate the total sum of squares (SST)

$$SST = \sum_{j=1}^{k} \sum_{i=1}^{n_j} \left(X_{ij} - \overline{\overline{X}} \right)^2$$

$$(9.4)$$

Where X_{ij} = i^{th} value of group j, n_j = number of values in group j, and k = number of groups.

Step 4 Calculate the between group sum of squares (SSG)

$$SSG = n \sum_{j=1}^{k} \left(\overline{X}_j - \overline{\overline{X}} \right)^2$$

$$(9.5)$$

Step 5 Calculate the within groups sum of squares (SSW)

$$SSW = SST - SSG \qquad (9.6)$$

These values can now be used to determine an estimate for the between and within group variances, as illustrated by equations (9.7)–(9.12):

Step 6 Calculate the degrees of freedom for SST, SSG, and SSW

$$df_T = (N - 1) = (nk - 1) \qquad (9.7)$$

$$df_G = (k - 1) \qquad (9.8)$$

$$df_W = (N - k) = (nk - k) \qquad (9.9)$$

Step 7 Estimate the variances between and within the groups

$$V_T = \frac{SST}{df_T} \qquad (9.10)$$

$$V_G = \frac{SSG}{df_G} \qquad (9.11)$$

$$V_W = \frac{SSW}{df_W} \qquad (9.12)$$

Step 8 Calculate F statistic

$$F_{cal} = \frac{\text{Variance between groups}}{\text{Variance within groups}} = \frac{V_G}{V_W} = \frac{s_G^{\,2}}{s_W^{\,2}} \tag{9.13}$$

If there are large differences among the treatment means, the numerator of F (and therefore F itself) will be inflated and the null hypothesis is likely to be rejected; but if there is no effect, the numerator and denominator should have similar values, giving F close to unity (1). A high value of F, therefore, is evidence against the null hypothesis of equality of population means. From equations (9.3)–(9.13) we can now construct the ANOVA summary table (Table 9.2):

Source of variation	Sum of squares	Degrees of freedom, df	Mean square (variance)	F
Between groups	SSG	df_G	V_G	F_{cal}
Within groups	SSW	df_W	V_W	
Total	SST	df_T		

Table 9.2

Excel will provide this table and includes a corresponding p-value for F_{cal} and a critical F value based upon a chosen significance level.

> **Note**
>
> 1. Excel one-way ANOVA procedure only works for an equal number of values in each group.
>
> 2. For groups with an unequal number of data values equation (9.5) requires modification to incorporate changing sample sizes (n_1, n_2, ..., n_k) into equation (9.5) to produce equation (9.14) as follows
>
> $$SSG = \sum_{k=1}^{k} n_k \times \left(\bar{X}_k - \bar{\bar{X}}\right)^2 \tag{9.14}$$
>
> All other values are calculated as above.

Step 9 Undertake a post hoc test to test which paired means are significant.

If the ANOVA F test gives significance, we know there is a difference somewhere among the means, but that does not justify us in saying that any particular comparison is significant. The F test tells us that at least two differ, but does not identify which two. In order to find out which of the two means differ, we must apply a further statistical test to our data. This type of comparison is called *post hoc*, or *a posteriori*, since we make the comparisons after the data has been collected.

> **Note**   It is important to note that we only perform this analysis if the F statistic result is significant.

To conduct a posteriori or post hoc analysis, a number of alternative tests are available, including Tukey's Honestly Significant test, Student Newman-Keuls, and Bonferroni t test (Table 9.3).

Post Hoc Test	When to use
Bonferroni t test	Wish to make planned comparison in all possible combinations (do not require ANOVA)
Tukey's Honestly Significant test	Large number of groups, wish to test all pairs
Scheffe test	Wish to test all possible combinations (not just pairs)
Newman-Keuls test	Small number of samples, wish to test all possible pairs for significant differences
Fisher's protected t test	Unequal samples sizes, wish to test all possible pairs

Table 9.3

The simplest approach is to perform a t test on every pair of group means in the data set. However, there is a problem with repeated t tests. If we have n groups and each group mean comparison t test is assessed at a significance level of α (probability α of a type 1 error—a false rejection of the null hypothesis) then we have $n(n-1)/2$ pairs to compare. We can show that an upper bound on the probability (P) of making at least one type 1 error during the **multiple comparisons** is given by equation (9.15):

$$P = 1 - (1-\alpha)^{\frac{n(n-1)}{2}}$$
(9.15)

As the number of means increases, this bound approaches 1. The **Bonferroni multiple comparison t test** is often used to address this problem as defined by equation (9.16).

$$t_{cal} = \frac{\bar{X}_L - \bar{X}_S}{\sqrt{V_W \times \left(\frac{1}{n_L} + \frac{1}{n_S}\right)}}$$
(9.16)

Where the t statistic is one tail, df = N−k, subscripts L and S represent the largest and smallest group means respectively. In the Bonferroni t test, the level of significance is divided by the number of means. This ensures that the probability of a type 1 error is no greater than the original level of significance. For the data example, we would compare the following group mean pairings: group 1–group 2, group 1–group 3, group 2–group 3. These group differences $(\bar{X}_L - \bar{X}_S)$ are then compared with the critical difference obtained from equation (9.16) to see which pairings are significantly different. The critical values for the Bonferroni t test are calculated as follows:

1. The critical value of t would be calculated with a significance level adjusted to significance level/number of pairs =TINV(α/n, df$_w$). If t < t$_{cri}$, reject H$_1$.

2. The p-value would be adjusted by muliplying the calculated p-value by the number of pairs =TDIST(t$_{cal}$, dfW, 2). If p < α/n, reject H$_0$.

Multiple comparisons
Multiple comparisons problem occurs when one considers a set, or family, of statistical inferences simultaneously.

Bonferroni t test The Bonferroni test is a statistical procedure that adjusts the alpha level to allow multiple t tests to be used following the ANOVA.

To summarize the one-factor ANOVA solution procedure consists of the following steps (Table 9.4):

A	Check normality assumption—see Section 5.2.4. Undertake a five-number summary or construct a normal probability plot.
B	Check variance assumption—see Excel solution below.
C	Perform one-factor ANOVA—see Excel solution below.
D	If significant difference run a comparison test (Bonferroni t test in our example)—see Excel solution below.

Table 9.4

How to apply ANOVA?

If we put the previous two sections into a practical context, it will become much more obvious how to use this powerful analysis tool. Let's take Example 9.1 and first check if the variances are the same.

Excel solution—Example 9.1—check variance assumption

Figure 9.7 illustrates the Excel solution.

	A	B	C	D	E	F	G	H	I
1	One-Way ANOVA								
2	Example 9.1								
3									
4									
5		A	B	C		State Hypothesis			
6		87	45	66			H_0: Group variances are equal		
7		55	60	50			H1: Group variances are different	1	
8		72	65	55					
9		76	50	88		Select Test			
10		48	55	72			Peform F test for variances	2	
11		67	78	65					
12		65	68	84		Set level of significance			
13		58	57	77			Significance α =	0.05	3
14		66	54	48					
15		71	80	56		Extract relevant statistic			
16		68	53	54			VAR (group A) =	111.4571429	=VAR(B6:B20)
17		73	45	72			VAR (group B) =	132.5714286	=VAR(C6:C20)
18		86	68	60			VAR (group C) =	155.352381	=VAR(D6:D20)
19		78	78	56			F_{max} =	1.393830642	=H18/H16
20		68	59	53			df_L =	14	=COUNT(D6:D20)-1
21						4	df_S=	14	=COUNT(B6:B20)-1
22							F_{cri} =	2.483725741	=FINV(H13,H20,H21)
23							P-value =	0.271306444	=FDIST(H19,H20,H21)
24									
25						Decision:			
26							Since $F_{max} < F_{cri}$ (P-value > 0.05), Accept H_0		5

Figure 9.7

→ Excel Solution

Group A Cells B6:B20	Values
Group B Cells C6:C20	Values
Group C Cells D6:D20	Values

Significance = Cell H13	Value
VAR1 = Cell H16	Formula: =VAR(B6:B20)
VAR2 = Cell H17	Formula: =VAR(C6:C20)
VAR3 = Cell H18	Formula: =VAR(D6:D20)
Fmax = Cell H19	Formula: =H18/H16
dfL = Cell H20	Formula: =COUNT(D6:D20)−1
dfS = Cell H21	Formula: =COUNT(B6:B20)−1
F_{cri} = Cell H22	Formula: =FINV(H13,H20,H21)
P-value Cell H23	Formula: =FDIST(H19,H20,H21)

(1) State hypothesis

H_0: Group variances are equal

H_1: Group variances are different

(2) Select test

Perform F test to test that the variances are not significantly different.

(3) Set level of significance (α) = 0.05

(4) Extract relevant statistic

The variance for each group can be calculated from equation (9.17):

$$\text{VAR(X)} = \frac{\sum\limits_{i=1}^{n} X_i^2 - \dfrac{\left(\sum\limits_{i=1}^{n} X_i\right)^2}{n}}{n-1} \tag{9.17}$$

Where n = number in each group (j = 1, k). From Excel the variance of each group is as follows: Group 1 variance = 111.457, Group 2 variance = 132.571, and Group 3 variance = 155.352. Calculate the F statistic, which is defined by the equation (9.13) as follows:

$$F_{cal} = \frac{\text{Largest Variance}}{\text{Smallest Variance}}$$

From Excel, F = 1.3938, p-value = 0.2713, and the critical value of F = 2.4837.

(5) Make a decision

Since $F_{cal} < F_{cri}$ (1.3938 < 2.4837) we accept H_0. The same conclusion would be made if you compared your significance level (α = 0.05) with the p-value (0.2713). In this case, p-value > significance level, accept H_0, reject H_1.

✻ **Interpretation** We may accept the null hypothesis that there is no significant difference among the group variances and we may, therefore, proceed with our one-factor analysis of variance. If we found a significant difference then we could use a non-parametric test (see Section 9.2.2).

Now let's embark on a proper ANOVA analysis and check if the means are the same.

Excel solution—Example 9.1—single-factor ANOVA

Figure 9.8 illustrates the Excel solution.

	J	K	L	M	N	O	P	Q	R	S
5		State Hypothesis								
6			H_0: Group means are equal							
7			H1: Group means are different		①					
8										
9		Select Test								
10			Peform One Factor ANOVA		②					
11										
12		Set level of significance								
13			Significance α =	0.05	③					
14										
15		Extract relevant statistic								
16										
17		Anova: Single Factor								
18										
19			SUMMARY							
20			Groups	Count	Sum	Average	Variance			
21			A	15	1038	69.2	111.4571			
22			B	15	915	61	132.5714			
23			C	15	956	63.73333333	155.3524		④	
24										
25										
26			ANOVA							
27			Source of Variation	SS	df	MS	F	P-value	F crit	
28			Between Groups	522.97778	2	261.4888889	1.964207	0.152941333	3.2199423	
29			Within Groups	5591.3333	42	133.1269841				
30										
31			Total	6114.3111	44					
32										
33		Decision:								
34			Since $F_{max} < F_{cri}$ (P-value > 0.05), Accept H_0		⑤					

Figure 9.8

→ **Excel Solution**

Using Excel ToolPak: Data Analysis and run the single-factor ANOVA test (Tools > Data Analysis > Anova: Single Factor).

Figure 9.9

In the input range enter B5:D20, choose columns for sample groups, click on 'labels in first row', choose significance 0.05, and select output range K5.

Click on OK to generate the results.

Figure 9.10

In this case, we have what we call a 'one-way ANOVA'. That is, there is one factor (stress) we are looking at across these 3 groups.

(1) State hypothesis

The null hypothesis in ANOVA is that the means of the groups are equal:

$$H_0 : \mu_1 = \mu_2 = \mu_3 = ... = \mu_n$$

H_1: At least one mean is different

(2) Select test

We now need to choose an appropriate statistical test for testing H_0. From the information provided we note:

- Number of samples—three samples.
- The statistic we are testing—testing for a difference between three sample means with one factor.
- Conduct one-way single-factor ANOVA test.

The test statistic in this case is an F test defined by equation (9.13):

$$F_{cal} = \frac{s_G^{\ 2}}{s_W^{\ 2}}$$

If the null hypothesis is true then each sample is from the same population with each sample mean representing a point value on the same sampling distribution. In this case, the 'between group variance' will be an estimate of the variance of the population. Finally, if the null hypothesis is true then the 'between group variance' is equal to the 'within group variance'. Thus, the null hypothesis and alternative hypothesis are equivalent to $S_G^{\ 2} = \alpha_w^{\ 2}$ and $S_G^{\ 2} > \alpha_w^{\ 2}$ respectively. Hence, analysis of variance is a one-sided test.

(3) Set level of significance $(\alpha) = 0.05$

④ Extract relevant statistic

$$\text{From Excel, } F_{cal} = \frac{\text{Variation between groups}}{\text{Variation within groups}} = \frac{261.488...}{133.126...} = 1.9642$$

⑤ Make a decision

As we can see, the mean level of stress reported by 'A' (69.2) is higher than that of either 'B' (61) or 'C' (63.7). But are these differences statistically significant? According to the test result $F_{cal} = 1.9642$. With a significance level of 0.05, the critical value of F, $F_{cri} = 3.2199$. Therefore, since $F_{cal} < F_{cri}$, we fail to reject the null hypothesis.

✳ **Interpretation**   The evidence suggests that, given the level of significance of 0.05, all three departments have the same level of stress.

Excel solution—Example 9.1—Bonferroni multiple comparison t test

Figure 9.11 illustrates the Excel solution.

	T	U	V	W
4	State Hypothesis			
5		$H_0: \mu_L = \mu_S$	①	
6		$H_0: \mu_L <> \mu_S$		
7	Select Test			
8		Bonferroni t test	②	
9	Set level of significance			
10		Signicance =	0.05 ③	
11	Extract relevant statistic			
12		V_W =	133.127	=N17
13		$n = n_1 = n_2 = n_3$ =	15	=L9
14		Number of pairs =	3	=COMBIN(3,2)
15				
16		Adjusted significance =	0.016667	=V10/V14
17		Within variance df_W =	42	=M17
18		t_{cri} =	2.493667	=TINV(V16,V17)
19		Grp A - Grp B		
20		M_L =	69.2	=N9
21		M_S =	61	=N10
22		t_{cal} =	1.946307	=(V20-V21)/SQRT(V12*(1/V13+1/V13))
23	④	P -value =	0.058328	=TDIST(V22,V17,2)
24		Grp A - Grp C		
25		M_L =	69.2	=N9
26		M_S =	63.73333	=N11
27		t_{cal} =	1.297538	=(V25-V26)/SQRT(V12*(1/V13+1/V13))
28		P -value =	0.201528	=TDIST(V27,V17,2)
29		Grp C - Grp B		
30		M_L =	63.73333	=N11
31		M_S =	61	=N10
32		t_{cal} =	0.648769	=(V30-V31)/SQRT(V12*(1/V13+1/V13))
33		P -value =	0.520019	=TDIST(V32,V17,2)
34				
35	Decision:			
36		All pairs are not different.	⑤	

Figure 9.11

→ **Excel Solution**

Significance = Cell V10	Values	
V_w = Cell V12	Formula: =N17	
$n = n_1 = n_2 = n_3$ = Cell V13	Formula: =N10	
Number of pairs = Cell V14	Formula: =COMBIN(3,2)	
Adjusted significance = Cell V16	Formula: =V10/V14	
Within variance df_w = Cell V17	Formula: =M17	
t_{cri} = Cell V18	Formula: =TINV(V16,V17)	
Grp A – Grp B		
M_L = Cell V20	Formula: =N9	
M_S = Cell V21	Formula: =N10	
t_{cal} = Cell V22	Formula: =(V20–V21)/SQRT(V12*(1/V13+	
	1/V13))	
P-value = Cell V23	Formula: =TDIST(V22,V17,2)	
Grp A – Grp C		
M_L = Cell V25	Formula: =N9	
M_S = Cell V21	Formula: =N11	
t_{cal} = Cell V27	Formula: =(V25–V26)/SQRT(V12*(1/V13+	
	1/V13))	
P-value = Cell V28	Formula: =TDIST(V27,V17,2)	
Grp C – Grp B		
M_L = Cell V30	Formula: =N11	
M_S = Cell V31	Formula: =N10	
t_{cal} = Cell V32	Formula: =(V30–V31)/SQRT(V12*(1/V13+	
	1/V13))	
P-value = Cell V33	Formula: =TDIST(V32,V17,2)	

We will now conduct one of the more popular a posteriori tests.

① State hypothesis

The null hypothesis in ANOVA is that the means of the groups are equal:

$$H_0 : \mu_L = \mu_S$$

$$H_1 : \mu_L \neq \mu_S$$

② Select test

If the null hypothesis was rejected then we would undertake a suitable multiple comparison test to test which of the paired samples are significantly different. From the information provided we note:

- Number of samples—three samples.

- The statistic we are testing—testing for a difference between three sample means using t test.

- Conduct Bonferroni multiple comparison t test.

③ Set level of significance ($\alpha = 0.05$). Adjusted significance (α_{adj}) = 0.05/3 = 0.0167.

④ Extract relevant statistic

$$t_{\frac{\alpha}{2},df_w} = \frac{(\overline{X}_L - \overline{X}_S) - (\mu_L - \mu_S)}{\sqrt{S_w^2\left(\dfrac{1}{n_L} + \dfrac{1}{n_S}\right)}}$$

(9.18)

Table 9.5 summarizes the results:

	Significance	t_{cri}	t_{cal}	P-value	Decision
Groups 1 and 2			1.9463	0.0558	Accept H_0
Groups 1 and 3	0.0167	2.494	1.2975	0.2015	Accept H_0
Groups 2 and 3			0.6487	0.5200	Accept H_0

Table 9.5

⑤ Make a decision

✻ **Interpretation**   The evidence suggests that, given the level of significance of α / n (= 0.0167), no significant differences are observed between all possible pairings of the group means.

Equation (9.18) can be rearranged to make $\mu_L - \mu_S$ the subject to give equation (9.19):

$$\mu_L - \mu_S = (\overline{X}_L - \overline{X}_S) \pm t_{\frac{\alpha}{2},df_w} \times \sqrt{S_w^2\left(\frac{1}{n_L} + \frac{1}{n_S}\right)}$$

(9.19)

Excel solution—Example 9.1—confidence interval

Figure 9.12 illustrates the Excel solution.

	X	Y	Z	AA
4		Confidence intervals		
5		V_w =	133.1269841	=N17
6		df_w =	42	=M17
7		$n = n_1 = n_2 = n_3$ =	15	=L9
8		Significance level =	0.05	
9		Two tail t_{cri} =	2.324620133	=TINV(Z8/2,Z6)
10		Error term =	5.50105527	=Z9*SQRT(Z6*(1/Z7+1/Z7))
11				
12		Grp A - Grp B =	8.2	=N9-N10
13		Upper CI =	13.70105527	=Z12+Z10
14		Lower CI =	2.69894473	=Z12-Z10
15		Grp A - Grp C =	5.466666667	=N9-N11
16		Upper CI =	10.96772194	=Z15+Z10
17		Lower CI =	-0.034388603	=Z15-Z10
18		Grp C - Grp B =	2.733333333	=N11-N10
19		Upper CI =	8.234388603	=Z18+Z10
20		Lower CI =	-2.767721936	=Z18-Z10

Figure 9.12

→ **Excel Solution**

V_w = Cell Z5	Formula: =N17
df_w = Cell Z6	Formula: =M17
$n = n_1 = n_2 = n_3$ = Cell Z7	Formula: =L9
Significance level = Cell Z8	Value
Two tail t_{cri} = Cell Z9	Formula: =TINV(Z8/2,Z6)
Error term = Cell Z10	Formula: =Z9*SQRT(Z6*(1/Z7+1/Z7))
Grp A − Grp B = Cell Z12	Formula: =N9−N10
Upper CI = Cell Z13	Formula: =Z12+Z10
Lower CI = Cell Z14	Formula: =Z12−Z10
Grp A − Grp C = Cell Z15	Formula: =N9−N11
Upper CI = Cell Z16	Formula: =Z15+Z10
Lower CI = Cell Z17	Formula: =Z15−Z10
Grp C − Grp B = Cell Z18	Formula: =N11−N10
Upper CI = Cell Z19	Formula: =Z18+Z10
Lower CI = Cell Z20	Formula: =Z18−Z10

Therefore, the 95% confidence intervals are as follows (Table 9.6):

Comparison	Difference between group means	Lower CI	Upper CI
$\mu_A - \mu_B$	8.2	2.70	13.70
$\mu_A - \mu_C$	5.47	−0.03	10.97
$\mu_C - \mu_B$	2.73	−2.77	8.23

Table 9.6

If the confidence interval includes zero, then we conclude that there is no difference between the two population means.

✳ **Interpretation** From the analysis we conclude that there is no significant difference between the group means (μ_A and μ_C, μ_C and μ_B) but we may have a significant difference between the group means μ_A and μ_B.

🖱 **Student Exercises**

X9.1 A manufacturing firm conducts a quality assurance test on five machines that are used to manufacture pins with a design pin diameter of 0.125 ± 0.005 cms:

Manufacturing Machine				
A	B	C	D	E
0.125	0.118	0.123	0.126	0.118
0.127	0.122	0.125	0.128	0.129
0.125	0.120	0.125	0.126	0.127
0.126	0.124	0.124	0.127	0.120
0.128	0.119	0.126	0.129	0.121

(a) Describe the one-way analysis of variance and list the model assumptions.

(b) Check that the model assumptions are not violated.

(c) Based upon the sample data collected can we assume that the machines are producing pin diameters with the same diameter?

(d) If the test results suggest a difference can we suggest where the difference between pairs is significant?

X9.2 A university department is undertaking a review of the delivery methods it uses to teach and assess a range of subject modules. The university department decides to undertake a series of controlled tests to assess the suitability of a particular method of delivery before implementing the new method across all subject modules. To test the hypothesis that the proposed method is successful at improving performance the department randomly placed four students into three different groups, where each student will experience one method of delivery only, and all sessions are taught by the same lecturer to reduce lecturer bias. The data set is as follows:

Student	Lecture + seminar	Workshop	Workshop and Virtual Learning Environment
1	16	19	24
2	21	20	21
3	18	21	22
4	13	20	25

(a) Describe the one-way analysis of variance and list the model assumptions.

(b) Check that the model assumptions are not violated.

(c) Based upon the sample data collected can we assume that the three methods have the same average mark?

(d) If the test results suggest a difference can we suggest where the difference between pairs is significant?

X9.3 A car magazine decides to conduct a test to test whether or not the average mileage per gallon between three four wheel drive cars are the same.

Car type A	Car type B	Car type C
15.2	14.8	15.1
15.4	14.4	14.3
14.8	14.3	14.6
14.4	14.1	13.9
14.7	14.4	14.6

(a) Describe the one-way analysis of variance and list the model assumptions.

(b) Check that the model assumptions are not violated.

(c) Based upon the sample data collected can we assume that the cars have the same average miles per gallon?

(d) If the test results suggest a difference can we suggest where the difference between pairs is significant?

X9.4   A new marketing strategy is being constructed on behalf of a national supermarket. To aid the development of this new strategy the marketing firm undertakes a survey to ask which issue is most important when purchasing products from the supermarket: convenience, quality, or price.

Convenience		Quality		Price	
491	464	677	689	575	803
712	559	627	650	614	584
558	759	590	704	706	525
447	557	632	652	484	498
479	528	683	576	478	812
624	670	760	836	650	565
546	534	690	628	583	708
444	657	548	798	536	546
582	557	579	497	579	616
672	474	644	841	795	587

(a) Describe the one-way analysis of variance and list the model assumptions.

(b) Check that the model assumptions are not violated.

(c) Based upon the sample data collected can we assume that the strategies have the same average response?

(d) If the test results suggest a difference can we suggest where the difference between pairs is significant?

9.2.2 Kruskal-Wallis test

Should the data be unsuitable for ANOVA (as when there is marked heterogeneity of variance, or the data are highly skewed), one should consider using a non-parametric (distribution-free) test, which require neither homogeneity of variance nor that the data be normally distributed. With ordinal data, the parametric ANOVA cannot be used in any case. The **Kruskal-Wallis test** uses group rank position to assess whether the group median values come from populations with the same global median.

H_0: The groups come from populations with the same median
H_1: The population medians are not all equal

> X
> Kruskal-Wallis test for
> > 2 medians Kruskal-
> Wallis test compares the
> medians of three or more
> independent groups.

The Kruskal-Wallis assumptions are as follows:

1. The groups are drawn at random from the population.
2. The groups are independent of each other.
3. The groups have similar distribution shape and variability.
4. The measured variable should be a continuous variable.

⌕ Example 9.2

In Example 9.1 we applied a one-way ANOVA test to test whether the population mean stress levels are the same across all groups. If we were concerned at the normality and variance assumptions we can use the Kruskal-Wallis non-parametric procedure to assess whether the median stress levels are equivalent. The Kruskal-Wallis test is an extension of the Mann-Whitney U test for two independent samples (see Section 8.2.3).

In the Kruskal-Wallis test we are testing the null hypothesis that the groups medians are all equal. The alternative states that at least one median pair are not equal.

The Kruskal-Wallis test is more flexible than the F test since it does not require the groups sampled from a population to be normally distributed and with equal variances.

Figure 9.13 represents the Example 9.1 data set.

	Groups j = 1, k		
	A	B	C
Values i = 1, n	87	45	66
	55	60	50
	72	65	55
	76	50	88
	48	55	72
	67	78	65
	65	68	84
	58	57	77
	66	54	48
	71	80	56
	68	53	54
	73	45	72
	86	68	60
	78	78	56
	68	59	53

Figure 9.13

If the F test assumptions hold, you should always use the F test which provides a more accurate test than the Kruskal-Wallis test. The Kruskal-Wallis test statistic is given by equation (9.20) as follows:

$$H = \frac{12}{N(N+1)} \sum_{j=1}^{k} \frac{R_j^2}{n_j} - 3(N+1)$$

(9.20)

Where k = number of groups, n_j = size of the jth group, N = total number of observations, and R_j = rank sum of the jth group. The value of the rank sums for each group can then be checked using the relationship given by equation (9.21):

$$\sum_{j=1}^{k} R_j = \frac{N(N+1)}{2}$$

(9.21)

Tied scores are given the mean of the ranks they would receive if they were not tied. The presence of tied scores does affect the variance of the sampling distribution of H. Equation (9.22) is a correction that can be applied in the case of tied scores:

$$H_c = \frac{1}{S^2} \left[\sum_{j=1}^{k} \frac{R_j^2}{n_j} - \frac{N(N+1)^2}{4} \right]$$

(9.22)

Where S^2 is given by equation (9.23) with r_{ij} = rank for the ith observation in the jth group, n_j = number of values in the jth group:

$$S^2 = \frac{1}{N-1}\left[\sum_{j=1}^{k}\sum_{i=1}^{n_j} r_{ij}^{2} - \frac{N(N+1)^2}{4}\right]$$

(9.23)

Therefore, if you are able to reject H_0 without correcting for ties, there is no need to do the correction. It should only be contemplated when you have failed to reject H_0. This serves to increase the value of H and make the result more likely to be significant. Why? Uncorrected scores are unnecessarily conservative. This is an example of how tied ranks makes it more difficult to distinguish between group medians. Multiple comparisons can be done using pairwise comparisons. For example, Mann-Whitney U test and adjust significance level with Bonferroni adjustment to access which pairs are significantly different.

Note

1. Each group size should have at least five data values although each group can have a different number of data values.

2. For two samples this is the same as the Mann-Whitney U test (see Section 8.2.3).

Excel solution—Example 9.2—Kruskal-Wallis test

Excel does not contain a function or ToolPak: Data Analysis tool to solve the Kruskal-Wallis non-parametric test. To aid understanding we have included a simple solution to enable users to solve these problems using Excel. The solution process can be split into a series of steps: rank data, calculate rank sums, calculate number of ties in groups, and calculate test statistic. These steps are illustrated in Figures 9.14–9.17:

Step 1 Input data into Excel

Step 2 Rank data

	A	B	C	D
1	Kruskal-Wallis test			
2	Example 9.2			
3				
4				
5		A	B	C
6		87	45	66
7		55	60	50
8		72	65	55
9		76	50	88
10		48	55	72
11		67	78	65
12		65	68	84
13		58	57	77
14		66	54	48
15		71	80	56
16		68	53	54
17		73	45	72
18		86	68	60
19		78	78	56
20		68	59	53

Figure 9.14

	A	B	C	D
22		STEP 2: Rank data		
23				
24		A	B	C
25		44	1.5	24.5
26		12	19.5	5.5
27		33	22	12
28		36	5.5	45
29		3.5	12	33
30		26	39	22
31		22	28.5	42
32		17	16	37
33		24.5	9.5	3.5
34		31	41	14.5
35		28.5	7.5	9.5
36		35	1.5	33
37		43	28.5	19.5
38		39	39	14.5
39		28.5	18	7.5

Figure 9.15

→ Excel Solution

Group A Cells B6:B20	Values	
Group B Cells C6:C20	Values	
Group C Cells D6:D20	Values	
Rank Cell B25	Formula: =0.5*(COUNT($B$6:$D$20)+1+	
	RANK(B6,$B$6:$D$20,1)–RANK(B6,$B$6:$D$20,0))	
	Copy formula B25:D39	

Step 3 Calculate H and critical values

Figure 9.16 illustrates the Excel solution.

	E	F	G	H	I
22		STEP 3: Calculate H and critical values			
23					
24			A	B	C
25		group n =	15	15	15
26		R =	423	289	323
27		(R^2)/n =	11928.6	5568.067	6955.267
28		Mean rank MR =	28.2	19.26667	21.53333
29		$\Sigma(R^2)$/n =	24451.93		
30		N =	45		
31					
32		H =	3.7503		
33		df =	2	④	
34		P value=	0.1533		
35		Significance =	0.05	area in right tail	
36		Chi critical =	5.991465		

Figure 9.16

→ Excel Solution

n_A = Cell G25	Formula: =COUNT(B25:B39)
n_B = Cell H25	Formula: =COUNT(C25:B39)
n_C = Cell I25	Formula: =COUNT(D25:B39)
R_A = Cell G26	Formula: =SUM(B25:B39)
R_B = Cell H26	Formula: =SUM(C25:C39)
R_C = Cell I26	Formula: =SUM(D25:D39)
$(R^2_A)/n_A$= Cell G27	Formula: =G26*G26/G25
$(R^2_B)/n_B$ = Cell H27	Formula: =H26*H26/H25
$(R^2_C)/n_C$ = Cell I27	Formula: =I26*I26/I25
MR_A= Cell G28	Formula: =G26/G25
MR_B = Cell H28	Formula: =H26/H25
MR_C = Cell I28	Formula: =I26/I25
$\Sigma (R^2)/n$ = Cell G29	Formula: =SUM(G27:I27)
N = Cell G30	Formula: =COUNT(B6:D20)
H = Cell G32	Formula: =(12/(G30*(G30+1)))*G29–3*(G30+1)
df = Cell G33	Formula: =COUNTA(B5:D5)–1
P-value = Cell G34	Formula: =CHIDIST(G32,G33)
Significance = Cell G35	Value
Chi critical = Cell G36	Formula: =CHIINV(G35,G33)

Step 4 Calculate adjustment for tied ranks and corrected test statistic

Figure 9.17 illustrates the Excel solution.

	J	K	L	M	N	O	P
22		Step 4 Calculate adjustment for tied ranks and corrected test statistic					
23							
24		A^2	B^2	C^2		$\Sigma\Sigma R_{ij}^2 =$	31378
25		1936	2.25	600.25		$S^2 =$	172.113636
26		144	380.25	30.25		$H_c =$	3.75875699
27		1089	484	144		P value=	0.1527
28		1296	30.25	2025		Chi critical =	5.991465
29		12.25	144	1089			
30		676	1521	484		④	
31		484	812.25	1764			
32		289	256	1369			
33		600.25	90.25	12.25			
34		961	1681	210.25			
35		812.25	56.25	90.25			
36		1225	2.25	1089			
37		1849	812.25	380.25			
38		1521	1521	210.25			
39		812.25	324	56.25			

Figure 9.17

→ **Excel Solution**

A^2 Cell K25   Formula: =B25^2
Copy formula K25:K39

B^2 Cell L25   Formula: =C25^2
Copy formula L25:L39

C^2 Cell M25   Formula: =D25^2
Copy formula M25:M39

$\Sigma\Sigma R_{ij}^2 =$ Cell P24   Formula: =SUM(K25:M39)
$S^2 =$ Cell P25   Formula: =(1/(G30−1))*(P24−G30*(G30+1)^2/4)
$H_c =$ Cell P26   Formula: =(1/P25)*(G29−G30*(G30+1)^2/4)
P value = Cell P27   Formula: =CHIDIST(P26,G33)
Chi critical = Cell P28   Formula: =CHIINV(G35,G33)

① State hypothesis
H_0: The population median stress levels are the same
H_1: At least one population median is different

② Select the test
Given the ANOVA assumptions (normality and variance) not valid we use the Kruskal-Wallis non-parametric test.

③ Set the significance level at 5%

④ Extract relevant statistic
Check ranks from equation (9.21):

$$\sum_{j=1}^{k} R_j = \frac{N(N+1)}{2} = 1035$$

From Excel, H = 3.7503, df = 2. It can be shown that if the group sizes are at least 5 then the distribution of H statistic is approximately a chi square distribution with df = k − 1. From Excel, p-value = 0.1527 and critical chi square value = 5.9915. Comparing H with the critical chi square value (3.7503 < 5.9915) and the significance level (0.05) with the p-value (0.1533 > 0.05) we conclude that we would accept H_0. Given that we have failed to reject H_0 and we have ties in the data we use the corrected H value, H_c. From Excel, H_c = 3.7588 < 5.9915 and we still fail to reject the null hypothesis.

⑤ Make a decision

> ✳ **Interpretation**   The evidence suggests that all three departments have the same level of stress.

Since we failed to reject the null hypothesis we do not need to undertake a post comparison test. If we had accepted the alternative hypothesis then we would undertake a comparison of all possible pairs of the departments to see which pairs are significantly different. This is beyond the scope of this text book.

Note   Manual Solution

Step 1 Rank Sample Data

A	B	C	Rank A	Rank B	Rank C
87	45	66	44	1.5	24.5
55	60	50	12	19.5	5.5
72	65	55	33	22	12
76	50	88	36	5.5	45
48	55	72	3.5	12	33
67	78	65	26	39	22
65	68	84	22	28.5	42
58	57	77	17	16	37
66	54	48	24.5	9.5	3.5
71	80	56	31	41	14.5
68	53	54	28.5	7.5	9.5
73	45	72	35	1.5	33
86	68	60	43	28.5	19.5
8	78	56	39	39	14.5
68	59	53	28.5	18	7.5
		N =	45		
		n =	15	15	15
		ΣR =	423	289	323
		Σ(R^2)/n =	11928.6	5568.06	6955.26
		Mean rank =	28.2	19.26667	21.53333

Step 2 Calculate the Kruskal-Wallis test statistic using equation (9.20):

$$H = \frac{12}{N(N+1)} \sum_{j=1}^{k} \frac{R_j^2}{n_j} - 3(N+1)$$

$$H = \frac{12}{N(N+1)} \left[\frac{R_A^2}{n_A} + \frac{R_B^2}{n_B} + \frac{R_C^2}{n_C} \right] - 3(N+1)$$

Substituting values into the equation gives

$$H = \frac{12}{45(45+1)} \left[\frac{(423)^2}{15} + \frac{(289)^2}{15} + \frac{(323)^2}{15} \right] - 3(45+1) = 3.7503$$

Step 3 Calculate critical value
This test statistic (H) follows a chi square distribution with the degrees of freedom given by the formula df = k − 1 = 3 − 1 = 2. The critical chi square test statistic (5%, 2 degrees of freedom) is $\chi_{cri}^2 = \chi^2(0.05) = 5.99$ (from tables).

Step 4 Compare the test statistic H with the critical value
Assuming no tied ranks we compare H (3.7503) with the critical chi square value (5.99). Given H < critical chi square value. Accept H_0 and reject H_1.

Step 5 Conclusion
The evidence suggests that all three departments have the same median level of stress.

The Kruskal-Wallis test is appropriate for comparing more than 2 treatment levels of a single factor. However, it is possible to modify this test to accommodate multiple factors (via the Scheirer-Ray-Hare extension of the Kruskal-Wallis test).

Student Exercises

X9.5 In Exercise X9.1 we employed one-factor analysis of variance to test the null hypothesis that the machines produce the same pin diameter. Describe the analysis of variance assumptions and list the assumptions that we could test statistically. If the assumptions are violated, which non-parametric test could we use to confirm that the pin diameters are the same? Undertake the appropriate non-parametric test to test this null hypothesis.

X9.6 A local airport authority is concerned at the service provided to customers by one of the airlines that uses the airport. To aid development the airport authority decides to randomly select 9 individuals to assess the three airlines who currently use the airport. The individuals rate only one airline and the data is as follows:

A rank	4	3	3	3	4	4	3	4	3
B rank	2	3	3	3	4	4	3	4	3
C rank	2	3	3	3	3	1	3	2	2

(a) Describe why the one-way analysis of variance is not appropriate to this data set.

(b) List the model assumptions.

(c) Based upon the sample data collected can we assume that the airlines are rated the same?

X9.7 In Exercise X9.3 we assumed that the one-factor assumptions were not violated. Describe and undertake an appropriate non-parametric test to test whether the cars have the same average miles per gallon.

X9.8 A journalist working for a television news programme is interested in comparing the predicted performance of four investment funds by a group of finance journalists. The finance journalists provide a forecast only for one of the investment funds (A, B, C, or D). Is there any evidence for the population average prediction to be equal for all funds?

A	B	C	D
4.2	3.3	1.9	3.5
4.6	2.4	2.4	3.1
3.9	2.6	2.1	3.7
4.0	3.8	2.7	4.1
3.7	2.8	1.8	4.4

9.3 Two-Factor Experiments with No Replication

In the previous section we explored the stress levels for three supermarkets with one factor (stress) being assessed and each participant being measured only once. But it is possible that we could change this scenario to include measuring stress across three supermarkets where staff are routinely moved between the three supermarkets. In this case the factor would be supermarket, with a treatment being the level of stress, and we would have a block design since each participant has worked in all three supermarkets.

Example 9.3

In a research project a human resource manager is concerned at the levels of stress within three supermarkets identified by analysing the number of sickness days reported. The human resource manager conducts a survey at the three supermarkets (A, B, C) and randomly selects 15 employees who routinely rotate which supermarket they are employed in and measures their stress levels (see Figure 9.18). In this case we have paired (or blocked) each staff member to each supermarket A–C (or group).

	A	B	C	D	E
1	Two-way ANOVA (Between or without replication)				
2	Example 9.3				
3					
4					
5		Staff Member	A	B	C
6		1	87	45	66
7		2	55	60	50
8		3	72	65	55
9		4	76	50	88
10		5	48	55	72
11		6	67	78	65
12		7	65	68	84
13		8	58	57	77
14		9	66	54	48
15		10	71	80	56
16		11	68	53	54
17		12	73	45	72
18		13	86	68	60
19		14	78	78	56
20		15	68	59	53

Figure 9.18

The following summary table may help you to choose a particular test when the samples are independent of each other (Table 9.7):

Data Type	Statistics Test
Interval or ratio	One-factor experiment with repeated measure (or two-way ANOVA without replication)
Ordinal	Friedman's test
Nominal	Cochran's Q test (not covered in this text)

Table 9.7

9.3.1 Two-way ANOVA with no repeated measures (or one-factor with repeated measures)

In one-factor ANOVA we have k groups in which we would like to test whether each of the population means are equal. In this case the relationship between the sum of squares is SST = SSG + SSW. In this case we have one factor (stress level). But consider Example 9.3 where 15 members of staff are to be assessed for stress level across each of the three departments A, B, and C. The null hypothesis in ANOVA is that the means of the groups $(j = 1, k)$ and means of the rows $(i = 1, n)$ are equal:

Test for difference between supermarkets (groups in columns):

$$H_0: \mu_1 = \mu_2 = \mu_3 = \text{.......} = \mu_k$$

H_1: At least one mean is different

Test for difference between supermarkets (subjects in rows):

$$H_0: \mu_1 = \mu_2 = \mu_3 = \text{.......} = \mu_n$$

H_1: At least one mean is different

Analysis of variance assumes: (1) interval or ratio level of measurement, (2) the samples should be randomly selected from the population, (3) the populations are not independent, (4) the population variances and co-variances are equal, (5) the populations are normally distributed for all block-column combinations, and (6) there are no **interactions** between the row and column variables. Assumptions 1, 2, 3, and 6 are design issues whilst assumptions 4 and 5 can be tested using a number of different methods. Should the data be unsuitable for ANOVA (as when there is marked heterogeneity of variance or the data are highly skewed), one should consider using non-parametric tests, which require neither homogeneity of variance nor that the data be normally distributed.

Step 1 Calculate the grand mean, $\bar{\bar{X}}$ —same as equation (9.2)

$$\bar{\bar{X}} = \frac{\left(\sum\limits_{j=1}^{k} \bar{X}_j \right)}{k}$$

(9.24)

Consider a table with k groups and n row values per group as illustrated in Figure 9.19. Each member of staff is then assessed across each of the departments A–C for stress. In this situation we can call the column variable the treatment and the row variable the level (or block). In this example we only have 1 data value per level.

In the ANOVA model we are concerned with exploring the differences between the groups and within the groups. This analysis of the differences between and within the groups will allow the group and subject means to be evaluated for equality.

Figure 9.20 graphically illustrates the difference in sample mean values for sample groups A–C.

We observe that the sample means are all different and we now wish to know whether or not this difference is statistically significant. To answer this question we apply ANOVA to the data set.

	Groups - Factor A j = 1, k		
Staff Member	A	B	C
1	87	45	66
2	55	60	50
3	72	65	55
4	76	50	88
5	48	55	72
6	67	78	65
7	65	68	84
8	58	57	77
9	66	54	48
10	71	80	56
11	68	53	54
12	73	45	72
13	86	68	60
14	78	78	56
15	68	59	53

(left margin: Levels - Factor B — One value for each level — i = 1, n)

Figure 9.19

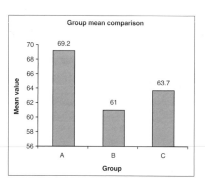

Figure 9.20

Interaction Two independent variables interact if the effect of one of the variables differs depending on the level of the other variable.

Figure 9.21 graphically illustrates the difference in sample mean values for each staff member across groups A–C.

We observe that the sample means are all different and we now wish to know whether or not this difference is statistically significant. To answer this question we apply ANOVA to the data set.

The sum of squares now needs to be modified to take into account this extra factor (staff member) as illustrated in equation (9.25):

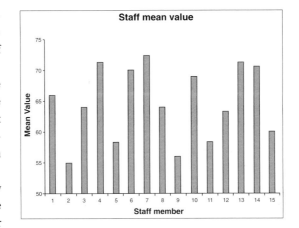

Figure 9.21

$$SST = SSG + SSB + SSW_2 \tag{9.25}$$

In this case we assume no interaction term between the column and row variables. Consider a table with k groups, n row values per group ($n = n_1 = n_2 = \ldots\ldots = n_k$) with each row measured across each group. The value of SST, SSG, SSB, and SSW are calculated using equations (9.26)–(9.37):

Step 2 Calculate the total sum of squares (SST)—same as equation (9.4)

$$SST = \sum_{j=1}^{k} \sum_{i=1}^{n_i} \left(X_{i,j} - \bar{\bar{X}} \right)^2 \tag{9.26}$$

Step 3 Calculate the between groups sum of squares for column (SSG)— same as equation (9.5)

$$SSG = n \times \sum_{j=1}^{k} \left(\bar{X}_j - \bar{\bar{X}} \right)^2 \tag{9.27}$$

Step 4 Calculate the between the row sum of squares (SSB)

$$SSB = k \times \sum_{i=1}^{n} \left(\bar{X}_i - \bar{\bar{X}} \right)^2 \tag{9.28}$$

Step 5 Calculate the within groups sum of squares (SSW_2)

$$SSW_2 = SST - SSG - SSB \tag{9.29}$$

These values can now be used to determine an estimate for the between and within group variances, as illustrated by equations (9.30)–(9.37):

Step 6 Calculate the degrees of freedom for SST, SSG, and SSW_2

$$df_T = (N - 1) = (nk - 1) \tag{9.30}$$

$$df_G = (k - 1) \tag{9.31}$$

Equations (9.30) and (9.31) are the same as equations (9.7) and (9.8).

$$df_B = (n-1) \tag{9.32}$$

$$df_{W_2} = (k-1)(n-1) \tag{9.33}$$

Step 7 Estimate the between and within variances

$$V_T = \frac{SST}{df_T} \tag{9.34}$$

$$V_G = \frac{SSG}{df_G} \tag{9.35}$$

Equations (9.34) and (9.35) are the same as equations (9.10) and (9.11).

$$V_B = \frac{SSB}{df_B} \tag{9.36}$$

$$V_{W_2} = \frac{SSW_2}{df_{W_2}} \tag{9.37}$$

Step 8 Calculate F statistic

At this stage we have two F test calculations to perform: (1) for the stress level factor (supermarket, G), and (2) one for the row factor (subject, B).

$$F_{cal,G} = \frac{V_G}{V_{W_2}} \tag{9.38}$$

$$F_{cal,B} = \frac{V_B}{V_{W_2}} \tag{9.39}$$

If there are large differences among the treatment means, the numerator of F (and therefore F itself) will be inflated and the null hypothesis is likely to be rejected; but if there is no effect, the numerator and denominator should have similar values, giving F close to unity (1). A high value of F, therefore, is evidence against the null hypothesis of equality of population means. From equations (9.26)–(9.39) we can now construct the ANOVA table (Table 9.8):

Source of variation	Sum of squares	Degrees of freedom, df	Mean square (variance)	F
Between groups	SSG	df_G	V_G	$F_{cal,\,G}$
Between blocks	SSB	df_B	V_B	$F_{cal,\,B}$
Within groups	SSW_2	df_{w2}	V_{w2}	
Total	SST	df_T		

Table 9.8

Excel will provide this table and includes a corresponding p-value for F_{cal} and a critical F value based upon a chosen significance level.

Step 9 Undertake a post hoc test to test which paired means (group, block) are significant.

The *Bonferroni multiple comparison t test* can be used to test which paired groups are significantly different and provide confidence intervals using a modified version of equation (9.13) to take into account all possible column and row comparisons. This test has been applied for the one-factor ANOVA test. To summarize the two-factor ANOVA solution procedure consists of the following steps (Table 9.9):

A	Check normality assumption—see Section 5.2.4. Undertake a five-number summary or construct a normal probability plot.
B	Check variance assumption—see Excel solution.
C	Perform two-factor ANOVA without replication—see Excel solution.
D	If significant difference run a comparison test (not covered in text for two-way ANOVA).

Table 9.9

Excel solution—Example 9.3—check variance assumption

Figure 9.22 illustrates the Excel solution.

	A	B	C	D	E	F	G	H	I	J
1	Two-way ANOVA (Between or without replication)									
2	Example 9.3									
3										
4										
5		Staff Member	A	B	C		State Hypothesis			
6		1	87	45	66			H_0: Group variances are equal	1	
7		2	55	60	50			H1: Group variances are different		
8		3	72	65	55					
9		4	76	50	88		Select Test			
10		5	48	55	72			Peform F test for variances	2	
11		6	67	78	65					
12		7	65	68	84		Set level of significance			
13		8	58	57	77			Significance α =	0.05	3
14		9	66	54	48					
15		10	71	80	56		Extract relevant statistic			
16		11	68	53	54			VAR (group A) =	111.45714	=VAR(C6:C20)
17		12	73	45	72			VAR (group B) =	132.57143	=VAR(D6:D20)
18		13	86	68	60			VAR (group C) =	155.35238	=VAR(E6:E20)
19		14	78	78	56			F_{max} =	1.3938306	=I18/I16
20		15	68	59	53			4 df_L =	14	=COUNT(E6:E20)-1
21								df_S=	14	=COUNT(C6:C20)-1
22								F_{cri} =	2.4837257	=FINV(I13,I20,I21)
23								P-value =	0.2713064	=FDIST(I19,I20,I21)
24										
25							Decision:			
26								Since $F_{max} < F_{cri}$ (P-value > 0.05), Accept H_0		5

Figure 9.22

→ Excel Solution

Group A Cells C6:C20	Values
Group B Cells D6:D20	Values
Group C Cells E6:E20	Values
Significance = Cell I13	Value
VAR1 = Cell I16	Formula: =VAR(C6:C20)
VAR2 = Cell I17	Formula: =VAR(D6:D20)

VAR3 = Cell I18	Formula: =VAR(E6:E20)
Fmax = Cell I19	Formula: =I18/I16
dfL = Cell I20	Formula: =COUNT(E6:E20)−1
dfS = Cell I21	Formula: =COUNT(C6:C20)−1
F_{cri} = Cell I22	Formula: =FINV(I13,I20,I21)
P-value Cell I23	Formula: =FDIST(I19,I20,I21)

① State hypothesis

H_0: Group Variances are Equal

H_1: Group Variances are Different

② Select test

Perform F test to test that the variances are not significantly different.

③ Set level of significance $(\alpha) = 0.05$

④ Extract relevant statistic

The variance for each group can be calculated from equation (9.13). From Excel the variance of each group is as follows: group 1 variance = 111.457, group 2 variance = 132.571, and group 3 variance = 155.352. Calculate the F statistic, which is defined by equation (9.14). From Excel, F = 1.3938, p-value = 0.2713, and the critical value of F_{cal} = 2.4837.

⑤ Make a decision

Since $F_{cal} < F_{cri}$ (1.3938 < 2.4837) we accept H_0. The same conclusion would be made if you compared your significance level $(\alpha = 0.05)$ with the p-value (0.2713). In this case, p-value > significance level, accept H_0, reject H_1.

✳ **Interpretation**   We accept the null hypothsis that there is no significant difference among the group variances. We may therefore proceed with our two-factor analysis of variance with no repeated measures. To complete the analysis one should check the co-variance assumption (beyond the scope of this text).

Excel solution—Example 9.3—two-way ANOVA (no repeated measures)

Figure 9.23 illustrates the Excel solution.

	K	L	M	N	O	P	Q	R	S
5		State Hypothesis							
6			H_0: Group means are equal		①				
7			H1: Group means are different						
8		Select Test							
9			Peform Two Factor ANOVA	②					
10		Set level of significance							
11			Significance α =	0.05 ③					
12		Extract relevant statistic							
13									
14									
15			Anova: Two-Factor Without Replication						
16			SUMMARY	Count	Sum	Average	Variance		
17			1	3	198	66	441		
18			2	3	165	55	25		
19			3	3	192	64	73		
20			4	3	214	71.3333333	377.3333		
21			5	3	175	58.3333333	152.3333		
22			6	3	210	70	49		
23			7	3	217	72.3333333	104.3333		
24			8	3	192	64	127		
25			9	3	168	56	84		
26			10	3	207	69	147		
27			11	3	175	58.3333333	70.33333		
28			12	3	190	63.3333333	252.3333		
29			13	3	214	71.3333333	177.3333		
30			14	3	212	70.6666667	161.3333		
31			15	3	180	60	57		
32									
33			A	15	1038	69.2	111.4571		
34			B	15	915	61	132.5714		
35			C	15	956	63.7333333	155.3524	④	
36									
37			ANOVA						
38			Source of Variation	SS	df	MS	F	P-value	F crit
39			Rows	1517.644	14	108.403175	0.745096	0.713944	2.063541
40			Columns	522.9778	2	261.488889	1.797312	0.184344	3.340386
41			Error	4073.689	28	145.488889			
42									
43			Total	6114.311	44				
44									
45		Decision:	Since $F_{max} < F_{cri}$ (P-value > 0.05), Accept H_0 ⑤						

Figure 9.23

→ Excel Solution

Using Excel ToolPak: Data Analysis and run the two-factor without replication ANOVA test (Tools > Data Analysis > Anova: Two-Factor Without Replication).

Figure 9.24

In the input range enter B5:E20, click on 'labels', choose significance 0.05, and select output range L5. Click on OK to generate the results.

Figure 9.25

In this case, we have what we call a 'two-way ANOVA without replication'. That is, there is one factor (stress) but each participant is measured across each of the 3 groups. Note that this is a special case for ANOVA where we have one data value per cell and no interaction. In other words, the model fit is testing for two factors (group, block) only.

(1) State hypothesis

The null hypothesis in ANOVA is that the means of the rows and column groups are equal:

Test for difference between groups (or columns):

$H_0: \mu_1 = \mu_2 = \mu_3 = ... = \mu_k$

H_1: At least one mean is different

Test for difference between levels or blocks (or rows):

$H_0: \mu_1 = \mu_2 = \mu_3 = ... = \mu_n$

H_1: At least one mean is different

(2) Select test

We now need to choose an appropriate statistical test for testing H_0. From the information provided we note:

- Number of samples—three samples.
- The statistic we are testing—testing for a difference between three sample means with one factor but measured across each of the three supermarkets.
- Conduct two-way ANOVA without replication test.

The test statistic in this case is an F test.

(3) Set level of significance ($\alpha = 0.05$)

(4) Extract relevant statistic

Test difference between groups (supermarket, factor A):

$$\text{From Excel, } F_{cal} = \frac{V_G}{V_{w_2}} = \frac{261.488...}{145.488...} = 1.7973$$

Test difference between levels (staff member, factor B):

$$\text{From Excel, } F_{cal} = \frac{V_B}{V_{w_2}} = \frac{108.403...}{145.488...} = 0.7450$$

(5) Make a decision

As we can see, the mean level of stress reported by the fifteen members of staff varies. But are these differences statistically significant?

Test difference between groups (supermarket, factor A):

From Excel, we see that $F_{cal} = 1.7973$. With a significance level of 0.05, the critical value of F, $F_{cri} = 3.3403$. Therefore, since the $F_{cal} < F_{cri}$, we fail to reject the null hypothesis. There is no evidence to suggest that the stress levels are different for the supermarkets.

Test difference between levels (staff member, factor B):

From Excel, we see that $F_{cal} = 0.7450$. With a significance level of 0.05, the critical value of F, $F_{cri} = 2.0635$. Therefore, since the $F_{cal} < F_{cri}$, we fail to reject the null hypothesis. There is no evidence to suggest that the stress levels are different for different members of staff.

✳ **Interpretation**

1. The evidence suggests that all fifteen members of staff have the same level of stress.

2. The evidence suggests that all three departments have the same level of stress.

Note   If we found a significant difference among the means of the groups, we would not know if all three means differ significantly from one another. The F test tells us that at least two differ, but does not identify which two. In order to find out which of the two means differ, we must apply a further statistical test to our data. As previously described, this type of comparison is called post hoc, or a posteriori, since we make the comparisons after the data has been collected. It is important to note that we only perform this analysis if the F statistic is significant. We already described how to use one of these a posteriori tests, i.e. Bonferrori multiple comparison test.

🖱 Student Exercises

X9.9 Suppose a car manufacturing company has three factories and each factory makes a range of car models. Car mileage varies from factory to factory due to a number of differences in the production methods between the three factories. The company has decided to test this hypothesis by asking 6 test drivers to drive the same model car produced by the three factories. The mileage data is as shown.

Is there a difference in the mean car mileage?

Driver	Factory		
	A	B	C
1	33.3	34.5	37.4
2	33.4	34.8	36.8
3	32.9	33.8	37.6
4	32.6	33.4	36.6
5	32.5	33.7	37.0
6	33.0	33.9	36.7

X9.10 A regional bus company is expanding the number of routes from city district X to the financial centre of a major city in England. The bus company have conducted several time tests to determine which route to adopt from four possible routes to the city centre.
To eliminate the effect of the driver, each driver was timed to travel each route (1, 2, 3, and 4).

Is there a difference in the mean travel time?

Driver	Route travel time (minutes)			
	1	2	3	4
1	18	17	21	22
2	16	23	23	22
3	21	21	26	22
4	23	22	29	25
5	25	24	28	25

X9.11 Six new fertilizers are to be tested on four farms growing oil seed rape. The company running the trial is interested in assessing whether the crop size (tons) is significantly dependent upon the type of fertilizer. On each farm six fields were used in the trial so it was only possible to use each of the six fertilizers once on each farm. The crop yields are given in the table, below.

Farm	Type of fertilizer					
	A	B	C	D	E	F
1	1130	1125	1350	1375	1225	1235
2	1115	1120	1375	1200	1250	1200
3	1145	1170	1235	1175	1225	1155
4	1200	1230	1140	1325	1275	1215

Is there a difference in the mean crop from the different fertilizers?

9.3.2 Friedman's test

This test is sometimes called the Friedman two-way analysis of variance by ranks. It is for use with n repeated measures where measurement is at least ordinal. The null hypothesis states that all k samples are drawn from the same population, or from populations with equal medians. Should the data be unsuitable for ANOVA (as when there is marked heterogeneity of variance, or the data are highly skewed), one should consider using non-parametric (distribution-free) tests, which require neither homogeneity of variance nor the data be normally distributed. With ordinal data, the parametric ANOVA cannot be used in any case. The assumptions made using this test are as follows: (1) the populations from which the samples are drawn have similar distributions, (2) the samples are drawn at random, and (3) the samples are independent of each other.

The Friedman test is designed for the case of related samples, e.g. where the same subjects are tested under a variety of experimental conditions. The Friedman test is a non-parametric statistical test developed by the U.S. economist Milton Friedman. Similar to the parametric repeated measures ANOVA, it is used to detect differences in treatments across multiple test attempts. The null hypothesis to be tested is that each of the population medians (M_1, M_2, M_3, ... M_k) are equal:

Null hypothesis

$$H_0: M_1 = M_2 = M_3 = \ldots\ldots = M_k$$

Alternative hypothesis

⟐ Example 9.4

In Example 9.3 the human resource manager was concerned that the ANOVA assumptions may not be valid and has requested that a non-parametric method be used to confirm the hypothesis outcome given by the application of ANOVA to the problem. Figure 9.26 screenshot illustrates the data set. In this case we have paired (or blocked) each staff member to each supermarket A–C. If the ANOVA assumptions are violated then we can use the Friedman two-way analysis of variance by ranks to answer the question. The Friedman test is an extension of the sign test for matched pairs.

Consider a table with k groups and n row values per group as illustrated in Figure 9.26. Each member of staff is then assessed across each of the departments A–C for stress. In this situation we can call the column variable the treatment and the row variable the level (or block). In this example we only have 1 data value per level. In this case the ranks replace the data values.

For each subject separately, rank the observations on each column (treatment or level) from 1 (lowest) to n (highest), where n is the number of treatments.

		Groups - Factor A $j = 1, k$	
Staff Member	A	B	C
1	87	45	66
2	55	60	50
3	72	65	55
4	76	50	88
5	48	55	72
6	67	78	65
7	65	68	84
8	58	57	77
9	66	54	48
10	71	80	56
11	68	53	54
12	73	45	72
13	86	68	60
14	78	78	56
15	68	59	53

Levels - Factor B
(One value for each level)
$i = 1, n$

Figure 9.26

H_1: at least one median pair significantly different.

As before, tied values are given the average of their ranks. Next, the ranks are totalled for each treatment to give values R_j. These are then combined to give equation (9.40) the Friedman statistic, G, as follows:

$$G = \frac{12}{nk(k+1)} \times \sum_{j=1}^{k} R_j^2 - 3n(k+1)$$

(9.40)

where k is the number of groups (or treatment, $j = 1, ..., k$), n is the number of subjects (or levels, $i = 1, ..., n$), and R_j^2 represents the square of the rank total for each column ($j = 1, 2, ..., k$). The test statistic distribution is approximated by the chi square distribution with degrees of freedom $df = k - 1$. For any particular value of k (the number of measures per subject), the mean of the ranks for any particular one of the k subjects is $(k + 1)/2$. Thus for k = 3, as in the present example, it is $(3 + 1)/2 = 2$. On the null hypothesis, this would also be the expected value of the mean for each of the n rows. Similarly, the expected value for each of the column sums (R_e) would be this amount multiplied by the number of subjects: $n(k + 1)/2$. For the present example, with n = 15, it would be $(15)(3 + 1)/2 = 30$. The ranks calculated can then be checked using the relationship given by equation (9.41):

$$\sum_{j=1}^{k} R_j = \frac{kn(k+1)}{2}$$

(9.41)

If there are ties among the ranks, the G statistic must be corrected, because the sampling distribution changes. The formula that corrects for tied ranks is actually a general formula that also works when there are no ties. When ties are present then equation (9.40) is modified to equations (9.42) and (9.43), as follows:

$$G_c = \frac{(k-1)\left[\sum_{i=1}^{k} R_j^2 - nC\right]}{\left[\sum_{j=1}^{k}\sum_{i=1}^{n} R_{ij}^2 - C\right]}$$

(9.42)

$$C = \frac{nk(k+1)^2}{4}$$

(9.43)

Therefore, if you are able to reject H_0 without correcting for ties, there is no need to do the correction. It should only be contemplated when you have failed to reject H_0. This serves to increase the value of G and make the result more likely to be significant. Why? Uncorrected scores are unnecessarily conservative. This is an example of how tied ranks makes it more difficult to distinguish between group medians. Multiple comparisons can be done using pairwise comparisons (for example using Wilcoxon signed-ranks tests)

Note

For two samples this is the same as the Wilcoxon signed rank sum test (see Section 8.2.2).

and using a correction to determine if the post-hoc tests are significant (for example a Bonferroni correction).

Excel solution—Example 9.4—Friedman's test

Excel does not contain a function or ToolPak: Data Analysis tool to solve the Friedman non-parametric test. To aid understanding we have included a simple solution to enable users to solve these problems using Excel. The solution process can be split into a series of steps: rank data, calculate rank sums, calculate number of ties in groups, and calculate test statistic, as follows:

Step 1 Input data into Excel

	A	B	C	D	E
1	Friedman two-way anova				
2	Example 9.4				
3					
4					
5		Staff Member	A	B	C
6		1	87	45	66
7		2	55	60	50
8		3	72	65	55
9		4	76	50	88
10		5	48	55	72
11		6	67	78	65
12		7	65	68	84
13		8	58	57	77
14		9	66	54	48
15		10	71	80	56
16		11	68	53	54
17		12	73	45	72
18		13	86	68	60
19		14	78	78	56
20		15	68	59	53

Figure 9.27

→ **Excel Solution**

Group A Cells C6:C20   Values
Group B Cells D6:D20   Values
Group C Cells E6:E20   Values

	A	B	C	D	E
23		STEP 2: Rank data			
24					
25		Staff Member	A	B	C
26		1	3	1	2
27		2	2	3	1
28		3	3	2	1
29		4	2	1	3
30		5	1	2	3
31		6	2	3	1
32		7	1	2	3
33		8	2	1	3
34		9	3	2	1
35		10	2	3	1
36		11	3	1	2
37		12	3	1	2
38		13	3	2	1
39		14	2.5	2.5	1
40		15	3	2	1
41					
42		rank sums R =	35.5	28.5	26
43		R^2 =	1260.25	812.25	676
44		Mean Rank =	2.366667	1.9	1.733333
45		Expected mean rank =	2	2	2
46		Expected row sum, Re =	30	30	30

Step 2 Rank data

Figure 9.28 illustrates the Excel solution.

Figure 9.28

→ Excel Solution

Rank A cells Cell C26 — Formula: =0.5*(COUNT($C6:$E6)+1+RANK(C6,$C6:$E6,1)−RANK(C6,$C6:$E6,0))
Copy formula Cells C26:E40

Rank sums R = Cell C42 — Formula: =SUM(C26:C40)
Copy formula Cells C42:E42

R^2 = Cell C43 — Formula: =C42^2
Copy formula Cells C43:E43

Mean rank = Cell C44 — Formula: =C42/COUNT(C26:C40)
Copy formula Cells C44:E44

Expected mean rank = Cell C45 — Formula: =($H$26+1)/2
Copy formula Cells C45:E45

Expected row sum Re = Cell C46 — Formula: =$H$27*($H$26+1)/2
Copy formula Cells C46:E46

	F	G	H
24		STEP 3: Calculate G and critical values	
25			
26		Number of groups, k =	3
27		Number of subjects, n =	15
28		ΣR^2 =	2748.5
29		Test statistic, G =	3.23333333
30		Significance =	0.05
31		df =	2
32		Critical chi square =	5.99146455
33		P-value =	0.19855946

Step 3 Calculate G and critical values

Figure 9.29 illustrates the Excel solution.

Figure 9.29

→ **Excel Solution**

k = Cell H26   Formula: =COUNTA(C25:E25)
n = Cell H27   Formula: =COUNT(B26:B40)
ΣR^2 = Cell H28   Formula: =SUM(C43:E43)
G = Cell H29   Formula: =(12/(H26*H27*(H26+1)))*
                                             H28−3*H27*(H26+1)

Significance = Cell H30   Value
df = Cell H31   Formula: =H26−1
Critical chi square = Cell H32   Formula: =CHIINV(H30,H31)
P-value = Cell H33   Formula: =CHIDIST(H29,H31)

Step 4 Calculate number of tied ranks and corrected test statistic

Figure 9.30 illustrates the Excel solution.

	J	K	L	M	N	O	P
24	Step 4 Calculate adjustment for tied ranks and corrected test statistic						
25							
26	Staff Member	A	B	C		C =	180
27	1	9	1	4		$\Sigma\Sigma$R2 =	209.5
28	2	4	9	1		G_c =	3.288136
29	3	9	4	1		Critical chi square =	5.991465
30	4	4	1	9		P-value =	0.193193
31	5	1	4	9			
32	6	4	9	1		4	
33	7	1	4	9			
34	8	4	1	9			
35	9	9	4	1			
36	10	4	9	1			
37	11	9	1	4			
38	12	9	1	4			
39	13	9	4	1			
40	14	6.25	6.25	1			
41	15	9	4	1			

Figure 9.30

→ **Excel Solution**

R_{ij}^2 Cell K27   Formula: =C26^2
                                             Copy formula Cells K27:M41
C = Cell P26   Formula: =H26*H27*(H26+1)^2/4
$\Sigma\Sigma R_i^2$ = Cell P27   Formula: =SUM(K27:M41)
G_c = Cell P28   Formula: =(H26−1)*(H28−H27*P26)/(P27−P26)
Critical chi square= Cell P29   Formula: =CHIINV(H30,H31)
P-value = Cell P30   Formula: =CHIDIST(P28,H31)

(1) State hypothesis
     H_0: The null hypothesis is that the stress levels are the same for all departments
     H_1: At least one population median stress level is different

(2) Select the test

Given the ANOVA assumptions (normality and variance) not valid we use the Friedman non-parametric test.

(3) Set the significance level at 5%

(4) Extract relevant statistic

Check ranks. From equation (9.41) we have: $\sum\limits_{j=1}^{k} R_j = \dfrac{kn(k+1)}{2} = 90$

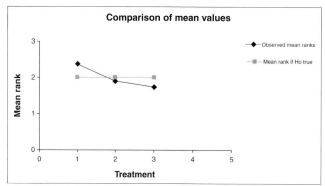

Figure 9.31

Figure 9.31 plots the expected value of the mean rank against the mean ranks for each of the treaments (A, B, C).

We observe that the means are different. Are they significantly different? The distribution of G is approximately a chi square distribution with df = n − 1. From Excel, G = 3.23, df = n − 1 = 2, critical chi square value = 5.99, and p-value = 0.1988. Comparing G with the critical chi square value we note that $G < \chi^2_{cri}$ (3.23 < 5.99), and conclude that we would fail to reject H_0 at a significance level of 5%. An alternative method is to use the p-value to make a decision is to compare the p-value with your significance level (α). In this case, p = 0.1932 > 0.05, and we fail to reject H_0. Given that we have failed to reject H_0 and we have ties in the data we use the corrected G value, Gc. From Excel Gc = 3.29 < 5.99 and we still fail to reject the null hypothesis.

(5) Make a decision

> ✳ **Interpretation**   The evidence suggests that all three departments have the same level of stress.

Since we failed to reject the null hypothesis we do not need to undertake a post comparison test. If we had accepted the alternative hypothesis then we would under-take a comparison of all possible pairs of the departments to see which pairs are signifi-cantly different. For example, Wilcoxon signed rank sum test and adjust significance with Bonferrori adjustment.

Student Exercises

X9.12 Repeat Exercise X9.9 but employ a suitable non-parametric test to test the null hypothesis that the average car mileage is the same.

X9.13 Repeat Exercise X9.10 but employ a suitable non-parametric test to test the null hypothesis that the average time travel is the same for the routes.

X9.14 Repeat Exercise X9.11 but employ a suitable non-parametric test to test the null hypothesis that the crop is the same.

9.4 Two-Factor Experiments with Equal Replication

In this section we consider the stress levels associated with three supermarkets (A, B, C) across two types of members of staff who work in different departments (Deli, Meat). In this situation we are dealing with two factors (supermarket with three supermarkets A–C, department with two departments). In this case observe that we have three staff values for each paired comparison. We say that we have three replications. In this case we would be looking for a **main effect** from the two factors: supermarket, department, and whether we have an interaction between the two main effects.

⇱ **Example 9.5**

The human resource manager conducts a survey at the three supermarkets (A, B, C) but decides to choose three randomly selected employees who routinely rotate which supermarket they are employed in but work in either the deli or meat departments. The stress levels recorded are provided in Figure 9.32.

	A	B	C	D	E
1	The Two-way ANOVA With Replication				
2	Example 9.5				
3					
4			A	B	C
5			87	54	68
6		Deli	50	56	70
7			58	57	67
8			67	61	56
9		Meat	48	54	61
10			59	52	65

Figure 9.32

9.4.1 Two-way ANOVA with equal replication

In two-way ANOVA with equal replication we have two factors (A, B) but each factor level has more than one value attached. For example, in Example 9.5 we observe that level 1 for supermarket (A) has 3 deli values and not just one data value as observed in Section 9.3. In this case, we say that each factor is replicated 3 times. The null hypothesis in ANOVA is that the means of the groups (j = 1, k) and means of the rows (i = 1, n) are equal:

Test for difference between supermarkets (groups or columns):

$$H_0: \mu_1 = \mu_2 = \mu_3 = \ldots\ldots = \mu_k$$

H_1: At least one mean is different

Main effect This is the simple effect of a factor on a dependent variable.

Test for difference between departments (or rows):

$$H_0: \mu_1 = \mu_2 = \mu_3 = \text{.......} = \mu_i$$

H_1: At least one mean is different

Test for interaction effect:

H_0: No interaction term between factor A and B

H_1: Interaction term is not zero

Analysis of variance assumes:

1. Interval or ratio level of measurement.

2. The samples should be randomly selected from the population.

3. The populations are not independent.

4. The population variances and co-variances are equal.

5. The populations are normally distributed for all block-column combinations.

6. There is an interaction between the row and column variables.

Assumptions 1, 2, and 3 are design issues whilst assumptions 4, 5, and 6 can be tested using a number of different methods. Should the data be unsuitable for ANOVA (as when there is marked heterogeneity of variance or the data are highly skewed), one should consider using non-parametric tests, which require neither homogeneity of variance nor that the data be normally distributed.

The model assumptions are as stated in Section 9.3 except that we now have an interaction term between factors A and B where the effect of factor A is dependent upon the level of factor B.

| | | Factor A j = 1, k | | |
		A	B	C
Factor B i = 1, n	Deli	87	54	68
		50	56	70
		58	57	67
	Meat	67	61	56
		48	54	61
		59	52	65

Figure 9.33

Condider a table with k groups, n row values per group, and each level with 3 data values as illustrated in Figure 9.33.

In all cases we observe that each combination of A and B is replicated 'r' times, where r = 3. In the ANOVA model we are concerned with exploring the differences between the groups and within the groups.

This analysis of the differences between and within the groups will allow the group and subject means to be evaluated for equality.

Step 1 Calculate the grand mean, $\overline{\overline{X}}$

$$\overline{\overline{X}} = \frac{\sum\limits_{j=1}^{k}\sum\limits_{i=1}^{n}\sum\limits_{p=1}^{r} X_{jip}}{knr}$$

(9.44)

Figure 9.34 graphically illustrates the difference in sample mean values for sample groups A–C.

We observe that the sample means are all different and we now wish to know whether or not this difference is statistically significant. To answer this question we apply ANOVA to the data set.

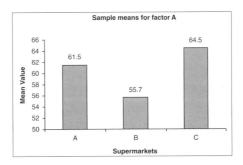

Figure 9.34

Figure 9.35 graphically illustrates the difference in sample mean values for each department (deli, meat).

We observe that the sample means are all different and we now wish to know whether or not this difference is statistically significant. To answer this question we apply ANOVA to the data set.

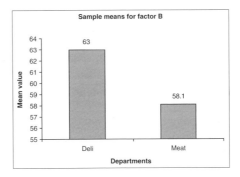

Figure 9.35

Figure 9.36 illustrates the interaction between the sample means for factor A and B.

We observe from this diagram that the sample means associated with each level of factor A changes depending upon the level of factor B.

If no interaction existed then we would expect these two lines to be parallel.

The sum of squares now needs to be modified to take into account this extra factor (staff member) as illustrated in equation (9.25):

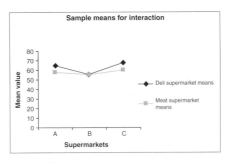

Figure 9.36

$$SST = SSG + SSB + SSGB + SSW_2 \tag{9.45}$$

In this case we assume an interaction term between the column and row variables. Condider a table with k groups, n row values per group ($n = n_1 = n_2 = \ldots\ldots = n_k$) with each row measured across each group. The value of SST, SSG, SSGB, and SSW$_2$ are calculated using equations (9.46)–(9.50):

Step 2 Calculate the total sum of squares (SST)

$$SST = \sum_{j=1}^{k} \sum_{i=1}^{n} \sum_{p=1}^{r} \left(X_{jip} - \overline{\overline{X}} \right)^2 \tag{9.46}$$

Step 3 Calculate the between groups sum of squares for column (SSG)

$$SSG = n \times r \times \sum_{j=1}^{k} \left(\overline{X}_{\bullet j \bullet} - \overline{\overline{X}} \right)^2 \qquad (9.47)$$

Step 4 Calculate the between the row sum of squares (SSB)

$$SSB = k \times r \times \sum_{i=1}^{n} \left(\overline{X}_{i \bullet \bullet} - \overline{\overline{X}} \right)^2 \qquad (9.48)$$

Step 5 Calculate interaction sum of squares (SSGB)

$$SSGB = r \times \sum_{i=1}^{n} \sum_{j=1}^{k} \left(\overline{X}_{ij\bullet} - \overline{X}_{i\bullet\bullet} - \overline{X}_{\bullet j\bullet} + \overline{\overline{X}} \right)^2 \qquad (9.49)$$

Step 6 Calculate the within groups sum of squares (SSW$_2$)

$$SSW_2 = SST - SSG - SSB - SSGB \qquad (9.50)$$

These values can now be used to determine an estimate for the between and within group variances, as illustrated by equations (9.51)–(9.60):

Step 7 Calculate the degrees of freedom for SST, SSG, SSGB, and SSW$_2$

$$df_T = (N - 1) = (nkr - 1) \qquad (9.51)$$

$$df_G = (k - 1) \qquad (9.52)$$

Equation (9.52) is the same as equation (9.8).

$$df_B = (n - 1) \qquad (9.53)$$

Equation (9.53) is the same as equation (9.32).

$$df_{GB} = (k - 1)(n - 1) \qquad (9.54)$$

$$df_{W_2} = nk(r - 1) \qquad (9.55)$$

Step 8 Estimate the variances between and within the groups

$$V_T = \frac{SST}{df_T} \qquad (9.56)$$

$$V_G = \frac{SSG}{df_G} \qquad (9.57)$$

Equations (9.56) and (9.57) are the same as equations (9.10) and (9.11).

$$V_B = \frac{SSB}{df_B} \qquad (9.58)$$

Equation (9.58) is the same as equation (9.36).

$$V_{GB} = \frac{SSGB}{df_{GB}} \qquad (9.59)$$

$$V_{W_2} = \frac{SSW_2}{df_{W_2}} \qquad (9.60)$$

Equation (9.60) is the same as equation (9.37).

Step 9 Calculate F statistic

At this stage we have three F test calculations to perform: (1) for the stress level (factor A), (2) one for the row (factor B), and (3) one for the interaction (A * B).

$$F_{cal,G} = \frac{V_G}{V_{W_2}}$$ (9.61)

$$F_{cal,B} = \frac{V_B}{V_{W_2}}$$ (9.62)

Equations (9.61) and (9.62) are the same as equations (9.38) and (9.39)

$$F_{cal,GB} = \frac{V_{GB}}{V_{W_2}}$$ (9.63)

If there are large differences among the treatment means, the numerator of F (and therefore F itself) will be inflated and the null hypothesis is likely to be rejected; but if there is no effect, the numerator and denominator should have similar values, giving F close to unity (1). A high value of F, therefore, is evidence against the null hypothesis of equality of population means. From equations (9.45)–(9.63) we can now construct the ANOVA table (Table 9.10):

Source of variation	Sum of squares	Degrees of freedom, df	Mean square (variance)	F
Between groups	SSG	df_G	V_G	$F_{cal,\,G}$
Between blocks	SSB	df_B	V_B	$F_{cal,\,B}$
Interaction	SSGB	df_{GB}	V_{GB}	$F_{cal,\,GB}$
Within groups	SSW_2	df_{w2}	V_W	
Total	SST	df_T		

Table 9.10

Excel will provide this table and include a corresponding p-value for F_{cal} and a critical F value based upon a chosen significance level.

Step 10 Undertake a post hoc test to test which paired means (factor A, factor B) are significant.

The *Bonferroni multiple comparison t test* can be used to test which paired groups are significantly different and provide confidence intervals using a modified version of equation (9.13) to take into account all possible column and row comparisons. This test has been applied for the one-factor ANOVA test. To summarize the two-factor ANOVA solution procedure consists of the following steps:

(a) Check normality assumption—see Section 5.2.4. Undertake a five-number summary or construct a normal probability plot.

(b) Check variance and co-variance (sphericity) assumptions.

(c) Perform two-factor ANOVA with replication—see Excel solution.

(d) If significant difference run a comparison test (not covered in text for two-way ANOVA).

Excel solution—Example 9.5—two-way anova with replication

Figure 9.37 illustrates the Excel solution.

	F	G	H	I	J	K	L	M	N	O
4		State Hypothesis								
5			H$_0$: Group means are equal							
6			H1: Group means are different		①					
7		Select Test								
8			Peform Two Factor ANOVA		②					
9		Set level of significance								
10			Significance α =	0.05	③					
11		Extract relevant statistic								
12			Anova: Two-Factor With Replication							
13			SUMMARY	A	B	C	Total			
14			Deli							
15			Count	3	3	3	9			
16			Sum	195	167	205	567			
17			Average	65	55.66667	68.33333	63			
18			Variance	379	2.333333	2.333333	128.25			
19										
20			Meat							
21			Count	3	3	3	9			
22			Sum	174	167	182	523			
23			Average	58	55.66667	60.66667	58.11111			
24			Variance	91	22.33333	20.33333	38.11111			
25										
26			Total							
27			Count	6	6	6				
28			Sum	369	334	387				
29			Average	61.5	55.66667	64.5				
30			Variance	202.7	9.866667	26.7			④	
31										
32										
33			ANOVA							
34			Source of Variation	SS	df	MS	F	P-value	F crit	
35			Sample	107.5556	1	107.5556	1.247423	0.285909	4.7472	
36			Columns	242.1111	2	121.0556	1.403995	0.283211	3.8853	
37			Interaction	54.11111	2	27.05556	0.313789	0.736491	3.8853	
38			Within	1034.667	12	86.22222				
39										
40			Total	1438.444	17					
41										
42		Decision:	Since F$_{max}$ < F$_{cri}$ (P-value > 0.05), Accept H$_0$ for all main effects and interaction						⑤	

Figure 9.37

→ **Excel Solution**

Using Excel ToolPak: Data Analysis and run the two-factor with replication ANOVA test (Tools > Data Analysis > Anova: Two-Factor With Replication).

Figure 9.38

In the input range enter B4:E10, enter 3 in the rows per sample, choose significance 0.05, and select output range G4.

Click on OK to generate the results.

Figure 9.39

In this case, we have what we call a 'two-way ANOVA with replication'. That is, there are two factors (supermarket, department) but each participant is measured across each of the 3 supermarkets but only in one of the departments.

(1) State hypothesis

The null hypothesis in ANOVA is that the means of the rows and column groups are equal:

Test for difference between groups (or supermarket):

$H_0: \mu_1 = \mu_2 = \mu_3 = ... = \mu_k$
H_1: At least one mean is different

Test for difference between subjects (or department):

$H_0: \mu_1 = \mu_2 = \mu_3 = ... = \mu_n$
H_1: At least one mean is different

Test for interaction effect:

H_0: No interaction term between factor A and B
H_1: Interaction term is not zero

(2) Select test

We now need to choose an appropriate statistical test for testing H_0. From the information provided we note:

- Number of samples—three samples.
- The statistic we are testing—testing for a difference between three sample means with two factors but measured across each of the three supermarkets but only for one department.
- Conduct two-way ANOVA with replication test.

The test statistic in this case is an F test.

③ Set the level of significance of 5%

④ Extract relevant statistic

Test difference between groups (supermarkets—factor A):

$$\text{From Excel, } F_{cal} = \frac{V_G}{V_{W_2}} = \frac{121.055...}{86.222...} = 1.404$$

Test difference between subjects (departments—factor B):

$$\text{From Excel, } F_{cal} = \frac{V_B}{V_{W_2}} = \frac{107.555...}{86.2222...} = 1.247$$

Interaction term between groups and subjects (A * B):

$$\text{From Excel, } F_{cal} = \frac{V_{AB}}{V_{W_2}} = \frac{27.055...}{86.222} = 0.313$$

⑤ Make a decision

As we can see, the mean level of stress reported by the fifteen members of staff varies. But are these differences statistically significant?

Test difference between columns (supermarkets):

From Excel, we see that $F_{cal} = 1.404$. With a significance level of 0.05, the critical value of F, $F_{cri} = 3.885$. Therefore, since the $F_{cal} < F_{cri}$, we fail to reject the null hypothesis. There is no evidence to suggest that the stress levels are different for the supermarkets.

Test difference between rows (department):

From Excel, we see that $F_{cal} = 1.247$. With a significance level of 0.05, the critical value of F, $F_{cri} = 4.747$. Therefore, since the $F_{cal} < F_{cri}$, we fail to reject the null hypothesis. There is no evidence to suggest that the stress levels are different for departments.

Interaction term:

From Excel, we see that $F_{cal} = 0.313$. With a significance level of 0.05, the critical value of F, $F_{cri} = 3.885$. Therefore, since the $F_{cal} < F_{cri}$, we fail to reject the null hypothesis. There is no evidence to suggest that the interaction term is significant.

✳ Interpretation

1. The evidence suggests that the stress levels across supermarkets are not significantly different.
2. The evidence suggests that the stress levels across departments are not significantly different.
3. The interaction term between the two factors is not significant.

Note   The *Bonferroni multiple comparison t test* can be used to test which paired groups are significantly different and provide confidence intervals using a modified version of equation (9.13) to take into account all possible column and row comparisons. This test has been applied for the one factor ANOVA test.

9.4.2 Friedman's test with equal replicates in each cell

For this case we can modify the Friedman equation (equation (9.40)) to take into account r replicates within each cell, as follows:

$$G = \frac{12}{nkr^2 (rk + 1)} \sum_{j=1}^{k} R_j^2 - 3n(rk + 1) \tag{9.64}$$

Where G is approximately a chi square distribution with df = k − 1.

🖱 Student Exercises

X9.15 In Exercise X9.4 we conducted a one-factor ANOVA to test whether or not we have equality of mean response. In this exercise we now have further information which consists of an extra factor: media type.

		Factor—Quality		
		Convenience	Quality	Price
Media type	TV	491	677	575
		712	627	614
		558	590	706
		447	632	484
		479	683	478
		624	760	650
		546	690	583
		444	548	536
		582	579	579
	Newspaper	672	644	795
		464	689	803
		559	650	584
		759	704	525
		557	652	498
		528	576	812
		670	836	565
		534	628	708
		657	798	546
		557	497	616
		474	841	587

(a) Is there a main effect based upon the quality factor?

(b) Is there a main effect based upon the media type factor?

(c) Is there an interaction between the two factors?

X9.16 In Exercise X9.10 the bus company driver travelled once on each of the possible bus routes. The possibility exists that the results may be affected by an interaction term between the route and the driver. To assess the extent of this interaction further information has been collected where each driver now repeats the trip to record 3 trips (or 3 replications) per route. The data set is as follows:

Driver	Route travel time (minutes)			
	1	2	3	4
1	18	14	20	19
	15	17	21	22
	21	20	22	25
2	19	20	24	24
	15	24	23	22
	14	25	22	20
3	19	23	25	23
	21	21	29	23
	23	19	24	20
4	24	20	30	26
	20	24	28	25
	24	22	29	24
5	27	24	28	28
	25	24	28	30
	23	24	28	26

(a) Is there a difference in the route mean travel time?

(b) Is there a difference in driver times?

(c) Is there a significant interaction between route and driver?

■ Techniques in Practice

1. CoCo S.A. is concerned at the time to react to customer complaints and has implemented a new set of procedures for its support centre staff (see Chapters 4 and 7 TP1). The customer service director has received a series of reports which directly links the complaints to one particular member of the support centre. To be fair to all the customer service director has requested that all support staff (A, B, C, D, E, and F) are

monitored and the time to respond for the first seven customer complaints is recorded as follows:

Time to respond to customer complaints (days)					
A	B	C	D	E	F
20	33	33	29	24	30
40	33	20	39	32	37
32	50	36	31	38	29
15	33	27	29	43	33
31	35	19	39	22	21
28	22	26	42	30	17
32	34	39	39	32	38

(a) Is the homogeneity of variance violated?

(b) Is the mean time to respond the same?

(c) If the result is significant describe a suitable multiple comparison test.

(d) Describe the non-parametric test you would apply if the assumptions were violated. Conduct the non-parametric test and comment on the results.

2. Bakers Ltd is currently undertaking a review of the delivery vans used to deliver products to customers. The company decides to review three possible new routes to a new superstore sited on the outskirts of the city. To remove driver variability each driver tests the same delivery van on each route and the time to complete the route is as follows:

Driver	Time (minutes)		
	A	B	C
1	17.7	15.8	19.5
2	18.7	20.1	22.4
3	26.5	24.5	24.5
4	26.6	28.0	29.3
5	19.6	25.5	23.4
6	22.4	28.1	26.6
7	20.3	22.4	23.1

(a) Is the homogeneity of variance violated?

(b) Is the mean route time the same?

(c) If the result is significant describe a suitable multiple comparison test.

(d) Describe the non-parametric test you would apply if the assumptions were violated. Conduct the non-parametric test and comment on the results.

3. Skodel Ltd is developing a range of low calorie lagers (type A, B, and C) for the European market. The new product development team are having problems with the calorie count

in each 100 ml bottle, and have decided to randomly sample four bottles from each plant for each type of lager. The data set is as follows:

Plant	Type of lager		
	A	B	C
1	49.7	39.4	45.2
	45.9	46.5	40.5
	37.7	36.2	31.9
	40.6	46.7	41.9
2	34.8	36.5	39.8
	51.4	45.4	54.0
	34.3	38.2	47.8
	63.1	44.1	26.3
3	41.2	58.7	31.7
	41.4	47.1	45.1
	41.1	59.7	47.9
	34.5	43.5	41.1

Conduct an appropriate ANOVA test for main factors and interaction.

■ Summary

In this chapter we have explored a range of statistical methods to conduct hypothesis tests on more than two population means or medians. Figure 9.40 compares the parametric and non-parametric tests described in this chapter.

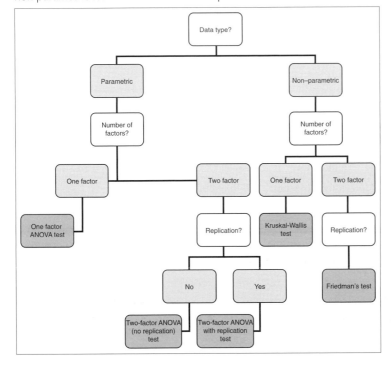

Figure 9.40

> **Note**   Excel ToolPak: Data Analysis will solve one and two factor problems only.

■ Key Terms

Analysis of variance
(ANOVA)
Between group degrees
of freedom (df_B)
Between group
variances (V_B)
Between groups sum
of squares (SSG)
Bonferroni t test
Confidence interval
Critical chi square
Critical F
Degrees of freedom
Excel ANOVA table
F distribution
F statistic (F_{cal})
Factor
Friedman's test for
> 2 medians
Homogeneity of variance

Independence
Interaction
Kruskal-Wallis test for >
2 medians
Level
Main effect
Mean square
Multiple comparisons
Normality
One-factor ANOVA
(or one-way without
replication)
One-factor ANOVA
within group degrees
of freedom (df_W)
One-factor ANOVA within
group variance (V_W)
Overall mean
Random error
Sample mean

Sample size
Subject
Tied ranks
Total degrees of freedom
(df_T)
Total sum of squares (SST)
Total variance (V_T)
Treatment
Two-factor ANOVA with
replication
Two-factor ANOVA within
group degrees of
freedom (df_{W2})
Two-factor ANOVA within
group variance (V_{W2})
Two-factor ANOVA without
replication
Within (error) groups sum
of squares (SSW)

■ Further Reading

Textbook Resources

1. Whigham, D. (2007) *Business Data Analysis using Excel*. Oxford University Press. ISBN: 9780199296286.

2. Lindsey, J. K. (2003) *Introduction to Applied Statistics: A Modelling Approach* (2nd Edition). Oxford University Press. ISBN: 978-0-19-852895-1.

Web Resources

1. StatSoft Electronic Textbook http://www.statsoft.com/textbook/stathome.html (accessed 28/1/2007).

2. HyperStat Online Statistics Textbook http://davidmlane.com/hyperstat/index.html (accessed 28/1/2007).

3. Eurostat—website is updated daily and provides direct access to the latest and most complete statistical information available on the European Union, the EU Member States, the euro-zone and other countries http://epp.eurostat.ec.europa.eu (accessed 28/1/2007).

4. Economagic—contains international economic data sets (http://www.economagic.com) (accessed 28/1/2007).

5. The ISI glossary of statistical terms provides definitions in a number of different languages http://isi.cbs.nl/glossary/index.htm

■ Formula Summary

$$\overline{X}_j = \sum_{i=1}^{n} \frac{X_{\bullet i}}{n_j} \tag{9.1}$$

$$\overline{\overline{X}} = \frac{\left(\sum_{j=1}^{k} \overline{X}_j \right)}{k} \tag{9.2}$$

$$SST = SSG + SSW \tag{9.3}$$

$$SST = \sum_{j=1}^{k} \sum_{i=1}^{n_j} \left(X_{ij} - \overline{\overline{X}} \right)^2 \tag{9.4}$$

$$SSG = n \sum_{j=1}^{k} \left(\overline{X}_j - \overline{\overline{X}} \right)^2 \tag{9.5}$$

$$SSW = SST - SSG \tag{9.6}$$

$$df_T = (N - 1) = (nk - 1) \tag{9.7}$$

$$df_G = (k - 1) \tag{9.8}$$

$$df_W = (N - k) = (nk - k) \tag{9.9}$$

$$V_T = \frac{SST}{df_T} \tag{9.10}$$

$$V_G = \frac{SSG}{df_G} \tag{9.11}$$

$$V_W = \frac{SSW}{df_W} \tag{9.12}$$

$$F_{cal} = \frac{V_G}{V_w} = \frac{S_G^2}{S_w^2}$$

(9.13)

$$SSG = \sum_{k=1}^{k} n_k \times \left(\bar{X}_k - \bar{\bar{X}}\right)^2$$

(9.14)

$$P = 1 - (1-\alpha)^{\frac{n(n-1)}{2}}$$

(9.15)

$$t_{cal} = \frac{\bar{X}_L - \bar{X}_S}{\sqrt{V_w \times \left(\frac{1}{n_L} + \frac{1}{n_S}\right)}}$$

(9.16)

$$VAR(X) = \frac{\sum_{i=1}^{n} X_i^2 - \frac{\left(\sum_{i=1}^{n} X_i\right)^2}{n}}{n-1}$$

(9.17)

$$t_{\frac{\alpha}{2}, df_w} = \frac{\left(\bar{X}_L - \bar{X}_S\right) - \left(\mu_L - \mu_S\right)}{\sqrt{S_w^2 \left(\frac{1}{n_L} + \frac{1}{n_S}\right)}}$$

(9.18)

$$\mu_L - \mu_S = \left(\bar{X}_L - \bar{X}_S\right) \pm t_{\frac{\alpha}{2}, df_w} \times \sqrt{S_w^2 \left(\frac{1}{n_L} + \frac{1}{n_S}\right)}$$

(9.19)

$$H = \frac{12}{N(N+1)} \sum_{i=1}^{k} \frac{R_j^2}{n_j} - 3(N+1)$$

(9.20)

$$\sum_{j=1}^{k} R_j = \frac{N(N+1)}{2}$$

(9.21)

$$H_c = \frac{1}{S^2} \left[\sum_{j=1}^{k} \frac{R_j^2}{n_j} - \frac{N(N+1)^2}{4} \right]$$

(9.22)

$$S^2 = \frac{1}{N-1} \left[\sum_{j=1}^{k} \sum_{i=1}^{n_j} r_{ij}^2 - \frac{N(N+)^2}{4} \right]$$

(9.23)

$$\bar{\bar{X}} = \frac{\left(\sum_{j=1}^{k} \bar{X}_j\right)}{k}$$

(9.24)

$$SST = SSG + SSB + SSW_2$$

(9.25)

$$SST = \sum_{j=1}^{k} \sum_{i=1}^{n_i} \left(X_{i,j} - \bar{\bar{X}} \right)^2 \tag{9.26}$$

$$SSG = n \times \sum_{j=1}^{k} \left(\bar{X}_j - \bar{\bar{X}} \right)^2 \tag{9.27}$$

$$SSB = k \times \sum_{i=1}^{n} \left(\bar{X}_i - \bar{\bar{X}} \right)^2 \tag{9.28}$$

$$SSW_2 = SST - SSG - SSB \tag{9.29}$$

$$df_T = (N-1) = (nk-1) \tag{9.30}$$

$$df_G = (k-1) \tag{9.31}$$

$$df_B = (n-1) \tag{9.32}$$

$$df_{W_2} = (k-1)(n-1) \tag{9.33}$$

$$V_T = \frac{SST}{df_T} \tag{9.34}$$

$$V_G = \frac{SSG}{df_G} \tag{9.35}$$

$$V_B = \frac{SSB}{df_B} \tag{9.36}$$

$$V_{W_2} = \frac{SSW_2}{df_{W_2}} \tag{9.37}$$

$$F_{cal,G} = \frac{V_G}{V_{W_2}} \tag{9.38}$$

$$F_{cal,B} = \frac{V_B}{V_{W_2}} \tag{9.39}$$

$$G = \frac{12}{nk(k+1)} \times \sum_{j=1}^{k} R_j^2 - 3n(k+1) \tag{9.40}$$

$$\sum_{j=1}^{k} R_j = \frac{kn(k+1)}{2} \tag{9.41}$$

$$G_c = \frac{(k-) \left[\sum_{i=1}^{k} R_i^2 - nC \right]}{\left[\sum_{j=1}^{k} \sum_{i=1}^{n} R_{ij}^2 - C \right]} \tag{9.42}$$

$$C = \frac{nk(k+1)^2}{4} \tag{9.43}$$

$$\overline{\overline{X}} = \frac{\sum_{j=1}^{k} \sum_{i=1}^{n} \sum_{p=1}^{r} X_{jip}}{knr} \tag{9.44}$$

$$SST = SSG + SSB + SSGB + SSW_2 \tag{9.45}$$

$$SST = \sum_{j=1}^{k} \sum_{i=1}^{n} \sum_{p=1}^{r} \left(X_{jip} - \overline{\overline{X}} \right)^2 \tag{9.46}$$

$$SSG = n \times r \times \sum_{j=1}^{k} \left(\overline{X}_{\bullet j \bullet} - \overline{\overline{X}} \right)^2 \tag{9.47}$$

$$SSB = k \times r \times \sum_{i=1}^{n} \left(\overline{X}_{i \bullet \bullet} - \overline{\overline{X}} \right)^2 \tag{9.48}$$

$$SSGB = r \times \sum_{i=1}^{n} \sum_{j=1}^{k} \left(\overline{X}_{ij\bullet} - \overline{X}_{i\bullet\bullet} - \overline{X}_{\bullet j\bullet} + \overline{\overline{X}} \right)^2 \tag{9.49}$$

$$SSW_2 = SST - SSG - SSB - SSGB \tag{9.50}$$

$$df_T = (N-1) = (nkr - 1) \tag{9.51}$$

$$df_G = (k-1) \tag{9.52}$$

$$df_B = (n-1) \tag{9.53}$$

$$df_{GB} = (k-1)(n-1) \tag{9.54}$$

$$df_{W_2} = nk(r-1) \tag{9.55}$$

$$V_T = \frac{SST}{df_T} \tag{9.56}$$

$$V_G = \frac{SSG}{df_G} \tag{9.57}$$

$$V_B = \frac{SSB}{df_B} \tag{9.58}$$

$$V_{GB} = \frac{SSGB}{df_{GB}}$$

(9.59)

$$V_{W_2} = \frac{SSW_2}{df_{W_2}}$$

(9.60)

$$F_{cal,G} = \frac{V_G}{V_{W_2}}$$

(9.61)

$$F_{cal,B} = \frac{V_B}{V_{W_2}}$$

(9.62)

$$F_{cal,GB} = \frac{V_{GB}}{V_{W_2}}$$

(9.63)

10 Linear Correlation and Regression Analysis

» Overview «

In this chapter we will explore methods that define possible relationships, or associations, between two interval, or ordinal, data variables. The issue of measuring the association between two nominal data variables was explored under cross tabulation and the chi square distribution. When dealing with two data variables we can explore visually the possibility of an association by plotting a scatter plot of one variable against another variable. Visually this will help to decide whether or not an association exists and the possible form of the association, e.g. linear or non-linear. The strength of this association can then be assessed by either calculating Pearson's correlation coefficient for interval data or Spearman's rank order correlation coefficient for ordinal data. If the scatter plot suggests a possible association then we can use least squares regression to fit this model to the data set. In this text we will focus on linear relationships but we have included sections introducing non-linear and multiple linear regression analysis. Excel can be used to calculate most of the terms using specific functions and we can access a data analysis macro called regression to calculate all the terms we would need to undertake the regression analysis described within this chapter.

» Learning Objectives «

On successful completion of this chapter, you will be able to:

» Understand the meaning of simple linear correlation and regression analysis.

» Apply a scatter plot to visually represent a possible relationship between two data variables.

» Calculate Pearson's correlation coefficient for interval data and provide meaning to this value.

» Calculate Spearman's rank correlation coefficient for ordinal ranked data and provide meaning to this value.

X

Least squares The method of least squares is a criterion for fitting a specified model to observed data. It refers to finding the smallest (least) sum of squared differences between fitted and actual values.

Linear relationship Simple linear regression aims to find a linear relationship between a response variable and a possible predictor variable by the method of least squares.

» Fit a simple linear regression model to the two data variables to be able to predict a dependent variable using an independent variable.

» Fit this simple linear model to the scatter plot.

» Estimate the reliability of this model fit to the dependent variable using the coefficient of determination and provide meaning to this value.

» Apply suitable inference tests to the simple linear model fit (t test and F test).

» Construct a confidence interval to the population parameter estimate.

» Assess whether the model assumptions have been violated that would undermine confidence in the models application to the data set.

» Extend the linear case to fitting a non-linear relationship and linear multiple regression models for interval data.

» Assess reliability and conduct inference tests to test suitability of the predictor variable (s).

» Solve problems using Microsoft Excel.

10.1 Linear Correlation Analysis

It seems obvious that sometimes there will be relationships between various sets of data and our aim is to discover if a relationship exists, and if so, how strong it is. In this section we shall:

- Apply a scatter plot to visually represent a possible relationship between two data variables.
- Understand the meaning of simple linear correlation analysis.
- Calculate Pearson's correlation coefficient for interval data and provide meaning to this value.
- Calculate Spearman's rank correlation coefficient for ordinal ranked data and provide meaning to this value.
- Undertake an inference test on the value of the correlation coefficients (r and r_s) to test for significance.

10.1.1 Scatter plot

Scatter plots are similar to line graphs in that they use horizontal and vertical axes to plot data points. However, they have a very specific purpose. Scatter plots show how much one variable is affected by another. The relationship between two variables is called their correlation. Scatter plots usually consist of a large body of data. The closer the data points come when plotted to making a straight line, the higher the correlation between the two variables, or the stronger the relationship.

X

Simple regression analysis
Simple linear regression aims to find a linear relationship between a response variable and a possible predictor variable by the method of least squares.

Multiple regression
Multiple linear regression aims to find a linear relationship between a response variable and several possible predictor variables.

Scatter plot
A scatter plot is a plot of one variable against another variable.

▷ Example 10.1

A large manufacturing firm with some 8,000 employees has designed a training programme that is supposed to increase the productivity of employees. The personal manager decides to examine this claim by analysing the data results from the first group of 20 employees that attended the course.

Table 10.1 provides the data set with the % raise in production (y) measured against a range of production values (x).

Employee Number	Production, x	% Raise in Production, y
1	47	4.2
2	71	8.1
3	64	6.8
4	35	4.3
5	43	5.0
6	60	7.5
7	38	4.7
8	59	5.9
9	67	6.9
10	56	5.7
11	67	5.7
12	57	5.4
13	69	7.5
14	38	3.8
15	54	5.9
16	76	6.3
17	53	5.7
18	40	4.0
19	47	5.2
20	23	2.2

Table 10.1

At this stage it is important to define what we mean by a dependent and independent variable:

a. Dependent variable—the variable that we wish to predict, in this case % raise in production or in general variable y.

b. Independent variable—in general labelled as variable x, or in this case production value. Independent variable provides the basis for calculating the value of the dependent variable:

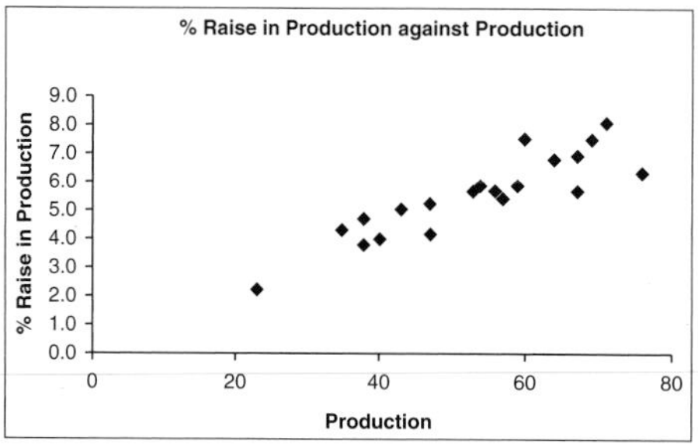

As a first stage to the analysis, the scatter plot would be plotted out and, as indicated in Figure 10.1, involves plotting each pair of values as a point on a graph. As can be seen from the scatter plot there would seem to be some form of relationship; as production increases then there is a tendency for % raise in production to increase.

Figure 10.1 Scatter plot

The data, in fact, would indicate a positive relationship. As we will see in the next section it is possible to describe this relationship by fitting a line or curve to the data set. In Figure 10.2 we modified the y-axis to run from 0 to 25 instead of 0 to 9. We also changed one point to illustrate the case of outliers. However, before we do this, just note how much impact the change in resolution (i.e. change in scale for y) has on the perceived pattern of the time series.

> **Note**   When scatter plots are used, like any other visualization method, make sure that the right resolution (the y-axis range) is used.

What are outliers?

The scatter plot can be used to identify possible outliers within the data set. We can see in Figure 10.2 the same data set as in Figure 10.1, but with one data value of y (22 approx) which is far greater than the other data point y values. The outlier could have undue influence on the value of the correlation and regression coefficients estimated in fitting a model to the data set.

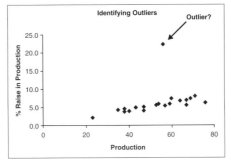

Figure 10.2

One of the solutions to this problem is to delete the value from the data set. Sometimes it might be that the outlier is not a true outlier but an extreme value of whatever you are measuring, or it could be that the data set consists of a small set of data values from the population being measured and the problem is due to having a small sample. There is no widely accepted method on how to deal with outliers. Some researchers use various methods to exclude outliers that lie beyond ±1.5 standard deviations around the mean value.

To decide on what type of relationship exists between the two variables (x, y) then we need to provide a numerical method to assess the strength of this potential relationship, rather than rely on just the scatter plot. The next three sections will explore three methods that can be used to measure the relationship between data values: covariance, **Pearson's coefficient of correlation**, and Spearman's rank correlation coefficient.

10.1.2 Covariance

A measure that tells us if the variables are jointly related is called **covariance**. Usually this implies that we measure if the two variables move together. The covariance takes either positive or negative values, depending if the two variables move in the

X

Pearson's coefficient of correlation Pearson's correlation coefficient measures the linear association between two variables that have been measured on interval or ratio scales.

Covariance Covariance is a measure of how much two variables change together.

same or opposite direction. If the covariance value is zero, or close to zero, then the two variables do not move closely together at all. Equation (10.1) defines the sample covariance:

$$\text{cov}(x, y) = \frac{\Sigma(x - \bar{x})(y - \bar{y})}{n - 1}$$

(10.1)

As it will be explained shortly, the covariance is an important building block for calculating the coefficient of correlation between two variables.

Excel Spreadsheet Function Solution—Covariance

	D25	▼	f_x =COVAR(C4:C23,D4:D23)		
	A	B	C	D	E
1	Covariance - % Raise in Production vs Old Production				
2					
3		Employee Number	Old Production, x	% Raise in Production, y	
4		1	47	4.2	
5		2	71	8.1	
6		3	64	6.8	
7		4	35	4.3	
8		5	43	5.0	
9		6	60	7.5	
10		7	38	4.7	
11		8	59	5.9	
12		9	67	6.9	
13		10	56	5.7	
14		11	67	5.7	
15		12	57	5.4	
16		13	69	7.5	
17		14	38	3.8	
18		15	54	5.9	
19		16	76	6.3	
20		17	53	5.7	
21		18	40	4.0	
22		19	47	5.2	
23		20	23	2.2	
24					
25			Covariance =	17.147	=COVAR(C4:C23,D4:D23)

Figure 10.3 Excel solution to calculate covariance

➜ **Excel Solution**

Covariance = Cell D25   Formula: =COVAR(C4:C23,D4:D23)

Note   From Excel the covariance is 17.147, implying that both variables are moving in the same direction (indicated by the positive value). A major flaw with the covariance is that the variable can take any value and you are unable to measure the relative strength of the relationship. For this value of 17.147 we do not know if this represents a strong or weak relationship between x and y. To measure this strength we would use the correlation coefficient or the coefficient of determination.

Correlation coefficient (ρ) can be calculated from standard deviations of each variable, as well as their covariance. A simple formula is:

$$\rho = \frac{\sigma_{xy}}{\sigma_x \sigma_y} \qquad (10.2)$$

Where σ_x is standard deviation of variable x, σ_y is standard deviation of variable y and σ_{xy} is the covariance between variables x and y. For practical purposes, this general formula can be modified and one of the most often used versions of it is called Pearson's correlation coefficient.

10.1.3 Pearson's correlation coefficient, r

A particular statistic that can be used to measure the strength of a linear relationship is the Pearson Product Moment Correlation Coefficient, r, which is defined as:

$$r = \frac{1}{n} \sum \frac{(x - \bar{x})(y - \bar{y})}{s_X \quad s_y} \qquad (10.3)$$

Where s_x is the standard deviation of the 'x' data, s_y is the standard deviation of the 'y' data, and 'n' is the number of paired values. The value of r will lie between -1 and $+1$.

Excel spreadsheet function solution—Pearson's correlation coefficient, r

	A	B	C	D
C25			f_x =PEARSON(C4:C23,D4:D23)	
1		Pearson - % Raise in Production vs Old Production		
2				
3		Employee Number	Old Production, x	% Raise in Production, y
4		1	47	4.2
5		2	71	8.1
6		3	64	6.8
7		4	35	4.3
8		5	43	5.0
9		6	60	7.5
10		7	38	4.7
11		8	59	5.9
12		9	67	6.9
13		10	56	5.7
14		11	67	5.7
15		12	57	5.4
16		13	69	7.5
17		14	38	3.8
18		15	54	5.9
19		16	76	6.3
20		17	53	5.7
21		18	40	4.0
22		19	47	5.2
23		20	23	2.2
24				
25		Pearson, r =	0.89	=PEARSON(C4:C23,D4:D23)
26			0.89	=CORREL(C4:C23,D4:D23)

Figure 10.4 Excel solution to calculate Pearson's correlation coefficient, r

Excel has two alternative functions to calculate correlation: = PEARSON( ) and CORREL ( ). The values they return are identical.

➜ **Excel Solution**

Correlation coefficient Cell C25   Formula: =PEARSON(C4:C23,D4:D23)
Alternative: Cell C26   Formula: =CORREL(C4:C23,D4:D23)

✳ **Interpretation**   In the above example the value of +0.89 would indicate a fairly strong positive linear association (or relationship), and this is borne out by the scatter plot of the data.

It should be noted that if you include the outlier illustrated in Figure 10.2 then the value of r would reduce to 0.3 and suggest very little correlation between the two variables.

Note

(a) If r lies between $-1 \leqslant r \leqslant -0.5$ or $0.5 \leqslant r \leqslant 1$ (large association).

(b) If r lies between $-0.5 \leqslant r \leqslant -0.3$ or $0.3 \leqslant r \leqslant 0.5$ (medium association).

(c) If r lies between $-0.3 \leqslant r \leqslant 0.1$ or $0.1 \leqslant r \leqslant 0.3$ (small association).

What does the value of 'r' not indicate?

1. Correlation only measures the strength of a relationship between two variables but does not prove a cause and effect relationship:

   a. Medical research suggests a strong correlation between the consumption of alcohol and alcohol induced liver disease. In this situation we have a cause and effect situation where increased alcohol consumption increases the risk of developing liver disease.

   b. But do we have a correlation between the amount of petrol sold and the consumption of ice cream during the summer months? In this case the increase in petrol consumption and ice cream sales is due to the fact that it is summer and (a) the holiday season has started and (b) the temperature is increasing.

   c. Even though we do not have a cause and effect between the variables it is possible that the association found might lead to what the true cause might be. For example, a new survey found that the more time people spent watching television the fatter they became. It could be that unemployed people spend more time watching television and at the same time they cannot afford to eat a healthy diet. In this case employment status would be the real cause. Remember it is usually more complicated then this simple example and the value of a dependent variable may depend on more than just one independent variable.

2. A value of $r \approx 0$ would indicate no linear relationship between x and y but this may indicate that the true form of the relationship is non-linear.

In Figure 10.5 we observe that in general as x increases, y increases. The correlation between x and y would be positive in this case.

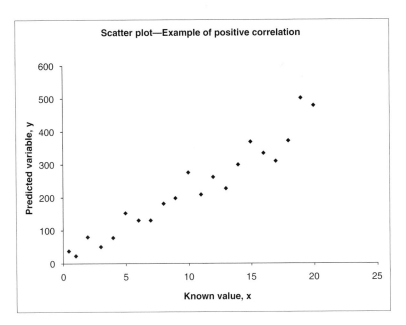

Figure 10.5

In Figure 10.6 the line goes from a high-value on the y-axis down to a high-value on the x-axis, the variables have a negative correlation.

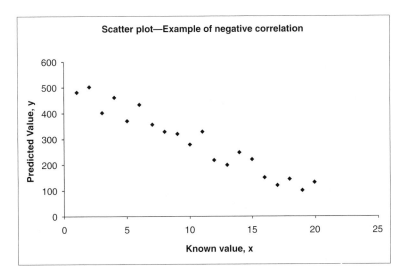

Figure 10.6

It is possible for all the data points to be lined up as if situated on a line. This is called *perfect correlation* and is illustrated in Figure 10.7. A similar straight line pointing downwards is an example of perfect negative correlation.

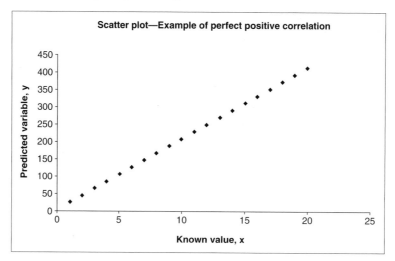

Figure 10.7 Example of perfect positive correlation, r = +1

A perfect positive correlation is given the value of 1 and a perfect negative correlation is given the value of –1. In reality the value of the correlation will lie between –1 and +1.

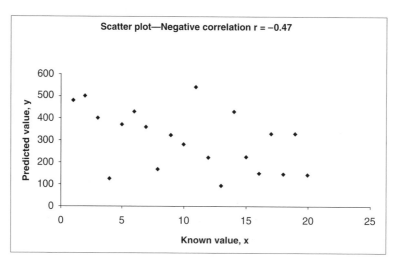

Figure 10.8

Figure 10.8 illustrates what the scatter plot would look like for correlation value of –0.47.

For example, Figure 10.1 is the scatter plot for % raise in production against production which, as we already know, suggests that as x increases, y increases and the values are increasing in the same direction. We will now show how to calculate Pearson's correlation coefficient, r, using a formula or manual approach in Excel.

Excel spreadsheet solution—formula method for r

Many textbooks show different formulae for the correlation coefficient. One of them is:

$$r = \frac{\sum xy - \dfrac{\sum x \sum y}{n}}{\sqrt{\left(\sum x^2 - \dfrac{(\sum x)^2}{n}\right)\left(\sum y^2 - \dfrac{(\sum y)^2}{n}\right)}} \qquad (10.4)$$

This is a modified version of equation (10.3). We will use this formula to demonstrate how to calculate the correlation coefficient in Excel using the formula in a manual way. Figure 10.9 illustrates the solution process:

D33		f_x =(D29-D27*D28/D26)/SQRT((D30-D27^2/D26)*(D31-D28^2/D26))						
	A	B	C	D	E	F	G	H	I	J
1	Pearson - % Raise in Production vs Old Production							
2								
3		Employee Number	Old Production, x	% Raise in Production, y	xy		x^2		y^2
4		1	47	4.2	197.4 =C4*D4		2209 =C4^2		17.64 =D4^2
5		2	71	8.1	575.1		5041		65.61
6		3	64	6.8	435.2		4096		46.24
7		4	35	4.3	150.5		1225		18.49
8		5	43	5.0	215		1849		25.00
9		6	60	7.5	450		3600		56.25
10		7	38	4.7	178.6		1444		22.09
11		8	59	5.9	348.1		3481		34.81
12		9	67	6.9	462.3		4489		47.61
13		10	56	5.7	319.2		3136		32.49
14		11	67	5.7	381.9		4489		32.49
15		12	57	5.4	307.8		3249		29.16
16		13	69	7.5	517.5		4761		56.25
17		14	38	3.8	144.4		1444		14.44
18		15	54	5.9	318.6		2916		34.81
19		16	76	6.3	478.8		5776		39.69
20		17	53	5.7	302.1		2809		32.49
21		18	40	4.0	160		1600		16.00
22		19	47	5.2	244.4		2209		27.04
23		20	23	2.2	50.6		529		4.84
24								
25								
26			n =	20.00	=COUNT(C4:C23)			
27			ΣX =	1064.00	=SUM(C4:C23)			
28			ΣY =	110.80	=SUM(D4:D23)			
29			ΣXY =	6237.50	=SUM(E4:E23)			
30			ΣX^2 =	60352.00	=SUM(G4:G23)			
31			Σy^2 =	653.44	=SUM(I4:I23)			
32								
33			r =	0.8902	=(D29-D27*D28/D26)/SQRT((D30-D27^2/D26)*(D31-D28^2/D26))			

Figure 10.9 Manual calculation of r using Excel

From Excel: n = 20, $\sum X$ = 1064, $\sum Y$ = 110, $\sum XY$ = 6237, $\sum X^2$ = 60352, and $\sum Y^2$ = 653.44. Substituting these values into equation 10.4 gives r = 0.89. As expected, we get the same value of 0.89 as calculated by Excel functions =PEARSON() or =CORREL(). We still have not examined how significant this linear correlation is, i.e. whether the conclusions we made about the sample data apply to the whole population. In order to do this we need to conduct a hypothesis test. The end result will confirm if the same conclusion applies to the whole company (population) and, more specifically, at what level of significance.

10.1.4 Testing the significance of Pearson's correlation coefficient, r

In Example 10.1 we found that the correlation coefficient was 0.89, which indicates a strong correlation between the two variables. Unfortunately, the size of the sample to provide this value of 0.89 is quite small (sample size n = 20 out of 8,000 total employee population) and we would now like to check whether or not this provides evidence of a significant association between the two variables in the overall population, i.e. among all 8,000 employees. Is this value of 0.89 due to sampling error from a population where no real association exists? To answer this question we need to conduct an appropriate hypothesis test to check if the population value of association is zero. In this hypothesis test we are assessing the possibility that $\rho = 0$ (the true population correlation coefficient). If the sample size is large ($n \geq 10$), then r is distributed as a t distribution with the number of degrees of freedom df = n − 2. It can be shown that the relationship between r, ρ, and n, is given by equation (10.5):

$$t_{cal} = \frac{r - \rho}{\sqrt{\frac{1 - r^2}{n - 2}}}$$

(10.5)

As per previous chapters on hypothesis testing, testing of the significance is done in 5 short steps:

① State hypothesis

② Select the test

③ Define the significance level

④ Extract relevant statistic, which will consist of three simple calculations:

    a.   Calculate the value of r (correlation coefficient)
    b.   Calculate test statistic t_{calc}
    c.   Determine the critical value t_{crit}

⑤ Make a decision

Excel spreadsheet function solution—checking significance of r

Figure 10.10 Inference test for correlation coefficient, r

→ **Excel Function Method**

	Value
Level of significance = Cell I10	
Pearson coefficient = Cell I13	Formula: =PEARSON(C4:C23,D4:D23)
n = Cell I15	Formula: =COUNT(B4:B23)
Degrees of freedom = Cell I16	Formula: =I15–2
t-calculated = Cell I17	Formula: =I13/SQRT((1–I13^2)/(I15–2))
Upper t-critical = Cell I18	Formula: =TINV(I10,I16)
Lower t-critical = Cell I19	Formula: =–TINV(I10,I16)

(1) State hypothesis

Null hypothesis $H_0: \rho = 0$ no population correlation exists

Alternative hypothesis $H_1: \rho \neq 0$ correlation exists

(2) Select test—in this case we already know that we are testing the significance of linear correlation and we use a t test to test for significance.

(3) Significance level. Set the significance level, $\alpha = 5\% \ (= 0.05)$

(4) Extract relevant statistics

   a.   Calculate the value of r. From Excel r = 0.89.

   b.   Calculate test statistic, t_{cal}, when H_0 true ($\rho = 0$).

$$t_{cal} = \frac{r}{\sqrt{\dfrac{1-r^2}{n-2}}}$$

(10.6)

Note   We note that the alternative hypothesis is ≠ and therefore we have not implied direction for the value of ρ. All we know is that it could be a significant correlation and that $\rho > 0$ or $\rho < 0$. In this case we have two directions where ρ would be deemed significant and this is called a two-tailed test.

In our case with the number of degrees of freedom df = n – 2. From Excel,

$$t_{cal} = \frac{r}{\sqrt{\dfrac{1-r^2}{n-2}}} = 8.3$$

   c.   Critical t value. From Excel we take that t_{cri} = TINV (I10, I16) = ±2.1

⑤ Make a decision

Given that t_{cal} (= 8.29) is greater than t_{cri} (= 2.10), the test statistic falls in the critical region. We reject H_0 and accept H_1.

✱ **Interpretation**   There is evidence to suggest a linear correlation between the two variables at the level of significance of 0.05.

📎 **Note**   One-tail tests

The preceding example illustrates a two-tailed test but one-tail tests can exist and will denote confidence in a specific relationship between X and Y. For example, in the previous example we are quite certain that we would expect the % raise in production and the original production value of the tested employees to be related and the association to be positive (as X increases Y increases). In this case we would conduct H_0: $\rho = 0$ and H_1: $\rho > 0$. If we then tested at 5% then all this 5% would be allocated to the right hand tail of the decision graph and t_{cri} would be positive. In this example the Excel solution would give t_{cri} = TINV (0.05*2, 18) = +1.73. If we reversed the test and assumed that the association was negative (as X increases Y decreases) then the alternative hypothesis would read H_0: $\rho = 0$ and H_1: $\rho < 0$, with a critical t value of $t_{cri} = -1.73$.

Summary:

Test for negative correlation	Test for positive correlation
H_0: $\rho = 0$	H_0: $\rho = 0$
H_1: $\rho < 0$	H_1: $\rho > 0$
Left-tailed test	Right-tailed test

10.1.5 Spearman's rank correlation coefficient, r_s

When data has been collected which is in *ranked form* then a ranked correlation coefficient can be determined. Equation (10.3) provides the value of Pearson's correlation coefficient between two data variables X and Y which are both at an interval level of measurement. The question then arises what do we do if the data variables are both ranked? In this case we can show algebraically that equation (10.3) is equivalent to equation (10.7) where r_s is known as Spearman's rank correlation coefficient.

$$r_s = 1 - \frac{6 * \Sigma (X_r - Y_r)^2}{n(n^2 - 1)}$$

(10.7)

Where X_r = rank order value of X, Y_r = rank order value of Y, and n = number of paired observations. The use of ranks allows us to measure correlation using characteristics that cannot be expressed quantitatively but that lend themselves to being ranked. This equivalence between equations (10.3) and (10.7) will only be true for situations where no tied ranks exist. When tied ranks exist then you will find discrepancies between the value of r

---

X

Rank coefficient of correlation
Spearman's rank correlation coefficient is applied to data sets when it is not convenient to give actual values to variables but one can assign a rank order to instances of each variable.

and r_s. As with the other non-parametric tests introduced in this text, ties are handled by giving each tied value the mean of the rank positions for which it is tied. The interpretation of r_s is similar to that for r, namely: (a) a value of r_s near 1.0 indicates a strong positive relationship, and (b) a value of r_s near –1.0 indicates a strong negative relationship.

❊ Interpretation

(a) If r_s lies between $-1 \leq r_s \leq -0.5$ or $0.5 \leq r_s \leq 1$ (large association).
(b) If r_s lies between $-0.5 \leq r_s \leq -0.3$ or $0.3 \leq r_s \leq 0.5$ (medium association).
(c) If r_s lies between $-0.3 \leq r_s \leq -0.1$ or $0.1 \leq r_s \leq 0.3$ (small association).

For pairs of data considered to have a strong relationship, just as in the case of Pearson's correlation coefficient, you will need to confirm that the value is significant (see Section 10.1.6).

Example 10.2

You are asked to decide whether the statistics rank correlates with the mathematics rank for seven students provided in Table 10.2. Since the information is ranked we use Spearman's correlation coefficient to measure the correlation between statistics and mathematics ranks.

Student	Statistics rank	Mathematics rank
1	2	1
2	1	3
3	4	7
4	6	5
5	5	6
6	3	2
7	7	4

Table 10.2

Excel spreadsheet solution—Spearman's correlation coefficient, r_s

F17 fx =1-6*F15/(F14*(F14^2-1))

	A	B	C	D	E	F	G	H	I
1	Spearman's rank correlation coefficient								
2									
3									
4		Student	Statistics rank, Xr	Mathematics rank, Yr		Xr - Yr		(Xr - Yr)^2	
5		1	2	1		1	=C5-D5	1	=F5^2
6		2	1	3		-2		4	
7		3	4	7		-3		9	
8		4	6	5		1		1	
9		5	5	6		-1		1	
10		6	3	2		1		1	
11		7	7	4		3		9	
12									
13									
14				n =		7		=COUNT(B5:B11)	
15				Σ(Xr - Yr)^2 =		26		=SUM(H5:H11)	
16									
17				rs =		0.535714		=1-6*F15/(F14*(F14^2-1))	

Figure 10.11 Calculation of Spearman's rank correlation coefficient using Excel

---

→ Excel Function Method

n = Cell F14   Formula: =COUNT(B5:B11)

Squared rank differences = Cell F15 Formula: =SUM(H5:H11)

Spearman's rank correlation = Cell C32 Formula: =1−6*F15/(F14*(F14^2−1))

✻ Interpretation   From Figure 10.11 the Spearman rank correlation is positive, $r_s = 0.54$, but indicating that there is only a mild positive rank correlation in this case. If this number was closer to +1, we would be able to claim much stronger positive rank correlation.

Note   Excel does not have a procedure for directly computing Spearman's ranked correlation coefficient. However, since the formula for Spearman's is the same as for the Pearson correlation coefficient, we can use it providing that we have first converted the x and y variables to rankings (Tools > Data Analysis > Rank and Percentiles).

10.1.6 Testing the significance of Spearman's rank correlation coefficient, r_s

In this section we need to undertake a hypothesis test to test whether the true correlation relationship between the population Y, X values is significant, based upon the sample data values y, x. Having found a correlation using Spearman, it is necessary to test it to discover whether or not it is significant. The hypothesis test takes the default form that there is no correlation and the alternative hypothesis that there is a positive or negative correlation. Not only do significance levels affect the critical value but so do the number of values in the sample. The smaller the sample, the higher the correlation must be for it to be significant. In this hypothesis test we are assessing the possibility that $\rho_s = 0$. If the sample size is large ($n \geqslant 10$), then r is distributed as a t distribution with the number of degrees of freedom df = n − 2. It can be shown that the relationship between r_s, ρ_s, and n, is given by equation (10.8):

$$t_{cal} = \frac{r_s - \rho_s}{\sqrt{\dfrac{1 - r_s^2}{n - 2}}}$$

(10.8)

The five step procedure we used in Section 10.1.4 is almost identical.

Excel spreadsheet solution—checking significance of r_s

	D9	▼	f_x =D8/SQRT(D8^2+D6-2)	
	A	B	C	D	E
1	Spearman's rank correlation coefficient				
2					
3		Critical rs:			
4					
5		sig =		0.05	
6		n =		10	
7		df =		8	
8		tcri =		2.31 =TINV(D5,D7)	
9		Critical rs =		0.63 =D8/SQRT(D8^2+D6-2)	

Figure 10.12 Critical value of Spearman's correlation coefficient

(1) State hypothesis

Null hypothesis $H_0: \rho_s = 0$ no population correlation

Alternative hypothesis $H_1: \rho_s \neq 0$ population correlation exists

(2) Select test—we already know that this is testing the significance of Spearman's rank correlation coefficient.

(3) Significance level. Set the significance level, $\alpha = 5\% \ (= 0.05)$

(4) Extract relevant statistic

    a. Calculate the value of r_s. From Excel, $r_s = 0.54$.

    b. Calculate test statistic from equation (10.8) with $\rho_s = 0$:

$$t_{cal} = \frac{r_s}{\sqrt{\dfrac{1 - r_s^2}{n-2}}}$$

       (10.9)

> **Note**   We note that the alternative hypothesis is $\neq$ and therefore we have no implied direction for the value of ρ_s. All we know is that it could be a significant correlation and that $\rho_s > 0$ or $\rho_s < 0$. In this case we have two directions where ρ would be deemed significant and this is called a two-tailed test.

    c. Determine the critical value

The critical value of r_s may be found either from:

    a) a table of values

    b) by calculation depending upon the size of the sample, n:

    a) Table of critical r_s values for $n \leq 10$

N	6	7	8	9	10
Significance Level 5%	0.829	0.759	0.738	0.666	0.632

Table 10.3 Critical values of Spearman's correlation coefficient

(b) If the sample size exceeds 10, the test statistic is approximated by a t statistic with n − 2 degrees of freedom, as shown in equation (10.10). The critical r_s value can be found by re-arranging equation (10.10) to make r_s the subject of the equation

$$r_s = \frac{t}{\sqrt{t^2 + n - 2}}$$

(10.10)

To find the critical r_s value: (i) find t_{cri}, (ii) substitute this value for t_{cri} into equation (10.10) to find the critical r_s value. For example, if the significance level is 5% two tail, then $t_{cri} = \pm 2.31$ and critical value of $r_s = \pm 0.63$.

Note For n > 20, r_s may be treated as normal (0, 1), where

$$z = r_s \sqrt{n - 1}$$

(10.11)

For example, if the significance level is 5%, two tail and n = 40, then $Z_{cri} = \pm 1.96$ and the critical value of $r_s = \pm 0.314$. In the comparison of marks example we have n = 7, significance level 5%, two tail, and the table critical r_s value is ± 0.759.

---

⑤ Make a decision

Given that 0.54 < 0.759 (see Table 10.3), the test statistic does not fall in the critical region. Therefore, we accept H_0 and reject H_1.

✳ **Interpretation** At the level of significance of 5%, there is insufficient evidence to suggest a significant correlation between the two variables.

Student Exercises

X10.1 In the course of a survey relating examination success, you have discovered a high negative correlation between students' hours of study and their examination marks. This is so at variance with common sense expectations that it has been suggested an error has been made in data collection. Do you agree?

X10.2 Construct a scatter plot for the following data and calculate Pearson's correlation coefficient, r. Comment of the strength of the correlation between x and y.

x:	40	41	40	42	40	40	42	41	41	42
y:	32	43	28	45	31	34	48	42	36	38

X10.3 Display the following data in an appropriate form and state how the variables are correlated.

x:	0	15	30	45	60	75	90	105	120
y:	806	630	643	625	575	592	408	469	376

X10.4 The following table indicates the number of vehicles and number of road deaths in 10 countries:

Countries	Vehicles per 100 population	Road deaths per 100,000 population
Great Britain	31	14
Belgium	32	30
Denmark	30	23
France	46	32
Germany	30	26
Ireland	19	20
Italy	35	21
The Netherlands	40	23
Canada	46	30
U.S.A.	57	35

(a) Construct a scatter plot and comment upon the possible relationship between the two variables.

(b) Calculate the product moment correlation coefficient between vehicle numbers and road deaths.

(c) Use your answers to (a) and (b) to comment upon your results.

X10.5 Samples of students' essays were marked by two tutors independently. The resulting ranks are shown below:

Tutor	A	5	8	1	6	2	7	3	4
	B	7	4	3	1	6	8	5	2

(a) Calculate the rank correlation coefficient.

(b) State any conclusions that you can draw.

X10.6 The mathematics and statistics examination marks for a group of ten students are shown below:

Mathematics	89	73	57	53	51	49	47	44	42	38
Statistics	51	53	49	50	48	21	46	19	43	43

(a) Find the product moment correlation coefficient for the two sets of marks.

(b) Place the marks in rank order and calculate the rank correlation coefficient.

(c) The following is a quotation from a statistics text: 'Rank correlation can be used to give a quick approximation to the product moment correlation coefficient.' Comment on this in the light of your results.

10.2 Linear Regression Analysis

In this section we shall extend the concept of measuring association to include a method for fitting a line equation to a data set. This will allow predictions to be provided for a dependent variable (y) given an independent (or predictor) variable (x). Linear regression analysis is one of the most widely used techniques for modelling a linear relationship between variables and is employed by a wide range of subjects (business, economics, psychology, social sciences) to enable models to be developed and levels of confidence to be provided in the model parameters. In later sections we will extend the linear case to briefly mention non-linear and multiple regression modelling. Regression models can be fitted to ordinal/categorical data but this is beyond the scope of this text book. Linear Regression Analysis attempts to model the relationship between two variables in the form of a straight line relationship of the form:

$$\hat{y} = b_0 + b_1 x + \text{error} \tag{10.12}$$

Where $\hat{y}$ is the estimated value of the dependent variable (y) at given values of the independent variable (x). As we are here taking a snapshot of the dataset, we are effectively dealing with a sample of a large dataset, or the whole population, as we called it in previous chapters. This implies that the true population relationship is defined by the equation:

$$\hat{Y} = \beta_0 + \beta_1 X \tag{10.13}$$

The values of constants b_0 and b_1 are effectively estimates of some true values of β_0 and β_1, and we'll also have to test to see how well they represent these true population values. In order to determine this relationship, the constants b_0 and b_1 have to be estimated from the observed values of x and y. To do this, regression analysis utilizes the method of least squares regression to provide a relationship between b_0, b_1 and the sample data values (x, y). The method assumes that the line will pass through the point of intersection of the mean values of x and y ($\bar{x}$, $\bar{y}$).

The method then pivots the line about this point until: (i) the sum of the vertical squared distance of the data points is a minimum, and (ii) the sum of the vertical distances of the data points above the line equals those below the line. This is described algebraically as $\sum(y - \hat{y})^2 = \text{minimum}$ and $\sum(y - \hat{y}) = 0$. From this concept two 'normal equations' are defined: $y = nb_0 + b_1 \sum x$ and $\sum xy = b_0 \sum x + b_1 \sum x^2$. By solving the above equations simultaneously, estimates of the constants b_0 and b_1 are determined to give the equation of the line of regression of Y on X, where Y is the dependent variable and X is the independent variable. The two 'normal equations' can be re-arranged so that a solution can be obtained as follows:

$$b_1 = \frac{n \sum xy - \sum x \sum y}{n \sum x^2 - (\sum x)^2} \tag{10.14}$$

$$b_0 = \frac{\sum y - b_1 \sum x}{n} \tag{10.15}$$

Excel can be used in a number of different ways to undertake regression analysis and calculate the required coefficients b_0 and b_1:

1. Excel Statistical Functions—Excel contains a range of functions that allow a range of regression coefficient calculations to be undertaken.

2. Excel functions—Standard Excel functions can be used to reproduce the manual solution e.g. SUM, SQRT functions.

3. Excel ToolPak Regression—This method provides a complete set of solutions.

The solution process can be split into a series of steps:

- Construct scatter plot to identify model.
- Fit model to sample data.
- Test model reliability using the coefficient of determination.
- Test whether the predictor variables are significant contributors, t test.
- Test whether the overall model is a significant contributor, F test.
- Construct a confidence interval for the population **slope**, β_1.
- Check model assumptions.

▷ Example 10.3

Consider the data set from Example 10.1. How to apply the above steps is described in the following sections (10.2.1–10.2.9).

10.2.1 Construct scatter plot to identify model

The first stage in undertaking regression analysis of a data set is to construct a scatter plot. We can see from the scatter plot that as x increases, y increases too, and in general the values are increasing in the same direction. If you identify outliers decide whether you plan to keep or remove them from the data set. Whatever you decide make sure you mention your outlier policy in your report.

Slope Gradient of the fitted regression line.

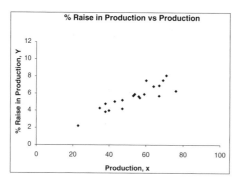

Figure 10.13 Scatter plot for % Raise in Production against Production

10.2.2 Fit line to sample data

Excel contains a number of functions that allow you to directly calculate the values of b_0 and b_1 in equation (10.12).

Excel spreadsheet solution—least squares regression coefficients b_0 and b_1

The Excel function to calculate the slope, b_1, and **intercept**, b_0, is as described below.

	C28	▾	ƒx =SLOPE(C5:C24,B5:B24)	
	A	B	C	D
1	Regression Analysis Example			
2				
3	Employee	Production	% Raise in Production	
4	Number	X	Y	
5	1	47	4.2	
6	2	71	8.1	
7	3	64	6.8	
8	4	35	4.3	
9	5	43	5.0	
10	6	60	7.5	
11	7	38	4.7	
12	8	59	5.9	
13	9	67	6.9	
14	10	56	5.7	
15	11	67	5.7	
16	12	57	5.4	
17	13	69	7.5	
18	14	38	3.8	
19	15	54	5.9	
20	16	76	6.3	
21	17	53	5.7	
22	18	40	4.0	
23	19	47	5.2	
24	20	23	2.2	
25				
26		Regression coefficients:		
27		b0 =	0.671189155 =INTERCEPT(C5:C24,B5:B24)	
28		b1 =	0.091519001 =SLOPE(C5:C24,B5:B24)	

Figure 10.14 Line fit to the data set using simple least squares regression

→ **Excel Solution**

b_0 = Cell C27   Formula: =SLOPE(C5:C24,B5:B24)
b_1 = Cell C28   Formula: =INTERCEPT(C5:C24,B5:B24)

X
Intercept Value of the regression equation (y) when the x value = 0.

From Excel: b_0 = 0.6712 and b_1 = 0.0915. The equation of the sample regression line is $\hat{y} = 0.6712 + 0.0915x$.

> ❊ **Interpretation**　The regression equation is % Raise in Production = 0.6712 + 0.0915*Production.

For every value of x (production) we can now calculate an estimated value of % raise in production. If we plotted these estimated values, they would represent a trend line, or a line of regression. The calculated trend line has been fitted to the scatter plot as shown in Figure 10.15.

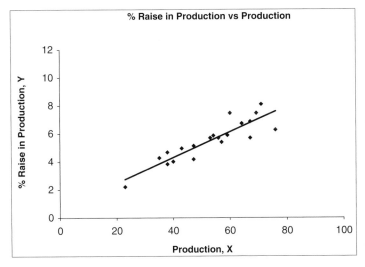

Figure 10.15

Observe that not all data points lie on the fitted line. In this case we can also observe an error (sometimes called a residual or variation) between the data y value and the value of the line at each data point. This concept of error can be measured using a variety of methods, including: coefficient of determination (COD), standard error of estimate (SEE), and a range of inference measures to assess the suitability of the regression model fit to the data set.

An alternative approach to calculating the regression line is to right-click on one of the data points in the graph and select Add Trendline option from the box.

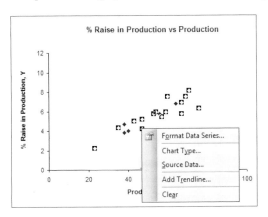

Figure 10.16　Using Excel to fit trend line

From the selection of curves that is presented after the Trendline option was selected, choose the first one, i.e. the linear option.

Excel will automatically insert the regression line in the graph. In order to see the actual equation that defines this linear regression, after you selected the type of regression, click on the Options tab and select 'Display equation on chart'.

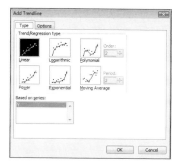

Figure 10.17 Select type of curve to fit to data

Figure 10.18 Displaying curve equation on scatter plot

We now get not just the regression line, but the equation, which is identical to the one we calculated using Excel functions SLOPE and INTERCEPT.

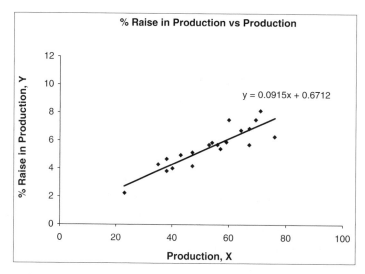

Figure 10.19 Trend line fit

In order to demonstrate the above points, we'll show here yet another method of calculating linear regression using the TREND() function.

E24	▼	_fx_ =TREND($C$5:$C$24,$B$5:$B$24,B24)					
	A	B	C	D	E	F	G
1	Regression Analysis Example						
2							
3	Employee	Production	% Raise in Production	Estimated y		Error	
4	Number	x	y	(ŷ)		e	
5	1	47	4.2	5.0	=TREND($C$5:$C$24,$B$5:$B$24,B5)	-0.8	=C5-D5
6	2	71	8.1	7.2	=TREND($C$5:$C$24,$B$5:$B$24,B6)	0.9	=C6-D6
7	3	64	6.8	6.5		0.3	
8	4	35	4.3	3.9		0.4	
9	5	43	5	4.6		0.4	
10	6	60	7.5	6.2		1.3	
11	7	38	4.7	4.1		0.6	
12	8	59	5.9	6.1		-0.2	
13	9	67	6.9	6.8		0.1	
14	10	56	5.7	5.8		-0.1	
15	11	67	5.7	6.8		-1.1	
16	12	57	5.4	5.9		-0.5	
17	13	69	7.5	7.0		0.5	
18	14	38	3.8	4.1		-0.3	
19	15	54	5.9	5.6		0.3	
20	16	76	6.3	7.6		-1.3	
21	17	53	5.7	5.5		0.2	
22	18	40	4	4.3		-0.3	
23	19	47	5.2	5.0		0.2	
24	20	23	2.2	2.8	=TREND($C$5:$C$24,$B$5:$B$24,B24)	-0.6	=C24-D24

Figure 10.20 Linear regression calculation using Excel =TREND() function

→ **Excel Solution**

Estimated y (ŷ) = Cell D5

Formula: =TREND($C$5:$C$24,$B$5:$B$24,B5)
Copy formula D5:D24

Error = Cell F5

Formula: =C5–D5
Copy formula F5:F24

Note   The syntax for the above Excel function is =TREND (known_y's, known_x's, New_x's, Const). We have ignored the constant element here, as it is not relevant. Known_x's is the set of all known production values, and as it does not change from cell to cell, we had to put the whole range as absolute references ($B$5:$B$24). Known_y's is the set of all known % raise in production values, and again as it does not change from cell to cell, we had to put the whole range as absolute references ($C$5:$C$24). The value of New_x's changes from cell to cell and it is therefore left as a relative reference in this formula.

There is obviously a degree of error between observed values of y and those estimated by the line (ŷ). This *error*, or difference, is known as the **residual** and is given by the formula:

$$\text{Residual} = y - \hat{y} \tag{10.16}$$

Where y is the actual observation and ŷ its estimated value obtained through regression equation.

X
Residual The residual represents the unexplained variation (or error) after fitting a regression model.

These errors, as we will discover shortly, are a very important part of regression analysis. An alternative is to use some general Excel functions to get even richer data. Excel also offers an even more comprehensive way to achieve the same task through the ToolPak, but we'll come back to it at the very end of this chapter. Let us return to the concept of error, we mentioned above, that can be measured using a variety of methods, including: coefficient of determination (COD), standard error of estimate (SEE), and a range of inference measures to assess the suitability of the regression model fit to the data set.

10.2.3 Sum of squares defined

When conducting regression analysis it is essential to be able to identify three important measures of variation: regression sum of squares (SSR), error sum of squares (SSE), and total sum of squares (SST).

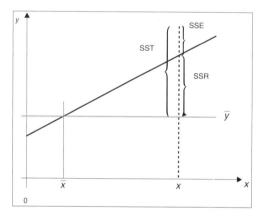

Figure 10.21 illustrates the relationship between these different measures which shows that the total variation can be split into two parts: explained and unexplained variation.

Figure 10.21 Understanding the relationship between SST, SSR, and SSE

Regression sum of squares (SSR)—sometimes called Explained variations:

$$SSR = \Sigma(\hat{y} - \overline{y})^2 \tag{10.17}$$

Error sum of squares (SSE)—sometimes called Unexplained variations:

$$SSE = \Sigma(y - \hat{y})^2 \tag{10.18}$$

Total sum of squares (SST)—sometimes called the Total variations:

$$SST = \Sigma(y - \overline{y})^2 \tag{10.19}$$

Or, an alternative expression:

$$SST = SSR + SSE \tag{10.20}$$

10.2.4 Regression assumptions

The four assumptions of regression are as follows: (1) linearity, (2) independence of errors, (3) normality of errors, and (4) variance constant.

1. Linearity

Linearity assumes that the relationship between the two variables is linear. To assess linearity, the residuals (or error) are plotted against the independent variable, x. Excel ToolPak Regression will automatically create this plot if requested (see Section 10.2.10). We observe that there is no apparent pattern between the residuals and x. Furthermore, the residuals are evenly spread out about error equal to zero.

For this example a line fit to the data set would appear appropriate. If the scatter plot suggests that the relationship is non-linear then you would have to identify and fit this relationship to your data set (see Section 10.3.1).

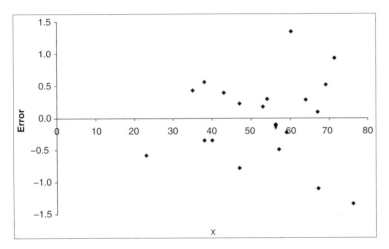

Figure 10.22 Residuals versus x

2. Independence of errors

The *independence of errors* assumption is a problem when data is collected over periods of time and the data value is not independent of the previous data value measured. This effect is called serial correlation and can be measured using the *Durbin-Watson statistic*. Another expression for serial correlation, though usually used in a different context, is autocorrelation. For Example 10.3, the data has been collected at the same time period and we do not need to consider serial correlation (independence of errors) as a problem. This topic is beyond the scope of this text book.

3. Normality of errors

The *normality assumption* requires that the measured errors (or residuals) are normally distributed for each value of the independent variable, X. If this assumption is violated then the result can produce unrealistic estimations for the regression coefficients b_0, b_1, and COD. Furthermore, any inference tests or confidence intervals calculated are dependent upon the errors being normally distributed. This assumption can be evaluated using two graphical methods: (i) construct a histogram for the errors against x and check whether the shape looks normal, or (ii) create a normal probability plot of the residuals (available from the Excel ToolPak Regression solution). Figure 10.23 illustrates a normal probability plot based upon the Example 10.3 data set.

We observe that the relationship is fairly linear and we conclude that the normal assumption is not violated.

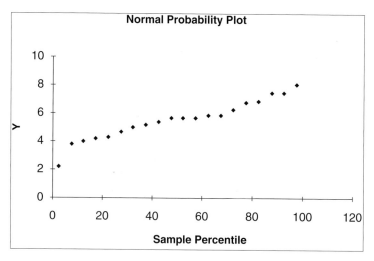

Figure 10.23

This problem can occur if the dependent and/or independent variables are not normally distributed, or the linearity assumption is violated. Like the t test, regression analysis is robust against departures from this assumption. As long as the distribution of error against X is not very different from a normal distribution then the inferences on β_0 and β_1 will not be seriously affected.

4. Variance constant

The final assumption of *equal variance* (or *homoscedasticity*) requires that the variance of the errors is constant for all values of X. This implies that the variability of Y values is the same for all values of X and this assumption is important when making inferences about β_0 and β_1. If there are violations of this assumption then we can use data transformations or weighted least-squares to attempt to improve model accuracy.

Figure 10.24 illustrates the Excel solution to check the variance assumption. We observe that the error is not growing in size as the value of X changes. This plot provides evidence that the variance assumption is not violated. If the value of error changes greatly as the value of X changes then we would assume that the variance assumption is violated.

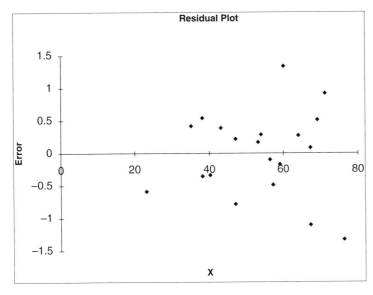

Figure 10.24

If any of the four assumptions are violated, we can only conclude that linear regression is not the best method for fitting the data set, and we need to find an alternative method or model.

10.2.5 Test model reliability

Of the many methods used to assess the reliability of a regression line we shall discuss: (a) Residuals and the standard error of the estimate (SEE) and (b) the coefficient of determination (COD).

Excel spreadsheet function solution—testing reliability

Figure 10.25 illustrates the Excel solution to calculate the coefficient of determination and standard error of the estimate.

	A	B	C	D	E	F	G
1	Linear Regression Analysis: Reliability						
2							
3	Employee	Production	% Raise in Production				
4	Number	X	Y	Line value, y^		Error	
5	1	47	4.2	5.0	=$C$27+$C$28*B5	-0.8	=C5-D5
6	2	71	8.1	7.2	=$C$27+$C$28*B6	0.9	=C6-D6
7	3	64	6.8	6.5		0.3	
8	4	35	4.3	3.9		0.4	
9	5	43	5.0	4.6		0.4	
10	6	60	7.5	6.2		1.3	
11	7	38	4.7	4.1		0.6	
12	8	59	5.9	6.1		-0.2	
13	9	67	6.9	6.8		0.1	
14	10	56	5.7	5.8		-0.1	
15	11	67	5.7	6.8		-1.1	
16	12	57	5.4	5.9		-0.5	
17	13	69	7.5	7.0		0.5	
18	14	38	3.8	4.1		-0.3	
19	15	54	5.9	5.6		0.3	
20	16	76	6.3	7.6		-1.3	
21	17	53	5.7	5.5		0.2	
22	18	40	4.0	4.3		-0.3	
23	19	47	5.2	5.0		0.2	
24	20	23	2.2	2.8	=$C$27+$C$28*B24	-0.6	=C24-D24
25					sum =	0.0	=SUM(F5:F24)
26		Regression coefficients:					
27		b0 =		0.671189155	=INTERCEPT(C5:C24,B5:B24)		
28		b1 =		0.091519001	=SLOPE(C5:C24,B5:B24)		
29							
30		Reliability:					
31		SEE =		0.675872845	=STEYX(C5:C24,B5:B24)		
32		COD =		0.79240371	=RSQ(C5:C24,B5:B24)		

Figure 10.25

→ **Excel Function Method**

b_0 = Cell C27	Formula: =INTERCEPT(C5:C24,B5:B24)
b_1 = Cell C28	Formula: =SLOPE(C5:C24,B5:B24)
Estimated y ($\hat{y}$) = Cell D5	Formula: =$C$27+$C$28*B5
	Copy formula D5:D24
Error = Cell F5	Formula: =C5−D5
	Copy formula F5:F24
Sum = Cell F25	Formula: =SUM(F5:F24)
Standard error of estimate = Cell C31	Formula: =STEYX(C5:C24,B5:B24)
efficient of Determination = Cell C32	Formula: =RSQ(C5:C24,B5:B24)

(a) Residuals and the standard error of the estimate, SEE

As before, we calculated errors, or residuals, and put them this time in column F. Plotting the regression line onto the scatter plot, as shown in Figure 10.26, reveals that many of the observed data points do not lie on the line. The values in column F show by how much the fitted data (estimated) are adrift from the observed data. Plotting the residuals against x values provides information about possible modifications of, or areas of caution in applying the regression line and the data from which it was formed. In plotting the residuals we would look for a random, even scatter about the zero residual line. This would indicate that the derived line was relatively free from error.

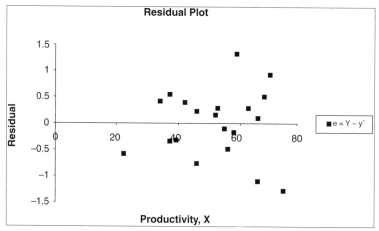

Figure 10.26 Residual plot

Deviations from such a pattern will help identify 'rogue' data points which might be taken out of the data set, *or* we might investigate possible data transforms to obtain a linear structure, *or* we might need to look for further explanatory variables (the province of multivariate linear regression analysis).

  If we were to determine all the residual values for the data then an interpretation of the error in predicting y from the regression equation could be obtained. This would be the standard deviation of actual y values from the predicted ŷ values and is known as the *standard error of the estimate* (SEE):

$$SEE = \sqrt{\frac{SSE}{n-2}}$$

(10.21)

Recall from equation 10.18 a formula for SSE. Therefore:

$$SEE = \sqrt{\frac{\Sigma\left(y - \hat{y}\right)^2}{n-2}}$$

(10.22)

This provides a measure of the scatter of observed values around the corresponding estimated ŷ values on the regression line and is measured in the same units as y. From the Excel solution (Figures 10.25 or 10.27) the value of the standard error of the estimate is 0.675%.

> ✳ **Interpretation**   The average difference between the actual and line y values is 0.675%. The unit of measurement for SEE is the same as the y variable.

Excel spreadsheet solution—calculation of standard estimate of the error

Figure 10.27 illustrates the Excel solution to calculate the standard error of the estimate.

	A	B	C	D	E	F	G	H	I
1	Linear Regression Analysis: Reliability								
2									
3	Employee	Production	% Raise in Production						
4	Number	X	Y	Line value, y^		y - y^		(y - y^)^2	
5	1	47	4.2	5.0	=$C$27+$C$28*B5	-1	=C5-D5	0.60	=F5^2
6	2	71	8.1	7.2		1		0.87	
7	3	64	6.8	6.5		0		0.07	
8	4	35	4.3	3.9		0		0.18	
9	5	43	5.0	4.6		0		0.15	
10	6	60	7.5	6.2		1		1.79	
11	7	38	4.7	4.1		1		0.30	
12	8	59	5.9	6.1		0		0.03	
13	9	67	6.9	6.8		0		0.01	
14	10	56	5.7	5.8		0		0.01	
15	11	67	5.7	6.8		-1		1.22	
16	12	57	5.4	5.9		0		0.24	
17	13	69	7.5	7.0		1		0.26	
18	14	38	3.8	4.1		0		0.12	
19	15	54	5.9	5.6		0		0.08	
20	16	76	6.3	7.6		-1		1.76	
21	17	53	5.7	5.5		0		0.03	
22	18	40	4.0	4.3		0		0.11	
23	19	47	5.2	5.0		0		0.05	
24	20	23	2.2	2.8		-1	=C24-D24	0.33	=F24^2
25						sum =	0	=SUM(F5:F24)	
26			Regression coefficients:						
27			b0 =	0.671189155	=INTERCEPT(C5:C24,B5:B24)				
28			b1 =	0.091519001	=SLOPE(C5:C24,B5:B24)				
29									
30			Reliability:						
31			Σ(y-y^)^2 =	8.22	=SUM(H5:H24)				
32			n =	20	=COUNT(A5:A24)				
33			SEE =	0.675872845	=SQRT(C31/(C32-2))				

Figure 10.27

The standard error of the estimate can also be calculated using standard Excel functions as described below.

➜ **Excel Manual Method**

Employee number Cells A5:A24	Values	
X Cells B5:B24	Values	
Y Cells C5:C24	Values	
$\hat{y}$ Cell D5	Formula: =$C$27+$C$28*B5	
	Copy formula: D5:D24	
$y - \hat{y}$ Cell F5	Formula: =C5–D5	
	Copy formula: F5:F24	
$(y - \hat{y})^2$ Cell H5	Formula: =F5^2	
	Copy formula H5:H24	
Sum = Cell F25	Formula: =SUM(F5:F24)	
b_0 = Cell C27	Formula: =INTERCEPT(C5:C24,B5:B24)	
b_1 = Cell C28	Formula: =SLOPE(C5:C24,B5:B24)	
Sum of squared differences = Cell C31	Formula: =SUM(H5:H24)	
n = Cell C32	Formula: =COUNT(A5:A24)	
Standard error of estimate = Cell C33	Formula: =SQRT(C31/(C32–2))	

(b) Coefficient of determination, COD

Given that the regression line effectively summarizes the relationship between x and y, then the line will only partially explain the variability of the observed values, and this has been seen when we examined the residuals. In fact, as we already explained, the total variability of Y can be split into two components: (i) variability explained or accounted for by the regression line, and (ii) unexplained variability as indicated by the residuals. It should be noted that the correlation coefficient provides a measure of the strength of the association between two variables but the issue of interpreting the value is a problem. After all what do we mean by strong, weak, or moderately associated? Fortunately, we do have a method that is easier to interpret: the **coefficient of determination (COD)**. The COD is defined as the proportion of the total variation in y that is explained by the variation in the independent variable x. This definition is represented by equations (10.23) and (10.24) below:

$$COD = \frac{\text{Regression sum of squares}}{\text{Total sum of squares}} = \frac{SSR}{SST}$$

(10.23)

$$COD = \frac{\Sigma(\hat{y} - \bar{y})^2}{\Sigma(y - \bar{y})^2}$$

(10.24)

By further manipulation of the above equation it can be shown that the coefficient of determination (COD) is given by the following formula:

$$COD = (\text{Correlation Coefficient})^2 = r^2$$

(10.25)

Coefficient of determination (COD) The proportion of the variance in the dependent variable that is predicted from the independent variable.

This is the reason why in Excel, the name for the coefficient of determination is R-squared. As we saw in Figure 10.28, the Excel function =RSQ() that calculates the coefficient of determination returned the value of 0.792.

> ❊ **Interpretation**   From Excel the coefficient of determination is 0.79 or 79%. This value tells us that 79% of the variation in the % raise in production is explained by the variation in the production variable. Conversely, this implies that 21% (i.e. 100–79) of the sample variability in the % raise in production is due to other factors than production and is not explained by the regression line.

> **Note**   The above formulae state that $r^2 = COD$ and that $r^2 = \dfrac{SSR}{SST}$. As SSR = SST−SSE, this means that the formula can also be written as $r^2 = \dfrac{SST - SSE}{SST} = 1 - \dfrac{SSE}{SST}$.

Excel spreadsheet solution—calculation of the coefficient of determination

Figure 10.28 illustrates the Excel solution to calculate the COD.

	A	B	C	D	E	F	G	H	I
1	Linear Regression Analysis: Reliability								
2									
3	Employee	Production	% Raise in Production						
4	Number	X	Y	Line value, y^		(y^-ybar)^2		(y-ybar)^2	
5	1	47	4.2	5.0	=$C$27+$C$28*B5	0.321963	=(D5-$C$31)^2	1.80	=(C5-$C$31)^2
6	2	71	8.1	7.2		2.653766		6.55	
7	3	64	6.8	6.5		0.976945		1.59	
8	4	35	4.3	3.9		2.774376		1.54	
9	5	43	5.0	4.6		0.871411		0.29	
10	6	60	7.5	6.2		0.387294		3.84	
11	7	38	4.7	4.1		1.935128		0.71	
12	8	59	5.9	6.1		0.281759		0.13	
13	9	67	6.9	6.8		1.595074		1.85	
14	10	56	5.7	5.8		0.065666		0.03	
15	11	67	5.7	6.8		1.595074		0.03	
16	12	57	5.4	5.9		0.120946		0.02	
17	13	69	7.5	7.0		2.090917		3.84	
18	14	38	3.8	4.1		1.935128		3.03	
19	15	54	5.9	5.6		0.005360		0.13	
20	16	76	6.3	7.6		4.354038		0.58	
21	17	53	5.7	5.5		0.000335		0.03	
22	18	40	4.0	4.3		1.459387		2.37	
23	19	47	5.2	5.0		0.321963		0.12	
24	20	23	2.2	2.8		7.638999		11.16	
25									
26		Regression coefficients:							
27		b0 =	0.671189155	=INTERCEPT(C5:C24,B5:B24)					
28		b1 =	0.091519001	=SLOPE(C5:C24,B5:B24)					
29									
30		Reliability:							
31		ybar =	5.5	=AVERAGE(C5:C24)					
32		Σ(y^-ybar)^2=	31.39	=SUM(F5:F24)					
33		Σ(y-ybar)^2=	39.61	=SUM(H5:H24)					
34		COD =	0.79240371	=C32/C33					

Figure 10.28

The coefficient of determination can also be calculated using standard Excel functions as described below.

➜ Excel Manual Method

Employee number Cells A5:A24	Values
X Cells B5:B24	Values
Y Cells C5:C24	Values
$\hat{y}$ Cell D5	Formula: =$C$27+$C$28*B5
	Copy formula: D5:D24
$(\hat{y} - \bar{y})^2$ Cell F5	Formula: =(D5–$C$31)²
	Copy formula: F5:F24
$(y - \bar{y})^2$ Cell H5	Formula: =(C5–$C$31)²
	Copy formula: H5:H24
b_0 = Cell C27	Formula: =INTERCEPT(C5:C24,B5:B24)
b_1 = Cell C28	Formula: =SLOPE(C5:C24,B5:B24)
Average y = Cell C31	Formula: =AVERAGE(C5:C24)
Sum of squared differences of predicted from average $\Sigma(\hat{y} - \bar{y})^2$ = Cell C32	Formula: =SUM(F5:F24)
Sum of squared differences of actual from average $\Sigma(y - \bar{y})^2$ = Cell C33	Formula: =SUM(H5:H24)
Coefficient of Determination = Cell C34	Formula: =C32/C33

10.2.6 Test whether the predictor variable is a significant contributor, t test

The true relationship between X and Y ($Y = \beta_0 + \beta_1 X$) is being estimated from the sample relationship ($\hat{y} = b_0 + b_1 x$). To determine the existence of a significant relationship between X and Y variables will require the application of a t test to check whether β_1 is equal to zero.

This is essentially a test to determine if the regression model is usable. If the slope is significantly different from zero then we can use the regression equation to predict the dependent variable for any value of the independent variable. If the slope is zero then the independent variable has no prediction value since for every value of the independent variable the dependent variable would be zero. Therefore, when this is the situation we would not use the equation to make predictions. For simple linear regression which has one independent variable the F test is equivalent to the t test (see Section 10.2.7). In this hypothesis test we are assessing the possibility that $\beta_1 = 0$. It can be shown that the relationship between b_1, β_1, and t_{cal}, is given by equation (10.26) which follows a t distribution with the number of degrees of freedom df = n – 2:

$$t_{cal} = \frac{b_1 - \beta_1}{s_{b_1}}$$

(10.26)

$$\text{Where } s_{b_1} = \frac{S_{xy}}{\sqrt{SSX}} = \frac{SSE}{\sqrt{(x - \bar{x})^2}}$$

(10.27)

> **Note** Hypothesis test
>
> H_0: no linear relationship exists, $\beta_1 = 0$.
>
> H_1: linear relationship exists, $\beta_1 \neq 0$ (or $\beta_1 < 0$, or $\beta_1 > 0$).

The five step procedure we used in Section 10.1.4 is almost identical.

Excel spreadsheet solution—t test

Figure 10.29 illustrates the Excel solution to calculate the regression equation.

	A	B	C	D	E	F	G	H	I	J	K	L
1	Linear Regression Analysis: t and F test											
2												
3												
4	Employee number	X	Y	Line value y^		(x - xbar)^2			Hypothesis Test			
5	1	47	4.2	5.0	=$C$27+$C$28*B5	38.44	=(B5-$C$32)^2		H_0 : no linear relationship β = 0			
6	2	71	8.1	7.2		316.84			H_1 : linear relationship exists β <>0			
7	3	64	6.8	6.5		116.64			Two tail test			
8	4	35	4.3	3.9		331.24						
9	5	43	5.0	4.6		104.04			Select Test t test			
10	6	60	7.5	6.2		46.24						
11	7	38	4.7	4.1		231.04			Set level of significance			
12	8	59	5.9	6.1		33.64				Level =	0.05	
13	9	67	6.9	6.8		190.44			Extract relevant statistic			
14	10	56	5.7	5.8		7.84				SEE =	0.68	=STEYX(C5:C24,B5:B24)
15	11	67	5.7	6.8		190.44				xbar =	53.20	=AVERAGE(B5:B24)
16	12	57	5.4	5.9		14.44				SSX =	3747.20	=SUM(F5:F24)
17	13	69	7.5	7.0		249.64				Sb1 =	0.01	=K14/SQRT(K16)
18	14	38	3.8	4.1		231.04				t =	8.29	=C28/K17
19	15	54	5.9	5.6		0.64						
20	16	76	6.3	7.6		519.84				n =	20.00	=COUNT(A5:A24)
21	17	53	5.7	5.5		0.04				k =	1.00	
22	18	40	4.0	4.3		174.24				df =	18.00	=K20-(K21+1)
23	19	47	5.2	5.0		38.44			Upper two taile tcri =		2.10	=TINV(K12,K22)
24	20	23	2.2	2.8		912.04			Lower two taile tcri =		-2.10	=-TINV(K12,K22)
25									Two tail p value =		1.473E-07	=TDIST(K18,K22,2)
26		Regression coefficients:							Decision:			
27		b0 =	0.67	=INTERCEPT(C5:C24,B5:B24)					Since t_{cal} > Upper t_{cri}, Accept H_1			
28		b1 =	0.09	=SLOPE(C5:C24,B5:B24)					Since p-value < α (1.47E-7 < 0.05), Accept H_1			

Figure 10.29

→ Excel Function Method

Employee number	Cells A5:A24	Values
X	Cells B5:B24	Values
Y	Cells C5:C24	Values
$\hat{y}$	Cell D5	Formula: =$C$27+$C$28*B5
		Copy formula: D5:D24
$(x - \bar{x})^2$	Cell F5	Formula: =(B5-$K$15)^2
		Copy formula:F5:F24
b_0 =	Cell C27	Formula: =INTERCEPT(C5:C24,B5:B24)
b_1 =	Cell C28	Formula: =SLOPE(C5:C24,B5:B24)
Level =	Cell K12	Value
SEE =	Cell K14	Formula: =STEYX(C5:C24,B5:B24)
Average x =	Cell K15	Formula: =AVERAGE(B5:B24)
SSX =	Cell K16	Formula: =SUM(F5:F24)
Sb_1 =	Cell K17	Formula: =K14/SQRT(K16)
t =	Cell K18	Formula: =C28/K17
n =	Cell K20	Formula: =COUNT(A5:A24)

k = Cell K21	Value
df = Cell K22	Formula: =K20–(K21+1)
Upper t_{cri} = Cell K23	Formula: =TINV(K12,K22)
Lower t_{cri} = Cell K24	Formula: =–TINV(K12,K22)
Two tail p-value = Cell K25	Formula: =TDIST(K18,K22,2)

A multi-step approach to conduct the test is applied here again.

(1) State hypothesis

$H_0: \beta_1 = 0$ no linear relationship

$H_1: \beta_1 \neq 0$ linear relationship exists and since we believe that the relationship is not zero (2 tail test)

(2) Select the test—we know that this is the t test for testing if the predictor variable is a significant contributor

(3) Significance level. Choose 5% (0.05)

(4) Extract relevant statistics

(a) Calculate the test statistic, t_{calc}

To test the possibility that H_0 is true we undertake a t test as follows:

$$t_{cal} = \frac{b_1}{s_{b_1}}$$

(10.28)

The test statistic t follows a t distribution with $n-2$ degrees of freedom. From Excel, t = 8.3 with 18 degrees of freedom

(b) Critical t value

We can now test to see if this sample t value would result in accepting or rejecting H_0. From Excel we see that the critical t value = ±2.1 at a 5% significance level (0.05). At this stage we need to remember that the hypothesis test implies no perceived direction for H_1 to be accepted.

(5) Make a decision

Since $t_{cal} > t_{cri}$ (8.3 > 2.1), then the test statistic lies in the rejection zone for H_0. Therefore, reject H_0 and accept H_1. Alternatively, the p-value < α (1.47E-7 < 0.05), reject H_0 and accept H_1.

✻ **Interpretation**   The sample data provides evidence that a significant relationship may exist between the two variables (% raise in production and production) at a 5% significance level.

Note   A similar procedure can be used to test the hypothesis on the intercept β_0. The test statistic $t_{cal} = \frac{b_0}{s_{b_0}}$, where b_0 is the least squares estimate of β_0, and s_{b_0} is its standard error.

10.2.7 Test whether the predictor variable is a significant contributor, F test

An alternative to the t test is the F test that can be used to determine whether the predictor variable (x) is a significant contributor to the value of $\hat{y}$. Recall in Section 10.2.3 that the total deviation in y, SST, can be partitioned between the deviation explained by the regression, SSR and the unexplained deviation, SSE. If the regression model fits the sample data then we would find that the value of the deviation explained by the regression (SSR) to be smaller then the value of the unexplained deviation (SSE). If we take the mean squares by dividing by their degrees of freedom, then the ratio MSR/MSE follows an F distribution and can be used to test for the overall significance of the relationship.

$$F_{cal} = \frac{\text{Mean square for model}}{\text{Mean square for actual error}} = \frac{MSR}{MSE} \tag{10.29}$$

$$F_{cal} = \frac{COD/k}{(1 - COD)/(n - (k + 1))} \tag{10.30}$$

Where n is the total number of paired values and k is the number of predictor variables. If the regression line fits the sample data (little scatter about line) then the value of F will be quite large. Conversely, if the regression line does not fit the sample data (increased scatter about line) then the value of F will approach zero.

Excel spreadsheet solution—F test

Figure 10.30 illustrates the Excel solution to calculate the F test statistic.

	A	B	C	D	E	F	G	H	I
1	Linear Regression Analysis: F test								
2									
3	Employee number	Production	% Raise in Production						
4		X	Y	Line value, y^		Hypothesis Test			
5	1	47	4.2	5.0			H_0 : no linear relationship $\beta = 0$		①
6	2	71	8.1	7.2			H_1 : linear relationship exists $\beta <> 0$		
7	3	64	6.8	6.5			Two tail test		
8	4	35	4.3	3.9					
9	5	43	5.0	4.6		Select Test	F test	②	
10	6	60	7.5	6.2					
11	7	38	4.7	4.1		Set level of significance		③	
12	8	59	5.9	6.1			Level = 0.05		
13	9	67	6.9	6.8		Extract relevant statistic			
14	10	56	5.7	5.8			n =	20 =COUNT(A5:A24)	
15	11	67	5.7	6.8			k =	1	
16	12	57	5.4	5.9			COD =	0.7924 =RSQ(C5:C24,B5:B24)	
17	13	69	7.5	7.0			F =	68.7068 =(H16/H15)/((1-H16)/(H14-(H15+1)))	
18	14	38	3.8	4.1		④			
19	15	54	5.9	5.6			df num =	1 =H15	
20	16	76	6.3	7.6			df denom =	18 =H14-(H15+1)	
21	17	53	5.7	5.5			Fcri =	4.4139 =FINV(H12,H19,H20)	
22	18	40	4.0	4.3			p-value =	1.473E-07 =FDIST(H17,H19,H20)	
23	19	47	5.2	5.0					
24	20	23	2.2	2.8		Decision:			
25						Since $F_{cal} > F_{cri}$, Accept H_1			⑤
26		Regression coefficients:				Since p-value < α (1.47E-7 < 0.05), Accept H_1			
27		b_0 =	0.6712 =INTERCEPT(C5:C24,B5:B24)						
28		b_1 =	0.0915 =SLOPE(C5:C24,B5:B24)						

Figure 10.30

> ➔ **Excel Function Method**
>
> Employee number Cells A5:A24   Values
> X Cells B5:B24   Values
> Y Cells C5:C24   Values
> $\hat{y}$ Cell D5   Formula: =$C$27+$C$28*B5
>   Copy formula: D5:D24
> b_0 = Cell C27   Formula: =INTERCEPT(C6:C25,B6:B25)
> b_1 = Cell C28   Formula: =SLOPE(C6:C25,B6:B25)
> Level = Cell H12   Value
> n = Cell H14   Formula: =COUNT(A5:A24)
> k = Cell H15   Value
> COD = Cell H16   Formula: =RSQ(C5:C24,B5:B24)
> F-cal = Cell H17   Formula: =(H16/H15)/((1−H16)/(H14−(H15+1)))
> df num = Cell H19   Formula: =H15
> df denom = Cell H20   Formula: =H14−(H15+1)
> F-critical = Cell H21   Formula: =FINV(H12,H19,H20)
> p-value = Cell H22   Formula: =FDIST(H17,H19,H20)

(1) Hypothesis test
   $H_0: \beta_1 = 0$ no linear relationship
   $H_1: \beta_1 \neq 0$ linear relationship exists and since we believe that the relationship is not zero (2 tail test)

(2) Select the test—which we know is F test testing whether the predictor variable is a significant contributor

(3) Significance level. We choose 5% (0.05)

(4) Extract relevant statistic
   Calculate the test statistic, F. From Excel, $F_{cal} = 68.71$
   Critical F value, F_{cri}
      Significance = 5% = 0.05
      Number of degrees on numerator, $df_n = k = 1$
      Number of degrees on denominator, $df_d = n - (k+1) = 20 - (1+1) = 18$
      From Excel, $F_{critical} = 4.41$ and p-value = 1.47E-7.

(5) Make a decision

> ✳ **Interpretation**   Conclude that the model is useful in predicting % raise in production at a 5% significance level.

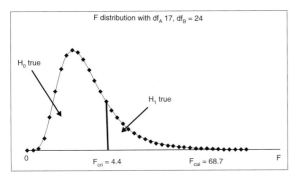

Figure 10.31 illustrates the shape of the F distribution and the relationship between the critical F value and H_0 and H_1 being true.

Since $F_{cal} > F_{cri}$ we reject H_0.

Figure 10.31

Note For one predictor models the t test and F test is essentially the same test. In fact, for a one predictor regression model the relationship between F and t is $t = \sqrt{F}$.

ANOVA table for testing the significance of the regression coefficient

Source	df	Sum of Squares	Mean Square (Variance)	F
Regression	k	SSR	$MSR = \dfrac{SSR}{k}$	$F = \dfrac{MSR}{MSE}$
Error	$n-k-1$	SSE	$MSE = \dfrac{SSE}{n-k-1}$	
Total		SST		

Table 10.4 ANOVA table

The completed ANOVA table is part of the Excel macro solution described in Section 10.2.10.

10.2.8 Confidence interval estimate for slope β_1

An alternative method to test whether or not a significant relationship exists is to find a confidence interval and see if the H_0: $\beta_1 = 0$ is included within the confidence interval. If we re-arrange equation (10.26) for b_1 we obtain equation (10.31):

$$\beta_1 = b_1 \pm t \times s_{b_1} \tag{10.31}$$

This equation implies two border values for β_1 with the confidence interval lying between these two values.

Excel spreadsheet solution—calculation of the confidence interval

Figure 10.32 illustrates the Excel solution to calculate the confidence interval.

	A	B	C	D	E	F	G
1	Linear Regression Analysis: Confidence Interval						
2							
3	Employee	Production	% Raise in Production				
4	Number	X	Y	Line value, y^		(x - xbar)^2	
5	1	47	4.2	5.0	=$C$27+$C$28*B5	38.44	=(B5-AVERAGE($B$5:$B$24))^2
6	2	71	8.1	7.2		316.84	
7	3	64	6.8	6.5		116.64	
8	4	35	4.3	3.9		331.24	
9	5	43	5.0	4.6		104.04	
10	6	60	7.5	6.2		46.24	
11	7	38	4.7	4.1		231.04	
12	8	59	5.9	6.1		33.64	
13	9	67	6.9	6.8		190.44	
14	10	56	5.7	5.8		7.84	
15	11	67	5.7	6.8		190.44	
16	12	57	5.4	5.9		14.44	
17	13	69	7.5	7.0		249.64	
18	14	38	3.8	4.1		231.04	
19	15	54	5.9	5.6		0.64	
20	16	76	6.3	7.6		519.84	
21	17	53	5.7	5.5		0.04	
22	18	40	4.0	4.3		174.24	
23	19	47	5.2	5.0		38.44	
24	20	23	2.2	2.8		912.04	
25							
26		Regression coefficients:					
27		b0 =	0.671189155	=INTERCEPT(C5:C24,B5:B24)			
28		b1 =	0.091519001	=SLOPE(C5:C24,B5:B24)			
29							
30		Confidence interval					
31		n =	20	=COUNT(A5:A24)			
32		level =	0.05				
33		df =	18	=C31-2			
34		t cri =	2.1	=TINV(C32,C33)			
35		SYX =	0.675872845	=STEYX(C5:C24,B5:B24)			
36		SSX =	3747.2	=SUM(F5:F24)			
37		sb1 =	0.01104108	=C35/SQRT(C36)			
38		Lower CI =	0.068322552	=C28-C34*C37			
39		Upper CI =	0.114715449	=C28+C34*C37			

Figure 10.32

→ Excel Function Method

Employee number Cells A5:A24	Values	
X Cells B5:B24	Values	
Y Cells C5:C24	Values	
$\hat{y}$ Cell D5	Formula: =$C$27+$C$28*B5	
	Copy formula: D5:D24	
$(x - \bar{x})^2$ Cell F5	Formula: =(B5−AVERAGE(B5:B24))^2	
	Copy formula: F5:F24	
b_0 = Cell C27	Formula: =INTERCEPT(C5:C24,B5:B24)	
b_1 = Cell C28	Formula: =SLOPE(C5:C24,B5:B24)	
n = Cell C31	Formula: =COUNT(A5:A24)	
level = Cell C32	Value	
d_f = Cell C33	Formula: =C31−2	
t_{cri} = Cell C34	Formula: =TINV(C32,C33)	
SYX = Cell C35	Formula: =STEYX(C5:C24,B5:B24)	

SSX = Cell C36	Formula: =SUM(F5:F24)
Sb1 = Cell C37	Formula: =C35/SQRT(C36)
Lower CI = Cell C38	Formula: =C28−C34*C37
Upper CI = Cell C39	Formula: =C28+C34*C37

✳ **Interpretation**   From Excel, the 95% confidence interval for Example 10.3 is between 0.06832% and 0.11471%. Because these values are above zero we conclude that there is a significant linear relationship between the two variables (% raise in production (y) and production (x)). If the interval had included zero then you would conclude no significant linear relationship exists. If we rescale the numbers, we can say that the confidence interval states that for production increase of 1000, the % raise in production is estimated to increase by at least 6.8 but no more than 11.5.

10.2.9 Prediction interval for an estimate of Y

The regression equation ($\hat{y} = b_0 + b_1x$) provides a relationship that can then be used to provide an estimate of y based upon an x value. For example, we may want to know what the % raise in production would be if production value was set at 30. The prediction interval for y at a particular value of x = xp is given by equation (10.32):

$$\hat{y} - e < y < \hat{y} + e \qquad (10.32)$$

Where the error term is calculated using equation (10.33)

$$e = t_{cri} * SEE * \sqrt{1 + \frac{1}{n} + \frac{n * \left(x_p - \overline{x}\right)^2}{n * \left(\sum x^2\right) - \left(\sum x\right)^2}} \qquad (10.33)$$

Excel spreadsheet solution—calculation of the prediction interval

Let's examine an Excel solution to calculate the prediction interval for $x_p = 30$. Figure 10.33 illustrates the Excel solution to calculate the predictor interval.

	A	B	C	D	E	F	G	H
1	Linear Regression Analysis: Prediction Interval							
2								
3	Employee	Production	% Raise in Production			Regression coefficients:		
4	Number	X	Y	x^2		b0 =	0.671189155	=INTERCEPT(C5:C24,B5:B24)
5	1	47	4.2	2209	=B5^2	b1 =	0.091519001	=SLOPE(C5:C24,B5:B24)
6	2	71	8.1	5041		Prediction interval		
7	3	64	6.8	4096		n =	20	=COUNT(A5:A24)
8	4	35	4.3	1225		level =	0.05	
9	5	43	5.0	1849		df =	18	=G7-2
10	6	60	7.5	3600		t cri =	2.10092	=TINV(G8,G9)
11	7	38	4.7	1444		x =	30.0	
12	8	59	5.9	3481		xbar =	53.2	=AVERAGE(B5:B24)
13	9	67	6.9	4489		y^ =	3.4	=G4+G5*G11
14	10	56	5.7	3136		Σx =	1064.0	=SUM(B5:B24)
15	11	67	5.7	4489		Σx^2 =	60352.0	=SUM(D5:D24)
16	12	57	5.4	3249		SEE =	0.675872845	=STEYX(C5:C24,B5:B24)
17	13	69	7.5	4761		E =	1.55135517	=G10*G16*SQRT(1+(1/G7)+(G7*(G11-G12)^2)/(G7*G15-G14^2))
18	14	38	3.8	1444		Lower PI =	1.865404	=G13-G17
19	15	54	5.9	2916		Upper PI =	4.968114	=G13+G17
20	16	76	6.3	5776				
21	17	53	5.7	2809				
22	18	40	4.0	1600				
23	19	47	5.2	2209				
24	20	23	2.2	529				

Figure 10.33

➜ **Excel Function Method**

Employee number Cells A5:A24	Values
X Cells B5:B24	Values
Y Cells C5:C24	Values
x^2 Cell D5	Formula: =B5²
	Copy formula: D5:D24
b_0 = Cell G4	Formula: =INTERCEPT(C5:C24,B5:B24)
b_1 = Cell G5	Formula: =SLOPE(C5:C24,B5:B24)
n = Cell G7	Formula: =COUNT(A5:A24)
level = Cell G8	Value
df = Cell G9	Formula: =G7−2
t_{cri} = Cell G10	Formula: =TINV(G8,G9)
x = Cell G11	Value
Xbar = Cell G12	Formula: =AVERAGE(B2:B24)
Y^ = Cell G13	Formula: =G4+G5*G11
Σx = Cell G14	Formula: =SUM(B5:B24)
Σx^2 = Cell G15	Formula: =SUM(D5:D24)
SEE = Cell G16	Formula: =STEYX(C6:C24,B6:B24)
E = Cell G17	Formula: =G10*G16*SQRT(1+(1/G7)+ (G7*(G11−
	G12)^2)/(G7*G15−G14^2))
Lower PI = Cell G18	Formula: =G13−G17
Upper PI = Cell G19	Formula: =G13+G17

From Excel: x_p = 30, n = 20, significance level = 5%, t_{cri} = 2.10092, SEE = 0.675872845, $\bar{x}$ = 53.2, Σx = 1064, and Σx^2 = 60352.

$$e = 2.10092 * 0.675872845 * \sqrt{1+\frac{1}{20}+\frac{20*(30-53.2)^2}{20*(60352)-(1064)^2}} = 1.551353666$$

Equation (10.32) then gives the 95% prediction interval for x_p = 30 to be between 1.87% and 4.97%.

✳ **Interpretation**   If the production level was at 30 units then we predict the value of % raise in production to be 3.4%. In fact, we can state with 95% confidence that this value of 3.4% will be somewhere between 1.87% and 4.97%. This shows that the actual value can vary from the predicted value of 3.4%.

10.2.10 Excel ToolPak regression solution

Most of the previous calculations (though not all of them) could be done automatically in Excel by the press of one single button. The Excel ToolPak regression solution provides a complete set of solutions, including:

- Calculate equation of line
- Calculate measures of reliability
- Check that the predictor is a significant contributor (T and F tests)
- Calculate a confidence interval for β_0 and β_1.

Figure 10.34 Data Analysis—Regression

Select Tools > Data Analysis > Select Regression

Y Range: C5:C24

X Range: B5:B24

Confidence Interval: 95%

Output Range: B36

Click on residuals, residual plots, and normal probability plot

Excel will now calculate and output the required regression statistics and charts as illustrated in Figure 10.35 below.

	B	C	D	E	F	G	H	I	J
36	SUMMARY OUTPUT								
37									
38	Regression Statistics								
39	Multiple R	0.890170607							
40	R Square	0.79240371							
41	Adjusted R Square	0.780870583							
42	Standard Error	0.675872845							
43	Observations	20							
44									
45	ANOVA								
46		df	SS	MS	F	Significance F			
47	Regression	1	31.38552615	31.3855262	68.706752	1.47315E-07			
48	Residual	18	8.222473847	0.4568041					
49	Total	19	39.608						
50									
51		Coefficients	Standard Error	t Stat	P-value	Lower 95%	Upper 95%	Lower 95.0%	Upper 95.0%
52	Intercept	0.671189155	0.606516188	1.10663024	0.2830246	-0.60305407	1.94543238	-0.60305407	1.94543238
53	X Variable 1	0.091519001	0.01104108	8.28895361	1.473E-07	0.068322552	0.114715449	0.06832255	0.114715449

Figure 10.35

Note We can also equate the printout in Figure 10.35 with the terms from Section 10.2.3. They are as follows:

Cell C40 = R Square, or COD

Cell C42 = Standard Error of Estimate (SEE)

Cell D47 = SSR

Cell D48 = SSE

Cell D49 = SST

Cell E47 = MSR (this is the result of D47/C47)

Cell E48 = MSE (this is the result of D48/C48). If you take a square root of this value, you get Standard Error of Estimate, as per Cell C42.

Cell F47 = F-statistic(this is the result of E47/E48)

$C52 = b_0$

$C53 = b_1$

$D52 = sb_0$ (Standard Error for b_0)

$D53 = sb_1$ (Standard Error for b_1)

$E52 = $ t-stat, or t-calc for b_0 (this is the result of C52/D52)

$E53 = $ t-stat, or t-calc for b_1 (this is the result of C53/D53)

From Figure 10.35 we can identify the required regression statistics:

Calculation	Regression statistic	Excel cell
Fit model to sample data	$b_0 = 0.67119$ $b_1 = 0.09162$	Cell C52 Cell C53
Test model reliability using the coefficient of determination and standard error of the estimate	COD = 0.79 SEE = 0.68	Cell C40 Cell C42
Test whether the predictor variables are significant contributors—t test $H_0: \beta_0 = 0$ vs. $H_1: \beta_0 \neq 0$ $H_0: \beta_1 = 0$ vs. $H_1: \beta_1 \neq 0$	$t = 1.11$, $p = 0.28$ $t = 8.29$, $p = 1.4732E\text{-}07$	Cells E52 and F52 Cells E53 and F53
Calculate the test statistics and p-values using Excel—F test $H_0: \beta_1 = 0$ vs. $H_1: \beta_1 \neq 0$	$F = 68.7$, $p = 1.473E\text{-}07$	Cells F47 and G47
Confidence interval for β_0 and β_1 95% CI for β_0 95% CI for β_1	$-0.63 - 1.84$ $0.06 - 0.11$	Cell G52 – H52 Cell G53 – H53

Table 10.5

What is the p-value in the above printout and how is it used and interpreted in Excel? This is the same statistic we have already used extensively in previous chapters on hypothesis testing. The Excel solution provides the t test values for each contributor (b_0 and b_1) and includes a statistic called the p-value. The p-value measures the chance (or probability) of achieving a test statistic equal to or more extreme than the sample value obtained, assuming H_0 is true. As we already know, to make a decision we compare the calculated p-value with your level of significance (say 0.05 or 5%) and if $p < 0.05$ then we would reject H_0.

The application of the t test tells us that the predictor variable (production) is a significant contributor to the value of y (% raise in production) given that p (=1.473E-7) < 0.05. Furthermore, it is observed that the constant is not a significant contributor to the value of y (p = 0.28 > 0.05) and this would suggest that the model should be of the form $\hat{y} = b_1 x$. This can easily be achieved in Excel by using constant = 0 in the Analysis ToolPak Regression solution. The F test confirms that the predictor variable is a significant contributor to the value of the dependent variable (p = 1.473E-7 < 0.05). This confirms the t test solution and we conclude that there is a significant relationship between the % raise in production and production variables. Remember that for a one predictor model, $t = \sqrt{F} = \sqrt{68.7} = 8.29$. The Regression ToolPak also helps with

	B	C	D
55	RESIDUAL OUTPUT		
56			
57	Observation	Predicted Y	Residuals
58	1	4.972582195	-0.772582195
59	2	7.169038215	0.930961785
60	3	6.528405209	0.271594791
61	4	3.874354184	0.425645816
62	5	4.606506191	0.393493809
63	6	6.162329206	1.337670794
64	7	4.148911187	0.551088813
65	8	6.070810205	-0.170810205
66	9	6.802962212	0.097037788
67	10	5.796253202	-0.096253202
68	11	6.802962212	-1.102962212
69	12	5.887772203	-0.487772203
70	13	6.986000213	0.513999787
71	14	4.148911187	-0.348911187
72	15	5.613215201	0.286784799
73	16	7.626633219	-1.326633219
74	17	5.5216962	0.1783038
75	18	4.331949189	-0.331949189
76	19	4.972582195	0.227417805
77	20	2.776126174	-0.576126174

Figure 10.36 Residual output

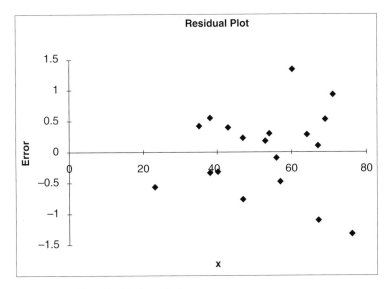

Figure 10.37 Plot of residuals against x

checking of some of the assumptions, namely: Linearity and constant variance, as illustrated in Figures 10.36 and 10.37 illustrated above:

We can see from Figure 10.37 that we have no observed pattern within the residual plot and we can assume that the linearity assumption is not violated. Furthermore, the residual and hence the variance are not growing in size and are bounded between a high and low point. From this we conclude that the variance assumption is not violated.

Assumption check: Normality

Figure 10.38 illustrates the normal probability plot.

From the normal probability plot we have a fairly linear relationship and we conclude that the normality assumption is not violated.

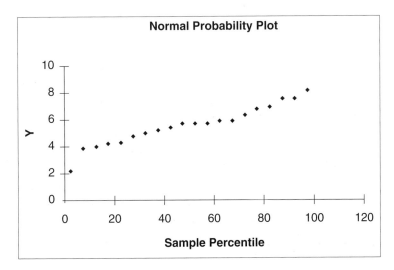

Figure 10.38

Student Exercises

X10.8 In the regression equation for $\hat{y} = b_0 + b_1 x$, the value of b_0 is given by which equation?

A. $b_0 = \dfrac{\Sigma Y - b_1^2 \Sigma X}{n}$

B. $b_0 = \dfrac{\Sigma Y - b_1 \Sigma X}{2n}$

C. $b_0 = \dfrac{\Sigma Y - b_1 \Sigma X}{n}$

D. $b_0 = \dfrac{\Sigma Y - n \Sigma X}{n}$

X10.9 In the regression equation for $\hat{y} = b_0 + b_1 x$, the value of b_1 is given by which equation?

A. $b_1 = \dfrac{n \Sigma XY^2 - \Sigma X \Sigma Y}{n \Sigma X^2 - (\Sigma X)^2}$

B. $b_1 = \dfrac{n \Sigma XY - \Sigma X \Sigma Y}{n \Sigma X^2 - (\Sigma X)^2}$

C. $b_1 = \dfrac{n \Sigma XY - \Sigma X \Sigma Y}{n \Sigma X - (\Sigma X)^2}$

D. $b_1 = \dfrac{n \Sigma XY - \Sigma X \Sigma Y}{n \Sigma X^2 - (\Sigma X)}$

Use the ANOVA table to answer exercise questions X10.10–X10.12:

ANOVA

	df	SS	MS	F	Significance F
Regression	1	3.76127E+11	3.76127E+11	162.7172745	7.34827E-16
Residual	41	94773006578	2311536746		
Total	42	4.709E+11			

X10.10 Which of the following is the coefficient of determination, COD?

A. 0.78   B. 1.80   C. 0.80   D. 1.80

X10.11 What is the value of Pearson's correlation coefficient, r?

A. 0.99   B. 1.89   C. 0.11   D. 0.89

X10.12 What is the value of the standard estimate of the error, SEE?

A. 84078   B. 84778   C. 48078   D. 48178

X10.13 In 2007 Pronto Ltd. ascertained the amount spent on advertising and the corresponding sales revenue by seven marketing clients:

Advertising (£000s), x	Sales (£000s), y
2	60
5	100
4	70
6	90
3	80
7	105
8	115

(a) Plot a scatter plot and comment on a possible relationship between the examination and assignment marks.

(b) Use Excel regression functions to undertake the following tasks:

    i. Fit linear model,

    ii. Check model reliability (r and COD),

    iii. Undertake appropriate inference tests (t and F test),

    iv. Check model assumptions (residual and normality checks),

    v. Provide a 95% confidence interval for the predictor variable.

X10.14 Fit an appropriate equation to the data set to predict examination mark given assignment mark for 14 undergraduate students.

Assignment	69	42	43	40	100	80	100	90	77	47	68	50	45	41
Examination	77	66	65	65	80	71	78	75	70	60	67	61	59	58

(a) Plot a scatter plot and comment on a possible relationship between the examination and assignment marks.

(b) Use Excel regression functions to undertake the following tasks:

    i. Fit linear model,

    ii. Check model reliability (r and COD),

    iii. Undertake appropriate inference tests (t and F test),

    iv. Check model assumptions (residual and normality checks),

    v. Provide a 95% confidence interval for the predictor variable.

10.3 Some Advanced Topics in Regression Analysis

In the previous two sections we have explored methods of measuring and fitting relationships between one variable and another variable. These one predictor models have assumed that the relationship between y and x is linear and this simple situation is known as simple linear regression modelling. In most cases the situation is more complicated and can include relationships that are non-linear between the dependent and independent variable and with a possibility that the dependent variable may also depend upon more than one independent variable.

10.3.1 Introduction to non-linear regression

In many situations we will find that the relationship between the dependent and independent variable is not necessarily linear. Some of the most popular curves that describe the shape of these relationships are:

a. **Line**

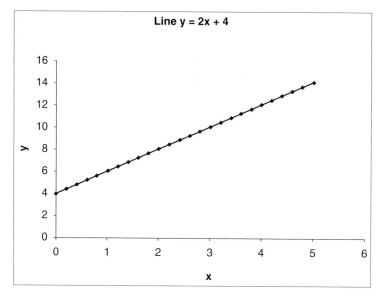

Figure 10.39 $y = b_0 + b_1 x$

b. **Parabola Curve**

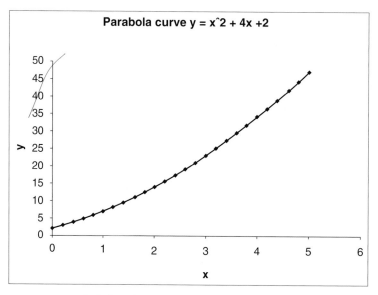

Figure 10.40 $y = b_2 x^2 + b_1 x + b_0$

c. **Hyperbola Curve**

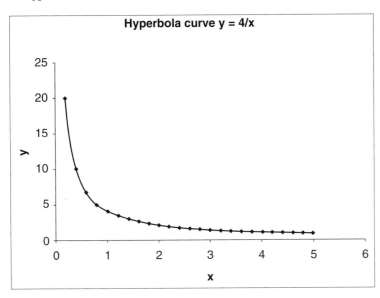

Figure 10.41 $y = b_0/x$

d. **Exponential Curve**

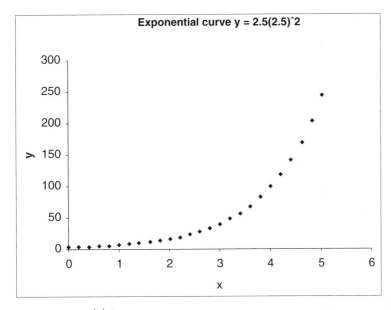

Figure 10.42 $y = b_0 b_1^{\,x}$

e. **Modified Exponential Curve**

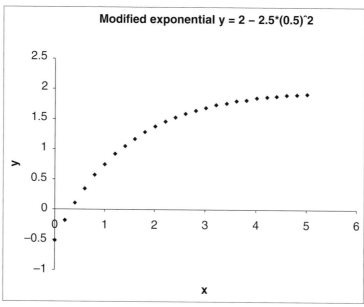

Figure 10.43 $y = b_2 + b_0 b_1{}^x$

f. **Logistic Curve**

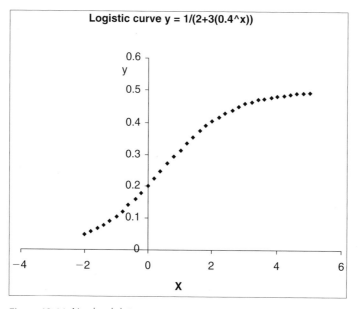

Figure 10.44 $1/y = b_2 + b_0 b_1{}^x$

g. Gompertz Curve

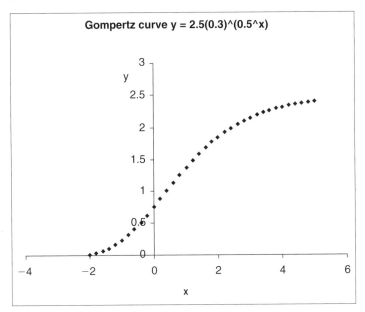

Gompertz curve y = 2.5(0.3)^(0.5^x)

Figure 10.45 $y = b_2 b_0^{b_1^x}$

Let's look at just one of these non-linear relationships. Equation (10.34) represents the equation of a parabola (or polynomial of degree 2):

$$\hat{y} = b_0 + b_1 x + b_2 x^2 \qquad (10.34)$$

The values of the parameters b_0, b_1, and b_2 can be determined using least squares regression by solving equations (10.35)–(10.38).

$$b_0 = \frac{\sum \hat{x}^4 \sum y - \sum \hat{x}^2 \sum \hat{x}^2 y}{n \sum \hat{x}^4 - \left(\sum \hat{x}^2\right)^2} \qquad (10.35)$$

$$b_1 = \frac{\sum \hat{x} y}{\sum \hat{x}^2} \qquad (10.36)$$

$$b_2 = \frac{n \sum \hat{x}^2 y - \sum \hat{x}^2 \sum y}{n \sum \hat{x}^4 - \left(\sum \hat{x}^2\right)^2} \qquad (10.37)$$

Where $\hat{x} = x - \overline{x}$ $\qquad (10.38)$

We will use Excel to show how to fit this curve to a data set, calculate the equation of the line, and calculate the coefficient of determination (though the data set is not shown here, just the principle of how to use Excel for this purpose).

Excel spreadsheet solution—fit parabola to a data set

Right click on a data point in the scatter plot and choose the 'Add Trendline' option and select Polynomial of Order 2.

Choose Options tab.

Select Display equation on chart and Display R-squared value on chart.

Click OK.

Figure 10.46 Fitting Trendline to scatter plot

Figure 10.47 Including trend equation and COD on the scatter plot

Linear models imposed on non-linear relationships will inevitably lead to errors. The extent of the errors will depend on the deviation of the data from the linear form.

> **Note**   If the relationship was non-linear we may still use linear regression as long as we are able to transform the non-linear data to a linear form.

Example 10.4

Price, x	Sales (£000's), y
0.30	100.00
0.40	95.00
0.50	93.00
0.58	90.20
0.60	90.00
0.65	88.00
0.70	85.00
1.10	86.00
1.15	83.00
1.40	82.00
1.80	80.00
2.60	81.00

The following sales and price data have been collected from a range of discount stores selling a particular product but using their own discount policy to price the product. The question is can we fit an appropriate relationship to predict sales given price?

The solution to this problem consists of identifying the type of relationship between the two variables. Figure 10.48 illustrates graphically the relationship between sales and price.

Table 10.6 Sales and price data

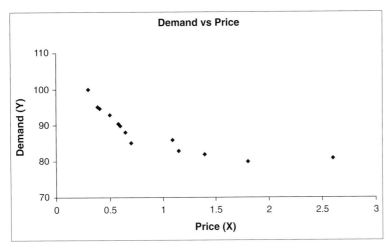

Figure 10.48

Figure 10.48 illustrates a scatter plot for demand vs. price with two possible models identified:

Model 1—line fit $y = b_0 + b_1 x$

Model 2—curve fit $y = b_0 + b_1/x$.

Table 10.7 shows the results of applying least squares regression for models 1 and 2. The results show that model 2 represents a better fit to the data set than model 1.

Model	Equation	COD
1	$\hat{Y} = -7.33 + 94.96x$	0.66
2	$\hat{Y} = 77.56 + \dfrac{6.95}{x}$	0.96

Table 10.7 Summary of results

✳ **Interpretation**   From the summary in Table 10.7 we can see that for the non-linear model 96% of the variations in one variable are explained by variations in another, whilst for the linear model only 66% of variations is explained by the model. Clearly, we are better off using the non-linear model.

To complete the solution you would then need to check the model assumptions and undertake an appropriate t test (or F test) to test whether the independent variable is a significant contributor to the dependent variable.

10.3.2 Introduction to multiple regression analysis

In many situations it is unlikely that a dependent variable (y) would depend upon only one independent variable (x) but on a number of independent variables (x_1, x_2, x_3, ..., and x_n). To solve problems with more than one independent variable we would be required to undertake multiple regression analysis. For example, house price might depend not only upon the land value but also upon the value of home improvements made to a property. The form of the population regression equation with 'n' independent variables can be written as:

$$\hat{y} = \beta_0 + \beta_1 x_1 + \beta_2 x_2 + \ldots\ldots\ldots\ldots\ldots + \beta_n x_n + \text{error} \tag{10.39}$$

The multiple regression models can be found using the Excel ToolPak Regression tool to provide the coefficients, assumption and reliability checks, and conduct appropriate inference tests.

▷ Example 10.5

Table 10.8 consists of data that has been collected by an estate agent who wishes to model the relationship between house sales price (£'s) and the independent variables: land value, LV (£'s) and the value of home improvements, IV (£'s). In order to fit the model the estate agent selected a random sample of size 20 properties from the 2000 properties sold in that year.

Selling Price (£'s), Y	Land Value (£'s), X_1	Home Improvements (£'s), X_2
68900	5960	44967
48500	9000	27860
55500	9500	31439
62000	10000	39592
140000	18000	72827
45000	8500	27317
115000	15000	60000
144000	23000	65000
59000	8100	39117
47500	9000	29349
40500	7300	40166
40000	8000	31679
135800	20000	75000
45500	8000	23454
40900	8000	20897
80000	10500	56248
56000	4000	20859
37000	4500	22610
50000	3400	35948
22400	1500	5779

Table 10.8 Sales and price data

The solution process includes:

- Construct scatter plot to identify relationships between the variables.
- Fit multiple regression models to the sample data.
- Check model assumptions.
- Using the multiple coefficient of determination and **adjusted r^2**.
- Test whether the predictor variables are a significant contributor to the overall model, F test.
- Test whether the predictor variables are significant contributors, t tests.
- Provide a 95% confidence interval for the population slopes.

Construct scatter plot to identify possible model

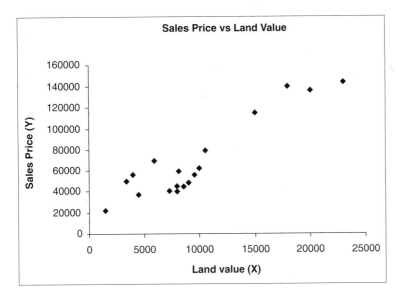

Figure 10.49 Scatter plot of sales price versus land value

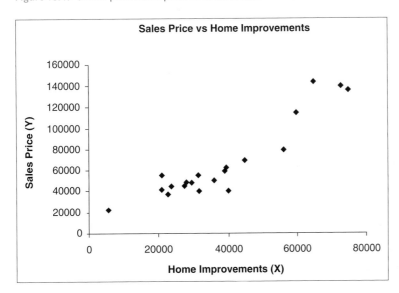

Figure 10.50 Scatter plot of sales price versus the value of home improvements

X

Adjusted r^2 Adjusted R squared measures the proportion of the variation in the dependent variable accounted for by the explanatory variables.

The two scatter plots suggest that a linear model would be appropriate for y vs. x_1 and y vs. x_2. It should be noted that in both scatter plots we do have some evidence that possible non-linear models may be more appropriate, given the observation that the data points are starting to decrease in y value at the top range for x. It should also be noted that the sample sizes are quite small and we will assume that both relationships are linear within the multiple regression model. From this analysis we can identify three possible models identified in Table 10.9.

	Population	Sample
Model 1	$Y = \beta_0 + \beta_1 X_1$	$y = b_0 + b_1 x_1$
Model 2	$Y = \beta_0 + \beta_2 X_2$	$y = b_0 + b_2 x_2$
Model 3	$Y = \beta_0 + \beta_1 X_1 + \beta_2 X_2$	$y = b_0 + b_1 x_1 + b_2 x_2$

Table 10.9 Appropriate models identified from scatter plots

Table 10.9 shows the results of applying least squares regression for models 1, 2, and 3. The results show that model 3 represents a better fit to the data than models 1 and 2.

Model	Equation	COD
1	$\hat{y} = 8263 + 6.11 x_1$	84%
2	$\hat{y} = -3703 + 1.83 x_2$	86%
3	$\hat{y} = -3187 + 3.07 x_1 + 1.05 x_2$	92%

Table 10.10 Summary of results

✳ **Interpretation**   From the summary in Table 10.10 we can see that the third model is the best fit as 92% of variations in selling price is explained by the combined effect of both the land value and home improvements. Clearly, this is the superior model.

As before, to complete the solution you would then need to check the model assumptions and undertake an appropriate t test (or F test) to test whether the independent variable is a significant contributor to the dependent variable. The examples given here serve just as an illustration to indicate that there is much more depth to multiple regression analysis technique.

🖰 **Student Exercises**

X10.15 An estate agent is interested in developing a model to predict the house sales price based upon two other variables: size of property (SF given in square feet), and age. His initial analysis suggests a multiple model regression would be appropriate with the relationship between the dependent and independent variables being linear.

Use Excel ToolPak Regression to undertake the following tasks:

i. Fit the multiple regression model

ii. Check model reliability

iii. Undertake appropriate inference tests (F and t tests)

iv. Check model assumptions

P	SF	Age
205000	2650	13
215000	2664	6
215000	2921	3
199900	2580	4
190000	2580	4
180000	2774	2
156000	1920	1
144900	1710	1
137500	1837	4
127000	1880	8
125000	2150	15
123500	1894	14
117000	1928	18
115500	1767	16
111000	1630	15

■ Techniques in Practice

1. Coco S.A. has requested that a local property company undertake an analysis of property prices. The initial data collection has been undertaken, independent variables identified: square feet (SF), age, and local property tax (PT), and Excel regression analysis performed with the results presented below:

SUMMARY OUTPUT

Regression Statistics	
Multiple R	0.9057464
R Square	0.820376542
Adjusted R Square	0.807844673
Standard Error	19704.49335
Observations	47

ANOVA

	df	SS	MS	F	Significance F
Regression	3	76251638632	25417212877	65.46322267	4.50863E-16
Residual	43	16695483496	388267058		
Total	46	92947122128			

	Coefficients	Standard Error	t Stat	P-value	Lower 95%	Upper 95%	Lower 95.0%	Upper 95.0%
Intercept	4834.308436	12279.91482	0.393676056	0.695765602	-19930.49967	29599.11654	-19930.49967	29599.11654
SF	40.88092148	11.99641734	3.40776086	0.00143248	16.68784051	65.07400244	16.68784051	65.07400244
Age	-176.7561806	266.9396479	-0.66215784	0.511403472	-715.0912794	361.5789182	-715.0912794	361.5789182
PT	51.57131245	20.27040468	2.544167878	0.014628263	10.69214598	92.45047893	10.69214598	92.45047893

Figure 10.51

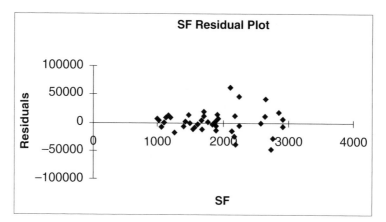

Figure 10.52

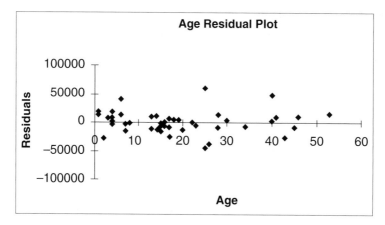

Figure 10.53

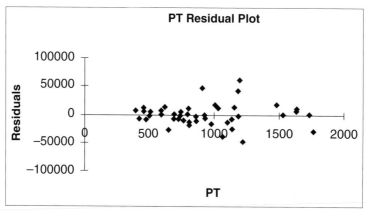

Figure 10.54

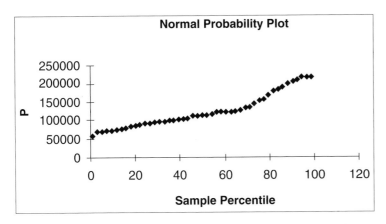

Normal Probability Plot

Figure 10.55

    i. State the least squares linear regression equation $\hat{y} = b_0 + b_1x_1 + b_2x_2$.

    ii. Comment on model reliability (r and COD).

    iii. Is the overall model significant (F test)?

    iv. Are the independent variables significant (t tests)?

    v. Check model assumptions (residual and normality checks).

2. Bakers Ltd is concerned at the possible relationship between the amount of fat (grams) and the number of calories in a popular pie.

Pie ID	Amount of Fat (grams)	Calories	Pie ID	Amount of Fat (grams)	Calories
1	19	410	16	33	597
2	31	580	17	31	583
3	34	590	18	37	589
4	35	570	19	39	640
5	39	640	20	23	456
6	39	680	21	43	660
7	43	660	22	22	448
8	22	465	23	30	577
9	28	567	24	34	594
10	38	610	25	35	590
11	35	576	26	41	638
12	22	434	27	34	560
13	40	690	28	43	660
14	43	660	29	45	680
15	21	435	30	29	587

(a) Plot a scatter plot and comment on a possible relationship between calories and the amount of fat in the pies.

(b) Use Excel Analysis ToolPak to undertake the following tasks:

    i. State the least squares regression model equation.

    ii. Comment on model reliability (r and COD).

iii. Is the independent variable significant (F or t test)?

iv. Check model assumptions (residual and normality checks).

3. Skodel Ltd employs a local transport company to deliver beers to local supermarkets. To develop better work schedules, the managers want to estimate the total daily travel time for their driver journeys. Initially the managers believed that the total daily travel time would be closely related to the number of miles travelled in making the daily deliveries.

Journey	Miles Travelled, x	Travel Time (hours), y	Journey	Miles Travelled, x	Travel Time (hours), y
1	100	9.3	11	85	7.4
2	50	4.8	12	62	6.4
3	100	8.9	13	98	8.4
4	100	6.5	14	58	4.9
5	50	4.2	15	73	6.8
6	80	6.2	16	81	7.8
7	75	7.4	17	66	6.2
8	65	6	18	72	7.3
9	90	7.6	19	53	4.4
10	90	6.1	20	56	4.6

(a) Plot a scatter plot and comment on a possible relationship between travel time and miles travelled.

(b) Use Excel Analysis ToolPak to undertake the following tasks:

i. State the least squares regression model equation.

ii. Comment on model reliability (r and COD).

iii. Is the independent variable significant (F or t test)?

iv. Check model assumptions (residual and normality checks).

■ Summary

In this chapter we have explored techniques that can be used to explore possible relationships between two variables using scatter plots and calculating appropriate numerical measures of association: Pearson and Spearman. The method used will depend upon the type of data within the data set as described in Table 10.11.

Data type	Statistic to measure association
Nominal (or category)	Chi square test (see Chapter 8)
Ordinal (or ranked)	Spearman's rank correlation coefficient
Interval (or ratio)	Pearson's correlation coefficient

Table 10.11 Using an appropriate measure to calculate association

If the initial data exploration shows that we have a possible relationship between y and x then we can attempt to fit an appropriate model to the data set using least squares regression. Within the chapter we have explored three methods: (i) fitting a line, (ii) fitting a curve and (iii) fitting linear multiple regression model to the data set. Excel will allow you to calculate the required statistics via its built in statistical functions or by making use of the Data Analysis ToolPak tool which includes the necessary statistics and appropriate assumption checking charts. The solution process consists of the following steps:

1. Construct scatter plot to visually assess the nature of a possible relationship between the variables.

2. Fit line or curve to data set using the identified relationship.

3. Calculate reliability statistics (COD and adjusted r^2 for multiple regression models).

4. For multiple regression models calculate the F test statistic to see if the combined model predictor coefficients are a significant contributor to the value of y.

5. Conduct appropriate t tests to check whether each predictor variable is a significant contributor to the value of y.

6. Conduct appropriate confidence intervals for the population slope.

7. Assess assumption violation checks.

■ Key Terms

Adjusted r^2	F test for simple regression models	Simple regression analysis
Assumptions		Slope
Autocorrelation	Homoscedasticity	Standard error of the estimate (SEE)
COD	Independence of errors	
Coefficient of correlation (Pearson)	Independent variable	Sum of squares for error (SSE)
	Interaction	
Coefficient of correlation (Spearman)	Interaction term	Sum of squares for regression (SSR)
	Least squares	
Coefficient of determination (COD)	Linear relationship	T test for multiple regression models
	Multiple regression model	
Coefficient of multiple determination	Normality	T test for simple regression models
	Outliers	
Confidence interval estimate of the mean value	Prediction interval for individual value	Total sum of squares (SST)
		Total variation
Dependent variable	Prediction line	Unexplained variation
Durbin-Watson	Regression analysis	Y intercept
Equal variance	Regression coefficient	
Explained variable	Residual	
Explanatory variable	Residual analysis	
F test for multiple regression models	Response variable	
	Scatter plot	

■ Further Reading

Textbook Resources

1. Whigham, D. (2007) *Business Data Analysis using Excel*. Oxford University Press. ISBN: 9780199296286.

2. Lindsey, J. K. (2003) *Introduction to Applied Statistics: A Modelling Approach* (2nd Edition). Oxford University Press. ISBN: 978-0-19-852895-1.

Web Resources

1. StatSoft Electronic Textbook http://www.statsoft.com/textbook/stathome.html (accessed 28/1/2007).

2. HyperStat Online Statistics Textbook http://davidmlane.com/hyperstat/index.html (accessed 28/1/2007).

3. Eurostat—website is updated daily and provides direct access to the latest and most complete statistical information available on the European Union, the EU Member States, the euro-zone and other countries http://epp.eurostat.ec.europa.eu (accessed 28/1/2007).

4. Economagic—contains international economic data sets (http://www.economagic.com) (accessed 28/1/2007).

5. The ISI glossary of statistical terms provides definitions in a number of different languages http://isi.cbs.nl/glossary/index.htm.

■ Formula Summary

$$\text{cov}(x, y) = \frac{\sum (x - \bar{x})(y - \bar{y})}{n - 1} \tag{10.1}$$

$$\rho = \frac{\sigma_{xy}}{\sigma_x \sigma_y} \tag{10.2}$$

$$r = \frac{1}{n} \sum \frac{(x - \bar{x})}{s_x} \frac{(y - \bar{y})}{s_y} \tag{10.3}$$

$$r = \frac{\sum xy \pm \dfrac{\sum x \sum y}{n}}{\sqrt{\left(\sum x^2 \pm \dfrac{(\sum x)^2}{n}\right)\left(\sum y^2 \pm \dfrac{(\sum y)^2}{n}\right)}} \tag{10.4}$$

$$t_{cal} = \frac{r - \rho}{\sqrt{\dfrac{1 - r^2}{n - 2}}} \tag{10.5}$$

$$t_{cal} = \frac{r}{\sqrt{\dfrac{1-r^2}{n-2}}} \qquad (10.6)$$

$$r_s = 1 - \frac{6 * \sum \left(X_r - Y_r\right)^2}{n\left(n^2 - 1\right)} \qquad (10.7)$$

$$t_{cal} = \frac{r_s - \rho_s}{\sqrt{\dfrac{1-r_s^2}{n-2}}} \qquad (10.8)$$

$$t_{cal} = \frac{r_s}{\sqrt{\dfrac{1-r_s^2}{n-2}}} \qquad (10.9)$$

$$r_s = \frac{t_{cal}}{\sqrt{t_{cal}^2 + n - 2}} \qquad (10.10)$$

$$z = r_s \sqrt{n-1} \qquad (10.11)$$

$$\hat{y} = b_0 + b_1 x + error \qquad (10.12)$$

$$\hat{Y} = \beta_0 + \beta_1 X \qquad (10.13)$$

$$b_1 = \frac{n\sum xy - \sum x \sum y}{n\sum x^2 - \left(\sum x\right)^2} \qquad (10.14)$$

$$b_0 = \frac{\sum y - b_1 \sum x}{n} \qquad (10.15)$$

$$Residual = y - \hat{y} \qquad (10.16)$$

$$SSR = \sum \left(\hat{y} - \bar{y}\right)^2 \qquad (10.17)$$

$$SSE = \sum \left(y - \hat{y}\right)^2 \qquad (10.18)$$

$$SST = \sum \left(y - \bar{y}\right)^2 \qquad (10.19)$$

$$SST = SSR + SSE \qquad (10.20)$$

$$SEE = \sqrt{\frac{SSE}{n-2}} \tag{10.21}$$

$$SEE = \sqrt{\frac{\Sigma(y - \hat{y})^2}{n-2}} \tag{10.22}$$

$$COD = \frac{\text{Regression sum of squares}}{\text{Total sum of squares}} = \frac{SSR}{SST} \tag{10.23}$$

$$COD = \frac{\Sigma(\hat{y} - \bar{y})^2}{\Sigma(y - \bar{y})^2} \tag{10.24}$$

$$COD = (\text{Correlation Coefficient})^2 = r^2 \tag{10.25}$$

$$t_{cal} = \frac{b_1 - \beta_1}{s_{b_1}} \tag{10.26}$$

$$s_{b_1} = \frac{S_{xy}}{\sqrt{SSX}} = \frac{SSE}{\sqrt{(x - \bar{x})^2}} \tag{10.27}$$

$$t_{cal} = \frac{b_1}{s_{b_1}} \tag{10.28}$$

$$F_{cal} = \frac{MSR}{MSE} \tag{10.29}$$

$$F_{cal} = \frac{COD/k}{(1 - COD)/(n - (k+1))} \tag{10.30}$$

$$\beta_1 = b_1 \pm t \times s_{b_1} \tag{10.31}$$

$$\hat{y} - e < y < \hat{y} + e \tag{10.32}$$

$$e = t_{cri} * SEE * \sqrt{1 + \frac{1}{n} + \frac{n*(x_p - \bar{x})^2}{n*(\Sigma x^2) - (\Sigma x)^2}} \tag{10.33}$$

$$\hat{y} = b_0 + b_1 x + b_2 x^2 \tag{10.34}$$

$$b_0 = \frac{\sum \hat{x}^4 \sum y - \sum \hat{x}^2 \sum \hat{x}^2 y}{n \sum \hat{x}^4 - \left(\sum \hat{x}^2\right)^2}$$

(10.35)

$$b_1 = \frac{\sum \hat{x} y}{\sum \hat{x}^2}$$

(10.36)

$$b_2 = \frac{n \sum \hat{x}^2 y - \sum \hat{x}^2 \sum y}{n \sum \hat{x}^4 - \left(\sum \hat{x}^2\right)^2}$$

(10.37)

(10.38)

$$\hat{x} = x - \overline{x}$$

$$\hat{y} = \beta_0 + \beta_1 x_1 + \beta_2 x_2 + \ldots\ldots\ldots\ldots + \beta_n x_n + error$$

(10.39)

11 Time Series Data and Analysis

The aim of this chapter is to provide the reader with a set of tools which can be used in the context of time series analysis and extrapolation. This chapter will allow you to apply a range of time series tools that can be used to tackle a number of business and other types of unrelated objectives (in economics, social sciences, etc.). These objectives range from calculating index changes, deflating prices and bringing the values to a constant value, extrapolating data, business forecasting, and reducing the uncertainty related to future events.

» Overview «

In this chapter we shall look at a range of methods that will be useful in helping us to solve problems using Excel, including:

- » Calculating and converting index numbers from one base to another.
- » Deflating prices and bringing them to a constant value.
- » Fitting a line to a time series.
- » Extrapolating the line in the future.
- » Using moving averages and exponential smoothing as forecasting methods.
- » Producing forecasts when dealing with the seasonal time series.
- » Learning how to calculate and interpret forecasting errors.
- » Learning how to assess the quality of forecasts by inspecting forecasting error.
- » Calculating the confidence interval for forecasts.

» Learning Objectives «

On successful completion of this chapter, you will be able to:

- » Understand how to use and recalculate index number.
- » Learn how to use indices to deflate prices.

» Understand the time series fundamentals.

» Inspect and prepare data for forecasting.

» Graph the data and visually identify patterns.

» Fit an appropriate model using the time series approach.

» Understand the concept of smoothing.

» Learn how to handle seasonal time series.

» Use the identified model to provide an extrapolation.

» Calculate a measure of error for the model fit to the data set.

» Learn how to calculate forecasting confidence interval.

» Solve time series related problems using Microsoft Excel.

11.1 Introduction to Time Series Data

Time series data are somewhat different from the majority of data sets we covered in this book. The chapter that deals with Linear Regression is the closest one to this one. So, what is a time series? A time series is a variable that is measured and recorded in equidistant units of time. A good example is inflation. We can record monthly inflation, quarterly inflation, or annual inflation. All three data sets represent a time series. In other words, it does not matter what units of time we use, as long they are consistent and sequential, then we will have time series data. By consistency we mean that we are not allowed to mix the units of time (daily with monthly data or minute with hourly data, for example). And by sequential we mean that we are not allowed to skip any data points and have zeros or empty values for this particular moment in time. Should this happen, we can somehow try to estimate the missing value by calculating the average of the two neighbouring values, or any other appropriate method. What is the purpose of time series analysis? Well, the main purpose of the majority of time series analysis methods is to predict the future movements of a variable. In other words, forecasting the future values is the main concern. In order to assess if the correct **forecasting** method has been used, a number of other auxiliary methods has been invented. They all fall in the category of time series analysis. Nevertheless, forecasting remains the main purpose.

11.1.1 Stationary and non-stationary time series

Example 11.1 consists of two different time series data sets. First of all, from column A we can see that in this case we have not specified the time units to which these two time series are referring to. In the text and the descriptor of the time series we would certainly do this, but for technical and calculation purposes this is not necessary. We can just use the words 'time period' and mark every observation with the sequential numbers starting from one onwards. This column will in fact become a variable, as we will see in the pages to follow, though a special kind of variable that contains sequential numbers. The second point to make here is that by just looking at the data, we can 'see' very little.

X

Time series A variable measured and represented per units of time.

Forecasting A method of predicting the future values of a variable, usually represented as the time series values.

Time period A unit of time by which the variable is defined (an hour, day, month, year, etc.).

▷ Example 11.1

The most important lesson here is: when dealing with the time series data, it is mandatory to *visualize* the data. Well, let's just do this. Figure 11.1 illustrates the two time series.

	A	B	C
	Period	Series 1	Series 2
1			
2	1	8	15
3	2	25	20
4	3	15	13
5	4	22	15
6	5	15	18
7	6	30	22
8	7	27	15
9	8	20	18
10	9	27	14
11	10	32	17

Figure 11.1

Figure 11.2 illustrates a time series plot for the Example 11.1 data set. What immediately jumps at us is that one of the time series seems to be moving upwards and the other one is following some horizontal line. The first time series is called **non-stationary**, whilst the second one, following a horizontal line, is called a **stationary time series**.

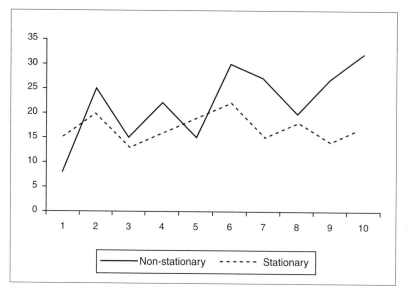

Figure 11.2

Figure 11.2 illustrates a graph of the two time series data sets.

In general, all time series will fall in the first or the second category. A variety of methods have been invented to handle either the stationary or non-stationary time series.

Non-stationary time series A time series that does not have a constant mean and oscillates around this moving mean.

Stationary time series A time series that does have a constant mean and oscillates around this mean.

> 📎 **Note**   Visualization and charting of a time series is not an optional extra, but one of the most essential steps in time series analysis. You can learn a lot about a variable by just looking at the time series graph.

11.1.2 Seasonal time series

In addition to the division above, every stationary and non-stationary time series can be either *seasonal* or *non-seasonal*. Again, a variety of methods exist to treat specifically **seasonal time series**. Here is an example of one seasonal stationary and one seasonal non-stationary time series.

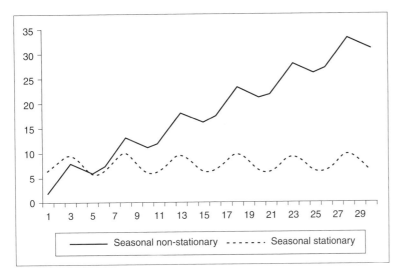

Figure 11.3

Figure 11.3 illustrates two seasonal time series data sets.

11.1.3 Univariate and multivariate methods

Besides the division to stationary and non-stationary time series and methods, the methods for handling time series can also be divided into univariate and multivariate methods. **Univariate** methods take just one single time series and try to produce a forecast for this time series independent of any other variable. The logic is that the influences of all other variables are already embedded into this single time series, so by just extrapolating it into the future, we extrapolate all the implicit influences of numerous other variables that have influenced this one. A good example would be taking the time series of the level of inventory for a particular product. We know that this inventory depends on many factors, such as the volume of sales (which depends on various market factors), speed of replenishment, etc. Rather than worrying about all these factors, we can say that they are implicitly embedded in our inventory time series. In other words, the history will tell us which way the future will unfold. This is the major assumption behind univariate time series methods, i.e. the history holds the clues for the future.

The opposite example is if we are trying to predict one variable by relating it to a number of other variables. We can take an example of inflation and try to predict this variable by anticipating how the interest rates will go, what will be the level of individual consumption, institutional investment, volume of money on the market, etc. If we have one variable that is dependent on a number of other variables that are treated as independent (often called the predictors), then the use of the so called **multivariate** methods is appropriate.

Seasonal time series A time series, represented in the units of time smaller than a year, that shows regular pattern in repeating itself over a number of these units of time.

Univariate methods Methods that use only one variable and try to predict its future values through some pre-defined method.

Multivariate methods Methods that use more than one variable and try to predict the future values of one of the variables by using the values of other variables.

> **Note**   Sometimes the methods that deal with time series are also divided into Causal
> regression methods and Time series methods. This is a bit of an old fashioned division as
> most of the methods have evolved to such a degree of complexity that it is difficult to say
> which one belongs where. Nevertheless, this chapter is dedicated only to a set of methods
> that belong to the family of time series methods.

11.1.4 Scaling the time series

We already emphasized that when dealing with time series, it is very important to chart the data and visually inspect the data set. Figure 11.4 illustrates how relevant this is.

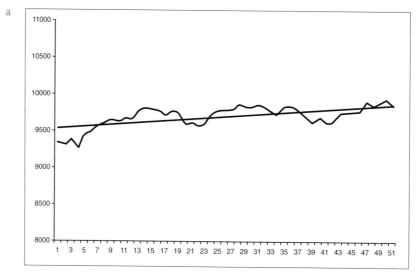

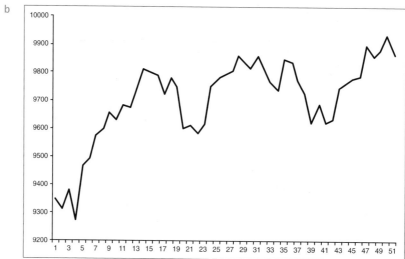

Figure 11.4 The same time series represented at two different scales

The above two time series are just one and the same time series, but visualized in two different ways. Both charts consist of the Dow Jones Industrial Average index arbitrarily taken between 25 Sep 2003 and 5 Dec 2003. However, the Y axis on the first chart is scaled to a smaller level of resolution and the second chart has a much larger scale. It is obvious that depending on the *scale*, we can 'see' almost two different time series. The way we visualize our time series and what our ultimate objectives are, will determine what method to apply. The first one could be approximated by some straight line, which is what we did, and the second one can be fitted with an nth term *polynomial line*.

> **Note**   The visual representation of the time series will often determine what method to use, although this is not the primary criterion. The choice of the method should be determined by the type of time series and the forecasting objectives.

The second example is also very illustrative. Let's look at the daily closing value of one of the companies quoted on the New York Exchange. The company is Emerson Electric (ticker EMR) and the daily closing values go from 5 Jan 1982 to 31 July 2008. The time series is 6700 observations long.

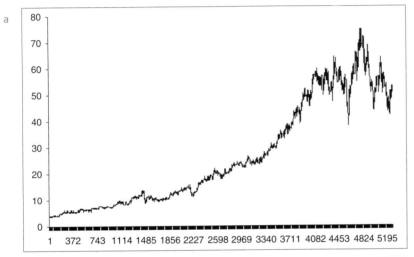

Figure 11.5 The same time series, one with normal scale and the other one at log scale

Again, two different charts showing the same data set. The first one is a normal line graph indicating that the closing daily stock values have grown almost exponentially with the exception of one part of time when the growth slowed down. The second graph shows the same data on a logarithmic scale, indicating a linear, steady growth of the closing stock values. The slowdown now looks less dramatic. As we can see, visualization is very important, as can be the transformation of the data, if necessary. **Transformations** can take various forms, such as taking the log values, calculating differences from the mean value of the series, simple differencing, etc. Most of these techniques are not described in this text, but some of the more basic are. It suffices to say that transformations help us with bringing our data in the shape so that a particular forecasting method can then be applied.

> **Note** A word about differencing as one of the more popular transformation methods. In certain instances we are compelled to use a method that is only applicable to stationary time series and the time series that we want to forecast is non-stationary. What do we do in this case? Most commonly used practice is to transform the non-stationary data series into a stationary one, then calculate the forecasts and then transform the forecasts back into the non-stationary values. How do we do this?
>
> One of the more often used transformation methods is to calculate the series mean and then subtract every value from the mean. If the newly created time series is stationary, we produce forecasts and then add them back to the mean value to recreate the non-stationary time series.
>
> Another even more often used method is differencing. The principle is to calculate the first differences of the series by subtracting every value from the preceding value and use this newly created series for forecasting. If the first differences do not convert the original non-stationary series into a stationary one (because the original time series is too dynamic), then the second differences are calculated. Second differences are differences of the differences. Here is a brief example of a differenced time series:

Y_t	Y_{t-1}	First difference $(Y_t - Y_{t-1})$		Second difference	
2	–	–		–	
3	2	1	$(3-2)$	–	
7	3	4	$(7-3)$	3	$(4-1)$
6	7	−1	$(6-7)$	−5	$(-1-4)$
9	6	3	$(9-6)$	4	$(3-(-1))$

X **Transformations** A method of changing the time series, usually to make it stationary. Most common method for transforming the time series is differencing or sometimes taking differences of every observation from the mean value.

Differencing A method of transforming a time series, usually to achieve stationarity. Differencing means that every current value in the time series is subtracted from the previous value.

Student Exercises

X11.1 Chart the following time series and decide if it is stationary and/or seasonal.

x	1	2	3	4	5	6	7	8	9	10
y	2	5	6	6	4	5	7	5	8	9

X11.2 The following time series is seasonal. What would you say is the periodicity of the seasonal component?

x	1	2	3	4	5	6	7	8	9	10	11	12	13	14	15
y	1	3	5	3	1	3	5	7	5	3	5	7	9	7	5

X11.3 Is it possible to have a time series that is non-seasonal and non-stationary? If so, what would you call it and can you draw a graph showing how such a series could look like?

X11.4 Go to one of the web sites that allow you to download financial time series (such as http://finance.yahoo.com/) and plot the series of your choice in several identical line graphs. Change the scale of the y-axis on every graph and make sure that they are radically different scales. What can you say about the appearance of every graph?

X11.5 Difference the time series from the exercise X11.1. Would you say that the differenced time series is stationary? If it was not what would you do to make it stationary?

11.2 Index Numbers

The simplest way to analyse time series data is to compare a value from one point in time with some other value at a different point in time. Example 11.2 represents average annual domestic crude oil prices in the USA from 1980–2007 (see Figure 11.6).

▷ Example 11.2

The price is given in $/bbl. In 1985, for example, the average price of oil was $26.92. In 2007, the same oil was priced at $64.20. The question we are interested in is: by how much has the 2007 nominal price changed when compared to the one from 1985?

Year	Average price of oil	Year	Average price of oil
1980	37.42	1994	15.66
1981	35.75	1995	16.75
1982	31.83	1996	20.46
1983	29.08	1997	18.64
1984	28.75	1998	11.91
1985	26.92	1999	16.56
1986	14.44	2000	27.39
1987	17.75	2001	23
1988	14.87	2002	22.81
1989	18.33	2003	27.69
1990	23.19	2004	37.66
1991	20.2	2005	50.04
1992	19.25	2006	58.3
1993	16.75	2007	64.2

Figure 11.6 Average annual domestic crude oil price in $/bbl

To answer this question we need to use index numbers.

Index numbers measure the change, typically expressed in percentages. To answer the question we introduced, all we have to do is to divide the price of oil from 2007 with the one from 1985 and multiply it by 100:

$$\text{Index change} = \frac{\text{Price from 2007}}{\text{Price from 1985}} \times 100 = \frac{64.20}{26.92} \times 100 = 238.00$$

Index number A value of a variable relative to its previous value at some base.

In other words, if the price in 1985 is treated as a **base index period** (which is equal to 100); then the price in 2007 is 138% higher than the one in 1985, i.e. $238 - 100 = 138$.

11.2.1 Simple indices

A general equation for calculating a **simple index** I_t at any point in time is:

$$I_t = \frac{y_t}{y_0} 100 \qquad (11.1)$$

Where y_t is the value for the year for which index is calculated and y_0 is the value for the base year. In our example above, this is:

$$I_{2007} = \frac{y_{2007}}{y_{1985}} 100 = \frac{64.20}{26.92} 100 = 238$$

Clearly it is easy to calculate indices in Excel. We show two examples using the same time series, one calculating indices for 1980 as the base year and the other one for 1992 as the base year. Figure 11.7 illustrates the Excel calculation procedure to calculate the required indices:

	A	B	C	D	E	F
		Average price	Index Year		Index Year	
1	Year	of oil in $/bbl	1980=100	Formulae	1992=100	Formulae
2	1980	37.42	100		194.39	=B2/$B$14*100
3	1981	35.75	95.54	=B3/$B$2*100	185.71	
4	1982	31.83	85.06	=B4/$B$2*100	165.35	
5	1983	29.08	77.71		151.06	
6	1984	28.75	76.83		149.35	
7	1985	26.92	71.94		139.84	
8	1986	14.44	38.59		75.01	
9	1987	17.75	47.43		92.21	
10	1988	14.87	39.74		77.25	
11	1989	18.33	48.98		95.22	
12	1990	23.19	61.97		120.47	
13	1991	20.2	53.98		104.94	=B13/$B$14*100
14	1992	19.25	51.44		100.00	
15	1993	16.75	44.76		87.01	=B15/$B$14*100
16	1994	15.66	41.85		81.35	
17	1995	16.75	44.76		87.01	
18	1996	20.46	54.68		106.29	
19	1997	18.64	49.81		96.83	
20	1998	11.91	31.83		61.87	
21	1999	16.56	44.25		86.03	
22	2000	27.39	73.20		142.29	
23	2001	23	61.46		119.48	
24	2002	22.81	60.96		118.49	
25	2003	27.69	74.00		143.84	
26	2004	37.66	100.64		195.64	
27	2005	50.04	133.73		259.95	
28	2006	58.3	155.80	=B28/$B$2*100	302.86	
29	2007	64.2	171.57	=B29/$B$2*100	333.51	=B29/$B$14*100

Figure 11.7 Index values of average oil price

Base index A value of a variable relative to its previous value at some fixed base.

Simple price index A value of a price for one item relative to the previous price for the same item at some base.

➔ **Excel Formula Method**

Index Value = Cell C3	Formula: =B3/$B$2*100
Cell C4	=B4/$B$2*100, etc.
Cell E4	=B2/$B$14*100
Cell E5	=B3/$B$14*100, etc.

✳ **Interpretation**

1. For the first index series: The price of oil in the year 2005, for example, was 33.73% (133.73 – 100) higher than the price of oil in 1980.

2. For the second index series: The price of oil in the year 1999, for example, was 13.97% (100 – 86.03) lower than the price of oil in 1992.

To convert indices from one year to another is very easy. Let's say that we want to know by how much the price of oil was higher in the year 2000 when compared to year 1990. Using the first series of indices, the one where 1980 is the base year, this is calculated as:

$$I_{2000} = \frac{I_{2000} - I_{1990}}{I_{1990}} \cdot 100 = \frac{73.20 - 61.97}{61.97} \cdot 100 = 18.12$$

If we tried to do the same for the second series of indices, the one where 1992 is the base year:

$$I_{2000} = \frac{I_{2000} - I_{1992}}{I_{1992}} \cdot 100 = \frac{142.29 - 120.47}{120.47} \cdot 100 = 18.11$$

The numbers behind the decimal point do not match due to the rounding error.

✳ **Interpretation**   Indices can be converted easily from one base to another. Regardless which series of indices we use, the price of oil in year 2000, for example, was 18% higher than the price of oil in 1990.

Rather than having a time series of indices on a fixed basis, i.e. starting from one particular year that is equal to 100, we can have indices on a year-to-year basis.

This effectively means that every previous year is equivalent to 100. Figure 11.8 illustrates the calculation procedure to calculate the average oil price and index values for oil prices.

	A	B	C	D
1	Year	Average price of oil in $/bbl	Index Change Year on Year	Formulae
2	1980	37.42	100	
3	1981	35.75	95.54	=B3/B2*100
4	1982	31.83	89.03	=B4/B3*100
5	1983	29.08	91.36	
6	1984	28.75	98.87	
7	1985	26.92	93.63	
8	1986	14.44	53.64	
9	1987	17.75	122.92	
10	1988	14.87	83.77	
11	1989	18.33	123.27	
12	1990	23.19	126.51	
13	1991	20.2	87.11	
14	1992	19.25	95.30	
15	1993	16.75	87.01	
16	1994	15.66	93.49	
17	1995	16.75	106.96	
18	1996	20.46	122.15	
19	1997	18.64	91.10	
20	1998	11.91	63.89	
21	1999	16.56	139.04	
22	2000	27.39	165.40	
23	2001	23	83.97	
24	2002	22.81	99.17	
25	2003	27.69	121.39	
26	2004	37.66	136.01	
27	2005	50.04	132.87	
28	2006	58.3	116.51	=B28/B27*100
29	2007	64.2	110.12	=B29/B28*100

Figure 11.8

→ **Excel Formula Method**

Index Value = Cell C3   Formula: =B3/B2*100
              Cell C4   =B4/B3*100, etc.

✳ **Interpretation**   The average oil price in 1985, for example, has dropped when compared to the previous year by 6.37% and the price in 2007, for example, has grown by 10.12% in comparison with the previous year.

The above series of numbers is very interesting as it actually shows us a percentage of change that takes place on a year-by-year basis. Using index numbers, we can calculate a number of other more complicated indices. This takes us to an example of aggregate price indices.

11.2.2 Aggregate indices

One of the best known **aggregate price indices** is the US Consumer Price Index (CPI). Similar aggregate indices exist in every country. This index is calculated every year (in fact it is calculated every month) by the US Bureau of Labor Statistics and it is a primary measure of changes in cost of living in the US. In fact, CPI measures changes in the cost of a typical market basket of goods and services. It is composed of housing prices, transportation, food, energy, medical care, etc. What is really important to understand is that CPI is a measure of inflation. Inflation is effectively calculated as the percentage change in the CPI from one year to the next (or one month to the next).

👆 **Example 11.3**

Figure 11.9 shows the value of CPI from 1980–2007 and they are calculated on the basis of year 2000.

Year	CPI 2000=100	Year	CPI 2000=100
1980	47.86	1994	86.08
1981	52.8	1995	88.49
1982	56.04	1996	91.09
1983	57.84	1997	93.22
1984	60.33	1998	94.66
1985	62.47	1999	96.73
1986	63.65	2000	100
1987	65.98	2001	102.83
1988	68.67	2002	104.46
1989	71.99	2003	106.83
1990	75.88	2004	109.69
1991	79.09	2005	113.41
1992	81.48	2006	117.07
1993	83.89	2007	120.41

Figure 11.9

Aggregate price index
A measure of the value of money based on a collection (a basket) of items and compared to the same collection of items at some base date or a period of time.

To calculate the value of CPI for year 2007, for example, when compared to the previous year, we can use the equation we have already introduced:

$$CPI_{2007} = \frac{I_{2007} - I_{2006}}{I_{2006}} 100 = \frac{120.41 - 117.07}{117.07} 100 = 2.85$$

✷ **Interpretation**   The annual inflation rate in the US, measured as CPI, in 2007 was 2.85%.

A more generic expression of the above equation is:

$$CPI_{YearA} = \frac{I_{YearA} - I_{YearB}}{I_{YearB}} 100 \qquad\qquad (11.2)$$

CPI has one very important quality and that is: it can be used as a price deflator. We can use CPI to convert (or deflate, hence the word deflator) prices from any year into the so called constant prices. This is sometimes called converting current dollars into real dollars, i.e. dollars free from the inflation.

11.2.3 Deflating values

Let's take the example of oil prices as before. Column B repeats the average annual price of the domestic crude oil in \$/bbl. These values are given in current dollars, i.e. the value of dollar in every given year. The second column shows us the values of the CPI index for every year, given on the basis of year 2000 = 100.

	A	B	C	D	E
1	Year	Oil Price	CPI 2000=100	Deflated to 2000 $ value	Formulae
2	1980	37.42	47.86	78.19	=B2*($C$22/C2)
3	1981	35.75	52.8	67.71	=B3*($C$22/C3)
4	1982	31.83	56.04	56.80	
5	1983	29.08	57.84	50.28	
6	1984	28.75	60.33	47.65	
7	1985	26.92	62.47	43.09	
8	1986	14.44	63.65	22.69	
9	1987	17.75	65.98	26.90	
10	1988	14.87	68.67	21.65	
11	1989	18.33	71.99	25.46	
12	1990	23.19	75.88	30.56	
13	1991	20.2	79.09	25.54	
14	1992	19.25	81.48	23.63	
15	1993	16.75	83.89	19.97	
16	1994	15.66	86.08	18.19	
17	1995	16.75	88.49	18.93	
18	1996	20.46	91.09	22.46	
19	1997	18.64	93.22	20.00	
20	1998	11.91	94.66	12.58	
21	1999	16.56	96.73	17.12	
22	2000	27.39	100	27.39	
23	2001	23	102.83	22.37	
24	2002	22.81	104.46	21.84	
25	2003	27.69	106.83	25.92	
26	2004	37.66	109.69	34.33	
27	2005	50.04	113.41	44.12	
28	2006	58.3	117.07	49.80	=B28*($C$22/C28)
29	2007	64.2	120.41	53.32	=B29*($C$22/C29)

Figure 11.10 Oil prices deflated with CPI

→ **Excel Formula Method**

Deflated Value = Cell D2   Formula: =B2*($C$22/C2)
                 Cell D3   =B3*($C$22/C3), etc.

To convert the prices of oil into a constant value, we need to deflate them. In our example we can **deflate** them by multiplying annual prices with their corresponding CPI that is divided by the base year, i.e. year 2000, as per our example: Price at time A = Price at time B x (CPI at time A/CPI at time B). In more general sense, this equation is:

$$P_A = P_B \frac{CPI_A}{CPI_B}$$

(11.3)

�֍ **Interpretation**   The price of oil in 2007, when expressed in constant dollar value for year 2000, was $53.32 (cell D29 in Figure 11.10). The price of oil in 1980, on the same basis, i.e. in constant year 2000 dollars, was $78.19 (cell D2 in Figure 11.10). This means that in real terms the price of oil in 1980 was much higher than in 2007.

Using the previously described technique for converting indices from one base to another, if we wanted to calculate the price of oil on the basis of constant value of US Dollar for the year 2007, the calculation is:

	A	B	C	D	E
1	Year	Oil Price	CPI 2000=100	Oil price in constant 2007 $	Formulae
2	1980	37.42	47.86	94.14	=B2*($C$29/C2)
3	1981	35.75	52.8	81.53	=B3*($C$29/C3)
4	1982	31.83	56.04	68.39	
5	1983	29.08	57.84	60.54	
6	1984	28.75	60.33	57.38	
7	1985	26.92	62.47	51.89	
8	1986	14.44	63.65	27.32	
9	1987	17.75	65.98	32.39	
10	1988	14.87	68.67	26.07	
11	1989	18.33	71.99	30.66	
12	1990	23.19	75.88	36.80	
13	1991	20.2	79.09	30.75	
14	1992	19.25	81.48	28.45	
15	1993	16.75	83.89	24.04	
16	1994	15.66	86.08	21.91	
17	1995	16.75	88.49	22.79	
18	1996	20.46	91.09	27.05	
19	1997	18.64	93.22	24.08	
20	1998	11.91	94.66	15.15	
21	1999	16.56	96.73	20.61	
22	2000	27.39	100	32.98	
23	2001	23	102.83	26.93	
24	2002	22.81	104.46	26.29	
25	2003	27.69	106.83	31.21	
26	2004	37.66	109.69	41.34	
27	2005	50.04	113.41	53.13	
28	2006	58.3	117.07	59.96	=B28*($C$29/C28)
29	2007	64.2	120.41	64.20	=B29*($C$29/C29)

Figure 11.11 Deflated oil prices with CPI

Deflating values
Converting current prices into constant prices by using one of the standard indices, such as CPI (Consumer Price Index).

The above table helps us with simple questions such as: Is the price of oil in 2007 of $64.20 higher in real terms than the price of oil of $37.42 in 1980? We can translate this into a question: how much is \$37.42 from 1980 worth in 2007 terms? This is calculated as: Adjusted Price = Old price * (CPI for 2007/CPI for 1980). In more general terms:

$$y_{t_{adj}} = y_t \left(\frac{CPI_{Fixed}}{CPI_t} \right) \tag{11.4}$$

✴ **Interpretation**   Given that the 2007 price of oil was \$64.20, this means that in 1980 the price of oil was equivalent to \$94.14. Using the constant value of dollars in 2007, the price of oil in 1980 was \$29.94 dollars more than the 2007 price of oil of \$64.20.

🖰 Student Exercises

X11.6 Calculate indices based on year 2000 for the series below. Could you convert them into indices based on year 2003?

Year	2000	2001	2002	2003	2004	2005	2006	2007	2008
Sales	230	300	290	320	350	400	350	400	420

X11.7 Use the CPI values from Figure 11.10 to convert the sales values from the student exercise X11.6 to a constant dollar value based on the 2004 value of the dollar.

X11.8 What is the real value of the sales value in 2007 if you put it on the constant year 2000 basis?

11.3 Trend Extrapolation

At the beginning of this chapter we classified not only the time series into various types but also various methods that deal with time series. It is our objective in this text to deal with univariate time series only and to describe just several basic time series analysis methods. **Classical time series analysis** starts with an assumption that every time series can be decomposed into four elementary components: (i) underlying **trend** (T), (ii) *cyclical* variations (C), (iii) *seasonal* variations (S), and (iv) **irregular** variations (I). Depending on a model, these components can be put together in different ways to represent the time series. The simplest of all is the so called *additive model*. It states that time series Y implicitly consists of the four components that are all added together:

$$Y = T + C + S + I \tag{11.5}$$

📎 **Note**   In addition to an additive model, a **multiplicative model** can also be used. Sometimes the most appropriate model is a **mixed** one. Here are two example of these models:

Multiplicative model: $Y = T \times C \times S \times I$
Mixed model: $Y = (T \times C \times S) + I$

The character of the data in time series will determine which model is the most appropriate.

Underlying trend is almost self explanatory, but we'll describe it further down. The **cyclical component** consists of the long-term variations that happen over a period of several years. If the time series is not long enough, sometimes we might not even be able to observe this component, because the cycle is either longer than our time series, or it is just not obvious. On the other hand, the seasonal component applies to seasonal effects happening within one year. Therefore, if the time series consists of annual data, there is no need to worry about the seasonal component. At the same time, if we have monthly data and our time series is several years long, then it will (potentially) consist of the seasonal as well as of the cyclical component. And finally, the irregular component is everything else that does not fit into any of the previous three components.

> **Note** A method of isolating different components in a time series, or decomposing the time series, is called the *classical time series decomposition* method. This is one of the oldest approaches to forecasting.

The whole area of classical time series analysis is concerned with the theory and practice of how to decompose a time series into these components, estimate them and then recompose to produce forecasts. We will not go into this method in any depth, but we'll look into the trend component.

11.3.1 A trend component

Let's say that, for practical purposes, we are only interested in estimating the trend and that all the remaining components can be grouped into something that we will call the **residuals** (R). In other words, time series Y in this simplified model now consists of only two components:

$$Y = T + R \qquad (11.6)$$

If a trend represents an underlying pattern that the time series follows, then the residuals are something that should **randomly** oscillate around the trend. In other words, if we can estimate the underlying trend of a time series, we will not worry about these random residuals fluctuating around the trend line. We can then extrapolate this trend. The trend becomes our forecast of the time series. Admittedly this forecast will not be 100% accurate as some residual value will be oscillating around the trend, but for all practical purposes, this might be exactly what we want. We are interested in just isolating the trend and extrapolating it into the future, which produces the forecast value for our time series.

> **Note** Fitting a trend to a time series and extrapolating it into the future is the most elementary form of forecasting.

Cyclical component A component in the classical time series analysis approach to forecasting that covers cyclical movements of the time series, usually taking place over a number of years.

Residuals The differences between the actual and predicted values. Sometimes called forecasting errors. Their behaviour and pattern has to be random.

Random component A component in time series analysis that has to act as a random variable, i.e. have some constant mean and the variance, as well as to exhibit no pattern.

11.3.2 Fitting a trend to a time series

If trend is the underlying pattern that indicates the general movements and the direction of time series, then this implies that a trend can be described by any regular curve. This usually means a smooth curve, either straight line, a parabola, a sinusoid, or any other well defined curve. Fortunately Excel is very well equipped to help us define the trend, fit it to time series, and extrapolate it into the future. Let's see what elementary types of trends are embedded in Excel and how to invoke them.

▷ Example 11.4

We'll use an artificially created time series that consists of only 30 observations.

Period	Series 1	Period	Series 1
1	8	16	38
2	25	17	43
3	15	18	55
4	22	19	54
5	15	20	56
6	30	21	49
7	27	22	46
8	20	23	58
9	27	24	60
10	32	25	59
11	30	26	62
12	35	27	65
13	39	28	60
14	35	29	58
15	55	30	62

Figure 11.12 A time series

When charted as a line graph, the time series looks as follows:

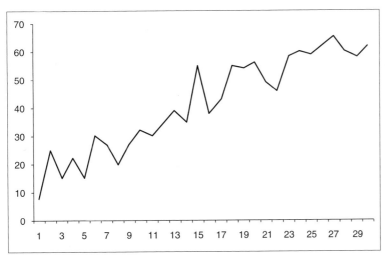

Figure 11.13

Figure 11.13 illustrates a time series graph based upon Example 11.4.

To find a trend that depicts any time series is a very easy graphical process in Excel, as we already demonstrated in Chapter 10 (see Figures 10.16–10.19). We right click anywhere on the time series. This invokes a dialogue box with several options included. We click on the one called 'Add Trendline...'. This invokes the next dialogue box, as below.

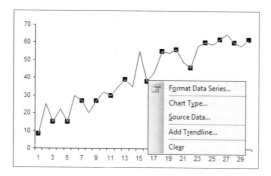

Figure 11.14 Getting Add Trendline function activated in Excel

We'll explain the meaning of the option tab, but at this point in time it suffices if we just select the Linear trend on the Type tab and click OK.

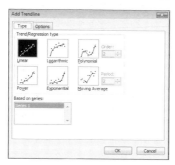

Figure 11.15 Selecting linear trend in Add Trendline option box

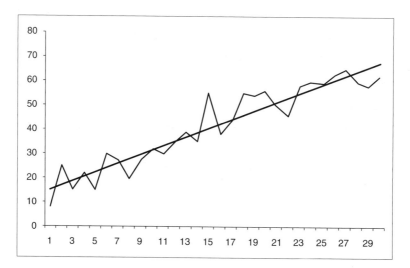

Figure 11.16 The final graph with the trend line automatically added

What we are getting here instantly is a straight line that describes the underlying movement and the direction of our time series.

11.3.3 Types of trends

Fitting a line to a time series is identical to establishing a regression line between two variables. The only difference is that in the case of time series analysis one of the variables has to be time. In Chapter 10 we reviewed briefly different types of curves that can be used to describe relationships between two variables. Before we go any further, let's look at all the options that Excel gives us. We can fit the following *types of trends* (or curves) to any data set: (a) linear trend, (b) logarithmic, (c) polynomial, (d) power, (e) exponential, and (f) moving average.

We'll go into a greater depth regarding the **linear trend**, but it suffices here to say that linear trend is described by a straight line equation, which is (following Excel notation):

$$Y = mx + b \qquad (11.7)$$

Logarithmic curve follows an equation such as:

$$Y = c \ln x + b \qquad (11.8)$$

Here c and b are constants and ln is natural logarithm function. The picture in the Excel dialogue box indicates that this trend has a form of an inverse exponential curve. The one that quickly reaches some high value, and then continues to grow much more slowly.

Polynomial curve comes in several degrees, i.e. 2nd, 3rd,..., all the way to 6th degree:

$$Y = b + c_1 x + c_2 x^2 + c_3 x^3 + c_4 x^4 + c_5 x^5 + c_6 x^6 \qquad (11.9)$$

In this case also b and c_1 to c_6 are constants. If you experiment with these curves, you will see that some of them translate into very dynamic curves making multiple turns and ups and downs.

Power function has a very simple equation, with c and b as constants:

$$Y = cx^b \qquad (11.10)$$

This trend is a parabolic trend that will continue to grow for ever.

Exponential trend also has two constants, c and b, and the equation is:

$$Y = ce^{bx} \qquad (11.11)$$

The symbol *e* is used for the basis of natural logarithms. Unlike the power trend which continues to grow at a constant rate, exponential trend moves slowly at the beginning and then resumes very fast change typified by exponential growth.

Moving averages trend is a special type of trend that we will cover further down as a separate heading, due to its special way of deployment.

11.3.4 Using a trend chart function to forecast time series

Earlier when we described how to right click on the time series chart to invoke the Trendline dialogue box, we did not describe what the Options tab means. Let's look at it and select several options. Figure 11.17 illustrates the Add Trendline dialogue box.

Figure 11.17

Linear trend model
A model that uses the straight line equation to approximate the time series.

Logarithmic trend
A model that uses the logarithmic equation to approximate the time series.

Polynomial trend
A model that uses an equation of any polynomial curve (parabola, cubic curve, etc.) to approximate the time series.

Power trend A model that uses an equation of a power curve (a parabola) to approximate the time series.

Exponential trend
An underlying time series trend that follows the movements of an exponential curve.

Moving averages
Averages calculated for a limited number of periods in a time series. Every subsequent period excludes the first observation from the previous period and includes the one following the previous period. This becomes a series of moving averages.

We have opted for automatic trend line that will move five periods in the future.

We also opted to display on the chart the trend equation as well as the R squared value. What will this look like and what is the meaning of all of this?

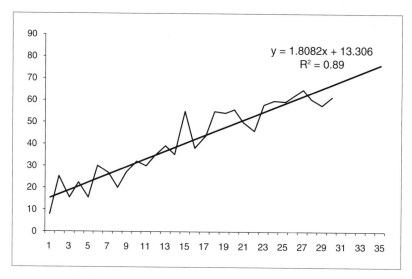

Figure 11.18 The final chart with the trend line, equation of the trend, and R squared value

First of all, we can see that the trend has now been extended five periods in the future, as expected. This is effectively our forecast.

We can see that the actual time series is not a smooth straight line, but it oscillates around one and we have identified it. By extrapolating our straight line, or linear trend in the future, we are stating that the actual line might be a bit adrift, but we believe that it will be inside some confidence factor, as we will describe later on. Excel does not just give us a pictorial of this trend line, but the actual equation of this line. By ticking an option in a dialogue box, we can see that this trend line is moving in accordance with the equation: $y = 1.802x + 13.306$. We'll explain this in a minute. The R squared (or R^2) value is 0.89. Let's refresh what we know about this statistic. When fitting a line to a data set, as we described in Chapter 10, we measure how closely the trend line fits the actual data. Every deviation is squared and all these values are summed to create Total Sum of Squares (SST). The theory suggests that the SST consists of the Regression Sum of Squares (SSR) and Residual Sum of Squares (SSE). R squared is a coefficient that measures how closely is the actual time series approximated (or fitted) by a trend line. The formula is:

$$R^2 = 1 - \frac{SSE}{SST}$$

(11.12)

R squared is actually the coefficient of determination (COD). As we know, the square root of this value would give us the coefficient of correlation. Clearly this coefficient is checking how closely the trend line and the actual time series are related. In effect it tells us how much of the time series variations are 'left out' after we fitted the trend line.

> **Note** The closer R^2 is to the value of 1, the better the fit of the trend to time series. In our case R squared is 0.89, which is very good. This confirms that our trend is approximating, or fitting, the data very well. Only 11% $(1 − 0.89 = 0.11)$ of data variations are not captured by the trend line. This is more than reasonable.

We said above that the trend line equation in this particular case was $y = 1.802x + 13.306$. Excel extrapolated five periods in the future for our trend line, but we do not know either the past values, or the future values of this trend line. All we have is the chart that does this for us. We need to learn how to calculate these values manually, or by using the built in Excel functions.

11.3.5 Trend parameters and calculations

The equation $y = 1.802x + 13.306$ is a specific case, fitted to our data set, of a generic Excel linear trend equation that we used before: $Y = mx + b$. In most of the textbooks this equation is written as $y = ax + b$ or $y = a + bx$. Whatever the case, the letter that stands alone (without x) is called an intercept and the other letter associated with x is called the slope. To avoid further confusion, let's standardize to a formula: $y = a + bx$. Clearly 'a' is an intercept and 'b' is a slope. In our case, the value of the intercept is 13.306 and the value of the slope is 1.802. Chapter 10 explains in greater depth the meaning of these two parameters, so let's go and just use them. To calculate our past and future trend values we just need these two parameters. The values of x are represented by the sequential numbers that represent time periods.

	A	B	C	D	E	F	G	H
1	Period	Series 1	Trend	Formulae			a=	13.306
2	1	8	15	=$H$1+$H$2*A2			b=	1.802
3	2	25	17	=$H$1+$H$2*A3				
4	3	15	19					
5	4	22	21					
6	5	15	22					
7	6	30	24					
8	7	27	26					
9	8	20	28					
10	9	27	30					
11	10	32	31					
12	11	30	33					
13	12	35	35					
14	13	39	37					
15	14	35	39					
16	15	55	40					
17	16	38	42					
18	17	43	44					
19	18	55	46					
20	19	54	48					
21	20	56	49					
22	21	49	51					
23	22	46	53					
24	23	58	55					
25	24	60	57					
26	25	59	58					
27	26	62	60					
28	27	65	62					
29	28	60	64					
30	29	58	66					
31	30	62	67	=$H$1+$H$2*A31				

Figure 11.19 illustrates the manual calculation of the trend. It indicates that we have put the value of the intercept in the cell H1 and the value of the slope in the cell H2.

Figure 11.19

→ **Excel Manual Method**

Intercept Value = Cell H1	Value = 13.306
Slope Value = Cell H2	Value = 1.802
Linear trend formula Cell C2	Formula: =$H$1+$H$2*A2
Cell C3	=$H$1+$H$2*A3, etc.

The forecasts are produced in the same way, as illustrated in Figure 11.20 which shows the calculation of the future values.

	A	B	C	D
1	Period	Series 1	Trend	Formulae
31	30	62	67	=$H$1+$H$2*A31
32	31		69	=$H$1+$H$2*A32
33	32		71	
34	33		73	
35	34		75	
36	35		76	=$H$1+$H$2*A36

Figure 11.20

Note   The future values of x should always be a sequential continuation of the period numbers used in the past. In our case, the last observation is for period 30, which means that the future values of x are 31, 32, ..., 35.

It is not necessary to use Excel graph function and chart the trend first to get the values of the intercept and the slope. Excel has built in function for both parameters. In cell H1 we could have invoked a function e.g. intercept.

Figure 11.21   Selection Intercept function

The slope function is invoked in exactly the same way and placed in cell H2. Both functions need to know the ranges for the values of y and x as follows: Y: B2:B31, and X: A2:A31.

Figure 11.22   Details for the Intercept function

Let's repeat that y represents the values of the time series and x represents the values of time period numbers. In Figure 11.19 the cells H1 and H2 could have been calculated as follows:

➜ **Excel Function Method**

Intercept Value = Cell H1   Formula: =INTERCEPT(B2:B31,A2:A31)
Slope Value = Cell H2   Formula: =SLOPE(B2:B31,A2:A31)
Linear trend formula Cell C2   Formula: =$H$1+$H$2*A2
                     Cell C3   =$H$1+$H$2*A3, etc.

Another approach is to use already 'pre-packaged' Excel functions dedicated to trend estimation, as already used in Chapter 11.

In cell C2, where we want the first value of trend to be calculated, we invoke the TREND function as illustrated in Figure 11.23.

This will trigger another dialogue box that needs to be completed. The values of *y*, as we said are the values of the time series (B2:B31) and the values of *x* are the values of time periods (A2:A31). New *x* is a specific period for which we are trying to calculate the trend value, which in our case is the period 1 (cell A2).

Figure 11.23

📎 **Note**   Pay attention to the values of *y* and *x*. They are entered as $B$2:$B$31 and $A$2:$A$31, respectively. They have to be referenced as fixed cells with the $ sign as otherwise if we copy down the formula, which we will, the range changes.

We can now copy the TREND function down from C2 all the way to C36, which will cover the historical and the future trend values.

📎 **Note**   As before, the values of *x* have to be the sequential numbers that continue from the last historical period number.

The future trend values are calculated just as in previous examples, i.e. by copying the TREND function all the way to the last future observation.

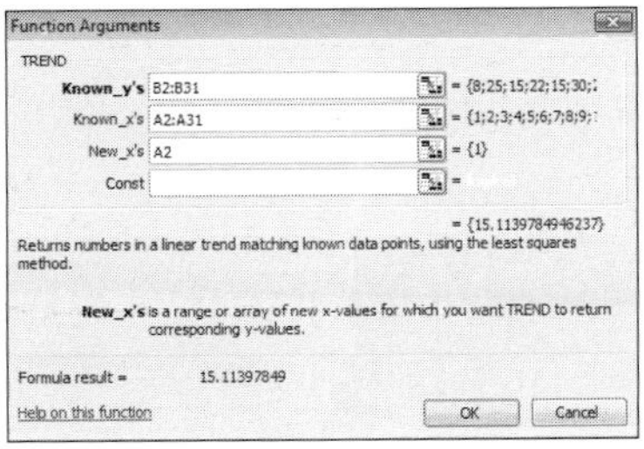

Figure 11.24 Using TREND function

→ **Excel Function Method 2**

Linear trend formula Cell C2   Formula: =TREND($B$2:$B$31,$A$2:$A$31,A2)

                     Cell C3   =TREND($B$2:$B$31,$A$2:$A$31,A3), etc.

Note The principles of calculating linear trend, as described here can be applied to other types of curves. The Manual and the Function method work with any curve. The Function method in addition to the TREND function can be applied to the GROWTH function. GROWTH is an Excel function that describes exponential trends. It is invoked and used exactly in the same way as the TREND function used for linear time series.

Student Exercises

X11.9 If the time series components were extracted as in the example below, how would you reconstruct the time series ($\hat{Y}$) using: a) additive model, b) mixed model?

T	90	95	100	105	110	115	120	125	130
C	2	4	6	4	2	4	6	4	2
I	5	3	4	6	5	6	4	5	4
$\hat{Y}$									

X11.10 If a time series can be best fitted with the trend whose equation is $y = a + bx + cx^2$, would you say that this is a linear model?

X11.11 R squared (R^2) is a measure of how closely a trend fits the time series. What is another expression for this statistic and in what context have we used it when discussing linear regression?

X11.12 Does R squared = 0.90 indicate a good fit? Why?

X11.13 Extrapolate the time series below three time periods in the future. Use TREND function. Why do you think it would not make sense to extrapolate this time series 10 time periods in the future?

X	1	2	3	4	5	6	7	8	9	10	11	12
Y	230	300	290	320	350	400	350	400	420			

11.4 Moving Averages and Time Series Smoothing

Let us use a simple Excel AVERAGE function to calculate the average value of a time series. We'll use a very short and artificial time series just for illustration purposes.

	A	B	C	D
1	Period	Series		
2	1	220		
3	2	250		
4	3	150		
5	4	220		
6	5	200		
7	Average	208	=AVERAGE(B2:B6)	

Figure 11.25

A very short time series in Figure 11.25 has an average value of 208. The above average value represents the series fairly well, because the series flows very much horizontally. Figure 11.26 depicts this.

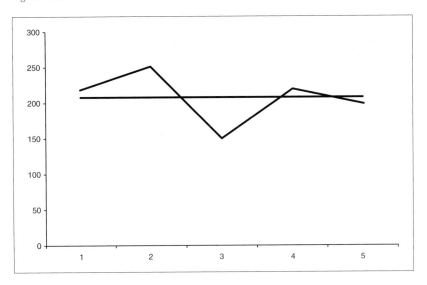

Figure 11.26 Time series and the mean value

As we know, the above sample time series can be called a stationary time series. However, if the series was moving upwards, or downwards, this average value would not be the best representation of the series. In this case a much more realistic representation would be some kind of moving average. We are effectively saying that in general a series of moving averages is a much more realistic representation for non-stationary time series.

11.4.1 Forecasting with moving averages

We'll show how to create *moving averages* and how to use this generic statistical tool for forecasting purposes.

We created another short time series and calculated moving averages in Figure 11.27.

	A	B	C	D	E
15	Period	Series	3MA	5MA	
16	1	150		252.0	
17	2	250	200.0	252.0	=SUM(B16:B18)/3
18	3	200	270.0	252.0	=SUM(B17:B19)/3
19	4	360	286.7	252.0	=SUM(B19:B20)/3
20	5	300		252.0	

Figure 11.27

→ **Excel Manual Method**

Moving average formula Cell C3   Formula: =SUM(B2:B4)/3

Cell C4   Formula: =SUM(B3:B5)/3, etc.

Moving averages are dynamical averages that change in accordance with the number of periods for which they are calculated. A general formula for moving averages is:

$$M_t = \frac{\sum_{i=t}^{t-N+1} x_i}{N}$$

(11.13)

In this formula t is the time period and N is the number of observations taken into calculation. It is clear that if we are using three observations as a basis for calculating moving averages then the first possible observation for which we can calculate the moving average is observation 3. The above formula can be simplified and expressed as:

$$M_t = \frac{x_t + x_{t-1} + x_{t-N+1}}{N}$$

(11.14)

The advantage of using an odd number for N and taking an odd number of elements into a formula, is that we can centre the moving average value in the middle of the interval, as per Figure 11.27. This implies that most of the time we'll use the odd number of interval, as it is easier to centre the values. In our case, the moving average for period two is calculated as:

$$M_2 = \frac{x_3 + x_2 + x_1}{3} = \frac{150 + 250 + 200}{3} = 200$$

Note   Formula 11.14 can also be rewritten as: $M_t = M_{t-1} + \frac{x_t - x_{t-N}}{N}$. In other words, if we do not know the value of the first observation in the moving average interval, we can still estimate the current moving average from the previous value of the moving average, plus the other value from the interval. Although this might appear to be a useless fact here, you will see why we mentioned it when we discuss exponential smoothing.

What happens if we extend the number of observations in the moving average interval? Let's look what happens if we take all the values from the series to constitute the interval.

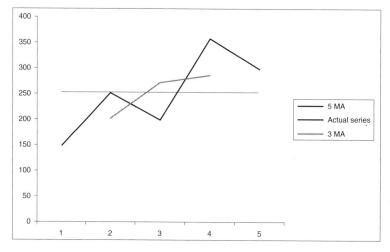

Figure 11.28

As Figure 11.28 shows, they simply became the overall average. This implies that the larger the number of observations used for calculating the moving average, the smoother and more horizontal the line representing it will be.

> 📎 **Note** It is a general principle that the larger the number of moving averages in the formula, the 'smoother', or less dynamic, the time series of moving averages will be.

Let us now use a little longer time series and see how to use moving averages for forecasting purposes. If a series is horizontal (stationary) and we just want to predict a single future value of this series, we already said that using a simple average value of the series is almost as good as any other method.

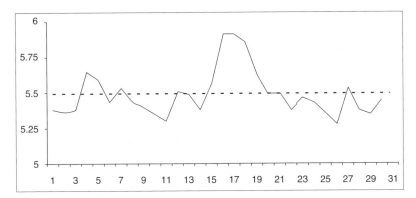

Figure 11.29

Figure 11.29 shows such a stationary series with 30 observations and its mean value that was used to predict the 31st observation.

The advantage of this simple method is that it can be extended further in the future. If we need to forecast for the next five observations, we just extend the mean line. By definition, if a series is stationary it fluctuates around its mean. Therefore, the mean is its best predictor. This method does not produce very accurate forecasts, but the results will be accurate enough. To add more sophistication to our forecasting and to try to emulate the movements of the original series, we need to see how to use the principle of moving averages. We'll use the same Excel method as in Chapter 11.3.2. To remind you how we added a trend line to a time series, we right click on the time series, which will invoke a dialogue box with several options included. We then click on the option called 'Add Trendline...'. This invokes the next dialogue box, and we select the moving averages option and change the number of periods to 3 as illustrated in Figure 11.30.

Excel will automatically start charting the moving average from the last observation in the period specified (in this case three). If we selected a 5-period moving average, then the moving average function would start from observation five. This is somewhat different to the advice we gave earlier when we recommended that moving average should be centred in the middle of the interval for which it is calculated. A simple reason for this is that here we are trying to predict the series, and this is going to help us to achieve this.

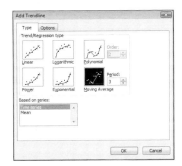

Figure 11.30

So, how is the moving average approach used to produce forecasts? All we need to do is to shift the moving average plot, as produced by Excel, by one observation. In other words, the moving average value for the first three observations (assuming we are using moving averages for three periods) becomes the forecast for the fourth observation. The fifth observation is predicted by using the second three-period moving average (observations two to four), etc. Figure 11.31 illustrates the point for three-period moving averages.

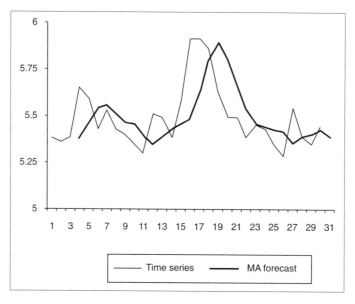

Figure 11.31

However, there are two difficulties associated with this approach. First of all, we cannot extend our forecast beyond just one future period, which means that this method can only be used as a short term forecasting method that predicts only one future observation.

	A	B	C	D
1	Period	Series	3MA	
2	1	5.38		
3	2	5.36		
4	3	5.38		
5	4	5.65	5.37	=AVERAGE(B2:B4)
6	5	5.59	5.46	=AVERAGE(B3:B5)
7	6	5.43	5.54	=AVERAGE(B4:B6)
8	7	5.53	5.56	=AVERAGE(B5:B7)
9	8	5.43	5.52	=AVERAGE(B6:B8)
10	9	5.4	5.46	
29	.	.	.	
30	28	5.38	5.39	
31	29	5.35	5.40	
32	30	5.45	5.42	=AVERAGE(B28:B31)
33	31		5.39	=AVERAGE(B30:B32)

Figure 11.32

The other issue is that Excel will not shift the moving average plot if we are using the Add Trendline wizard. We need to calculate moving averages manually. Figure 11.32 shows how they were calculated in this particular case.

➡ **Excel Formula Method**

Moving averages Cell C5   Formula: =AVERAGE(B2:B4)

            Cell C6   =AVERAGE(B3:B5), etc.

Forecast Cell C33   Formula: =AVERAGE(B29:B32)

As stated earlier, we need to remember that the more we extend the number of periods used for calculating the moving average, the smoother the curve will be. If we take into account all the observations in the series, needless to say, we will have only one moving average value and it will be identical to the mean value of the overall time series.

> **Note** Moving averages are acceptable forecasting technique, providing we are interested in forecasting only one future period.

11.4.2 Exponential smoothing concept

In order to introduce the **exponential smoothing** method, we need to assume that one of the ways to think about observations in a time series is to say that the previous value in the series, plus some error element, is the best predictor of the current value (in particular if we are dealing with a stationary time series) as given by equation (11.15):

$$\hat{y}_t = y_{t-1} + e_t \tag{11.15}$$

With a bit of imagination, we can say that every forecasted value in the series is built that way, i.e. it depends on the previous forecasted value, plus some error term. The error term is, as specified in Chapter 10, defined as a difference between the actual value and the forecasted value, i.e. $e_t = y_t - F_t$. This means we can rewrite the above formula as:

$$F_t = F_{t-1} + (y_{t-1} - F_{t-1}) \tag{11.16}$$

Let us now assume that the error element, i.e. $(y_t - F_t)$ is zero. In this case the future forecast is the same as the present forecast. However, if it is not zero, then under certain circumstances we might be interested in taking just a fraction of this error, i.e.:

$$F_t = F_{t-1} + \alpha(y_{t-1} - F_{t-1}) \tag{11.17}$$

> **Note** Why a fraction of an error? If every current forecast/observation depends on the previous one and this one depends on the one before etc., then all the previous errors are in fact embedded in every current observation/forecast. By taking a fraction of error, we are in fact discounting the influence that every previous observation and its associated error has on current observations/forecasts.

We use letter α to describe the fraction and the word 'fraction' implies that α takes values between zero and one. If $\alpha = 0$, then current forecast is the same as the previous one. If $\alpha = 1$, then current forecast is also the same as the previous one, plus the full amount of the deviation between the previous actual and forecasted value. In order to take just a fraction of that deviation, α has to be greater than zero and smaller than one, i.e. $0 < \alpha < 1$. The forecasts calculated in such a way are in fact smoothing the actual observations. If we plot both the original observations and these newly calculated 'back-forecasts' of the series, we'll see that the back-forecast curve is eliminating some of the dynamics that the

Exponential smoothing
One of the methods of forecasting that uses a constant (or several constants) to predict future values by 'smoothing' the past values in the series. The effect of this constant decreases exponentially as the older observations are taken into calculation.

original observations exhibit. It is a smoother time series. We'll change the notation and start referring to F_t as S'_t, or the smoothed values. The previous formula is in this case:

$$S'_t = S'_{t-1} + \alpha(y_{t-1} - S'_{t-1}) \qquad (11.18)$$

The above formula can be rewritten differently, which is often used, as:

$$S'_t = \alpha y_t + (1 - \alpha) S'_{t-1} \qquad (11.19)$$

> **Note** We could have derived to the above formula in a different way. You will recall from the section on moving averages that we've said that: $M_t = M_{t-1} + \dfrac{y_t - y_{t-N}}{N}$, which can be rewritten as $M_t = \dfrac{1}{N} y_t + (1 - \dfrac{1}{N}) M_{t-1}$. If we say $\alpha = \dfrac{1}{n}$ that and that M_t is another expression for S_t, then we can see how we got equation (11.19).

Equations (11.18) and (11.19) are identical and it is a matter of preference which one to use. They both provide identical smoothed approximations of the original time series. This approach to forecasting is called the single exponential smoothing method, and we will explain shortly why the word 'exponential' is used.

> **Note** We implied that the smaller the α (i.e. the closer α to zero), the smoother the series of newly calculated values is. Conversely, the larger the α (i.e. the closer α to one), the more impact the deviations have and potentially the more dynamic the fitted series is. When $\alpha = 1$, the smoothed values are identical to the original values, i.e. no smoothing is taking place.

The smoothing constant α and the number of elements in the interval for calculating moving averages are in fact related. The formula that defines this relationship is:

$$\alpha = \frac{2}{M + 1} \qquad (11.20)$$

In the formula above, M is a number of observations used to calculate the moving average. The formula indicates that the moving average for three observations that we used earlier is equivalent to $\alpha = 0.5$. Equally, $\alpha = 0.2$ is equivalent to M = 9, etc. So, the smaller the value of the smoothing constant, the more horizontal the series will be, just like in the case when larger number of moving averages is used.

> **Note** If we substituted in the formula for exponential smoothing all the previous values from the series we would see that effectively we are multiplying the newer observations with higher values of α and the older data in the series with the smaller values of α. By doing this we are in effect assigning a higher importance to the more recent observations. As we move further in the past, the value of α falls exponentially. This is the reason why we call it exponential smoothing. In essence, every value in the series is affected by all those that precede it, but the relative weight (importance) of these preceding values declines exponentially the further we go in the past.

11.4.3 Forecasting with exponential smoothing

The formula for exponential smoothing can easily be applied in Excel. As an example, we can use the same short time series we used to demonstrate how to use moving averages, illustrated in Figure 11.33.

	A	B	C	D
1	Period	Yi	Si'	
2	1	150	150	=B2
3	2	250	180	=$B$7*B3+(1-$B$7)*C2
4	3	200	186	=$B$7*B4+(1-$B$7)*C3
5	4	360	238.2	=$B$7*B5+(1-$B$7)*C4
6	5	300	256.74	=$B$7*B6+(1-$B$7)*C5
7	$\alpha =$	0.3		

Figure 11.33 Applying simple exponential smoothing

→ **Excel Formula Method**

Constant α Cell B7		Value = 0.3
Exponential smoothing Cell C3		Formula: =$B$7*B3+(1-$B$7)*C2
	Cell C4	Formula: =$B$7*B4+(1-$B$7)*C3, etc.

As was the case with moving averages, in order to forecast one value in the future, we need to shift the exponential smoothing calculations by one period ahead. The last exponentially smoothed value will in effect become a forecast for the following period.

Note Simple exponential smoothing, just like the moving averages method is an acceptable forecasting technique, providing we are interested in forecasting only one future period.

As an alternative to this formula method, Excel gives us an option to use exponential smoothing method from the Data Analysis add-in pack. To apply it, we need to go to the Tools menu, and select the Data Analysis option. In the dialogue box that follows, select Exponential Smoothing, as illustrated in Figure 11.34.

Figure 11.34 Activating the Data Analysis add-in pack

Selecting the Data Analysis option will trigger another dialogue box in which some of the parameters need to be defined. Figure 11.35 shows an example of selecting a data range A1:A30.

Note WARNING: Excel uses the expression 'Damping factor', rather than smoothing constant, or α. Damping factor is defined as $(1-\alpha)$. In other words, if you want α to be 0.1, you must specify in Excel the value of damping factor as 0.9.

If in the dialogue box we select the options to display the chart as well as the standard errors.

Figure 11.35 Selecting data set for exponential smoothing from Data Analysis add-in

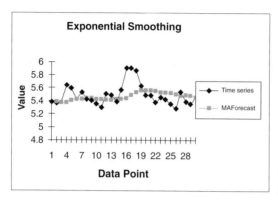

Figure 11.36 Data analysis chart output for exponential smoothing option

Part of the Excel output is also the spreadsheet, and Figure 11.37 displays the formulae contained in this spreadsheet (only the first 15 cells are shown here).

	A	B	C
1	5.38	#N/A	#N/A
2	5.36	=A1	#N/A
3	5.38	=0.1*A2+0.9*B2	#N/A
4	5.65	=0.1*A3+0.9*B3	#N/A
5	5.59	=0.1*A4+0.9*B4	=SQRT(SUMXMY2(A2:A4,B2:B4)/3)
6	5.43	=0.1*A5+0.9*B5	=SQRT(SUMXMY2(A3:A5,B3:B5)/3)
7	5.53	=0.1*A6+0.9*B6	=SQRT(SUMXMY2(A4:A6,B4:B6)/3)
8	5.43	=0.1*A7+0.9*B7	=SQRT(SUMXMY2(A5:A7,B5:B7)/3)
9	5.4	=0.1*A8+0.9*B8	=SQRT(SUMXMY2(A6:A8,B6:B8)/3)
10	5.35	=0.1*A9+0.9*B9	=SQRT(SUMXMY2(A7:A9,B7:B9)/3)
11	5.3	=0.1*A10+0.9*B10	=SQRT(SUMXMY2(A8:A10,B8:B10)/3)
12	5.51	=0.1*A11+0.9*B11	=SQRT(SUMXMY2(A9:A11,B9:B11)/3)
13	5.49	=0.1*A12+0.9*B12	=SQRT(SUMXMY2(A10:A12,B10:B12)/3)
14	5.38	=0.1*A13+0.9*B13	=SQRT(SUMXMY2(A11:A13,B11:B13)/3)
15	5.57	=0.1*A14+0.9*B14	=SQRT(SUMXMY2(A12:A14,B12:B14)/3)

Figure 11.37 Exponential smoothing Data Analysis add-in sheet output

First of all, Excel always ignores the first observation and produces exponential smoothing from the second observation. It also cuts short with the exponential smoothing values, as the last exponentially smoothed value corresponds with the last observation in the series. You can easily extend the last cell one period in the future to get a short term forecast.

The second thing that becomes obvious is that you cannot change the values of α and see automatically what effect this has on your forecasts. This means that you would be better off producing your own set of formulae, as shown in Figure 11.38.

	A	B	C	D
1	Period	Data	Exp. Smoothing	0.1
2	1	5.38		
3	2	5.36	=B2	
4	3	5.38	=$D$1*B3+(1-$D$1)*C3	
5	4	5.65	=$D$1*B4+(1-$D$1)*C4	
6	5	5.59	=$D$1*B5+(1-$D$1)*C5	
7	6	5.43	=$D$1*B6+(1-$D$1)*C6	
8	7	5.53	=$D$1*B7+(1-$D$1)*C7	
9	8	5.43	=$D$1*B8+(1-$D$1)*C8	
10	9	5.4	=$D$1*B9+(1-$D$1)*C9	
11	10	5.35	=$D$1*B10+(1-$D$1)*C10	
12	11	5.3	=$D$1*B11+(1-$D$1)*C11	
13	12	5.51	=$D$1*B12+(1-$D$1)*C12	
14	13	5.49	=$D$1*B13+(1-$D$1)*C13	
15	14	5.38	=$D$1*B14+(1-$D$1)*C14	
16	15	5.57	=$D$1*B15+(1-$D$1)*C15	

Figure 11.38 Manual calculations for exponential smoothing

The advantage of our formulae approach is that, providing we have a chart open that includes the data from the column B and exponentially smoothed values from the column C, we can see immediately the effects of changing the value of α (Cell D1) on our overall forecast.

Figure 11.39 shows the impact two different values of α have on forecasts. As expected, smaller α makes forecasts smoother and larger α makes them more dynamic.

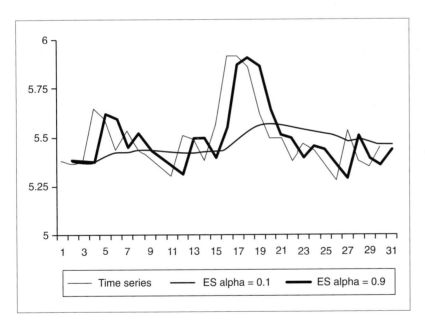

Figure 11.39

The formulae in column B in Figure 11.37 are Excel equivalent of equation (11.19). This essentially means that the current smoothed value is the forecast for the next period, or: $S_t = \hat{Y}_{t+1}$. In this case we can rewrite the equation as:

$$\hat{Y}_{t+1} = \alpha y_t + (1 - \alpha)\hat{Y}_t \qquad (11.21)$$

Another way to express the same equation is:

$$\hat{Y}_{t+1} = \hat{Y}_t + \alpha e_t \qquad (11.22)$$

Or, indeed, yet another way to say the same is:

$$\hat{Y}_{t+1} = y_t - (1 - \alpha)e_t \qquad\qquad (11.23)$$

This last equation takes us back to equation (11.21), confirming that the forecasts in this method are exponentially weighted moving averages. The word weighted is equivalent of saying discounted, where $(1 - \alpha)$ is the discount factor (or, a damping factor as it is termed in Excel).

> **Note**　It is important to remember that equation (11.18), (11.19), (11.21), (11.22), and (11.23) all say the same thing and we are free to use whichever we think is easiest to implement.

If we go back to Excel's printout (Figure 11.37) we will see that it does provide one interesting and useful piece of information, that is, we automatically get the value of the standard error. The formula that Excel uses to calculate this starts in cell C5 as: =SQRT(SUMXMY2(A2:A4,B2:B4)/3) and the value in the last cell, i.e. cell C31 is: =SQRT(SUMXMY2(A28:A30,B28:B30)/3). What is the meaning of this formula, why is it different from the formula for standard error we used in Chapter 10 and is this the only way to calculate the standard errors? There are several ways of calculating standard error. We will cover this topic in Section 11.6.

Student Exercises

X11.14　By including more observations in a moving average interval, would you say that it will 'smooth' the time series more than moving averages calculated on the basis of the fewer observations included in the moving average interval?

X11.15　Can you extrapolate a time series 5 time periods in the future using the moving average forecasting method? What is the reason?

X11.16　Is there a difference between the two expressions: $S'_t = S'_{t-1} + \alpha(y_{t-1} - S'_{t-1})$ and $S'_t = \alpha y_t + (1 - \alpha)S'_{t-1}$? Why is it called exponential smoothing?

X11.17　If the value of the smoothing constant α is 0.25, what is the corresponding number of moving averages that has the same effect on the time series when approximated?

X11.18　Produce two forecasts for the enclosed time series using exponential smoothing. Use $\alpha = 0.1$ for the first set of forecasts and $\alpha = 0.9$ for the second set of forecasts. What can you conclude?

X	1	2	3	4	5	6	7	8	9
Y	230	300	290	320	350	400	350	400	420

X11.19　If the Damping Factor in Excel Data Analysis add-in is defined as 0.65, what is the equivalent value of the smoothing constant (α)?

X11.20 Produce forecasts for the time series in Exercise X11.18 by using exponential smoothing formula in the format: $\hat{Y}_{t+1} = \hat{Y}_t + \alpha e_t$. Make sure that you first write the formula for the forecasts and errors just for the first row. Once you see the values in the spreadsheet, copy down both cells simultaneously. If you try to enter the forecasts first, you will get errors, as the formula requires inclusion of the errors.

11.5 Seasonal Models

We mentioned briefly that time series can also be **seasonal** in nature. Seasonality is measured by the number of periods after a particular pattern repeats itself. It does not mean that the values will be identical, just that the pattern will have similar features. Using classical methods, such as time series decomposition, we could break the time series down into its constituent components, such as trend, **seasonal component** and the irregular component. According to this classical method, we can then recompose the time series using one of the models (additive, multiplicative, or mixed). In this section we will use a different approach. We will combine exponential smoothing with some of the model re-composition methods.

Earlier in this chapter we fitted a time series using linear trend. The equation for the straight line used as a trend was: Y = a + bx. You will also recall that we said that various time series components (trend, cyclical, seasonal, and irregular) can be added together to form a time series decomposition model. As we said, this additive relationship is only one of several possible. In fact, sometimes the components form not an additive, but a multiplicative model. Which one is the correct one is beyond the scope of this book but it suffices to say that it will primarily depend on the type of time series used. In order to introduce one of the possible approaches to handling the seasonal time series, we need to accept that we can use either an additive or a multiplicative model. They are defined as follows:

$$F_{t+m} = a_t + S_{t-s+m} \tag{11.24}$$

$$F_{t+m} = a_t S_{t-s+m} \tag{11.25}$$

> **Note** As a general guidance, multiplicative models are better suited for time series that show dramatic growth or decline, whilst additive models are more suited for less dynamic time series.

Seasonal correlation A correlation between the observations given in the corresponding units of time within which the seasonality repeats itself.

Seasonal component A component in the classical time series analysis approach to forecasting that covers seasonal movements of the time series, usually taking place inside one year's horizon.

Classical additive time series model One of the models in classical time series analysis that assumes that components (trend, cyclical, seasonal, and random component) need to be added to compose the time series.

Just as with the linear trend, the coefficient a_t is an intercept of the series, but in this case a dynamic one. We'll explain this. S_{t-s+m} have a function of a slope, but it is called a seasonal component. The meaning of the symbols s and m in the subscript $t+m$ and $t-s+m$ is: $s=$ number of periods in a seasonal cycle, and $m=$ number of forecasting periods (forecasting horizon). The main feature of this approach is that we can use exponential smoothing to estimate dynamical values of not just the seasonal component, but of the intercept too. For an additive model, these two factors are calculated as follows:

$$a_t = \alpha(y_t - S_{t-s}) + (1 - \alpha)a_{t-1} \tag{11.26}$$

$$S_t = \delta(y_t - a_t) + (1 - \delta)S_{t-s} \tag{11.27}$$

For a multiplicative model, these two factors are calculated as follows:

$$a_t = \alpha\left(\frac{y_t}{S_{t-s}}\right) + (1 - \alpha)a_{t-1} \tag{11.28}$$

$$S_t = \delta\left(\frac{y_t}{a_t}\right) + (1 - \delta)S_{t-s} \tag{11.29}$$

As we can see, unlike the simple exponential smoothing which required only one smoothing constant, here we are using two smoothing constants, alpha (α) and delta (δ). In both cases we need to initialize the values of a_t and S_t. This is achieved, for additive models, by calculating a_s, from equation (11.30):

$$a_s = \frac{\sum_{t=1}^{s} y_t}{s} \tag{11.30}$$

Where, $t = 1, 2, ..., s$ and $a_t = a_s$. In other words, the first s number of a_s are calculated as an average of all the corresponding actual observations. The initial values of S_t are calculated as:

$$S_t = y_t - a_t \tag{11.31}$$

For the multiplicative model a_s is calculated in the same way as in (11.31) and S_t is calculated as:

$$S_t = \frac{y_t}{a_t} \tag{11.32}$$

The forecasts are produced as follows. To produce back forecasts (i.e. m = 0) for a current period, for example at $t = 15$, and assuming that $s = 4$, we would use the following equation:

$$F_{15+0} = a_{15} + S_{15-4+0} = a_{15} + S_{11}$$

If the series has only twenty observations, for example, and we want to produce the forecast for the 23rd period, the forecast is calculated as:

$$F_{20+3} = a_{20} + S_{20-4+3} = a_{20} + S_{19}$$

For a multiplicative model we use the same principle, except that the components are not added but multiplied. Figure 11.40 gives an example of an additive model.

	A	B	C	D	E	F	G	H
1	Period	Quarter	Series	a_t	S_t	Seas. Forec.	0.5	=alpha
2	1	Q1	17.15	17	-0.06		0.50	=delta
3	2	Q2	19.87	19	1.04		2.036	=MSE
4	3	Q3	20.53	21	-0.39			
5	4	Q4	20.78	22	-0.97			
6	5	Q1	16.80	19	-1.28	19.25		
7	6	Q2	15.87	17	-0.08	18.11		
8	7	Q3	17.13	17	-0.28	16.90		
9	8	Q4	18.11	18	-0.52	17.22		
10	9	Q1	13.85	17	-2.05	15.38		
11	10	Q2	19.67	18	0.69	18.13		
12	11	Q3	20.29	19	0.31	19.11		
13	12	Q4	20.94	20	0.00	19.90		
14	13	Q1	16.99	20	-2.39	17.68		
15	14	Q2	18.96	19	0.33	19.69		
16	15	Q3	24.84	22	1.70	22.08		
17	16	Q4	23.11	22	0.33	22.43		
18	17	Q1	21.12	23	-2.12	20.58		
19	18	Q2	21.03	22	-0.24	22.17		
20	19	Q3	24.55	22	1.95	24.04		
21	20	Q4	25.90	24	1.14	24.29		
22	21	Q1	17.35	22	-3.25	19.59		
23	22	Q2	17.57	20	-1.22	19.52		
24	23	Q3	18.19	18	1.07	19.95		
25	24	Q4	21.66	19	1.77	20.40		
26	25	Q1				19.20		
27	25	Q2				20.30		
28	25	Q3				18.87		
29	25	Q4				18.29		

Figure 11.40 Calculating seasonal forecasts using the simple seasonal additive exponential smoothing model

→ **Excel Formula Method—seasonal additive exponential smoothing method**

Alpha α Cell G1	Value = 0.5
Delta δ Cell G2	Value = 0.5
MSE Cell G3	Formula: =SUMXMY2(C6:C21,F6:F21)/COUNT(C6:C21)
a_t Cells D2:D5	Formula: =(C2+C6+C10+C14+C18+C22)/6
	=(C3+C7+C11+C15+C19+C23)/6
	=(C4+C8+C12+C16+C20+C24)/6
	=(C5+C9+C13+C17+C21+C25)/6
Cells D6:D25	=$G$1*(C6–E2)+(1–$G$1)*D5
	=$G$1*(C7–E3)+(1–$G$1)*D6, etc.
S_t Cells E2:E5	Formula: =C2–D2
	=C3–D3, etc.
Cells E6:E25	Formula: =$G$2*(C6–D6)+(1–$G$2)*E2
	=$G$2*(C7–D7)+(1–$G$2)*E3, etc.
Forecast F_t Cells F6:F25	Formula: =D6+E2
	=D7+E3, etc.
Cells F26:F29	Formula: =$D$25+E2
	=$D$25+E3, etc.

Cells G1 and G2 contain the values of constants alpha and delta, whilst cell G3 contains MSE (Mean Square Error). We assigned the initial values to both alpha and delta as 0.5 each.

By inputting manually the value of 0.5 in cells G1 and G2 as the values of constants alpha and delta, in cell G3 we automatically get the value of MSE to be 2.036.

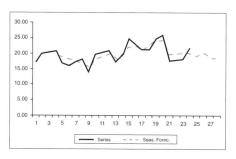

Figure 11.41 Initial forecast chart

Cell G3 contains MSE (Mean Square Error) and the Excel formula we used for MSE is: =SUMXMY2(C6:C21,F6:F21)/COUNT(C6:C21). This formula will be fully explained in the next section and we'll use it here just as a method for estimating the values of alpha and delta. We used Excel's solver function to find the optimum values of alpha and delta. Let us explain how this is done. We put manually any value to cells G1 and G2, in our example 0.5 in each cell. After that we put together all the formulae and calculate forecasts. Once this is done, we click on cell G3 where the formula for MSE resides. From the Tools pop-down menu we select Solver... function (Figures 11.42–11.43).

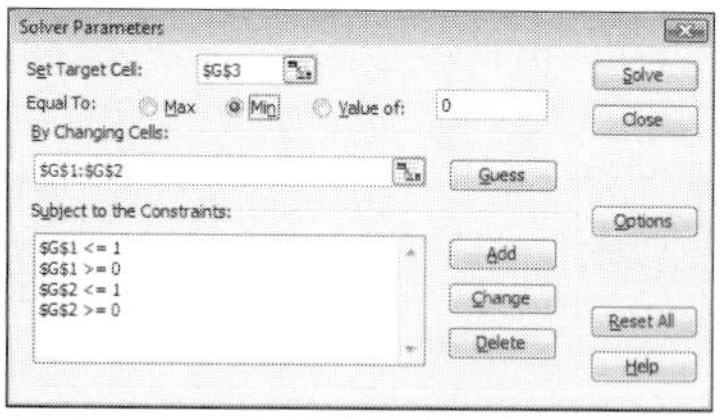

Figure 11.43 Solver parameters dialogue box

Figure 11.42 Solver function

In the solver dialogue box we specify that we want cell G3 to take the minimum value, by changing cell G1 and G2, under the condition that both cells G1 and G2 should never exceed zero or 1.

Note   If the Solver add-in does not show in the Tools menu go to Tools > Add-Ins and switch on the Solver add-in.

This changes all the calculated cells automatically and produces the forecast as per Figure. 11.44. As we can see, the Solver has changed the values of alpha and delta, which in turn had an effect on all our formulae and forecast.

	A	B	C	D	E	F	G	H
1	Period	Quarter	Series	a_t	S_t	Seas. Forec.	1	=alpha
2	1	Q1	17.15	17	-0.06		0.57	=delta
3	2	Q2	19.87	19	1.04		0.000	=MSE
4	3	Q3	20.53	21	-0.39			
5	4	Q4	20.78	22	-0.97			
6	5	Q1	16.80	17	-0.06	16.80		
7	6	Q2	15.87	15	1.04	15.87		
8	7	Q3	17.13	18	-0.39	17.13		
9	8	Q4	18.11	19	-0.97	18.11		
10	9	Q1	13.85	14	-0.06	13.85		
11	10	Q2	19.67	19	1.04	19.67		
12	11	Q3	20.29	21	-0.39	20.29		
13	12	Q4	20.94	22	-0.97	20.94		
14	13	Q1	16.99	17	-0.06	16.99		
15	14	Q2	18.96	18	1.04	18.96		
16	15	Q3	24.84	25	-0.39	24.84		
17	16	Q4	23.11	24	-0.97	23.11		
18	17	Q1	21.12	21	-0.06	21.12		
19	18	Q2	21.03	20	1.04	21.03		
20	19	Q3	24.55	25	-0.39	24.55		
21	20	Q4	25.90	27	-0.97	25.90		
22	21	Q1	17.35	17	-0.06	17.35		
23	22	Q2	17.57	17	1.04	17.57		
24	23	Q3	18.19	19	-0.39	18.19		
25	24	Q4	21.66	23	-0.97	21.66		
26	25	Q1				22.57		
27	25	Q2				23.67		
28	25	Q3				22.24		
29	25	Q4				21.66		

Figure 11.44 Revised forecast

Figure 11.45 illustrates the forecast using the seasonal exponential smoothing method.

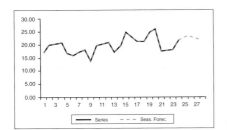

We observe from Figure 11.45 that the forecast values are a good fit to the actual data values. As we can see this method, although fairly simple, produces impressive results.

Figure 11.45

🖱 Student Exercises

X11.21 For what kind of time series would you use a multiplicative vs. additive seasonal exponential smoothing model?

X11.22 Why are seasonal parameters a_t and S_t in the seasonal exponential smoothing method called dynamic parameters?

X11.23 What is the role of MSE in the seasonal exponential smoothing method?

11.6 Forecasting Errors

11.6.1 Error measurement

One of the primary reasons for using forecasting as a tool is to try to reduce uncertainty. The better the forecasts, the lower the uncertainty that surrounds the variable we forecast. We can never eliminate uncertainty, but good forecasts can reduce it to an acceptable level. What would we consider to be a good forecast? An intuitive answer is that it has to be the one that shows the smallest error when compared with an actual event. The problem with this statement is that we cannot measure the error until the event happened, by which time it is too late to say that our forecast was, or was not, good. In a way, we would like to measure the error before the future unfolds. How do we do this? As we demonstrated in this chapter, when forecasting, we always used the model to back-fit the existing time series. This is sometimes called back-casting, or more appropriately, ex-post forecasting. Once we produced **ex-post forecasts**, it is easy to measure deviations from the actual data. These deviations are **forecasting errors** and they will tell us how good our method or model is.

> ✳ **Interpretation**   The main assumption we make here is: whichever model shows the smallest errors in the past, it will probably make the smallest errors when extrapolated in the future. In other words, the model with smallest historical errors will reduce the uncertainty that the future brings. This is the key assumption.

Calculating errors, or engaging in **error measurement**, is one of the easiest tasks. We can define an error as a difference between what actually happened and what we thought would happen. In the context of forecasting time series and models, error is the difference between the actual data and the data produced by a model, or ex-post forecasts. This can be expressed with an equation:

$$e_t = A_t - F_t, \quad \text{or} \quad e_t = y_t - F_t \tag{11.33}$$

Where e_t is an error for a period t, A_t is the actual value in a period t and F_t is forecasted value for the same period t. Figure 11.46 shows an example of how to calculate forecasting errors.

×
Ex-post forecasts Values produced from a forecasting model that are fitted to historical data.

Forecasting errors A difference between the actual and the forecasted value in the time series.

Error measurement A method of validating the quality of forecasts. Involves calculating the mean error, the mean squared error, the percentage error, etc.

	A	B	C	D
1	Period	Actual	Forecast	Error
2	1	100	130	-30
3	2	250	150	100
4	3	150	210	-60
5	4	220	250	-30
6	5	320	320	0
7	Sum	1040	1060	-20

Figure 11.46

In the above example, using some simple method, we produced back-forecasts that clearly deviate from the actual historical values. Figure 11.47 shows the results in a graphical way.

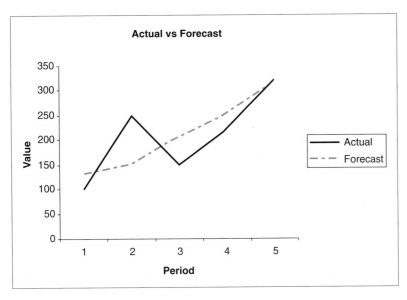

Figure 11.47 A chart showing actual and forecasted values

For period 1 (t = 1) our method exceeded actual values, which is presented as –30, because errors are calculated as actual minus forecasted. For period t = 2, our method underscored by 100. For period 6 (t = 6), for example, our method was perfect and it had not generated any errors. What can we conclude from this? If these were the first five weeks of our new business venture, and if we add all these numbers together, then our cumulative forecast for these five weeks would have been 1060. In reality the business generated 1040. This implies that the method we used made a cumulative error of –20, or given the above formula, it overestimates the reality by 20 units. If we divide this cumulative value by the number of weeks to which it applies, i.e. 5, we get the average value of our error:

$$\bar{e} = \frac{\Sigma\left(A_t - F_t\right)}{n} = \frac{-20}{5} = -4$$

✳ **Interpretation**   The average error that our method generates per period is –4 and because errors are defined as differences between the actual and forecast values, this means that on average the actual values are by 4 units *higher* than our forecast. Given earlier assumptions that the method will probably continue to perform in the future as in the past (assuming there are no dramatic or step changes), our method will probably generate similar errors in the future.

Assuming that we decided to experiment with some other method and assuming that the average error that this other method generated was 2, which method would you rather use to forecast your business venture? The answer, hopefully, is very straightforward. The second method is somewhat pessimistic (the actual values are by 2 units per period *below* the forecasted values), but in absolute terms 2 is less than 4. Therefore we would recommend the second method as a much better model for forecasting this particular business venture. In the above example, we have not only decided which forecasting method reduces uncertainty more, but we have also learned how to use two different ways of measuring this uncertainty. Using errors as measures of uncertainty, we learned how to calculate an average, or mean error, and we implied that an absolute average error also makes sense to be estimated. In practice, other error measurements are used too.

11.6.2 Types of errors

In fact, many error measurements are used to assess how good the forecasts are. The four more commonly used error measurements are the **mean error (ME)**, the mean absolute error (sometimes called the **mean absolute deviation** and abbreviated as **MAD**), the **mean square error (MSE)**, and the **mean percentage error (MPE)**. These errors are calculated as follows:

$$ME = \frac{\Sigma\left(A_t - F_t\right)}{n} = \frac{\Sigma e_t}{n} \tag{11.34}$$

$$MAD = \frac{\Sigma\left|A_t - F_t\right|}{n} = \frac{\Sigma\left|e_t\right|}{n} \tag{11.35}$$

$$MSE = \frac{\Sigma\left(A_t - F_t\right)^2}{n} = \frac{\Sigma e_t^2}{n} \tag{11.36}$$

$$MPE = \frac{\Sigma\left(\dfrac{A_t - F_t}{A_t}\right)}{n} = \frac{\Sigma\left(\dfrac{e_t}{A_t}\right)}{n} \tag{11.37}$$

Sometimes MPE causes problems in Excel (due to negative values), in which case it is better to estimate the **mean absolute percentage error (MAPE)**:

$$MAPE = \frac{\Sigma\left(\dfrac{\left|A_t - F_t\right|}{A_t}\right)}{n} = \frac{\Sigma\left(\dfrac{\left|e_t\right|}{A_t}\right)}{n} \tag{11.38}$$

In Excel it is very easy to calculate these errors. Using our previous short example, these errors are calculated as shown in Figure 11.48.

	A	B	C	D	E	F	G	H	I
1	Period	Actual	Forecast	Error	MAD	MSE	MPE	MPE %	MAPE
2	1	100	130	-30	30	900	-0.3	-30	0.3
3	2	250	150	100	100	10000	0.4	40	0.4
4	3	150	210	-60	60	3600	-0.4	-40	0.4
5	4	220	250	-30	30	900	-0.1	-13.6	0.1
6	5	320	320	0	0	0	0	0	0
7	Sum	1040	1060	-20	220	15400	-0.43636	-43.6363636	1.236364
8	Average	208	212	-4	44	3080	-0.08727	-8.72727273	0.247273

Figure 11.48 Calculating various errors

Mean error (ME) The mean value of all the differences between the actual and forecasted values in the time series.

Mean absolute deviation (MAD) The mean value of all the differences between the actual and forecasted values in the time series. The differences between these values are represented as absolute values, i.e. the effects of the sign are ignored.

Mean square error (MSE) The mean value of all the differences between the actual and forecasted values in the time series. The differences between these values are squared to avoid positive and negative differences cancelling each other.

Mean percentage error (MPE) The mean value of all the differences between the actual and forecasted values in the time series. The differences between these values are represented as percentage values.

Mean absolute percentage error (MAPE) The mean value of all the differences between the actual and forecasted values in the time series. The differences between these values are represented as absolute percentage values, i.e. the effects of the sign are ignored.

→ **Excel Formula Method**

ME Cells D2:D6	Formula: =B2–C2	
	=B3–C3, etc.	
MAD Cells E2:E6	Formula: =ABS(D2)	
	=ABS(D3), etc.	
MSE Cells F2:F6	Formula: =D2^2	
	=D3^2, etc.	
MPE Cells G2:G6	Formula: =D2/B2	
	=D3/B3, etc.	
MPE % Cells H2:H6	Formula: =D2/B2*100	
	=D3/B3*100, etc.	
MAPE Cells I2:I6	Formula: =E2/B2	
	=E3/B3, etc.	
SUM Actual Cell B7	Formula: =SUM(B2:B6)	
Average Actual Cell B8	Formula: =AVERAGE(B2:B6)	
SUM Forecast Cell C7	Formula: =SUM(C2:C6)	
Average Forecast Cell C8	Formula: =AVERAGE(C2:C6)	
SUM ME Cell D7	Formula: =SUM(D2:D6)	
Average ME Cell D8	Formula: =AVERAGE(D2:D6)	
SUM MAD Cell E7	Formula: =SUM(E2:E6)	
Average MAD Cell E8	Formula: =AVERAGE(E2:E6)	
SUM MSE Cell F7	Formula: =SUM(F2:F6)	
Average MSE Cell F8	Formula: =AVERAGE(F2:F6)	
SUM MPE Cell G7	Formula: =SUM(G2:G6)	
Average MPE Cell G8	Formula: =AVERAGE(G2:G6)	
SUM MPE % Cell H7	Formula: =SUM(H2:H6)	
Average MPE % Cell H8	Formula: =AVERAGE(H2:H6)	
SUM MAPE Cell I7	Formula: =SUM(I2:I6)	
Average MAPE Cell I8	Formula: =AVERAGE(I2:I6)	

The column H in Figure 11.48 is identical to the column G. The only difference is that we used Excel percentage formatting to present the numbers as percentages, rather than decimal values. Rather than calculating individual errors (as in columns D to I) and adding all the individual error values (as in row 7) or calculating the average (as in row 8), we could have calculated all these errors with a single formula line for each type of error. Using some of the built-in Excel functions, these errors can be calculated as:

→ **Excel Formula Method—Alternative**

ME Cell D8	Formula: =(SUM(B2:B6)–SUM(C2:C6))/COUNT(B2:B6)
MAD Cell E8	Formula: ={SUM(ABS(D2:D6))/COUNT(D2:D6)}
MSE Cell F8	Formula: =SUMXMY2(B2:B6,C2:C6)/COUNT(B2:B6)
MPE Cell G8	Formula: ={SUM(((B2:B6)–(C2:C6))/(B2:B6))/COUNT(B2:B6)}
MAPE Cell I8	Formula: ={SUM(ABS((B2:B6)–(C2:C6))/(B2:B6))/COUNT(B2:B6)}

> **Note** Note that MAD, MPE, and MAPE formulae have curly brackets on both sides of the formulae. Do not enter these brackets manually. Excel enters the brackets automatically if after you typed the formula you do not just press the Enter button, but CTRL+SHIFT+ENTER buttons (i.e. all three at the same time). This means that the range is treated as an *array*.

Just for the sake of clarity, Figures 11.49 and 11.50 reproduce the spreadsheet as it should look like if the single cell formulae for the error calculations were used. Again, note that the curly brackets for MAD, MPE, and MAPE are not visible by observing formulae in cells D10, D12, and D13. However, they are visible in the formula bar.

	A	B	C	D	E	F
				fx {=SUM(ABS(D2:D6))/COUNT(D2:D6)}	C11	
1	Period	Actual	Forecast	Error		
2	1	100	130	-30		
3	2	250	150	100		
4	3	150	210	-60		
5	4	220	250	-30		
6	5	320	320	0		
7	Sum	1040	1060	-20		
8	Average	208	212	-4		
9						
10			ME =	-4		
11			MAD =	44		
12			MSE =	3080		
13			MPE =	-0.08727		
14			MAPE =	0.247273		

Figure 11.49

	A	B	C	D
	C11		fx {=SUM(ABS(D2:D6))/COUNT(D2:D6)}	
1	Period	Actual	Forecast	Error
2	1	100	130	=B2-C2
3	2	250	150	=B3-C3
4	3	150	210	=B4-C4
5	4	220	250	=B5-C5
6	5	320	320	=B6-C6
7	Sum	=SUM(B2:B6)	=SUM(C2:C6)	=SUM(D2:D6)
8	Average	=AVERAGE(B2:B6)	=AVERAGE(C2:C6)	=AVERAGE(D2:D6)
9				
10			ME =	=(SUM(B2:B6)-SUM(C2:C6))/COUNT(B2:B6)
11			MAD =	=SUM(ABS(D2:D6))/COUNT(D2:D6)
12			MSE =	=SUMXMY2(B2:B6,C2:C6)/COUNT(B2:B6)
13			MPE =	=SUM(((B2:B6)-(C2:C6))/(B2:B6))/COUNT(B2:B6)
14			MAPE =	=SUM(ABS((B2:B6)-(C2:C6))/(B2:B6))/COUNT(B2:B6)

Figure 11.50 Single cell formulae for calculating the ME, MAD, MSE, MPE, and MAPE

The ability to calculate all these aggregate errors with a single formula will become one of many useful features that will be explored later on when we start comparing forecasts.

11.6.3 Interpreting errors

How do we interpret the above five different error measurements? We have already said that ME indicates that the actual data are on average 4 units per period above the forecasted values. This is a good indication, but the problem is that positive and negative deviations eliminate each other, so we might end up with a forecast that jumps up and down around the actual values, never providing exact forecasts, yet the ME could be zero. To eliminate the above problem with ME, we can calculate MAD. MAD indicates that if we eliminate overestimates and underestimates of our forecasts, a typical bias that our method shows (regardless whether it is positive or negative) is 44 units per period. This is typical error, regardless of the direction in which our forecasts went when estimating the actual values.

The meaning of the MSE is more difficult to interpret, for a simple reason that we have taken the square values of our errors. What is a square value of something? The rational is as follows: if there are some big deviations of our forecast from the actual values, then in order to magnify these deviations we need to square them. Let's take an example of two hypothetical errors for a period. Let one error reading show 2 and the other one 10. The second error is 5 times larger than the first one. However, when we square these two numbers, number 100 (10 x 10) is 25 times larger than number 4 (2 x 2). This is what we mean by magnifying large errors. So, the higher the MSE, the more extreme deviations from the actual values are contained in our forecast. This is particularly useful when comparing two forecasts. If MSE obtained from the first forecast is larger than the MSE from the second, then the first forecast contains more extreme deviations than the second one.

The interpretation of the MPE is very intuitive. It tells us that on average an error constitutes x% of the actual value, or as in our case, MPE = −8.73%. This means that on average our forecasting errors overshot the actual values by 8.73% (remember that negative error means forecasts overshooting the actual values and positive error means undershooting). However, this implies that just like with the ME we could have a series of overshoots and undershoots (as in our example), yet gaining an average value of almost zero. The mean absolute percentage error (MAPE) addresses this problem. It shows us the value of 0.2473. In other words, if we disregard positive and negative variations of our forecasts from the actual values, we are on average making an absolute error of 24.73%.

11.6.4 Error inspection

At the beginning of this chapter on time series, we mentioned that forecasting errors should be treated as the residual element, in other words, something that is moving completely randomly when observed visually. Regardless of the forecasting method, errors should always be calculated and inspected. Should these errors follow any kind of pattern, the forecasting method must be treated as suspect. In fact, forecasting errors are often required to adhere to some formal assumptions, such as: independence, normality, and homoscedasticity (see Chapter 10.2.4 for full explanation). The meaning of some of these terms is not just that we do not want to see any pattern among the errors (residuals), but also that they should be independent of each other, normally distributed, and have a constant variance (homoscedasticity). Some rigorous tests exist to help us determine if the residuals violate any of these assumptions, but they are beyond the scope of this book. One of the most elementary steps to take after we produced our forecasts is to visually check the residuals/errors. Figure 11.51 shows an example of plotting forecasting errors. It appears that the residuals are flowing in a random fashion and do not show any pattern, which is exactly what we wanted.

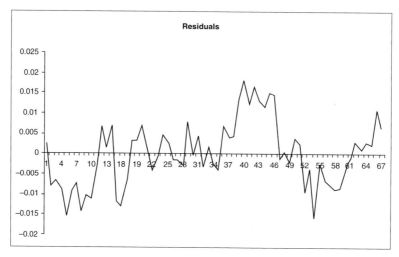

Figure 11.51 Error/residual plot

In addition to visually checking that forecasting errors are behaving randomly, we also need to ensure that they are not dependent of one another. In other words, errors must not be correlated. There are other properties that errors need to comply with, but this is beyond the scope of the chapter on basic forecasting.

> **Note** One of the methods of verifying whether residuals are correlated is the auto-correlation plot. Autocorrelations are the coefficients that we calculate and they form an autocorrelation function. They can be used for various purposes, but here we are referring to the series of autocorrelations of residuals. Essentially, we lag the residuals by one time period, then by another and another, etc., and then measure correlations between all these lagged series of residuals. This is called a residual autocorrelation function.

Student Exercises

X11.24 Could you explain the difference between accuracy and precision? What are the consequences if your forecasts are precise, but not accurate? Could you have accurate forecasts that are not precise?

X11.25 Why is MAD type of error measurement preferred over the ME type of error?

X11.26 Two forecasts were produced, as shown below. The ME for the second forecast is some seven times larger than the ME for the first forecast. However, the MSE is some twenty times larger. Can you explain?

Autocorrelation
Autocorrelation is the correlation between members of a time series of observations and the same values shifted at a fixed time interval.

X	Y	$\hat{Y}_1$	$\hat{Y}_2$	e_1	e_2
1	230	230	230	0	0
2	300	305	305	−5	−5
3	290	295	295	−5	−5
4	320	320	320	0	0
5	350	345	345	5	5
6	400	402	350	−2	50
7	350	355	355	−5	−5
8	400	395	395	5	5
9	420	420	420	0	0
	ME =	−0.78	5.78		
	MSE =	14.33	291.67		

X11.27 Is it acceptable to see some regularity in pattern when examining the series of residuals, or forecasting errors?

X11.28 The closer the actual observations, when compared with forecasted values on a scatter diagram, are to the diagonal line, the better the forecasts. Is this correct?

11.7 Confidence Intervals

11.7.1 Population and sample standard errors

We need to remind ourselves from the sampling chapter that the standard error (SE) of the mean is calculated as:

$$\sigma_{\bar{x}} = \frac{\sigma}{\sqrt{n}} \qquad (11.39)$$

We also said that when dealing with a normal distribution, we expect 68.3% of all the values to be within $\bar{x} \pm 1\sigma$, 95.4% of all the values to be within $\bar{x} \pm 2\sigma$, and 99.7% to be within $\bar{x} \pm 3\sigma$. We also said that to change any distribution into a standard distribution, standardized z units need to be calculated, and this is done as:

$$z = \frac{X - \mu}{\sigma} \qquad (11.40)$$

Z-values are used for estimating the *confidence interval* (CI) of the estimate of the mean:

$$CI = \bar{x} \pm z\,SE \qquad (11.41)$$

Where, SE is the standard error. Depending on the value of z, we get different confidence intervals (CI). For: (a) $z = 1.64$ for 90% CI, (b) $z = 1.96$ for 95% CI, and (c) $z = 2.58$ for 99% CI. It is important to also remind ourselves that most of the time we cannot calculate the SE as in equation 11.39, for a simple reason that we do not know the population standard deviation (σ). In this case, *the sample standard deviation* is calculated as:

$$s = \sqrt{\frac{\sum\limits_{i=1}^{n} (x_i - \bar{x})^2}{n-1}}$$

(11.42)

Now we have the standard deviation of the sample (the data set, or the time series) we can modify the formula for the standard error (SE) as:

$$SE = \frac{s}{\sqrt{n}}$$

(11.43)

How do we estimate the confidence interval of the sample mean? First of all, if the time series is relatively short and just a small sample of the true variable, then the *t*-distribution is used for the computation of the confidence interval, rather than the *z*-value. The formula is:

$$\bar{x} \pm t_{value}\, SE, \quad \text{or} \quad \bar{x} \pm t_{value}\, (s/\sqrt{n})$$

(11.44)

The only difference between equations (11.44) and (11.41) is that the *t*-value in the above formula will be determined not just by the level of significance (as it was the case with the *z*-values), but also by the number of degrees of freedom.

> **Note**   A general rule is that for larger samples, the *z*-values and the *t*-value produce similar results, so it is discretionary which one to use. A large sample in time series analysis is a series with more than 30 observations.

If we take a sample of 20 observations, all the values mentioned above can easily be calculated. Figure 11.52 shows the calculations.

The value of alpha in cell B1 should not be confused with the smoothing constant (α). The value used here has the same letter, but this is a traditional way for the statisticians to describe the level of significance. As the formula in cell C2 explains, the confidence interval is calculated as: $(1 - \text{level of significance}) \times 100$.

	A	B	C
1	Alpha	0.01	
2	Confidence Interval (CI) %	99	=100*(1-B1)
3	No of observations	20	=COUNT(F2:F21)
4	Degrees of Freedom	18	=B3-2
5	Sample Mean	5.3500	=AVERAGE(F2:F21)
6	Standard Deviation	1.5652	=STDEV(F2:F21)
7	Z-value	2.58	=NORMSINV(1-(B1/2))
8	CI Value	0.9015	=B7*(B6/SQRT(B3))
9	Lower Limit	4.4485	=B5-B8
10	Upper Limit	6.2515	=B5+B8
11	t-value	2.88	=TINV(B1,B4)
12	CI value	1.0075	=B11*(B6/SQRT(B3))
13	Lower Limit	4.3425	=B5-B12
14	Upper Limit	6.3575	=B5+B12

Figure 11.52

> ➡ **Excel Formula Method**
>
> | | |
> |---|---|
> | z-value Cell B7 | Formula: =NORMSINV(1−(B1/2)) |
> | CI value Cell B8 | Formula: =B7*(B6/SQRT(B4)) |
> | Lower CI Cell B9 | Formula: =B5−B8 |
> | Upper CI Cell B10 | Formula: =B5+B8 |
> | t-value Cell B11 | Formula: =TINV(B1,B4−B3) |
> | CI value Cell B12 | Formula: =B11*(B6/SQRT(B4)) |
> | Lower CI Cell B13 | Formula: =B5−B8 |
> | Upper CI Cell B14 | Formula: =B5+B8 |

The above equation (11.44) is used when the mean value of a sample is estimated. However, in order to use these formulae with time series, they need to be modified.

11.7.2 Standard errors in time series

In equation (11.42) we measured the differences between every observation and the mean. This was the basis for calculating the standard deviation. When dealing with time series, it would seem logical to use the same principle, but rather than calculating deviations from the mean, we calculate deviations between the actual and predicted values. We can modify equation (11.42) and instead of the mean value use the predicted values:

$$SE_{y,\hat{y}} = \sqrt{\frac{\sum_{i=1}^{n}(y_i - \hat{y}_i)^2}{n-2}}$$

(11.45)

Here y_i are the actual observations and $\hat{y}_t$ are the predicted values. The Excel version of this formula is =SQRT(SUMXMY2(array_x, array_y)/n−2). Actually Excel offers an even more elegant function as a substitute for this formula. The function is called: =STEYX (known_y's, known_x's). This function returns the standard error of the predicted y-value for each x in the regression, or the **standard error of forecast**. If you look into Excel's Help file, you will see that this function is a very elegant representation of a monstrous looking formula:

$$SE_{y,x} = \sqrt{\left(\frac{1}{n(n-2)}\right)\left(n\sum y^2 - (\sum y)^2 - \frac{[n\sum xy - (\sum x)(\sum y)]^2}{n\sum x^2 - (\sum x)^2}\right)}$$

(11.46)

> 📎 **Note**   Remember that these two formulae are identical:
> =SQRT(SUMXMY2(array_x, array_y)/n−2)
> and
> =STEYX(known_y's, known_x's)
> They both return the standard error for the predicted values, or standard error of forecast.

Standard error of forecast The square root of the variance of all forecasting errors.

If the standard error $SE_{y,x}$ is a measure of the amount of error in the prediction of y for an individual x. This means we can modify equation (11.44) into:

$$\hat{Y} \pm t_{value} \, SE_{y,\hat{y}} \qquad\qquad (11.47)$$

$\hat{Y}$ are the predicted values, $SE_{y,x}$ is the standard error of prediction and t_{value} is the t-value from the table. We can recap that, depending on what is the desired confidence interval (CI), the values for z are as follows: (a) CI = 90% for $z = 1.64$ and $t = 1.73$, (b) CI = 95% for $z = 1.96$ and $t = 2.09$, and (c) CI = 99% for $z = 2.58$ and $t = 2.86$. The values of t are not fixed as they depend on the number of degrees of freedom and the size of the sample.

> **Note**   The t-values above are not universal for these given levels of confidence. The calculation of the t-values depends on a number of degrees of freedom. The above t-values are only valid for eight degrees of freedom, which is the length of our time series minus 2.

Figure 11.53 illustrates the technique using a very short time series.

	A	B	C	D	E	F	G	H
1	X	Y	Trend	- Interval	+ Interval		3.227	=Standard Error SE
2	1	2	1.47	-5.9682	8.9137		0.05	=Level of significance (alpha)
3	2	1	2.41	-5.0289	9.8531		8	=degrees of freedom
4	3	1	3.35	-4.0895	10.7925		2.306	=t-value
5	4	4	4.29	-3.1501	11.7319			
6	5	13	5.23	-2.2107	12.6713			
7	6	3	6.17	-1.2713	13.6107			
8	7	8	7.11	-0.3319	14.5501			
9	8	6	8.05	0.6075	15.4895			
10	9	9	8.99	1.5469	16.4289			
11	10	10	9.93	2.4863	17.3682			
12	11		10.87	3.4257	18.3076			
13	12		11.81	4.3651	19.2470			
14	13		12.75	5.3045	20.1864			
15	14		13.68	6.2439	21.1258			
16	15		14.62	7.1833	22.0652			

Figure 11.53

We have a very short time series with only ten observations and we used the TREND function to produce forecasts. This trend function was extrapolated 5 periods in the future.

> **→ Excel Formula Method**
>
> | | | |
> |---|---|---|
> | Trend function | Cell C2 | Formula: =TREND($B$2:$B$11,$A$2:$A$11,A2) |
> | | Cell C3 | Formula: =TREND($B$2:$B$11,$A$2:$A$11,A3), etc. |
> | Standard Error | Cell G1 | Formula: =STEYX($B$2:$B$11,$C$2:$C$11) |
> | Alpha | Cell G2 | Constant = 0.05 |
> | Degrees of f. | Cell G3 | Formula: =COUNT(B2:B11)–2 |
> | t-value | Cell G4 | Formula: =TINV(G2,G3) |
> | CI Interval – | Cell D2 | Formula: =C2–($G$1*$G$4), etc. |
> | CI Interval + | Cell D2 | Formula: =C2+($G$1*$G$4), etc. |

Figure 11.54 illustrates the graph for the prediction and the corresponding confidence interval.

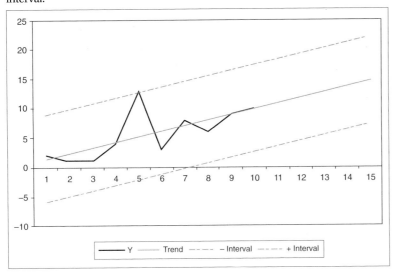

Figure 11.54

The above calculations, as well as the graph, indicate that we are on the right track as far as the confidence interval is concerned, except that it does not comply with one intuitive assumption. It is intuitive to think that the confidence interval is not constant and that it should change with time. In other words, the further we go in the future, the wider the interval should be as the uncertainty increases. As we can see from the above example, the level of confidence here is a constant value. In order to make the confidence level change with time, in addition to equation (11.45), we'll need another formula:

$$SE_{y,x} = SE_{y,\hat{y}} \sqrt{1 + \frac{1}{n} + \frac{(x_i - \bar{x})^2}{\sum (x_i - \bar{x})^2}} \qquad (11.48)$$

This is exactly the same equation as equation (10.33) from Chapter 10. The only exception is that in Chapter 10 we included t_{cri}-value in the formula, whilst here it is included in the procedure. We'll use exactly the same example to demonstrate the effects of this additional equation. Figure 11.55 contains the details.

Figure 11.55 illustrates the Excel solution to calculate interval estimate.

	A	B	C	D	E	F	G	H	I	J	K
1	X	Y	Trend	Mean X	SE(Y)	Interval +	Interval -		0.05	=Level of significance (alpha)	
2	1	2	1.472727	5.5	1.159937	10.104	-7.158		8	=degrees of freedom	
3	2	1	2.412121	5.5	1.117356	10.726	-5.902		2.306	=t-value	
4	3	1	3.351515	5.5	1.084324	11.420	-4.717	3.22678	=SE_pred	
5	4	4	4.290909	5.5	1.061731	12.191	-3.609				
6	5	13	5.230303	5.5	1.050252	13.045	-2.585				
7	6	3	6.169697	5.5	1.050252	13.985	-1.645				
8	7	8	7.109091	5.5	1.061731	15.009	-0.791				
9	8	6	8.048485	5.5	1.084324	16.117	-0.020				
10	9	9	8.987879	5.5	1.117356	17.302	0.674				
11	10	10	9.927273	5.5	1.159937	18.558	1.296				
12	11		10.86667	5.5	1.21106	19.878	1.855				
13	12		11.80606	5.5	1.269693	21.254	2.358				
14	13		12.74545	5.5	1.334848	22.678	2.813				
15	14		13.68485	5.5	1.405616	24.144	3.226				
16	15		14.62424	5.5	1.481195	25.646	3.603				

Figure 11.55

The only difference to Figure 11.53 is that we had to introduce two additional columns, one for $SE_{y,x}$ and the other one for the mean value (column D). This column, as we will see below, will help us with some of the formulae.

→ Excel Formula Method

Trend function	Cell C2	Formula: =TREND($B$2:$B$11,$A$2:$A$11,A2)
	Cell C3	Formula: =TREND($B$2:$B$11,$A$2:$A$11,A3), etc.
Average value	Cell D2	Formula: =AVERAGE($B$2:$B$11), etc.
Standard Error	Cell E1	Formula: =SQRT(1+(1/COUNT($A$2:$A$11))+(A2−AVERAGE($A$2:$A$11))^2/SUMXMY2($A$2:$A$11,$D$2:$D$11))
	Cell E2	Formula: =SQRT(1+(1/COUNT($A$2:$A$11))+(A3−AVERAGE($A$2:$A$11))^2/SUMXMY2($A$2:$A$11,$D$2:$D$11)), etc.
Alpha	Cell H1	Constant = 0.05
Degrees of f.	Cell H2	Formula: =COUNT(B2:B11)−2
t-value	Cell H3	Formula: =TINV(G2,G3)
SE_{pred}	Cell H4	Formula: =STEYX(B2:B11,A2:A11)
CI Interval −	Cell D2	Formula: =C2−($H$3*$H$4*E2), etc.
CI Interval +	Cell D2	Formula: =C2+($H$3*$H$4*E2), etc.

Figure 11.56 illustrates the Excel graphical solution.

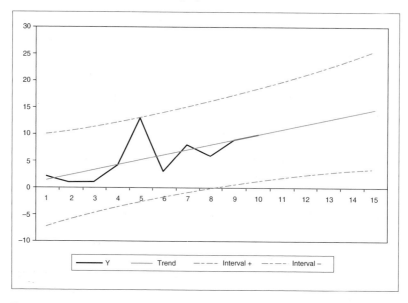

Figure 11.56

As we can see the confidence interval gets wider the further we go into the future. This is quite intuitive as it implies that the uncertainty increases as we move further and further into the forecasting horizon.

Student Exercises

X11.29 How would you describe the concept of confidence interval in the context of precision in forecasting?

X11.30 Would you use the z-values or t-values to calculate the confidence interval for a time series that has 200 observations?

X11.31 Why is it logical to expect that the confidence interval should get wider and wider the further we go in the future with our forecasts?

■ Techniques in Practice

1. Coco S.A. is considering diversifying and entering the housing market in the USA. It is only interested in a short term investment. To help it with the decision and assess the market, its US analyst extracted a time series that covers US Months Supply of Houses For Sale at Current Sales Rate. The time series is not adjusted for seasonality and the data set reflects true market movements. The table below covers data from January 2004 till June 2008 (Year Y, Month M, Value V).

Y	M	V	Y	M	V	Y	M	V	Y	M	V	Y	M	V
2004	01	4.2	2005	01	4.8	2006	01	5.9	2007	01	8.2	2008	01	11
2004	02	3.6	2005	02	4	2006	02	6.1	2007	02	8	2008	02	10
2004	03	3	2005	03	3.5	2006	03	5.1	2007	03	6.8	2008	03	10
2004	04	3.5	2005	04	3.8	2006	04	5.6	2007	04	6.5	2008	04	9
2004	05	3.3	2005	05	3.7	2006	05	5.5	2007	05	6.9	2008	05	9
2004	06	3.7	2005	06	4	2006	06	5.8	2007	06	7.5	2008	06	9
2004	07	4.2	2005	07	3.9	2006	07	6.9	2007	07	8	2008	07	
2004	08	4	2005	08	4.3	2006	08	6.5	2007	08	8.9	2008	08	
2004	09	4.4	2005	09	5	2006	09	7	2007	09	9.9	2008	09	
2004	10	4.1	2005	10	4.7	2006	10	7.5	2007	10	9	2008	10	
2004	11	5	2005	11	5.9	2006	11	7.8	2007	11	11	2008	11	
2004	12	5.2	2005	12	5.9	2006	12	7.6	2007	12	11	2008	12	

Analyse the data and produce a forecast. Pay specific attention to:

• Graphing the time series.
• Deciding the type of time series.
• Using the best suited method and produce forecasts until end of 2008 (six time periods in the future).
• Measuring the quality of your forecast.
• Decide what would be your recommendations, from the data analysis point of view, to Coco S.A.

2. Bakers Ltd is concerned about the influence of petrol prices on their profit margins. The owner of the company looked at weekly petrol prices (pence per gallon) just for London

and compiled a time series. The series starts from 14 November 2005 and it goes until 4 August 2008. The data in pence per gallon are shown below in columns:

250.1	238.6	291.5	269.1	249.7	296.2	296.1	330.9	334.2	423.8
241.6	244.3	287.9	261.5	245	302.6	293.2	331	335.7	423.5
235.8	245.6	283.7	255.9	240.2	304.4	290.7	328.9	341.1	424.7
232.2	261.6	290.5	251.7	237.6	307.1	288.6	328.5	338.5	424.8
234.3	261.7	295.8	247.4	236.2	313.5	287.3	327.8	340.1	424.2
236.8	273.7	299.3	243	236.2	315.1	287.5	327.6	342.9	421.9
238.1	279.7	302	239.9	239.6	313.1	288.9	329.4	349.8	412.7
244.2	292	305.2	239.1	246.6	313.5	293.8	334	362.6	405.1
254	306.4	307.6	238.5	268	310.4	293.2	332.4	375.3	
254.8	304.9	309.1	242.8	271.3	307.6	292.7	329.1	376.9	
257.7	303.6	305.3	248.9	273.4	307.5	292.5	328.7	385.9	
255.6	301.6	300	247.6	275.9	306.6	298.6	326	393.1	
253.1	298.9	294.4	252.2	281.4	307	304	326.1	408.3	
248.8	296.4	287.5	253.9	287.3	303.6	319.6	327.4	412.1	
242.4	292.5	279.3	253.5	295.7	300.4	328.6	333.2	418.3	

The owner is not too familiar with forecasting, but knows how to use trending function. Put yourself in his shoes and do the following:

- Chart the time series.
- Pick the best suitable curve to fit to the data set.
- Extrapolate the data another 20 time periods in the future.
- Calculate the confidence interval.
- What do you think you need to do to preserve your profit margins?

3. Skodel Ltd is considering investing into technology stocks. As a test case, it looked at Microsoft adjusted monthly closing values of stocks between 1 March 2001 and 1 August 2008. The time series is given in columns below:

26.21	30.25	26.02	25.57	22.5	21.52
25.72	29.42	27.17	23.93	22.4	22.09
27.51	27.38	25.24	23.66	21.75	25.5
28.32	27.68	26.72	23.36	20.88	24.67
28.42	30.22	24.73	24.3	21.69	26.94
28.28	29.24	24.76	24.36	20.54	28.01
27.1	28.75	26.35	22.38	20.1	27.15
32.35	28.02	24.57	22.29	20.07	24.59
35.33	26.69	23.83	21.27	21.86	21.63
33.35	25.08	24.76	22.63	24.39	24.12
36.41	23.39	24.2	23.59	22.61	27.98
29.14	22.65	23.12	23.35	18.49	30.86
28.42	22.02	24.07	21.93	20.75	29.25
28.58	23.39	25.06	22.3	20.29	28.64
29.05	26.35	25.48	23.58	23.13	23.12

Use exponential smoothing method and experiment with various levels of constant α. See what impact it has on your forecasts and how it changes the forecasting errors. Make recommendation as to what approach to forecasting would you use and why.

■ Summary

In this chapter we focused on univariate time series analysis as a primary tool for extrapolating time series and forecasting. We described what are the prerequisites before we start selecting a forecasting method, namely: ensuring that all the observations were rerecorded in the same units of time, that no observation was missing, that we do not have unexpected outliers and that the time series is transformed, if necessary, and that we produce the time series graph before proceeding. We explained the concept of indices and how to convert them from one base to another. This was linked with aggregate indices and we introduced CPI as a major method of deflating the value related time series. We also showed how to convert the values into constant dollars.

Various trend models were introduced as well as how to fit them to time series, producing the ex-post forecasts. Other alternative methods to trend fitting and extrapolation were introduced, such as the moving average method and exponential smoothing. The relevance of the smoothing constant α was explained. This was followed with the introduction of how to apply exponential smoothing to seasonal time series. Once we mastered various forecasting methods and techniques, we focused on forecasting errors and how to measure them. The relevance of various error indicators (ME, MSE, MAD, etc.) was introduced, as well as how to interpret them to select the best forecast.

The final element introduced was the confidence interval, which brings together extrapolation and error measurement. We explained how to apply confidence measurement to our forecasts and what are the limitations.

■ Key Terms

Aggregate price index
Array range
Base index period
Causal forecasting methods
Classical additive time
  series method
Classical time series
  decomposition
Classical time series
  mixed method
Classical time series
  multiplicative method

Coefficient of
  determination
Confidence intervals
Cyclical component
Deflating values
Differencing
Error measurements
Exponential smoothing
Exponential trend
Forecasting
Forecasting errors
Forecasting horizon

Index numbers
Irregular component
Linear trend model
Logarithmic trend
Mean absolute
  deviation (MAD)
Mean absolute percentage
  error (MAPE)
Mean error (ME)
Mean percentage
  error (MPE)
Mean square error (MSE)

Mixed time series model

Moving averages

Multivariate

Non-stationary time series

Polynomial trend

Population standard deviation

Power trend

Price index

Random component

Residuals

Sample stan dard deviation

Scale

Seasonal component

Seasonal correlation

Seasonal time series

Simple price index

Standard error

Stationary time series

Time period

Time series

Time series forecasting

Time series smoothing

Transformations

Trend component

Types of trend

Visualization

Univariate

■ Further Reading

Textbook Resources

1. Brown, R. G. (2004) *Smoothing, Forecasting and Prediction*. Dover Publications.

2. Chatfield, C. (2004) *The Analysis of Time Series: An Introduction*. Boca Raton, Fla.; London, Chapman & Hall/CRC.

3. Hanke, J. E. and Wichern, D. W. (2005) *Business Forecasting*. Upper Saddle River, Pearson/Prentice Hall.

4. Newbold, P. and Bos, T. (1994) *Introductory Business & Economic Forecasting*. Cincinnati, South-Western Pub.

5. Evans, M. K. (2003) *Practical Business Forecasting*. Malden, Mass.; Oxford, Blackwell Publishers.

Web Resources

1. Engineering Statistics Handbook http://www.itl.nist.gov/div898/handbook/pmc/section4/pmc4.htm.

2. Economagic—contains numerous economic data sets http://www.economagic.com/.

3. Wikipedia articles on time series http://en.wikipedia.org/wiki/Time_series.

4. Statsoft Electronic Textbook http://www.statsoft.com/textbook/sttimser.html.

5. A private collection by Rob Hyndman http://www.robjhyndman.com/TSDL/.

■ Formula Summary

$$I_t = \frac{y_t}{y_0} 100 \tag{11.1}$$

$$CPI_{YearA} = \frac{I_{YearA} - I_{YearB}}{I_{YearB}} 100 \tag{11.2}$$

$$P_A = P_B \frac{CPI_A}{CPI_B} \tag{11.3}$$

$$y_{t_{adj}} = y_t \left(\frac{CPI_{Fixed}}{CPI_t} \right) \tag{11.4}$$

$$Y = T + C + S + I \tag{11.5}$$

$$Y = T + R \tag{11.6}$$

$$Y = mx + b \tag{11.7}$$

$$Y = c \ln x + b \tag{11.8}$$

$$Y = b + c_1 x + c_2 x^2 + c_3 x^3 + c_4 x^4 + c_5 x^5 + c_6 x^6 \tag{11.9}$$

$$Y = c x^b \tag{11.10}$$

$$Y = c e^{bx} \tag{11.11}$$

$$R^2 = 1 - \frac{SSE}{SST} \tag{11.12}$$

$$M_t = \frac{\sum_{i=t}^{t-N+1} x_i}{N} \tag{11.13}$$

$$M_t = \frac{x_t + x_{t-1} + x_{t-N+1}}{N} \tag{11.14}$$

$$\hat{y}_t = y_{t-1} + e_t \tag{11.15}$$

$$F_t = F_{t-1} + (y_{t-1} - F_{t-1}) \tag{11.16}$$

$$F_t = F_{t-1} + \alpha(y_{t-1} - F_{t-1}) \tag{11.17}$$

$$S'_t = S'_{t-1} + \alpha(y_{t-1} - S'_{t-1}) \tag{11.18}$$

$$S'_t = \alpha y_t + (1 - \alpha) S'_{t-1} \tag{11.19}$$

$$\alpha = \frac{2}{M+1} \tag{11.20}$$

$$\hat{Y}_{t+1} = \alpha y_t + (1 - \alpha) \hat{Y}_t \tag{11.21}$$

$$\hat{Y}_{t+1} = \hat{Y}_t + \alpha e_t \tag{11.22}$$

$$\hat{Y}_{t+1} = y_t - (1 - \alpha)e_t \tag{11.23}$$

$$F_{t+m} = a_t + S_{t-s+m} \tag{11.24}$$

$$F_{t+m} = a_t S_{t-s+m} \tag{11.25}$$

$$a_t = \alpha(y_t - S_{t-s}) + (1 - \alpha)a_{t-1} \tag{11.26}$$

$$S_t = \delta(y_t - a_t) + (1 - \delta)S_{t-s} \tag{11.27}$$

$$a_t = \alpha\left(\frac{y_t}{S_{t-s}}\right) + (1 - \alpha)a_{t-1} \tag{11.28}$$

$$S_t = \delta\left(\frac{y_t}{a_t}\right) + (1 - \delta)S_{t-s} \tag{11.29}$$

$$a_s = \sum_{t=1}^{s} \frac{y_t}{s} \tag{11.30}$$

$$S_t = y_t - a_t \tag{11.31}$$

$$S_t = \frac{y_t}{a_t} \tag{11.32}$$

$$e_t = A_t - F_t, \text{ or } e_t = y_t - F_t \tag{11.33}$$

$$ME = \frac{\sum(A_t - F_t)}{n} = \frac{\sum e_t}{n} \tag{11.34}$$

$$MAD = \frac{\sum|A_t - F_t|}{n} = \frac{\sum|e_t|}{n} \tag{11.35}$$

$$MSE = \frac{\sum(A_t - F_t)^2}{n} = \frac{\sum e_t^2}{n} \tag{11.36}$$

$$MPE = \frac{\sum\left(\frac{A_t - F_t}{A_t}\right)}{n} = \frac{\sum\left(\frac{e_t}{A_t}\right)}{n} \tag{11.37}$$

$$MAPE = \frac{\sum\left(\frac{|A_t - F_t|}{A_t}\right)}{n} = \frac{\sum\left(\frac{|e_t|}{A_t}\right)}{n} \tag{11.38}$$

$$\sigma_{\bar{x}} = \frac{\sigma}{\sqrt{n}} \tag{11.39}$$

$$z = \frac{X - \mu}{\sigma} \tag{11.40}$$

$$CI = \bar{x} \pm z\,SE \tag{11.41}$$

$$s = \sqrt{\frac{\sum_{i=1}^{n}(x_i - \overline{x})^2}{n-1}} \qquad (11.42)$$

$$SE = \frac{s}{\sqrt{n}} \qquad (11.43)$$

$$\overline{x} \pm t_{value}SE, \quad \text{or} \quad \overline{x} \pm t_{value}SE(s/\sqrt{n}) \qquad (11.44)$$

$$SE_{y,\hat{y}} = \sqrt{\frac{\sum_{i=1}^{n}(y_i - \hat{y}_i)^2}{n-2}} \qquad (11.45)$$

$$SE_{y,x} = \sqrt{\left(\frac{1}{n(n-2)}\right)\left(n\Sigma y^2 - (\Sigma y)^2 - \frac{[n\Sigma xy - (\Sigma x)(\Sigma y)]^2}{n\Sigma x^2 - (\Sigma x)^2}\right)} \qquad (11.46)$$

$$\hat{y} \pm t_{value} SE_{y,\hat{y}} \qquad (11.47)$$

$$SE_{y,x} = SE_{y,\hat{y}}\sqrt{1 + \frac{1}{n} + \frac{(x_i - \overline{x})^2}{\Sigma(x_i - \overline{x})^2}} \qquad (11.48)$$

Chapter 1

X1.1 b   X1.2 a   X1.3 c   X1.4 b   X1.5 c   X1.6 a

X1.7 c   X1.8 71%   X1.9 b   X1.10 c   X1.11 b   X1.12 d

Chapter 2

X2.1   (a) 27,   (b) 1/27,   (c) 4,   (d) 2.

X2.2   (a) £105,   (b) £37.50,   (c) £40.62 to the nearest penny,   (d) 3.33333'% pa,   (e) 2.5 years,   (f) £1000.

X2.3   (a) £123.60,   (b) £5832,   (c) £17705.27,   (d) £23380.18 to the nearest penny, £3107.69, £2851.09,   (e) £79.72,   (f) £1012.46 to the nearest penny, £1038.74 to the nearest penny, is the greater sum,   (g) £27674.10 to the nearest penny,   (h) £1356.08 to the nearest penny,   (i) £3015.26 to the nearest penny, £4642.86 to the nearest penny,   (j) £8830.97 to the nearest penny, £93945.95 to the nearest penny.

X2.4   1. Q (−2, 4),   2. R (2, 4),   3. S (3, −3),   4. T (−2, −4).

X2.5   (a) Y = 3x + 1,   (c) Intercept = +1, coordinate of intercept point = (0, 1).

X2.6   (a) Gradient m = 5 and y-intercept c = +1,   (b) Gradient m = −3 and y-intercept c = +5,   (c) Gradient m = ½ and y-intercept c = +3.

X2.7   (a) Intercept = 1 and slope = 5. Yes,   (b) Intercept = 5 and slope = −3. Yes,   (c) Intercept = 3 and slope = 1/2. Yes.

Chapter 3

X3.1   No title, no source mentioned, class unclear, group differentiation unclear.

X3.2   Grouped frequency distribution

Bin	Frequency		Class	Frequency
49.5	0			
54.5	1		50–54	1
59.5	2		55–59	2
64.5	13		60–64	13
69.5	10		65–69	10
74.5	12		70–74	12
79.5	21		75–79	21
84.5	5		80–84	5
89.5	9		85–89	9
94.5	3		90–94	3
99.5	4		95–99	4
More	0			

Figure AX3.2

X3.3   Bar chart

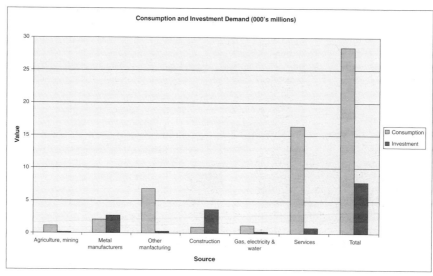

Figure AX3.3

X3.4   Pie chart

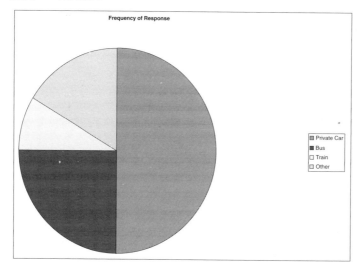

Figure AX3.4

X3.5   Pie chart

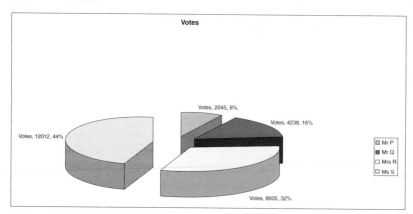

Figure AX3.5

X3.6   Histogram

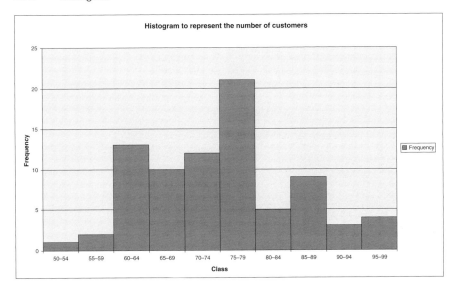

Figure AX3.6

X3.7   Histogram

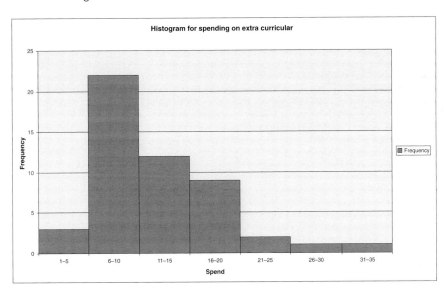

Figure AX3.7

X3.8   Frequency polygon for X3.2

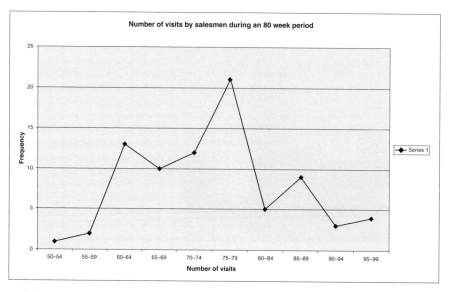

Figure AX3.8

X3.9   Scatter plot for road deaths against the number of vehicles

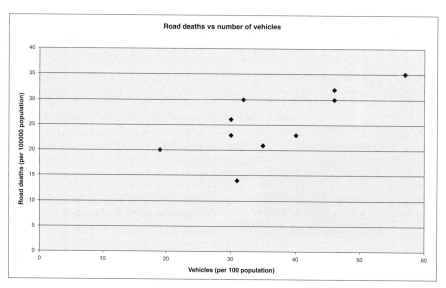

Figure AX3.9

X3.10   Time series graph of passenger miles flown against time

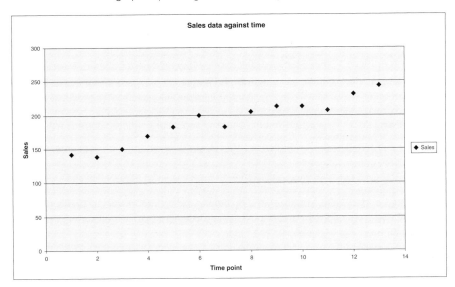

Figure AX3.10

We can see from the graph that the passenger miles fluctuate over time with two peaks identified at quarter 3 for 2003 and 2004.

Chapter 4

X4.1   Mean = 44 and Median = 48. Note the large difference in the two values. Provide an explanation for the difference.

X4.2   Mean = 100 and Median = 99. Both measures of average support the I. Q. statement. Note that the sample size is small. The issue of sample size will be discussed in Chapter 6.

X4.3   Mean = 54.5 and Median = 55. The calculation of each average assumes: (i) mean—uses all data values with no extreme values identified,   (ii) median is the 50th percentile value and can be used if extreme values are identified. In this question the two values are approximately equal and we can say that there is no evidence of extreme values in the data set.

X4.4   Mean = 2.9, Median = 3, and Mode = 2.

X4.5   Mean salary £6700.

X4.6   (a) We can see from the histogram that we have a slightly skewed distribution.

(b) Mean = 23.5, Median = 22.

(c) In this case we would use the median rather than the mean as the measure of average.

X4.7   Mean = 27.

X4.8   (a) Mean nail length = 5.1 mm,   (b) Median from CF graph = 5.18 mm,   (c) Median from formula = 5.18.

X4.9   (a) Mean from formula = 49.2,   (b) From CF graph: Median = 46.5, Upper Quartile = 62.5, Lower Quartile = 36.5.

X4.10   Mean = 2.97, Standard Deviation = 1.8.

X4.11   Range = 21, Mean = 66.98, Standard Deviation = 4.33.

X4.12   See instructor manual for the two frequency polygons plotted on the same graph. Distribution A: Mean = 27.3, Standard Deviation = 4.73, and Distribution B: Mean = 27.3, Standard Deviation = 9.03. We can see from the frequency polygons that the distributions have the same mean average value but distribution B is more dispersed than distribution A.

X4.13   (a) We can see from the histogram that the pattern consists of an uneven pattern in the data.

(b) From Excel mean = 132.1, median = 136, standard deviation = 24, semi interquartile range = 16.

(c) From the histogram we have no evidence of extreme values within the data set and we have a range of data values between the minimum and maximum values. In this case we can see that the mean and median are approximately equal and therefore we would use the mean to represent the average miles travelled.

(d) From Excel skewness = −0.298 (values slightly bunched up to the higher end of the data values) and kurtosis = −0.542 (evidence of a slightly flat distribution). Compare these two values with the error equations for skewness ($\pm 2\sqrt{\dfrac{6}{45}} = \pm 0.73$) and kurtosis ($\pm 2\sqrt{\dfrac{24}{45}} = \pm 1.46$). We can see that we do not have a problem with either skewness or kurtosis within the data set.

X4.14   (a) Five-number summary: Q1 = 1.085, minimum = 0.27, median = 1.395, maximum = 4.89, Q3 = 1.765.

(b) Distance from Q3 to the median (1.765 – 1.395 = 0.37) is approximately equal to distance from Median − Q1 (1.395 – 1.085 = 0.31). Distance from largest value to Q3 (4.89 – 1.765 = 3.125) is greater than between Q1 and minimum value (1.085 – 0.27 = 0.815) which indicates right skewness.

(c) We can see from this screenshot that the value of skewness is 2.33. This value is greater than the error measurement of $\pm 2\sqrt{\dfrac{6}{40}} = \pm 0.77$ and we conclude that the data distribution is significantly skewed to the right.

(d) Given that this data set is heavily skewed we would use the median to represent the average and semi interquartile range to represent the measure of spread.

X4.15   (a) Five-number summary: Q1 = 156312.75, minimum = 123636, median = 175144, maximum = 214563, Q3 = 191975.

(b) Distance from Q3 to the median (= 16831) is approximately equal to distance from Median − Q1 (= 18831). Distance from largest value to Q3 (= 22588) is less than between Q1 and minimum value (= 32677) which indicates left skewness.

(c) We can see from this screenshot that the value of skewness is −0.16. This value is less than the error measurement of $\pm 2\sqrt{\dfrac{6}{50}} = \pm 0.69$ and we conclude that the data distribution is not significantly skewed to the left.

(d) Given that this data set is not significantly skewed we would use the mean to represent the average and standard deviation to represent the measure of spread.

Chapter 5

X5.1 (a) Set of 52 playing cards, (b) gender of males and females, (c) sample space consists of 9 sample points (*) is as follows:

		1st Game		
		Win	Draw	Lose
2nd Game	Win	*	*	*
	Draw	*	*	*
	Lose	*	*	*

X5.2 Only events A and B are mutually exclusive.

X5.3 Use official records to correlate the number of 25 year olds passing a driving test at the first attempt with the total number sitting the test. This would be undertaken for a particular time frame and the probability would represent the probability for this time frame only. This is likely to change if you were to repeat the calculation for a different time frame (different sample).

X5.4 (a) 4/25, (b) 7/10, (c) 43/50, (d) 5/8, (e) 7/100.

X5.5 (a) 0.024, (b) 0.452.

X5.6 20.

X5.7 (a) E(A) = E(B) = £10000, (b) A yields a better profit profile—variance lower for A compared to B—reduces overall risk.

X5.8 (a) $P(X \leq 95) = 0.1587$, (b) $P(95 \leq X \leq 105) = 0.6826$, (c) $P(105 \leq X \leq 115) = 0.1574$, (d) $P(93 \leq X \leq 99) = 0.3399$. Shaded regions accessible via text book web site.

X5.9 (a) $P(Z \leq -1) = 0.1587$, (b) $P(-1 \leq Z \leq 1) = 0.6826$, (c) $P(1 \leq Z \leq 3) = 0.1574$, (d) $P(-1.4 \leq Z \leq -0.2) = 0.3399$.

X5.10 (a) $P(X \geq 11) = 0.4207$, (b) $P(X \leq 11) = 0.5793$, (c) $P(X \leq 5) = 0.1587$, (d) $P(X \geq 5) = 0.8413$, (e) $P(5 \leq X \leq 11) = 0.4207$.

X5.11 P(replaced) = 0.1814 (18.14%).

X5.12 (a) P(reject) = 0.1686, (b) P(reject) = 0.0956, (c) Adjust standard deviation to 2.13 ohms.

X5.13 (a) 3, (b) 120, (c) 1.

X5.14 (a) Probability distribution: P(0) = 0.0256, P(1) = 0.1536, P(2) = 0.3456, P(3) = 0.3456, P(4) = 0.1296, (b) Histogram for probability distribution data accessible via text book web site.

X5.15 (a) P(All women) = 0.004096, (b) P(3 men) = 0.27648, (c) P(less than 3 women) = 0.54432.

X5.16 P(production line stopped) = 0.02034.

X5.17 P(at least 3 voted) = 0.6768.

X5.18 (a) P(no accidents) = 0.3164, (b) P(at least two accidents) = 0.2617, (c) Expected cost is £18066.41, (d) Reject bid based upon expected cost.

X5.19   Mean = 1.2, Variance = 1.2.

X5.20   (a) P(One machine not working) = 0.2707,   (b) P(More than one not working) = 0.5940.

X5.21   P(One or more defective) = 0.3935 = 39.35%.

X5.22   (a) P(free from faults) = 0.6703,   (b) Length > 0.5129m.

X5.23   (a) P(0) = 0.1353, P(1) = 0.2707, P(2) = 0.2707, P(3) = 0.1804, mean = 1.3533,   (b) Expected daily profit = £27.07.

X5.24   (a) P(no accidents in month) = 0.074,   (b) P(More than one accident per month) = 0.733.

X5.25   Costs: method A = £134, method B = £208. Use method A—cheaper.

X5.26   (a) $np \geq 5$, use normal approximation,   (b) $np < 5$, do not use normal approximation,   (c) $np < 5$, do not use normal approximation.

X5.27   (a) P(less than 30 per week) = 0.1587,   (b) P(more than 40 per week) = 0.25143,   (c) P(between 30 and 40 births per week) = 0.5899.

Chapter 6

X6.1   (a) $\mu = 800$ and $\bar{\bar{X}} = 800$,   (b) $\sigma = 303.3150178$, n = 2 and $\sigma_{\bar{x}} = 214.476$.

X6.2   (a) $\bar{X} \sim N(10,2)$,   (b) $\bar{X} \sim N(10,1)$,   (c) $\bar{X} \sim N(10,0.25)$. Increased sample size reduces the size of the error ($\sigma_{\bar{x}}$).

X6.3   (a) $\bar{X} \sim N(63,2.5)$,   (b) $\bar{X} \sim N(63,5/3)$,   (c) $\bar{X} \sim N(63,1)$.

X6.4   See Section 6.2.8.

X6.5   (a) Expected number n = 3400 items,   (b) 34%,   (c) For n = 10, $\sigma_{\bar{x}} = 0.9487$. If n = 40, $\sigma_{\bar{x}} = 0.4743$.

X6.6   (a) Sample mean = 512, $\sigma_{\bar{x}} = 4.24$,   (b) Sample mean = 564, $\sigma_{\bar{x}} = 4.74$.

X6.7   (a) $P(0.4 \leq p \leq 0.6) = 0.9544$,   (b) $P(0.35 \leq p \leq 0.65) = 0.9973$,   (c) $P(0.5 \leq p \leq 0.65) = 0.4987$.

X6.8   P(Labour win) = 0.0207 or 2%.

X6.9   (a) P(desired accuracy) = 0.6826 or 68%,   (b) P(desired accuracy) = 0.98758 or 99%.

X6.10   P(average cost exceeds £11.10) = 0.00256 or 0.26%.

X6.11   Population estimates: mean = 6.54, standard deviation = 1.2361…, standard error = 0.553.

X6.12   Population estimates: mean = 8.7, standard deviation = 0.2808.

X6.13   Unbiased population estimates: mean = 0.2538, variance = 0.011.

X6.14 $P(12.12 \leq \bar{X}_{B} \leq 12.14) = 0.4762$.

X6.15   Population estimates: proportion = 0.6, standard error = 0.1.

X6.16   Estimate number of fish in lake = 10000.

X6.17   90% CI for population mean is 1.1218 → 1.1382.

X6.18   (a) 90% CI for D is 9.5 → 10.5,   (b) sample size = 553.

X6.19   95% CI for population mean is 23.21 → 25.21.

X6.20   Sample size = 6.

Chapter 7

X7.1   (i) Mean quantity from sample (μ_s) = Mean quantity within contract (μ_c),   (ii) $H_0: \mu_s = \mu_c$, $H_1: \mu_s \neq \mu_c$,   (iii) Two tail test.

X7.2

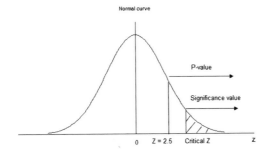

X7.3   (i) ±2.326, (ii) −2.054, (iii) +2.054.

X7.4   p-value = 0.00028.

X7.5   Accept H_0 (Z_{cal} = 1.77, two tail p-value = 0.076, Z_{cri} = ±1.96).

X7.6   Accept H_1 (Z_{cal} = 2.83, two tail p-value = 0.0047, Z_{cri} = ±1.96).

X7.7   (i) ± 2.681, (ii)−2.303, (iii) +2.303.

X7.8   (i) when σ unknown, n small, population normally distributed (or approximately), (ii) p-value = 0.032564.

X7.9   Accept H_0 (t_{cal} = −2.073, two tail p-value = 0.06246, t_{cri} = ±2.201).

X7.10   Accept H_1 at 5% (t_{cal} = −2.37, two tail p-value = 0.038, t_{cri} = ±2.145).

X7.11   Accept H_0 (Z_{cal} = 0.688, two tail p-value = 0.4917, t_{cri} = ±1.96).

Accept H_0 (Z_{cal} = 1.567, two tail p-value = 0.1171, t_{cri} = ±1.96).

X7.12   Accept H_1 (Z_{cal} = 2.1, two tail p-value = 0.035, t_{cri} = ±1.96 [borderline decision]).

X7.13   Accept H_1 (Z_{cal} = −2.32, two tail p-value = 0.02, t_{cri} = ±1.96).

X7.14   Accept H_0 (Z_{cal} = 1.628, two tail p-value = 0.104, t_{cri} = ±1.96).

X7.15   Accept H_1 (t_{cal} = −2.42, two tail p-value = 0.02, t_{cri} = ±2.018).

X7.16   Accept H_1 (t_{cal} = 5.78, upper one tail p-value = 0.000005, upper t_{cri} = 1.72).

X7.17   Accept H_1 ($t_{cal} = -2.15$, two tail p-value = 0.04, $t_{cri} = \pm2.069$ [borderline decision]).

X7.18   Accept H_1 ($t_{cal} = 5.64$, upper one tail p-value = 0.000018, upper $t_{cri} = 1.75$).

X7.19   5%—Accept H_1 ($t_{cal} = -2.204$, lower one tail p-value = 0.022, lower $t_{cri} = -1.76$).

    1%—Accept H_0 $t_{cal} = -2.204$, lower one tail p-value = 0.022, lower $t_{cri} = -2.62$).

X7.20   Accept H_1 ($t_{cal} = -4.003$, two tail p-value = 0.0013, $t_{cri} = \pm2.145$).

X7.21   5%—Accept H_1 ($F_{cal} = 3.04$, two tail p-value = 0.0115, upper $F_{cri} = 2.36$, lower $F_{cri} = 0.38$).

    1%—Accept H_1 ($F_{cal} = 3.04$, two tail p-value = 0.0115, upper $F_{cri} = 3.1$, lower $F_{cri} = 0.28$ [borderline decision]).

X7.22   Accept H_0 ($F_{cal} = 0.8$, two tail p-value = 0.69, upper $F_{cri} = 4.16$, lower $F_{cri} = 0.29$).

Chapter 8

X8.1   (i) 24,   (ii) 12.59, 16.81,   (iii) 0.18.

X8.2 $\chi^2_{cal} = 28.88$, $\chi^2_{cri} = 9.49$, p-value = 8.28E-6. Association exists between industrial class and level of risk.

X8.3 $\chi^2_{cal} = 48.07$, $\chi^2_{cri} = 12.59$, p-value = 3.14E-8. Association exists between shift and defect type.

X8.4 $\chi^2_{cal} = 7.35$, $\chi^2_{cri} = 12.59$, p-value = 0.29. No association exists between optimism level and type of business.

X8.5 $\chi^2_{cal} = 10.8$, $\chi^2_{cri} = 9.49$, p-value = 0.029. Association exists between performance in English and German (borderline decision—alternative decision if 1% significance).

X8.6   (i) p-value = 0.089,   (ii) 1.7,   (iii) 2.58, 1.96.

X8.7   Proportion p = 0.67, $\chi^2_{cal} = 0.77$, $\chi^2_{cri} = 3.84$, p-value = 0.37. Accept H_0. No evidence that customers are taking into account petrol prices when buying cars.

X8.8   Proportion p = 0.66, $\chi^2_{cal} = 4.04$, $\chi^2_{cri} = 3.84$, p-value = 0.044. Reject H_0. Evidence that campaign has altered the proportion voting yes (borderline decision).

X8.9   Upper one sided p-value = 0.000488. Accept H_1. Evidence suggests that p > 0.5.

X8.10 H_0: Median difference = 0, H_1: Median difference ≠ 0, Median d = +1.000. Correct direction so continue with test. Binomial: n = 32, x = 26, upper one sided p-value = $P(X \geq 26) = 0.0003$. Normal: $\mu = 16$, $\sigma = 2.8284$, $X_c = 25.5$, $z_{cal} = 3.3588$, upper one tail critical = 1.65, and upper one tail p-value = 0.0004. In both cases accept H_1. Results are significantly different.

X8.11 H_0: Median difference ≤ 0, H_1: Median difference > 0, Median d = +1.000. Correct direction so continue with test. Binomial: n = 14, x = 10, upper one sided p-value = $P(X > 10) = 0.0287$. Accept H_1. Class sizes are significantly larger.

X8.12   The Wilcoxon signed rank sum test is used to test the null hypothesis that the median of a distribution is equal to a particular value. This is what the sign test measures but the Wilcoxon test also takes into account the magnitude of the number values. Given that it uses more information from the data set it is therefore considered to be more powerful. The sign test only uses the signs of the differences but the Wilcoxon test ranks the data and then measures the difference in the rank values.

X8.13 H_0: Median difference $A - B \leq 0$, H_1: Median difference $A - B > 0$. Normal: $\mu = 105$, $\sigma = 26.8$, $z_{cal} = 2.859$, upper one tail critical $= 1.65$, and upper one tail p-value $= 0.0020$. Accept H_1. New packaging more favourably received. Note: Ties have not been accommodated within this solution.

X8.14 H_0: Median difference $B - A \leq 0$, H_1: Median difference $B - A > 0$. Normal: $\mu = 233$, $\sigma = 48.6$, $z_{cal} = 4.2165$, upper one tail critical $= 1.65$, and upper one tail p-value $= 0.0000$. Accept H_1. Significant reduction in the number of errors made. Note: Ties have not been accommodated within this solution.

X8.15   Mann-Whitney U test assumptions: (1) Samples are random and independent,   (2) Sample distributions are continuous,   (3) Data scale at least ordinal so that you can put a meaning to 'less than', 'equal', or 'greater than'.

X8.16   Given the sample sizes we should solve using the exact method. If we assume a normal approximation: $\mu = 36$, $\sigma = 10.39$, $Z_{cal} = 0.6255$, upper one tail $Z_{cri} = 1.65$, upper one tail p-value $= 0.2658$. Accept H_0. No evidence of an improvement in performance.

X8.17   Given sample size apply a normal approximation: $\mu = 65$, $\sigma = 16.1245$, $Z_{cal} = -3.0078$, two tail $Z_{cri} = \pm 1.96$, upper one tail p-value $= 0.0026$. Accept H_1. Evidence suggests interest rates are significantly different. (If you changed to a 1% significance level then you would reverse this decision.)

Chapter 9

X9.1   (a) See Section 9.2.1.   (b) Homogeneity of variance test: Fmax $= 17.3 >$ Fcri $= 6.4$. Accept H_1. Evidence suggests variance significantly different ($p = 0.0009 < 0.05$)—use non-parametric test.   (c) One-way ANOVA results: Fcal $= 5.2 >$ Fcri $= 2.87$ (p-value $= 0.005 < 0.05$). Therefore, there is sufficient evidence to reject the hypothesis that the levels are all the same.   (d) Bonferroni t test significant differences: A-B, B-D.

X9.2   (a) See Section 9.2.1.   (b) Homogeneity of variance test: Fmax $= 17 >$ Fcri $= 9.3$. Accept H_1. Evidence suggests variance significantly different ($p = 0.02 < 0.05$)—use non-parametric test.   (c) One-way ANOVA results: Fcal $= 7.04 >$ Fcri $= 4.3$ (p-value $= 0.014 < 0.05$). Therefore, the proposed method is successful.   (d) Bonferroni t test significant differences: A-C.

X9.3   (a) See Section 9.2.1.   (b) Homogeneity of variance test: Fmax $= 3 <$ Fcri $= 6.4$. Accept H_0. Evidence suggests variance not significantly different ($p = 0.12 > 0.05$)—use parametric test.   (c) One-way ANOVA results: Fcal $= 2.5 < 3.88$ (p-value $= 0.124 > 0.05$). Therefore, the average mileage is the same.   (d) Bonferroni t test not required—if you undertook the test you would find all comparisons not significant.

X9.4   (a) See Section 9.2.1.   (b) Homogeneity of variance test: Fmax $= 1.28 <$ Fcri $= 2.17$. Accept H_0. Evidence suggests variance not significantly different ($p = 0.30 > 0.05$)—use parametric test.   (c) One-way ANOVA results: Fcal $= 5.46 >$ Fcri $= 3.16$ (p-value $= 0.007 < 0.05$). Therefore, significant differences observed.   (d) Bonferroni t test significant differences: A-B.

X9.5   See Section 9.2.1 for one-way ANOVA assumptions. Kruskal-Wallis: $Hc = 12.152 >$ critical chi square $= 9.49$ (p-value $= 0.016 < 0.05$). Accept H_1. Therefore, there is sufficient evidence to reject the hypothesis that the levels are all the same.

X9.6   (a) Ranked data.   (b) See Section 9.2.1 for one-way ANOVA model assumptions. (c) Kruskal-Wallis: $Hc = 8.47 >$ critical chi square $= 5.99$ (p-value $= 0.015 < 0.05$). Accept H_1. Therefore, the airlines are not rated the same by the nine individuals.

X9.7   Kruskal-Wallis: $Hc = 4.288 <$ critical chi square $= 5.99$ (p-value $= 0.117 > 0.05$). Accept H_0. Therefore, the average mileage is the same.

X9.8   Kruskal-Wallis: $Hc = 13.86 >$ critical chi square $= 5.99$ (p-value $= 0.004 < 0.05$). Accept H_1. Therefore, the performances are significantly different.

X9.9   Two-factor anova (no replication):   (i) Homogeneity of variance—$Fcal = 2.12 <$ critical $F = 5.05$ (p-value $= 0.21 > 0.05$) not significantly different—use parametric test,   (ii) $Fcal = 244.98 >$ critical F value $= 4.10$ (p-value $= 0.000 < 0.05$). Accept H_1. Evidence suggests significant difference in mean car mileage.

X9.10   Two-factor anova (no replication):   (i) Homogeneity of variance—$Fcal = 4.93 >$ critical $F = 6.39$ (p-value $= 0.076 > 0.05$) not significantly different (borderline)—use parametric test,   (ii) $F = 7.25 >$ critical F value $= 3.49$ (p-value $= 0.005 < 0.05$). Accept H_1. Evidence suggests significant difference in mean travel time.

X9.11   Two-factor anova (no replication):   (i) Homogeneity of variance—$Fcal = 20.63 <$ critical $F = 9.28$ (p-value $= 0.017 < 0.05$) significantly different—use non-parametric test,   (ii) $F = 2.58 >$ critical F value $= 2.9$ (p-value $= 0.071 > 0.05$). Accept H_0. No evidence to suggest a significant difference in crop size.

X9.12   Friedman: $G = Gc = 12$ (no ties) $>$ critical chi square $= 5.99$, df $= 2$, p-value $= 0.002 < 0.05$. Accept H_1. Evidence suggests significant difference in mean car mileage.

X9.13   Friedman: $G = 8.7$, $Gc = 9.26 >$ critical chi square $= 7.81$, df $= 3$, p-value $= 0.026 < 0.05$. Accept H_1. Evidence suggests significant difference in mean travel time.

X9.14   Friedman: $G = 10.32$, $Gc = 10.39 <$ critical chi square $= 11.07$, df $= 5$, p-value $= 0.065 > 0.05$ (borderline). Accept H_0. No evidence to suggest a significant difference in crop size.

X9.15   Two-factor anova (with replication):   (a) factor Quality ($Fcal = 5.33 >$ critical F value $= 3.17$ (p-value $= 0.008 < 0.05$), significant main effect for Quality),   (b) factor Media Type ($Fcal = 1.42 <$ critical F value $= 4.02$ (p-value $= 0.491 > 0.05$), no significant main effect for Media Type),   (c) interaction Quality * Media type ($Fcal = 0.087 <$ critical F value $= 3.17$ (p-value $= 0.917 > 0.05$), no significant interaction between the two factors).

X9.16   Two-factor anova (with replication):   (a) factor Route ($Fcal = 16.9 >$ critical F value $= 2.83$ (p-value $= 0.000 < 0.05$), significant main effect for Route),   (b) factor Driver ($Fcal = 20.88 >$ critical F value $= 2.6$ (p-value $= 0.000 < 0.05$), significant main effect for Driver),   (c) interaction Route * Driver ($Fcal = 2.134 >$ critical F value $= 2.00$ (borderline) (p-value $= 0.036 < 0.05$), significant interaction between the two factors).

Chapter 10

X10.1   Have the students been truthful? Is the sample large enough or are the results just a fluke?

X10.2   r = 0.84. Scatter plot and Pearson's correlation coefficient seems to suggest a strong positive correlation but look at the scatter plot and how the data points are lined up with only
three x values (40, 41, 42).

X10.3   r = −0.93. Scatter plot and Pearson's correlation coefficient suggest a strong −ve
correlation.

X10.4   r = 0.72. Scatter plot and Pearson's correlation coefficient suggest a strong +ve
correlation.

X10.5   Spearman's rank correlation coefficient r_s = 0.12. Calculation suggests little association
between the two markers. Note that this result may be due to the small sample.

X10.6   Pearson's correlation coefficient r = 0.47 and Spearman's rank correlation coefficient
r_s = 0.81. The two values are quite different and care should be taken using the rank correlation coefficient to provide an approximation for Pearson's product moment correlation
coefficient.

X10.7   Spearman's rank correlation calculation r_s for each pair are as follows: PQ 0.75, PR 0.32, QR
0.57. The results suggest that pair PQ are more likely to agree.

X10.8   C.   X10.9   B.   X10.10   C.   X10.11   D.   X10.12   C.

X10.13   To solve this problem use Analysis ToolPak—Regression to provide the following set of
solutions: line equation $\hat{y} = 46.6 + 8.4x$, r = 0.91, cod = 0.81 or 81%, for b_1 coefficient: F =
27.14, p = 0.0034, t = 5.21, p = 0.0034. Predictor variable is a significant contributor to the
value of the dependent variable. 95% CI is 4.35 − 12.53. Assumption checks:

(a) We can see from the scatter plot that we have no observed pattern within the residual
plot and we can assume that the linearity assumption is not violated. Furthermore, the
residual and hence the variance are not growing in size and are bounded between a high
and low point. From this we conclude that the variance assumption is not violated.

(b) We can see from the scatter plot that we have no observed pattern within the residual
plot and we can assume that the linearity assumption is not violated. Furthermore, the
residual and hence the variance are not growing in size and are bounded between a high
and low point. From this we conclude that the variance assumption is not violated.

(c) From the normal probability plot we have a fairly linear relationship and we conclude
that the normal assumption is not violated.

X10.14   To solve this problem use Analysis ToolPak—Regression to provide the following set of
solutions: Line equation $\hat{y} = 49.65 + 0.29x$, r = 0.88, cod = 0.78 or 78%, for b_1 coefficient
F = 27.14, p = 0.000029, t = 6.49, p = 0.000029. Predictor variable is a significant contributor
to the value of the dependent variable. 95% CI is 0.19 − 0.38. Assumption checks:

(a) We can see from the scatter plot that we have no observed pattern within the residual
plot and we can assume that the linearity assumption is not violated. Furthermore, the

residual and hence the variance are not growing in size and are bounded between a high and low point. From this we conclude that the variance assumption is not violated.

(b) From the normal probability plot we have a fairly linear relationship and we conclude that the normal assumption is not violated.

X10.15   To solve this problem use Analysis ToolPak—Regression to provide the following set of solutions: Line equation: $\hat{y} = 16017.7 + 70.95SF - 1702.85Age$, Multiple r = 0.94, cod = 0.89 or 89% (or adjusted r^2 = 0.87 or 87%), F = 46.36, p = 2.265E-6 < 0.05 significant, for b_1 coefficient: t = 7.68, p = 5.66E-6 < 0.05 significant, for b_2 coefficient: t = −2.55, p = 0.026 < 0.05 significant. Both predictor variables are significant contributors to the value of the dependent variable. Assumption checks:

(a) We can see from the scatter plots that we have no observed pattern within the residual plot and we can assume that the linearity assumption is not violated. Furthermore, the residual and hence the variance are not growing in size and are bounded between a high and low point. From this we conclude that the variance assumption is not violated.

(b) From the normal probability plot we have a fairly linear relationship and we conclude that the normal assumption is not violated.

Chapter 11

X11.1   The time series is non-stationary, but we cannot tell if it is seasonal too. First of all, we do not clearly see the pattern, but more importantly, the time units have not been defined. If the time units are not less than annual, we cannot talk about seasonality.

X11.2   The seasonality is 5 as the pattern seems to repeat itself every five time periods.

X11.3   Yes, it is. A non-seasonal and non-stationary time series is a simple stationary time series, oscillating around some fixed horizontal value.

X11.4   See instructor manual for graphs.

X11.5   Yes, the differenced time series appears to be stationary.

X11.6   The answer is:

Year	2000	2001	2002	2003	2004	2005	2006	2007	2008
Sales	230	300	290	320	350	400	350	400	420
I_{2000}	100	130.4	126.1	139.1	152.2	173.9	152.2	173.9	182.6
I_{2003}	71.88	93.75	90.63	100	109.4	125	109.4	125	131.3

X11.7   We took CPI values from Fig. 11.10 and recalculated Sales in constant 2004 dollar value. Year 2008 was not included as the CPI value for that year was missing.

Year	2000	2001	2002	2003	2004	2005	2006	2007
Sales	230	300	290	320	350	400	350	400
CPI	100	102.8	104.5	106.8	109.7	113.4	117.1	120.4
$Fixed_{2004}$	252.3	320	304.5	328.6	350	386.9	327.9	364.4

X11.8 The value of sales in 2007, which is $400, when converted to constant dollars from year 2000, becomes $332.2.

X11.9 Two different models generate two different sets of values:

T	90	95	100	105	110	115	120	125	130
C	2	4	6	4	2	4	6	4	2
I	0.55	0.3	0.4	0.6	0.5	0.6	0.4	0.5	0.4
$\hat{Y}_{Additive}$	92.6	99.3	106.4	109.6	112.5	119.6	126.4	129.5	132.4
$\hat{Y}_{Multiplicative}$	99.0	114.0	240.0	252.0	110.0	276.0	288.0	250.0	104.0

X11.10 No, the stated formula is not a linear trend formula, but a quadratic equation formula. The corresponding trend for this equation has a parabolic shape.

X11.11 Another expression for R squared is the coefficient of determination (COD). When discussing linear regression, we used it as a measure of how closely the two variables track each other's movements.

X11.12 Yes, R squared of 0.90 is a very good fit. It indicates that the trend line accounts for 90% of the variations in the time series and that only 10% is attributed to some other factors that are not captured by the trend line.

X11.13 The trend is calculated and extrapolated. The TREND function for the first cell, for example is: =TREND($B$17:$J$17,$B$16:$J$16,B16), etc.

X	1	2	3	4	5	6	7	8	9	10	11	12
Y	230	300	290	320	350	400	350	400	420			
Trend	256	277	298	319	340	361	382	403	424	445	466	487

It would not make sense to extrapolate the time series much further in the future. A general rule is that we cannot go too far in the future, as it becomes meaningless, in particular if the history is not long enough. A rule of thumb says that the future extrapolation should be a maximum of one third of the historical time series. In our case, this is only up to three future observations.

X11.14 Yes, the more observations we include in the moving average interval, the more 'smooth' this newly calculated time series of moving averages will be. In the extreme, if we take all the values of the time series in the moving average, we eventually get just a standard average, which is a very 'smooth' horizontal line.

X11.15 It is not feasible to extrapolate a time series using simple moving average method more than one time period in the future. The whole 'forecasting' approach of using moving averages is based on a simple principle that we just shift the moving average value of the previous interval to the time period that follows the time interval. It would make no sense to extend this further in the future.

X11.16 The equation $S'_t = S'_{t-1} + \alpha(y_{t-1} - S'_{t-1})$ can be written as $S'_t = S'_{t-1} + \alpha y_{t-1} - \alpha S'_{t-1} = \alpha y_{t-1} + S'_{t-1}(1-\alpha)$, which is identical to $S'_t = \alpha y_{t-1} + (1-\alpha)S'_{t-1}$. The reason it is called exponential smoothing is twofold.

Exponent smoothing method is based on the principle that every observation in the time series has an influence on the value of the forecast. However, the effect that every observation has on the future forecasts drops exponentially with the age of the historical observation. In other words, an observation at the very beginning of the time series will have much smaller influence on the future forecast than the latest observation in the series. This combined influence of historical observations on the future forecasts is 'managed' via the constant α. The value of α will determine how much are the newly calculated values 'smoother' than the original time series. Effectively, it is the constant α that determines how smooth the new series will be and how rapidly (exponentially) will the effects of older observations drop as we use them to produce current forecasts.

X11.17   The value of $\alpha = 0.25$ corresponds to MA = 7. This is calculated using formula 11.20: $\alpha = \dfrac{2}{M+1}$, from which $M = \left(\dfrac{2}{\alpha}\right) - 1$.

X11.18   The two forecasts, each with a different value of α are as follows:

X	1	2	3	4	5	6	7	8	9
Y	230	300	290	320	350	400	350	400	420
$\hat{Y} \alpha = 0.1$	230	230	237	242	250	260	274	282	293
$\hat{Y} \alpha = 0.99$	230	230	293	290	317	347	395	354	395

We observe that the small value of α has a greater effect on smoothing of the time series. The conclusion is that for non-stationary and more dynamic time series a larger value of α is probably more appropriate.

X11.19   If Excel Damping Factor is 0.65, then the value of alpha is 0.35 ($\alpha = 1 - $ Damping Factor).

X11.20   The result is as follows:

	A	B	C	D	E	F
1	X	Y	$\hat{Y}$	e	$\alpha =$	0.1
2	1	230	230	0		
3	2	300	230	70		
4	3	290	237	53		
5	4	320	242	78		
6	5	350	250	100		
7	6	400	260	140		
8	7	350	274	76		
9	8	400	282	118		
10	9	420	293	127		

The formulae are as follows:

C2=B2   D2=B2−C2
C3=C2+$F$1*D2   D3=B3−C3
C4=C3+$F$1*D3   D4=B4−C4
etc.

X11.21   Multiplicative seasonal exponential smoothing model is better suited for very dynamic movements of the time series, whilst the additive model is better suited for less dramatic changes in time series. In general the additive model performs better with stationary time series, whilst the multiplicative model is better suited for non-stationary time series.

X11.22   The parameters a_t and S_t are called a dynamic intercept and dynamic slope, respectively, because they serve the same purpose as the intercept and slope in a standard regression, or trend equation, with the exception that they change with every observation in the series. Unlike the regression intercept and slope which are constant for all observations, these ones dynamically change.

X11.23 The role of the mean square error (MSE) in the seasonal exponential smoothing method is to ensure the convergence of the smoothing constants to optimum value. Using Excel function Solver, we use MSE to find the best value of α and δ that minimizes differences between the actual and forecasted values.

X11.24 If we take the analogy of shooting at a target, then we can say that we are accurate if all our shots are inside the target. However if they are scattered around the target, then we are not precise. Clearly we want all the shots clustered as narrowly as possible around the middle of the target. The same applies to forecasting. Our ex-post forecasts might not be identical to actual observations, i.e. we are not accurate, but they closely follow the actual observations, which means we are precise. Conversely is not possible, i.e. we cannot have accurate forecasts that are not precise as this makes no sense.

X11.25 Mean error (ME) is a result of adding up all errors and dividing them by the total number of errors. If some errors are positive and some negative, when we add them up we might end up with zero sum (positives cancelling out the negatives). We do not have this problem if we use the mean absolute error (MAD), as all the values will be positive.

X11.26 MSE is very sensitive to large errors. In our example only one forecasted value in the second forecast is radically different from the same value in the first forecast. However, the error that this one forecast creates is quite large. The ME is not so sensitive to these individual extremes and shows the ME for the second forecast only seven times higher. The MSE, on the other hand, is very sensitive to large deviations and it 'penalizes' the second forecast with much larger value.

X11.27 No, it is not acceptable to see any pattern in residuals. If there is any pattern, then this means that we have not used the most adequate model. Effectively, in this case our forecasting method is not adequate and we need to find another one that will represent the dynamics of the time series better.

X11.28 Yes, this is correct. The diagonal line between the actual vs. ex-post forecasted values is the ideal line.

X11.29 Confidence interval is a measure of precision. The narrower the confidence interval, the more precise the forecasts are.

X11.30 For a time series that is 200 observations long it does not matter if we use either the t-values or z-values. The t-value distribution is more appropriate for shorter time series (less than 100 observations), but for longer ones it is irrelevant which one we use. However, z-values are easier to use as they do not require the number of degrees of freedom.

X11.31 The further we go in the future, the more uncertain it gets and it is logical to expect that our forecasts will be less precise, i.e. the confidence interval will be wider.

Glossary

The ISI glossary of statistical terms provides definitions in a number of different languages: http://isi.cbs.nl/glossary/index.htm

Adjusted r^2 Adjusted R squared measures the proportion of the variation in the dependent variable accounted for by the explanatory variables.

Aggregate price index A measure of the value of money based on a collection (a basket) of items and compared to the same collection of items at some base date or a period of time.

Alpha, α Alpha refers to the probability that the true population parameter lies outside the confidence interval. Not to be confused with the symbol alpha in a time series context i.e. exponential smoothing, where alpha is the smoothing constant.

Alternative hypothesis (H_1) The alternative hypothesis, H_1, is a statement of what a statistical hypothesis test is set up to establish.

Analysis of variance (ANOVA) Analysis of variance is a method for testing hypotheses about means.

Arithmetic mean The sum of a list of numbers divided by the number of numbers.

Autocorrelation Autocorrelation is the correlation between members of a time series of observations and the same values shifted at a fixed time interval.

Base index A value of a variable relative to its previous value at some fixed base.

Beta, β Beta refers to the probability that a false population parameter lies inside the confidence interval.

Binomial distribution A Binomial distribution can be used to model a range of discrete random data variables.

Bonferroni t test The Bonferroni test is a statistical procedure that adjusts the alpha level to allow multiple t tests to be used following the ANOVA.

Box plot A box plot is a way of summarizing a set of data measured on an interval scale.

Box-and-whisker plot A box-and-whisker plot is a way of summarizing a set of data measured on an interval scale.

Categorical variable A set of data is said to be categorical if the values or observations belonging to it can be sorted according to category.

Causal forecasting methods Methods that forecast one variable on the basis of relating it to another variable.

Central Limit Theorem The Central Limit Theorem states that whenever a random sample is taken from any distribution (μ, σ^2), then the sample mean will be approximately normally distributed with mean μ and variance σ^2/n.

Central tendency Measures the location of the middle or the centre of a distribution.

Chi square distribution The chi square distribution is a mathematical distribution that is used directly or indirectly in many tests of significance.

Chi square test Apply the chi square distribution to test for homogeneity, independence, or goodness of fit.

Classical additive time series model One of the models in classical time series analysis that assumes that components (trend, cyclical, seasonal, and random component) need to be added to compose the time series.

Classical time series analysis Approach to forecasting that decomposes a time series into certain constituent components (trend, cyclical, seasonal and, random component), makes estimates of each component and then re-composes the time series and extrapolates into the future.

Classical time series mixed model One of the models in classical time series analysis that assumes that components (trend, cyclical, seasonal, and random component) need to be added and multiplied to compose the time series.

Classical time series multiplicative model One of the models in classical time series analysis that assumes that components (trend, cyclical, seasonal, and random component) need to be multiplied to compose the time series.

Coefficient of determination (COD) The proportion of the variance in the dependent variable that is predicted from the independent variable.

Coefficient of variation The coefficient of variation measures the spread of a set of data as a proportion of its mean.

Confidence interval $(1 - \alpha)$ A confidence interval gives an estimated range of values which is likely to include an unknown population parameter.

Contingency table A contingency table is a table of frequencies classified according to the values of the variables in question.

Continuous probability distribution If a random variable is a continuous variable, its probability distribution is called a continuous probability distribution.

Continuous variable A set of data is said to be continuous if the values belong to a continuous interval of real values.

Covariance Covariance is a measure of how much two variables change together.

Critical test statistic The critical value for a hypothesis test is a limit at which the value of the sample test statistic is judged to be such that the null hypothesis may be rejected.

Cumulative frequency distribution The cumulative frequency for a value x is the total number of scores that are less than or equal to x.

Cyclical component A component in the classical time series analysis approach to forecasting that covers cyclical movements of the time series, usually taking place over a number of years.

Deflating values Converting current prices into constant prices by using one of the standard indices, such as CPI (Consumer Price Index).

Degrees of freedom Refers to the number of independent observations in a sample minus the number of population parameters that must be estimated from sample data.

Differencing A method of transforming a time series, usually to achieve stationarity. Differencing means that every current value in the time series is subtracted from the previous value.

Directional test Implies a direction for the implied hypothesis (one tailed test).

Discrete probability distribution If a random variable is a discrete variable, its probability distribution is called a discrete probability distribution.

Discrete variable A set of data is said to be discrete if the values belonging to it can be counted as 1, 2, 3, ...

Dispersion The variation between data values is called dispersion.

Error measurement A method of validating the quality of forecasts. Involves calculating the mean error, the mean squared error, the percentage error, etc.

Estimate An estimate is an indication of the value of an unknown quantity based on observed data.

Event An event is any collection of outcomes of an experiment.

Expected frequency In a contingency table the expected frequencies are the frequencies that you would predict in each cell of the table, if you knew only the row and column totals, and if you assumed that the variables under comparison were independent.

Expected value The expected value of a random data variable indicates its population average value.

Exponential smoothing One of the methods of forecasting that uses a constant (or several constants) to predict future values by 'smoothing' the past values in the series. The effect of this constant decreases exponentially as the older observations are taken into calculation.

Exponential trend An underlying time series trend that follows the movements of an exponential curve.

Ex-post forecasts Values produced from a forecasting model that are fitted to historical data.

Factor A factor of an experiment is a controlled independent variable; a variable whose levels are set by the experimenter.

Five-number summary A five-number summary is especially useful when we have so many data that it is sufficient to present a summary of the data rather than the whole data set.

Forecasting A method of predicting the future values of a variable, usually represented as the time series values.

Forecasting errors A difference between the actual and the forecasted value in the time series.

Forecasting horizon A number of the future time units until which the forecasts will be extended.

Frequency distributions Systematic method of showing the number of occurrences of observational data in order from least to greatest.

Frequency polygon A graph made by joining the middle-top points of the columns of a frequency histogram.

Friedman's test for > 2 medians The Friedman rank test is primarily used to test whether c sample groups have been selected from populations having equal medians.

F test for variances Tests whether two population variances are the same based upon sample values.

Grouped frequency distributions Data arranged in intervals to show the frequency with which the possible values of a variable occur.

Histogram A histogram is a way of summarizing data that are measured on an interval scale (either discrete or continuous).

Homogeneity of variance Population variances are equal.

Hypothesis test procedure A series of steps to determine whether to accept or reject a null hypothesis, based on sample data.

Independent events Two events are independent if the occurrence of one of the events has no influence on the occurrence of the other event.

Index number A value of a variable relative to its previous value at some base.

Interaction Two independent variables interact if the effect of one of the variables differs depending on the level of the other variable.

Intercept Value of the regression equation (y) when the x value = 0.

Interquartile range The interquartile range is a measure of the spread of or dispersion within a data set.

Interval scale An interval scale is a scale of measurement where the distance between any two adjacent units of measurement (or 'intervals') is the same but the zero point is arbitrary.

Irregular component A component in the classical time series analysis approach to forecasting that is uncovered by other components. It has to be random in shape.

Kruskal-Wallis test for > 2 medians The Kruskal-Wallis test compares the medians of three or more independent groups.

Kurtosis Kurtosis is a measure of the 'peakedness' or the distribution.

Least squares The method of least squares is a criterion for fitting a specified model to observed data. If refers to finding the smallest (least) sum of squared differences between fitted and actual values.

Level The number of levels of a factor or independent variable is equal to the number of variations of that factor that were used in the experiment.

Level of confidence The confidence level is the probability value $(1 - \alpha)$ associated with a confidence interval.

Linear relationship Simple linear regression aims to find a linear relationship between a response variable and a possible predictor variable by the method of least squares.

Linear trend model A model that uses the straight line equation to approximate the time series.

Logarithmic trend A model that uses the logarithmic equation to approximate the time series.

Main effect This is the simple effect of a factor on a dependent variable.

Mann-Whitney U test The Mann-Whitney U test is used to test the null hypothesis that two populations have identical distribution functions against the alternative hypothesis that the two distribution functions differ only with respect to location (median), if at all.

McNemar's test for matched pairs McNemar's test is a non-parametric method used on nominal data to determine whether the row and column marginal frequencies are equal.

Mean The mean is a measure of the average data value for a data set.

Mean absolute deviation (MAD) The mean value of all the differences between the actual and forecasted values in the time series. The differences between these values are represented as absolute values, i.e. the effects of the sign are ignored.

Mean absolute percentage error (MAPE) The mean value of all the differences between the actual and forecasted values in the time series. The differences between these values are represented as absolute percentage values, i.e. the effects of the sign are ignored.

Mean error (ME) The mean value of all the differences between the actual and forecasted values in the time series.

Mean percentage error (MPE) The mean value of all the differences between the actual and forecasted values in the time series. The differences between these values are represented as percentage values.

Mean square error (MSE) The mean value of all the differences between the actual and forecasted values in the time series. The differences between these values are squared to avoid positive and negative differences cancelling each other.

Median The median is the value halfway through the ordered data set.

Mode The mode is the most frequently occurring value in a set of discrete data.

Moving averages Averages calculated for a limited number of periods in a time series. Every subsequent period excludes the first observation from the previous period and includes the one following the previous period. This becomes a series of moving averages.

Multiple comparisons Multiple comparisons problem occurs when one considers a set, or family, of statistical inferences simultaneously.

Multiple regression Multiple linear regression aims to find a linear relationship between a response variable and several possible predictor variables.

Multivariate methods Methods that use more than one variable and try to predict the future values of one of the variables by using the values of other variables.

Nominal scale A set of data is said to be nominal if the values belonging to it can be assigned a label rather than a number.

Non-parametric Non-parametric tests are often used in place of their parametric counterparts when certain assumptions about the underlying population are questionable.

Non-stationary time series A time series that does not have a constant mean and oscillates around this moving mean.

Normal distribution The normal distribution is a symmetrical, bell-shaped curve, centred at its expected value.

Normal probability plot Graphical technique to assess whether the data is normally distributed.

Null hypothesis (H_0) The null hypothesis, H_0, represents a theory that has been put forward but has not been proved.

Observed frequency In a contingency table the observed frequencies are the frequencies actually obtained in each cell of the table, from our random sample.

Ogive (or cumulative frequency polygon) A distribution curve in which the frequencies are cumulative.

One tail test A one tail test is a statistical hypothesis test in which the values for which we can reject the null hypothesis, H_0, are located entirely in one tail of the probability distribution.

Ordinal variable A set of data is said to be ordinal if the values belonging to it can be ranked.

Outlier An outlier is an observation in a data set which is far removed in value from the others in the data set.

Parametric Any statistic computed by procedures that assume the data were drawn from a particular distribution.

Pearson's coefficient of correlation Pearson's correlation coefficient measures the linear association between two variables that have been measured on interval or ratio scales.

Point estimate A point estimate (or estimator) is any quantity calculated from the sample data which is used to provide information about the population.

Poisson distribution Poisson distributions model a range of discrete random data variables.

Polynomial trend A model that uses an equation of any polynomial curve (parabola, cubic curve, etc.) to approximate the time series.

Population mean The population mean is the mean value of all possible values.

Population standard deviation The population standard deviation is the standard deviation of all possible values.

Population variance The population variance is the variance of all possible values.

Power trend A model that uses an equation of a power curve (a parabola) to approximate the time series.

Probability A probability provides a number value to the likely occurrence of a particular event.

P-value The p-value is the probability of getting a value of the test statistic as extreme as or more extreme than that observed by chance alone, if the null hypothesis is true.

Qualitative variable Variables can be classified as descriptive or categorical.

Quantitative variable Variables can be classified using numbers.

Quartiles Quartiles are values that divide a sample of data into four groups containing an equal number of observations.

Random component A component in time series analysis that has to act as a random variable, i.e. have some constant mean and the variance, as well as to exhibit no pattern.

Random sample A random sample is a sampling technique where we select a sample from a population of values.

Rank coefficient of correlation Spearman's rank correlation coefficient is applied to data sets when it is not convenient to give actual values to variables but one can assign a rank order to instances of each variable.

Ranks List data in order of size.

Range The range of a data set is a measure of the dispersion of the observations.

Ratio variable Ratio data are continuous data where both differences and ratios are interpretable and have a natural zero.

Region of rejection The range of values that leads to rejection of the null hypothesis.

Residual The residual represents the unexplained variation (or error) after fitting a regression model.

Residuals The differences between the actual and predicted values. Sometimes called forecasting errors. Their behaviour and pattern has to be random.

Sample space The sample space is an exhaustive list of all the possible outcomes of an experiment.

Sampling distribution The sampling distribution describes probabilities associated with a statistic when a random sample is drawn from a population.

Sampling error Sampling error refers to the error that results from taking one sample rather than taking a census of the entire population.

Scatter plot A scatter plot is a plot of one variable against another variable.

Seasonal component A component in the classical time series analysis approach to forecasting that covers seasonal movements of the time series, usually taking place inside one year's horizon.

Seasonal correlation A correlation between the observations given in the corresponding units of time within which the seasonality repeats itself.

Seasonal time series A time series, represented in the units of time smaller than a year, that shows regular pattern in repeating itself over a number of these units of time.

Significance level, α The significance level of a statistical hypothesis test is a fixed probability of wrongly rejecting the null hypothesis, H_0, if it is in fact true.

Sign test The sign test is designed to test a hypothesis about the location of a population distribution.

Simple price index A value of a price for one item relative to the previous price for the same item at some base.

Simple regression analysis Simple linear regression aims to find a linear relationship between a response variable and a possible predictor variable by the method of least squares.

Skewness Skewness is defined as asymmetry in the distribution of the data values.

Slope Gradient of the fitted regression line.

Standard deviation Measure of the dispersion of the observations (A square root value of the variance)

Standard error of forecast The square root of the variance of all forecasting errors.

Stated limits The lower and upper limits of a class interval.

Statistic A statistic is a quantity that is calculated from a sample of data.

Statistical independence Two events are independent if the occurrence of one of the events gives us no information about whether or not the other event will occur.

Stationary time series A time series that does have a constant mean and oscillates around this mean.

Student's t distribution The t distribution is the sampling distribution of the t statistic.

Symmetrical A data set is symmetrical when the data values are distributed in the same way above and below the middle value.

Test of association The chi square test of association allows the comparison of two attributes in a sample of data to determine if there is any relationship between them.

Test statistic A test statistic is a quantity calculated from our sample of data.

Tied ranks Two or more data values share a rank value.

Time period An unit of time by which the variable is defined (an hour, day, month, year, etc.).

Time series A variable measured and represented per units of time.

Time series plot A chart of a change in variable against time.

Transformations A method of changing the time series, usually to make it stationary. Most common method for transforming the time series is differencing or sometimes taking differences of every observation from the mean value.

Trend component A component in the classical time series analysis approach to forecasting that covers underlying directional movements of the time series.

Two tail test A two tail test is a statistical hypothesis test in which the values for which we can reject the null hypothesis, H_0, are located in both tails of the probability distribution.

Type I error, α A type I error occurs when the null hypothesis is rejected when it is in fact true.

Type II error, β A type II error occurs when the null hypothesis, H_0, is not rejected when it is in fact false.

Unbiased When the mean of the sampling distribution of a statistic is equal to a population parameter, that statistic is said to be an unbiased estimator of the parameter.

Univariate methods Methods that use only one variable and try to predict its future values through some pre-defined method.

Variable A variable is a symbol that can take on any of a specified set of values.

Variance Measure of the dispersion of the observations.

Wilcoxon signed rank t test The Wilcoxon signed ranks test is designed to test a hypothesis about the location of the population median (one or two matched pairs).

Index